THE REMNANTS OF THE RECHTSSTAAT

The Remnants of the Rechtsstaat

An Ethnography of Nazi Law

JENS MEIERHENRICH

OXFORD
UNIVERSITY PRESS

OXFORD
UNIVERSITY PRESS

Great Clarendon Street, Oxford, OX2 6DP,
United Kingdom

Oxford University Press is a department of the University of Oxford.
It furthers the University's objective of excellence in research, scholarship,
and education by publishing worldwide. Oxford is a registered trade mark of
Oxford University Press in the UK and in certain other countries

First Edition published in 2018

Published in the United States of America by Oxford University Press
198 Madison Avenue, New York, NY 10016, United States of America

British Library Cataloguing in Publication Data
Data available

Library of Congress Control Number: 2017960273

ISBN 978–0–19–881441–2

For Shan

Preface

This book was a pleasure to write. The research for it was by turns sobering and awe-inspiring. The book's key protagonist was a courageous man in dark times. Ernst Fraenkel is his name. On September 20, 1938, this otherwise ordinary man fled the Third Reich. From the safety of his exile in the United States, he published *The Dual State*, an English-language edition of his remarkable account about the legal origins of dictatorship. Fraenkel, a German labor lawyer and social democrat of lapsed Jewish faith, had secretly drafted the original manuscript between 1936 and 1938, the only such account written inside the Hitler state. Due to the book's clandestine origins, some consider *The Dual State* the ultimate piece of intellectual resistance to the Nazi regime. Ernst Fraenkel is the name of its author. The name is worth introducing twice, for it is all but forgotten.

What follows is a book of legal theory and intellectual history. It revolves centrally around Fraenkel's life and *magnum opus*, but I also travel farther afield, to chart the changing character of law in the transition from Weimar democracy to Nazi dictatorship. Through the lens of what I call Fraenkel's ethnography of law, I reflect on the historiography of the Third Reich, as well as on the study of the authoritarian rule of law in the twenty-first century. With a bit of luck, readers will come away sharing my admiration for Ernst Fraenkel's extraordinary achievement, and be convinced by my argument about its contemporary relevance.

I am glad to have an opportunity to express my appreciation to those who helped me to bring *The Dual State* back in. At Oxford University Press, Merel Alstein responded enthusiastically to my proposal for preparing a new edition of Fraenkel's classic. OUP had published the first edition in 1941. The second edition was released in 2017, and I am grateful to Anthony Hinton and Emma Endean-Mills who oversaw that volume's publication, and the three anonymous reviewers who encouraged it. More recently, Jamie Berezin, also of OUP's law team, was receptive to turning my excavation of Fraenkel's ethnography of law into a book. I am grateful to him for believing in the project from the get-go, for responding to any and all queries with speed and kindness, and for finding three anonymous reviewers whose comments were thoughtful and important. Eve Ryle-Hodges assisted reliably with the book's production. For facilitating access to primary documents, I especially thank the staff in the

Manuscripts and Archives Division of New York Public Library and in Archives and Special Collections at the London School of Economics and Political Science.

It is a particular pleasure to acknowledge my debt to colleagues who commented on parts of the manuscript and thereby improved it. David Dyzenhaus, Martin Krygier, and Martin Loughlin provided useful feedback on Chapter 9. Horst Dreier, William Scheuerman, Michael Stolleis, Dan Stone, and Jakob Zollmann all read earlier versions of Chapters 3, 6, and 7. I am grateful to them all for taking time out of their busy schedules to help me hone my argument and analysis. Kenneth Ledford is owed thanks for trawling through the entire draft of the penultimate manuscript. To my relief, he came up with no major errors. His kind words and encouragement meant a great deal as the book was about to go to print. The most substantial contribution to my revision came from Douglas Morris, who deserves special mention. A legal historian whose insightful articles about Fraenkel in recent years have done their share to draw attention to this important cause lawyer-turned-legal ethnographer, Morris went beyond the call of collegiality. His close scrutiny of the completed manuscript produced invaluable commentary: He shared with me no less than twenty-one single-spaced pages of questions and suggestions for revision. These nearly 10,000 words of feedback were so carefully (and sensitively) phrased and so extraordinarily useful that I have serious doubt about whether I will ever be able to repay the debt I incurred.

Interrupted by illness, my research and writing were delayed by a few years. I am grateful to Christopher Hughes in the Department of International Relations at the LSE for his care and support during this difficult time. I will not forget it. Nor will I forget the loyal friends who saw me through my own darkness: the late Heather Adams in Boston, Ben and Jodie Elley in Wendover, Alex Krämer and Malte Stellmann in Berlin, Dirk Moses in Florence and Sydney, Angelo Pacillo and Anke Rose in Cologne, Oliver Simons and Michelle Tihal in New York, and Roz Ghosh, Stephen Richards, John Sidel, and Dan Stone in London. I am lucky to have them in my life. Equally deserving of gratitude are my parents, Friedel and Christa Meierhenrich, who made it all possible, as well as my parents-in-law, Shiu Cho and Woon Hing Lam. The latter contributed immeasurably to my happiness by allowing me to marry their daughter, Shan Lam. To her go my deepest thanks. She is one of the most delightful, fun, and thoughtful people you will ever meet, and Shan's support these last few years has been generous and unwavering, which is why this book is dedicated to her.

Contents

1

The Idea of Lawlessness

> The claim that no legal order exists under despotism,
> that the ruler's arbitrary will governs,
> is utterly nonsensical.
>
> Hans Kelsen[1]

One can be forgiven for thinking that the man whose portrait adorns this book's cover was a loyal servant of the *Rechtsstaat*, the German variant of the rule of law. The man's enigmatic gaze as well as his robe suggest that he took seriously legal norms and institutions, that he had faith in the authority of law. Upon closer inspection of the photograph one notices the insignia pinned to the jurist's cloth: a *Reichsadler*, or Reich Eagle, crouched on a swastika enveloped by an oak wreath—the emblem of Nazi dictatorship.[2]

The man on the cover has one of the most iconic faces of the Third Reich. He is Roland Freisler, from 1942 until 1945 the president of Nazi Germany's *Volksgerichtshof*, its notorious "people's court." One of the earliest members of the *Nationalsozialistische Deutsche Arbeiterpartei* (NSDAP), the National Socialist German Workers' Party, Freisler eagerly helped to hollow out the *Rechtsstaat* in Nazi Germany, first in his roles as a bureaucrat in the Reich Ministry of Justice and a scholarly protagonist of racial law (notably in the realm of criminal law), later, and most infamously, during his tenure at the helm of the *Volksgerichtshof*.[3] Consider the following statistic: whereas the extraordinary tribunal handed down 191 death sentences in the period 1939–1941, the number rose exponentially under Freisler's stewardship. Between 1942 and 1944, the court's jurisprudence turned considerably more violent, as a large number of the proceedings before the *Volksgerichtshof* ended with the imposition of one or more death penalties. Out of 10,289 defendants who stood trial in this period, 4,951 were sentenced to death.[4] Freisler was an ardent advocate of what Max Weber, the Germany lawyer and sociologist, a few decades earlier had termed "substantively irrational law."[5] Freisler's ideological fervor and blatant careerism earned him the nickname "racing Roland" ("*rasender Roland*").[6] Given his disdain for "formally rational law," another of Weber's ideal types, why does Freisler's ignoble persona illustrate a book about the remnants of the *Rechtsstaat*? This begs further questions: What was Nazi law? What authority—if any—did it have in the Third Reich? Which functions did it serve, what effects did it have, whose lives did it alter?

IN THE IMAGE OF JANUS

The choice of cover illustration was deliberate. I selected the little-known image of Freisler because it signifies dissonance. It is suggestive of conflicting imperatives—of a schizophrenic identity—at the heart of one of the Nazi state's major institutions: the law. As we shall see, Freisler, one of the major representatives of the authoritarian and later totalitarian administration of justice, was himself at first of two minds about the nature of Nazi law and how best to advance it. Unlike other fervent supporters of racial supremacy, Freisler for a while even clung to the language of the *Rechtsstaat*.[7] He continued to do so even when the term had long been jettisoned, replaced in Nazi discourse by that of the "*völkischer Führerstaat*," the concept of Hitler's racial state. For reasons to be explained in this book, Freisler, this loyal servant of the Nazi state, for a while showed a grudging respect for a truncated idea of the *Rechtsstaat*. Inasmuch as his donning of the judicial robe was a façade, a superficial remnant of the *Rechtsstaat*, the pride Freisler so evidently felt when he performed the role of the guardian of Nazi law for the photographer in the cover image is suggestive of something deeper, something rooted in the cultural foundations of law.[8] Freisler's persona—like his portrait—was Janus-faced.[9]

According to Cicero, Ovid, and other ancient sources, Janus was the Roman god of transitions (*eundo*). Myth has it that his double-head served a purpose. In his role as guardian of the heavenly gates (*caelestis ianitor aulae*), Janus was said to simultaneously keep watch over both the eastern and western gates of heaven. As a god of motion, he is also believed to have presided over all beginnings and transformations, whether abstract or concrete, sacred or profane.[10] Among other states of flux, Janus, who is sometimes referred to as the "god of gods" ("*diuom deo*"), was seen as holding the middle ground between civilization and barbarism. The image of the two-headed Janus—looking in two directions at once—is a useful metaphor for thinking about the nature of the state in the Third Reich.

I argue in this book that the Nazi state was inherently bifurcated—and that it remained so for much longer than previously thought. It housed, notably in the pre-war years, two subsidiary states with conflicting imperatives. The dispensation's inherent doubleness gave rise to two contending practices of Nazi rule: a *legal* way of doing things and a *violent* way of doings things. This "dual state," as a brave contemporary observer dubbed it, occupied a liminal position in the transition from authoritarianism to totalitarianism in the late 1930s. Comprised of a "normative state" and a "prerogative state," it presided over a critical juncture in the making of Nazi dictatorship.[11] It both hastened *and* retarded the country's brownshirt revolution. Although agents of the prerogative state helped to gradually dismantle the normative state, remnants of the latter continued to have a structuring effect on social outcomes in the Third Reich, especially at the level of everyday law. I suggest that this diminished, rudimentary *Rechtsstaat* was crucial in the creation and maintenance of Nazi dictatorship. The legal norms and institutions that it comprised sustained the regime not only in peacetime, but in wartime as well. The idea of "Nazi law," then, is not an oxymoron but was a fact of everyday life—a claim at odds with a prominent supposition in legal philosophy.

RADBRUCH'S FORMULA

It is sometimes said that the law of the Third Reich was not law, properly understood. This view has its roots in an influential jurisprudential argument from 1946, formulated by the legal philosopher Gustav Radbruch, about the relationship between law and morals in times of injustice.[12] The article in which he first developed this claim has been hailed as "one of the most important texts in 20th century legal philosophy."[13] Aside from decisively influencing the jurisprudence of postwar Germany's two highest courts, that of the *Bundesgerichtshof* (Federal Supreme Court) and the *Bundesverfassungsgericht* (Federal Constitutional Court), it gave rise to one of the most important debates in legal philosophy, the so-called Hart-Fuller debate, which played out in the pages of the *Harvard Law Review* and has been revisited in a plethora of publications since.[14] Entitled "Gesetzliches Unrecht und übergesetzliches Recht" ("Statutory Lawlessness and Supra-Statutory Law"), Radbruch's article set out what has since become known as "Radbruch's formula" ("*Radbruch'sche*

Formel"), an idea that has shaped legal theory and practice in highly significant ways.[15] It can be summarized as follows:

> Where there is not even an attempt at justice, where equality, the core of justice, is deliberately betrayed in the issuance of positive law, then the statute is not merely "flawed law", it lacks completely the very nature of law. For law, including positive law, cannot be otherwise defined than as a system and an institution whose very meaning is to serve justice. Measured by this standard, whole portions of National Socialist law never attained the dignity of valid law.[16]

Radbruch's was a normative intervention that sought to overcome the legacies of Nazi dictatorship by strengthening the philosophical foundations of the rule of law, in postwar Germany and elsewhere: "In the face of the statutory lawlessness of the past twelve years, we must seek now to meet the requirement of justice with the smallest sacrifice of legal certainty."[17] Radbruch had no doubts about what needed to be done in the wake of war and genocide: "[W]e must build a *Rechtsstaat*, a government of law that serves as well as possible the ideas of both justice and legal certainty."[18] The prescription was reasonable, laudable even, considering that many of Radbruch's fellow citizens were not at all enamored with the new, democratizing order imposed on a defeated Germany from the outside. But the simplifying language of morality sits uneasily with the complex nature of reality. An abundance of microhistorical evidence contradicts Radbruch's macrotheoretical argument about the nature of Nazi law. Available data about everyday law in Nazi Germany cast doubt on the utility of Radbruch's famous formula as "a test for the validity of statutory enactments."[19] It has even been suggested that his philosophical intervention has not helped but hindered analyses of his country's legal development in the period 1933–1945, and, as a concomitant consequence, also undermined postwar efforts at coming to terms with the contribution of lawyers to dictatorship.[20]

The trouble with Radbruch's formula is that it linked two questions that should not be conflated: the question of law's nature and the question of law's practice. The former is a philosophical question, the latter an empirical one. The former demands an abstract answer, the latter a concrete one. Because Radbruch was put on a pedestal in the transition from Nazi dictatorship, his voice was amplified: "After World War II, Radbruch's reputation and good will endowed his reflections with gravitas. Contemporaries and later scholars have admired a revived spirit who, despite years of quiescence and physical debility, energetically engaged a dawning era."[21] By contrast, the voices of contemporaries who had been forced into exile such as Hans Kelsen and Franz Neumann—both of whom shared Radbruch's social-democratic leanings but were more circumspect about his faith in natural law—were drowned out. Because Radbruch's formula paved the way for the kinds of reductionist representations of Nazi law at which I take aim in this book, it deserves a closer look.[22]

Radbruch theorized "lawlessness" as a pervasive feature of Nazi law. His argument comprised two sub-theses, sometimes described in the literature as the "causal thesis" and the "exoneration thesis." According to the causal thesis, legal positivism was responsible for the damage done to Weimar Germany's *Rechtsstaat*, and its eventual destruction in Nazi Germany. The exoneration thesis followed from the causal thesis. It held that the power of legal positivism in the Third Reich left the regime's judges normatively defenseless against the immoral content of Nazi legislation. Their professional socialization under the influence of the theory of legal positivism, so the argument goes, left them no choice but to apply statutory law. As Radbruch explained in 1947, "The proponents of this theory were compelled to recognize even the most unjust statute as law. [...] [And it is] precisely because of his positivistic legal training that the judge is not to be held personally responsible for the injustice of a sentence based on an unjust statute."[23]

We now know that Radbruch's categorical statements about the nature of law in the Third Reich were empirically ill-informed, his pronouncements "far off the mark."[24] Stanley Paulson and others have persuasively shown that it was not judges' adherence to statutory law that was a causal factor in the gradual destruction of the *Rechtsstaat* in the mid-1930s but their departure from it: "Statutory law that had been valid before 1933 remained for the most part on the books. Rather than waiting for the introduction of new statutory law, judges and other officials in Nazi Germany simply departed from the language of existing law whenever and wherever that was called for."[25] Paulson supports this argument with an instructive example:

> The principle *nulla poena sine lege*, found in section 2 of the German Penal Code of 1871, had been interpreted in Wilhelminian [*sic*] Germany as including certain more determinate principles, including the prohibition of ex post facto law and of applications of criminal law by analogy. These time-honored guarantees of the rule of law or *Rechtsstaat* were eliminated in one full swoop—not legislatively, but rather in the judicial practice of the new regime.[26]

It will come as no surprise that Carl Schmitt applauded the regime's boldness, declaring in 1933 "the fiction of a normative commitment of the judge to a statute has, for substantial areas of legal life (*Rechtsleben*), become theoretically and practically untenable."[27] The institution of the statute, he claimed, could no longer guarantee the predictability ("*Berechenbarkeit*") and security ("*Sicherheit*") of law in the country's *Rechtsstaat*.[28] This brings us back to Roland Freisler.

Echoing justice minister Otto Georg Thierack's pronouncement in one of his *Richterbriefe*, letters addressed to Nazi judges to guide their jurisprudence, that statutes represented unnecessary "crutches," Freisler jumped on the post-positivist bandwagon, insisting in 1935 that the commitment of judges to statutory criminal law had been foreign to German jurisprudence prior to the Enlightenment, and, as such, deserved to be excised from it because it unduly "binds" ("*fesselt*") the regime's judges.[29] Unsurprisingly, given these intellectual foundations, judges, in the everyday operation of Nazi law, tended to dispose of criminal cases, especially if they had a political dimension, "by appeal to the precepts of the Nazi regime—the '*Führerprinzip*', the program of the Nazi Party, the '*Geist* of National Socialism', the 'moral sentiments' of the people, and the like."[30] And yet court decisions were not always substantively irrational, for reasons to be explained. In one of its most important judgments, postwar Germany's Federal Constitutional Court found that *even* legally invalid norms had created social facts in the period 1933–1945. This judicial observation is highly relevant to the issue at hand because it speaks to the relationship between facts and norms in the practice of Nazi law.[31]

In the case in question, a seven-judge panel in 1980 declared invalid the Eleventh Decree (*Verordnung*) relating to the 1935 Reich Citizenship Law (*Reichsbürgergesetz*), dated November 25, 1941, which had led to the expulsion of the plaintiff, identified in the court documents only as "Herr Karl St."[32] The judgment reaffirmed key tenets of the court's longstanding jurisprudence on the validity of Nazi law, that is, to declare invalid, drawing on Radbruch's formula, those "National Socialist 'legal' provisions" that "so evidently contradict fundamental principles of justice that a judge who tried to apply them, or to acknowledge their legal effects, would declare lawlessness instead of law (*Unrecht statt Recht*)."[33] More interesting for our purposes is the judges' finding that the organs of the postwar German state were "incapable of undoing *the facts* that the Nazis' lawless practices created."[34] As the judges opined: "The 'expatriation' of Jews pursuant to National Socialist legislation remains a *historical fact*, which, this being the case, cannot retrospectively be expunged [from the empirical record]."[35] By highlighting and explicitly recognizing not once but repeatedly the facticity of this statutory lawlessness ("*faktische[s] gesetzliche[s] Unrecht*"), the *Bundesverfassungsgericht* honored Radbruch's formula while simultaneously transcending it. Let me explain, as the point is significant for what is to come.

In the proceeding before us, BVerfGE 54, 53 (the so-called *Ausbürgerung II* Case), the Constitutional Court revisited its earlier jurisprudence, notably BverfGE 23, 98 (its *Ausbürgerung I* Case) of February 14, 1968 and BVerfGE 3, 58 (the *Beamtenverhältnisse* Case) of December 17, 1953. The latter case centered on the legality of Nazi Germany's civil service law (*Beamtenrecht*), but the details need not concern us here. The judgment is significant for our purposes because the chamber introduced a distinction between a normative (what it called "philosophical") and a factual (what it termed "sociological") approach to Nazi law—and tried to do justice to both. It is worth quoting from the judgment verbatim, not least because key portions of it resurfaced decades later as *obiter dicta* in *Ausbürgerung II*:

> It may be the case, in this instance, as in other areas, that the law created by National Socialism, amounts, in a higher philosophical sense, to "lawlessness." But it would be unrealistic ("*unrealistisch*") in the highest degree to develop this idea, in a legal positivistic manner, such that the (formal) law [of Nazi Germany] would *ex post facto* be regarded as null and void [. . .]. Such a perspective would overlook that a "sociological" validity of legal norms exists, which only ceases to be meaningful where such provisions stand in so evident a contradiction ("*in so evidentem Widerspruch*") to the principles of justice which govern formal law, that the judge who wanted to apply them or acknowledge their legal effects, would render lawlessness instead of law.[36]

I am suggesting that BVerfGE 3, 58 was a judicial attempt at *précising* Radbruch's formula, at making it *practically* usable for adjudicating between the conflicting imperatives of morality and reality. In the case at hand, the judges found that Nazi Germany's civil service law had, in fact, constituted valid law, as defined by Radbruch, in the Third Reich. They gave three reasons for their finding: first, the constitutional foundations of the *Beamtenrecht* had been adopted in a procedurally correct manner in Nazi Germany; second, the beneficiaries of the law had accepted its authority; and, third, its rules and procedures had been in force for years and not met opposition, let alone resistance. Taken together, the chamber reasoned, these "legally relevant facts" ("*rechtserheblichen Tatsachen*") had created legal expectations on the part of the population that the Constitutional Court could not disappoint without simultaneously violating the norm of legal certainty (*Rechtssicherheit*). That norm had gained in importance a few years earlier when it was folded into the *Rechtsstaatsprinzip*, the new and fundamental constitutional principle set out in Article 20(3) of the *Grundgesetz*, or Basic Law, postwar Germany's interim democratic constitution of 1949.

A few years later the court reiterated its idea of the "sociological validity" ("*soziologische Geltungskraft*") of Nazi law in its *Gestapo* Case (BVerfGE 6, 132) of February 19, 1957. In this Gestapo-related ruling, it introduced further nuance into its interpretation of Radbruch's formula, this time distinguishing explicitly between the validity of a specific law and the validity of the legal order as a whole. The judges also pronounced on the applicability of Radbruch's formula, declaring it the "outermost limit" ("*äußerste Geltungsgrenze*") for assessing the validity of Nazi law, thereby effectively casting it as a principle of last resort.[37] By trying to do justice to both facts and norms, the constitutional jurisprudence of postwar Germany took on a schizophrenic quality whenever it was concerned with cases arising from the law of the Third Reich. The *Bundesverfassungsgericht* repeatedly declared portions of Nazi law *normatively invalid*, but, on occasion, it found the same legal norms, rules, or procedures to have nonetheless been *factually valid*—and thus impossible to disregard in its adjudication of Nazi dictatorship.[38] Although this squaring of the circle was "logically untidy," as one commentator put it, it led to an improved understanding of the everyday life of Nazi law.[39] In operationalizing Radbruch's formula, the court tempered the morality of Radbruch's formula with a dose of reality, allowing for the kind of critical legal history of the Nazi dictatorship that eventually emerged in Germany at century's end.

Taking a leaf from the jurisprudence of Germany's *Bundesverfassungsgericht*, I treat Nazi law in this book as an observable social phenomenon. I follow in a long line of scholars, the best known of whom is the legal historian Michael Stolleis. He was one of the first postwar analysts to focus on the day-to-day operation of Nazi law rather than the question of its morality.[40] Convinced that moral outrage contributed little to understanding the legal determinants of Nazi rule, he went archival. For him "National Socialist law" encompassed the following, a yardstick that I also adopt:

> (1) in the narrow sense, the law that was strongly influenced by National Socialist ideology (racial laws, marriage and family laws, the Hereditary Farm Law, labor law); (2) all the statutory and case law that was newly created under National Socialist rule and superseded the older legal order; (3) the entire legal order that was in force, practiced, and taught between 1933 and 1945.[41]

To be sure, Stolleis, like Radbruch, *was* morally outraged by Nazi dictatorship, war, and genocide, as am I. He felt "a sense of shared responsibility for that period and its crimes" even though he was born only in 1941.[42] But he also wanted to *understand*, in the Weberian sense, the law of the swastika, and therefore warned, rightly in my view, of falling prey to "limits of perception" ("*Schranken der Wahrnehmung*").[43] Cognizant of this danger, he implored scholars to

> take into account the inner make-up of the actors, and, above all, avoid reading the texts of the period as though their authors knew or foresaw what is easy to know today. [...] Analytical understanding does not exclude the question of morality, in fact it can deepen it, for example by making clear how closely related writing and doing can be. [...] The conditions of this dictatorship provide an especially good model for studying how traditional legal doctrine was distorted and devalued by a result-oriented vulgar jurisprudence, how [...] scholarly networks were transformed, and how the individual processing of reality was deformed by external and internal pressure.[44]

Stolleis was interested in historical analysis, not philosophical judgment. Horst Dreier joined him in the quest for an empirical approach to the study of Nazi law. Dreier in turn cautioned scholars not to be misled by outcome knowledge: "One must not interpret everything that was written in Weimar and in the early years of the Third Reich from the knowing vantage point of those who were born later (*Nachgeborenen*), and thus from the perspective of the evil end (*bösen Ende*). Instead one must be cognizant of the contingency of the historical situation (*der Offenheit der historischen Situation bewußt bleiben*) in which, and in response to which, [historical actors] thought, spoke, wrote, and acted."[45]

The historical study quickly superseded the philosophical study of Nazi law. Stolleis, Dreier, and other progressive historians in the 1980s advanced the kind of critical legal history of Nazi law for which Dieter Simon had been calling in the 1970s.[46] Seeing that my training is not just in law but also in the social sciences, my analytical interest is different from that of Stolleis; it has a theoretical dimension. It is rooted in the so-called new institutionalism that emerged in the 1980s and by now has engulfed disciplines from economics to sociology via history and political science. It is surprisingly rewarding, as I hope to show, to think of the law of the Third Reich in *institutional* terms, as understood by new institutionalists. James March and Johan Olsen, who invented the label for the theoretically rigorous study of institutions, have offered this definition of what social scientists have in mind when they talk about institutions:

> An institution is a relatively enduring collection of rules and organized practices, embedded in structures of meaning and resources that are relatively invariant in the face of turnover of individuals and relatively resilient to the idiosyncratic preferences and expectations of individuals and changing external circumstances.[47]

Unlike Radbruch's philosophical take on the institution(s) of Nazi law, this definition, which I adopt in this book, is agnostic on the question of institutional morality.[48] The main concern of all of the various new institutionalisms (rational choice institutionalism, sociological institutionalism, historical institutionalism, discursive institutionalism) is to figure out why institutions matter, how, when, and to whom. If a new institutionalist is historically inclined, she might also want to know where institutions come from and how they evolve over time. One of the core assumptions of this book is that regardless of their moral purpose "institutions create elements of order and predictability. They fashion, enable, and constrain political actors as they act within a logic of appropriate action. Institutions are carriers of identities and roles and they are markers of a polity's character, history, and visions."[49]

With this approach to law in mind, I analyze the institutional foundations of Nazi order, with particular reference to the legal determinants of dictatorship. I conceive of law as a normative idea that comes to life—most notably as practices, rules, institutions, traditions, and cultures—in response to the exigencies of politics and society. My approach is an inductive one; for me law is what actors, individual and collective, make of it. It is "an intrinsically moral idea," for the reasons that Nigel Simmonds elaborates, but one caught up in a given society's webs of significance.[50] The German idea of the *Rechtsstaat* was an attempt to turn a moral idea into a foundational principle of rule, into a tool of institutional regulation and self-binding. We shall see that the appeal of this idea was not lost on the Nazi regime—the remnants of the *Rechtsstaat* also bound it, and even after its leading jurists abandoned the term itself. "[T]he fact that the Nazi government was possessed of unlimited power does not in itself preclude a presumption of legality, nor does it establish a presumption of arbitrariness."[51] H. O. Pappe's observation cuts to the heart of my analysis of the institutional development of the *Rechtsstaat* in Nazi Germany, its uses and abuses in legal theory and practice.

Coined in the late eighteenth century by conjoining the nouns "*Recht*" ("law") and "*Staat*" ("state"), the idea of the *Rechtsstaat* originally served as a rallying cry in the run-up to the German revolutions of 1848–1849. Although ultimately unsuccessful, the calls by insurgent social movements in post-Napoleonic Germany for parliamentary government, written constitutions, and "a secular, liberal state based on the recognition of fundamental rights like freedom of movement, economic liberty and freedom of the press, constitutional guarantees for the independence of the courts, and trial by jury" found expression in the idea of the *Rechtsstaat*, as first imagined by Robert von Mohl, of whom more in Chapter 4.[52] It was the enlightened ideas of von Mohl and like-minded reformers that shaped Radbruch's postwar conception of the *Rechtsstaat*, and its antonym: the "*Unrechtsstaat*."[53] However, Radbruch's idea of the *Rechtsstaat* was an invented tradition of—and for—the postwar world. It served as an animating idea for the theory of democracy, and found its expression in Germany's postwar constitution. Few thinkers in late nineteenth and early twentieth century Germany thought a substantive conception of the *Rechtsstaat* like that in Article 20(3) of the *Grundgesetz* was either necessary or appropriate. For them, a *Rechtsstaat* was just that: a state of law, that is, a law-governed state in which public affairs were regulated by rules and regulations with no regard to their content. "The *Rechtsstaat* was, literally, a state that operated within the realm of legality. Historically, the concept of the *Rechtsstaat* was associated as well with an independent judiciary and a neutral and predictable set of procedures for applying the law. But the term is not identical with the English phrase 'rule of law.'"[54]

In the post-revolutionary world, law and morals came (once again) to be seen as ontologically distinct. As Rainer Grote writes, "The end of the nineteenth century [...] witnessed the gradual transformation of the concept of the '*Rechtsstaat*' into a mere principle of legality."[55] This fact is of crucial significance for understanding the transformation of law in the period 1933–1945. That a separation of law and morals was germane to German legal thought no-one expressed more forcefully than Hans Kelsen, who, in 1925, insisted it was "utterly nonsensical" ("*vollends sinnlos*") to claim that authoritarianism and law were incompatible:

> Even a despotically governed state represents a form of social order. [...] This order is a legal order. To deny its legal character is naïveté or an exaggeration owing to natural-law thinking. [...] What is interpreted as wanton rule is merely the authoritarian's legal authority to make all decisions, to determine unconditionally all behavior of subordinate organs, and to rescind or alter existing norms [...] at any time. Such an order is a legal order, even if it is perceived to be disadvantageous.[56]

This book seeks to prove Kelsen right for the case under investigation. When I speak of "the remnants of the *Rechtsstaat*," what I have in mind are legal practices and legal consciousness(es) carried forward from an *ancien régime* that continue to structure the politics of authoritarian rule. In the case of Nazi Germany, the preservation of such remnants of law was sometimes strategic, that is, intended by the country's self-styled revolutionaries; at other times, it was the result of habituation. For some practitioners, they were habits of the heart, the cultural remains of governing by way of rules rather than rifles—a sticky political practice that had become so pervasive in the late nineteenth century that it amounted to a veritable logic of rule, with long-run consequences for legal development.

By advancing an ideal theory of law, Radbruch obscured the persistence of legal practices in everyday life. This was likely not his intention. He only believed that "whole portions"—not the totality—of Nazi law were devoid of legal validity. Radbruch also did not think that evidence of injustice alone was sufficient to invalidate law. Lest such a determination unnecessarily create legal uncertainty, "[t]he positive law, secured by legislation and power, takes precedence even when its content is unjust and fails to benefit the people, unless the conflict between statute and justice reaches such an intolerable degree that the statute, as 'flawed law', must yield to justice."[57] Only in these exceptional circumstances, Radbruch argued, would law lose its validity and cease to be law, philosophically defined. In an attempt to salvage and improve Radbruch's formula, Robert Alexy has elaborated on the implication of this threshold condition, sometimes referred to as "the collapse thesis": "Even when a great many individual norms are denied legal character on the grounds of morality, including many that are important to the character of the system, even then the system can continue to exist as a legal system. This presupposes that a minimum complement of norms, the minimum necessary for the existence of a legal system, retain legal character."[58] This raises the question of how one is to measure the justice of a given legal system. Alexy has a solution:

> Take a legal system whose constitution empowers a dictator to issue norms without constraints. Thirty per cent of the norms issued by the dictator on the basis of this empowerment are unjust in the extreme, 20 per cent are unjust but not in the extreme, 20 per cent are neither unjust nor required by justice, and 30 per cent are required by justice. The 30 per cent that are unjust in the extreme are the norms that lend to the rogue system its specific character. The 30 per cent that are required by justice are, say, norms of contract law, tort law, and social security law. According to Radbruch's formula, legal character is to be denied only to that 30 per cent of norms that are unjust in the extreme. The formula does not apply to the remaining 70 per cent. Thus, the existence of the legal system would be endangered only if the 30 per cent of norms that are unjust in the extreme were to have such an effect on the empowering norm that, as a norm of extreme injustice, it forfeited its legal character over its entire range. For then the remaining 70 per cent of the norms of the system would also forfeit the basis of their validity. And then the legal system, as a hierarchically constructed system, would forfeit its existence and in this sense collapse.[59]

It is worth drawing attention to Radbruch's caveat that a substantial subset of Nazi legal practices likely amounted to law. This important qualification is often overlooked in critiques of his work. Given the prominence, at least in the English-speaking world, of the Hart-Fuller debate—for which Radbruch's formula gave the impetus—a simplified interpretation of Nazi law (and of Radbruch's formula) has seized the legal imagination.[60] Regardless, in everyday life, on the ground, in the cities and countryside, the law of Nazi Germany was a far more dynamic institution than Radbruch's philosophical account allows. Radbruch's failure to come to terms with the complexity of Nazi law reminds us of Neil MacCormick's quip that "the theorist's position is in the sense that of an outsider to any particular practice except that of theorising."[61] Ernst Fraenkel, a German labor lawyer of Jewish background, by contrast, was an insider. He showed us decades before anyone else would that Nazi law was neither stable nor were its institutional effects uniform. In this book, I tell the history of his forgotten theory. With it he brought into view the heterogeneity and changing character of law in the Third Reich. Developed in the mid-1930s, Fraenkel constructed his parsimonious, institutional theory of dictatorship on the foundation of some of the most daring field research ever undertaken.

INSIDE DICTATORSHIP

In the early years of Nazi rule Ernst Fraenkel set out to analyze—clandestinely—the logic of domination in the country of his birth, to make "a contribution," as he put it in *The Dual State* in 1941, "to the theory of dictatorship."[62] And a lasting contribution he did make. He may well have written the single-most important book on the topic to date. Though rarely invoked nowadays, Fraenkel's analytic narrative once was regarded as a canonical work in disciplines ranging from law to history, and from political science to sociology. It is unfortunate that *The Dual State* is largely forgotten these days because Fraenkel achieved the nigh impossible—he crafted a veritable ethnography of Nazi law. His singular achievement is not usually considered in anthropological terms, although it should be and I will.

As a field of study the anthropology of law emerged in the early twentieth century, although one of its earliest (now discredited) publications, by Sir Henry Maine, a former colonial official in Victorian Britain, actually dates back to the mid-nineteenth century.[63] The hallmark of the anthropological study of law remains ethnographic field research. Ethnographers of law pride themselves on understanding law—its agents, norms, customs, rules, procedures, institutions, organizations, discourses, practices—from the inside out. They "examine law as a social form, along with the assumptions and ideas that give it meaning."[64] The preferred method for this inquiry continues to be participant observation, which involves a researcher's immersion, over an extended period of time, in a legally relevant social setting to understand up close and personally the lifeworlds of the actors who inhabit it and the modes of their interaction. Its purpose is to describe and inscribe socially meaningful legal practices in an effort to convey their significance for the creation and maintenance of social order in a given, particular setting.[65] "Of fundamental importance to the ethnographic imagination," Paul Willis believes, "is comprehending creativities of the everyday as indissolubly connected to, dialectically and intrinsically, wider social structures, structural relations and structurally provided conditions of existence."[66]

Studying law in the field also means separating "the emic" from "the etic," that is, research subjects' own understandings of the world from the ethnographer's theoretical perspective. The legal anthropologist Paul Bohannan was more adamant than most in maintaining that the emic/etic distinction was of utmost methodological relevance to participant observation. As he put it in his most famous work, "the cardinal error of ethnographic and social analysis [...] [is] the grossly ethnocentric practice of raising folk-systems like 'the law,' designed for social action in one's own society, to the status of an analytical system, and then trying to organize the raw social data from other societies into its categories."[67] In other words, a scholar of the law of the Third Reich would be well advised not to mistake accounts derived from, say, Radbruch's formula for the reality of Nazi law.

Legal anthropologists are particularly interested in slippage between law's formalities and its realities. Fernanda Pirie, for one, believes that ethnographers of law "need to ask what it is about law that means it can be used to both exercise and resist power; how does it come to be turned back against those who would employ it to dominate and control?"[68] The kinds of answers that legal ethnographers give to these and related questions tend to look different than those produced in other fields, including legal philosophy, where alternative methodologies are preferred. As Pirie writes about her approach: "We are not seeking to perfect a philosophically refined model: we promise less than the legal theorist, but our accounts should be richer, more detailed, and more nuanced."[69] The legal historian Lawrence Friedman, not himself an ethnographer of law, described the analytical value of immersion aptly: "It is a technique of considering, observing, co-living with human beings of some society, or some piece of society. It uses a microscope, not a telescope."[70]

The Dual State sheds light on another cutting edge topic in the study of authoritarianism: the relationship between nondemocratic regimes and the production of knowledge. As Ariel Ahram and Paul Goode write, "authoritarian regimes constrain the selection of research tools and especially the conduct of fieldwork. The agnotological properties of authoritarian regimes generate three major challenges for research, relating to the practical question of access, the methodological question of data validity, and the ethical question of avoiding harm or damage to human sources."[71] Ernst Fraenkel considered, observed, and co-lived with those who regarded him as "the other" almost up until World War II. Like all of Germany's Jews, he was marked for defamation, discrimination, and, ultimately, destruction. Not all Germans wanted to see him dead, but there cannot have been much solace in this. An erstwhile insider, Fraenkel was reimagined as an outsider by almost everyone he met—neighbors, lawyers, strangers. He drafted the first iteration of *The Dual State* when he was at once insider and outsider. In those years he languished on the precipice of otherness, in a liminal state half way between his old identity and his new: allowed to practice law longer than other Jews on account of his military service in World War I, but still subject to the rest of the dehumanizing practices that the racial state had invented to violently torment the country's Jewish population. He was an outsider on the inside of Nazi dictatorship, a barely concealed thorn in its side. From this precarious position he embarked on long-term, focused participant observation of the law of the Third Reich, which makes his intellectual achievement even more remarkable. The analytical payoff was considerable, as I hope to demonstrate in this book. This is not entirely surprising, for as Friedman reminds us,

> One of classic ethnography's greatest contributions to our understanding of human societies was its outsider perspective: a stranger's cool, impassive, sympathetic view of life inside some community or culture. Each culture no doubt guards some secrets from the outside; each has a kind of wordless language that no stranger can ever hope to penetrate. There are, in other words, *limits*, borders, frontiers, that no ethnographer can pass. But there is far more that can and will yield to objective research. The best of the classic anthropologists were very skilled at deciphering the codes of a culture and transmitting their knowledge to the world at large.[72]

Friedman almost certainly did not have Nazi Germany's *Volksgemeinschaft* in mind when he wrote the above lines, but he might as well have, for some of the limits that Fraenkel encountered in the mid-1930s were not dissimilar to those any anthropologist in an unfamiliar culture faces, except that the stakes for Fraenkel were infinitely higher than they are for most of us studying law in the field. *The Dual State*, then, is not just a major contribution to the theory of dictatorship but also a feat of extraordinary human courage.

The innovative nature of Fraenkel's endeavor is even more striking, methodologically speaking, if we consider that the anthropology of law had only just been invented (and probably without his realizing) when he opted to become, by necessity more than choice, a participant observer of Nazi legal practices.

Bronislaw Malinowski, widely regarded as the founding father of cultural anthropology, had only just published his landmark studies of the Trobriand Islanders, *Argonauts of the Western Pacific* and *Crime and Custom in Savage Society*, in 1922 and 1926 respectively.[73] The former is widely regarded as the first ever ethnography of any kind, the latter as the first ever ethnography of law.[74] In *Argonauts of the Western Pacific*, Malinowski famously described the essentials of the emergent ethnographic method:

> First of all he [the researcher] has to find out that certain activities, which at first sight may seem incoherent and not correlated, have a meaning. He then has to find out what is constant and relevant in these activities, and what accidental and inessential, that is to find out the laws and rules of all the transactions. [...] [T]he Ethnographer has to *construct* the picture of the big institution, very much as the physicist constructs his theory from the experimental data, which always have been within reach of everybody, but needed a consistent interpretation.[75]

Malinowski believed that if scholars studied the "imponderabilia of everyday life," they would acquire a new way of seeing, a tool with which to take the measure of the world more meaningfully—and thus more accurately.

Without realizing it, Fraenkel was following in the footsteps of Malinowski. It was a case of methodological learning by doing. Unwittingly, he advanced legal anthropology. Yet throughout his life, he remained unaware of this contribution. Up until now he has never been credited for it. The first generations of anthropologists of law habitually looked outward—toward "savage" or otherwise ostensibly "primitive" societies—rather than inward, to their own polities.[76] Perhaps this is the reason why there is no mention of Fraenkel in the annals of anthropology. But like the best ethnographers of the twentieth century, he was adept at making the strange familiar, and the familiar strange, in his first, all-important book.

Fraenkel's use of court records as ethnographic data is methodologically innovative even by twenty-first century standards. In addition to "the insights into the functioning of the Hitler regime that I gleaned from my legal practice," Fraenkel in the 1930s relied on "hard-to-find judgments that had been published in official law reports and learned journals to see whether they offered insights into *societal* ('*gesellschaftliche*') processes in the Third Reich, which, in turn, would allow for the drawing of inferences about the everyday practices of the statist ('*staatlichen*') organs of the National Socialist executive and judiciary" and combined this with his observational data.[77] He thereby made a lasting contribution to legal anthropology, for as Pirie recently complained, "textual laws have rarely been at the heart of anthropological studies" even though they "constitute an important set of resources through which people make sense of their worlds, and for the anthropologist [...] provide rich material with which to explore the nature of law."[78] Sally Engle Merry, a few years earlier, had published a similar critique, presenting a methodological case for "doing ethnography in the archives."[79] As she wrote: "Ethnography in the archives means setting the caseloads of the courts in the context of the people who were running them, and those caught in them, as well as within the context of broader economic and political changes."[80] But what exactly does this methodological technique entail, and why is it superior to conventional approaches in legal anthropology? Merry's argument is simple:

> [I]n order to investigate social change, archival research is essential. Historical data provides clear evidence of changes in the kinds of problems in court[s] and links these changes to shifts in the personnel running the courts and the political currents of the time. [...] An historical approach is necessary to demonstrate the linkages between court processes and the changing social order. On the other hand, ethnography is necessary to situate these changes in a local place and with a cast of characters. An ethnographic approach to history unveils everyday behavior rather than only dramatic historical events taking place in capital cities. Much as [Michel] Foucault argues for attention to the microphysics of power embedded in the margins and interstices of institutions, ethnography based on archives such as court records [...] provides a way of looking at the everyday exercise of power and resistance.[81]

Fraenkel was one of the first-ever legal ethnographers of the archive. Because he studied the imponderabilia of everyday life in *both* the courtroom *and* the archive—he was well ahead of his time. He contextualized Nazi law like none of his contemporaries managed to, and very few—if any—scholars have done since. Numerous examples exist of more comprehensive, more fine-grained, more up-to-date, or more theoretical treatments of Nazi law, but none to date has integrated theory, history, and practice as compellingly as *The Dual State* in 1941. It is for this reason that Fraenkel, not Radbruch, should be our guide through the thicket of Nazi law.

Because Fraenkel's approach was factual, not formulaic, it has largely stood the test of time. Lest I be misunderstood, although I consider Fraenkel's intellectual achievement to be greater (albeit less influential) than Radbruch's, the relationship between legal philosophy and legal anthropology is not zero-sum. Radbruch's formula and Fraenkel's ethnography—the nomothetic and the ideographic—can be profitably *combined* in attempts to make sense of law's role(s) in the Third Reich. Legal anthropologists "produce accounts that are less philosophically tidy, but detailed and nuanced, and these, in turn, enrich the empirical material available to philosophers of law."[82] Fraenkel's ethnography of Nazi law is rich in examples that would undoubtedly lend themselves to a philosophical restatement of Radbruch's famous formula.

I do not with this book propose to make such a contribution, however. My objectives, rather, are these: (1) to craft an intellectual history of Fraenkel's theory of dictatorship; (2) to take seriously the Nazi concept of law and chart its development in theory and practice; (3) to shed light on the formation and deformation of the *Rechtsstaat*, this misunderstood pendant to the idea of the rule of law; (4) to contribute to the literature on nondemocratic regimes in political science by making the concept of the dual state usable for the twenty-first century; and (5) to advance the idea of the authoritarian rule of law.

Fraenkel's closely observed, institutional analysis is not only essential to the long-standing and continuing debate over the legal origins of Nazi dictatorship—which, as I explain in the next chapter, is a part of the larger debate over the nature of the Nazi state—it also has much to offer the study of the rule of law and its promotion, especially given the rise of authoritarian legalism, a topic of growing interest in law-and-society scholarship with obvious policy implications.[83] I therefore develop in this book an argument for bringing the dual state back in, for reconfiguring it as a conceptual variable in the study of nondemocratic regimes. Because transitions to authoritarian rule are once again on the rise in both the industrialized and developing world, the imperative to grasp the institutional logic(s) of nondemocratic regimes is an urgent, policy-relevant one.[84] The historical institutional analysis of legal norms and institutions is particularly relevant given "the revival of the use of law in international politics," especially since the end of the Cold War, a development that is sometimes described as the rise of legalization in the international system.[85] Cognizant of this trend, I have positioned this book at the intersection of law and the social sciences. Cutting across disciplines and sub-fields, and eventually also space and time, I blend legal theory and intellectual history as well as insights from the various new institutionalisms to make a contribution to the study of authoritarian rule—then and now.[86] If recent scholarship is to be believed, "the new cutting edge" of this literature "is dissecting the authoritarian genus."[87] Fraenkel's ethnography of law speaks uniquely to this agenda. I extrapolate from its theory and findings and develop a new subtype of authoritarianism suitable for comparative historical analysis.

OUTCOME KNOWLEDGE

The Dual State is worth revisiting for many reasons, but one stands out. Like Karl Schleunes's pioneering *The Twisted Road to Auschwitz*, first published in 1970, Fraenkel's erstwhile classic sensitizes us to the problem of outcome knowledge in historical analysis.[88] Investigations that are anchored in outcome knowledge run the risk of distorting the interaction effects in social life among agents, preferences, strategies, and outcomes. Experimental research has shown that subjects tend to overestimate what they would have known without outcome knowledge as well as what others actually did know without outcome knowledge.[89] This hindsight bias has been shown to be responsible not only for misunderstanding the past, but also for drawing inappropriate lessons from a misconstrued past for the future.[90] Whenever outcomes are perceived as having been inevitable, teleological explanations result. What were twisted paths in real life are analytically straightened. Empirical complexity is reduced and contingent outcomes are reframed, and misleadingly so, as deterministic outcomes.

By re-reading Fraenkel, and by comparing his account in *The Dual State* with those published in the wake of war and genocide, it becomes apparent that most of the postwar studies of the transition to authoritarian rule in Weimar Germany—and the concomitant destruction of the *Rechtsstaat*—have been clouded by outcome knowledge. Like the evolution of the Holocaust, the rise and expansion of Nazi dictatorship was neither inevitable nor smooth. A twisted road led not only to Auschwitz, but also to the totalitarian state that made the destruction of the European Jews conceivable in the first place. As the late Hans Mommsen observed, "Not until November 1938 did Hitler decide in favor of a centralized and coordinated procedure in the Jewish question."[91] The year 1938, to which I will return repeatedly in this book, represents a critical juncture in the transition from authoritarianism to totalitarianism in Nazi Germany. This transition was structurally contingent on the institutional reconfiguration of the racialized polity. Its transformation from a dual state into a totalitarian state meant that the institutional determinants of Nazi behavior were *fundamentally different* in the period 1939–1945 than in the years 1933–1938.

The Dual State continues to make for fascinating reading because it is not clouded by outcome knowledge. At the time of his participant observation in Nazi courtrooms, Fraenkel had no way of knowing that the dictatorship he was studying in secret would turn into what his law partner, Franz Neumann, in 1942, likened to a "behemoth," the mythical beast described in Job 40:15-24.[92] *The Dual State* reminds us that the institutional transformation of the Nazi state was non-linear. It was not at all obvious in the mid-1930s that the authoritarian regime that persecuted the Jews of Germany would turn into a fully-fledged genocidal regime.[93] Historical institutionalists for decades now have insisted that specifying why particular paths were *not* taken is methodologically as important as tracing the actual course of history. Revisiting Mommsen's explanation of democratic breakdown in interwar Germany, the historian Eric Weitz has rightly observed that in his colleague's influential account "the republic appears dreary from the outset, and everyone feels beleaguered. [...] One reads *The Rise and Fall of Weimar Democracy* hoping for some evaluation of possibilities, of the roads not taken, yet it never comes."[94] Peter Fritzsche reached a similar conclusion about Mommsen's deterministic account: "[F]or most German historians the plot that holds the story together has been fragile democracy and its demise. 'Weimar' is, as numerous subtitles inform us, the 'history of the first German Democracy,' the site where democracy surrendered or failed. The drama of twentieth-century Germany has largely turned on the failure of the Weimar Republic."[95] With Weitz and Fritzsche, I believe it is essential for scholars not just to assert this failure but to account for it; to reconstruct the road from constitutional to genocidal dictatorship with an acute awareness of the challenges involved in working with outcome knowledge.

On September 20, 1938, Fraenkel fled the Nazi dictatorship.[96] Three years later, from the safety of his exile in the United States, he published, with Oxford University Press, an English-language edition of his pioneering account about the complicated relationship between legalism and authoritarianism in the early years of Hitler's Germany. Fraenkel had secretly drafted the original manuscript in Germany between 1936 and 1938. Because of these clandestine origins, one commentator recently described *The Dual State* as "the ultimate piece of intellectual resistance" to the Nazi regime.[97] An ethnography of law crafted in the most forbidding of circumstances, *The Dual State* was the first comprehensive, institutional analysis of the rise and nature of National Socialism, and it was the only such analysis written from within Germany. Fraenkel's dispassionate analysis chronicled the long and winding denaturation of the *Rechtsstaat*, which brings me once again to Roland Freisler.

Freisler and Fraenkel represent two very different faces of the Third Reich. Like Fraenkel, Freisler grew up in northern Germany. He, too, served in World War I, was briefly under the spell of Marxism, and the law also became his vocation. But differences in Freisler and Fraenkel's intellectual socialization and professional ambitions catapulted one into the Nazi regime and the other into the intellectual resistance. They travelled along paths that could not have been more divergent: the one hell-bent on racializing the *Rechtsstaat*, the other risking his life to make use of its surviving remnants. By the time Hitler appointed Freisler to the *Volksgerichtshof*, on August 20, 1942, to succeed Otto Georg Thierack—who replaced Franz Schlegelberger as Reich minister of justice—the *Rechtsstaat* was a mere shell of its former self. Key planks had been removed and dismantled. Fraenkel was safe in the United States.

During his march in goose-step through the Nazi institutions, Freisler had quickened his step. He played an ever more visible role in the transition from authoritarianism to totalitarianism in Nazi Germany, as his role in the Wannsee Conference of January 20, 1942, at which he provided expert advice on the legal dimensions of making genocide work, attests.[98] He had arrived where he longed to be. By now a faithful and ardent servant of the prerogative state, for Freisler the judicial robe was no longer symbol but disguise. His arrival at the helm of the *Volksgerichtshof* ushered the country into a veritable age of lawlessness. The "islands of 'injustice'" that some, like Stolleis, saw floating in the early years of Nazi dictatorship "within a system that, on the whole, still functioned as 'law,'" had grown into an archipelago.[99] Yet notwithstanding the supremacy and expansion of the prerogative state in the 1940s, and despite the verbal tirades that made infamous Freisler's performances at the helm of Nazi Germany's most politicized court, the normative state did not entirely disappear. It continued to exercise a modicum of authority and control, also in wartime. Occasionally it even interfered with the all-powerful prerogative state. Why these remnants of the *Rechtsstaat* survived, and how they mattered, is the subject of this book.

OVERVIEW OF THE BOOK

The book is organized into seven substantive chapters on the law of the Third Reich, its logic, antecedents, and aftermath. They are framed by an extended introduction and elaborate conclusion that look farther afield and situate my undertaking theoretically, relating ethnography to philosophy (this chapter), and the past to the present (Chapter 9). The empirical chapters oscillate between intellectual biography and legal history. The red thread connecting them is Fraenkel's institutional theory of dictatorship, on which I rely to build the microfoundations for the metatheoretical arguments that I critique in this book.

Chapter 2 accounts for the neglect of law in the historiography of the Third Reich, which it traces to the success of Franz Neumann's *Behemoth*, first published in 1942. Through a sustained critique of Neumann's political economy of dictatorship, I show that his argument about the ostensible lawlessness of Hitler's rule gave rise in the 1950s and 1960s to an intellectual trajectory in scholarship on the Third Reich that has done a fair amount to obscure—rather than illuminate—the logic of Nazi dictatorship. Chapter 3 turns from Neumann to Fraenkel. The chapter provides the biographical and historical context necessary for understanding the author of *The Dual State* and his time. I trace Fraenkel's upbringing in a secular household influenced by the *Haskalah*, the so-called Jewish Enlightenment, explain his life-long predilection for social democracy, and reconstruct his education and socialization as a young lawyer. Through a close reading of Fraenkel's most important Weimar-era writings, I reconstruct the intellectual antecedents of *The Dual State*. The analysis provides clues as to why Fraenkel, in the 1930s, turned to what we now call historical institutionalism whereas Neumann gravitated toward historical materialism.

Chapter 4 surveys the long and winding history of the idea of the *Rechtsstaat*, laying additional groundwork for the analysis to come. I trace the evolution of the term from its emergence in the late eighteenth century until 1933. In my intellectual history of the *Rechtsstaat*, I relate the ideas of Immanuel Kant to those of Adam Müller and Carl Theodor Welcker; juxtapose the legal thought of Robert von Mohl and that of Friedrich Julius Stahl and Rudolf Gneist; consider the role of Carl Friedrich von Gerber, Paul Laband, and Georg Jellinek in the legal theory of empire; and introduce readers to Weimar legal thought by comparing and contrasting ideas about the *Rechtsstaat* by some of that era's most glittering thinkers: Hans Kelsen, Hermann Heller, Carl Schmitt, and Rudolf Smend, among others. This sketch of the *Rechtsstaat*'s intellectual foundations and discursive development sets the stage for my analysis in the next chapter of the concept's manipulation by legal theorists in Nazi Germany. Chapter 5 is an account of Nazi legalism. I reconstruct a little known, but telling, debate among Nazi theorists and practitioners of law about the nature and virtues of the *Rechtsstaat*. I find that the debate is indicative of a degree of legal consciousness in the Third Reich, which, in turn, is useful for explaining why, and, how, remnants of the *Rechtsstaat* mattered in the transition to authoritarian rule.[100]

Relying on primary documents, Chapter 6 reconstructs the gestation of the first, German-language manuscript of *The Dual State*, known as the *Urdoppelstaat* of 1938, and charts the transformation of this unpublished manuscript into the 1941 book. The analysis shows that Neumann and Fraenkel, erstwhile law partners in Berlin, arrived at increasingly divergent interpretations of the Nazi dictatorship. Whereas Neumann radicalized his argument as time went on, Fraenkel toned down his, largely eschewing the moralizing commentary that runs like a red thread through *Behemoth*. Chapter 7 turns from the making of *The Dual State* to the findings of the ethnography of law that it houses. Through a critical engagement with the strengths—and weaknesses—of Fraenkel's pioneering analysis, I prepare the ground for the extensions of (and friendly amendments to) his institutional theory of dictatorship that I offer in my treatment of the authoritarian rule of law (see Chapter 9). Chapter 8 explores the uneven reception of Fraenkel's classic, with particular reference to the book's fortunes in the United States and postwar Germany. I account for the international recognition bestowed on Fraenkel in the early 1940s, and its subsequent status as an obligatory, but rarely noticed footnote—a forgotten classic. In Chapter 9, I consider the theoretical and empirical significance of my analysis by turning from the twentieth century to the twenty-first. In addition to this temporal leap, I make another: from the *Rechtsstaat* to the rule of law. I reconfigure the concept of the dual state and relate it to the idea of the authoritarian rule of law. Through a series of empirical vignettes, I show that Fraenkel's ethnography of Nazi law is relevant beyond borders. What I offer is an in-depth concept analysis of the idea of the authoritarian rule of law. Mine is a tentative effort to make the unwieldy term usable for comparative historical research.

Born of analytical eclecticism, this book, like the concept at its heart, is of a hybrid nature. In part intellectual biography, in part legal history, and grounded in legal and institutional theory, it is the result of my desire to put Ernst Fraenkel on a pedestal. I have felt for a long time that it is a sad irony that Carl Schmitt's oeuvre has been studied ad nauseam, while the work of one of his most learned, Jewish interlocutors is virtually unknown.[101] I have derived some consolation from the fact that Judith Shklar, the eminent theorist of legalism, also deeply admired *The Dual State*, remarking in 1987 that it was "one of the few older studies of the Third Reich that remain valid."[102] By situating Fraenkel's ethnography of law in the historiography of the Third Reich as well as in the new institutionalism in the social sciences, mine is an attempt to resurrect a theoretically sophisticated, methodologically innovative theory of dictatorship, one with immediate relevance for coming to terms with twenty-first century authoritarianism. But it is not just that. This book is also an effort to stem the tide of forgetting the guardians of the *Rechtsstaat* in the 1930s, these defenders of light in a dark time. Ernst Fraenkel served valiantly in a forlorn army of fearless jurists. For this contribution alone he is deserving of our respect and remembrance.

2

Behemoth and Beyond

There is no single phenomenon in our time
so important for us to understand
as the one which identified itself in Germany
during the 1920s, 30s and 40s as
National Socialism.

Karl A. Schleunes[1]

It is difficult to overstate the appeal
of a two-dimensional portrait of Nazi power
based entirely on brute force applied ruthlessly
against the will of all people.
This simplified version of the Reich
is illustrated all around [...].

Nathan Stoltzfus[2]

Few issues in the historiography of the Third Reich have provoked as much ire and acrimony in the academy as the debate over the nature of the Nazi state. Sir Ian Kershaw, in his preface to the latest edition of *The Nazi Dictatorship*, revisited an infamous conference at Cumberland Lodge, where, in 1979, leading English and German historians had gathered to compare research findings on what was known as the *Führerstaat*, or Hitler state. Those who had made their way to Windsor Great Park were at loggerheads over the question of how exactly to categorize the supremely violent, institutional entity that Hitler's ambitions had spawned over the course of his twelve-year rule. Agreement was not to be had. Kershaw previously pointed to "chasmic divisions of interpretation among leading historians."[3] It appears irreconcilable views provoked vociferous arguments. "The intensity and vehemence of the discussions at the Cumberland Lodge conference struck me forcibly," Kershaw recalled.[4] "These were heated, uncompromising and sharply

The Remnants of the Rechtsstaat: An Ethnography of Nazi Law. Jens Meierhenrich.

polarized exchanges which went to the heart of attempts to understand the Nazi regime."[5]

With the retirement or passing of leading members of this first generation of historians of Nazi dictatorship—Karl Dietrich Bracher, Martin Broszat, Saul Friedländer, Tim Mason, Hans Mommsen, Detlev Peukert—many erstwhile "chasmic divisions" have been bridged, or at least narrowed. More recent generations of historians of the Third Reich, among them Christopher Browning, Jane Caplan, Richard Evans, Robert Gellately, Ulrich Herbert, Ian Kershaw, Claudia Koonz, Michael Wildt, and Nikolaus Wachsmann, have approached the subject matter with a greater detachment, an achievement undoubtedly made possible by their biographical remove from the violent conflagration of the 1930s and 1940s.[6]

Although tempers rarely flare anymore when historians of Nazi Germany gather, this does not mean that the debate over the nature of the phenomenon of National Socialism has been settled. Scholars continue to argue over the terms and concepts most—and least—appropriate for capturing the anatomy of Nazi dictatorship. This book contributes to the debate by focusing on one determinant of Nazi dictatorship that was absent entirely from the proceedings at Cumberland Lodge, and which influential analyses by leading historians continue to ignore into the present—the institution of law. Although Broszat in his classic, if controversial, study of the Nazi state devoted an entire chapter to the legal foundations of dictatorship, the large majority of scholars of the Third Reich, with the exception of legal historians such as Lothar Gruchmann, a doctoral student of Fraenkel's, and Martin Stolleis, have paid scant attention to the role of legal norms and institutions in the transition to authoritarianism and eventually to totalitarianism in Germany.[7]

Kershaw's aforementioned textbook, now in its fifth edition, neither addresses the contribution of law to Nazi dictatorship, nor has it made an appearance in Jane Caplan's useful collections, *Reevaluating the Third Reich*, which she co-edited with Thomas Childers, and *Nazi Germany*, a volume in the "Short Oxford Histories" series.[8] But the institution of law is not just missing from introductory volumes. Major works on the Third Reich have also ignored it. It is absent from Peter Fritzsche's *Life and Death in the Third Reich* as well as from Richard J. Evans's *The Third Reich in Power 1933-1939*, and it plays but a minor role in Hans-Ulrich Wehler's *Der Nationalsozialismus* and in Thomas Childers's survey *The Third Reich*. Two of the few books to have addressed the topic in more depth are Robert Gellately's *Backing Hitler* and Claudia Koonz's *The Nazi Conscience*.[9] Yet these scholars' treatments of law are incidental to their respective research designs. The widespread neglect of law in the study of the Third Reich has to do in part with the tremendous success of Franz Neumann's *Behemoth*, first published in 1942, and in an enlarged edition in 1944.[10]

The rise of *Behemoth* corresponded directly with the decline of *The Dual State* in the final war and early postwar years. I devote an entire chapter to the argument and reception of Neumann's book for two reasons. First, *Behemoth*, which has never gone out of print, exemplifies major shortcomings—theoretical, empirical, methodological—in early studies of Nazi rule. I argue that it gave rise in the 1950s and 1960s to an intellectual trajectory in scholarship on the Third Reich that has done a fair amount to obscure—rather than illuminate—the logic of Nazi dictatorship, including law's role in it. Reductionist perspectives like Neumann's continue to hold sway today, but a less dogmatic approach is called for, especially when it comes to making sense of authoritarian rule at home: "While his dictatorship murdered millions in the name of ideology, Hitler managed his relationship with the Germans of the Reich in ways that place him among those whom scholars now identify as 'soft' dictators, who prefer the tactics of persuasion, enticement, cooptation, and compromise to work their will."[11]

The law was one instrument in Hitler's strategy of conflict. But the reasons why remnants of the *Rechtsstaat* survived, and structured authoritarian politics, have to do not just with means and ends, but also with norms and values. Law was a weapon, but it also was a tradition. I will show in Chapter 5 that some Nazis were more reluctant than others to abandon what they had learned to respect. This does not mean that the nineteenth-century tradition of the *Rechtsstaat* survived the Nazi revolution. It did not. But a subset of its norms and institutions left a mark on the dictatorship for longer than conventional wisdom would have us believe. As Nathan Stoltzfus has shown, "Hitler's willingness to compromise with the people, particularly when the people were drawing upon their traditions, continued up until some point very late in the war when he became convinced that Germany would be forced to surrender unconditionally."[12]

A close reading of *Behemoth* also illuminates the personal relationship and intellectual affinities between Fraenkel and Neumann. Business partners at *Fraenkel & Neumann*, their Berlin-based law firm, until Neumann's sudden and involuntary emigration to London in May 1933, the two close friends for several years fought as comrades-in-arms in the struggle to defend Weimar democracy. My analysis of the gestation of *Behemoth* shows why, how, and when the two friends nonetheless arrived at vastly divergent interpretations of the phenomenon of National Socialism.

THE POLITICAL ECONOMY OF DICTATORSHIP

Fraenkel's *The Dual State*, released by Oxford University Press in 1941, was the first learned and comprehensive analysis of the Nazi state. In the historiography of the Third Reich, Neumann's *Behemoth* soon eclipsed it. The memorable metaphor of the behemoth conjured an image of institutional anarchy in Germany that proved irresistible, especially abroad. Neumann came up with the language of the "non-state" to capture the extent of the lawlessness that he saw.[13] Here is how Neumann explained his book's pithy title:

> In the Jewish eschatology—of Babylonian origin—Behemoth and Leviathan are two monsters, Behemoth ruling the land (the desert), Leviathan the sea, the first male, the second female. [. . .] Both are monsters of the Chaos. [. . .] St. Augustine saw in the Behemoth the Satan. It was [Thomas] Hobbes who made both the Leviathan and the Behemoth popular. His *Leviathan* is the analysis of a state, that is a political system of coercion in which the vestiges of the rule of law and of individual rights are still preserved. His *Behemoth*, or the *Long Parliament*, however, discussing the English civil war of the seventeenth century, depicts a non-state, a chaos, a situation of lawlessness, disorder, and anarchy. Since we believe National Socialism is—or tending to become—a non-state, a chaos, a rule of lawlessness and anarchy, [. . .] we find it apt to call the National Socialist system *The Behemoth*.[14]

Unlike Fraenkel, Neumann denied that law mattered, that it could be analytically relevant for making sense of Nazi dictatorship. It was not a variable worth taking seriously in his view.[15] He claimed it had neither an enabling nor a constraining effect on political outcomes: "It has been maintained that National Socialism is a dual state, that is, in fact, one state within which two systems are operating, one under normative law, the other under individual measures, one rational, the other the realm of prerogative. We do not share this view because we believe that there is no realm of law in Germany, although there are thousands of technical rules that are calculable."[16]

This book seeks to prove Neumann wrong. I show that his account of the structure and practice of "the phenomenon of National Socialism," as Schleunes called it, is deeply flawed. Neumann erected a rickety theoretical argument on a weak empirical foundation. An unreliable structure for interpretation, it distorted for years the truth about the destruction of the *Rechtsstaat* in Nazi Germany—and the impact of its surviving remnants on everyday life. Neumann's failing would be negligible were it not for the fact that his book made a splash, especially in policy circles. It was the talk of the town in Washington, D.C., where it influenced quite significantly U.S. planning for the military occupation of a defeated Germany. *Behemoth* was "a book that had consequences," is how the historian Peter Hayes has put it:

> In 1943–1945, while Neumann was serving in Washington, D.C., in the Office of Strategic Services, the forerunner of the Central Intelligence Agency, his work strongly influenced the formulation of America's goals for postwar Germany as the "four Ds," each directed at one of the colluding groups he had highlighted: denazification, democratization (including the recruitment and training of civil servants), demilitarization, and decartelization. Immediately after the war, when Neumann was a member of the prosecution staff preparing the Nuremberg Trials of major war criminals, *Behemoth* stamped both the conception of the American case and the organization of its supporting documents.[17]

What, exactly, was Neumann's argument? And what accounts for the tremendous impact of *Behemoth*—and the corresponding decline in the reception of *The Dual State* that, on my argument, it hastened?[18]

In *Behemoth*, Neumann developed a political economy of dictatorship. Unlike more recent approaches to the political economy of dictatorship, almost all of which are based on rational-choice assumptions, Neumann's was indebted to the Marxist understanding of political economy.[19] What positive and normative approaches to political economy have in common is their treatment of economic ideas and behavior not as beliefs and actions to be explained but as independent variables.[20] Their major difference is ontological: rational-choice theorists are beholden to methodological individualism, critical theorists like Neumann are wedded to methodological structuralism.[21] What their 1930s representatives, from Friedrich Pollock and Max Horkheimer to Neumann and Otto Kirchheimer, believed central to accounting for the political and economic malaise of the interwar period was "an epochal transformation of capitalism": "The general analysis by these theorists of contemporary historical changes in the relation of state and society was, in part, consonant with mainstream Marxist thought. The new centralized bureaucratized configuration of polity and society was seen as a necessary historical outcome of liberal capitalism, even if this configuration negated the liberal order that generated it."[22] The principal argument in *Behemoth* reflects this general way of seeing the world.

Neumann argued that the Nazi dictatorship could only be grasped if its economic determinants were foregrounded in any explanatory account. But not just any economic interpretation would do. For Neumann, the Third Reich was the natural and "pragmatic" outgrowth of a particular variety of capitalism: monopoly capitalism.[23] He identified the monopolization of business and the cartelization of politics as the twin social mechanisms that gave birth to the Nazi behemoth.[24] The interaction of business and politics resulted in a dual economy: "It is a monopolistic economy—*and* a command economy. It is a private capitalistic economy, regimented by the totalitarian state. We suggest as a name best to describe it, 'Totalitarian Monopoly Capitalism.' "[25] What Neumann sketched was a far-reaching structural transformation of the economic sphere, one that gave rise to a self-reinforcing dictatorship. A new kind of enemy, he was certain, was presiding over this dictatorship.

Neumann's behemoth was hydra-headed. Four "totalitarian bodies" conspired to dominate "over the ruled classes": the Nazi party, the bureaucracy, the military, and big business.[26] What has been referred to as "[a] sort of institutional Darwinism" governed the operation of this "cartel."[27] "[T]he whole of society is organized in four solid, centralized groups, each operating under the leadership principle, each with a legislative, administrative, and judicial power of its own."[28] Unsurprisingly, given his premise, Neumann found it "difficult to give the name state to four groups entering into a bargain."[29]

What did the monopolists want? For Neumann the answer was obvious. Corporations and companies like Flick, Thyssen, Krupp, Quandt, Mannesmann, Reemtsma, and the like were utility-maximizers. The utility they wanted to maximize was profit. Theirs was a quest for absolute *and* relative gains, which is why, according to Neumann, "big business" as a collective agent of the four-power cartel had no compunction about sacrificing morality for the economy. If we believe Neumann, it was solely the distribution of power among interacting agents in this domestic system that governed politics and society in the "Third Reich." No sovereign reigned supreme: "There is no need for a state standing above all groups; the state may even be a hindrance to the compromises and to domination over the ruled classes. [...] It is thus impossible to detect in the framework of the National Socialist political system any organ which monopolizes political power."[30] Jürgen Bast has proposed the apt term "totalitarian pluralism" to describe the theoretical model presented in *Behemoth*.[31]

In Neumann's institutional analysis, Hitler was not the *Führer*, the omnipotent leader, but *primus inter pares*. He was one power broker among four: "The decisions of the Leader are merely the result of the compromises among the four leaderships."[32] For Neumann, as Chris Thornhill has pointed out, the Nazi dictatorship was "not political at all, but a mere sporadic refraction of economic interests. It [...] triumphed because of the absence, not the primacy, of the political."[33]

With his argument Neumann challenged conventional wisdom on the left. His principal target was Pollock whose argument at the time was dominating the conversation among the Frankfurt School theorists in American exile. "Whereas Neumann saw National Socialism as a totalitarian form of monopoly capitalism, Pollock thought that it had [...] mutated into a state capitalism with the attendant central features of vast state planning buttressed by an all-powerful bureaucracy."[34] Neumann was not convinced that the neologism "state capitalism" at all captured what was going on in Nazi Germany. Moreover, he thought the concept was a contradiction in terms. He believed it was nonsensical to describe in economic categories a political order in which the state was the sole owner of the means of production. In support, he invoked Eberhard Barth, a civil servant in the *Reichswirtschaftsministerium*, the Nazi ministry of economic affairs: "Once the state has become the sole owner of the means of production, it makes it impossible for a capitalist economy to function, it destroys the mechanism which keeps the very processes of economic circulation in active existence."[35] Added Neumann: "Such a state is therefore no longer capitalistic. It may be called a slave state or a managerial dictatorship [...], that is, it must be described in political and not in economic categories."[36]

This brings us back to the corporatist element in Neumann's political economy of dictatorship: the institution of the cartel. Neumann, in sharp contrast to Pollock, believed the capitalism of old continued to govern in Nazi Germany, though less unfettered than under "democratic monopoly capitalism."[37] As he put it in *Behemoth*, "Entrepreneurial initiative is not dead; it is as vital as ever before and perhaps even more so."[38] But to what end was the capitalist machinery running? Neumann was convinced that the four members of the cartel that constituted the Nazi behemoth had but one ambition—to wage expansionist war:

> National Socialism has co-ordinated the diversified and contradictory state interferences into one system having but one aim: the preparation for imperialist war. [...] With regard to imperialist expansion, National Socialism and big business have identical interests. National Socialism pursues glory and the stabilization of its rule, and industry, the full utilization of its capacity and the conquest of foreign markets. [...] National Socialism utilized the daring, the knowledge, the aggressiveness of the industrial leadership, while the industrial leadership utilized the anti-democracy, anti-liberalism and anti-unionism of the National Socialist party, which had fully developed the techniques by which masses can be controlled and dominated.[39]

Neumann made a distinctive and still influential contribution to the political economy of dictatorship.[40] Unfortunately, the validity of his argument has been widely called into question, especially insofar as it relates to the role of business in the Third Reich. Hayes, who has made major contributions to this line of scholarship, is blunt in his critique of *Behemoth*:

> Neumann was inclined not only to conflate outcomes and causes but also on occasion to misrepresent even the evidence he had. Historians now generally concur that German corporate leaders played little part in bringing Hitler to power except insofar as they helped create and prolong the economic catastrophe from which he profited politically. Specialists also agree that German industry and finance adapted their business strategies to the goals of Hitler's foreign policy, rather than vice versa; the pursuit of living space was his, not their, idea. Thus, though Neumann was no doubt right to emphasize that the productive power of German industry became one of the pillars of the Third Reich, and that the importance of that power gave business a strong bargaining position on some matters of policy, he goes too far when he depicts business as an equal partner of the Nazi state and party.[41]

The gist of extant critiques: Neumann's political economy of dictatorship suffers from structural determinism to such an extent that the thrust of his theoretical argument is all but impossible to sustain empirically. Appropriately, Alfons Söllner has described the period 1933–1942, in which the ideas expressed in *Behemoth* took shape, as Neumann's "materialist decade."[42] The label draws our attention to the book's strong Marxist undercurrents—and to what I analyze in the next section as Neumann's *radical legalism*. They have left indelible blemishes on his political economy of dictatorship. Like Pollock's approach, to which it is often compared, *Behemoth* has "the unintended heuristic value of revealing the problematic character of traditional Marxist presuppositions."[43] It advanced critical theory but contributed little to our knowledge about the Nazi dictatorship. And, as we shall see, Neumann's take on the law of the Third Reich was even more problematic than his account of its economics.

RADICAL LEGALISM

Despite Neumann's dismissal of *The Dual State*, Fraenkel was kind in his public assessment of *Behemoth*. In fact, he was downright effusive in his praise for his former business partner. In a review for the *Neue Volks-Zeitung*, published on May 16, 1942, Fraenkel elevated Neumann's book to the status of an instant classic, declaring it an "encyclopedia of National Socialism."[44] He applauded the "tremendously clear x-ray image" ("*ungemein klare Röntgenaufnahme*") of the dictatorship that his friend had supposedly produced.[45] But Fraenkel was not shy either about making his reservations publicly known. He chided Neumann for the excessive amount of descriptive material that he felt cluttered *Behemoth*. Fraenkel bemoaned that Neumann had repeatedly given short shrift to essential questions and pursued marginal matters instead. Fraenkel's verdict: Neumann had failed to craft a full account of the dictatorship.

As Fraenkel saw it, Neumann had succeeded in analytical "deconstruction" ("*Zergliederung*") but struggled to paint "a uniform picture" ("*einheitliches Bild*") of how the Nazis ruled.[46] Fraenkel also criticized Neumann's inattention to what some today would call the dynamics of contention in the Third Reich.[47] In particular, he wanted to know more about the normalization ("*Veralltäglichung*") of Hitler rule, the mechanisms and processes by which it became embedded in the fabric of everyday life.[48] How *exactly*, he asked, did the Nazi revolutionaries and the bureaucrats of old come to terms with one another? And by what means *exactly* did the barons of industry and Nazi careerists manage to find common ground?[49] To Fraenkel's frustration, Neumann was silent about all of these matters. There was too much macro-politics, not enough micro-politics, in *Behemoth* for his liking. The picture that Neumann presented of the Third Reich was uniform because he had painted it in broad strokes, with little attention to detail. This lack of nuance is hard to miss in Neumann's analysis of law, in which he caricatured the institution in an unhelpful way. The difference in approach by the onetime business partners requires some unpacking, as it speaks to the larger debate over the relationship between law and morals in the study of the Third Reich.

Neumann and Fraenkel worked with two competing concepts of law. For Neumann, the law of the *Rechtsstaat* was a *discrete variable*: it could only take on two values. This dichotomous approach ran counter to Fraenkel's concept of law. For Fraenkel, the law of the *Rechtsstaat* was a *continuous variable*, that is, an explanatory factor that has an infinite number of possible values. Fraenkel allowed for the conceptual and empirical possibility of *degrees* of *Rechtsstaatlichkeit*. He was interested in really existing varieties of the *Rechtsstaat*. By contrast, Neumann's *Rechtsstaat* was not an analytical but a normative category; it revolved around a substantive definition of law that conjured a legal utopia. It was an effort "to realize the original promises of enlightened liberalism, and to give substance to the formal emancipatory claims of liberal thought."[50] Or, as Duncan Kelly phrased it, Neumann "wished to radicalize the *Rechtsstaat*."[51]

Like all of the Frankfurt School theorists, Neumann felt disdain for the dominance of technical rationality, a type of rationality that, from the vantage point of critical theory, benefitted only the haves, not the have-nots.[52] This aversion to formal rationality helps explain why he, unlike the ideologically more moderate Fraenkel, saw no value in thinking about the remnants of the *Rechtsstaat*.[53] Neumann took Weber's argument about the dark sides of rationality to its extreme, seeing disenchantment wherever he looked. Given these assumptions, law to him was "nothing but an *arcanum* for the maintenance of power."[54] He was convinced that Carl Schmitt's theory of decisionism (which Schmitt abandoned in 1934) amounted to an accurate portrayal of Nazi legal practice.[55] It is therefore not surprising that the account of the Third Reich in *Behemoth* included a dystopian portrayal of law. Neumann's bleak rendering of law is logically related to his classification of the Nazi polity as a non-state: where there was no state, there presumably could not be meaningful law, as *he* used the term. "The system of coercion under Hitler's rule is instead [...] a structure of direct and institutionally fluid compulsion, which lacks both the sovereign authority of universal law and the unified character of a rational state."[56] But not everyone looked at Nazi law the way Neumann did—least of all Fraenkel.

Gray Law

Where Neumann saw uniformity and sameness in the law of the Third Reich, Fraenkel noticed diversity and variation, complexity and contingency. Not content to paint in broad strokes only, he saw the value of applying a finer brush. Unlike Neumann, the émigré, Fraenkel, the practicing lawyer who had stayed behind in Hitler's Berlin, existed for eight years in a "gray zone" of sorts. In Primo Levi's use of the term, which I am mindful to not overstretch, it described a reality so extreme that any victims of Nazism who have not experienced it are said to have no right to judge those that did.[57] If we take the metaphor of the gray zone out of its original context—the concentration camp universe for which Levi had invented it—and apply it to the realm of law, it brings into view a poorly understood aspect of the violence of everyday life under the Nazi dictatorship: that the law of the Third Reich, at least for some its victims, occasionally served as a valuable sword and shield. Fraenkel was one of those victims. To be sure, the law, like the concentration camp, was an inverted moral universe. And yet, despite the dehumanizing racial ideology that served as its principal ideational foundation in the period 1933–1945, outcomes were not always predictable.

Where Neumann and Radbruch saw only black and white—law or lawlessness—Fraenkel noticed shades of gray. He was a quintessential theorist of gray law. He saw for himself, especially in the early years of the dictatorship, that the law (as well as the state in which it was applied) was alive and in reasonably good condition, all things considered, despite the Nazi onslaught on the *Rechtsstaat*.[58] It would not have occurred to him to conclude, as Neumann did, and much later also Hannah Arendt, that a non-state was governing the dictatorship and that law had ceased to exist. Neumann's was a world of certainty, one he felt compelled to capture in binaries—not unlike Carl Schmitt whose work he both admired and reviled.[59] Unlike his friend, Fraenkel allowed for ambiguity and the existence of institutional hybridity.

Out of necessity, *Behemoth* was the result of desk research. What Neumann took to be the state of law in the Third Reich was a figment of his imagination. Neumann's ideologically derived assumptions about what made the world hang together in the 1930s blinded him to the reality of authoritarian rule—in economics *and* in law. His progressive fervor undermined the empirical validity of his argument. Because *The Dual State* grew out of participant observation, Fraenkel was more attuned than Neumann to the many different and contradictory roles that law played in the transition from democracy to authoritarianism and from authoritarianism to totalitarianism in interwar Germany.

It is ironic that Neumann, the consummate lawyer, should be remembered for getting the law wrong.[60] And yet I am not the first scholar to cast doubt on his empirical understanding of the law of the Third Reich as well as on the concept of law that underpinned Neumann's sweeping analysis. Joachim Perels, for example, has faulted Neumann for equating the concept of law with statutory law. He derides Neumann's twin assumptions that the institution of the "general statute" ("*allgemeines Gesetz*") represented the "fundamental form of law" ("*Grundform des Rechts*"), and that the generality of law was a reliable indicator of law's rationality.[61] Neither assumption is borne out by historical evidence. Both are also "theoretically wrong" ("*theoretisch falsch*"), according to Perels.[62] He makes the important point—self-evident to law-and-society scholars the world over—that law's intended function is not always the function that law *actually* serves in politics and society.[63] A preconceived, simplistic, and "rather artificial" understanding of law, one that mostly ignored legal practice, blinded Neumann.[64] Perels has therefore rightly cautioned against an uncritical reception of Neumann's oeuvre. He considers much if it is to be a model for "moralizing commentary" rather than for analytically sophisticated socio-legal scholarship.

Interestingly, Neumann and Fraenkel at one point had a very similar understanding of the logic of authoritarian legalism. But divergent trajectories in the two friends' biographies account for what Alfred Söllner has described as Neumann's rapid theoretical radicalization after 1933.[65]

A sense of impending doom appears to have persuaded Neumann to fundamentally rethink the nature and function of law in society. He gave "Weber's views on legal development a radical gloss."[66] This widened considerably the intellectual distance between him and Fraenkel.[67] For Fraenkel remained beholden to Weber's concept and theory of law, which is why, according to William Scheuerman,

> Neumann harshly criticizes Ernst Fraenkel's [*The*] *Dual State*, which anticipates many features of Neumann's own study but insists on a dualistic face of Nazi law [. . .]. But like Weber, Fraenkel believes that capitalism presupposes a high degree of legal regularity and, hence, some features of the liberal rule of law. Insofar as German fascism remains capitalist, Fraenkel concludes, it preserves certain minimal characteristics of modern legal rational authority that can be identified in the sphere of private law. In contrast, Neumann traces the disintegration of rational law to the socioeconomic sphere itself. Consequently, Neumann must embrace a more radical and disturbing picture of the Nazi legal order than his friend and colleague.[68]

Marx to Fuller

To the extent that Fraenkel wrote like a Weberian, Neumann's style resembled that of a Marxist. Fraenkel compared the Third Reich to an ideal type, Neumann to an ideal. Because the reality of Nazi rule did not correspond to his preferred idea of state, Neumann drew the only conclusion that seemed logical to him: he denied that the racial polity was a state at all. "[I]t is difficult to give the name state to four groups entering into a bargain."[69] Neumann reasoned in analogous fashion when it came to the concept of law: "If general law is the basic form of right, if law is not only *voluntas* but also *ratio*, then we must deny the existence of law in the fascist state. Law, as distinct from the political command of the sovereign, is conceivable only if it is manifest in general law, but true generality is not possible in a society that cannot dispense with power."[70] In some respects, Neumann's position anticipates Radbruch's formula, which I critiqued in the previous chapter. Like Radbruch, Neumann was only concerned with the general thrust of law, not its particulars.[71] Neumann and Radbruch were meta-theoretical thinkers not overly concerned with the empirical validity of their far-reaching claims. Whereas most anthropologists of law would operate with a broad conception of what law is, and what it is not, Neumann began and ended with a preconceived, reductionist notion of this complicated phenomenon. To be deserving of the name, a *Rechtsstaat*, for Neumann, had to be a progressive *Rechtsstaat*.[72] He enumerated its defining attributes in a key essay, "Types of Natural Law," published in 1939: "the generality of law, the equality of men, the prohibition of individual legislative decisions, the impossibility of retroactive legislation, especially in penal law, and an independent judiciary."[73] The list is reminiscent of an influential postwar perspective on the relationship between law and morals: Lon Fuller's argument about the inner or internal morality of law.

In his 1965 book *The Morality of Law*, Fuller, a professor of law at Harvard Law School, introduced a procedural concept of law founded on a secular version of natural law theory. It revolved around eight "principles of legality," which, Fuller wrote, embodied the moral essence of the rule of law. They demanded, *inter alia*, that legal rules be sufficiently general, publicly promulgated, prospective, minimally clear, relatively constant, and administered in a predictable fashion.[74] Fuller's philosophical inquiry, directly inspired by Radbruch's formula and the case of the Third Reich, cast doubt on the legal quality—the "lawness"—of Nazi law. But not everyone was convinced that the issue was an important one to explore. Ronald Dworkin was among them: "[Fuller] asserts that to the *extent* to which lawmaking is subject to internal immorality of the sort common under tyrannies like Nazi Germany, it fails, and its product is to this extent less law. Fuller has toiled in this vineyard before. He shares with many an obsessive ambition to lessen the horror of tyranny by arguing it into anarchy, or at least partial anarchy."[75] Neumann is guilty of precisely this ambition. His radical legalism paved the way for Radbruch and Fuller who followed in his wake.

All three theorists proved more comfortable with the purity of philosophy than the reality of history—to the detriment of empirical understanding. "There is no available shortcut of the sort Fuller assumes," Dworkin pointed out: "[A]lthough we should certainly agree that some political outrages involving secret legislation, or retroactivity, or whatever, are also cases in which an attempt to produce or apply law must be said to abort, it would not follow that every such outrage, or even most such outrages, have some effect on legality. Nor would it follow that there is any connection between the gravity of the moral wrong and the extent of the legal impairment involved."[76] This echoes the observation by Hans Kelsen with which I opened this book: "The claim that no legal order exists under despotism, that the ruler's arbitrary will governs, is utterly nonsensical."[77] But unlike Kelsen, who penned his remark in 1925, Dworkin addressed explicitly the case of Nazi Germany, calling into question not only Fuller's—and thus Neumann's—conclusions about the law of the Third Reich but also their approach to it:

> An apparatus of government dressed in legal forms and vocabulary may so far fail to meet Fuller's [principles of legality] that it falls below the threshold

> of our concept of law. Perhaps the Nazi governmental system is a case in point; perhaps it was not only immoral, but also not quite law. One cannot prove this by showing that it differed from our own in the dimensions these [principles of legality] present. To prove it one would have to refine and to some extent calibrate the concept of law formed by the [principles] and then document the application of this concept to Nazi history. I doubt that the game would be worth the candle, or that this calculation serves any important purpose. I regard most arguments as to whether the Nazi system was "law" as having little point. But the conclusion that it was *less* law than ours, on the basis of Fuller's argument that because it had more retroactivity it must have been, is in addition illogical.[78]

Fraenkel's litigation experience in the Third Reich illustrates the power of Dworkin's theoretical argument. Douglas Morris recently surveyed half a dozen of Fraenkel's Nazi-era cases. He finds that "[i]n representing political defendants, Fraenkel assumed a hard but not hopeless task. Political prosecutions usually yielded convictions, but not always."[79] Although his court cases informed Fraenkel's argument in *The Dual State*, he did not rely explicitly on any of them in support of his argument.[80] They nonetheless provide evidence for his theoretical claim that law and lawlessness existed side by side—albeit to different degrees and in changing permutations—during the span of the dictatorship. As Morris writes, "Using their skills as legal technicians, lawyers on occasion could turn [courtroom] procedures [...] to their clients' advantage."[81] On occasion they were even able to "challenge in court not only National-Socialist brutality but also National-Socialist deceit."[82] Sebastian Haffner's recollections from the early years of the Nazi dictatorship, during which he was a legal trainee in Berlin, bear out this finding:

> In the *Kammergericht*, the highest court in Prussia, where I worked as a *Referendar* at that time, the process of law was not changed at all by the fact that the interior minister enacted ridiculous edicts. The newspapers might report that the constitution was in ruins. Here every paragraph of the Civil Code was still valid and was mulled over and analysed as carefully as ever. Which was the true reality? The Chancellor could daily utter the vilest abuse against the Jews; there was none the less still a Jewish *Kammergerichtsrat* (*Kammergericht* judge) and member of our senate who continued to give his astute and careful judgements, and these judgements had the full weight of the law and could set the entire apparatus of the state in motion for their enforcement—even if the highest office-holder of that state daily called their author a "parasite", a "subhuman" or a "plague". [...] I must admit that I was inclined to view the undisturbed functioning of the law, and indeed the continued normal course of daily life, as a triumph over the Nazis.[83]

What Haffner, who left Nazi Germany for Britain in 1938, the same year as Fraenkel, described was nothing other than a bifurcated state, a dual state. The glimpses into the workings of the *Kammergericht* that he provided are suggestive of more institutional continuity than Neumann's non-state model allows. Though he did not use Fraenkel's terminology, Haffner's sketches of everyday law point to the co-existence of a prerogative state and a normative state, at least at the outset of the dictatorship.[84]

An inductive thinker, Fraenkel was the methodological opposite of Neumann. He quickly developed a knack for ideographic reasoning—in spite of his professional training as a lawyer. Although he took concepts very seriously, Fraenkel was less hung up than Neumann on permanently fixing the meaning of terms. Ever the careful student of Weber, Fraenkel put the still relatively new ideal type method to use, albeit implicitly. In *The Dual State*, he used the conventional, positivist understanding of law that was dominant in his time as an analytical standard against which to measure the everyday life of Nazi law. Instead of thinking in binaries, as Neumann was wont to, Fraenkel embraced a non-dichotomous approach to the meaning of law. This intellectual flexibility meant that he was well equipped to theorize innovatively about institutional hybridity and liminal states when it mattered, an ability that Neumann lacked.

In Neumann's view, law had "concealing functions" and was thus epiphenomenal: "Law is now a technical means for the achievement of specific political aims. It is merely the command of the sovereign. To this extent, the juristic theory of the fascist state is decisionism. Law is merely an *arcanum dominationis*, a means for the stabilization of power."[85] Neumann was not wrong, of course. Fraenkel had already made a similar point the previous year. It did not follow, however, that all law was repressive: "Fraenkel showed not that some core of the normative state was impervious to the prerogative state but rather that the normative and prerogative states interacted dynamically with each other within a dictatorial regime. He made clear that the dual state, taken as a whole, that is the combination of the normative and prerogative states, had replaced the rule of law, and that this National-Socialist dual state had been conceived in unlawfulness."[86] This is why I speak of the remnants of the *Rechtsstaat*. I find the phrase useful to convey my argument that although in Nazi Germany the reign of the *Rechtsstaat* as such was over, some of the norms and institutions associated with it survived, if in heavily circumscribed form. They continued to matter, structuring politics and society on the margins of dictatorship. Sometimes the legal system had the institutional effects that its Nazi guardians intended, at other times it produced unintended consequences, including some that undermined the dictatorship.

This brings us back to Fuller who believed that law existed on a continuum and thus was always a matter of degree. Neumann, by contrast, was a far more categorical thinker. Where even Fuller was willing to see gray, or degrees of *Rechtsstaatlichkeit*, for Neumann the question of the law of the Third Reich was a black-and-white issue. Thinking about remnants of the *Rechtsstaat* was anathema to Neumann, which explains his vehement critique of *The Dual State*: either law was both formally *and* substantively rational, or it did not qualify as law at all. Even a cursory look at Fraenkel's experience as a cause lawyer in the 1930s suggests that Neumann missed the trees for the forest when it came to Nazi law. Fraenkel's court appearances alone lend credence to the notion that in the early years of the dictatorship "defendants could still counter National-Socialist arguments in some courtrooms."[87] As Morris writes, "At least for a while, the normative state provided a place where National-Socialist opponents could speak, even if they could not launch a counter-attack."[88]

This anecdotal evidence, in conjunction with more comprehensive data on the law of the Third Reich now available, indicates that Neumann overstated his case when he claimed "[t]here is complete agreement in the literature that the law is nothing more than the command of the Leader."[89] No such agreement existed. But not only *The Dual State*, even some of the empirical data in *Behemoth* itself contradicted Neumann's assertion. Consider the following example. Immediately after stating, not incorrectly, that "[t]he main function of National Socialist law is to preserve racial existence," Neumann conceded that the regime's instrumental use of law was not absolute. Even at the time of his writing, in 1941, Neumann held that the Nazi machinery of law had "not yet fully developed" its principles and practices: "The law is still in a state of flux, the judiciary not yet fully synchronized. The trends are unmistakable, however, and during the war, the law reached its full development as an instrument of violence."[90] This interpretation is nearly identical to Fraenkel's, whose account Neumann dismissed so cavalierly.[91]

But Neumann was out of step with the majority of practicing lawyers, not just with Fraenkel. Weimar-era lawyers were not convinced by Neumann's claim that the existence of "calculable and predictable rules" of law as well as of legal "competences, jurisdictions, regularities" did not constitute prima facie evidence of the continued operation of remnants of the *Rechtsstaat*.[92] The vast majority of them worked with a more conservative, procedural concept of law than Neumann. To conceive of the *Rechtsstaat* in procedural rather than substantive terms was the norm in the early twentieth century. Inasmuch as the negation and destruction of some of these procedures persuaded Neumann to deny the existence of law—to extol the end of the *Rechtsstaat tout court*—not everyone agreed that the deformation of law was akin to its destruction. As one contemporary of Neumann's wondered at the time: "Must we really say that a bottle is empty when the labels at our disposal cannot properly describe its contents?"[93] Neumann answered in the affirmative, Fraenkel in the negative. With *Behemoth* and *The Dual State* the two friends wrote competing titles, arriving at diametrically opposed answers to the question of whether the law of the Third Reich mattered.

Neumann and Fraenkel occupied different positions on the analytical spectrum of their time. Whereas Neumann looked for macrofoundations of the Nazi dictatorship, Fraenkel appreciated that mesofoundations as well as microfoundations also had to be factored into any explanatory account of Nazi rule. While not entirely innocent of a reductionist reading of reality, especially of the economics of dictatorship, Fraenkel by and large avoided the crude holism and functionalism that characterized Neumann's argument in *Behemoth*.[94] Instead of singling out supraindividual entities and aggregate evolutionary patterns as the sole drivers of authoritarianism, Fraenkel was attuned to what political scientists call structured contingency, that is, situations in which agents act voluntaristically but within the limitations imposed by structural constrains.[95] It is a less deterministic version of Marx's adage in *The Eighteenth Brumaire of Louis Bonaparte*, where he famously proclaimed that

> Men make their own history, but not of their own free will; not under circumstances they themselves have chosen but under the given and inherited circumstances with which they are directly confronted. The tradition of the dead generations weighs like a nightmare on the minds of the living.[96]

Speaking of Marx, the difference between Neumann and Fraenkel is not dissimilar to that between the author of *The Eighteenth Brumaire of Louis Bonaparte* and Alexis de Tocqueville.[97] Whereas Neumann, inspired by Marx, was beholden to historical materialism, Fraenkel, like de Tocqueville, was a historical institutionalist *avant la lettre*. Initially united by Sinzheimer's faith in the liberating potential of progressive legalism, Fraenkel and Neumann came to stand for two opposing tendencies in the intellectual resistance to Nazi dictatorship: Neumann's was marked by radicalization, Fraenkel underwent a deradicalization. The former embraced radical legalism, the latter a reformist variant thereof.[98] Their mutual disenchantment with each others' responses to the challenge of Hitler rule is remarkable considering that at one point the two of them saw eye to eye on the Third Reich. Both emphasized the economic origins of dictatorship, and—more important—*both* believed its law to be bifurcated.

One of the most remarkable aspects of *Behemoth* is the fact that much of it betrayed Neumann's long-standing thinking about the nature of the Third Reich. To some extent, in *Behemoth*, Neumann repudiated ideas that he himself developed. In other words, a noticeable tension runs through Neumann's treatment of law. Or, as one reviewer put it, "Dr. Neumann seems at times not too convinced of his own thesis."[99] This tension tells us a great deal about intellectual affinities between him and Fraenkel—common points of view that their famous books at first glance conceal.[100] For it turns out that the principal conceit in *The Dual State*—the idea of institutional hybridity—has intellectual antecedents in Neumann's prewar work, and even resurfaces in *Behemoth*. Like Fraenkel, Neumann saw a dual state at work in the Third Reich. He, too, believed that the Nazi state was a schizophrenic institutional creature—a hybrid comprised of independent but mutually constitutive halves. Here is Neumann himself:

> Two notions of law must be distinguished, a political and a rational notion. In a political sense, law is every measure of a sovereign power, regardless of its form or content. Declarations of war and peace, tax laws, civil laws, police measures and court attachments, court decisions and legal norms applied in the decisions, all these are law simply because they are expressions of sovereignty. Law is then will and nothing else. The rational concept of law, on the other hand, is determined by its form and content, not by its origin. Not every act of the sovereign is law. Law in this sense is a norm, comprehensible by reason, open to theoretical understanding, and containing an ethical postulate, primarily that of equality. Law is reason and will.[101]

In the section immediately preceding this theoretical discussion, Neumann, although refusing to call the transactions by their name, acknowledged that a legal way of doing things nonetheless existed in Nazi Germany:

> The average lawyer [. . .] will point out that hundreds of thousands, perhaps millions, of transactions in Germany are handled according to calculable and predictable rules. That is true. Any society based on a division of labor will necessarily produce competences, jurisdictions, regularities, which give the appearance of a functioning legal system. Traffic must move to the right or the left; houses are to be painted green or white; groups and chambers may raise this or that fee. These and thousands of other questions are dealt with rationally, even in the so-called "prerogative" state—the S.S., the S.A. and the Gestapo. But they are, in the words of my late teacher Max E. Mayer, "culturally indifferent rules" of a predominantly technical character.[102]

The discussion is telling. For Neumann, " 'culturally indifferent rules' of a predominantly technical character" were not law, did not qualify as law. But even he conceded that "the average lawyer" would disagree with his understanding of law. Fraenkel was one such lawyer. He had no illusions about the morality of Nazi law, but he was cognizant that law remains a medium of, and stage for, social interaction even when it is honored in the breach or flooded with inhumane content, as was the case in the period 1933–1945.

Neumann was a thought-provoking theorist, but not much of a social scientist. He was model-driven, not too curious about the real world. His "England problem" illustrates the point.[103] Roger Cotterrell has shown that Neumann, like Weber before him, relied on "unrecognisable descriptions of actual judicial practice" in order to sustain empirically, in the context of the common law, his theoretical argument about the generality of law that he had developed based on his personal experience in the civil law tradition.[104] The target of Cotterrell's critique is the publication in English of Neumann's 1936 doctoral dissertation, "The Governance of the Rule of Law," which the émigré scholar completed at the London School of Economics and Political Science under the supervision (and demonstrable influence) of Harold Laski.[105] In it, Neumann developed his quintessential argument about the function of law in society, one that "ascribed a historically transcendent *ethical* function to general law," regardless of empirical context.[106]

"Neumann is forced to claim," Cotterrell points out, "that despite all doctrinal differences there are no significant functional differences between the common law and the continental code systems, insofar as both correspond to the political, economic and social order of the competitive society."[107] It followed from this that "both kinds of legal order have to be seen as rational in the sense demanded by the rule of law."[108] The problem, however, is this: the historical record does not support Neumann's claim. His idiosyncratic interpretations of institutions such as the doctrine of *stare decisis* bespoke an incomplete grasp of the history and practice of the English rule of law, which Neumann erroneously conflated, like so many others, with that of the German *Rechtsstaat*.[109] In Weber's typology of law, which informed Neumann's classificatory scheme, the common law of England "is 'irrational' rather than formally rational—based in empirical law-finding rather than the systematic elaboration of formal concepts."[110] Despite admiration for Neumann's oeuvre, Cotterrell is blunt in his assessment: "[H]is discussion of English law in terms of the thesis of *The Rule of Law* is ultimately confused and unsatisfactory."[111] If Cotterrell is to be believed, Neumann's concept of law does not easily travel. He points out that even though Neumann declared open-ended legal standards (called *Generalklauseln* in German) "in the Weimar context as antithetical to the rule of law," such open-ended legal standards had the opposite effect in England where they contributed to the advancement of the rule of law.[112] But let us return from England to Germany, where Neumann's argument about general law has also been challenged. According to Ulrich Preuß, detailed and empirical studies have shown the institution of the statute—defined as an abstract and general norm—never enjoyed the kind of standing that Neumann attributed to it. Preuß has disputed that a strong, let alone widespread, theoretical or empirical commitment to general law ever existed in nineteenth century Germany. He concludes that Neumann mistook "the loud, liberal propaganda of pre-constitutional times for [...] social reality."[113]

My larger point is this: Had Neumann had the opportunity to delve into the thorny thicket of Nazi law, the chance to experience for years on end the everyday life of dictatorship, he would have found incontrovertible evidence that aspects of the law, regardless of its fractured appearance, mattered in the Third Reich. It enjoyed facticity; it had an empirical presence and produced innumerable institutional effects, intended and otherwise, as postwar Germany's Federal Constitutional Court confirmed.[114] The law of the Third Reich structured politics and society, not all of politics and society, but a significant chunk of both. It did so prior to the war but also in diminished form throughout. By writing law out of existence as a structural parameter to choice, Neumann did a disservice to scholarship about the nature of Nazi rule. He retarded the production of knowledge about the transition to, and consolidation of, the Third Reich by clinging to an ideologically charged way of seeing the world.[115]

If the institution of Nazi law was as inconsequential as Neumann claimed, why did a group of courageous Germans, fully aware of the ongoing destruction of the *Rechtsstaat* around them, seize opportunities to resist the rise and expansion of the prerogative state in the courtrooms of the Third Reich? Though their number was shamefully small, these "fearless jurists," as a 2017 study conducted under the auspices of Germany's Ministry of Justice christened them, risked their careers, some their lives, to fight the Nazi dictatorship by legal means.[116] Highly accomplished and reflective, these jurists were no fools. If the state of lawlessness had been as pervasive as Neumann claimed, the pursuit of legal resistance as futile from as early as 1933 as he implied, would these attorneys and judges have chosen to engage in kamikaze legalism? The most principled ones would likely have done: out of human decency or a commitment to their vocation. But is it reasonable to assume that the majority would have been willing to become martyrs for an impossible mission? Judging by the archival evidence, most of Germany's resisting jurists acted strategically, not wantonly. They pursued a strategy of lawfare.[117] It was not naïvité but a clear-eyed assessment of the promise—and limits—of legal resistance in the evolving dictatorship that persuaded them to become lawyers with a cause.

SLAYING *BEHEMOTH*

At the dawn of his life the Holocaust historian Raul Hilberg had a complaint: "[O]ne can pick up a work of even a thousand pages with two thousand footnotes, presenting a complete assessment of Nazi Germany, and not find Neumann in any footnote."[118] These were the grateful words of Neumann's star student. As a Ph.D. candidate at Columbia University in the late 1940s, Hilberg fell under the spell of his charismatic supervisor.[119] It was there that Hilberg laid the foundations for what would turn into the first institutionalist interpretation of the Holocaust—the three-volume *The Destruction of the European Jews*.[120] The publication inaugurated a functionalist (or structuralist) approach to the study of Nazi Germany, one that influenced historians from Hans Mommsen to Christopher Browning.[121] However, *pace* Hilberg, *Behemoth* is not at all underrepresented in scholarship on the Third Reich and never was. Quite the opposite: Neumann's *Behemoth* has always enjoyed a prominent place in that literature—arguably too prominent a place: "Neumann was so overwhelmingly successful in his attempt [to lay bare the character of the Nazi dictatorship] that *Behemoth* is recognized, even today, as the first comprehensive interpretation of National Socialism, a work which has served several generations of researchers in contemporary history as the benchmark for their own work."[122]

The extraordinary reception of *Behemoth* has cast a long shadow over that era's other, better study of Nazi dictatorship—*The Dual State*. To the detriment of scholarship, it has distracted from key parts of the anatomy of this scariest of bodies politic.[123] Hyperbolic assessments like Hilberg's ensured that it did. They came quick and fast in the wake of the book's publication. A gander at these reviews helps us understand why *Behemoth* rose, despite the long list of shortcomings that I have identified, to the rank of a classic.

Locus Classicus

The publication of *Behemoth* was greeted with fanfare. The *New York Herald* tribune advertised the book as "a scholarly and brilliant study," and the reviewer for the *Saturday Review of Literature* was certain that it represented "by a wide margin the most illuminating and the most learned analysis yet written of Nazi political theory, of Nazi economics, and of the Nazi social order," one that offered "an intellectually exciting experience of the first order."[124] In his estimation, the book was quite simply "dynamite."[125] Learned assessments quickly followed on the heels of the popular reviews. In August 1942, Oscar Jászi credited Neumann in the *American Political Science Review* with having produced

> an almost encyclopedic survey of the development and present functioning of Nazi Germany. In the enormous flood of literature now covering the most spectacular dictatorship of our period, there is no treatise which offers such an amount of facts and critical evaluation as does this one. It is not too much to say that there is no single aspect of the German problem to which the author does not contribute some important facts, interesting sidelights, or a new hypothesis.[126]

Harvard University's Paul Sweezy chose equally ebullient prose: "Franz Neumann's *Behemoth* is unquestionably the best work on the subject that has yet appeared, and it sets a very high standard for future writers to live up to. [...] Neumann has given us the first genuinely scientific interpretation of Nazi ideology in terms of the antagonisms and compulsions of the system as a whole."[127] In the *Review of Politics*, Waldemar Gurian was convinced that "No student of political and social trends of our time can afford to let this book go unnoticed," and George Sabine, in the *Philosophical Review*, declared *Behemoth* to be "one of the most thorough and judicious accounts of National Socialism so far produced. [...] The treatment is in all cases as thorough as the space permits and as objective as is possible under present circumstances."[128]

Economists, too, took note. From the University of California at Berkeley, Robert Brady bestowed plaudits in the *American Economic Review*: "The careful reader [...] will be richly paid for the time he invests in *Behemoth*, not only for the grasp it will give him of the [N]azi system as a whole, but also for the profoundly disturbing parallels it suggests to developments in other sections of the world—not excluding many of those at home."[129] For Brady, Neumann's treatise represented "by a large margin the most powerful and masterly exposition of the origin, functions, and outlook of the [N]azi system yet to appear in print."[130] The reviewer for the *Political Science Quarterly*, despite some misgivings, acknowledged that the volume provided "a far better insight into what has been happening during these nine long years of Nazi rule than the surface observations of so-called first-hand reporters arriving from the Reich."[131] But one review stood out for the lavish praise that it heaped upon Neumann's analysis.

C. Wright Mills, the American sociologist, wrote a paean to *Behemoth* in the *Partisan Review*.[132] He saw in Neumann a radical brother-in-arms: "The analysis of *Behemoth* casts light upon capitalism in democracies. To the most important task of political analysis Neumann has contributed: if you read his book thoroughly, you see the harsh outlines of possible futures close around you. With leftwing thought confused and split and dribbling trivialities, he locates the enemy with a 500 watt glare. And Nazi is only one of his names."[133] The tone of Mills's extended review is adulatory throughout, despite minor gripes. He hailed Neumann's book as "a fresh intellectual act" and "a definitive analysis" of Germany's descent into violence. But he appreciated even more its universalizing normative argument, to wit: the moral warning that *Behemoth* contained about the economic origins of dictatorship elsewhere: "Franz Neumann's is not only the most important book to appear about Germany; it is a live contribution to all leftwing thinking today. His book will move all of us into deeper levels of analysis and strategy. It had better. *Behemoth* is everywhere united."[134]

The adulation is not difficult to understand. "[T]he more conjectural frame [of *Behemoth*] fascinated younger political writers, such as C. Wright Mills," who were clamoring for "a fresh, unhackneyed start for [the] leftist diagnosis of trends that were not limited to Germany."[135] *Behemoth* was a highly policy-relevant book, as we shall see in more detail in a moment. What Mills's review makes abundantly clear is that *Behemoth* was also advocacy-relevant. Years later, in his bestselling *The Sociological Imagination*, Mills reiterated his earlier praise and upped the ante when he compared *Behemoth* favorably to another influential mid-century treatise: Talcott Parsons's *The Social System*. Mills was convinced that Parsons had misunderstood the structural determinants of Nazi dictatorship. He therefore urged readers to turn to Neumann's rather than Parsons's *locus classicus*: "[O]ne *Behemoth* is worth, to social science, twenty *Social Systems*."[136] Ironically, given my argument about *Behemoth*'s weak theoretical, empirical, and methodological foundations, Mills presented *Behemoth* as a "truly splendid model of what a structural analysis of an historical society ought to be."[137]

Not a single of the aforementioned book reviews mentioned *The Dual State*, which had appeared in the previous year. Within the span of twelve months, *Behemoth*'s historical materialism had supplanted Fraenkel's historical institutionalism as the modal approach in the theory of dictatorship, with far-reaching consequences for the study of the Third Reich. This does not mean that critical voices could not be heard. They existed but were drowned out by those who, like Mills, heaped praise upon *Behemoth*. Especially circumspect in his assessment was Moritz Julius

Bonn of Hamilton College. Until 1933, Bonn, a leading macroeconomist and influential Weimar politician, had served as rector of Berlin's *Handelshochschule*, a prominent business school where Carl Schmitt, upon Bonn's recommendation, became a professor in 1928.[138] In his 1943 review of the first edition of *Behemoth*, published in the *Journal of Political Economy*, Bonn did not mince his words.

He criticized the simplistic reading on offer and complained that Neumann's inattention to conceptual and empirical nuances had "prevented him from making the useful contribution which his wide reading might have made possible. He nowhere reaches the profound understanding of the dynamic forces at work [in Nazi Germany]."[139] Bonn was especially critical of Neumann's habit to substitute assertion for argumentation: "Many of the author's historical statements are but half-truths. He does not look to history for the raw material from which he might attempt to draw generalizations; it is to him a card index from which he can get references to facts useful for proving preconceived theories."[140]

Others concurred. Writing in the *American Historical Review*, Dwight Lee also thought that Neumann was "not always convincing."[141] He criticized him for attempting "too much by arguments too dependent upon a preconceived thesis."[142] Lee noted that Neumann's "social philosophy often seems too metaphysical and his conclusions too doctrinaire" and wondered whether "that what might be obvious to the naked eye may have escaped him."[143] Frederick Cramer's evaluation of *Behemoth* in the *Journal of Modern History* pushed in the same direction. It panned the "somewhat arbitrary manner in which the materials were selected for use" and, like Lee, concluded "[t]he author's desire for clear-cut conclusions not infrequently goads him into oversimplification."[144] Paul Sweezy, who, as we have seen, was generally fond of *Behemoth*, nonetheless took Neumann to task for the logic of his argument, notably the social mechanisms that were driving it: "Bureaucracy, party, army and industrialists are all, of course, important but the crucial questions are precisely what are the relations among them and what role do they play in the developmental tendencies of National Socialism. To lump them together as coordinate rulers of Germany avoids these questions; it does not answer them."[145] Instead of opening the black box of Nazi dictatorship, Neumann merely repackaged it.

He failed to notice or left unexplored the many contradictions and countervailing tendencies associated with the transition from authoritarianism to totalitarianism. For someone who is credited in the historiography of the Third Reich with having laid the theoretical foundations for the postwar concept of polycracy (*Polykratie*), Neumann was remarkably uninterested in the historicity of institutions, by which I mean institutional variation across space, time, and Nazi organizations.[146] The sociologist C. H. Pegg accordingly was not persuaded by Neumann's "rather obvious attempt to make National Socialism conform to some sort of Marxist pattern," and concluded that *Behemoth* was, as a result, "marred."[147] This critique of Neumann's political economy of dictatorship ushered in the review's most damning line: "It led him to conclusions which are not in line with the facts presented."[148] The more discerning among the book's many reviewers homed in on precisely this weakness. According to Charles Robson, who weighed in for the *Journal of Politics*, "the author frequently makes statements unsupported by his evidence and inconsistent with his own conclusions."[149] Even the Princeton historian Carl Schorske, a colleague at the Office of Strategic Services (OSS), where Neumann was headed, in retrospect remarked rather damningly that *Behemoth* combined evidence-based research and speculation ("*eine Kombination von Quellenstudium and Spekulation*").[150]

Already at an earlier stage of Neumann's career, Hugo Sinzheimer, his mentor, had criticized the "quick, apodictic judgments" ("*rasche, apodiktische Urteile*") for which his student, *Referendar*, and *Assistant* was developing a reputation.[151] It would be uncharitable, but not unreasonable, to think of *Behemoth* as a quick, apodictic judgment in long form. Neumann was an exciting but rigid thinker. The absolute certainty with which he advanced his radical argument is astounding, especially given how much conflicting empirical evidence already existed at the time of his research and writing in New York City and later in Washington, D.C.[152]

The publication of the second, enlarged edition of *Behemoth* in 1944 provoked one of the most damning reviews. Written by Josef Kunz of the University of Toledo, for the *American Political Science Review* no less, it inveighed against the famous book's reductionist argument and in particular its retrospective determinism. Although Kunz acknowledged Neumann's achievement in data collection, he concluded that *Behemoth* left much to be desired: "[T]he facts he gives not only present the most detailed analysis of National Socialism, but are undistorted, true, complete, and reliable. But his interpretation of these facts is open to the most serious doubt and criticism. It is not only that he says little about the reasons why National Socialism rose to power—and this is indispensable to a full understanding—but he suffers from a double prejudice: an over-rationalistic and a Marxist prejudice [...]."[153] Or, as Gurian memorably put it, "Neumann uses the term Monopoly Capitalism as a kind of *passe-partout*, a key opening all doors."[154]

These assessments remind of Fraenkel's review in the *Neue Volks-Zeitung*. But Gurian and Kunz went further in their critiques than Fraenkel. Gurian called out Neumann for trying "too much to fit concrete events and theoretical trends into abstract patterns," and opined that "[i]t would have been more simple and more satisfactory to put a stronger emphasis on German traditions than upon economic systems."[155] Critiquing Neumann's penchant for historical materialism, Kunz went as far as stating that "the Marxist 'economic interpretation of history' " he considered to be driving *Behemoth* was "scientifically and philosophically absolutely untenable."[156] Seven decades of research on the Nazi dictatorship have proved both Kunz and Gurian right. Yet the passage of time has done little to tarnish the mythology of *Behemoth*.

Behemoth in Washington, D.C.

Despite its conceptual, theoretical, empirical, and methodological flaws, Neumann's *Behemoth* informed U.S. policy planning for a defeated Germany. The rave reviews of the book (few of the critical ones appear to have at all registered) opened doors for its author in New York City and Washington, D.C.[157] As Scheuerman writes,

> Lavishly praised by reviewers when it first appeared in 1941, [*Behemoth*] catapulted Neumann into a position of prominence in comparison with his colleagues at the Institute for Social Research. While they remained obscure figures on the intellectual scene in the United States, it helped him gain a position at prestigious Columbia University. Neumann, and not [Max] Horkheimer or [Theodor] Adorno, was the first of the Frankfurt émigrés to receive such an offer. Soon thereafter, the American government asked Neumann to participate in coordinating the Office of Strategic Services' crucial Research and Analysis Bureau, a division of the federal government given the task of analyzing the political situation in Nazi Germany and providing policy proposals to elected officials and military authorities.[158]

More significant, not to mention disconcerting, than Neumann's entry into government service, is the fact that his *Behemoth* "played a central role in the Research and Analysis Bureau, where the empirical work undertaken by the German émigrés and their American coworkers at times represented little more than an attempt to elaborate on its main theses and make them palatable to government officials otherwise unfamiliar with twentieth-century radical thought, let alone known for their Hegelian-Marxist sympathies."[159] Barry Katz, author of the leading study on the OSS, has come to a similar conclusion: "Neumann's monumental study of the National Socialist 'Behemoth,' completed shortly before he entered the government, informed much of the [OSS's Central European] Section's ongoing research (which in turn filled in many of its omissions and contributed to the extensive appendix to the second edition [of *Behemoth*] that appeared in the summer of 1944)."[160] Aside from other real-world effects, Neumann's book decisively shaped the Central European Section's preparation for what became the Trial of the Major War Criminals at the International Military Tribunal at Nuremberg: "The structure of their case against the Nazi Behemoth grew out of Neumann's claim that it was a tightly integrated system, a corporate state managed by an interlocking directorate of political, military, and economic leaders."[161] The "émigré socialists" led by Neumann "treated National Socialism as the negative realization of the Marxist eschatology that had permeated their prewar theoretical work: a social totality that transcends the alienation of inner and outer, public and private, civil society and the state."[162] Take Irving Dwork's draft memorandum on the criminal responsibility of German individuals and collectivities for the destruction of the European Jews. It bore "the indelible stamp of Neumann's influence."[163] As Katz writes, "The brief was in fact an elaboration of the so-called spearhead theory of anti-Semitism that Neumann had worked out some two years before and which appears to have served the Section as a feeble beacon against the blackness of fascist irrationalism."[164]

Remembering his OSS days, the political scientist Harold Deutsch recalled, "It did not even take me a day to recognize that Franz Neumann was by far the most significant personality among its members."[165] Others have described the organization as a "permanent historical convention" ("*amerikanischer Historikertag in Permanenz*") dominated by Neumann whose charisma and growing influence in Washington, D.C., ensured that he "influenced an entire generation of future historians" at the OSS.[166] If the Bible's behemoth is a mythical creature, Neumann's *Behemoth* in 1944 attained the status of a nigh mythical book. Faith in Neumann's political economy of dictatorship was so strong that it drowned out dissenting voices. Because he also headed the "chairborne division," as the Research and Analysis Bureau was teasingly known, Neumann's opinion enjoyed greater authority than Fraenkel's.[167] It is an irony of history that Neumann's radical legalism was popular in U.S. foreign policy circles. But the reason for its appeal is not difficult to understand: "[T]he publication of *Behemoth* was an important event from a political standpoint [...] because it analysed the inner structure of National Socialism at a moment when the United States was about to enter the war against the Axis Powers and when everything depended upon revealing in its entirety the aggressive dynamism and the destructive potential of the enemy they had to overcome."[168]

It has been said that Neumann's vantage point as an outsider looking in was the root cause for his simplistic view of the law of the Third Reich.[169] The argument goes that Fraenkel had a more differentiated sense of law's role in Nazi Germany because he was subjected to Nazi domination for several years longer than Neumann, who had been forced to flee in 1933. Five additional years of limited access to surviving remnants of the *Rechtsstaat* certainly afforded Fraenkel glimpses into the everyday life of Nazi law that Neumann never had. What counts against Neumann is not that he was not privy to this trove of data, but that he apparently had no curiosity in finding out more about it. He was dismissive of his friend's clandestine research when he should have been inquisitive.

Neumann to Arendt

Notwithstanding the aforementioned shortcomings, mystique surrounds Neumann's *Behemoth* to this day. It has to do in part with the perception that the book was an important forerunner of Hannah Arendt's *The Origins of Totalitarianism*, an equally problematic and even more influential treatise from the middle of the twentieth century.[170] Vicky Iakovou, for one, believes that Neumann's "pathbreaking approach" put him "among those theorists who, very early, recognized the novelty of Nazi domination."[171] This innovation, Iakovou believes, got Arendt's attention and shaped the argument of her most important work: "*Behemoth* proves to be a permanent and privileged—albeit often implicit—reference in *The Origins of Totalitarianism*, as if it contained an analysis touching the nodal points of totalitarianism."[172] In particular, Neumann's concept of the non-state, though, as we have seen, of questionable theoretical and empirical value, left a mark on *The Origins of Totalitarianism*.[173] William Selinger has gone as far as suggesting that *Behemoth* served as "[t]he most important [...] historical account in America when Arendt was composing *Origins*."[174] Selinger, like Hilberg and Iakovou, was either unaware or unperturbed by *Behemoth*'s significant methodological flaws even though a long line of Neumann's contemporaries, as we have seen, had painstakingly enumerated them upon publication in 1942.

Other admirers of *Behemoth* have claimed an even greater impact for the work: "Neumann's assumptions concerning the functions of violence for Nazi Germany have been the basis of *all* historical research on this regime."[175] Many twenty-first century readings of *Behemoth* are similarly hyperbolic. Fueling this tendency toward hagiography was the *Times Literary Supplement*. At the close of the twentieth century, its editors included Neumann's best-known work in the TLS's list of "The Hundred Most Influential Books since the War," a decision that further enhanced the mythology of *Behemoth*. The TLS ranked the book at no. 13 on its list of twenty-one titles from the 1940s. It deemed *Behemoth* more influential than George Orwell's *Nineteen Eighty-Four*, which came in at no. 15 on the TLS list, as well as Karl Popper's *The Open Society and Its Enemies* (no. 17) and Joseph Schumpeter's, *Capitalism, Socialism, and Democracy* (no. 20).[176]

Behemoth has cast a long shadow over the study of the Third Reich. Due to its extraordinary reception in the early 1940s, it has attained the status of an instant classic in scholarship on the Nazi dictatorship. It has left an indelible mark on the way generations of scholars have come to view the nature and determinants of the Hitler regime.[177] It has inspired critical theories of law but also done lasting damage, which is why, to speak metaphorically, *Behemoth* needs slaying.

From the perspective of this book, one of the most troublesome legacies of *Behemoth*'s enormous success has been its contribution to the marginalization of law in the study of the Third Reich. Neumann's flawed argument about the non-state and its supposed logic of anarchy obscured the many different institutional determinants of the Nazi dictatorship. "Abstraction, reification, and oversimplification were the frequent results, particularly when Neumann purported to be providing historical explanations" is how one scholar summarized the value of *Behemoth*.[178] Neumann correctly perceived the fractured nature of power in the Third Reich but failed to identify its most important loci and divisions. His obsession with the economics of dictatorship caused him to give short shrift to the politics of dictatorship. And his faith in functional explanation meant that he was ill equipped to make sense of contingent outcomes.[179] Neumann's firm commitment to structuralism blinded him to the possibility of voluntarism in the Third Reich. Or, as Peter Hayes put it, "Neumann contributed something indispensable, then overreached."[180]

3

The Making of a Cause Lawyer

In the late twentieth century, legal scholars invented the "cause lawyer" as a type. But while the term was new, the strategy was not. Cause lawyering refers to the age-old set of practices that lawyers have employed in the furtherance of social change for centuries. "At its core," Austin Sarat and Stuart Feingold write, "cause lawyering is about using legal skills to pursue ends and ideals that transcend client service—be those ideals social, cultural, political, economic or, indeed, legal."[1] Lisa Hajjar clarifies: "What distinguishes cause lawyers from 'conventional lawyers' is that the former apply their professional skills in the service of a cause other than—or greater than—the interests of the client in order to transform some aspect of the status quo, where the latter tailor their practices to accommodate or benefit the client within the prevailing arrangements of power."[2] Ernst Fraenkel was a consummate cause lawyer—half a century before the term was invented.

THE JEWISH CONSCIENCE

Ernst Fraenkel was born in Cologne on December 26, 1898. His father, Georg Fraenkel, a merchant, and his mother, Therese Epstein, both hailed from bourgeois households that practiced enlightened forms of Judaism. Influenced by the so-called Jewish Enlightenment, or *Haskalah*, Fraenkel's parents and their relatives regarded skeptically the role of traditional religious rules and rites. They were part of a loose but sizable movement of European Jews that practiced a more secular, a more rational kind of Judaism. With origins in Germany, this ideational revolution actively promoted integration of Jews into Gentile societies.[3] The philosopher Moses Mendelssohn was the most important advocate of leaving behind the segregated communities in which Jews had historically lived in

The Remnants of the Rechtsstaat: An Ethnography of Nazi Law. Jens Meierhenrich.

Germany. In the eighteenth century, and with his own life as an example, Mendelssohn—who, among many other intellectual accomplishments, translated the *Torah* into German—encouraged *Maskilim*, as leaders of the *Haskalah* movement were called, to set their sights on vocational callings other than the rabbinate, whether in the arts, the professions, or public life. It was a call to intellectual arms. As the poet and writer Heinrich Heine, a contemporary, memorably put it: "As Luther overthrew the Papacy, so Mendelssohn overthrew the Talmud, and in exactly the same way: by rejecting tradition, declaring the Bible to be the source of religion, and translating its most important part. He thus destroyed Jewish Catholicism as Luther destroyed the Christian version. Indeed, the Talmud is the Catholicism of the Jews."[4] In the wake of this far-reaching rejection of orthodox faith, the number of Jews making important and lasting contributions to non-religious areas of life grew steadily. This form of cultural assimilation, in turn, contributed to other forms of social integration in Germany.

Though archival sources are scant, it appears that Fraenkel's parents approved of the teachings of Mendelssohn and raised their children in their spirit. As a result, he and his two elder siblings grew up in a religiously progressive home. As Fraenkel later recalled: "My education transpired under the influence of the Enlightenment, which also informed my family's attitude toward Judaism. My mother's siblings felt even less in touch with Jewish religion than my parents. In accordance with their total assimilation, they thought of themselves without reservation as Germans."[5]

Yet Fraenkel's upbringing, though comfortable, was far from easy. Early on in life, Fraenkel lost both of his parents and one sibling. His father and brother, Maximilian, died in 1909, his mother in 1915. After these losses, Fraenkel and his older sister, Marta, relocated to Frankfurt am Main, where they lived with their uncle Joseph Epstein, a physics graduate, not far from the city's university.[6] As he had in Cologne, Fraenkel enjoyed the comforts of a progressive household and continued his secondary education at the *Musterschule*, a grammar school in the city center. Fraenkel later remarked that the teaching of history at this school had been heavily influenced by the writings of Heinrich von Treitschke, the German nationalist historian whose rabid antisemitism and ardent calls for colonial expansionism was very much at odds with Fraenkel's emerging view of the world.[7] We can glean as much from a student essay in which Fraenkel was asked to debate Helmuth von Moltke's contention that "The idea of perpetual peace is a dream—and not even a pleasant one." The dismissive attitude toward Immanuel Kant's philosophical treatise implicit in the essay topic apparently incensed the young Fraenkel.

In response, he composed an imaginary dialogue between a pacifist and a militarist in which the former outwitted the latter. Fraenkel's teacher deemed the effort "impossible to grade" ("*unzensierbar*").[8] The anecdote permits a glimpse into the political socialization of the lawyer as a young man. Fraenkel's parents had laid the foundation for this socialization by instilling in their young son a social consciousness. He recalled that conversations about social problems of the time were taboo in school; in the family home, they were the order of the day and deemed a "humanitarian" issue that demanded rational reflection.[9]

Of greatest significance for Fraenkel's political maturation was probably the influence of Wilhelm Epstein, who, together with his wife, assisted his brother Joseph—the legal guardian—with the raising of the two Fraenkel children. The elder Epstein, a doctor by training but chemist by vocation, was very active in adult education. A pacifist and admirer of the Fabian Society, he helped build the *Frankfurter Ausschuß für Volksvorlesungen*, a local, private organization associated with the trade unions, where he also taught to make education accessible to the masses.[10] Discussions with his uncle about the nature and purpose of the educational reform project, which Fraenkel in retrospect described as "politically neutral" and "not Marxist" in orientation, may well have laid the foundations for his life-long predilection for social democracy as a political ideology.[11] His political socialization was given another boost by the coming war.

World War I cut short Fraenkel's secondary schooling. He graduated in November 1916 and immediately joined the ongoing war effort, for which he had volunteered. Fraenkel later remarked that in the beginning he was caught up in the general enthusiasm for the war, not least because "it was a war against Czarism."[12] As was the case with many of the country's Jews, the bellicose atmosphere made Fraenkel feel more German than ever: "Whatever Jewish consciousness I might have possessed, it was pushed into the background with the outbreak of war. I was deeply convinced that the war would mean the end of antisemitism."[13]

On April 3, 1917, Fraenkel was ordered to join an infantry reserve unit stationed in Jablonna, Poland, the *Infanterie-Ersatztruppe Warschau*. Sequestered in a camp eighteen kilometers north of Warsaw, Fraenkel's unit underwent basic military training to get the young recruits ready for the Western front to where they were dispatched in July 1917. Before they got there, however, the newly trained soldiers were put on a two-month hiatus in Prez, in the Ardennes. The entire unit was quarantined in a military hospital in order to contain a diptheria outbreak. Suspected of having contracted the infectious disease, Fraenkel and his comrades had to entertain themselves. It so happened that Fraenkel during this time discovered Max Weber's political writings, notably a series of newspaper articles that the famous German lawyer and sociologist had written for the *Frankfurter Zeitung*. Entitled "Parliament and Government in Germany under a New Political Order," the article series left a deep impression on the young Fraenkel.[14] As he recalled many years later, "Reading it introduced me to a scholarly perspective on politics."[15] But not just that: "The more frequently I read in the following months Weber's additional articles in the *Frankfurter Zeitung*, the more I came to regard him as my intellectual mentor."[16]

After having been laid up for two months, Fraenkel's unit finally arrived on the frontlines in August 1917. It was a momentous juncture in his life. As he noted in one of the very few personal letters from his military service that have survived: "I remembered the date on which we arrived in the trenches: It was August 1, 1917."[17] Fraenkel talked about his wartime experience as a soldier only reluctantly. It was a disorienting time for the young man. He jettisoned what he called the "uncritical pacifism" of his youth, but he was no less perturbed by the rise of nationalism and the glorification of war.[18] The experience of several months of trench warfare for him was "soul destroying and intellectually sterile."[19] In the dying days of World War I, Fraenkel personally encountered the one person who had kept his intellectual curiosity alive during the war. In the fall of 1918, on temporary military leave, Fraenkel accompanied his uncle Wilhelm to a private lecture by Max Weber. Deeply impressed, Fraenkel spent the night committing to paper Weber's key observations from memory. Yet despite admiration for the man's scholarly work and political advocacy, Fraenkel, apparently like most of the other audience members, felt alienated by what he perceived to be Weber's reactionary perspective on the question of peace. While emphasizing the importance for Germany of accepting territorial losses in order to end the war, Weber argued that a punitive peace was unacceptable. If the terms of a peace settlement were unreasonable, Weber insisted, the war simply had to go on. Fraenkel, who had experienced the death and destruction of World War I firsthand, was not convinced.[20] Aside from the more obvious forms of suffering in times of war, he and his fellow soldiers had endured extreme hunger when they engaged the enemy near Reims, in the Champagne, in Laon, and near Cambrai, and no other topic of discussion was as popular among soldiers as the prospects for peace.[21]

Up until January 1918, Fraenkel's unit fought to hold the *Siegfriedstellung*, usually referred to in English as the "Hindenburg Line," a supposedly impenetrable system of defences beyond which some of the German forces had retreated in the wake of the Battle of the Somme. Although the British Army's major offensive of July 1916 ground to a halt almost immediately, the devastating war of attrition that ensued caused Germany to reinforce their defensive fortifications. From this part of the front, Fraenkel also participated in the German spring offensive of 1918, notably in "Operation Michael" (*Michael-Offensive*). The largest of four attempted German advances, it was designed to penetrate the Allied lines and drive the British Army into the sea. In the course of the unsuccessful military operation, 239,800 German soldiers, 178,000 British soldiers, and 43,000 French soldiers are believed to have died.[22] The eventual failure of the spring offensive spelled the beginning of the end of World War I.

Despite staggering casualty figures, Fraenkel survived the carnage. On April 1, 1918, he sustained injuries from a hand grenade and spent several months recovering, initially in a military hospital in Sachsen, then in Darmstadt as part of a *Genesungskompanie*, or convalescent company, a military unit of wounded troops on the road to recovery.[23] The episode is noteworthy because it is in Darmstadt that Fraenkel, as he put it, became "witness to the revolution."[24] There he first encountered the revolutionary fervor of his time. Courtesy of the hopeful stories that prisoners of war returning from Russia were telling about the revolutionary upheaval there, Fraenkel became acquainted with, and even briefly drawn into, the contentious politics that would usher in, later that year, the German Revolution of 1918–1919. Yet the revolution was not for him, not least because he felt ill-equipped intellectually to make sense of what was happening around him.[25] Left traumatized by the war and confused by the revolution, Fraenkel was keen to start his university education and acquire the analytical tools necessary for making sense of the uncertain times in which he found himself.

LAW AS VOCATION

Fraenkel left military service on January 28, 1919. In conversations with his uncle Joseph Epstein, it was decided that Fraenkel would study law with a minor in history at the University of Frankfurt, a progressive, privately funded institution that had opened its doors just a few years earlier, in 1914. Even though Fraenkel had originally set his heart on reading history, he never regretted the decision to switch to law. Many years later, he even remarked that his dual training in law *and* history proved essential for developing his research trajectory in political science.[26]

In addition to his compulsory courses, Fraenkel attended lectures on Prussian legal history, the jurisprudence of the *Reichsgericht* as well as on British and American civil law in pursuit of his law degree.[27] Interestingly, at Frankfurt, the compulsory law curriculum included a course on "*Öffentliches Recht*," or "public law," in which Fraenkel enrolled in the summer semester 1921.[28] The title of the course is unusual because in the 1920s it was the norm for law students to be instructed only in "*Staatsrecht*," which literally translates as "state law" and of which constitutional law forms an important part. The teaching of public law rather than a narrower focus on *Staatsrecht*, or state law, is suggestive of a fairly progressive conception of law on the part of the Frankfurt faculty. It is also noteworthy because in the teaching of public law, the concern is not only with the organization of the state, but also with the rights and roles of individuals in relation to this state. In other words, whereas the relationship between state and society is at the heart of a university course on *Öffentliches Recht*, it was traditionally of secondary or no importance in courses on *Staatsrecht*, and certainly not at Fraenkel's time.[29] Having become acquainted with a more progressive legal conception of the political than was the norm in Weimar Germany, Fraenkel was primed for, and receptive to, additional influences.

While enrolled in Frankfurt, he also attended courses at the University of Heidelberg, mostly in law.[30] It was there that he met Otto Kahn-Freund, who would become one of his closest friends and who subsequently transferred to Frankfurt. It appears there the lectures of Hugo Sinzheimer left the deepest impressions on them. Sinzheimer had joined the law faculty in 1920 to take up the first chair in Germany in the new field of labor law (*Arbeitsrecht*). Aside from advancing this new field, and his related interest, the sociological study of law, it was Sinzheimer's ambition to help train a new generation of lawyers, one that would be socially aware and committed to creating a fair and equitable society.[31] To this end, Sinzheimer also founded, and edited between 1925 and 1931, the journal *Die Justiz,* a publication of the Republican Federation of Judges (*Republikanischer Richterbund*) that sought to push against the dominance of doctrinalism and legal positivism in the legal profession. In substantive terms, he headed a fledgling intellectual movement committed to the creation of a social *Rechtsstaat*, an idea that that, following the Nazi conflagration, grew into the mainstay of twentieth century German politics and society.[32]

Sinzheimer's commitment to social justice—and his conception of labor law as a tool to advance it—influenced Fraenkel enormously. As he once remarked, "In Frankfurt, my teacher, the lawyer and professor Hugo Sinzheimer [...] contributed to my understanding of trade unions, social policy, the political workers' movement, the sociology of law, and, most importantly, collective labor law."[33] Fraenkel described Sinzheimer admiringly as "a political *homo novus*"—a reference to his teacher's quest to make a contribution to both theory *and* practice, and an intellectual trait that Fraenkel chose to emulate in his own life.

But Fraenkel was not the only notable German whose intellectual development Sinzheimer shaped. Fellow students included Hans Morgenthau, who, with the publication in 1948 of the first edition of *Politics among Nations*, became one of the founders of the paradigm of classical realism in the political science sub-field of International Relations, and Carlo Schmid, who went on to become a professor of law and is widely credited as one of the main architects of post-war Germany's constitution, the *Grundgesetz*, or "Basic Law."[34] Franz Neumann, who, only a few years later, became Fraenkel's partner in law in Berlin was also a member of the Sinzheimer circle.[35] Fraenkel's extracurricular interactions with like-minded students further contributed to his gradually developing a distinctly social democratic conception of law.[36] Together with fellow students, Fraenkel formed a book club in which they debated major works of the leading scholars and intellectuals of their time. The authors they subjected to analysis were drawn from various parts of the political spectrum and included, most important, Karl Marx and Max Weber, whose contending analytical frameworks deeply informed the book club's efforts at making sense of Weimar's fledgling experiment with democracy. But other thinkers such as Karl Renner, Ferdinand Tönnies, Hans Kelsen, and Carl Schmitt were read as well—always with an eye toward deriving prescriptions for action in support of a more egalitarian society.[37]

Not surprisingly, given these influences, Fraenkel, in 1921, joined the *Sozialdemokratische Partei Deutschlands* (SPD), Germany's Social Democratic Party, as did most of the other members of the book club. The University of Frankfurt in the 1920s was also home to the Marxist-oriented *Institut für Sozialforschung*, the incubus for what would become the so-called Frankfurt School of critical theory.[38] More so than other German universities at the time, Fraenkel's *alma mater* was awash with a very broad spectrum of progressive and leftist ideas—ideas that sensitized the young lawyer to the social dislocations that can result from unfettered capitalism.

After completing the first part of his law degree (*Erstes Staatsexamen*) on December 17, 1921, Fraenkel embarked on the various stations of his legal traineeship, known as the *Referendariat*. Then and now, this mandatory program requires law graduates to spend up to two years honing their legal skills in different types of legal institutions—courts, prosecutors' offices, administrative agencies, and in private practice. In Fraenkel's case, the applied phase of his legal education first took him to the district court (*Amtsgericht*) in Weilburg, a small town located some fifty kilometers north of Frankfurt, where he spent six months becoming acquainted with the practice of law. While stationed in the countryside, he clashed with, and lodged a formal complaint against, a young judge over the latter's lack of political neutrality and display of arch conservative insignia on his judicial robe. To Fraenkel's consternation, the complaint went nowhere.[39]

Fraenkel subsequently spent three months training at the regional court (*Landgericht*) in Frankfurt and another three months in the prosecutor's office there. On May 9, 1923, he began a four-month stint as a *Referendar*, or lawyer-in-training, in Sinzheimer's law firm, during which he likely laid the groundwork for his doctoral dissertation, entitled "*Der nichtige Arbeitsvertrag*" ("The Nugatory Employment Contract"), which Sinzheimer supervised and Fraenkel submitted in December that year.[40] Between September 1923 and January 1924, Fraenkel continued with his traineeship, gaining experience in the Frankfurt district court. The final stop en route to becoming a fully qualified lawyer was a six-month stint at the regional court of appeal (*Oberlandesgericht*), also in Frankfurt. After the completion of his applied training, Fraenkel sat for, and passed, the second part of his law degree (*Zweites Staatsexamen*) on January 12, 1925. Now a qualified civil servant, he gained the title of *Assessor* and initially remained in the employ of the state. Almost immediately, however, Fraenkel applied for leave from what could have been a judicial career as a judge. Instead, he turned to private practice and briefly worked in a small law firm in Saarbrücken, *Sender & Lehmann*. Around this time, Fraenkel began to contribute more regularly commentary to left-leaning publications such as *Die Tat*, *Vorwärts*, and the *Jungsozialistische Blätter* as well as to more specialized scholarly outlets like *Arbeitsrecht*. His passion for social causes in general, and labor law in particular, netted him invitations to workshops and conferences. It followed ever closer contact with the trade union movement.[41] Fraenkel had found his cause. He began dedicating his career to lawyering in pursuit of social justice, especially on behalf of Germany's working class. The strategies Fraenkel deployed saw him representing his cause in both commentary and courtrooms. He embodied a subtype of cause lawyering that Thomas Hilbink has dubbed "vanguard lawyering"—a habitus that Fraenkel would be forced to abandon less than a decade later.[42]

LAWYER WITH A CAUSE

In February 1926, Fraenkel extended his civil service leave to take up a position as legal adviser to the German Metalworkers Union

(*Deutscher Metallarbeiterverband*). It must have been a perfect match because only four weeks into his new job, Fraenkel asked to be permanently released from his position as *Assessor*, thus foregoing a potential career in the Weimar judiciary. Under the auspices of the German Metalworkers Union, Fraenkel took up a teaching position in Bad Dürrenberg, near Leipzig, where the trade union had just opened a *Wirtschaftsschule*, an educational institution aimed at instructing metalworkers in questions of law and economics as well as at introducing them to more general subjects.[43] Fraenkel saw his mission as that of contributing to "the struggle for the emancipation of the proletariat."[44] Groups of approximately fifty union functionaries, aged between twenty and forty-five years of age, would spent three or four weeks in Bad Dürrenberg to complete the full course of instruction. In 1926, the *Wirtschaftsschule* offered nine such courses; in 1927 already thirteen.[45] Fraenkel is said to have enjoyed his time as a lecturer and was apparently effective and well liked, if distant.[46] During his foray into teaching, he continued to publish widely on the social questions of the time. He also completed his longest publication to date, the forty-five page pamphlet *Zur Soziologie der Klassenjustiz* (*On the Sociology of Class Justice*), first published in 1927.[47] It was an attempt to draw attention to structural determinants of Weimar jurisprudence, notably the reification of capitalist values in the education of judges. Although his essay bore the mark of Marxist ideas, his aim, Fraenkel wrote in the pamphlet's preface, was "not to indict, but to explain."[48] In fact, he explicitly distanced himself from the unreflective use of the notion of "class justice" that was popular in socialist and communist circles at the time. He was keen to temper the revolutionary zeal of the German left. To bridge ideological cleavages, he looked for commonalities. For Fraenkel, as Udi Greenberg points out,

> both workers and the bourgeoisie were heirs to the tradition of a rational "natural law." Both believed that laws should reflect universal moral truths, not power relations or class interests. Consequently, workers were not as radically different from the bourgeoisie as Communists or Marxist Social Democrats often believed. While they disagreed on economy policies, they still shared a similar conviction that the *Rechtsstaat* had to serve universal justice. Workers, in this line of thought, were not obliged to overthrow the entire bourgeois legal system. They merely had to expand it to create what Fraenkel termed "proletarian natural law."[49]

Drawing on the ideas that had been percolating in the Sinzheimer circle, Fraenkel made the case for a social *Rechtsstaat*, the idea of which Hermann Heller had introduced in 1930 and theorized as the only alternative to authoritarian rule.[50] Here is Greenberg summarizing Fraenkel's train of thought:

> According to Fraenkel, the parliamentary system established in the Weimar Republic, like the *Rechtsstaat*, drew from nineteenth-century bourgeois principles and social conditions that predated the industrial revolution and the creation of the Socialist movement. Fraenkel therefore claimed that, like the *Rechtsstaat*, the German parliamentary system had to be reformed and fused with Socialist ideas to create a hybrid, Socialist-liberal democracy.[51]

With this argument, Fraenkel turned Carl Schmitt's critique of liberalism, much of which he admired, on its head. Instead of seeing the institution of parliament as mere problem, he saw in it potential, a solution even to Germany's woes. The only adjustment to be made to the practice of parliamentary democracy, according to Fraenkel, was a strengthening of the social foundations of democracy, most notably by institutionalizing collective logics of representation.

The publication of *Zur Soziologie der Klassenjustiz* marked Fraenkel's transition from lecturer to lawyer in private practice. Though he retained close ties with the German Metalworkers Union, Fraenkel, in March 1927, opened a private law firm in Berlin. In the late 1920s, the city was known as a thriving, but increasingly competitive, marketplace for lawyers. But Fraenkel did not have to struggle to attract clients. Located at Tempelhofer Ufer 16a, in Kreuzberg, Fraenkel specialized in labor law and represented private clients as well as the German Metalworkers Union. He appears to have been a regular at the *Landesarbeitsgericht*, Berlin's regional labor court.[52] This time was also an intellectually rewarding and productive one for Fraenkel. He continued to write on topics in labor law, though mostly from a strictly doctrinal legal perspective. In 1928, he managed to publish seventeen essays and articles and eleven in 1929.[53] The most prominent of these pieces were his articles on "Kollektive Demokratie" ("Collective Democracy") and on "Rechtssoziologie als Wissenschaft" ("The Sociology of Law as Science").[54] The former appeared in the widely read journal *Die Gesellschaft*, an outlet for theoretical analyses of contemporary politics. Edited by Rudolf Hilferding and subsequently by Albert Salomon, the journal was published under the auspices of the SPD leadership and attracted contributors ranging from Hannah Arendt to Walter Benjamin, from Emil Lederer to Ferdinand Tönnies, and from Herbert Marcuse to Gustav Radbruch. The staff of *Die Gesellschaft* became Fraenkel's most important social circle in Berlin.[55] Later in life he remembered fondly the regular interactions and stimulating discussions he had in *Café Dümichen*, a coffee shop located not far from the Potsdamer Platz: "Never before or since have I been part of a more inspired and inspiring circle."[56] Franz Neumann, Fraenkel's university friend, was a regular member of this group, and his Charlottenburg apartment served as a regular meeting place. Inasmuch as Fraenkel was wary of Germany's *Kommunistische Partei* (Communist Party), the KPD, he displayed a fondness for Marxism in these years, even borrowing the ideology's concepts and language for some of his publications.[57] This notwithstanding, Fraenkel's article "Kollektive Demokratie" is hardly revolutionary in either tone or claim. He was concerned with enhancing democracy rather than overthrowing it. More specifically, Fraenkel identified defects in the operation of Weimar's constitutional framework, notably the dependence of the country's parliament on the bureaucracy. Because the parliamentary supremacy envisaged by the drafters of the constitution had not materialized, according to Fraenkel, it was essential, or so he claimed, to supplement—though not supplant—the existing dispensation with elements of collective democracy, by which he meant the systematic involvement of civil society organizations, notably economic associations ("*wirtschaftliche Vereinigungen*"), in the administration of politics.[58] An increased practice of collective democracy, Fraenkel argued, would not only lead to the "democratization of administration" but also help combat what he diagnosed as "*Parlamentsverdrossenheit*," that is, a general disillusionment with parliament that he detected in the population.[59]

His other publication from 1929, "Rechtssoziologie als Wissenschaft" ventured in a slightly different direction. Here Fraenkel was primarily concerned with the political utility of the social sciences, notably Sinzheimer's preferred methodology for understanding legal developments: the sociology of law. This article is one of the most insightful of Fraenkel's shorter contributions. Though the argument, from our vantage point in the twenty-first century, may at first glance seem unremarkable, it is important to recognize the continued dominance of doctrinal analysis in the study of law in the early twentieth century, in Germany and elsewhere. Critical approaches to the law, especially mixed or non-legal methodologies, were the exception—far from established as a legitimate way of exploring law and society.[60] But Fraenkel's 1929 article was not just pioneering, it was also programmatic, a sketch of Fraenkel's analytical trajectory to come. This point is of immediate significance for our discussion of *The Dual State*, notably of its interdisciplinary nature.

With his article, Fraenkel sought to establish "*Rechtssoziologie*" ("sociology of law") as a legitimate approach to the study of legal phenomena. He proposed that it was as valuable as—and therefore should be seen as methodologically equal to—the conventional approach of "*Rechtswissenschaft*" ("legal science") as well as to established auxiliary approaches in the subfield of "*Rechtstheorie*" ("legal theory"), namely "*Rechtsphilosophie*" ("legal philosophy"), "*Rechtsgeschichte*" ("legal history"), and "*Rechtspolitik*" ("legal politics").[61] Fraenkel did not think legal science, as practiced in his time, had much to offer to the production of knowledge about law-in-society. For him it was mere "*Rechtsanwendungslehre*," nothing more than the tallying and interpretation of black-letter-law in the service of legal practice.[62] For Fraenkel, it was an applied approach, not a learned one. He wanted to work with data, not doctrine. He held in higher regard the auxiliary approaches in the subfield of legal theory. And yet, Fraenkel did not think that the philosophical, historical, and political study of law as such were sufficient as analytical approaches either. A distinctly sociological approach was also needed, he claimed. He positioned this approach in direct opposition to Paul Laband's brand of legal positivism, which was still very influential at that time.[63]

According to Laband, "[a]ll historical, political, and philosophical considerations" were "without significance" in the study of law. His legal positivism (known as *Staatsrechtspositivismus*, or state law positivism) was wary of extra-legal considerations and advocated a "retracing of individual [legal] norms to general [legal] concepts."[64] Laband's was legal science par excellence. As Stefan Korioth writes, "For the first time, attempts were made to offer a state law theory that could provide rational, logically grounded, and reliable answers in the field of constitutional law; in short, positivism established a doctrine of constitutional law. In addition, positivist procedure linked the field of law with the methods of the expanding natural sciences and the tendency, characteristic of nineteenth century thought, to turn all of life into science. The positivist trust in 'what is' corresponded to the general trend in the humanities that followed the collapse of philosophical idealism in the first half of the century."[65]

Methodologically, Fraenkel objected to the theoretical reductionism at the heart of *Staatsrechtspositivismus*; politically, he objected to its built-in status-quo bias. Throughout his long life and far-reaching thought, Fraenkel was driven by, to borrow a phrase of Karl Jaspers, "the unqualified will to know."[66] As a result of his social democratic upbringing, he also never ceased to question the status quo. He had internalized the lesson that it was usually the haves—rarely the have-nots—who benefitted from it. It is for these reasons that Fraenkel responded so strongly, in methodological terms, to Laband's legal positivism. In an effort to upend it, Fraenkel invoked with admiration the achievements of Anton Menger, Eugen Ehrlich, and Karl Renner.[67] He considered the three leading Austrian jurists to be at the forefront of the sociology of law—the kinds of scholars that Germany lacked. It did not hurt that Ehrlich held a theoretical position that was, at the time at least, also Fraenkel's: "The law and thus also legal rules are merely a superstructure of the economic order."[68] This article of faith served as the normative foundation for many of Fraenkel's occasional writings (as well as of the *Urdoppelstaat*) in the Nazi years.

Of greater relevance for understanding his interpretive approach is Fraenkel's distinction among three subtypes of the legal sociological method: (1) "descriptive sociology of law ("*deskriptive Rechtssoziologie*"); (2) "analytical sociology of law" ("*analysierende Rechtssoziologie*"); and (3) "constructive sociology of law" ("*konstruktive Rechtssoziologie*").[69] Here is how he imagined the contribution of each to the critical study of law: "The analytical sociology of law shows us the lawmaker's dependence on the societal forces of the time; the descriptive sociology of law reveals the limited reach of the lawmaker's commands ('*Anordnungen*'); the constructive sociology of law demonstrates completely the lawmaker's powerlessness ('*Ohnmacht*')."[70] Fraenkel proposed that a combination of the three approaches ought to be seen as a *sine qua non* of sophisticated legal scholarship, that is, a literature that aims to do more than just train the next generation of status-quo-oriented lawyers. As he put it: "The sociology of law is a political science ('*eine politische Wissenschaft*'), not only because it is relevant to the politician, but also because its subject matter is a political one."[71]

The influence of Fraenkel's 1929 article on his various accounts of the dual state in the period 1937–1941 was considerable, as I explain in more detail in Chapter 6. For now, consider for example the organization and structure of the 1941 English edition of *The Dual State*. Part I was entitled "The Legal System of the Dual State," Part II "The Legal Theory of the Dual State," and Part III "The Legal Reality of the Dual State."[72] True to his call in 1929 for an interdisciplinary approach to the study of law, Fraenkel combined, and fully integrated, insights from legal science, legal theory, legal philosophy, and legal history to arrive at his sociological account of Nazi law. He also unwittingly relied on techniques from the emerging anthropology of law. Fraenkel's use of ethnographic data about the role(s) of law in everyday life—culled from his own legal practice—underlined the analytical value of participant observation as yet another useful methodological approach to the study of law in society.[73] *The Dual State*, in other words, was an early and pioneering example of interdisciplinary legal scholarship, daringly conceived and masterfully crafted in extraordinary times.

In the late 1970s, Roger Cotterrell, a prominent exponent of the sociology of law in the latter half of the twentieth century, appraised the role of interdisciplinary legal scholarship: "The list of great men in the history of scholarship who have refused to limit their vision within the confines of the disciplinary boundaries of their era is sufficiently impressive to reassure modern teachers and researchers that, despite all the problems involved in interdisciplinarity, it has a sound and respectable history as one of the eminently productive and innovatory varieties of intellectual non-conformity."[74] We know from his postwar statements that for Fraenkel, the writing of the *Urdoppelstaat*, and subsequently of *The Dual State*, were such acts of non-conformity. Except that Fraenkel's non-conformity was more dangerous than interdisciplinary research should be. Fraenkel's was a valiant act of resistance couched in the form of an ethnography of law.

But before Fraenkel was forced to turn his life over to the analysis of the law of the Third Reich—which, in the late 1920s, was still but a distant fear—he stayed true to the practice of labor law. Fraenkel joined forces with Neumann and opened a law firm in the newly built headquarters of the German Metalworkers Union at Alte Jakobstraße 148–55. Designed by the architect Erich Mendelsohn, and completed in 1930, the imposing building allowed for continued access to one of Fraenkel's most important clients.

When Sinzheimer, disillusioned by the state of democracy in Weimar Germany, relinquished, in 1931, the lead editorship of *Die Justiz*, Fraenkel continued in his stead and published, until the journal ceased publication in 1933, sharply worded commentary in support of his ideal of a democratic society.[75] In eleven incisive essays in total, Fraenkel analyzed legal and intellectual developments ranging from proposals for a reform of civil procedure to the increasing use of the notorious Article 48 of the Weimar Constitution, what he termed the "*Diktaturparagraphen*," or "dictator's provision"; and from the implications of Carl Schmitt's "friend-enemy" distinction for the administration of criminal justice to the political fallout of the important 1932 proceeding *Preussen contra Reich* before the *Staatsgerichtshof*, the ad hoc constitutional tribunal in Weimar Germany's *Reichsgericht*, the Republic's Federal Supreme Court in Leipzig, which adjudicated in cases of organizational conflict.[76] Fraenkel grew increasingly concerned about the "crisis of state" ("*Staatskrise*") in which his country was finding itself, not least because the NSDAP had secured the majority of votes in the parliamentary elections of July 30, 1932. It garnered thirty-seven percent of the vote and increased its number of seats in the *Reichstag*, the country's federal parliament, from 107 to 230. To preserve the constitutional integrity of Weimar democracy in these trying times—in which unstable parliamentary majorities and the quick succession of chancellors were the order of the day—Fraenkel proposed an ingenious institutional safeguard. He saw the need for an "operation" on "the heart of the constitution" ("*das Herzstück der Verfassung*"), by which he meant a reconfiguration of Article 54.[77]

This constitutional provision had been a major advance for democracy because it provided that the chancellor and his ministers needed to have the confidence of the *Reichstag*, the German parliament. As soon as parliament withdrew its confidence by adopting a resolution to this effect, the chancellor or individual(s) had to resign. A good idea in theory; in practice, however, the proliferation of political parties made the creation of stable majorities unexpectedly difficult, with the result that chancellors were losing parliament's confidence, both de jure and de facto, at an alarming rate. Even though, as the historian Karl Dietrich Bracher reminded us, only two of the seventeen different cabinets that governed Weimar Germany in the period 1919–1930 fell apart as a result of a successful vote of no confidence, the specter of dissolution added a great deal of uncertainty to the already contentious politics of the time.[78] Fraenkel maintained that "a parliament that is incapable of approbation, loses its right of reprobation."[79] He made a case for curtailing the hard-won parliamentary right to recall the executive. In his argument, parliament should only be entitled to force the resignation of a chancellor or minister if it combined its call for dismissal with the election of a replacement candidate. The innovative solution, though never tried, was a forerunner of the famous Article 67 in postwar Germany's constitutional text, the *Grundgesetz*, which enshrined the institution of the *konstruktives Mißtrauensvotum* ("constructive vote of no confidence"). This crucial institutional plank of the 1949 constitutional order has been widely lauded as a harbinger of institutional stability since the end of World War II and thus as an important corrective to the logic of non-sustainable democracy in the 1920s. Though inspired by ideas of Heinrich Herrfahrdt, Carl Schmitt, and Erich Kaufmann, it sprang in the main from Fraenkel's institutional thought.

INTO THE ABYSS

Just before the burning of the Reichstag in Berlin, on February 27, 1933, Fraenkel threw down the gauntlet, issuing a daring challenge to the incoming Nazi regime. In his final article for *Die Justiz* he voiced in no uncertain terms his opposition to the impending Nazi revolution: "We proudly fly the flag. On this flag these words are written: Against arbitrary rule!"[80] We now know that Fraenkel at the time underestimated the threat that the Nazis posed. He misjudged how few adherents the democratic ideal truly had in his native Germany and how irreparably divided the fledgling anti-Nazi alliance was. The gravity of the situation was driven home on a personal level at the end of March, when police detained Hugo Sinzheimer, Fraenkel's mentor, in Frankfurt, and placed him in *Schutzhaft*, ostensibly for his own protection.[81] It was the beginning of the destruction of Jewish life and thought in Nazi Germany.[82]

On May 2, 1933, the new regime outlawed the country's trade unions, including the German Metalworkers Union. SA forces stormed the headquarters at Alte Jakobstra*ße* and systematically rounded up suspected enemies of the state, including Franz Neumann. On May 9, Fraenkel received his *Vertretungsverbot*, an official notification that he, as a Jew, was henceforth prohibited from representing clients in a German court of law.[83] Neumann received the same notice and took the opportunity to flee abroad before things could get worse. Neumann built a new life in London, where he enrolled at the London School of Economics and Political Science, studied under Harold Laski and Karl Mannheim, and completed a second doctoral dissertation (this time in political science) on "The Governance of the Rule of Law."[84] Fraenkel, by contrast, decided to stay in Berlin. He appealed his prohibition to practice law, as did around 1,700 other Jewish lawyers in the city. Although the Nazis were only tolerating Jewish lawyers with a *Frontkämpfer*-background, that is, individuals who had been involved in military combat on the frontlines of World War I, Fraenkel was able to provide the requisite testimonies and the prohibition against him was lifted on May 11, 1933.[85] Thus began Fraenkel's adventure inside the belly of what would become, in the late 1930s, the Nazi behemoth.

Though his file was reviewed once more in 1934, this time for suspected "communist activity," Fraenkel managed to muddle through, taking on ever more sensitive cases. While his roster of clients had previously centered on those caught up in labor law-related disputes, Fraenkel in the following years became increasingly involved in the legal representation of political activists on the left.[86] He later recalled that it was common, even for defense attorneys, to push for lengthy prison sentences in order to spare clients the terror of the Nazi concentration camps to where they would likely have been sent in the event of an acquittal or lesser sentence. Fraenkel readily acknowledged the collusion of "humane judges" ("*humane Richter*") who for the same reason imposed lengthy prison sentences on defendants who stood to otherwise fall into the hands of the prerogative state.[87]

But Fraenkel resisted the regime not just in the courtroom but also in print. In 1934, under the pseudonym "Frank III," he published a provocative analysis of Nazi criminal justice in the *Sozialistische Warte*, the periodical of the *Internationaler Sozialistischer Kampfbund* (International Socialist Militant League).[88] It recounts, *pars pro toto*, the criminal proceeding against Oskar Schulze, a metalworker from Berlin, its perverse outcome, and the investigation and adjudication that directly led to it. For Fraenkel, it was meaningful, and thus important to publicize, because as an example of political justice it represented "an everyday occurrence" ("*eine alltägliche Geschichte*").[89] In 1935, this time under the pseudonym "Fritz Dreher," Fraenkel published again in the *Sozialistische Warte*.[90] This time it was a rallying cry. Fraenkel was seized by a desire to energize and fortify resistance to Nazi rule. His biographer has observed that it was at this moment in time that Fraenkel gave up his analytical detachment and "political action became the center" of his depleted life.[91] During this more overt phase of his resistance, Fraenkel called upon "socialist workers" to take on a leadership role.[92] Reminding his readers of socialism's "inglorious" implosion in 1933, he outlined in his article the need and opportunities for "insurgent work." Fraenkel had in mind any and all underground activities that were both highly "visible" and capable of spreading unease and "a sense of uncertainty" on the part of the Nazi regime.[93] It would count as a success, proclaimed Frankel, if insurgent socialist action managed to provoke a continuation of Nazi rule by exception.[94] Why? Because Fraenkel was convinced that ordinary Germans would eventually tire of a regime that interfered too much with "*Gemütlichkeit*," that is, the calm, comfortable, and cozy state of being that is said to represent an ideal of ordinary life in Germany.[95] Fraenkel wanted to do damage to the, in his eyes, still tenuous connecting tissue between "people" and "government" ("*Volk und Regierung*").[96] To win allies in the struggle against Nazism, Fraenkel invoked the "liberating effect" ("*befreiende Wirkung*)" of insurgent action, the purpose of which, he concluded with rhetorical flair, was as follows: "to give strength to the workers, confidence to the weary, hope to those who are suffering, and to put the fear into those who govern" ("*den Arbeitenden Kraft geben, den Schwankenden Vertrauen, den Leidenden Hoffnung und den Herrschenden Furcht einzuflößen*").[97]

Fraenkel's passionate article, printed in the Netherlands via Switzerland and France, was also distributed as a flyer of the resistance. Had Nazi authorities uncovered Fraenkel's pseudonymous identity, he would most certainly have been tried—and sentenced—for high treason. His legal practice on behalf of the resisting Jews of Berlin was already a thorn in the side of Nazi authorities.[98] In the fall of 1938, the Fraenkels left Nazi Germany in great haste. Fraenkel's name had appeared on a Gestapo list. His life was now in danger.[99] However, he was allowed to leave the country legally and on September 20 boarded a plane for London at Berlin's Tempelhof Airport.[100] He was among 33,000–40,000 Jews who managed to emigrate that year. See Table 3.1.

Table 3.1 Jewish emigration from Nazi Germany, 1933–1941

Year	Number of Émigrés
1933	37,000–38,000
1934	22,000–23,000
1935	20,000–21,000
1936	24,000–25,000
1937	23,000
1938	46,000
1939	75,000–80,000
1940	15,000
1941	8,000

Source: Wolfgang Benz, *Die Juden in Deutschland 1933–1945*, Third edition (Munich: Beck, 1993), p. 738. Benz reported an estimated 33,000–40,000 émigrés for 1938. I substituted Michael Wildt's higher figure, culled from an annual report of the *Sicherheitsdienst* (SD), or Security Service. See Michael Wildt, ed., *Die Judenpolitik des SD 1935 bis 1938* (Munich: Oldenbourg, 1995), p. 202. A comprehensive analysis is available in Herbert Strauss, "Jewish Emigration from Nazi Germany," *Leo Baeck Institute Yearbook*, Vol. 25 (1980), pp. 313–61.

After a brief spell in Great Britain, Fraenkel and his wife emigrated to the United States. They started out in New York, where Fraenkel hoped to secure employment at the New School for Social Research. Modeled after the LSE, the New School, as it was known then and still is today, had been founded in 1918 and during the interwar years developed into a veritable "university in exile." In 1935/1936 alone, it received some 5,000 requests for teaching positions from international scholars at risk.[101] Like many of his compatriots, Fraenkel was unsuccessful with his application. It was an extraordinarily trying time for him. His professional life was in tatters, income meager or non-existent. With no other prospects, he decided to become a student again. In the fall of 1939, he enrolled for a J.D. at the University of Chicago Law School. To finance his studies, Fraenkel applied and received a competitive scholarship from the American Committee for the Guidance of Professional Personnel (ACGPP). As part of his application, Fraenkel included the second English-language draft of *The Dual State*.

Before I elaborate further on Fraenkel's years in exile, I chart the long and winding road that led to the publication of *The Dual State*. Fraenkel certainly took the one less traveled by, and I show why this made all the difference. It resulted in the making of a slow-burning classic, the intellectual significance of which far surpasses that of the other, more influential book about the Nazi dictatorship that appeared in the early 1940s—Franz Neumann's better-known *Behemoth*, which we encountered in Chapter 2. Fraenkel's unique experiences and dangerous encounters in Nazi Germany alienated him from most of the German Jewish refugees with whom he crossed paths in the United States. But his fiercely independent streak and intellectual confidence ensured that he weathered unharmed the criticism with which some of the cognoscenti in New York—especially at the New School for Social Research—greeted his ideas about the logic of Nazi rule.

4

Mr. von Mohl's Term of Art: A History of the *Rechtsstaat*, 1798–1933

> One has to assume that the word and concept
> of the "*Rechtsstaat*" are uniquely German.
> Neither exists in a non-German literature,
> nor can they be expressed correctly
> in a non-German language.
>
> Lorenz von Stein[1]

The *Rechtsstaat* crafted in postwar Germany must not be confused with earlier incarnations. Theodor Maunz and Reinhold Zippelius put it succinctly in a well-known textbook: "In today's conception, the '*Rechtsstaat*' is not only a *Rechtsstaat* in a formal sense (a state of law), but also a *Rechtsstaat* in a material sense (a state of justice)."[2] It was not always thus.

This chapter tells a brief history of the idea of the *Rechtsstaat* in Germany.[3] I trace the evolution of the term from its emergence in the late eighteenth century until 1933. Its intellectual trajectory raises questions about the long-run consequences of legal development in modern Germany. It sets the stage for my analysis in the next chapter of the term's manipulation by legal theorists in Nazi Germany.

AN INSURGENT IDEA, 1798–1871

The idea of the *Rechtsstaat* has revolutionary origins. It was a creature of the nineteenth century. Robert von Mohl crafted it under the influence of the Enlightenment. The term itself, however, was not von Mohl's. It was the brainchild of Johann Wilhelm Petersen, better known as Johann

The Remnants of the Rechtsstaat: An Ethnography of Nazi Law. Jens Meierhenrich.

Wilhelm Placidus. A trained lawyer and professor of, among other subjects, diplomacy, Placidus, in 1798 published his *Litteratur der Staatslehre*, a reflection on extant theories of the state.[4] In it, he set out liberal critiques of the *Polizeistaat*, the concept of the police state, that was providing the intellectual foundation for the regimes of enlightened despotism that governed most of continental Europe at the time. It was an era in which, especially in Germany, the codification of everyday life meant that the state was the sole source of law. A prominent example of this legalization drive is the 1794 *Allgemeines Landrecht für die Preußischen Staaten*. Organized into twenty substantive parts and some 17,000 provisions, this General Law Code for the governance and administrative of the states of Prussia firmly cemented the idea of rule by law. It was by all accounts a staggering achievement to which Alexis de Tocqueville testified: "This law code is a real constitution, in the sense that was then attributed to that word; its purpose was not only to regulate relations among citizens but between citizens and the State; it is simultaneously a civil code, a criminal code, and a political constitution."[5] Commissioned by Frederick II but completed only after his death, this institutional design of a genuinely "public law" for the states of Prussia was a blueprint for a total state, a state penetrating society deeply. Although the *Allgemeines Landrecht* placed certain limits on the sovereign, Prussia's experiment with authoritarian legalism established a bona fide police state. As Elisabeth Zoller observes, "With this document, not only does the police power enter into the law; the entire law falls under its control."[6] And despite his praise for some of its provisions, such as the emphasis on "the general rights of men," de Tocqueville's overall judgment was damning: "After having laid out these great principles, the legislator, rather than drawing from them as in the [French] constitution of 1791 the dogma of the sovereignty of the people, and the organization of a popular government in a free society, makes a quick turn back and heads for another equally democratic, *but not liberal*, conclusion; he considers the ruler to be the sole representative of the state, and gives him all the rights that were just recognized as belonging to society."[7]

What emerged in Prussia was an institutional ancestor of the dual state. Madame de Staël was the first to comment on the state's bifurcated structure: "[T]he image of Prussia offers a double face, like that of Janus, one of which is military, the other philosophical."[8] De Tocqueville described it with similar anatomical flair: "Beneath [a] completely modern head we will see a totally gothic body appear; Frederick [II] had only eliminated from it whatever could hinder the action of his own power, and the whole forms a monstrous being which seems to be in transition between one shape and another."[9] Heinrich Treitschke,

Hans Rosenberg, and Reinhart Koselleck endorsed these nineteenth century portrayals in the twentieth century and Christopher Clark reaffirmed them in the twenty-first.[10]

The rise, in Prussia and elsewhere, of the *Polizeistaat*, or a very limited rule by law, was the target of Placidus's pamphlet in 1798. Authoritarian legalism for him was still authoritarianism, which is why, in a play on words, he distinguished in his book between "*Staats-Rechts-Lehrer*," or theorists of the state for whom law was always subservient to the interests of the sovereign, a school of thought that dominated the study of public law, and "*Rechts-Staats-Lehrer*," that is, theorists of the state according to whom law, not the state, should rank supreme in the governance of social life, a progressive school of thought that revolved around the enlightened ideas of Immanuel Kant.[11] Courtesy of Placidus's rhetorical flourish, a neologism was born: the *Rechtsstaat*.

In the early nineteenth century, Adam Müller and Carl Theodor Welcker, representing very different ends of the political spectrum—one a reactionary, the other a revolutionary—laid sturdy intellectual foundations for the long and winding development of the idea of the *Rechtsstaat*. Both conceived of it, in the Kantian fashion, as a state of reason. But theirs were not yet times of revolution but of re-equilibration, it was a period in which a number of nondemocratic regimes made adjustments to the ways of their authoritarian rule.[12] The English rule by law was the animating idea for these institutional re-designs.

In the early 1800s, Müller and Welcker, for very different reasons, believed that institutional self-binding by way of law could be to the benefit of ongoing projects of state redevelopment. Müller, a leading representative of Romanticism, reckoned that institutionalizing the idea of law ("*Rechts-Idee*") would enhance the state's longevity and ideological stance ("*Dauer und wahre Haltung*").[13] In keeping with the tenets of *Staatsrechtslehre*, he regarded law as a tool of statecraft: it was a regulatory device, not a check on state power. With a similar talent for performing (rather than making a sustained contribution to the theorization of) the idea of the *Rechtsstaat* as Müller, but with a rather different ambition, Welcker sought to infuse the nascent concept with the values of liberty, justice, and nationhood. The result, published in 1813, was an amalgam of ideas culled from the natural law tradition and theories of statehood inspired by more pragmatic considerations.[14] For both men, the idea of the *Rechtsstaat* "was a category of philosophical politics through which the raw material of the French Revolution was ordered. [...] It was oriented toward the recently realized facts of individual liberties, and it distinguished the kind of states that did from the kind of states that did not account for them."[15]

It was not until Robert von Mohl seized the word *Rechtsstaat* in the run-up to the revolutions of 1848/1849 that it became a term of art. For Mohl, the *Rechtsstaat* was the name for a revolutionary institution dedicated to the pursuit of ends that are at once "sensual" ("*sinnlich*") and "reasonable" ("*vernünftig*").[16] Not unlike Müller and Welcker, he derived the concept of the *Rechtsstaat* from reasons of state; his was an argument from substance rather than institutional form. The sole purpose of a *Rechtsstaat*, according to Mohl, was to "order" ("*ordnen*") a *Volk*'s social existence ("*Zusammenleben des Volkes*") in such a manner that its members were free to pursue their individual life goals unperturbed.[17] The role of the state was to create negative freedom: it was responsible for the "removal" ("*Wegräumung*") of any barriers that stood in the way of citizens' private enterprise.[18] That was the "basic idea" ("*Grundidee*") of the *Rechtsstaat*, though Mohl hastened to add that this idea could find expression in "all kinds of forms" ("*in mancherlei Formen*").[19]

In Mohl's hands the *Rechtsstaat* stood for a state that revolved around the protection of individual rights. "He grafted individualism in purpose upon lawfulness as form," as Leonard Krieger put it, and thereby "he made the liberal state a matter not of constitution but of definition [...]."[20] But as Ingeborg Maus has shown, in Mohl's conceptualization of the *Rechtsstaat*, its substantive dimensions ultimately remain slight.[21] Here is a statement by Mohl himself in 1859, a quarter of a century after he first began to think about the concept: "The frequently misunderstood and erroneously applied concept of the *Rechtsstaat* conveys an order not to act beyond what is required by statute."[22] But, in an important qualification, he added that the statute "will command the minimal, but not the maximal."[23] It stands to reason that the failure of the revolutionary movement for liberal nationhood (in what soon would become a unified German empire) was partially responsible for Mohl's shift to a substantively less demanding idea of the *Rechtsstaat.*

In his post-revolutionary writings, Mohl continued to dwell on the purpose of the *Rechtsstaat*. He now emphasized that the idea was compatible with more than one "form of government" ("*Form der Regierung*").[24] In fact, maintained Mohl, *any* kind of institutional design could turn a state into a *Rechtsstaat* provided this design was geared toward promoting and enabling all humanly pursuits.[25] Note that Mohl, in the German original, wrote "*rechtlich*," not "*rechtsstaatlich*," to qualify the nature of the institutional design.[26] The difference is more than semantic. It supports the interpretation that Mohl was the advocate of far less radical a concept of the *Rechtsstaat* than he is often made out to be. He saw not only democracy as being compatible with the *Rechtsstaat*, far from it. "It is entirely wrong," he wrote, "to regard democratic rule as the only completely justified manifestation of the *Rechtsstaat*."[27] Instead he believed that the *Rechtsstaat* could thrive in monarchy, aristocracy, as well as democracy, that is, in all three forms of the ancient state.

It appears what Mohl hoped to accomplish with his revised theory of the *Rechtsstaat* was to establish the supremacy of legality without paying all too much heed to morality. Otto Mayer echoed this sentiment a few decades later when he chronicled the discourse of the *Rechtsstaat* in the revolutionary struggles of the nineteenth century that was then drawing to a close: "The most important thing, what mattered first and foremost [to insurgent liberals], was [to establish the principle of] statutory rule."[28] This principle—the so-called *Herrschaft des Gesetzes*—is a defining attribute of Fraenkel's concept of the normative state. It also played an important role, as we shall see, in the Nazi debate about the *Rechtsstaat*. But first I must reconstruct the antecedents of that debate—the discursive transition from the idea of the liberal *Rechtsstaat* to the idea of the authoritarian *Rechtsstaat*.

EMPIRE OF LAW, 1871–1918

In the post-revolutionary period, these years of authoritarian renewal, a reactionary idea of the *Rechtsstaat* took root in Germany. The concern for law and liberty, the hallmark of the liberal idea of the *Rechtsstaat*, was pushed to the margins of legal theory and practice. No longer a "*Staatsgattung*," or type of state, as envisaged by Mohl, the role of the *Rechtsstaat* was reduced to that of a guarantor of institutional form. It was no longer seen as a purveyor of substance. Ernst-Wolfgang Böckenförde has argued that this transformation in the discourse about the *Rechtsstaat* was in part a consequence of the fact that some of the goals of its liberal proponents had been achieved.[29] Inasmuch as there is merit to the argument that the demands of administrative law were responsible for the rise in formal (as opposed to substantive) conceptions of the *Rechtsstaat* in the late nineteenth century, it is important to not gloss over the considerably more conservative orientation of influential legal thinkers, notably Friedrich Julius Stahl and Rudolf Gneist.

The religious Stahl, who detested the revolutionary furor of 1830 and 1848, was a declared intellectual enemy of Mohl's. Viewed by some contemporaries as an arch conservative advocate of a Christian state, as someone willing to administer freedom only in "homeopathic drips" ("*homöopathischen Tropfenteilchen*"), Stahl described the idea of the *Rechtsstaat* thus: "The state shall be a *Rechtsstaat*, that is the slogan, and in reality, also the impulse of our time. It shall determine with precision and firmly secure the nature and boundaries of its reach as well as the free sphere of its citizens. [...] That is the concept of the *Rechtsstaat*. [...] It does not at all denote the goal (*Ziel*) and content (*Inhalt*) of the state, but only the nature (*Art*) and character (*Charakter*) required to realize them," that is, the state's substance.[30] Taking a leaf from Stahl, Gneist called for "government by statute" ("*Regierung nach Gesetzen*").[31] He helped popularize the notion that the achievement of procedural justice was more important than the pursuit of more far-reaching, substantive forms of justice. Gneist is most famous for conceiving and promoting a system of administrative law courts, what became known as *Verwaltungsgerichtsbarkeit*. The institutional design was progressive without being radical. Adopted in Prussia between 1872 and 1886, it created a multilayered framework for reviewing the legality of administrative acts in order to place a check on the discretion of government officials and protect individuals against abuses by the executive. But despite this liberty-enhancing response to the supremacy of bureaucracy, Gneist was an unapologetic statist who condoned few of the revolutionary ideas of 1789.[32] Kenneth Ledford has summarized well the effects of the failed revolution of 1848: "After 1850, German thought conceived of the *Rechtsstaat* as the 'state of well-ordered administrative law,' including the availability of meaningful review of all administrative actions in judicial form."[33]

A new era of the *Rechtsstaat* began in the late 1870s.[34] Increased state interventionism spelled a rapid expansion of public law that lasted up until World War I. The authoritarian *Rechtsstaat*, with its quest for law and order, became the modal institutional design of the times. It was the intellectual product of concerted resistance by reactionary forces in all the states of the German empire to the idea of the rule of law, as practiced in the kingdoms of England and Scotland, and a vote in favor of the separation of law and morals in the governance of politics and society.

In this period, Paul Laband, the influential jurist, distinguished the concept of the *Rechtsstaat* from what he believed to be its antonym: despotism (*Despotie*). Whereas rules of law ("*Rechtsregeln*") governed the *Rechtsstaat*, arbitrariness ("*Willkühr*") held sway in a despotic state.[35] And yet, Laband was no liberal reformer. For him, as for other prominent legal theorists of the time, the *Rechtsstaat* was a state of law, but not necessarily one of morals. Laband saw no need for adding substance to his institutional design for the Wilhelmine *Rechtsstaat*. This is no wonder considering that he served as an important norm entrepreneur for Carl Friedrich von Gerber's theory of legal positivism, which supplied the legal tapestry for the newly established empire.[36] Unsurprisingly, Laband wrote of "subjects" ("*Unterthanen*"), not "citizens" ("*Bürger*"), as Mohl had. Their station in life he deemed subordinate to that of the state and its officials: "The state does not face its members as an equal subject, but as a gentleman equipped with *imperium*," by which Laband meant the power to command.[37]

In this historical period, the concept of the *Rechtsstaat* was stripped of most of the substance with which its liberal theorists had sought to equip it. "Beginning with Carl Friedrich von Gerber, passing through Paul Laband up to Georg Jellinek, the conception of the *Rechtsstaat* underwent a profound transformation that marked the definitive defeat of the liberal standpoint."[38] Martin Loughlin explains why: "The Kantian liberal approach whereby individuals are bearers of rights by virtue of their humanity and which therefore impose specific limits on the authority of the state had, as a logical necessity, to be rejected. Within the frame of this positivist jurisprudence [advocated by von Gerber and Laband], rights are created only through objective law: they therefore are entirely conventional concepts. Once this manoeuvre was set in place, the concept of [the] *Rechtsstaat* itself could be subsumed in the concept of *Staatsrecht*."[39]

This brings us back to Placidus, for whom the supremacy of "*Staats-Rechts-Lehrer*" in the late eighteenth century, and their reverence for the law of the state as opposed to the state of law, as we have seen, was deeply troubling. By the late nineteenth century, the concept of the *Rechtsstaat* had come full circle. It was once again reduced to the idea that law created the rules of the game for politics, but that the substance of these rules was up for grabs. "The predominance of legal positivism in late-nineteenth-century public law thought meant that the *Rechtsstaat* concept emerged in twentieth-century German jurisprudence as a purely formal principle. [...] The idea of 'the rule of law' implicit in the [late-twentieth-century] concept of the *Rechtsstaat* [was in the early-twentieth-century] limited to that of 'rule by law.' "[40] In this formally rational understanding, the *Rechtsstaat* was about procedures, not about rights. "*Gerber-Labandscher Positivismismus*" was the term that contemporaries gave to this approach to the concept of law.[41] It was a far cry from the *Rechtsstaat* that Robert von Mohl had dreamt up half a century earlier. Not states of reason, but states crammed full with rules (and sometimes rifles) governed the lands. "[I]n German state practice, adherence to the principle of legality became the price rulers paid for the maintenance of authoritarian systems of government. Kantian formulations incorporated significant conservative aspects and under its influence early elaborations of the *Rechtsstaat* concept could not be assumed to rest on liberal foundations."[42] Authoritarian legalism was the order of the day.

But a small band of reformers kept the ideal of a substantive *Rechtsstaat* alive. In 1881, Otto von Bismarck, in a letter to Prussia's minister of culture, Gustav von Goßler, even predicted a "lively struggle" ("*lebhaften Kampf*") with proponents of the liberal *Rechtsstaat*. The German chancellor was wary of "von Mohl's invented term of art" ("*dem von Robert von Mohl erfundenen Kunstausdruck*") and bemoaned its lack of settled meaning.[43] He complained that no definition capable of "satisfying a political mind" ("*einen politischen Kopf befriedigende*") existed.[44] Although Bismarck fancied his chances in the conflict with "those people who want to do politics according to mathematical rules" ("*mit den Leuten, welche Politik wie nach mathematischen Sätzen treiben wollen*"), his correspondence suggests a begrudging respect for the *Rechtsstaat* as an institutional ideal with which to tangle—and one that *Realpolitik* might be able to usurp.[45] Bismarck was right to take seriously the force of law. As Ledford's important analysis of the law as a vocation in the German lands has shown, despite the authoritarian renewal of the preceding decades,

> [i]n the 1870s, lawyers could bask in the widespread liberal assessment of their profession as a sort of Hegelian "general estate," representing the general interest and the common good and entitled to respect, deference, and leadership. Opinion leaders believed that reform of the legal profession formed the touchstone of success in the project of the liberal *Bürgertum* to bring into existence its chief goal of the *Rechtsstaat*, the state rule by law. Lawyers and liberals achieved almost all of their aims for the legal professiona in 1878, carving out a space for the bar to create its own institutions, to govern its internal affairs, and to assume the important public role that theory ascribed to it.[46]

The creation of the Bar in Wilhelmine Germany was a critical juncture in the consolidation of a normative state. It was one of the institutional foundations upon which Fraenkel's cause lawyering in the mid-1930s rested. In the late nineteenth century "training as lawyers instilled in them a reverence for procedure, for values of uniformity, regularity, and certainty in decision making, values that form the basis both of the 'rule of law' and of the German concept of the *Rechtsstaat*."[47] The professionalization of lawyers was one of the institutional foundations of the *Rechtstaat*, and one of the remnants that withstood the destruction of democracy in the 1930s. And yet the claim by historian David Blackbourn that the idea of the *Rechtsstaat* was so cherished that it helped the German *Bürgertum* to unleash a bourgeois revolution from above, overstates the reach and relevance of law.[48] Michael John has shown why.

Revisiting the making of the 1896 Civil Code, the *Bürgerliches Gesetzbuch*, or BGB, which still governs private relations in Germany today, John found that law's institutional effects were contingent. A monumental achievement, the code brought national legal unity, thus helping to realize a bourgeois demand. As such, the BGB played in the hands of national sentiment, for as John puts it, "law was second only to language as an expression of the *Volksgeist*, the 'spirit' of a people."[49] And yet, the Civil Code was less revolutionary an accomplishment for the liberal *Bürgertum* as Blackbourn believed. Moreover, it only represented a fraction of the legal system at the time. As John concludes, "there is no necessary correlation between the success of 'bourgeois' values in the sphere of law and the success of liberal constitutionalism in the political sphere. Indeed, in many cases it was the most reactionary states in political terms, which first introduced 'liberal' systems of civil law."[50] One might say that institutional hybridity was a defining feature of the empire of law. These structural limits of law had effects on the socialization of lawyers in the late nineteenth and early twentieth centuries; they, too, were leading hybrid lives: Ledford is convinced that "[t]he belief in the efficacy and primacy of procedures that their legal education imprinted upon them linked them with liberal theory but constrained their imagination and vocabulary of discourse as they faced the massive changes of 1878 to 1933."[51]

From the perspective of the everyday life of law, political turmoil in the Reich meant, among other things, that the Wilhelmine judge "no longer saw himself as a subsuming automaton," as Laband had portrayed him, "and did not recognize himself in Laband's depiction."[52] This points to a correlation between the transformation of legal practice(s) and the transformation of legal thought at the turn of the century:

> It makes complete sense that a new characterization of judicial activity—between faithfulness to statute and freedom from it—was sought at the end of Empire: with the onset of rapid industrialization in the second half of the nineteenth century, the need for norms and the density of norms regulating individual spheres of life had grown steeply. At the same time, the state developed into an interventionist entity that sought to, and had to, regulate social processes more intensely. The increased density of norms—their proliferation and extension throughout society—led, on the one hand, to increasing judicialization; judges became more important. On the other hand, increased production of norms in legislation did not mean that judges could find ready-made solutions to legal conflicts in statutes.[53]

In Germany's great transformation, legal certainty was a scarcer commodity than many a legal formalist would have liked. A "'gapless' system of legal propositions" the law of empire was no longer, if it ever was.[54] Steadily growing gaps in the law meant a rise in judicial activism, as a result of which German legal thought found itself increasingly out of step with legal practice. Enter Carl Schmitt. His theoretical intervention, which "declared the judge to be empowered to create law outside given norms and emphasized the autonomy of legal practice (as against the codifying legislature and systematizing scholarship) filled precisely this vacuum."[55] With his first book, *Gesetz und Urteil* (*Statute and Judgment*), Schmitt in 1912 took aim at Laband's idea of the judge as *viva vox legis*.[56] He strove to elevate the role of the judge from that of an interpreter to that of a decider. This is why he implored his readers not to confuse a correct *interpretation* of law with a correct *decision* about law.[57] Or, as he quipped, "a correct opinion is not yet an insight."[58] Rightness of legal interpretation was an incorrect standard by which to measure legal validity, according to Schmitt. Instead of their assessing law abstractly, Schmitt wanted judges to foreground the rightness of a legal decision in practice ("*Entscheidung in der Praxis*").[59] He made a case for adjudication as an "intellectual" vocation.[60] A fervent believer in the "*Verstandestätigkeit*" of judges—by which he meant their reliance on rational and instinctual faculties as well as "life experience" ("*Lebenserfahrung*")—Schmitt theorized them as indispensable agents of law. "For Schmitt," writes John McCormick, "between the law and concrete reality, there will always be a gap that must be mediated by a judge."[61] In his little-known monograph on judging, Schmitt laid out ideas about the promise—and limits—of the liberal *Rechtsstaat* that a few years later resurfaced, more fully formed and robustly argued, in his legal theory of the sovereign exception.[62] The tropes of decisionism and personalism were already prominent in *Statute and Judgment*. However, in his early work he still attempted "to mediate between the irrational position of sheer judicial prerogative and the hyperrational position of legal formalism," a position he soon resolved decisively in favor of the former, as I explain in Chapter 5.[63]

In the context of imperial decline, the late Wilhelmine state was turning dualistic. Not yet under siege, the authoritarian *Rechtsstaat* was heaving under the practical demands—and theoretical expectations—that an epoch of confusing turmoil was beginning to place upon it. The need for adaptive legal thought caused a shattering of methods in early twentieth-century Germany. As Arthur Jacobson and Bernhard Schlink write, "The realist or idealist, normative and positivist, or anti-normative and anti-positivist theoretical tendencies of state law theory were [. . .] reactions to and recognitions of the political changes—various attempts to grasp and master them. State law theory in the Empire had already been geared to this political situation—to the specific, precarious balance of power that the bourgeoisie, the monarch, and the aristocracy had found in the Empire. After the collapse of this balance of power, a new constellation of power had to be found."[64] The brightest star to emerge in this constellation was the Weimar Constitution.

RIGHTSIZING THE *RECHTSSTAAT*, 1919–1933

Adopted in 1919, the *Weimarer Reichsverfassung*, as the constitutional document was known, inaugurated a new era for the *Rechtsstaat*.[65] By enhancing its normative reach, the founding fathers of Germany's first democracy endeavored to put authoritarian legalism on a leash.

> The Constitution of the Empire had contained only laws of organization; the Weimar Constitution [...] also contained basic rights. In its laws of organization, the constitution of the Empire had left state power in the hands of the monarchic executive, granting the Reichstag only limited shares; the Weimar Constitution developed a complicated interplay among the Reichstag, the president of the Reich [*Reichspräsident*] and the government of the Reich [*Reichsregierung*]. The constitution of the Empire had not known any sort of constitutional jurisdiction; the Weimar Constitution assigned the Federal Supreme Court [*Reichsgericht*] as the court for disputes over the law of the state [*Staatsgerichtshof*], at least the beginnings of a constitutional jurisdiction.[66]

Another notable difference between the empire of law and the republic of law: in the former, an autocrat (Bismarck) served as the architect of the constitution; in the latter, it was an academic (Hugo Preuss). This change signaled an attempt to establish the supremacy of the normative state over the roving remnants of Wilhelmine Germany's prerogative state.[67] "The new constitution represented a rupture in German constitutional history; for the first time, a German state was constituted on the basis of the principle of popular sovereignty."[68] The state was a mystical existence no more; no longer was it prior to, and above, the law. Not it ranked supreme, but the *Volk*. Most advocates of the *Rechtsstaat* conceived of the *Volk* in more inclusionary terms than the Nazis who took it away from them.[69] The commitment of Weimar republicans to a rights-based constitutionalism in the interwar period, though unsustainable in the 1920s and 1930s, was so innovative that postwar republicans in occupied Germany reinvented the short-lived tradition and, over time, even inspired what Jürgen Habermas speaks of as "constitutional patriotism" ("*Verfassungspatriotismus*"), an emotional attachment rooted in civil (and inclusionary) values, not national (and exclusionary) ones.[70] But let me stay with Weimar Germany.

It has been said that by reducing the concept of the *Rechtsstaat* to that of the *Gesetzesstaat* (legislative state), its late-nineteenth-century theorists made it harder for subsequent thinkers to make a case for attaching substantive values to the idea of the *Rechtsstaat*.[71] Or, to put it in the language of the Hart-Fuller debate, by insisting on a separation of law and morals, the late-nineteenth-century *Rechtsstaat* left itself open to a

Nazi assault on its substantive vacuity. For Ulrich Schellenberg, the imperial *Rechtsstaat* of Wilhelmine Germany was "the prototype of a society without honor and dignity" ("*Prototyp einer Gemeinschaft ohne Ehre und Würde*").[72] Hermann Heller also called into question its strict separation of law and morals. In opposition to Hans Kelsen, who prized the legal certainty that any positive law provided, Heller "thought that certainty cannot by any means exhaust the meaning of the *Rechtsstaat*. Certainty is a legal value that can come into conflict with other legal values, most notably the substantive ideas of justice on which law's claim to legitimacy must be based."[73] Law without values, the argument went, spelled the specter of decline—an argument that in the 1930s found adherents not only on the left but also on the right. David Dyzenhaus has located the precise vantage point that Heller claimed for himself: "Heller argued with Schmitt and against Kelsen that all conceptions of law are fundamentally political and tied to particular historical and social contexts. However, he shared with Kelsen a commitment to democracy, to the liberty of the individual and to social equality. And, for want of any better way to describe a further similarity, he also shared Kelsen's respect for law, for the idea that it is important for a decent political society to make sense of the constraints of legality."[74]

Heller was one of the most prominent theorists of the *Rechtsstaat* in Weimar Germany. Perturbed by the resurgence of collective violence in the wake of World War I and authoritarian renewal throughout interwar Europe, he asked with concern in 1929 whether the rise in dictatorships on the continent spelled "the end of the *Rechtsstaat*."[75] His response was a profound meditation on the idea of the *Rechtsstaat*, but one in which his defense of the idea came with a call for the transformation of the institution. Heller's was a plea for a substantive conception of the *Rechtsstaat* that was capable of aligning liberty and identity, but also sovereignty and equality, to sustain the reeling republic.

"Statutory rule" ("*Herrschaft der Gesetze*") was a load-bearing beam in Heller's blueprint for the *Rechtsstaat*. Rulers and ruled were subject to its legal authority. Heller put it succinctly: "In a *Rechtsstaat*, the act should follow the norm."[76] Equally fearful of liberals and fascists, of "bloodless rationalists" ("*blutlose Rationalisten*") as well as "bloodthirsty irrationalists" ("*blutgierige Irrationalisten*"), he invented the concept of the "social *Rechtsstaat*" ("*sozialer Rechtsstaat*"), with which he injected a considerable amount of substance into Mr. von Mohl's term of art, thereby inventing it anew.[77] He appended the adjective "social" to the concept to communicate his belief in the importance of achieving a measure of social homogeneity among the population within reach of that state. Absent such homogeneity, or so he argued, any *Rechtsstaat* would be diminished.

As Dyzenhaus writes, "Heller argues that the sociological basis for the legitimation of legal order has to figure in an account of the validity of law. His central insight here is contained in his claim that what might appear from above to rulers as a command that they wish to issue through the legal system must appear from below as a norm if it is to succeed. That is, it must appear from below as a sound standard of conduct."[78]

In Heller's account, the Weimar *Rechtsstaat* was on the verge of losing its "soul."[79] He decried an "emptying out of all meaning" ("*Entleerung aller Sinngehalte*") and layed the blame for this predicament squarely at the door of the Vienna School of legal positivism over which Kelsen presided. Not afraid of hyperbole, Heller even conjured the prospect of law turning into a kind of "maths of the humanities" ("*Mathematik der Geisteswissenschaften*").[80] His antidote to law's de-politicization: socialization and concretization. An admirer of the Fabian Society, like Wilhelm Epstein, who helped raise the young Fraenkel, Heller was convinced that the creation of a "*Staatsvolk*," a unified people bound by culture and history, would generate "social consciousness."[81] This we-feeling, he reckoned, would inspire loyalty to a given *Rechtsstaat*. Why? Because the latter would no longer be seen by its citizens as an octroyed abstraction, but as a concrete expression of the *Volk* that it serves. Heller was well aware that any *Volk* needed symbols to affect belonging, which is why he regretted so dearly the loss of a "subjective metaphysics of justice" ("*'subjektive Metaphysik' einer Gerechtigkeit*") in Weimar legal thought.[82] For him "equality" ("*Gleichheit*") was worth little unless it was valuable not just when viewed from a logic of consequences, but also, and more importantly, when seen from a logic of appropriateness.[83] He bemoaned the fact that the achievement of equality, once assessed in terms of "qualitative rightness" ("*qualitative Richtigkeit*"), now was measured by a standard of "quantitative logical generality" ("*quantitative logische Allgemeinheit*").[84] Not unlike Schmitt, Heller detested the rise of the "formalist-technical" ("*Formalistisch-Technische*") in his time and took a stance against law as technology.[85] Heller's dream was law of the *Volk*, by the *Volk*, for the *Volk*. But unlike the Nazi legal conscience that was forming in the shadows of the Weimar state at the time of Heller's writing, his conscience was clean. Heller's idea of *Volk* was not race-based. Quite the contrary. In 1932, he agitated for a "socialist *Rechtsstaat*," radicalizing his position in view of the specter of "fascist" dictatorship.[86]

Heller's idealized *Rechtsstaat* inspired compliance with its laws; it did not command it. Unlike Weber, he did not think that the legality of law was enough to generate its legitimacy. But make no mistake: Heller was a legal positivist—and a committed statist. Whereas Kelsen, "saw the primary task of constitutional jurisdiction in annulling unconstitutional sovereign acts," Heller maintained "that sovereignty is still something that transcends the positive law in that the state can decide to act legally against the law for the sake of law."[87] Here is Heller in his own words, channeling Georg Jellinek: "[T]he power of the state does not exhaust itself in positive law."[88] Heller conceded that until "humans and history" became "predictable," the "*summa potestas*" of the state would be "*legibus soluta*," its total powers not bound by laws.[89] All that could be done in the meantime, or so he seemed to think, was to acculturate the state, to socialize the *Rechtsstaat*.

The turn to "concreteness" in philosophical thought, a concern with the situatedness of life, was part and parcel of this effort. The war against abstraction, first declared by Hegel, in Weimar Germany was often fought with the weapon of concreteness.[90] Heller's call for concreteness in German legal thought and practice reminds of Schmitt's call for the same, with the important difference that Heller's concern with the composition of the *demos* stemmed from an effort to deepen the *Rechtsstaat* and strengthen parliamentary democracy, while Schmitt's interest in institutional identity was the manifestation of a pragmatist (and later extremist) institutionalism that hoped to transcend the *Rechtsstaat* and weaken parliamentary democracy.[91]

As I intimated above, Heller's take on the *Rechtsstaat* drew on Jellinek's legal thought. By successfully synthesizing in his account Jellinek's discrete insights about the "normative force of the factual" ("*normative Kraft des Faktischen*") and the "factual force of the normative" ("*faktische Kraft des Normativen*"), Heller, in Wolfgang Schluchter's estimation, advanced with the idea of the social *Rechtsstaat* a unified, superior theory of law.[92] The innovation becomes even more relevant, in the context of this book, once we appreciate that Fraenkel's metaphor of the dual state has conceptual affinities with Jellinek's *Zwei-Seiten-Lehre*, his two-sided theory of the state. Or, as one scholar recently put it, Jellinek's concept "reveals the dual nature of the state."[93] Jellinek did not theorize two discrete concepts of state but, like Fraenkel, worked with a Janus-faced conception of two indivisible halves based on two rival—and seemingly irreconcilable—epistemological phenomena: facts and norms.[94]

Deeply admired by Weber, Jellinek developed his theory of a dual state in 1900, in *Allgemeine Staatslehre*, his magnum opus: "The state is on the one hand a societal structure; a legal institution on the other. Consequently, *Staatslehre* is divided into *soziale Staatslehre* and *Staatsrechtslehre*."[95] He intended the study of empirical statehood to become the preserve of socio-legal studies, and the study of juridical statehood to remain the focus of doctrinal legal studies. Jo Murkens has summarized Jellinek's contribution neatly:

> Jellinek accepted the need for a differentiated juristic method, but rejected both a [purely] scientific sociological approach (of which Max Weber was the latest exponent) and a [purely] scientific legal approach (Laband) as erroneous approaches. The historical and ontological existence of the state ("*[d]as An-sich des Staates*") could not be [addressed] by legal positivism, and the legal nature of the state could not be [addressed] by sociological positivism. The state could neither be understood in purely normative-juristic terms nor in purely socio-politico-historical terms. The state could only be conceptualized by a custom-made "two-side" theory of the state [...].[96]

Jellinek's mission, in other words, was "to relate 'will' and 'norm' on the abstract level of the state as a whole."[97] His intervention must not be confused with Fraenkel's, however. The similarities are slight, but important. Notwithstanding divergent analytical concerns, Jellinek and Fraenkel (unlike their most important detractors—Kelsen and Neumann respectively) recognized the importance of supplying the philosophy of law with microfoundations. They must therefore be located on the same trajectory of legal thought. At the beginning of the twentieth century, Jellinek's *Allgemeine Staatslehre* operated as an intellectual beacon for theorists adrift in the sea of legal positivism. It inspired a whole range of attempts to open the black box of the state, to take the institution seriously as an "actual factor in the life of the *Volk*" ("*tatsächlicher Faktor im Volksleben*").[98] Jellinek refused to accept that it was enough to imagine an ideal state without studying the real state. Part of recognizing the reality of law's rule meant acknowledging the reserve power of the sovereign. In the final analysis, statutory positivism was a contingent force of law: its normative exercise was dependent on the state's "directing and coercive force," as Jellinek observed in one of his Wilhelmine-era writings on international law.[99] This is "Jellinek's paradox": his *Rechtsstaat* needed an omnipotent state to ensure compliance, but the existence of an omnipotent state undermined the independence of the *Rechtsstaat*.[100] Although facts and norms were mutually constitutive, their relationship, he found, was asymmetrical.

Fraenkel thought similarly about the world. As we will see, he, too, acknowledged a structural asymmetry between the normative state and the prerogative state when he formulated his dual state concept in the mid-1930s. Jellinek and Fraenkel also shared a penchant for inter- and transdisciplinary theorizing. Jellinek was a trailblazer in this regard; one of the many reasons why Weber felt inspired by this interlocutor of his.[101] A member of the vanguard of Neo-Kantians in late nineteenth century legal theory, Jellinek imagined a new approach to studying the state.[102] Epistemological advances in philosophy trickled down to the discipline of law and there came upon a reservoir of discontent about the supremacy of legal positivism. This encounter inspired a gradual methodological turn from purity to reality in the study of law, and from the formulaic to the factual in theories of the *Rechtsstaat*. One way of thinking of *The Dual State*, then, is as an addition to a long shelf of books written by members of an epistemic community who had become disenchanted with what they perceived as law's detachment from life. In response to this disenchantment, Jellinek called for an overhaul of universalizing concepts of state. The idea of the state, he claimed, could only ever be understood "subjectively," not objectively.[103] The essence of the state, for Jellinek, was to be found in the particular, not the general. We now see why Jellinek was important for Fraenkel's legal thought but not for Neumann's.[104]

Heller also incorporated a notion of institutional hybridity into his theory of state. Although, normatively speaking, he was intent on preserving an idea of the *Rechtstaat* as a unified institution, analytically speaking, he recognized the importance of proceeding sociologically: by trying to understand the "is" not the "ought" of the interplay between what Fraenkel with some modifications three decades later would theorize as the normative state and the prerogative state. In Heller's sketch of a dual state, its two halves were drawn less sharply. Like Jellinek, Heller distinguished between a "normative sphere of law" ("*normative Rechtssphäre*") and a "factual sphere of power" ("*faktische Machtsphäre*").[105] The dialectical relationship of these halves was a given in Heller's institutional theory, a constitutive feature of the state as a living organism. Problems only arose if the equilibrium was under threat of being disturbed. As a solution to the problem of social order, Heller, as we have seen, made a case for the social *Rechtsstaat*. It promised to solve what I have elsewhere called the trilemma of justice: the real-world challenge of optimizing the relationship among legality, morality, and reality in the design of a polity's institutional framework.[106]

The idea of the social *Rechtsstaat* deepened the intellectual gulf between Heller and Kelsen. The Vienna School assumed a diametrically opposed position on the question of law's nature. Intellectual barbs about contending concepts of law were traded in the *Methodenstreit*, the drawn-out dispute over methods in German legal thought that unfolded between 1925 and 1929 and engulfed all influential *Staatsrechtler* in German-speaking Europe.[107]

Flying the flag for legal positivism—and calling for constitutional loyalty to the Weimar Constitution were, aside from Kelsen, Gerhard Anschütz, Hans Nawiasky, Fritz Stier-Somlo, Richard Thoma, and other so-called *Vernunftrepublikaner*, or republicans of reason.[108] Kelsen's position was the most extreme, philosophically speaking: He rejected the view that a legal order has a normative and a factual dimension. Legal validity was a purely philosophical question for Kelsen; for Weber, Jellinek, and Heller, as we have seen, it was also an empirical one. "The legal order," Weber argued, ought to be understood "not in the legal, but in the sociological sense, i.e., as being *empirically* valid. In this context, 'legal order' thus assumes a totally different meaning [than in legal positivism]. It refers not to a set of norms of logically demonstrable correctness, but rather to a complex of actual determinants (*Bestimmungsgründe*) of human conduct."[109] Fraenkel's approach to the study of law was rooted in Weber's sociology of law, with sociology being an example of what Kelsen described as "explanatory" disciplines.[110] These disciplines he distinguished from his own, the law, a "normative" discipline.

Kelsen viewed the "push toward reality" by some jurists of his generation with great skepticism. He was unsure whether their "metalegal" scholarship "even falls within the scope of law."[111] But Kelsen was in the minority at the time of his writing (in all senses of the word). "The pure theory of law was a radical and incisive answer" to the question of law's nature, as Stolleis points out, "but it did not accord with the prevailing psychological need in Germany for a metaphysical grounding, for a fusion of law and morality, for the overcoming of the separation between Is and Ought."[112] A brilliant theorist, Kelsen failed to address the vital question of his time: the question of belonging. It was a politically pertinent question about the cement of society, about what makes the world hang together. Not only Schmitt was fearing the disorder of things, a considerable number of legal theorists in the interwar period saw a need for a less detached *Rechtsstaat*, a need to ground law in life.[113]

The examples of two other prominent legal positivists illustrate the transformation of German legal thought in the wake of imperial decline. "Even positivists such as Anschütz and Thoma no longer supported the positivism of the Empire, which Kelsen had shattered. Their positivism was no longer a legal positivism [*Rechtspositivismus*], but a statutory positivism [*Gesetzespositivismus*]. Statutory positivism as practiced by Anschütz and Thoma no longer put the needs of the system before the actual norms of positive law, as Laband's legal positivism had done, but made interpretation of these norms its focus. However, unlike the statutory positivist Kelsen, Anschütz and Thoma made free use of historical and political arguments in interpretation."[114]

Facing this coalition of legal traditionalists was a variegated group of anti-positivists, most notable among them Heller, Erich Kaufmann, Hugo Preuss, Heinrich Triepel, and Rudolf Smend. But it also included representatives of the "Young Right," notably strivers such as Schmitt, Ernst Forsthoff, and Ernst Rudolf Huber. Some of these anti-positivists supported the Weimar Republic (e.g., Heller, Preuss), others sought to put an end to parliamentary rule (e.g., Schmitt, Forsthoff). What united them was a rejection of *Gesetzespositivismus* in all of its varieties.[115]

The period from 1871 to 1933 was not a monolithic era of legal thought. Neither legal positivism nor any other philosophy of law dominated the academy.[116] This helps explains why there is "no simple pattern" into which the participants and positions in the *Methodenstreit* can be slotted.[117] Not unlike the Nazi debate about the *Rechtsstaat*, the Weimar debate about *Staatsrecht* was a genuine contest about the concept of law.[118] One that was politically charged, but intellectually grounded. Described as "a jurisprudence of crisis" by some, it not only offers a glimpse of shifting patterns of elite legal consciousness during Germany's first democratic experiment, it also testifies to the centrality of the *Rechtsstaat* in Weimar Germany.[119] The notion of the *Rechtsstaat* had the status of an essentially contested concept, but one solidly incorporated into the country's edifice. This fidelity to the *Rechtsstaat* was about to be tested.

Before I turn to this contest over the *Rechtsstaat*, I would be remiss if I did not also mention Rudolf Smend in my brief history of Weimar legalism. Also inspired by Weber, Smend in 1928 developed an ideal typical theory of integration (*Integrationslehre*).[120] Harshly criticized by Kelsen for ostensibly laying the intellectual foundations of dictatorship, Smend's efforts were aimed at uprooting legal positivism, especially Laband's "empty formalism."[121] Disturbed by Laband's supposed depoliticization of law, he accused him of painting a "strange picture of a meaningless system of competencies and power with no relation to life itself" ("*seltsames Bild eines sinnentleerten Systems von Kompetenz- und Machtparzellen, das zum Leben keine Beziehung hat*").[122] Smend was a legal organicist; he believed in taking seriously the life of institutions, in making law culturally meaningful.[123] For him, doing so required accepting the changing character of law—an assumption utterly alien to legal formalism.

Otto von Gierke had been one of the first to challenge, in the nineteenth century, the predominance of legal positivism. He did so under the cover of the Historical School of Law (*historische Rechtsschule*). For him no legal method was "scientific" ("*wissenschaftlich*") unless it included tools to study law "genetically" ("*genetisch*"), by which he meant contextually and historically.[124] Gierke, like some of the anti-positivists who followed in his footsteps, was beholden to a substantive concept of the *Rechtsstaat*.[125] Gierke's target was Friedrich Puchta's conceptual jurisprudence (*Begriffsjurisprudenz*) rather than Kelsen's pure theory of law.[126] But the pandectists around Puchta to a large extent anticipated the logical and conceptual parsimony that would come to define Kelsen's seminal contribution.[127] This means that Gierke's critique from the late nineteenth century still resonated in the early twentieth. Among the many legal theorists Gierke influenced was Hugo Sinzheimer—whom we got to know in the previous chapter as Fraenkel's *Doktorvater* and a formative influence on our protagonist's intellectual development. More disconcertingly, as we shall see in the next chapter, both Gierke's organicist theory of the state (which rejected the, at the time increasingly prominent, idea of the state as a mere formal institution, or *Anstalt*) and his doctrine of the "*Rechtsidee*," or idea of law, some of the participating jurists in the Nazi debate about the *Rechtsstaat* borrowed. This outcome is ironic because Gierke had predicted that Nazi jurists would *exploit* the substantive vacuity of legal formalism—not *appropriate* the substantive verity of legal organicism.

But let me return to Smend's theory of integration, which in the final years of the Weimar Republic was "the subject of lively debate."[128] I mention it here because it represents an intellectual bridge to the Nazi debate about the *Rechtsstaat* to which I am about to turn. Although the archconservative Smend was immune to the lure of National Socialism (he was removed from his professorship in Berlin in 1935 and forced to accept a chair in law at Göttingen), his anti-positivist concept of the constitution ensured that Nazi theorists of law discovered his theory of integration and sought to appropriate it.[129] "After 1933," Stefan Korioth writes, "scattered attempts were made to use a modified version of Smend's concept of integration to explain the Nazi state, presenting it as an example of a functioning system of integration."[130] The appeal is immediately understandable. Legal post-positivism is *precisely* what the Nazi concept of law was all about, as I will now explain.

5

The Debate about the *Rechtsstaat* in Nazi Germany, 1933–1936

One can be forgiven for thinking that the *Rechtsstaat* ceased to exist in Germany when the Nazis grabbed the reins of government in the course of their so-called *Machtergreifung* of January 30, 1933.[1] This narrative is prevalent in scholarly and popular accounts alike. And yet it distorts historical reality. It misconstrues not only the meaning of the concept of the *Rechtsstaat* in the early twentieth century but also the institutional development of the Nazi state in the early years of the Third Reich. In this chapter I correct these distortions of the theoretical and empirical record by analyzing in depth the debate about the *Rechtsstaat* in Nazi Germany that took place in the first years of the dictatorship. The debate was not just window dressing to placate the international community, although that was part of it. In the main it was a genuine battle over, about, and with ideas, abhorrent ideas, but ideas nonetheless.

In a review of Edgar Tatarin-Tarnheyden's 1934 book *Werdendes Staatsrecht*, Otto Koellreutter, a key participant in the Nazi debate about the *Rechtsstaat*, held that the role of scholarship in the Third Reich was a critical one. To devise genuine solutions to the problems of the times, "slogans alone" ("*bloß Phrasen*") were not enough, he insisted: "Aside from the right attitude, the scholarly toolbox is required."[2] The debate about the *Rechtsstaat* was a serious intellectual contest among regime sympathizers, loyalists, and stalwarts—all of them jurists—concerning the contours and ideological foundations of the new state and its uses of law. Ideas mattered to almost all of the Nazis involved. The debate is indicative of a degree of legal consciousness that goes a long way toward explaining why, and, how, remnants of the *Rechtsstaat* mattered in the transition to authoritarian rule. In the midst of the debate, in June 1935, Carl Schmitt, Koellreutter's longstanding adversary in the legal academy, maintained that their "philosophical efforts [were] not non-legal ruminations, but an

The Remnants of the Rechtsstaat: An Ethnography of Nazi Law. Jens Meierhenrich.
 Published 2018 by Oxford University Press.

immediately necessary part of the legal work involved in the clarification of a consequential and fateful concept" such as the *Rechtsstaat*.[3] His virulent antisemitism notwithstanding, Schmitt was right.

The debate about the *Rechtsstaat* was symptomatic of the institutional development to come. Like so many things at the time, it too was Janus-faced. The debate pitted against one another, on the one hand, theorists and practitioners who sought to retain, within Nazi reason, the terminology of the *Rechtsstaat*, and, on the other, far more extremist norm entrepreneurs who were insistent on doing away with the old nomenclature and keen to invent a new language to capture the revolutionary overhaul of the institutions of state. In the latter camp, however, disagreement was deep over which of the many proposed neologisms accommodated best the ideology of National Socialism. From administrative law to constitutional law, "[t]he clashes between party and state, between the prerogative state and the normative state, and between authoritarian and totalitarian currents were [. . .] played out in the terminology of [. . .] law. As in other areas, they remained unresolved right up to the end of the regime. However, the front lines shifted in tandem with the developmental phases of the entire regime."[4] The Nazi dictatorship was a dynamic institution, not a static one. Because legal practices were subject to, and crucial factors in, the institutional formation, deformation, and transformation of Nazi governance, it is essential to inquire into the changing character of law in the Third Reich, at the level of both theory and practice. Before I turn in subsequent chapters to everyday *practices* of Nazi law, I delineate in this chapter rival *theories* of Nazi law.

The analysis complements that in Chapter 2 and continues the intellectual history of the idea of the *Rechtsstaat* that I began in Chapter 4. I illuminate the dynamics of contention inside the dictatorship in an effort to debunk the myth of a Nazi behemoth. By examining in depth an important arena of Nazi intellectual life—legal thought—during the transition to and consolidation of authoritarian rule in Germany, I demonstrate that the law of Nazi dictatorship—at the moment of its most significant theorization—was not as uniform as we have been led to believe. I suggest that the Nazi debate about the *Rechtsstaat* bears out a number of claims of Fraenkel's theory of dictatorship. It epitomizes the struggle between (Nazi theorists of) the normative state and (those advocating for the expansion of) the prerogative state in the 1930s, thus mirroring key findings of Fraenkel's ethnography of law. I find that not just the *practice* of Nazi law was dual in nature, but that the *theory* of Nazi law was schizophrenic as well. Remnants of both the liberal *Rechtsstaat* and of the authoritarian *Rechtsstaat* were visible in everyday life up until 1938, and some of them were operational well into the war years. An improved understanding of Nazi legal thought in the mid-1930s is useful for thinking about Nazi legal practice, which is why I take this detour before turning in detail to the findings Fraenkel derived from his research on, and participant observation in, the courts of the Third Reich. It is part of the historicization of law that I am attempting in this book, which for me is the task "of accurately describing the developments leading from one situation to another, or from one mindset to another."[5]

Although the shifting discourse about the nature and purpose of the *Rechtsstaat* in the period 1933–1936 contributed to its immediate devaluation and eventual destruction, it would be a mistake to dismiss the reflections about the concept of law in Nazi Germany as only a façade. On the one hand, Nazi stalwarts certainly advocated loudly for an abandonment of what they deemed a perversely liberal concept. More moderate Nazis, on the other hand, were reluctant to give up completely on the norms and institutions of the *Rechtsstaat*. They recognized their value for governing the dictatorship. For those among them who reasoned from a logic of consequences, the value of *Rechtsstaat* was purely instrumental; for others who argued from a logic of appropriateness, it was also the expressive function of the *Rechtsstaat* that in their eyes accounted for its value. To them, the *Rechtsstaat* was a cultural achievement, its formal embodiment of Germanic values appealing. These Nazis wanted to change the content of the form, not the form itself.

In order to make the idea of the *Rechtsstaat* usable in the Third Reich, both of these groups of Nazi legal theorists modified von Mohl's term of art with adjectives ranging from "national" to "National Socialist." In what follows, I reconstruct the convoluted three-year intellectual struggle to define the boundaries of authoritarian legalism as a practice of Nazi rule. Inasmuch as this struggle was, for most of those who partook, about ideas, it would be naïve to think that intellectual edification was the only motivation in play. Peter Caldwell's take on the logic of Nazi scholarship also applies to the discipline of law: "The 'theory industry' under Nazism was itself one of the areas of ravenous, opportunistic struggle among factions."[6]

The analysis is organized into four parts. I begin with an analysis of the Nazi concept of law, elaborating key tropes in Nazi critiques of the nineteenth century idea of the *Rechtsstaat*. I then disentangle the intellectual positions of those Nazi legal theorists who were inclined to retain the idea of the *Rechtsstaat*. The third part turns to their intellectual foes, comparing calls for the rejection of the *Rechtsstaat* as a conceptual—and political—variable. With the help of this juxtaposition I explain why the Nazi debate about the *Rechtsstaat* "was more than a mere disagreement over words," why it represented in fact "a fight over the very nature of

Nazi politics."[7] Carl Schmitt and his ilk won the battle for the Nazi legal conscience: in the late 1930s, the term *Rechtsstaat* was purged from what Victor Klemperer had begun to call "LTI," the language of the Third Reich, or *lingua tertii imperii*.[8]

THE NAZI CONCEPT OF LAW

The debate about the *Rechtsstaat* in Nazi Germany got underway not long after the creation of the dictatorship. It centered on the question of whether the concept of the *Rechtsstaat* should be abandoned—or appropriated—to meet the demands of the "German revolution," as Nazi hardliners and sympathizers were wont to describe Hitler's seizure of power in the spring of 1933. Almost all of the protagonists of the Nazi debate about the *Rechtsstaat* were representatives of the subfield of *Staatsrechtslehre*, this peculiar theoretical branch of public law scholarship that dominated the German legal tradition in the early twentieth century.[9] Because the theory of law in the 1930s was "dictatorially homogenized," archconservative and extremist law scholars possessed the "interpretive power" ("*Interpretationsherrschaft*") to rethink the state in whichever way they saw fit.[10] Important intellectual (and other) cleavages divided these jurists, but what bound them together was a disdain for the idea of the nineteenth century *Rechtsstaat*, which they referred to as the "liberal" or "bourgeois" *Rechtsstaat*. This part analyzes the most important tropes in Nazi critiques of the nineteenth century idea of the *Rechtsstaat*. A trifecta of tropes stands out: (1) antiliberalism, (2) antiformalism, and (3) antisemitism. When considered in conjunction, they reveal a great deal about the Nazi concept of law.

Antiliberalism

The intellectual theme uniting all of the protagonists in the Nazi debate about the *Rechtsstaat* was antiliberalism. Deep-seated and longstanding, the virulence of antiliberalism increased in the transition from democracy to dictatorship in the late 1920s and early 1930s. It reached its apotheosis in the immediate aftermath of the *Machtergreifung*, when the figurative and literal destruction of anything that smacked of liberalism was high on the Nazi agenda. The adjective "liberal" acquired a pejorative connotation, and with it anything that the ultimately unsuccessful revolutions of the previous century had introduced into politics, including parliaments, tolerance, and the rights of individuals.

The rise of individualism in particular irked the legal theorists for the Reich. One of the first to revive the state as a conceptual variable was Julius Binder, a leading representative of Neo-Hegelianism in interwar legal thought.[11] In an extended meditation on the authority of the state, Binder critiqued the contractual tradition according to which statehood was a collective bargain, entered into by individuals seeking to escape Hobbes's *bellum omnium contra omnes*. This account of the state's authority was unconvincing, according to Binder: "[F]or us, the state is, in essence, authority. The state's rule over its citizens is unconditional and categorical. [. . .] [T]his authoritative nature of state power [. . .] [is] fundamental, original, and not at all derivative: it is not bestowed or derived or dependent on any earthly power. The state is not a means to an end, but is end in itself."[12] Binder's critique of individualism was partially inspired by Rudolf Smend, notably by the idea that the state is a living entity, an organic whole that can be traced back to an origin myth in response to which it also evolves and inspires commitment, and thus acquires legitimacy. This leads us back to the relationship between the individual and the state. Binder was convinced that the liberal turn had led to a categorical misunderstanding of this relationship. Liberals had imagined the individual as existing apart from the state, when, in fact, its existence was entirely contingent upon it. In Binder's argument, man is not the individual being that he thinks he is: the individual is only individual qua his group membership ("*er in seiner Einzelheit nur die Besonderheit eines Allgemeinen, ein Mensch als Glied seines Volkes ist*").[13] According to Binder, individuals are creatures of blood and soil. The formation of their interests is mediated by the culture of the state on the territory of which they live. Their preferences therefore are "concretely identical" ("*konkret identisch*") with the national interest of the state.[14] For Binder the state was the manifestation of a *Volk*'s will, an integrated and indivisible whole with a capacity for inspiring collective identity. He believed this idea of state was infinitely superior to that of the laissez-faire state favored by liberals.

The new statism in the interwar period had far-reaching consequences. As Heinrich Lange wrote gleefully at the time: "The new value system has pushed the individual off his throne. He is not valuable for his own sake. He is a serving member of society ('*Glied der Gemeinschaft*'), is of, and subordinate to, it."[15] Otto Koellreutter embraced "the idea of 'us' as the unity of a *Volk*" as the first and foremost attribute of statehood.[16] The mythology of community would eventually culminate in the invention of the *Volksgemeinschaft*, an ominous Nazi institution that received a great deal of scholarly attention in recent years.[17] By placing the interests of the community ahead of those of its individual members, Nazi jurists radically reimagined the *Rechtsstaat*. In the racial imaginary, its purpose was not to protect the individual from the state, but the state from the individual; its nature was not passive, but interventionist. The Nazi theorist Wilhelm Glungler clarified this intellectual tenet during World War II: "Law's purpose is not to secure the so-called individual sphere and thus private life. The law of the state as the foundation of life for the *Volksgemeinschaft* has priority."[18]

There was widespread agreement among Nazi legal theorists that the function of law in the Nazi dictatorship was to create the conditions for the creation and maintenance of a strong state, one unencumbered by special interests, one not hamstrung by a liberal institutional design like von Mohl's. Liberal theories of law, according to this argument, had betrayed the achievements of German idealism and paved the way for unbridled decadence, as exemplified by the rampant rise of individualism and, in the words of Hans Frank, the "crassest materialism" ("*krassesten Materialismus*").[19] Nazi critics in the legal establishment disparaged the idea of freedom as an example of narcissistic self-interest pursued by moneyed classes. A supposed sense of entitlement had led to the legalization of politics in Weimar Germany, which in turn had resulted in a depoliticization of politics, an unacceptable condition that required a radical cure.[20] Depending on who made the diagnosis, the cure involved either the racialization of the *Rechtsstaat* or its abandonment.

Helmut Nicolai posited that the prevalent commitment to legal positivism in Weimar Germany had resulted in the comprehensive destruction of law as a moral idea ("*zu einer vollständigen Erschlagung des sittlichen Gedankens*"), not to mention the most awful materialism ("*übelstem Materialismus*").[21] The only way to combat the risk of arbitrariness that legal positivism was said to have created, according to Nicolai, was to look beyond the written law and let the underlying moral idea of law ("*den zentralen, ethischen Rechtsgedanken*") be the guide for assessing the validity of law, and thus its suitability for the creation and maintenance of Nazi order.[22] Carl Schmitt heaped additional scorn on the laissez-faire nature of the "bourgeois *Rechtsstaat*," as the liberal instantiation of von Mohl's neologism was often described in conservative and right-wing circles. But as Peter Caldwell has persuasively shown,

> The key to Schmitt's notion of the bourgeois *Rechtsstaat* is to be found as much in the adjective "bourgeois" as in the term "*Rechtsstaat*" itself. The bourgeoisie was, for Schmitt, more a moral and political stance than a social group. Its essential characteristics were individualism, liberalism, and support for government by parliament. It yearned for the "eternal conversation" of parliamentary debates rather than concrete decision. It was indecisive and unable to act. It avoided the "real" world of politics in favor of "political

romanticism." Schmitt saw an intrinsic connection between the effeminate and indecisive bourgeoisie and the *Rechtsstaat*.[23]

Schmitt was opposed to the limited nature of the liberal *Rechtsstaat*, which he saw falsely enshrined by the institutional separation of powers, a principle he detested. Prior to the Nazi dictatorship, in his constitutional treatise the *Verfassungslehre*, published in 1928, Schmitt had chronicled in great detail his reservations about the "bourgeois *Rechtsstaat*," and without giving it a name, the key features of the more authoritative (and authoritarian) state he was after—in both theory and practice. At the time, his assessment was critical but not yet disparaging. His summary of key tenets of the liberal *Rechtsstaat* was admirably clear and concise:

> The fully realized ideal of the bourgeois *Rechtsstaat* culminates in the conformity of the entire state life to *general judicial forms*. Under this *Rechtsstaat* ideal, there must be a procedure for every type of disagreement and dispute, whether it is among the highest state officials, between officials and individuals, or, in a federal state, between the federation and the member states or among the member states, without regard for the type of conflict and object of dispute, a process in which decisions are reached according to a procedure in accordance with legal forms. [...] [T]he most important presuppositions of this type of procedure are valid, general norms. For the judge is "independent" only so long as there is a valid norm on which he is unconditionally dependent, whereby under "norm" is understood only a general rule determined in advance.[24]

This state of affairs was unacceptable to Schmitt, not least because it meant that the state was mere "*Gesetzesstaat*" ("legislative state"), a pejorative term that was popular among conservatives at the time to denote a state lacking in soul, one that churned out legislation but neither housed nor inspired metaphysical meaning. The equation of law with statute was anathema to all Nazi legal theorists. Martin Wittig, for example, was convinced that statutory rule was arbitrary rule. His logic: Because any form of parliamentary representation was by definition temporary, any legislative act could only ever be an ad hoc solution to a political problem.[25] For Wittig, the problem was exacerbated by the fact that the political compromise that lay at the heart of any statute was invariably negotiated by a random selection of individuals and groups serving in parliament at a given time. Heinrich Lange also rejected the liberal idea of representation and claimed that the rise of statutory rule had marginalized such "eternal values" ("*Ewigkeitswerte*") as "God, *Volk*, homeland, blood, honor, duty."[26] By establishing a supremacy of facts, and by introducing a strict separation between "is" (*Sein*) and "ought" (*Sollen*), Nazi legal scholars believed, liberal theorists of law had rendered law meaningless—in all senses of the word. As long as the "ought" was separated from the "is," Günther Krauß argued, it was impossible to account for either the origins of law, the substance of law, its binding character, or the purpose of law.[27]

Schmitt likewise was convinced that the state was "not merely a judicial organization," as he put it in one of his Weimar-era writings: "It is also something other than a merely neutral member of a conflict resolution body or an arbitrator. Its essence lies in the fact that it reaches the *political decision*."[28] Five years later, in 1933, Schmitt reconfigured his institutional theory to legitimate the emerging racial state, this "*Weltanschauungsstaat*."[29] All Nazi legal theorists desired an ideological state. All of them sought to overcome the separation of law and morals, which they portrayed (erroneously) as the common denominator of liberal theories of the *Rechtsstaat*.

Nazi theorists also worried about the effects of practices associated with the idea of the liberal *Rechtsstaat* in specific areas of the law. In the case of criminal law and procedure, for example, Schmitt objected to resolving the trade-off between liberty and security in favor of the individual rather than society. Referencing Friedrich von Liszt's quip that the principle of *nullum crimen, nulla poena sine lege* represented the "criminal's magna carta" ("*Magna Charta des Verbrechers*"), Schmitt argued the eighteenth century "positivistic" principle had fatefully supplanted the "just" principle of *nullum crimen sine poena*, or no crime without punishment.[30] For Schmitt, this state of law was to the detriment of the *Volksgemeinschaft* and incompatible with "today's National Socialist predicament" ("*heutige nationalsozialistische Problemstellung*").[31] Nicolai echoed this assessment, declaring that liberalism "due to its tolerance" was no longer capable of distinguishing "law and lawlessness" ("*Recht und Unrecht*").[32] By legalizing the state, so the argument went, liberals had taken "the lightness and nimbleness" ("*Leichtigkeit und Wendigkeit*") out of politics.[33]

Antiformalism

For the protagonists in the Nazi debate about the *Rechtsstaat*, Friedrich Julius Stahl was the enemy personified. He was the intellectual "other" whose institutional theory they sought to discredit, uproot, and overcome. Stahl's famous definition of the *Rechtsstaat* revolved around a strict separation of law and morals, which is why it was inherently objectionable to all legal theorists in the Third Reich.

In the mid-nineteenth century, Stahl described the idea of the *Rechtsstaat* as one that did not "denote the goal (*Ziel*) and content (*Inhalt*) of the state, but only the nature (*Art*) and character (*Charakter*) required to realize them."[34] This conceptual reduction of the idea of the *Rechtsstaat* was unacceptable to a racist movement dedicated to ideological projection. It is therefore not surprising that all of our protagonists, albeit to different degrees, wanted to jettison the procedural concept of law that had dominated the late nineteenth and early twentieth centuries and establish in its stead a substantive concept of law, one infused with Nazi ideology. They imagined a state that would be receptive to, and reflective of, "higher values," as Ernst Forsthoff put it in his widely read pamphlet, *Der totale Staat* (*The Total State*).[35] With Schmitt they believed that the laws and statutes of the liberal *Rechtsstaat* amounted to nothing more than the "timetable of the bureaucratic machine" ("*Fahrplan der bürokratischen Maschine*").[36]

This empty formalism was anathema to the Nazi project, least of all due to the latter's insistence on the supremacy of the *Führerprinzip*, that is, the principle of Hitler's legitimate authority qua charismatic leadership. By subordinating legal authority, what they decried as "rule of statutes" ("*Herrschaft der Gesetze*"), to charismatic authority, Nazi theorists stood the idea of the liberal *Rechtsstaat* on its head. A ruler, not rules, was the apex of power. The principle of institutional self-binding was, at least in the highest echelon of power, discarded. Hitler was the final arbiter of law. It does not follow that law was meaningless, however. As we shall see, up to a point, legal norms and institutions mattered in the Third Reich. They enabled and constrained and were honored in the breach. They courted violence, sometimes muted it. They made dictatorship possible, and, on occasion, resistible. The effects of legal norms and institutions were contradictory: they governed and legitimated the Nazi dictatorship but every now and then also stood in its way. In other words, Nazi law was Janus-faced, which is why Fraenkel's institutional theory of dictatorship is so insightful.

The regime's legal theorists embraced antiformalism as a way to undermine the constraining effects of legal norms and institutions. The institutional validation of the *Führer* in Nazi legal theory was, among other things, a denigration of Kelsen's concept of the *Rechtsstaat*, in which "*Führerlosigkeit*," or lack of leadership, was a defining feature.[37] Inasmuch as Kelsen's concept was acknowledged to hold arbitrariness in check, the protagonists in the Nazi debate about the *Rechtsstaat* firmly believed that the achievement of legal certainty came at too high cost: at the price of leaving no room for the "genuine passion and genius virtue of the true statesman" ("*echter Leidenschaft und genialer Tugend des wahren Staatsmannes*").[38] Unless the ruler was left unmoored, the potential of his charismatic leadership could not be harnessed. He was, as Lange wrote in a reference to Jonathan Swift, a "bound Gulliver" ("*gefesselter Gulliver*").[39]

One cost of formalism that several of the Nazi legal theorists highlighted was the existing *Rechtsstaat*'s supposed inability to govern the exception, or *Ausnahmezustand*, by which they meant, as one of them put it, "a case of extreme peril, a danger to the existence of the state, or the like."[40] Re-enter Schmitt, for whom "there exists no norm that is applicable to chaos."[41] Unsurprisingly, his institutional prescription was as straightforward as it was reactionary: "The precondition as well as the content of jurisdictional competence in such a case must necessarily be unlimited."[42] This contradicted von Mohl's concept of the *Rechtsstaat*: "When Robert von Mohl said that the test of whether an emergency exists cannot be a juristic one, he assumed that a decision in the legal sense must be derived entirely from the content of a norm. But this is the question. In the general sense in which Mohl articulated his argument, his notion is only an expression of constitutional liberalism and fails to apprehend the independent meaning of the decision."[43] In this argument, politics trumped law, and decisions were more important than norms. If we use Fraenkel's categories, we might say that Schmitt, the arch conservative-turned-Nazi, in his Weimar-era writings articulated a clear preference for a prerogative state over a normative state. Or, as Schmitt put it in 1922, "Like every order, the legal order rests on a decision and not on a norm."[44] For him, maintaining political order in extraordinary times was more important than preserving a given legal order, even though he recognized the contribution of legal norms and institutions to the maintenance of social order in ordinary times. The *Rechtsstaat* (with or without adjectives) was for Schmitt a relic of a bygone era.[45] He was after "politonomy," to use Martin Loughlin's useful term:

> [Schmitt] is to be situated within a tradition of understanding public law as political jurisprudence. This body of thought recognizes the necessity of addressing the relationship between the legal within the political for the purpose of explaining the constitution of modern political authority. Rather than postulating the autonomy of law, thereby cutting off inquiry into the nature of the relationship between law and politics, political jurisprudence insists on the necessity of undertaking an inquiry into the character of the fundamental laws of the political. In this sense, political jurisprudence is an alternative formulation of the discipline of politonomy.[46]

For Schmitt and others, "all law is situational law."[47] And only an almighty leviathan could ensure that social order was preserved. "For Schmitt, a monstrous state of affairs ensued when society presumed to enter the state, dictate the state's will, and thereby alter the abstract norms regulating society itself."[48] The idea of the *Rechtsstaat*, according to him, exemplified such an entry—society's invasion of the sacred state space. Already in 1930, Schmitt had likened liberal theorists of the state, like von Mohl, to "a great band of robbers": "When the 'earthly God' tumbles from his throne and the realm of objective reason and ethics [*Sittlichkeit*] becomes a '*magnum latroconium*,' then the political parties butcher the mighty Leviathan and each cut their piece of flesh from his body."[49] The metaphor of the state being devoured by societal actors cuts to the heart of Schmitt's critique of liberalism.[50] It also sheds light on his reasons for rejecting the *Rechtsstaat* as an institutional design for orderly rule. For Schmitt, as for other hardliners in the debate about the *Rechtsstaat*, the idea of institutionally limiting the sovereign—whether king or *Führer*—was tantamount to treason. To take the place of "functional legality" ("*funktionale Legalität*"), Nazi legal theorists endeavored to institutionalize "substantive legitimacy" ("*substantzhafte Legitimität*"). All of these institutional designs started from the premise of antisemitism.

Antisemitism

Most of the contributors to the Nazi debate about the *Rechtsstaat* were convinced that liberalism's concern with legality and normativity was a manifestation of "Jewish legal thought" ("*jüdischen Rechtsdenkens*").[51]

The legal theorist most frequently targeted with antisemitic slurs in the debate about the *Rechtsstaat* was Stahl. According to Günther Krauß, Stahl's idea of the *Rechtsstaat* posed a "danger" ("*Gefährlichkeit*") to the incumbent regime.[52] Although the religious Stahl, who detested the revolutionary furor of 1830 and 1848, was a declared intellectual enemy of von Mohl's, and an advocate of an authoritarian *Rechtsstaat*, he was held responsible for having inspired Christian legal thought in Weimar Germany, the kind of conservative perspectives on law that theorists of the Third Reich condemned.[53] Krauß singled out Stahl for opprobrium because of the latter's rejection of Hegel. He put an antisemitic twist on the argument by claiming that Stahl had "chased the German," by which he meant Hegel, "out of his homeland" ("*den Deutschen aus seiner Heimat vertrieben*") which, by implication, meant that Germany was not Stahl's country.[54] In this antisemitic argument, the Nazi Reich belonged to Hegel's descendants, not Stahl's.

Binder also singled out Stahl. In a widely read article that he had completed before but published only after the *Machtergreifung*, in 1933, Binder spelled out the ideational and institutional demands of the authoritarian state of the future as he imagined it. He charged Stahl with having distorted "the true essence of the conservative and national concept of the state," and for having paved the way for liberalism and democratization through his advocacy for a monarchical principle on Christian foundations.[55] Others concurred, writing with concern about the fact that Stahl's arguments had become staples ("*Gemeinplätze*") of Weimar legal thought.[56] Given the influence he was said to posthumously have wielded, Stahl's scholarship was consistently derided, as was his character: he was pejoratively referred to as "Stahl-Jolson," "Jolson-Stahl," or just "Jolson."

Born Julius Jolson to Jewish parents in 1802, Stahl converted to Protestantism at the age of seventeen and assumed the name Friedrich Julius Stahl.[57] The explicit references in Nazi Germany to Stahl's pre-Christian surname were a blatant attempt at "othering," a hateful tactic to denigrate Stahl's intellectual contribution by reminding readers, in a time when antisemitism was a widely accepted societal norm, of his erstwhile Jewish faith.[58] Günther Krauß fanned the flames of antisemitism when he insisted that "Stahl" was a fake name ("*Tarnungsname*") behind which "Jolson" hid his supposedly wicked Jewish character.[59] Schmitt, more than anyone, took aim at Stahl, borrowing heavily from the antisemitic repertoire of legal contention. As Heinrich Meier writes, "From 1933 to 1938 Stahl is the enemy whom Schmitt most frequently attacks by name and reviles personally."[60] The matter is far from trivial, and Schmitt's antisemitism far from incidental. We now know that Schmitt was a lifelong antisemite; his hatred of Jews was not a phase but a constant.[61] During the period under investigation, "enmity towards 'the Jews' is what binds Schmitt to National Socialism the longest."[62] He and many other Nazi legal theorists used the adjective "Jewish" and the noun "Jew" as intellectual weapons. Schmitt explained at some length why the weaponization of language was called for. He illustrated the issue with reference to what he termed "the problem of citations" and pointed to the example of Stahl:

> A Jewish author to us has no authority, not even "purely scholarly" authority. [...] A Jewish author, if he is even cited, is to us [nothing more than] a Jewish author. The addition of the word and label "Jewish" is not a minor point, but something essential [...]. Otherwise the cleansing of our legal literature is impossible. Whoever today writes "Stahl-Jolson" has, in a truly scientific manner, accomplished more than [he could] with grand observations directed against Jews that stay at a general level of abstraction, and, as a result of which, not a single Jew feels addressed *in concreto*.[63]

Schmitt uttered these words at the infamous 1936 conference "*Das Judentum in der Rechtswissenschaft*" which he convened in October of that year, among other things, to curry favor with the new authoritarians. In addition to Stahl, Schmitt singled out Paul Laband, Erich Kaufmann, Hans Kelsen, and Hermann Heller as legal scholars to be shunned.[64] "If for a substantive reason it is necessary to cite Jewish authors," Schmitt instructed his audience, "then only with the addition 'Jewish.' The mere mention of the word 'Jewish' will bring about a healing exorcism."[65]

Although some of Schmitt's rivals in the Nazi legal academy did not attend the 1936 conference, another important protagonist in the debate about the *Rechtsstaat* did participate: Edgar Tatarin-Tarnheyden.

The focus of Tatarin-Tarnheyden's intervention, subsequently published as a monograph, was the role of Jewish thought in the theory and practice of the German state.[66] The "Jewish question" ("*Judenfrage*"), as he referred to it, was of critical significance to him because of the supposedly "fateful" ("*verhängnisvoll*") role that non-Aryan scholars had played in the development of nineteenth but especially twentieth century law. Tatarin-Tarnheyden's diagnosis: Jewish influences had "swamped" ("*überfremdet*") German legal thought, thereby soiling it.[67] Like Schmitt, he singled out Stahl, although he conceded that other scholars probably had more directly influenced Weimar legal culture. But Tatarin-Tarnheyden offered an extensive reading of Stahl's oeuvre nonetheless, one full of racial epithets, because, as he observed, in the writings of the nineteenth century conservative theorist "the Jewish" ("*das Jüdische*") was not always immediately noticeable—and thus important to bring to the attention of readers in the Third Reich who might otherwise mistake Stahl for one of their own.[68]

Among the many failings attributed to Stahl was his disregard of the *Volk* as a living organism. It was in this context, claimed Tatarin-Tarnheyden, that "his Jewish thinking" was "doubly evident."[69] Stahl was targeted because he thought the *Volk* was not a providential community, but simply another word for a population subject to the authority of the state. For Stahl it was indeed a descriptive designation, not a constitutive one. He thought in societal, not communal terms, which is why the Nazi institution of the *Volksgemeinschaft* ran afoul of his institutional belief in a separation between state and society. For this point of view, his "formal-statist" ("*formal-etatistisch*") concept of the *Volk*, Stahl was called to task in the Nazi debate about the *Rechtsstaat*. Stahl's legal thought as well as that of Kelsen and Laband and some of the other influential lawyers that we encountered in the previous chapter, the racial state deemed dispensable. It was described as lacking in "natural and cultural substance" ("*frei von aller naturhaften and kulturhaften Substanz*"), and, consequently, the "substantive ethos" ("*substanzhafter Ethos*") that the governance of a purified Germany required.[70] This pervasive lack of conviction, or moral hollowness, Tatarin-Tarnheyden claimed, had, in the cases of Kelsen, Laband, and "Stahl-Jolson," led to an objectionable dogmatism. In practical terms, he claimed, it had spawned two phenomena that needed to be uprooted: "*Gesetzespositivismus*" and "*Begriffsjurisprudenz*," or "statutory positivismus" and "conceptual jurisprudence."[71]

According to virtually every Nazi legal theorist writing at the time, the emphasis on formality and generality, on logic and abstraction, were quintessentially Jewish preoccupations that deserved to be condemned and eradicated from the theory and practice of law. Krauß, for example, argued that Stahl was predestined "by race" ("*seiner Rasse nach*") to believe in a normative state.[72] Such crude essentialism was commonplace in the debate about the *Rechtsstaat*. Nazi intellectuals also invoked the metaphor of a "phalanx" of Jewish legal theorists to exaggerate the supposed onslaught from legal positivism—the unified front of the invented other in law.[73] Tatarin-Tarnheyden's antisemitic pamphlet even announced a destructive ambition: After likening Germany's Jews to "parasitic" climbing plants that were tarnishing Aryan trees, he warned they should not be surprised if the weakened and exhausted tree trunk rose ("*aufbäumt*") to fight for its survival.[74] This slur is a quintessentially "chimerical assertion," as defined by the historian Gavin Langmuir.

In his effort to comprehend the precise function of communication in antisemitic utterances, Langmuir has distinguished among realistic, xenophobic, and chimerical assertions. He takes the latter to refer to "propositions that grammatically attribute with certitude to an outgroup and all its members characteristics that have never been empirically observed."[75] Schmitt, Krauß, Tatarin-Tarnheyden, and the other participants in the Nazi debate about the *Rechtsstaat* compiled a large repertoire of chimerical assertions about a group within the outgroup: lawyers. Despite important and obvious epistemological, theoretical, and methodological differences among German lawyers of Jewish ancestry, the distinguishing factors of their professional identities were erased, their individual selves violently reduced to an imagined, chimerical essence.[76] This essence was said to have undermined the long legal tradition of the "Nordic Urvolk," for whom, according to some of the Nazi legal theorists, law represented an indivisible trinity of race, law, and *Sittlichkeit*.[77] Helmut Nicolai in particular mythologized a "Germanic" way of law. By appropriating Friedrich Savigny's idea of the *Volksgeist*, or "spirit of the Volk," and declaring it a fundamental and perennial source of German law, he charted a course for the racialization of law.

According to Nicolai, the concept of the *Volksgeist* had temporarily—and unjustly—fallen out of favor because of a missing ingredient: race. Race was the animating idea behind Nicolai's idea of the *Volksgeist*. He drew inspiration especially from ancient German law in which, he claimed, race and law had existed in such a tight and mutually constitutive relationship that "the entire legal order was arranged along *völkisch*, racial, and biological lines."[78] Schmitt was looking in the same murky corners for ingredients with which to strengthen the cement of society: "We are looking for a bond that is more credible, more alive, and deeper than the treacherous commitment to the twistable letters of the law contained in thousands of statutory provisions. Where else could this bond be found if not in ourselves and in our kind?"[79] Schmitt left no doubt that by "kind," he meant the Aryan race. In his pamphlet *Staat, Bewegung, Volk*, first published in 1933, he produced a forty-six-page justification of the Nazi racial order. In it, he insisted, among other things, that "racial equality" ("*Artgleichheit*") was a *sine qua non* of Nazi dictatorship.[80] I have elsewhere described this line of reasoning as "racial institutionalism": "What previously had been 'just' an example of extremist institutionalism [Schmitt] retrofitted with the trappings of National Socialism, including some of the ideological tenets that combined with the regime's 'eliminationist racism.'"[81]

However, antisemitic tropes were more prevalent in some of the contributions to the Nazi debate about the *Rechtsstaat* than in others. In the writings of Otto Koellreutter, Julius Binder, and Otto von Schweinichen, for example, anti-Jewish propaganda, although ever present, was communicated less virulently than in the contributions of Helmut Nicolai and Hans Frank—to draw attention to two Nazi theorists for whom the category of race was not of incidental but of central import. Nicolai was an ardent advocate of what he called "*rassengesetzliche Rechtslehre*," or "racial legal studies."[82] In his manifesto, Nicolai was quick to invoke recent advances in eugenics and race science ("*Erkenntnisse der neueren Vererbungs- und Rassenwissenschaft*") to lay the foundations for his racial theory of law.[83] For him law was a question of genetics. Respect for it was transmitted by blood, not statutes. Better humans, not better institutions, improved the law, or so he thought.[84] Nicolai was convinced that the idea of freedom of will was a smokescreen. In his argument, criminal behavior was always a consequence of genetic predisposition never the result of individual choice. Consequently, Nicolai favored severe punishment for any transgressions of the law. The notion that perpetrators could be rehabilitated, he dismissed as the brainchild of "democratic Jewry" ("*demokratischen Judentums*").[85] Because race determined being, the purpose of punishment had to be the removal of transgressive beings, either, in major cases, by elimination ("*Ausmerzung*"), or, in minor ones, by deterrence.[86]

At the time of the Nazi debate about the *Rechtsstaat*, Hans Frank was the most visible (though not the most influential) legal practitioner in the Third Reich. On April 25, 1933, Reich President Paul von Hindenburg had appointed him to the position of Reich Commissioner for the Centralization of the Judiciary and the Renewal of the Legal Order (*Reichskommissar für die Gleichschaltung der Justiz und für die Erneuerung der Rechtsordnung*). In June of that year, Frank founded the *Akademie für Deutsches Recht*, the Berlin-based Academy of German Law, and in 1936 construction began in Munich on the *Haus des Deutschen Rechts*, a monumental building designed as a stage for his legal performances on behalf of the dictatorship.[87] Frank was an early ally of Hitler's. Starting in 1927, he defended Hitler in court on several dozen occasions, and in 1929 became the NSDAP's legal counsel. He also had a hand in the creation of the *Bund Nationalsozialistischer Deutscher Juristen* (BNDJ, Association of National Socialist German Jurists), and the *Leipziger Juristentage*, annual conventions of the country's Aryan lawyers that sought to mimick, on a smaller scale, the regime's Nuremberg rallies.[88]

Frank's hatred of Jews was often on display. In an address to jurists on May 12, 1933, he declared that the BNDJ "will never cease until all Jews are completely purged from legal life," a statement for which, according to the transcript, he earned strong applause.[89] Later that year, Frank introduced a number of principles meant to guide the purification of Nazi law. He decreed that legal scholarship was the sole preserve of German men ("*deutschen Männern vorbehalten*").[90] Moreover, publishers were barred from publishing new editions of law books by Jewish authors, and any existing such editions were to be removed from public libraries.[91] Reiterating a position he had first formulated ten years earlier, Frank, in 1936, declared that law was what benefitted the German *Volk*, and that whatever was to the detriment of the *Volk*, by definition, constituted lawlessness ("*Unrecht*"), a view that moderates and hardliners in the Nazi debate about the *Rechtsstaat* ultimately shared.[92] However, the "*Neue Rechtswissenschaft*," or "New Legal Science," a programmatic term that the so-called *Kieler Schule*, an influential stream within the Nazi legal academy, had invented, was more convincing at performing acts of "demarcation" ("*Abgrenzung*") than acts of constitution. Its members were adept at describing the kind of law they did *not* want to practice, but far less so at articulating a coherent conception of Nazi law.[93] Horst Dreier has used the term "negative consensus" ("*Negativkonsens*") to describe this predicament.[94]

A few dozen legal theorists and practitioners participated in the Nazi debate about the *Rechtsstaat*. All of them were "frightful jurists" ("*furchtbare Juristen*"), to borrow Ingo Müller's well-worn formulation. Unfortunately, the label, as befitting as it is, tells us little about the fierce infighting that divided the Nazi legal establishment in both the academy and government, and the consequences thereof for the legal terminology and institutional development of the Third Reich, including its normative state. With good reason, the legal philosopher Edin Šarčević has therefore implored scholars not to dismiss authoritarian critiques of the liberal *Rechtsstaat* and their efforts to advance a Nazi concept of law. With Šarčević I believe it important to subject these critiques to analytical scrutiny so as to understand better than we currently do the legal origins of dictatorship, then and now.[95] In an effort to cut through the cacophony of voices in the Nazi debate about the *Rechtsstaat*, I distinguish two competing preferences on the part of the participating jurists: (1) racializing the *Rechtsstaat*; and (2) replacing the *Rechtsstaat*. As so often in life, the devil is in the details.

RACIALIZING THE *RECHTSSTAAT*

It has been said that Nazi jurists retained the language of the *Rechtsstaat* in the early years of the dictatorship for strategic reasons, to curry favor with an international community in which some governments feared a return of German militarism and a renewed quest for mastery in Europe.[96] According to this rationalist argument, the Nazi debate about the *Rechtsstaat* was purely performative, not at all substantive. Several observers have pointed to the "legitimating" effects of an internationally recognizable "political-constitutional achievement."[97] It is also undeniable that some Nazi advocates of the *Rechtsstaat* hoped to appease the country's anxious monied classes, notably those who were concerned about the right to property and related protections of commercial activity.[98] And yet, it would be wrong to assume that this was the only, let alone, the most important reason for the Nazi debate about the *Rechtsstaat* to take place. In accounting for its emergence and the vigor (as well as the intellectual rigor) with which (much of) it was conducted, we need to consider a constructivist explanation as well. I propose that some Nazi legal theorists debated the *Rechtsstaat* at the highest level of abstraction also because it was socially meaningful for them to do so. Many of the elite jurists in the Third Reich were genuinely committed to broadening their country's legal imagination—however repulsive this Nazi legal conscience is by almost any standard. They certainly were self-interested actors, but whether as nemesis or katechon, the *Rechtsstaat* mattered to almost every one of them expressively. It gave social meaning to their intellectual struggle in the service of a dehumanizing ideology. It was a contest over identity: the collective identity of Nazi law, certainly, but also the individual and professional identities of theorists and practitioners of Nazi law, all of whom needed to come to terms—inwardly and outwardly—with the confusing signs of the times.[99]

Legalizing the *Volk*

The most notable defender of the language of the *Rechtsstaat* was Otto Koellreutter. Koellreutter proposed to retain and modify the concept because he considered it a *general* category of analysis and practice. In a 1932 contribution, he proffered the concept of the "national *Rechtsstaat*." With it he hoped to uproot the liberal connotation of von Mohl's idea of the *Rechtsstaat*. According to Koellreutter, a national *Rechtsstaat* related "legal value" ("*Rechtswert*") to "political value" ("*politischen Wert*"), though the latter would always rank supreme. He attributed an explicit ordering function to this *Rechtsstaat*, which centered on the provision of legal formality and legal certainty. His idea of a racial *Rechtsstaat*, which he theorized further in 1933 and again in 1934 and 1935, was an "authoritarian state" ("*autoritärer Staat*") that, in Nazi Germany, he re-christened "authoritarian *Führerstaat*" ("*autoritärer Führerstaat*"). In Koellreutter's conception, this state was held together by an expressive "idea of law" ("*Rechtsidee*") derived from a constitutive "experience of community" ("*Gemeinschaftserlebnis*") and made possible by the *völkisch* "ideology" ("*Weltanschauung*") underpinning it. This idea of law was ingrained in and supported by a "legal order" ("*Rechtsordnung*"), a formal but weakly institutionalized structure designed to reduce transaction costs but *not* to constrain the racial dictatorship. In his 1933 textbook, he noted that the function of any legal order—its only function—was to give shape and form to the "energy field" ("*Kräftefeld*") where social and political forces meet.[100] This was the be-all and end-all of the Nazi *Rechtsstaat*, according to Koellreutter's vision: it enabled, but it did not constrain. His quest for an authoritarian state that was *authoritative* was not dissimilar to Binder's understanding of the adjective, of whom more below. For both theorists, an authoritarian state was a powerful state that governed through strength but primarily by way of the legitimacy that it acquired through the confidence vested in it by its people, the *Volk*.[101]

For Koellreutter the existence of the Nazi legal order was predicated exclusively on the will of the *Volksgemeinschaft*, as expressed in its "*Rechtsgefühl*," the community's sense of law, by which he meant everyday attitudes toward law's rightness. Immanent in it, according to Koellreutter, were the self-evident, "moral demands of justice" ("*ethische Forderungen der Gerechtigkeit*"), by which he meant not universal imperatives in the Kantian fashion but moral imperatives derived solely from the demands of the political.[102] Nazi justice was political justice. Or, to paraphrase Schmitt, Koellreutter's fiercest rival on the Nazi firmament: just is he who decides on the norm.[103] In 1934, Koellreutter coined the label "National Socialist *Rechtsstaat*" to bring his expressivist institutional design even further in line with the precepts of Nazi ideology.[104] He declared that the supreme source of Nazi law was not legislation, that is, formally rational law, but the law itself ("*das Recht*"), by which he meant, in Weber's parlance, substantively irrational law.[105] In the transition from his concept of the "national *Rechtsstaat*" to that of the "National Socialist *Rechtsstaat*," Koellreutter altered his understanding of law in subtle but noteworthy ways. Whereas he previously worked with a non-positivist concept of law, he now relied on a "supra-positivist" ("*überpositiv*") one.[106] In his elaboration of the idea of the "national *Rechtsstaat*," Koellreutter had argued that a relationship of polarity ("*Polaritätsverhältnis*") existed between the "ethical" demands and "political necessities" of lawmaking.[107] By placing the binary of law/politics at the heart his concept of the *Rechtsstaat*, Koellreutter laid intellectual foundations for the emergence of a dual state *in practice*. By subsequently theorizing the "*völkisch* idea of law" ("*völkische Rechtsidee*") as the foremost *source* of law, rather than merely a guide for interpretation, as he had done previously, Koellreutter hollowed out the idea of the *Rechtsstaat* in a very particular way. His was a theoretical argument for removing the institutional separation that he maintained still kept law and politics apart. The so-called *Röhm Putsch* of 1934 illustrates the practical significance of this theoretical move. To use Fraenkel's terms, it exemplifies the normative state acting on behalf of the prerogative state.

In Koellreutter's reading, the violent intra-regime purge that took place between June 30 and July 2—in which extrajudicial death squads had assassinated Ernst Röhm, the leader of the SA, as well as other figures marked as troublesome—was legal because it was retroactively legalized.[108] Koellreutter was not in the least concerned with the ex post facto legalization of the killing spree. The legislation in defense of the state exemplified to him the regime's commitment to *both* formally rational law and substantively irrational law. The exception became the norm, so to speak, and in more senses than one. The violence of the 1934 exception, in Koellreutter's view, "positivized" itself, it acquired formal legality after the fact.[109] Substantive legality, to stay with Weber's terminology, the purge possessed all along, at least in Koellreutter's interpretation: "The law of exception (*Staatsnotrecht*) positivizes itself (*positiviert sich*) whenever the preservation of a *Volk*'s order of life is concerned (*Lebensordnung*), the preservation of which is the highest political and simultaneously a legal value (*Rechtswert*)."[110] Koellreutter's second revision of the *Rechtsstaat*-concept—his institutional sketch of the "National Socialist *Rechtsstaat*"—allowed him to legitimate the violent foray of Hitler's prerogative state in terms of law.

Because he had turned the *völkisch* idea of law into a fully-fledged source of law, any act or omission carried out in accordance with this supra-positivist principle enjoyed legal validity in Koellreutter's world. With this theoretical construction, Koellreutter hoped to show that the Nazi state was a genuine state of law, a *Rechtsstaat*, albeit one with racial overtones. Like previous incarnations of the *Rechtsstaat*, he argued, the Nazi state was institutionally bound by law, except that in this latest manifestation, law's constitutive and constraining force derived from the *völkisch* idea of law and no longer the "rigid forms of statutory rule" ("*starren Formen des Gesetzes*").[111] In 1942, Koellreutter looked back upon the Nazi debate about the *Rechtsstaat* with regret.[112] Intellectually defeated, he bemoaned the inability of his intellectual (and professional) rivals to recognize the "eternal value" ("*Ewigkeitswert*") of the *Rechtsstaat*, which, he was still certain, fulfilled essential ordering functions in any polity, including the Nazi one.[113] Koellreutter was not the only Nazi theorist who tried to combine his trust in law with his faith in race.

Despite reservations about the idea of the *Rechtsstaat*, a notable number of Nazi intellectuals at first clung to the concept. Some did so out of an expressive conviction; others saw its instrumental value, from its regulatory power to its "suggestive power."[114] Regardless, "[m]uch was still up in the air during this first phase [of theoretical reflection about the concept of Nazi law], which lasted from January 1933 to about the summer of 1934. Still dominant was the hope," on the part of some participants and observers, "that the regime, after overcoming the revolutionary phase of transition, would set up a 'national *Rechtsstaat*.' "[115] Indeed, the 1934 edition of Germany's most trusted encyclopedia, the multi-volume *Brockhaus*, described the Hitler state as a "national *Rechtsstaat*."[116]

A Nazi Leviathan

Bodo Dennewitz, a Koellreutter student, built on the foundation of his mentor's conceptual innovation. His was by the far the most lucid and thoughtful contribution to the Nazi debate about the *Rechtsstaat*. It was not marred by the ideological fervor, opportunistic or otherwise, that was germane even to more moderate contributions, including, as we have seen, those by Koellreutter. He may not have felt the same professional pressures as his mentor, whose competition with Schmitt in the early years of dictatorship was not just a defining feature of Nazi legal thought but had surfaced in the conservative currents of the so-called *Staatsrechtsdebatte* during the breakdown of democracy in Weimar Germany.[117] Judging by his modest output and professional conduct, Dennewitz may also have been less committed a Nazi than Koellreutter, who was considerably quicker (like Schmitt) to lace his scholarly publications with the language of the Third Reich. To be sure, Dennewitz was by no means a liberal thinker. But neither was he an ideologue, nor a theorist of the prerogative state, which is presumably why his attempt to reconfigure the *Rechtsstaat* for the "national revolution" ("*nationale Revolution*") found few adherents in the 1930s. To understand why the Nazi revolution left him, and his conservative ideas, behind, we must focus on Dennewitz's belief in what he called, unusually for the time, the "institutionalism of the *Rechtsstaat*" ("*rechtsstaatlichen Institutionalism*").[118] His was a sketch for a Nazi leviathan, a *völkisch* variant of Hobbes's institutional ideal of the all-powerful state.

Dennewitz began his defense of the *Rechtsstaat* with a bold assertion. Not only was the idea of the *Rechtsstaat* compatible ("*existenzfähig*") with the Nazi revolution, he claimed, its norms and institutions were "necessary" ("*notwendig*") to preserve the achievements of this revolution.[119] Like his mentor, Dennewitz thought of the national *Rechtsstaat* in terms of two institutions that made up its essence: a "neutral, legal factor" and a "political factor" that invested the former with meaning. The legal half in this dual state of Dennewitz's design represented the stable essence, the eternal value ("*unveränderten Grundton, den Ewigkeitswert*") of the idea of the *Rechtsstaat.*[120] Two attributes of this normative state stood out for him: first, and most important, that the exercise of state power was "bound by law and statute" ("*an Recht und Gesetz gebunden*"); and, second, that individuals possessed rights vis-à-vis the state.[121] The "protection" ("*Schutz*") of citizens from the state was a fundamental mark of Dennewitz's legal institutionalism. He believed the existence of a *Rechtsstaat* could be gleaned from the distribution of power in a polity, which is why he took the existence of a separation among judiciary, legislature, and executive in an institutional framework as an indicator of a "fundamental recognition" ("*grundsätzliche Anerkennung*") of the *Rechtsstaat.* The adjective "institutional" was crucial to Dennewitz. He reserved it to denote stable patterns of behavior, that is, institutional practices that evolved over time and gradually grew into defining attributes of state.[122] However, for Dennewitz, normative statehood was but one half of his national *Rechtsstaat*, a necessary but by no means sufficient attribute. Only the injection of political values was capable of turning an otherwise neutral institutional structure into a truly sovereign state.[123] For him, legal institutions made states useful, but only political ideas rendered them meaningful. It is worth noting that Dennewitz's conception of the national *Rechtsstaat* bears a striking resemblance to what Fraenkel a few years later came to theorize as the dual state.

Importantly, for Dennewitz as well as for Koellreutter, the precise content of the state's political value could not be fixed at the conceptual level. It will always be the expression of a given era of politics, a "concrete historical epoch" ("*konkreten historischen Epoche*"), which is precisely why both of these legal thinkers attributed eternal value to the *Rechtsstaat*.[124] In the logic of their respective theories, the national *Rechtsstaat* of the 1930s *happened* to be National Socialist in character, but this was a reflection of the times, not a defining feature of the concept they were promoting. Dennewitz's metaphors of the state as a "living organism" and the "living embodiment of the *Volk* as a whole" give credence to this reading.[125] The language implicitly rendered the Nazi dictatorship as a stage in the institutional development of the German state, not a case *sui generis*.

Dennewitz's response to Koellreutter's modification of the *Rechtsstaat* concept resulted in its further diminuation. Unlike his erstwhile teacher, Dennewitz did not subscribe to the idea that the *Rechtsstaat* ought to fulfill a protective and ordering function (think Koellreutter's "*Sicherheits- und Ordnungselement*") that ensured legal security and legal predictability for the citizens of the Third Reich. Incorporating insights from Ernst Rudolf Huber's lengthy and contemporaneous critique of "*Grundrechte*," or basic rights, Dennewitz's was an argument for drastically curtailing the realm and the protection of individual freedom.[126] He summarized his concept of law in terms of three interrelated binaries. He insisted that it (1) be grounded in reality not abstract principles; (2) be dynamic, not static; and (3) be communitarian, not individual or formal.[127]

Although Dennewitz did not want to jettison the hard-won legalization of fundamental rights (*Grundrechte*) enshrined in the Weimar constitution, he argued that their legal status needed to be altered. He proposed to subordinate them to new, unwritten principles of constitutional law.[128] Dennewitz rejected the equation of law and statute, which he believed to be the essence of the "bourgeois-liberal" *Rechtsstaat*, because it took insufficient cognizance of the distribution of power in the national system, or the state's "*nationale Machtposition*."[129] Deeply skeptical of legal positivism, Dennewitz argued that the validity of constitutional law had to be interpreted through the lens of constitutional reality, notably what he called "constitutional life" ("*Verfassungsleben*").[130] Put differently, he did not seek to destroy the normative state of old, but to roll it back. The goal was to infuse the norms and institutions of law with a corporate spirit.[131] In cases of conflict between law on the books and the law of politics, "*Volksrecht*" was to automatically supersede positive law, which meant that the protection of the rights of individuals vis-à-vis the state were considerably weaker in Dennewitz's vision for the "national *Rechtsstaat*" than in Koellreutter's. As Christian Hilger writes, "The limits of state power [...]

are not immediately recognizable for the individual, which has a negative effect on legal security and legal predictability."[132] At the same time, Dennewitz did believe in placing legal limits on the Nazi state (writing as he did of a "*begrenzte Machtbefugnis des Staates*"). Rather than calling for a prerogative state tout court, he insisted that the Nazi state action required legitimation by either law or statute.[133] He described the institutional function of the national *Rechtsstaat* as the "neutral regulation of responsibilities" ("*neutrale Zuständigkeitsregelung*") in accordance with formal principles of organizational design ("*Organisations- und Zuständigkeitsprinzip*").[134] It is also significant that Dennewitz, despite the standard overtures, was not obsessed with race as a defining attribute of his reconfigured *Rechtsstaat*.

Gesetzesstaat to *Rechtsstaat*

Like Koellreutter and Dennewitz, Heinrich Lange and Otto von Schweinichen too saw a possibility of retaining the *Rechtsstaat* as a term of art, provided that the concept was reimagined "in a concrete sense" ("*im konkreten Sinne*").[135] However, unlike Koellreutter and Dennewitz, neither Lange nor von Schweinichen were willing to concede that the liberal *Rechtsstaat* ever represented a valid historical instantiation of the more general idea of the *Rechtsstaat*.

Lange, a private law scholar, dismissed the "bourgeois-liberal" *Rechtsstaat* as the outer shell of an empty legislative state ("*Gesetzesstaat*") whose legitimacy derived in large part from its exercise of power ("*Machtstaat*").[136] He contrasted this formal instantiation of the idea of the *Rechtsstaat* with the substantive one that, or so he claimed, the "National Socialist *Rechtsstaat*" had established, an institutional design that appealed to him because of the "inner value" ("*inneren Wert*") that it projected.[137] Lange's *Rechtsstaat* was an expression of the "*Volksgeist*," an amorphous term that he took to refer to a nation's "absolute spirit" (though he used the term in a non-Hegelian sense), the eternal values toward the realization of which the *Volk* is oriented.[138]

Although reminiscent of Koellreutter's "*völkische Rechtsidee*," Lange did not regard the *Volksgeist* as a source of law; it merely informed the "legal consciousness of the *Volk*" ("*Rechtsempfinden des Volkes*"), which itself was rooted in blood and soil.[139] In Lange's theoretical argument, the legal consciousness of the *Volk* represented the essence of law (*Recht*) and was institutionally superior to statute (*Gesetz*). He applauded the achievements of the Nazi revolution because it had, in his opinion, transformed the concept of law, from a "technology of statutory thought" ("*Technik des Gesetzesdenkens*") into an "ethics of legal consciousness" ("*Ethik des

Rechtsempfindens").[140] But we must be careful not to read too much into Lange's critique of statutory rule: he retained a firm belief in the centrality of some form of normative state. Like Koellreutter, he emphasized the ordering function of law, which he saw fulfilling, in addition to the inculcation of Nazi morals, an important regulatory function in the racialized *Rechtsstaat*. Statutes spelled out the fundamental rules of the game. Enacted in accordance with the ruling ideology, they demarcated the institutional "boundaries, paths, and forms" ("*Grenzen, Bahnen und Formen*") of Nazi dictatorship.[141]

Lange used the same language as Koellreutter to advance his argument. The state was not mere "apparatus" ("*Apparat*") but the guardian of the *Volk*'s order of life ("*Lebensordnung*"). It was not sovereign but subordinate to the *Volk*. Governed by the *Führer* from the regime's helm, the Nazi movement and the state, according to Lange, were manifestations of *völkisch* rule, "the movement more in the realm of morals, the state more in that of technology" ("*die Bewegung mehr auf dem Gebiet des Ethischen, der Staat mehr auf dem des Technischen*").[142] Decisions of the "political leadership," he hastened to add, were not subject to the reach of the *Rechtsstaat*.[143] In a formulation that justified the rise of the prerogative state, Lange held that "no hard stop [exists] for the state as organized *Volksgemeinschaft*" ("*kein hartes Halt für den Staat als organisierte Volksgemeinschaft*").[144] And yet, in the same breath, he also acknowledged the value of remnants of the *Rechtsstaat*. Some institutions of the normative state, such as individual rights, Lange wrote, were not violated "without necessity" ("*ohne Not*").[145] Although his argument is vague, he insisted that such far-reaching infractions required legal authorization and could not be undertaken wantonly. However, the kind of normative restraint that Lange saw operating in the "National Socialist *Rechtsstaat*" was a watered-down version from that associated with previous incarnations of the *Rechtsstaat*. The normative protections that Lange had in mind were not enshrined in constitutional documents or legislative acts, but underwritten exclusively by the "healthy legal consciousness of the *Volk*."[146] In this conception of the *Rechtsstaat*, even the concentration camp was just another institution capable of protecting the law of the *Volk* ("*Rechtswahrung*").[147] For Lange, the Nazi state remained a *Rechtsstaat* as long as its conduct was oriented toward the *Volksgeist*, which is where elective affinities with Dennewitz come into view. The existence and operation of a normative state (with its emphasis on statutory rule) alongside a prerogative state (with its penchant for violent rule) for Lange was an incidental consequence of stable governance, not a defining attribute of his racialized *Rechtsstaat*. Lange's theoretical design, although a minority view in the Nazi debate about the *Rechtsstaat*, bears a notable resemblance to the everyday life of Nazi law, especially in the period 1933–1938, as captured by Ernst Fraenkel's metaphor of the dual state.

Otto von Schweinichen also saw value in the concept of the *Rechsstaat*. Like Lange, he took aim at the *Gesetzesstaat*, or legislative state, of the Weimar Republic, which, or so he claimed, had encapsulated but a fraction of the idea of the *Rechtsstaat* as it *ought* to be understood.[148] The essence of the kind of law-governed state that he envisaged was its rejection of abstract formalism. The question of whether law was just did not at all concern von Schweinichen.[149] For him this was a nonsensical question because law (*Recht*) as an institution was inherently just. Encasing a polity's fundamental norms, it served as a "pure guideline" ("*reine Richtschnur*") for politics and society from which "factual guidelines" ("*tatsächliche Richtschnuren*") were derived. As a given polity's "highest normative principle" ("*höchste Normprinzip*"), law, thus defined, was binding on whoever lived within its reach. Forged out of historical experience, it defined "true" duties and permissions ("'*echtes*' *Sollen oder Dürfen*"), giving expression to an ideational universe ("*ideell Angehendes*") that is culturally appropriate to the polity in question.[150] Von Schweinichen theorized law as a concrete abstraction.

Significantly, von Schweinichen, unlike prominent Nazi legal theorists like Larenz and Binder, drew a clear distinction between law (*Recht*) and statute (*Gesetz*). Although he recognized the regulative importance of "rules" ("*Bestimmungen*"), he was careful not to attribute a defining role to these institutions. He described statutes, directives, decrees, custom, and the like as de facto concretizations of a polity's fundamental norms. As "mere facts" ("*bloße Tatsächlichkeiten*"), their normative significance was regulative, not constitutive.[151] They existed, but they only made social life possible, not meaningful. Meaningful norms, what von Schweinichen theorized as "true norms" ("*echte Normen*") reflected a polity's ideational universe, its moral imperative. Proto-norms ("*Normanmaßungen*") such as those contained in statutes were capable of becoming true norms.[152] But only pure law—not the mere application of law—generated rights and obligations, according to von Schweinichen: law was normative, statutes were not. Law, thus defined, was to be found not in procedure, but in substance. Law for him was the essence of morality ("*der Inbegriff des Sittlichen*"), and, as such, supra-positivist in nature. Statutes might well *attain* "the character of supra-positivity" ("*den Charakter des Überpositiven*"), but they do not inherently possess it.[153] Conceptually speaking, statutes were auxiliary to law, not institutions of it.

The conceptual point held theoretical as well as political significance for von Schweinichen who had little patience for what he decried as Larenz and Binder's uncritical use of the language of liberalism. Von

Schweinichen believed it was but a short step from exaggerating the normative import of statutes to resurrecting legal positivism. On his interpretation, Larenz and Binder erroneously equated norms and statutes (whereas he subordinated the latter to the former).

When it comes to analyzing the relationship between law and statute in Nazi legal thought, it is important to distinguish between two dimensions of statutory law: the *primacy of statute* (what is known as *Vorrang des Gesetzes* in German law) and the *principle of legality* (*Vorbehalt des Gesetzes*). Both were defining features of the administration of justice in Wilhelmine Germany and Weimar Germany alike. A commitment to the primacy of statute means that a legal order regards statutes as the foremost source of law; it trumps utterances about the law emanating from other organs of state. It follows from this commitment that all branches of government, including the judiciary, are statutorily bound. Next, a commitment to the principle of legality means that all administrative action must be authorized *ex ante* by statute. Without prior statutory authorization, an administrative action would be legally invalid.[154] The legalization of administrative action was a gradual outgrowth of the rise of the *Rechtsstaat* as an idea in the nineteenth century. As Stolleis writes, "The constitutional movement and the interest of a society that was becoming more autonomous economically and politically gave rise to the call for the *Rechtsstaat*. Concretely, it meant that the administration should act in accordance with the rules of law, and that it should be subject to oversight by the courts in this regard."[155]

The distinction between the primacy of statute and the principle of legality is crucial for the analysis to come. In the Nazi debate about the *Rechtsstaat*, some participants—despite their unified rejection of the so-called *Gesetzesstaat*—attacked one, others none, and yet others both of the aforementioned dimensions of statutory rule. The variation is noteworthy because it illustrates the heterogeneity of Nazi legal thought. The greater a theorist's faith in statutory rule, the more likely he was, on balance, to invoke the language of the *Rechtsstaat*. Let me illustrate the point with reference to Carl Schmitt, who was vehemently opposed to retaining the language of the *Rechtsstaat*.

Schmitt initially argued that a resort to Nazi principles (as laid out in the NSDAP platform) in the adjudication or application of law was invalid unless authorized by statute. He first articulated this position in an address at the 1934 convention of the Association of National Socialist German Legal Professionals (*Bund Nationalsozialistischer Deutscher Juristen*, or BNSDJ) in Cologne. Schmitt, echoing Freisler, argued that judges were bound by Hitler's "enacted norms" ("*durch den Führer gesetzten Normen*").[156] A year earlier, he had written that a commitment to statutory rule was required to preserve the independence of judges in the Third Reich.[157] Schmitt's was a fleeting commitment to formality that co-existed with his faith in Nazi ideology. Despite his remarks about the utility of statutory form, Schmitt, like most of the dictatorship's legal intelligentsia, denied that Nazi statutes or otherwise enacted norms could be subject to judicial review.[158] In line with his vanishing commitment to the statute as an institutional constraint on authoritarian rule, Schmitt also began to reinterpret the statute as a concept. In 1935 he announced that, henceforth, statutory rule no longer meant normative rule but prerogative rule. "For us," he wrote, a statute ceased to be an abstract norm that gave institutional form to a preference of the past. Instead, he argued, the idea of statute was now synonymous with Hitler's "plan and will" ("*Gesetz ist Plan und Wille des Führers*").[159]

Because not all extant statutes could be revoked or rewritten in these early years of Nazi dictatorship, Schmitt (building on Freisler) theorized a compromise. Unless explicitly revoked, all statutes enjoyed bounded validity, according to this proposal. Statutes continued to matter as regulatory norms but were emptied of the substantive values that had informed them at the moment of their adoption. What Schmitt proposed was that a given statute from the Wilhelmine or Weimar eras could be retained in Nazi Germany provided it operated only as a "functional norm of the bureaucratic apparatus" ("*Funktionsnorm des staatlichen Behördenapparates*") and was neither applied nor adjudicated in accordance with the values that had prevailed "in the old state."[160] The so-called *Generalklauseln* are a case in point. General clauses are responses to gaps in the law.[161] They serve as placeholders in statutes, and the notion of *Treu und Glauben* is the most prominent *Generalklausel* in German private law. Others include *Billigkeit* and *Sittenwidrigkeit*. Because much hinges on the interpretation of general clauses, Schmitt called for judges to interpret "absolutely and unreservedly" ("*unbedingt und vorbehaltlos*") all of Germany's *Generalklauseln* and through the lens of Nazi ideology.[162] The promotion of general clauses as a tool of Nazi law found many adherents in the regime, which is why Bernd Rüthers identified them as "gateways" ("*Einfallstore*") through which Nazi legal thought entered the edifice of the *Rechtsstaat*, dismantling it from within.[163]

Mind you, Schmitt did not deny the relevance of statutory rule as such, but he radically reimagined what it meant to act in accordance with statute.[164] He debased the nineteenth century conception of statutory rule because it, or so he claimed, was backward-looking, informed by the concerns of a distant past, not the immediate present and the all-important future, as the Nazi dictatorship purported it was. The notion of statutory self-binding, key to both the liberal and conservative ideas of formally rational law, Schmitt regarded as unnecessarily inhibiting. How is the Nazi sovereign supposed to "plan," he asked, if he is constrained by legislative responses to long forgotten challenges from the past? How could the *Führer* be ready for governing the exception—and defending the realm—if his hands are tied by the principle of legality? Schmitt's solution: abandon the separation of powers. Planning, he argued, required a fusion of powers. Borrowing from René Capitan the aphorism "*gouverner c'est légiférer*" ("governing is legislating"), Schmitt claimed that the positivist idea of statutory rule was on its way out, and not just in Germany but the world over.[165] In support of this bold claim, Schmitt singled out the example of the U.S. Supreme Court, which in 1935 had declared unconstitutional President Franklin D. Roosevelt's National Industrial Recovery Act (NIRA), the well-known legislative effort to attenuate (in conjunction with other pieces of New Deal legislation) the economic effects of the Great Depression. Schmitt pitied FDR's inability to engage in long-term policy planning without legislative oversight and judicial review. Because the *Führer*, by contrast, possessed both executive and legislative power (and was not subject to judicial checks or balances either), Schmitt had no doubt that this state of affairs placed Nazi Germany in the vanguard of legal innovators in the international system.[166] As Hitler's "plan and will," a statute in Nazi Germany was what the *Führer* made of it. Or, as Ernst Rudolf Huber put it in 1939: "[O]nly one legislator [exists] in the German Reich: that is the Führer himself."[167] No longer a backward-looking, abstract norm, Schmitt and others redefined the law as a forward-looking concrete decision.[168]

The Content of the Form

Facticity trumped formality in the Nazi concept of law. Legality continued to matter, but it was beginning to mean something different from what German jurists had been taught to believe for generations. Horst Dreier has come up with the useful term "*Formindifferenz*" ("indifference to form") to describe this attitudinal shift. The Nazi scholar Ulrich Scheuner exemplified it, when, in 1940, he maintained that all forms of Hitlerian lawmaking were of the "same standing" ("*gleichen Ranges*"), their authority indistinguishable.[169] The Nazi indifference to form eventually led to a "*Formverlust*" ("loss of form"). This loss was most noticeable when it came to law's publicity. Over time the number of promulgated statutes and related instruments decreased steadily *despite* an increase in the number of such instruments, especially of so-called *Führererlasse* (*Führer* decrees), that were issued.[170] Theodor Maunz and Johannes Heckel were among those who defended the practice.

Taking inspiration from Scheuner, Maunz distinguished four equal modes of lawmaking: "*Gesetzgebungsverfahren*" (formal enactment), "*Normenschöpfungsverfahren*" (norm creation), "*Einzelweisung*" (singular directive), and "*Einzelbilligung*" (singular authorization). Because the will of the *Führer* was, in his eyes, the only arbiter of law, Maunz was unperturbed by the decline in legal promulgation. Heckel, by contrast, defended the lack of publicity in lawmaking by citing the security interests of the state, which, he proposed, justified keeping "state law" under lock and key ("*Staatsrecht im Panzerschrank*").[171]

Maunz and Heckel legitimated what was impossible to stop. With Nazi Germany's turn to aggressive war, the prerogative state was in full control of the normative state. The *Rechtsstaat* was hollowed out, a mere shell of its former self. And yet, Nazi legal thought was not as cohesive as one might expect. Werner Weber, Otto Koellreutter, and Ernst Rudolf Huber each called into question the wisdom of undermining the publicity of law—and thus the professional judgments of their colleagues. It is worth recalling their arguments because they complicate conventional wisdom about norm entrepreneurs in the legal academy of the Third Reich. Like the Nazi state, a significant number of Nazi lawyers also possessed split personalities and responded differently to conflicting imperatives, just like the dual state itself.

Werner Weber, a former doctoral student of Schmitt's, is a case in point. He was the first to critique the secrecy of Nazi lawmaking. In a 1942 monograph he reminded his readers that in the tradition of the occident (*Abendland*) the public promulgation of laws was a defining feature of legal order. The belief that publicity was indispensable to law acquiring validity, he argued, was an "old truth" ("*alte Wahrheit*"), thereby implying that the Nazi dictatorship would do well to act on it.[172] And just in case his message was not received as clearly as intended, he added that *Führer* decrees had to be published in the *Reichsgesetzblatt*, the official gazette, to be legally valid.[173] At the height of totalitarianism, Koellreutter also rediscovered his respect for the *Rechtsstaat*, echoing Weber's concerns. He even warned that Nazi law was subject to a "cold Bolshevikization" ("*kalte Bolschewisierung*").[174] Dreier has drawn attention to the rhetorical power of this metaphor, for it was Koellreutter who, almost ten years earlier, had held up the Soviet Union as an example of a "*Nichrechtsstaat*," a lawless state, that is, the kind of unworthy polity that he contrasted with the national *Rechtsstaat* of Nazi Germany.[175] Raising the specter of lawlessness in 1942, Koellreutter appears to have lost faith in the Nazi way of law. Also inching toward a *volte face* was Ernst Rudolf Huber. His enthusiasm for the Nazi project, like Koellreutter's, had also waned, as evidenced by a sympathetic review from 1944 of Weber's little book. It served him as a platform from which to critique vehemently the neglect of meaningful statutory rule. Huber's argument was simple: because lawmaking had been steadily deformalized, it was teetering on the verge of arbitrariness. It was hanging by a thread—and the promulgation of laws was this thread. As he punchily put it,

> The promulgation [of statutes and comparable instruments] has therefore increased in importance; it now bears responsibility alone for fulfilling certain functions that previously were distributed among a number of institutional forms. The [act of] promulgation is today the minimum of form, which cannot be dispensed with unless the statute as a manifestation of law as such is to be destroyed.[176]

One reason for Koellreutter's disillusionment with Nazi law in what we now know to have been the final years of the dictatorship, may have to do with the fact that the regime did not just destroy the idea of the *Rechtsstaat* but eventually also assaulted the more fundamental idea of the orderly state, the *Ordnungsstaat*.[177] For many conservative theorists and practitioners felt an allegiance to this idea of state, a commitment that preceded, and sometimes rivaled, their loyalty to the *Führer*. There are reasons to think that some Nazi jurists—Weber, Koellreutter, and Huber are but examples—were willing to countenance (and help legitimate) totalitarian rule, but were too conservative in their legal imagination to lend a hand to the construction of wanton rule. The idea of form is capable of separating one from the other. In fact, for many thinkers of the early twentieth century, the degree of institutionalization in a given state spelled the difference between anarchy and order.[178] Weber, Koellreutter, and Huber can be counted among this group, which explains why the impending death of one of the last surviving remnants of the *Rechtsstaat* caused these three unlikely rebels to voice their dissent in the early 1940s.

The episode underscores the processual and gradual character of the Nazi reconstruction of the legal system. It shows why Fraenkel's metaphor of the dual state is so helpful for capturing the liminality of law in the mid-1930s, by which I mean the ambiguity and disorientation that characterized defining stages in the legal development of the Third Reich, especially the long and winding consolidation of the dictatorship that took place in the period 1933–1938. Like everyone else in Germany, Nazi jurists stood at the threshold, facing the unknown. To steady themselves, some held on to remnants of the *Rechtsstaat* of old; others dove straight into the abyss and emerged with genuinely new (if reprehensible) solutions to the problem of legal order. Always the maverick, Schmitt belonged to the latter group.

"Collaborators of the *Führer*"

In theorizing the role of adjudication in the racial state, Schmitt described judges as "collaborators of the *Führer*'s will and plan" ("*Mitarbeiter des Führerwillens und -planes*").[179] It was a broadside against the liberal *Rechtsstaat.* In one sense, it amounted to an intellectual demotion of judges, whom Schmitt put in their new, marginal place. In another sense, he elevated the role of judges. By calling for politicized judges, Schmitt emboldened the regime's adjudicating jurists. Whereas judges in Wilhelmine and Weimar Germany subsumed facts under abstract and publicized norms, Nazi judges faced no such straitjacket. With great powers of discretion at their disposal, they were allowed, in fact encouraged, to become activist judges. Schmitt regarded judicial restraint as an indefensible remnant of the liberal *Rechtsstaat.* For him judicial activism was indispensable to the Nazi way of law. As collaborators of the *Führer*, he expected the regime's judges to fill any and all gaps in the law, all the while being mindful of Hitler's will. In practice, this meant reading his mind: by concretizing deliberately broad principles of law and by anticipating his expectations in hard cases. One might say, with a nod to Adam Smith, that Nazi judges had to adjudicate with a *partial spectator* in mind: they needed to possess the ability to stand outside themselves and see their judicial behavior as if through Hitler's eyes.[180] As the "man within," this imaginary Aryan spectator represented the voice of Nazi conscience.[181] In deciding cases, judges were expected to let their racial imagination roam. As "guardians of the law" (*Rechtswahrer*), their function was to render racially appropriate judgments, by which I mean judgments in keeping with the spirit of Nazi ideology. In the province of law, as in other areas of the Third Reich, uncertainty was a deliberate feature of institutional design. It created room for maneuver, which accounts for (and legitimated at the time) the rise of judicial activism, defined as adjudication based on political considerations.

Schmitt had two policy prescriptions for how to establish the "new" statutory rule in judicial practice. He rejected both codification (*Kodifikation*) and amendment (*Novellierung*) for the legalization of Nazi mores, as he feared that they could give rise to a new era of normativism and rule by the "twistable letters of a thousand laws" ("*verdrehbaren Buchstaben von tausend Gesetzesparagraphen*").[182] Better suited to the demands of dictatorship, Schmitt argued, were guiding principles (*Leitsätze*) and the modification of select statutory provisions.[183] Schmitt turned to the so-called *Analogieverbot*, the prohibition of analogical reasoning in German law, to illustrate the latter technique. On June 28, 1935, an amendment to the *Strafgesetzbuch*, the country's criminal code, had retired the prohibition. The motivation for the institutional re-design was obvious: to enable judges to *make* law. The return of analogical reasoning meant that activist, politicized judges in the mid-1930s were empowered to construe crimes in the *Strafgesetzbuch* far more broadly than the drafters of that document had intended in 1871. As a result, the character of criminal law was unrecognizable. By overturning the *Analogieverbot*, the regime had not just dismantled a disliked provision; it had struck a blow to—and fatally damaged—the liberal architecture of the *Strafgesetzbuch* as a whole. This fundamentally transformed the institutional foundations of Nazi criminal law, further weakening the remnants of the *Rechtsstaat*.[184] It is easy to understand why Schmitt advocated surgical strikes like the one just described: their institutional effects could be more easily concealed—and more quickly brought about—than legal alterations by codification or more comprehensive amendments. The practice of appending guiding principles (*Leitsätze*) to legislation, of which Schmitt also approved, was another feature of the "new" statutory rule in the Third Reich. The inclusion of guiding principles—say in the form of preambles (*Vorsprüche*)—ensured that formal law was saturated with substantive values, that is, the regime's racial ideology. Related tools such as *Auslegungsregeln*, or rules of interpretation, as well as the notorious *Richterbriefe*—monthly missives sent by the Ministry of Justice between October 1942 and December 1944 to all of the country's judges to streamline the administration of Nazi justice—served the same function as *Leitsätze*: they contributed to the Nazi unification of law and morals.[185] Bernd Rüthers has come up with a moniker for the practice of Nazi adjudication that the imposition of guiding principles inaugurated: "interpretation without limits" ("*die unbegrenzte Auslegung*").[186]

It is one thing to put Hitler on a pedestal and present theoretical justifications for the concentration of executive, legislative, and judicial power in his person, as Schmitt, Larenz, and many others jurists did. However, it is quite another to make such an institutional framework work *in practice*.[187] Huber, among other Nazi theorists, conceded that an informal proceduralism—the so-called *Umlaufverfahren*—regularly stood in for Hitler's sovereign will in the legalization of the racial order, even during the war years.[188] What this means is that the everyday demands of dictatorship appear to have placed an informal, temporary limit on the rise of the prerogative state. Another way of saying this is that proceduralism and decisionism co-existed, albeit in different ways and to different degrees depending on the area of law concerned.

Even though Hitler was omnipotent de jure, he was de facto dependant on those who did, or did not, involve him in the process of legalization, as even Schmitt acknowledged after the war, in 1947. In his autopsy of the dead Nazi body politic, Schmitt shone light on the regime's institutional "abnormality" ("*Abnormität*").[189] Most relevant for our discussion is his claim that the Hitler regime experienced an "emerging compulsion to forms and norm-creation" ("*eintretenden Zwang zu Formen und Normierungen*").[190] A consequence of this revival of formality, Schmitt suggested, was a return, at least in part, to a legal way of doing things ("*zu einer gewissen Legalität der Methoden*"): "Legality is the functional mode of any bureaucracy. For this reason the need for a modicum of at least outward legality entered the Hitler regime at precisely this point," where it connected "with the grand command apparatus of the 'state.' "[191] Even though the NSDAP as the political party was supposed to hover over the state (which in the language of the Third Reich included only the civil service), Schmitt held that at this time of the dictatorship the administrative state "was still the true executive" ("*war immer noch die eigentliche Exekutive*").[192] Why? Because ensuring the effectiveness of the Nazi dictatorship demanded that the state govern efficiently and expeditiously, which meant that the bureaucrats staffing it had, for the most part, little choice but to respond to the multitude of governance tasks in a quasi-formally rational way.[193] And respond they did, which is why "[t]he civil service, far from having been integrated into the National Socialist community, appeared to its political masters an alien, and to its own leaders an alienated institution."[194] Even though checks and balances were a thing of the past, it dawned on the architects of dictatorship that even arbitrary rule required a modicum of formalization if it was to be sustainable. Schmitt points to the promulgation of laws and ordinances in the *Reichsgesetzblatt* as an example of how form continued to play an integral part in the Nazi theater of law—and *despite* Hitler's reported hatred of formalization.[195]

It was not unusual for judges and bureaucrats in the Third Reich to be left to their own devices. As Jane Caplan has found, depite the institutional sketches of Nazi jurists like Koellreutter and Schmitt, many functionaries of the Nazi state were left to muddle through as best they could, certainly in "less critical areas."[196] The imperative to govern meant legal theory and practice diverged in the administration of justice when the demands of dictatorship required it. Another way of putting this is to say that the powers that were could not afford to rid themselves of *all* remnants of the *Rechtsstaat*. As Caplan writes,

> As far as any shared conclusions were reached at a theoretical level, the tendency was to argue that although the separation of powers, administrative law, and individual rights in the liberal sense had clearly been superseded by the conditions of the National Socialist state, this did not necessarily mean either that laws as such were no longer needed, or that all forms of

> administrative law were nugatory. Typically, this argument involved reformulating the principle of the separation of powers and the consequent relationship between individual and state in terms more appropriate to Nazi ideology. [...] The most common solution was to argue that administrative law did not protect the rights of individuals, but the needs of the community; the administrative court system could be seen as the "guardian of objective order", therefore, and continue to function. This contrivance represented an acceptable theoretical justification for the persistence of administrative review, while explaining why its sphere of application was more narrowly constructed under National Socialism than before.[197]

Fraenkel found an appropriate label for this contrivance: the dual state. But as we shall see in more detail in the chapters to come, this institutional hybrid was partly the result of institutional design and partly the product of institutional practice. It appears to have been mostly "defenders of traditional legal means and institutions" who were willing to adjust to this new reality, many of them mid-level bureaucrats.[198] According to the historian Hans Mommsen, the bureaucracy of Nazi Germany remained an instantiation of the normative state, one that continued to function "until the end of the Third Reich."[199] He believed that its "technical, routinely functioning and self-sufficient apparatus" provided a counterweight to the NSDAP's vision of the prerogative state.[200] Michael Stolleis in his study of administrative courts (*Verwaltungsgerichte*) has come to a similar conclusion. As in the case of many ministries, institutional continuity was pervasive in the administrative courts, which the stalwarts of the Nazi dictatorship therefore viewed with suspicion. In their eyes, the administrative courts were decidedly liberal remnants of the *Rechtsstaat* and one that impeded the racial revolution.[201] This is not to say that these quasi-normative institutions did not also aid the Third Reich. They certainty did. In fact, the arrangement was mutually beneficial: the leadership of the regime co-opted nationalist and conservative judges—many of whom were beholden to the ideal of the nineteenth century *Rechtsstaat*—by tolerating a rudimentary normative state in select areas. Where it threatened to thwart ambitions of the Nazi elite, the prerogative state stepped in to re-equilibrate the dictatorship, aligning norms with facts.

Eventually the abolition of the principle of legality and the expanded duty to obey (*Gehorsamspflicht*) for civil servants hollowed out the legal foundations of Nazi administration, resulting in a "corrosion of the state's substance."[202] When the representatives of the prerogative state turned on the functionaries of the normative state, what had functioned for a while as a "well-organized chaos" led to "the decline of the state as such."[203] Such are the legacies of the Nazis' degenerate law.

Degenerate Law

After this analysis of the transformation and deformation of statutory law in Nazi Germany, we are in a position to return to the debate about the *Rechtsstaat.* Like Koellreutter, von Schweinichen argued that the concept of the *Rechtsstaat* was not just an "*Individualbegriff*," a term applicable only to the nineteenth century, as some Nazi theorists vehemently insisted at the time, but a valid concept usable for comparative historical analysis ("*Analogiebegriff* ").[204] Yet for von Schweinichen, the liberal *Rechtsstaat* was not a *Rechtsstaat* "in the true sense" ("*im wahren Sinne*") because it constrained the state. In a "true" *Rechtsstaat,* he argued, law was not "limit" ("*Schranke*"), but merely form.[205] For this reason, the Nazi *Rechtsstaat* had nothing in common with the liberal *Rechtsstaat*; it was "something fundamentally different" ("*etwas wesentlich anderes*").[206] The liberal *Rechtsstaat,* he claimed, was a degenerate example ("*Entartungserscheinung*") of the *Rechtsstaat* as a conceptual type.[207] A "true" *Rechtsstaat,* as von Schweinichen conceived of it, was a "*Volksstaat,*" not mere "*Gesellschaftsstaat.*"[208] It satisfied the concrete needs of a homogenous *Volk*; it did not cater to the abstract demands of a heterogeneous society. In the Nazi *Rechtsstaat,* fostering collective identity was essential, not accommodating individual interests. Applying his distinction, Schweinichen concluded that nineteenth century Prussia had not been a *Rechtsstaat* in the true sense, which is why he described the institutional structure variously as a "non-*Rechtsstaat*" ("*Nichtrechtsstaat*") and a "state of lawlessness" ("*Staat des Unrechts*").[209]

Von Schweinichen was convinced the institution of the *Rechtsstaat* needed to be theorized as a form *of* rule, not a constraint *on* rule.[210] It was by definition an enabler, not a limit. In order to avoid any confusion with the liberal *Rechtsstaat,* he recommended that theorists and practitioners in the Third Reich speak of a "concrete *Rechtsstaat*" ("*konkreter Rechtsstaat*") when describing the institutional form that Nazi legalism was taking.[211] Krauß, von Schweinichen's intellectual rival, was not persuaded by these conceptual acrobatics. He complained that efforts to recycle the language of the *Rechtsstaat* were born of "laziness" ("*Bequemlichkeit*"), that they amounted to an objectionable "habit" ("*Angewohnheit*") inculcated into young minds by three generations of liberals.[212]

However, even a Nazi practitioner as radical as Roland Freisler apparently was unable to kick the habit. Time and time again he borrowed the language of the *Rechtsstaat,* relying upon it until 1937, by which time the Nazi debate about the concept had been concluded and the word all but banished. Freisler had first pronounced on the subject in 1931, in the *Völkischer Beobachter,* where he sketched a biopolitical concept of the *Rechtsstaat.*[213] It took him six years to complete his sketch.[214] For Freisler, as for numerous other Nazi legal theorists, the law was not an end in itself, but simply a means for the advancement of the *Volk*. Accordingly, he declared the "healthy consciousness of the *Volk*" ("*gesundes Volksempfinden*") to be the only true source of law.[215] Like Koellreutter and Dennewitz, before him, he imagined a concept of Nazi law in which the validity of its norms and institutions was contingent upon their being in concordance with political perceptions of what is just and proper. The purpose of law, argued Freisler, was to advance "substance justice" ("*materielle Gerechtigkeit*"), not "Shylock justice" ("*Shylockgerechtigkeit*"), an antisemitic swipe at defenders of nineteenth century varieties of the *Rechtsstaat*, both liberal and conservative.[216] He crafted a qualified argument for racializing the concept of the *Rechtsstaat*: "Adolf Hitler's National Socialist state is [...] not a *Rechtsstaat* in [the liberal] sense. But a *Rechtsstaat* it is nonetheless, albeit in a very different [...], higher, internal, natural, and thus true sense."[217] Freisler bolted a racial superstructure onto the foundation of an anthropomorphic conception of the *Volk*, the natural interest and protection of which are served by the state.

Not unlike von Schweinichen, he was convinced that the Nazi debate about the *Rechtsstaat* could be settled easily: by retaining the language of the *Rechtsstaat* and downplaying the significance of its institutions and its norms in the administration of justice. As he put it, "That this state [the Nazi state] is a *Rechtsstaat*, is a given [...], but not more."[218] The state's essence, Freisler insisted, no longer revolved around law but Hitler and the *Volk*. To bolster his argument, he invoked Gustav Adolf Walz's widely used concept of the "*völkischer Führerstaat*," which had become a calling card for the highflying international lawyer and likely contributed to Walz's surprising appointment, in December 1933, as rector of Breslau University, in Lower Silesia, which the Nazi regime a few years later designated as a storm-trooping institution ("*Stoßtruppfakultät*").[219] Although Freisler and Walz emphasized to a greater degree than Koellreutter and von Schweinichen legal discontinuity in the transition from democracy to dictatorship (with Walz advocating to jettison the language of the *Rechtsstaat* altogether), it bears pointing out that both nonetheless conceded that a nominal *Rechtsstaat* was buried in the depths of the dictatorship from where it occasionally reared its head. The persistence of this institutional remnant troubled neither of them, which is where we notice intellectual affinities between them and the later concerns of Weber, Koellreutter, and Huber. Walz, for one, exclaimed that "the new Reich [was] a *Rechtsstaat* in two senses" ("*das neue Reich ein Rechtsstaat im doppelten Sinn*").[220] For him the Nazi polity was a *Rechtsstaat* in a conventional sense because it complied with the norms, rules, and statutes that it enacted; it was a *Rechtsstaat* in a second sense because its principal mission was the pursuit of *völkisch* justice, which for Walz was synonymous with and identical to law, its raison d'être, so to speak. The incorporation of the institution of the "*Führer*" into the concept of statehood itself was crucial for Walz (as well as for other theorists of various neologisms, as we shall see) because he was keen to stress the plenipotentiary nature of the state's institutional apex, which he labored hard to distinguish from the institution of the king (in the Wilhelmine *Rechtsstaat*) on the one hand, and from the institution of the president (in the Weimar *Rechtsstaat*) on the other.

Freisler and Walz explicitly rejected Koellreutter's and Dennewitz's talk of a "national *Rechtsstaat*." Freisler's argument was simple: the term reified the idea of statehood. By so doing, it distorted the essence of Nazi dictatorship, sacrificing what really mattered to Hitler and the NSDAP—"the dynamic, the lively, the moving, the power of struggle" ("*das Dynamische, Lebende, Sichbewegende, die kämpferische Kraft*")—to safeguard what was dispensable—"the stationary, the organized, the formal" ("*dem Stationären, Organisierten, Formalen*").[221] Walz concurred, adding that, in contrast to Italian fascism, which worshipped the state, National Socialism gave greater priority to race, what he called "the *völkisch*" ("*das Völkische*").[222] The language of the Third Reich thus needed to find a way to express what for him was the defining feature of Nazi statehood—its pursuit of racial purity ("*Reinheit des Volkes*").[223] But Walz was wary of the label "authoritarian state" that was making the rounds.[224] It smacked too much of the "Weimar system" for his liking.[225] Walz argued that the concept of the authoritarian state "had specific, recent political connotations, namely reliance on presidential power as enshrined in the Weimar constitution [...]. The underlying point was that the concept [...] conjured up the viewpoint of those who had sought to establish an authoritarian alternative to *both* the democratic order of Weimar *and* to the National Socialist."[226]

The cases of Walz and Freisler are illuminating because they show that even some of the staunchest Nazi functionaries saw a modicum of value in the *Rechtsstaat* as an institutional structure, however perverted their constructions of the underlying idea ultimately became. Freisler in particular saw not just instrumental value, but demonstrated varying degrees of expressive commitment to the idea of the *Rechtsstaat* and for a whole host of reasons. In 1933, for example, he defended a quasi-liberal conception of statutory law. When he declared that Nazi judges were *bound* by statute, and had to follow the letter of the law regardless of whether this letter was of liberal or National Socialist origin, Freisler showed a certain appreciation for the legacies of law.[227]

Such commitments to the idea of the *Rechtsstaat* surely are significant because there was no shortage of alternative monikers for the Nazi polity, as demonstrated by Walz's innovation. They also are noteworthy because they cut against the grain of the general Nazi discourse in the 1930s in which the concept of the state was increasingly being replaced by the concept of community, specifically that of the *Volksgemeinschaft*. This goes to show that the distribution of preferences in the debate about the *Rechtsstaat* cut across a whole array of cleavages in Nazi Germany.

Regulating the Race

It would be a mistake to assume that the intellectual positions that jurists assumed in the Nazi debate about the *Rechtsstaat* could be mapped easily onto a continuum ranging from hardliners to moderates in the regime. The Freisler example illustrates as much.[228] Freisler's intervention is not only remarkable for its timing, but also for its revival of *another* deeply contested concept in Nazi Germany—that of the state itself. In the early years of the dictatorship, the idea of the racial community, the *Volksgemeinschaft*, was fast replacing that of the racial state. By bringing the state back in, Freisler found himself at loggerheads with another ardent Nazi intellectual: Reinhard Höhn. Höhn won the intellectual tussle, but Freisler prevailed as far as the everyday law of the Third Reich was concerned: "[F]or all jurists who thought in practical terms the state seemed indispensable as a personal point of attribution, whether as a tax authority, as the responsible agent for administrative acts, or in international law."[229] This pragmatism was especially pronounced in the area of administration, despite attempts to de-legalize it. The Nazification of administrative law was more difficult to accomplish than the overhaul of Germany's *Staatsrecht*, or state law. As Stolleis writes, "administrative law proved tenacious and so strongly tied to practice that it could not be so readily shunted aside."[230] The extraordinary planning needs of an expanding state meant that remnants of the *Rechtsstaat* related to aspects of administration survived until 1939:

> Administrative law was not only an ideological battleground, but also a place of refuge for objective contributions of the kind that was [*sic*] no longer possible in state law. Here one could still write in a more or less neutral fashion about issues of communal and tax law, questions of building and planning law, expropriation law or trade law.[231]

To be sure, these remnants of the *Rechtsstaat* served the dictatorship. And their theorists facilitated Nazi criminality: "[L]ike other branches of the legal sciences, the discipline of administrative law was [...] part of the system; it supported the functioning of the administration in theory and practice, it created the semblance of the normality of an administration that operated according to the law and was controllable, and in this way it solidified the temporary pact between the Nazi state and the world of civil values."[232]

Positioned closest to this "world of civil values" were Martin Wittig, Hans Helfritz, Edgar Tatarin-Tarnheyden, and Kurt Groß-Fengels. These four theorists of the *Rechtsstaat* borrowed most heavily from the existing reservoir of legal norms and values.

Wittig was the most moderate of the bunch.[233] His 1933 doctoral dissertation performed a variation on the theme of the "national *Rechtsstaat*." Interestingly, Wittig was beholden to key tenets of the liberal *Rechtsstaat*. He singled out three and welded them into a tripartite concept with universal reach: (1) the legality of administration ("*Gesetzesmäßigkeit der Verwaltung*"); (2) the legality of the administration of justice ("*Gesetzesmäßigkeit der Rechtspflege*"); and (3) the legality of lawmaking ("*Bindung des Gesetzgebers an das Recht*"). Such were, for Wittig, the defining attributes of "*Rechtsstaatlichkeit*."[234] He was in no doubt that the newly created Nazi state conformed to the first two criteria.[235] The third criterium proved trickier, but he persevered. To this end, Wittig, who was keen to keep "arbitrariness" ("*Willkür*") in check, reinterpreted its meaning. Whereas for Fraenkel, a decline in formally rational law was an indicator of arbitrary rule, Wittig gave the concept of arbitrariness a decidedly substantive gloss.

This brings us back to *Behemoth*.[236] Like Neumann, Wittig objected to law as technology. He saw it as essential to jettison the idea of law's "technical" validity. Like Neumann, he believed in the ethical function of law (though in pursuit of a vastly different normative project). Law's "ethos" ("*Ethos*"), as Wittig saw it, was bound up with the "life and flourishing of the nation" ("*Leben und Gedeihen der Nation*").[237] In this sense, he approved of Koellreutter's rendering of the national *Rechtsstaat*. More specifically, and inspired by Plato, Wittig prized the satisfaction of collective wants over the protection of individual rights. To this end, he outlined a series of key functions for which the sovereign state, in his view, had "definite responsibility" ("*unbedingte Verantwortlichkeit*").[238] As long as the state protected the integrity of its borders, safeguarded the *Volk*'s existence, maintained the population's "racial purity" ("*rassenmäßige Reinheit*"), and preserved its "soil" ("*Boden*"), Wittig argued, its actions, or those of its organs, would be legal. It would be a true *Rechtsstaat*. All that was required was conformity with the Nazi ethos, which he equated with existential security for the *Volk* ("*Sicherheit der nationalen Lebensordnung*").[239] In this idea of the *Rechtsstaat*, substance mattered more than form. Wittig's was a racial (and racist) argument for the unification of law and morals, albeit one that borrowed heavily from pre-Nazi mores. Perhaps most interesting in this context was Wittig's policy proposal to balance the *Führerprinzip*, the leadership principle, with a corporatist principle, specifically a *Ständestaat*. The point of the latter, wrote Wittig, was to pre-empt the "isolation and alienation" ("*Abkapselung und Entfremdung*") of governing elites in the national *Rechtsstaat*.[240] Wittig entertained limits for the Nazi *Rechtsstaat*, which meant he cut a lonely figure in the Nazi debate, although Hans Helfritz, leader of the arch-conservative *Deutschnationale Volkspartei* (DNVP) in Breslau, saw eye to eye with him in some respects.[241]

In fact, Helfritz held on to more of the essence of the liberal *Rechtsstaat* than Wittig. Perhaps due to this political leanings, Helfritz did not seem to think the protection of racial purity was a desirable raison d'état. A fervent monarchist, he certainly was comfortably countenancing, within limits, prerogative excess. For example, he thought it possible that executive action could be legal even without statutory authorization, provided that such overreach was the exception, not the norm.[242] This position indicates a preference for positive law. Much of what the other contributors to the Nazi debate about the *Rechtsstaat* theorized as a new form of law, for Helfritz was something else: "*Rechtspolitik*," or "legal politics." He was unequivocal that the noun "*Recht*" was reserved for law on the books ("*wie es ist*").[243]

How did Helfritz's idea of the *Rechtsstaat* differ from the "liberal-bourgeois" variant? Two aspects are worth mentioning. First, he rejected a purely procedural conception of the *Rechtsstaat*. To define the nature and purpose of the *Rechtsstaat* solely in terms of the legal rules of the game that it provided struck him as ludicrous and ahistorical: "No state has [ever] been content with offering its members nothing more than a legal order and its maintenance."[244] Consequently, Helfritz dismissed the concept of the *Rechtsstaat* "in this older sense" ("*in diesem älteren Sinne*").[245] He also found wanting (his interpretation of) Friedrich Darmstädter's well-known Weimar-era attempt to conceptually demarcate the *Rechtsstaat* from the "*Machtsstaat*," that is, the idea of a law-governed state from that of a power-driven state.[246] Helfritz did not think that law and power were incompatible or that they could be easily disentangled in real life. Indeed he believed that law possessed "physical" ("*physisch*") and "psychological" ("*psychisch*") power, the former visible in the enforcement of norms, the latter more amorphous.[247] Because Helfritz also believed that not all politics could be conducted by way of law, he rejected calls for an "absolute concept" ("*absoluter Begriff*") of the *Rechtsstaat*.[248] The concept of the *Rechtsstaat*, or so he argued, needed to accommodate both legalism ("*Entscheidung nach Rechtssatz*") and decisionism ("*Ermessensentscheidung*").[249] He was willing to concede that cost-benefit analysis ("*Zweckmäßigkeitsabwägungen*") sometimes trumped the demands of legality.[250] Helfritz's concept accommodated *degrees* of *Rechtsstaatlichkeit*.[251] For Helfritz the *Rechtsstaat* was a continuous variable of politics, which reminds of Fraenkel's approach.

Like Wittig before him, Helfritz placed great importance on the legality of administration as well as the legality of the administration of justice, both of which, together with a system of administrative courts (*Verwaltungsgerichtsbarkeit*), he regarded as fundamental institutions of the *Rechtsstaat*. And like Wittig, Helfritz too was optimistic in his assessment of the extent to which the law of the Third Reich met his criteria of the *Rechtsstaat*. He believed that the administration of justice in the areas of civil and criminal law continued to be governed by statute, and he took public pronouncements by Hans Frank and Carl Schmitt about the independence of Nazi judges at face value. He also did not think the legality of administration diminished, though he acknowledged that in the transition to authoritarianism, what he termed the "transitional period" ("*Übergangszeit*"), not all administrative measures had had a basis in statute.[252] This was par for the course, he thought, because, on balance, the national interest was of greater political significance than any rights of individuals that might be abrogated in its defense. Unlike Wittig, Helfritz did not set limits on this exceptionally powerful *Rechtsstaat*. His scholarship leaves little doubt that he regarded near limitless discretion as a necessary attribute of Nazi legalism, which is why Hilger concluded that Helfritz's concept of the *Rechtsstaat*, though indebted to nineteenth century norms and value, muddies the dividing line between law and lawlessness.[253] Another way of putting this is that Helfritz noticed early on, like Fraenkel would a little later, that the Nazi dictatorship was governed by a dual state whose constitutive halves operated in accordance with two different—but often complementary—logics of rule. Helfritz assumed the rectorship of Breslau University in the spring of 1933 but was removed barely half a year later, likely because his enthusiasm for the Nazi dictatorship was muted.[254] Walz, a considerably more radical contributor to the Nazi debate about the *Rechtsstaat* succeeded him at the university's helm.[255]

Hard, Unrelenting Legal Norms

Elements of a radical legalism can also be found in the writings of Edgar Tatarin-Tarnheyden, whose perspective on the *Rechtsstaat* had much in common with those of Wittig and Helfritz, but whose racialization of the term also meant that he straddled the border between the two camps in the Nazi debate, occupying a rather unique position that combined aspects of legal positivism and biological racism. To begin with, Tatarin-Tarnheyden believed in a separation of law and morals, and he deemed both to be distinct from politics.[256] For him law was about the regulation of wants in society, morals about the regulation of wants in the minds of individuals, and politics about the "crafting of a social totality" ("*Gestaltung einer sozialen Ganzheit*").[257] He distanced himself from Schmitt, whose distinction between law and politics he thought misleading. While recognizing that law and politics "in practice often overlap," Tatarin-Tarnheyden argued that fundamental differences in the nature of both phenomena made it impermissible to conflate them conceptually.[258] This assumption made it possible for him to distinguish two stages of revolutionary activity in Nazi Germany. He claimed that at the time of his writing, in 1934, the Nazi revolution had come to an end ("*beendet*") but was not yet complete ("*vollendet*").[259] Still to come in the institutional development of Nazi dictatorship was what he dubbed the "stage of legal construction" ("*Stadium gesetzmäßiger Aufbauarbeit*").[260] He believed, mistakenly as we now know, that the " 'wild' actions" of roving revolutionaries and their "transgressions of legality" were a thing of the past, that the foundations of a "new legality" ("*neue Legalität*") had been laid.[261] His commitment to the *Rechtsstaat*-tradition of old is evident in his insistence that "henceforth [the revolutionizing] must proceed in a 'legal' framework" ("*von nun an muß sich [die Revolutionierung] in 'legalem' Rahmen abspielen*").[262] But not just any legal framework would do. Tatarin-Tarnheyden, consummate legal positivist that he was, expected more than that: "It is essential to create norms, that is, [. . .] to place the new state on a well-balanced, statutory foundation [. . .]. Formal legal norms should not be disrespected."[263]

Tatarin-Tarnheyden's unusual commitment to achievements of an earlier era of the *Rechtsstaat* becomes understandable once we appreciate the cultural value he attributed to law. He considered the institution of the *Rechtsstaat* "one of the greatest socio-cultural goods of a *Volk*," which is why, in 1934, he had high hopes for legal "self-binding" ("*Selbstbindung*").[264] He was convinced that "legality" ("*Rechtmäßigkeit*"), especially in the form of "firm statutoriness" ("*fester Gesetzlichkeit*"), was an indispensable feature of a *Volk*'s cultural order ("*Kulturbau*").[265] The binding nature of "hard, unrelenting" ("*harte, unnachsichtlich* [*sic*]") legal norms applicable equally to all persons for Tatarin-Tarnheyden cut to the heart of the *Rechtsstaat* as a universal institution. The independence of the judiciary was another attribute of *Rechtsstaatlichkeit* that he elevated to the rank of a defining feature. This faith in law brings us to

Tatarin-Tarnheyden's unusual call for the protection of individual rights, which set him apart from almost all of the other protagonists in the Nazi debate about the *Rechtsstaat*, notably from Helmut Nicolai, whose scholarship he critiqued.[266]

Tatarin-Tarnheyden felt that the attack on individual rights was ill-advised, least of all because it discouraged entrepreneurship, economic and otherwise. Some the worst ills of the Weimar Republic, according to his diagnosis, were servility, selfishness, and a general lack of ambition.[267] Favoring the collective over the individual, he reasoned, would be counterproductive. It could worsen the *Volk*'s lackluster condition, which is why he proposed to re-invent individual rights as "national individual rights" ("*nationale persönliche Rechtsgüter*").[268] Three in particular were deserving of legal protection, according to Tatarin-Tarnheyden: honor, freedom, and property.[269] He intended these hybrid rights to protect the kind of space necessary to encourage individual creativity and the commercial activity to which it might lead. Or, as Tatarin-Tarnheyden put it, "the new state has no need for vassals" ("*der neue Staat kann keine Knechte brauchen*").[270] He invoked Ernst Forsthoff in support, who in the previous year had made the case for preserving a realm for private decision-making ("*persönlicher Handlungsspielraum*").[271] He even adorned his plea for private property with a surprising reference to Immanuel Kant. But by involving Richard Wagner's epic *The Ring of the Nibelung* (*Der Ring des Nibelungen*), Tatarin-Tarnheyden immediately tempered the progressiveness of his stance on individual rights. It led to this caveat: To enjoy legal protection, all private economic activity had to contribute to the *völkisch* public good. If it did not, Tatarin-Tarnheyden was willing to "limit" the exercise of national individual rights, and even thought expropriation appropriate.[272] This brings us to the darker side in Tatarin-Tarnheyden's *Rechtsstaat*-concept: his biological racism.

Tatarin-Tarnheyden's economic worldview may have been progressive, but his politics were that of a Nazi hardliner. His progressive ideas co-existed with a reactionary streak in his legal thought. Whereas Wittig resembled a run-of-the-mill conservative legalist, Tatarin-Tarnheyden was a racist legalist par excellence. This becomes immediately clear if we turn to his notion of the "*Rechtsidee*," by which he meant law's underlying morality. This "idea of law" to him was "always concrete, always blood-based, always morally grounded," unlike the abstract "concept of law," or "*Rechtsbegriff*," favored in the nineteenth and early twentieth century by adherents of the rationalist-deductive movement of the so-called *Begriffsjurisprudenz*, a polemical moniker for the legal idealism that Christian Wolff inspired.[273] Echoing Binder's rejection of this variant of legal positivism, Tatarin-Tarnheyden introduced the concept of the "*Ur-Nomos*," or original nomos, which he described as the moral foundation, the "base value of the state" ("*staatlicher Grundwert*").[274] The Nazi "revolution," he argued, had given rise to a new *Rechtsidee*. This "new spirit of state" ("neuer *Staatsgeist*") was the "highest norm" for the interpretation of Nazi law, especially in the operation of *Generalklauseln* and ad-hoc decisions.[275] Whenever pre-Nazi norms were in conflict with Nazi norms, Tatarin-Tarnheyden theorized, reference to the *Ur-Nomos*, his version of a basic norm, would either infuse, in "galvanizing fashion," pre-Nazi norms with new meaning, or it would put Weimar-era norms "on ice" ("*lethargischen Gefrierzustand*").[276] The latter, in other words, would not be rescinded or destroyed, merely incapacitated. What Tatarin-Tarnheyden had in mind, though he never used the term, was a dual state: He was certain that the *Ur-Nomos* could co-exist with what had preceded it. In *Werdendes Staatsrecht*, he argued that the *Rechtsstaat* as a guarantor of social order required precisely formed law.[277] His vision was to erect in the ruins—and with the remnants—of Weimar law a racial *Rechtsstaat*. For he abhorred nothing more than arbitrariness. He relied on metaphors from architecture to get his point across indirectly, presumably so as to not run afoul of other Nazi hardliners. He told his readers that a "complete plan" ("*Gesamptlan*") was needed for the institutional development of the Nazi dictatorship.[278] Elsewhere, he reminded them that, the progress during the insurgent phase revolution notwithstanding, future additions to the institutional design ought to follow an "integrated blueprint for construction" ("*einheitlichen Bauplan*").[279] This blueprint needed to achieve a harmony of its parts.[280] Tatarin-Tarnheyden's qualified defense of the *Rechtsstaat* was in the main an argument from the logic of appropriateness. He was the embodiment of a Nazi legal conscience.

Kurt Groß-Fengels, finally, is important to include in this analysis of Nazi jurists who expressed a rudimentary respect for the idea of the *Rechtsstaat* because his concept of Nazi law, which he developed in a 1936 doctoral dissertation, had more in common with liberal concepts of law than that of any other participant in the debate about the *Rechtsstaat*.[281] Unlike his colleagues, Groß-Fengels hoped to preserve a surprising number of legal innovations from the Wilhelmine and Weimar eras, including, *inter alia*, the separation-of-powers doctrine, the principle of statutory rule, the catalogue of fundamental rights, and the system of administrative courts.[282] His has been described as an attempt to approximate ("*Versuch einer Annäherung*") the liberal *Rechtsstaat*, and the description is accurate. Groß-Fengels too had faith in the *Rechtsstaat* as an eternal idea. He had no doubt that some legacies of liberalism could help to realize certain goals of antiliberalism. As late as 1936, he made a case for the economic utility of legal predictability ("*Vorraussehbarkeit*") and legal certainty ("*Rechtssicherheit*"), both quintessentially liberal values.[283] By endorsing, naively or daringly, "the justice of positivity" ("*Gerechtigkeit der Positivität*"), he contradicted a key tenet of Nazi legalism: antiformalism.[284]

Groß-Fengels was a lone proceduralist. In his institutional design for the Nazi dictatorship, substantive justice did not trump procedural justice, as it did in contending conceptions of Nazi law. For Groß-Fengels, the achievement of substantive justice was impossible without institutional foundations that were stable and reliable. Legal predictability was a *sine qua non* of his racial *Rechtsstaat*. To claim otherwise, or so he wrote, would destroy the "bases for a healthy development of the life of the *Volk*" ("*Grundlagen für eine gesunde Lebensentwicklung des Volkes*").[285] Yet he conceded that "revolutionary transformations" ("*revolutionäre Umgestaltungen*") may require a temporary suspension of the supremacy of legality. In times of transition, statutory compliance *could* spell injustice, according to Groß-Fengels, especially if the substantive content of law (*Recht*) and statute (*Gesetz*) are incongruent.[286] This sentiment is similar to that of other jurists discussed in this section. What distinguishes Groß-Fengels from all of them, however, are the qualms he had about trampling on rules. He was not fond of the prospect of a commissarial dictatorship. Indeed, he argued that any authoritarian rule by exception had to be strictly limited, and a return to normalcy promptly pursued. As he saw it, no victorious revolution could afford to dispense with statutory rule.[287] To not diminish the value of law in the long-run, a period of strict compliance, Groß-Fengels argued, was needed in the aftermath of any state of exception (*Ausnahmezustand*), to compensate for the reputational costs of non-compliance. It comes as no surprise that Groß-Fengels was a critic of Schmitt's. He rejected Schmitt's "concrete-order thinking" ("*konkretes Ordnungsdenken*") with the argument that it was unfit for everyday life. It provided no basis for reliable governance. Logically underdeveloped, Schmitt's institutional design, in Groß-Fengels's reading, would invariably lead to "rulelessness" ("*Regellosigkeit*"), and, as a direct consequence, "disorder" ("*Unordnung*").[288]

In most respects, Groß-Fengels's argument for reconfiguring the *Rechtsstaat* was that of a conservative rather than a bona fide Nazi jurist. Although his dissertation included a series of stated commitments to a *völkisch* way of life, his institutional design contained so many prescriptions for self-binding, and protections of individual freedom, that it stands out in the Nazi debate about the *Rechtsstaat* for its continuation of liberalism by other means. He was the only jurist, aside from Koellreutter and Tatarin-Tarnheyden, who contemplated the value of *Volksgenossen*, who saw individuals, not just comrades. Theirs were efforts to keep "arbitrary decisionism" in check.[289] But progressive ideas for the protection of *Volksgenossen* from the *Volksgemeinschaft* was not what the victors in the Nazi debate about the *Rechtsstaat* were after.

REPLACING THE *RECHTSSTAAT*

Around 1936 the essentially contested, nineteenth century concept of the *Rechtsstaat* began to disappear from Nazi legal discourse. Those jurists who argued for replacing—rather than reconstituting—the concept of the *Rechtsstaat*, won the day. Most of them we have already encountered, which means a brief analysis will suffice to complete my intellectual history of select Nazi legal thought.

For three years, Carl Schmitt and like-minded legal theorists battled their intellectual rivals inside the dictatorship. It was a fierce battle over the meaning of law's vocabulary. Most adamant in their rejection of the *Rechtsstaat* as a category of practice as well as of analysis, aside from Schmitt, were Günther Krauß, Ernst Forsthoff, Helmut Nicolai, Hans Frank, and Werner Best. Reinhard Höhn and Wilhelm Stuckart also intervened to help purge Mr. von Mohl's term of art from the language of the Third Reich. Considering who they were up against inside the dictatorship, the efforts by advocates of a racialized *Rechtsstaat*, from Koellreutter to Groß-Fengels, is remarkable. Koellreutter and others were, without a doubt, reprehensible scholars. But it was their intellectual rivals who truly unleashed the violence of law.[290]

Law's Violence

As so often in those years, Schmitt was one of the first to nail his colours to the mast. In May 1933, in a contribution to the Nazi broadsheet *Westdeutscher Beobachter*, Schmitt opined that anyone who invoked the idea of the *Rechtsstaat* was only after one thing: retarding the "German revolution" ("*zur Hemmung der deutschen Revolution*").[291] Schmitt's fear was partially rooted in his conceptual thought. In 1930, he had famously declared, "Every political concept is a polemical concept. It has a political enemy in mind and, with respect to its intellectual rank, intellectual force, and historical significance, it is determined by this enemy."[292] The political enemies *he* mobilized against in the Nazi debate about the *Rechtsstaat* were liberals, Jews, and his intellectual rivals in the Nazi regime. The most formidable of them was Otto Koellreutter, who, as we have seen, saw value in the *Rechtsstaat*, eternal value, in fact. Schmitt was having none of it.

He saw no point in racializing the *Rechtsstaat*. For him the term was of, and for, a bygone era.[293] In von Schweinichen's parlance, the *Rechtsstaat* for Schmitt was "*Individualbegriff*," not "*Analogiebegriff*."[294] He made known his reservations about the language of the *Rechtsstaat* with fanfare from the outset of the Nazi dictatorship, when he very briefly entertained the idea of reconfiguring the concept: "Whoever uses the word *Rechtsstaat* will have to be clear about what he understands by it, how his *Rechtsstaat* is different from the liberal *Rechtsstaat*, and the extent to which his *Rechtsstaat* is meant to be a *National Socialist* one or one of the many other types of *Rechtsstaat*."[295] For Schmitt, conceptual imprecision spelled "the danger of political abuse."[296] If the concept of the *Rechtsstaat* was not right away imbued with Nazi morals, he prophesized, "the enemies of the National Socialist state" would seize it to bring alternative conceptions in position and challenge "the law and justice of the National Socialist state" ("*das Recht und die Gerechtigkeit des nationalsozialistischen Staates*").[297] But Schmitt's doubts persisted. Sooner than most of the participants in the debate about the *Rechtsstaat* in Nazi Germany, he made a case for abandoning the concept altogether, asking rhetorically, in 1935: "Does not the word '*Rechtsstaat*' also belong to those indestructible words of German legal and *Volk* history?"[298] His answer was unequivocal: "I do not think so."[299]

For Schmitt, the *Rechtsstaat* possessed no intrinsic value; it was a mere *Gesetzesstaat*, a legislative state. Instead of waging lawfare with a blunt instrument forged in Weimar, he was keen to battle liberals, Jews, and other supposed enemies with a sharp weapon made in Nazi Germany.[300]

A new language was needed to prepare for this violent struggle. As Peter Stirk writes, "Even the once-favored *Allgemeine Staatslehre*," as a field of study and instruction, "was consigned to the past. Carl Schmitt dismissed this 'category' as a 'typical concern of the liberal nineteenth century'. The very word *allgemein* (general) suggested a form of state of universal validity. That was incompatible with the idea that the National Socialist state was distinctive and distinctively German."[301] Schmitt believed it was "no historical coincidence" that "the word and concept of the *Rechtsstaat*" ("*Wort und Begriff des Rechtsstaates*") emerged in Germany "only around 1830."[302] He cast aspersions on the term's valence in German legal thought. A concept of such recent pedigree as the *Rechtsstaat*, he implied, could not possibly be culturally meaningful and thus was semantically inappropriate. He was convinced it lacked the gravitas to demand obedience, the metaphysical air to inspire loyalty; it was a manifestation of degenerate law. The Nazi debate about the *Rechtsstaat* epitomizes the quest to overhaul the vocabulary of law. "The more ambitious, both personally and intellectually, staked everything on

National Socialist victory."[303] These thinkers, and the few practitioners among their ranks, further radicalized the Nazi concept of law. In their obsessive quest for an organic way of law, they cobbled together an ideology of *extremist legalism*.[304]

Günther Krauß, a onetime student of Schmitt's, fired a notable salvo in the battle for rhetorical mastery in Nazi Germany. Like his mentor, he objected to the idea that being a *Rechtsstaat* could be a legitimate reason of state. The raison d'être of statehood, he was convinced, had to be sought elsewhere. Because the liberal *Rechtsstaat*, according to Krauß, artificially juxtaposed law and state power, law had become associated with powerlessness in the interwar period. This he deemed unacceptable, which is why he argued stridently in favor of abandoning the idea of the *Rechtsstaat* and everything associated with it: "Language usage in the nineteenth century has fixed the meaning of the concept *Rechtsstaat*, word and concept are inextricably intertwined. It is essential to prevent both from infiltrating the twentieth century state courtesy of dull nominalist thinking and technology."[305] Whereas Koellreutter as well as Wittig, Helfritz, and Tatarin-Tarnheyden regarded the concept of the *Rechtsstaat* as a general category with lasting value, Krauß refused to accept that it could amount to a valid term of art, let alone an eternal one. He denied its utility for the Nazi revolution, insisting that the word for, and concept of, law had to be indivisible.

Where Koellreutter, von Schweinichen, Lange, and Dennewitz all attempted—in different ways and to different degrees—to racialize the *Rechtsstaat*, Krauß dismissed such efforts on ontological grounds. He believed that his intellectual adversaries were misguided in tearing apart a social phenomenon that existed as an organic whole. Where they searched for differentiation, he saw natural unity. He faulted not only the distinction between word and concept, but also that between form and substance, the letter of the law and its spirit, as well as body and soul. Krauß spoke of "*Trennungs- und Zergliederungsdenken*" and attributed it to the supposedly pernicious legacies of legal positivism.[306] The notion of the *Rechtsstaat* was useless in the Third Reich, he reasoned, because, in addition to subverting the idea of the law of the Swastika, it kept alive the modernist imagination: not only did it promote an inorganic way of law, it also perpetuated an inorganic way of life. The conceptual binary of the *Rechtsstaat/Gesetzestaat* to which some of the Nazi proponents of a racialized *Rechtsstaat* clung, Krauß dismissed as pointless ("*sinnlos*").[307] For him, the "retrospective" ("*nachträglich*") reinterpretation of the *Rechtsstaat* into an "other" of the legislative state for the sole purpose of utilizing Mr. Mohl's term of art in the Nazi revolution was akin to denying the victory of this revolution in the first place.[308]

Given the fact that Krauß was after an unfettered state, the language of law had to be scrubbed clean of all liberal and legal positivist stains. As he put it: "If we retain the concept of the *Rechtsstaat*, we relativize the *Führerstaat*. For 'law' will once again be defined as self-constraint of the leadership, conformity with statutory law [...]."[309] From this vantage point, all talk of a "National Socialist *Rechtsstaat*" was both tautological and inappropriate. In Krauß's reading, the addition of the adjective "National Socialist" was tautological because it précised the Nazi state and thus served as a superfluous descriptor; it was inappropriate because it qualified the *Rechtsstaat*, thereby making the contested noun the new term's principal referent and elevating it to a prominence that Krauß felt it did not deserve in Nazi dictatorship. As he wrote: "National Socialism is primary, not the *Rechtsstaat*."[310]

Ernst Forsthoff, a doctoral student of Schmitt's in the Weimar Republic, covered his supervisor's flank. Although not a direct participant in the Nazi debate about the *Rechtsstaat*, he jumped into the breach on the side of the hardliners with a highly critical review of Koellreutter's treatise *Der deutsche Führerstaat*. According to Forsthoff, the concept *Rechtsstaat* was a semantic invention that could be traced back exclusively to liberal thought ("*rein aus dem liberalen Denken hervorgegangen*").[311] It was impossible to purge it of the legacies of liberalism. This being so, "whoever deliberately appropriates or retains such a word, is guilty of more than a terminological error (*terminologischen Mißgriff*); he invariably unleashes the connotations and emotions that are associated with a word such as the *Rechtsstaat*."[312] Dangerous minds think alike: Schmitt and Krauß and Forsthoff were, at this juncture at least, in complete agreement in their rejection of the *Rechtsstaat*. They desired a new vocabulary of law.

This brings us to Reinhard Höhn and Werner Best, whose intellectual contributions to the Nazi debate about the *Rechtsstaat* were slight, but whose positions as central cogs in the wheel of the dictatorship meant their political influence was considerable—and quickly felt in everyday life. In October 1936, Best, who with Heinrich Himmler and Reinhard Heydrich formed the triumvirate at the helm of the German Police, from where the expansion of the prerogative state was orchestrated, became chairman of a working group on police law at the Academy of German law.[313] This *Ausschuß für Polizeirecht*, which Höhn supported as Best's deputy, is pertinent to this analysis because its (incomplete) work accelerated the destruction of the *Rechtsstaat*. It ensured that the most radical arguments in Nazi legal thought found expression in the real world. And Best was the leader of the pack. Although his tortuous definition of what the concept of policing entailed found no adherents in the working group, and was not adopted, select aspects are worth pondering because their spirit informed the deliberations—and determined their outcome. First, policing, according to Best, comprised "all state activity" that used coercive violence in pursuit of "the preservation and development of the *Volk*."[314] Best wanted police violence to be directed at any individuals or collectivities who posed a threat to "the *Volk*'s leadership and communal order."[315] In order to stave off "disturbance" and "destruction" of these orders, Best wanted his organization to be the sole arbiter of deciding when police violence was called for. He wanted his organization to be in charge of judging the necessity of the use of force.[316] It was a push for autonomy.

And even though Best's definitional foray was quashed by the other members of his working group, he won the battle over substance. His principal objective after all was to free policing practices in the Nazi dictatorship from as many remaining constraints of the *Rechtsstaat* as possible. Best had his sights set especially on statutory limits placed on police powers as well as on what he considered the inhibiting demands of administrative law. But it was *not* rampant lawlessness that he was after. What Best envisaged was a dual state. He wanted legalism for Aryans, and decisionism for their enemies. As he wrote in 1937, summarizing the results of his working group, "The state's normative self-binding [...] is generally appropriate vis-à-vis all positive and constructive forces of the *Volk*."[317] But, as Best hastened to add, in confronting the "destructive forces" ("*zerstörende Kräfte*"), that is, the dictatorship's enemies, legal constraints that would limit the choice of "necessary defensive measures" ("*notwendigen Abwehrmaßnahmen*") were out of the question.[318]

Best's resistance to the codification of *Polizeirecht*, or police law, was rooted in a fear of unnecessary self-binding, which is why the inability of the *Polizeirechtsausschuß*, the working group on which he served, to make progress with the legalization of police affairs, was not an institutional failure, but a success. It represented a resounding victory of the regime's praetorians over its bureaucrats. Rather than contributing to the regulation of the police, the working group facilitated its deregulation. It effectively exempted the police from the remnants of the *Rechtsstaat*. The police were the face of the prerogative state. Its reconstitution as "*innere Wehrmacht*," or internal army, meant that the realm of law had shrunk quite significantly. For Best, the re-equilibration of the dual state represented revolutionary progress. By balancing rifles and rules, he was convinced, the Nazi dictatorship was sustainable.[319]

Ulrich Herbert has credited Best with intellectual sophistication, and with good reason. Absent scholarly sensibilities and experience of legal reasoning, he argued, Best would have been hardpressed to legitimate law's violence in the face of more moderate Nazi functionaries in the police apparatus, which, in 1937, was still that of an authoritarian—not yet of a totalitarian—regime.[320] Best's was an effort to make lawlessness appear legal, to cultivate it, but within limits. It was about keeping up appearances, and to not unduly interfere with the Aryan way of life.

Best was among those who advanced the expansion of the prerogative state, notably "Himmler's attempts to free the political police from all irksome legal bonds."[321] In a series of articles in *Deutsches Recht*, the official journal of the Academy of German Law of which Frank served as editor-in-chief, Best, in spring and summer 1936, provided the intellectual underpinnings for the marginalization of the normative state. It is therefore not surprising that Best belonged to the hardliners in the Nazi debate about the *Rechtsstaat*. The most vociferous participants were jurists on the payroll of the NSDAP or the SS, that is, stalwarts of the new "movement." No mere sympathizers of the Nazi cause, their zeal was fuelled by ideological faith in the *Volksgemeinschaft*, this imagined community of race. Foremost among them was Reinhard Höhn, a member of both NSDAP and SS and an ambitious and rambunctious jurist who relished taking on the likes of Koellreutter, Scheuner, Schmitt, and Tatarin-Tarnheyden all of whom he believed insufficiently committed to the racial order. Koellreutter voiced very publicly his doubts about "whether Höhn and Maunz are correct in their belief that our entire existing stock of legal tools must be smashed because it has been compromised as a result of having been taken over by liberalistic conceptions," accusing his rivals of peddling "legal astrology."[322] Höhn was one of the reasons why Koellreutter was defeated and legal astrology won the day.

A onetime protégé of Schmitt's, Höhn was a newly minted professor of law when the debate about the *Rechtsstaat* was in full swing. With a 1934 *Habilitation* from Heidelberg, he began teaching in Berlin in 1935, where he succeeded Rudolf Smend, who had been forced out. But Höhn was an intellectual with ambitions. His goal was to outperform both of the two leading lights on the Nazi legal stage: Schmitt and Koellreutter. He attacked the latter by talking about the decline of the state as a conceptual—and political—variable.

An important dividing line between Nazi moderates and Nazi radicals in the debate about the *Rechtsstaat* revolved around their diametrically opposed thinking regarding the nature of the newly emerging polity: was it a racial *state* or a racial *community*? As a term of art, the *Rechtsstaat* was unacceptable to any Nazi jurist who thought the concept of the state had outlived its relevance. Hans Helfritz, among others, criticized the political use of legal language and the hollowing out of legal instruments, notably the attempt to turn the *Volksgemeinschaft* into a legal person (*juristische Person*) and to have it take the place of the state as the fundamental reference point of the new public law.[323] Koellreutter agreed and in a slew of publications objected to Höhn's aggressive "scientific campaign" ("*wissenschaftlichen Feldzug*").[324] Stolleis has described the substantive difference between these two lawyers of the Nazi dictatorship in terms of their contending conceptions of self: Koellreutter, as a nationalist, was oriented toward the state; Höhn, as a revolutionary, wanted to transcend it.[325] Consequently, it was inherently impossible for them to agree on a law of the Third Reich that served both goals, though the dual state may have existed for as long as it did in order to create space for a rapprochement between opposing camps. Eventually, however, time ran out. The sword proved mightier than the pen: Höhn managed to overcome intellectual opposition to his ideas with a show of force. "He constantly harried those whom he suspected, rightly or wrongly, of less-than-wholehearted commitment to the new order."[326]

It did not hurt that Höhn had friends in high places, which brings me to his silencing of Schmitt, who had supported his appointment in Berlin.[327] Between 1933 and 1935, Höhn served as a department head in the Main Office of the *Sicherheitsdienst*, the Security Service of the SS, known by its acronym SD. In the Berlin-based *Hauptamt*, his immediate superior was Heydrich. We already saw that Höhn also had Best's support, as whose deputy he served in the earlier mentioned working group on the legalization of police affairs. In October 1936, he used his expanding authority in the security services to open an intelligence file on "Prof. Dr. Carl Schmitt." By December of the same year, *Das Schwarze Korps*, the official mouthpiece of the SS, had published two articles calling into question Schmitt's Nazi credentials, which ended his rise through the ranks of the dictatorship, though it did not end his intellectual services to it.[328]

The Nazi debate about the *Rechtsstaat* ended better for those who were able to wield real and not just symbolic power. Best and Höhn were among them, as were Frank and Freisler. As servants of the prerogative state, these men's concept of law placed close to no value on formal rationality or legal certainty. It was not a *Rechtsstaat* these "150-percenters" were after.[329] The all-encompassing rule of which they dreamt knew no bounds, which is why they managed to defeat advocates of the *Rechtsstaat* inside the dictatorship so soundly despite starting out in the minority.

Having reconstructed the contours of the debate about the *Rechtsstaat* in the Third Reich, what is its relevance? Why should anyone care about the disagreements among a handful of despicable Nazi intellectuals? What difference, if any, did their extended ruminations make to the presentation of law in everyday life?[330] My answer revolves around the expressive function of law.

THE EXPRESSIVE FUNCTION OF LAW

In a frequently cited article, Cass Sunstein reasoned constructively about the law. In the late twentieth century, he reminded his colleagues in U.S. law schools of what social scientists have known at least since the posthumous publication of Max Weber's *Wirtschaft und Gesellschaft* at the beginning of that century: "Actions are expressive; they carry meanings."[331] Starting from this deceptively simple premise, Sunstein developed a new answer to the question of why law is invented and obeyed. As he wrote, "sometimes people support a law, not because of its effects on norms, but because they believe that it is intrinsically valuable for the relevant 'statement' to be made."[332] According to Sunstein, "Many debates over the appropriate content of law are really debates over the statement that law makes, independent of its (direct) consequences."[333] The Nazi debate about the *Rechtsstaat* is evidence of this proposition. Although law's consequences were clearly on the minds of many of the participating jurists, it is immediately apparent how much importance most of the Nazi jurists involved also placed on law's meaning.

Meanings matter to agents, individual and otherwise, as social constructivists across the disciplines have made abundantly clear. Kenneth Ledford has staked a similar claim for a subset of agents in the case at hand, contending that "explanations of the behavior of lawyers in 1933 must move beyond analyses based upon economic exigency, deprofessionalization, or moral and ethical failure."[334] In Ledford's important analysis, liberal and conservative lawyers in the transition to authoritarian rule failed to develop an alternative legal conscience, a legal imaginary capable of rivaling the emerging Nazi concept of law: "[L]awyers demonstrated the limited integrative power of procedural conceptions of liberalism and its inherent weakness in the face of opponents mobilized by substantive ideas of justice."[335]

If we believe Michael Stolleis, the Nazi debate about the *Rechtsstaat* "ended in a grotesquerie and was soon abandoned."[336] This assessment is not wrong. The debate's sophistication declined as some of the participants were marginalized (or took themselves out of the crosshairs of the NSDAP and SS who were gunning for them) and the racial dictatorship consolidated itself. And yet Stolleis's perfunctory assessment—he only devotes two pages to it in his magisterial, four-volume history of German public law—risks our bypassing a large window into the "Nazi conscience." The historian Claudia Koonz, who came up with the heuristic, has peered through this window.[337] But her eye caught something else than mine. Koonz focused on the substance of Nazi law, the invention of racial categories by "ethnocrats" like Hans Globke, one of the co-drafters of the Nuremberg Race Laws of 1935, and the bureaucratic infighting that accompanied this "incremental racialization."[338] A focus on substantive law is the mainstay of scholarship on Nazi law by non-legal scholars. By contrast, I am more concerned with practices of formation, deformation, and transformation of Nazi law. I consider the long-run consequences of its procedures, as well as their emotional import, including the various conceptions of it that leading intellectuals debated in the formative years of the Third Reich in their quest to provide the Hitler regime with an institutional design for a sustainable dictatorship. Where Koonz historicized law's substance, I inquire into law's form, the media through which jurists communicated its abhorrent content to the *Volk*, and the social meaning(s) it had for those performing the law.

Nazi Legal Conscience

Much has been written in recent years about Nazi morality.[339] It is at once enlightening and utterly disturbing to think that policies which culminated in the destruction of the European Jews could have started out as moral sentiments. And yet they did, which is precisely what Koonz wants us to appreciate. And her evidence is convincing:

> The Final Solution did not develop as evil incarnate but rather as the dark side of ethnic righteousness. Conscience, originally seen to protect the integrity of the individual from the inhumane demands of the group, in the Third Reich became a means of underwriting the attack by the strong against the weak. To Germans caught up in a simulacrum of high moral purpose, purification of racial aliens became a difficult but necessary duty. [...] In offering the faithful a vision of sanctified life in the *Volk*, it resembled a religion. Its condemnation of egotism and celebration of self-denial had much in common with ethical postulates elsewhere.[340]

The discourse about law in the 1930s was fueled by expressions or extensions of neo-conservative patterns of thought.[341] Neo-Hegelianism was one such pattern that informed the new legal imagination.[342] It supplied a respected philosophical foundation for the intellectual struggle over the meaning of Nazi law. The debate about the *Rechtsstaat* was but one battle, if a major one, in this larger struggle. It was not without significance that the year 1931 marked the 100th anniversary of Hegel's death; it rejuvenated the reception of his philosophy. Julius Binder, whom I already discussed, brought the "Hegel renaissance" to law.[343] Together with Karl Larenz and a small band of like-minded jurists—Walther Schönfeld, Martin Busse, Gerhard Dulckeit, Carl August Emge, and Wilhelm Sauer—he outlined a moral philosophy of Nazi law.[344] They desperately wanted their colleagues in the legal profession to recognize that an appreciation of "true reality" ("*wahre Wirklichkeit*") was more important for advancing the *Volk* than positive law.

A defining feature of neo-Hegelian thought was the redefinition of the philosophical notions of "*Begriff*" ("concept"), "*Wirklichkeit*" ("reality"), and "*Idee*" ("idea"). In contrast to legal positivists, neo-Hegelians like Binder and Larenz regarded law's reality as a social construct whose existence could not be grasped by mere description. Rather, they were certain that reality was more than what was observable in the real world; it referred to a higher reality. In his most important works, the 1935 *Grundlegung zur Rechtsphilosophie* and the 1937 *System der Rechtsphilosophie*, Binder therefore developed arguments about the nature of law from what he termed "absolute idealism" ("*absoluter Idealismus*").[345]

Unlike Neo-Kantians, Neo-Hegelians did not use concepts to describe or categorize this reality. Why? Because in the latter interpretation concepts were not analytical tools but philosophical states. For Binder and Larenz, the concept was the form that human understanding (*Begreifen*) took when it captured an objectively ideal reality.[346] Put differently, "the real" and "the ideal" were indivisible for neo-Hegelians. The idea, next, Larenz defined as a "creative force" ("*schöpferische Macht*").[347] Alive and perpetually in motion, ideas are not norms, wrote Larenz, nor are they valid or purposive; rather, they represented "*das in Wahrheit Seiende*," that which truly exists.[348] Reality in this system of thought referred to more than a state of bare existence ("*äußerliches Dasein*"); reality was the idea's "manifestation" ("*Erscheinung*"), its "concretion" ("*Konkretion*").[349] Because an idea is one with reality ("*mit ihr eins*"), for Binder and Larenz, Nazi legal concepts such as *Vertrag* (contract), *Strafe* (punishment), *Gemeinschaft* (community), or *Führerstaat* (Hitler state) were not in need of exhaustive definitions.[350] Because only "one reality" existed under this extreme form of philosophical idealism, disagreements were logically inconceivable. Given its absolutist claims, Oliver Lepsius has written of the "revolutionary ambition" of neo-Hegelian legal thought in Nazi Germany.[351] This ambition was not of the Nazis' making, but the neo-Hegelian philosophical agenda in the interwar period coincided (and subsequently became enmeshed) with the revolutionary ethos of Hitler's NSDAP.

The example of Neo-Hegelianism is immediately relevant to the idea of a Nazi legal conscience because for Binder and Larenz—who in my analysis only stand in as examples for the various intellectual efforts in the Third Reich to legitimate Nazi legality philosophically—thinking about the Nazi concept of law was primarily an expressive act, and only secondarily an instrumental one. By appropriating from the early 1920s to the late 1930s neo-Hegelian ideas for their evolving legal thought, Binder and Larenz adumbrated the emergence of a Nazi legal conscience. And yet, although Neo-Hegelianism undeniably played a major role in legitimating Nazi legalism, Steffen Kluck has shown that this effect was not always "intentional."[352] We must thus be careful to avoid retrospective determinism when studying the development of legal norms and institutions in the Third Reich. Neither Nazi legal thought nor Nazi legal practice were as uniform as they are often portrayed to be. Nor was either fully Nazified, as Stolleis made clear in his 1974 *Habilitation*. His analysis of the Nazi reconstitution of the idea of the *Gemeinwohl*, or public good, showed that the legal system of the Third Reich consisted "primarily" ("*überwiegend*") of norms that antedated the Nazi dictatorship, remnants of the *Rechtsstaat* all.[353] While the bulk of valid law stemmed from the Wilhelmine and Weimar eras, numerous legal norms were enacted in earlier periods.[354] Despite constant propaganda to the contrary, Nazi law in the main was old law, a product of the *Rechtsstaat* desperately needed "to avoid chaos."[355] Nazi jurists refurbished the existing norms and legal instruments, putting on them a racial gloss in keeping with absolute idealism.[356] The result was a dual state.

The instrumentalization in the law of the Third Reich of the concept of the *Gemeinwohl* shows as much. Stolleis unearthed evidence of both "radicalism" and a "continuity of the *Rechtsstaat*" in the process of its legalization.[357] The example of the Nazi appropriation of the idea of the *Gemeinwohl* illustrates why the concept of Nazi legal conscience has analytical purchase: it accommodates the real and the ideal, "*Anspruch*" and "*Realität*."[358] *Gemeinwohlformeln*, these vague formulas of the public good, undeniably undermined law's positivity regularly and often in Nazi Germany, thereby fulfilling the intended purpose of their institutional design. The institutional effect was not anomie, however; *pace* conventional wisdom, law was not just façade. *Gemeinwohlformeln* at times had unintended consequences that were at odds with the dictatorship.

This brings into view a causal link between the Nazi debate about the *Rechtsstaat* and the dual state, between legal thought and legal practice. Variation in the usage of *Gemeinwohlformeln* especially by courts, Stolleis argues, is evidence of what he calls "hidden pluralism" ("*verdeckter Pluralismus*").[359] This "factual pluralism" ("*faktischer Pluralismus*"), which the regime's propaganda concealed, in Stolleis's estimation, ringfenced a "field of battle" ("*Kampffeld*") in the struggle against the Nazi dictatorship.[360] At the level of the everyday, the reach of the will of the *Führer* was more limited than at the elite level, which meant that the influx and impact of *Gemeinwohlformeln* was less absolute than imagined at the moment of institutional design. Legal practitioners in the periphery were able to exploit interpretive disagreements ("*Divergenzen*") among legal theorists at the center. It gave them room for maneuver in "enclaves of freedom" ("*Freiheitsräume*").[361] In key respects, the everyday law that Stolleis studied was more polycratic law than it was totalitarian. His 1974 study remains important because it exposed the Hitler myth in law. The evidence he presented lent support to Fraenkel's argument about institutional hybridity. It showed that Hitler's will may have ranked supreme in Nazi legal thought, but it did not in Nazi legal practice. This dissonance should not, however, affect our sense of the moral guilt that intellectuals who pledged their allegiance to Nazi law incurred.

Schreibtischtäter

The intellectual heterogeneity among the *dramatis personae* in the Nazi debate about the *Rechtsstaat* must not distract from the reactionary values around which their contending conceptions of law converged. Hans Helfritz, one of the participating Nazi jurists, put it memorably: "In dispute was not the issue, but the name" ("*Strittig war nicht die Sache, sondern ihr Name*").[362]

Virtually all of the participants in the Nazi debate about the *Rechtsstaat* were members of the "*Neue Rechtswissenschaft*," the aforementioned judicial network of lawyers formed to cultivate a new legal science.[363] These reactionary modernists were *Schreibtischtäter*. A quintessentially German expression, the term refers to a perpetrator of large-scale violence, like Adolf Eichmann, who orders, plans, administers, or otherwise contributes to mass death without directly participating in the act of killing.[364] Many of the *Schreibtischtäter* in the Third Reich did not act out of base motives but—disturbingly—in keeping with what they considered a higher morality. Their attachments to the law of the Third Reich were emotional as well as instrumental.

The example of Franz Gürtner, Reich minister of justice in the Third Reich between 1932 and 1941 is a case in point. The hold that the memory of the *Rechtsstaat* appears to have had on Gürnter meant that he played the role of Freisler's nemesis when, in June 1934, the task arose to criminalize the supposed offense of *Rassenschande*, or racial treason. Along with other "ethnocrats," all of them lawyers, Gürnter for a short while retarded Freisler's ambition to racialize the law at breakneck speed. "Despite the obvious pressure from Freisler, they [...] forestalled the criminalization of 'mixed-race' intercourse, thwarted a law against criticism of racial dogma, and headed off further encroachment on Jews' civil rights."[365] Their behavior, Koonz believes, was suggestive of "unease with the ethical and legal issues engaged by sweeping proposals for racial persecution."[366] The reason? "As trained jurists, these ethnocrats thought analogically and reasoned from precedent."[367] Whereas Freisler, though also a lawyer, placed more stock in race than in law, Gürnter and like-minded colleagues apparently were still flying a tattered flag for the conservative tradition of the *Rechtsstaat*. This is remarkable, but not entirely surprising, considering that Gürnter had served the Weimar *Rechtsstaat* for more than ten years, first as Bavarian minister of justice between 1922 and 1932, and then, from 1932, as Reich minister of justice. However, he and other moderate Nazi practitioners came around, and it did not take long. Attitudinally and behaviorally, they transitioned from extremist institutionalism to racial institutionalism within less than two years.[368] After deliberations that lasted from April 1933 until September 1935, Freisler's investment in the racialization of the *Rechtsstaat* had paid off. A large practical step away from the normative state and toward the prerogative state had been taken.[369]

If one compares the making of the Nuremberg Race Laws and the Nazi debate about the *Rechtsstaat*, one notices a striking similarity between the behavior of Koonz's ethnocrats and that of the Nazi jurists discussed in this chapter. In both instances, the lawyers involved eventually "behaved as Max Weber had predicted they ought to: they internalized commands from a legitimate authority."[370] Virtually all "accommodated themselves to a Nazi conscience appropriate to the tasks ahead."[371] Nazi jurists in favor of appropriating the language of the *Rechtsstaat* acquiesced. They tacitly accepted the dominant view, which may or may not have been the majority view among them at the time. Years of tense exchanges in numerous fora and across multiple intellectual and other divides had created, if not unanimity, at least a working consensus between institutional extremists and institutional pragmatists. Like Koonz's ethnocrats, the defeated jurists in the Nazi debate about the *Rechtsstaat* "could think of themselves as moderates because they endorsed orderly methods and eschewed vulgar racism."[372]

In the legalization of his dictatorship, Hitler "endorsed both bureaucratic and radical goals."[373] It was the dual state in operation, its two constituent halves working in unison to consolidate the racial order. Inside the normative state, the excesses of the prerogative state were denied. The regime's bureaucratic functionaries, or "ethnocrats," as Koonz calls them, displayed extraordinary levels of cognitive dissonance: "Ineluctably, networks had coalesced and collegiality drew them into a shared bureaucratic space. In place of the fundamental ethical questions that plagued them in the early years of the Third Reich, by the late 1930s ethnocrats' moral field narrowed to questions of definitional and procedural consistency."[374] The prerogative half of the dual state loomed over the normative half. The structural imbalance between them grew in the war years. It was Heinrich Himmler whose drive to expand his institutional authority and access to levers of infrastructural power was chiefly responsible for this final gutting of the *Rechtsstaat*. The manufactured judicial crisis ("*Justizkrise*") of 1942, which led to the appointment of Otto Georg Thierack as minister of justice, was his doing. Most significantly, the intensification of law's totalization meant an even greater dependence of judges. Thierack's tactics to bring the judiciary fully in line with the totalitarian dictatorship included an increase in individual directives to steer judicial behavior, the above mentioned *Richterbriefe* with which the regime leaned on its judges, pre- and reviews of their judgments, a reporting requirement, and inspection visits.[375] The abandoning of the *Rechtsstaat* on the theoretical level did not augur well for its remnants in the real world. It precipitated the decline of the normative state in the life of the dictatorship. Among other violence this institutional development caused, it forced Ernst Fraenkel to flee the increasingly violent Reich.

The Legal Imaginary

By feeling the dictatorship in 1938, Fraenkel followed in Franz Neumann's footsteps. In his 1942 book *Behemoth*, Neumann put to use Hobbes's interpretation of the mythical land monster. It served him as the linchpin in his analysis of "the structure and practice of National Socialism." In Job 40: 15-24, the beast is described thus:

> Look at Behemoth,
> which I made just as I made you;
> it eats grass like an ox.
> Its strength is in its loins,
> and its power in the muscles of its belly.
> It makes its tail stiff like a cedar;
> the sinews of its thighs are knit together.
> Its bones are tubes of bronze,
> its limbs like bars of iron.[376]

Hobbes, as Stephen Holmes reminds us, "employed Leviathan as a symbol for the peacekeeping state and Behemoth as a symbol for rebellion and civil war."[377] A year before Fraenkel's flight from the Reich, Karl Loewenstein, like Neumann in 1942, also borrowed from Hobbes to describe the state of the Third Reich. But he chose the sea monster as his metaphor. He considered the creature of the leviathan a more befitting metaphor than that of the behemoth: "National Socialism in its present aspect is certainly the most thoroughgoing organization of social life, the most omnipotent leviathan, in Hobbes' phrase, known in modern history."[378] Assuming that Loewenstein knew his Hobbes, he had a less dystopian outlook on the Nazi dictatorship than Neumann. Even more striking about Loewenstein's speech act is that the Nazi phenomenon he identified in 1937 bears a close resemblance to the institutional structure that Fraenkel had begun to describe thickly around the same time: "Paradoxically," Loewenstein wrote, "it is the most notable feature of the Third Reich that it has succeeded in organizing arbitrariness in the form of law."[379]

To better understand the origins and effects of this remarkable institutional development, I excavated in this chapter and in the one preceding it the intellectual history of the *Rechtsstaat* up until the late 1930s. A purely rationalist approach to authoritarian legalism in the Third Reich would have missed the cultural dimensions that accompanied the gradual destruction in the 1930s of the nineteenth century *Rechtsstaat* that von Mohl had invented. I wrote of the expressive function of Nazi law in order to draw attention to these normative roots, and also to the continuity of law across the 1933 juncture. Lepsius has argued that the majority of Germany's legal theorists and practicing lawyers—those whose lives the Nazis had not threatened or diminished or taken—experienced the onset of authoritarian legalism not as a *novum* but as the completion of an incipient reality.[380]

This strengthens the case for taking seriously Nazi legal conscience as a useful *explanandum*. The case becomes even stronger if we remind ourselves of the role that conservative revolutionaries such as Martin Heidegger, Ernst Jünger, and Carl Schmitt played in the transition to authoritarian rule. Let us not forget that "they were viewed and they viewed themselves as a cultural elite with a special responsibility and ability to work with traditions, ideas, symbols, and meanings in an effort to make sense of their times."[381] A sizable army of German intellectuals was seized by the idea of Nazi dictatorship, eager to contribute their brain power.[382] A veritable labor front, they were united by a faith in "*Sittlichkeit*," or ethicality, Hegel's term for a distinctly German form of morality, and an interest in those aspects of German tradition that were compatible with the kind of exclusionary nationalism that they wanted to see realized, "namely, romanticism, *völkisch* ideology, the existentialist language of the self and authenticity, a widespread acceptance of social Darwinism, *Lebensphilosophie*, Wagnerian visions of apocalypse and transformations, Nietzsche's amoral celebration of aesthetics, and a general antipathy to Enlightenment thought and morality."[383] "Like so many of their peers," Koonz writes, with Heidegger and Schmitt in mind, they "welcomed ethnic solidarity in a time of political confusion, economic dislocation, and cultural pluralism. In their lecture halls and scholarship they had expressed a vague longing for a harmonious community (*Gemeinschaft*). After watching politics from the sidelines, these [...] powerful thinkers cast their lot with a former front-fighter who represented stridently masculine values and ethnic authenticity. It is a mark of success of Hitler's public persona" that Heidegger and Schmitt "not only fell in with the mood of ethnic solidarity in 1933 but elaborated their own very different visions of what might be accomplished. Succumbing to the atmosphere of battle—against Communism, cultural decadence, and Jews—they embraced a virile ethos."[384]

Even after a cursory look at the Nazi debate about the *Rechtsstaat*, and the variation—sometimes dramatic, but often subtle—among the many voices that made themselves heard during the four years that it took to settle it, one would be hard-pressed to miss the expressive energy that went into it. The jurists involved "celebrated the heroic values that elevated the community over the individual, instinct over reason, authenticity over rationality, and hardness over empathy."[385] What Koonz wrote about Heidegger and Schmitt's conduct in 1933 applies to virtually all of the participants whose contributions I discussed in this chapter:

> At this critical juncture, while Hitler himself was silent on the subject, [they] stepped in to translate the Nazis' crude slogans and repellant images into intellectual respectable justifications not only for dictatorship but also for antisemitism. [...] They advanced the values of the Nazi conscience in their praise of a communitarian ethnic utopia. Each, in his own way, contributed to the redefinition of courage as the capacity to harm the vulnerable without shirking, in the name of the *Volk*.[386]

This, then, is why the Nazi debate about the *Rechtsstaat* matters. It points to a neglected social mechanism in the making of the Nazi dictatorship: the reconstitution of legal norms. By acknowledging the Nazi quest for normativity (to which the phenomenon of ideology is related but from which it must be analytically distinguished), we are in a position to understand better why remnants of the *Rechtsstaat* survived, at least for a while, the Nazi assault on liberal legalism. The social construction of the Nazi concept of law, which gained new and sharper contours in the period 1933–1937, amounted to a legal imaginary, which gradually took hold of the Nazi legal conscience.

Few theorists have done more to advance the idea of the "social imaginary" ("*l'imaginaire social*") than the Greek-French philosopher Cornelius Castoriadis.[387] Even though the notion originated in the early work of Jacques Lacan in the 1950s, it was Castoriadis's rendering of it that convinced social theorists to take note. Pathbreaking about Catoriadis's contribution was his assertion that the imaginary element of the social world represented not a reflection of reality, "a specular image of what is already there," as mainstream thought had long assumed, but a reality in its own right.[388] The imaginary, in this account, is an elementary form of social life. According to Castoriadis,

> This element, which endows the functionality of each institutional system with its specific orientation, which overdetermines the choice and connections of symbolic networks, which creates for each historical period its singular way of living, seeing and making its own existence, its world and its relations to it, this originary structuring, this central signifier-signified, source of what is each time given as indisputable and indisputed sense, support of the articulations and distinctions of what matters and of what does not, origin of the augmented being (*surcroit d'être*) of the individual or collective objects of practical, affective and intellectual investment—this element is nothing other than the *imaginary* of the society or period concerned.[389]

Elsewhere Castoriadis described "the central imaginary significations of a society" memorably as "the laces which tie a society together and the forms which define what, for a given society, is 'real.' "[390] If we accept this premise, the Nazi debate about the *Rechtsstaat* tells us a great deal more about life in the Third Reich than it should, and than Radbruch's formula or Neumann's *Behemoth* arguably ever could.[391] Rather than representing an insignificant sideshow, it is a rich (and largely untapped) source for prima facie evidence of the "pre-reflexive parameters" within which Nazi jurists imagined their legal existence.[392]

In this sense, law was what Nazis made of it. This is the reality of law at the level of *legal theory*. The self-understandings of agents matter apart from the conduct in which individual or collective agents might engage. "[I]n this context one looks at the ways in which lawyers, judges and other participants in the 'interpretive community', law, understood what they were doing between 1933 and 1945. Did they act as if they were still lawyers and judges, within a 'legal' system, albeit a new or revolutionary Nazi legal system? On this question, there can be little debate."[393] The Nazi debate about the *Rechtsstaat* shows that even the most hardened jurist thought of himself as an agent of law. Authoritarian legalism in the Third Reich, in short, was invented but meaningful. If we take Peter Winch's idea of social science as our guide, the fact that Nazi legalism was an invented tradition is of secondary significance. For as Winch writes, "[a]ll behaviour which is meaningful (therefore all specifically human behaviour) is *ipso facto* rule-governed."[394] When speaking of "rule-governed" behavior, what Winch had in mind were any and all social practices that were based on common understandings.[395] Despite the myriad differences and disagreements among the participants in the Nazi debate about the *Rechtsstaat*, their habitual invocation in critiques of the nineteenth century idea of the *Rechtsstaat* of what I have called the trifecta of tropes—antiliberalism, antiformalism, and antisemitism—is indicative of the strength of the repugnant ideas that bound them together. Because the intentions of their scholarly contributions to the Nazi debate about the *Rechtsstaat* were discernable to anyone who cared to pay attention, the participating jurists, in Winch's definition, reasoned not wantonly but in accordance with revised rules of the game. Nazi legal thought, then, was an activity like any other.[396]

But law was real in a second sense as well. This is the reality of law at the level of *legal practice*. We must consult both dimensions of legal reality if we hope to make reliable inferences about the state of law—and the law of the state—in the Third Reich. David Fraser rightly cautions that "all who reject the 'legality' of Nazi Germany are still faced with the existential reality of a legal system which continued to function much as it had before."[397] The tradition of legalism in Germany, which dates back to a time before von Mohl invented the idea of the *Rechtsstaat*, exercised an ideational pull on a subset of Nazi intellectuals that partially constrained the theory and practice of authoritarian rule. As Karl Loewenstein remarked from the safety of his American exile, "Bent upon the creation of fundamentally new legal concepts, National Socialist constitutional jurisprudence takes pride in pretending that it has established a legal system which is *sui generis* and beyond the reach of comparative standards."[398] It is an apt summary of the Nazi legal conscience in 1937, the year in which the debate about the *Rechtsstaat* was settled. Friedrich Roetter, writing in 1945, when Radbruch's philosophical interest was also peaked, did not see any reason to disagree with Loewenstein's prewar finding. Himself a refugee from the Reich and erstwhile insurgent lawyer, he summarized succinctly the contribution that the Nazi legal imaginary in the preceding twelve years had made to the dictatorship:

> Although Nazi doctrines may have been conceived in cool calculation as a means to power and nurtured through emotion, the point of interest to the lawyer is that the acts of the Nazi regime were committed under law. The Nazis recognized the necessity of law. But their law had little in common with what lawyers had theretofore called law.[399]

For Roetter, just as for Fraenkel, as we shall see in more detail in the next few chapters, Nazi legalism was neither law (*Recht*) nor lawlessness (*Unrecht*), but gray law. Both thought it important, for all the suffering that Germany's Nazis made them endure, to recognize and try to understand the operation of law amidst lawlessness. Because the demand for legalization was considerable in the early life of the Third Reich, it was impossible to purge the Nazi legal system of all norms and institutions of the ancien régime(s). And because Nazi legalism was predicated on new, racialized legal norms, the existing institutions into which these norms were transplanted came to be seen as less threatening by Nazi functionaries than they had in the run-up to dictatorship, when they appeared to represent bastions of liberalism. It was thus that remnants of the *Rechtsstaat* came to govern the Nazi dictatorship, where they gave hope to a lawyer with a cause.

6

An Ethnography of Nazi Law: The Gestation of *The Dual State*, 1936–1941

Ernst Fraenkel completed the manuscript for the English edition of *The Dual State* on June 15, 1940.[1] Oxford University Press published it in early 1941. But the journey from the book's conception to its eventual publication was arduous and probably more so than Fraenkel anticipated when he first began his research in Nazi Germany in 1936, when the Nazi debate about the *Rechtsstaat* was nearing its end.

Fraenkel was one of the most visible jurists in Weimar Germany.[2] As a veteran of World War I, a so-called *Frontkämpfer*, he was allowed to practice law until November 30, 1938, when all remaining lawyers of Jewish ancestry were banned from their profession.[3] With the Fifth Ordinance of the Reich Citizenship Law (*Fünfte Verordnung zum Reichsbürgergesetz*) of September 27, 1938, the Nazi regime completed its purge of the legal profession.[4] The first, partial purge took place shortly after Hitler's seizure of power in 1933, when the newly installed regime, in connection with the more general Law for the Restoration of the Professional Civil Service (*Gesetz zur Wiederherstellung des Berufsbeamtentums*), on April 7, 1933, adopted a law mandating the disbarment of Jewish lawyers by September 30 of that year.[5] At the time, the 4,394 German lawyers of Jewish faith or background accounted for twenty percent of the approximately 19,500 members of the Bar in Germany.[6]

Yet to the chagrin of various legal representatives of the Nazi regime, Fraenkel and a considerable number of other Jewish lawyers were exempt from the provisions of this Law on Admission to the Bar (*Gesetz über die Zulassung zur Rechtsanwaltschaft*).[7] Either they had, like Fraenkel, contributed to the war effort, had lost fathers or sons in World War I, or they had opened their legal practice prior to 1914, in which case they were classified as *Altanwälte* ("Old Lawyers") and thus also entitled to continued Bar membership.[8] Konrad Jarausch estimates that sixty percent of all Jewish lawyers fell into one of these categories and thus outside of the purview of the legal ban.[9] Ingo Müller found that an even larger percentage escaped the draconian legislation: He calculated that 2,900 Jewish lawyers, or sixty-five percent of their total number, "were still permitted to practice," whereas 1,500 were stripped of their Bar membership during this first concerted effort at displacing Germany's Jews from legal life.[10] Saul Friedländer, finally, suggests that as many as seventy percent of Jewish lawyers were nominally allowed to continue to work in their chosen profession.[11] Whatever the exact figure may be, a substantial number of Jewish lawyers remained visible in public life, if only for a few more years. But this visibility must not be misinterpreted, and even it declined almost immediately. As Friedländer writes, "Though still allowed to practice, Jewish lawyers were excluded from the national association of lawyers and listed not in its annual directory but in a separate guide; all in all, notwithstanding the support of some Aryan institutions and individuals, they worked under a 'boycott by fear.' "[12]

Interestingly, it was Hitler himself who initially called for restraint in the purification of the professions. Possibly wary of an international outcry in response to a complete purge, he instructed his cabinet "only to regulate what is necessary at this time. For attorneys, a solution similar to the law on the restoration of professional civic service ought to be found."[13] In accordance with these wishes, Franz Gürtner, the minister of justice at the time, "forestalled complete exclusion by drafting a more moderate national law" than many of his legal contemporaries were hoping for.[14] In fact, Gürtner's legislative intervention from the center came in response to vociferous and violent initiatives in the *Länder*, that is the constitutive states of the German Reich. In the aftermath of the far-reaching regime change on January 30, 1933, the so-called *Machtergreifung*, roving Nazi supporters as well as SA and police units took it upon themselves—sometimes nudged, at other times instructed—to abuse and physically remove Jewish lawyers from courts around the country or otherwise interfere with their legal practice.

In early March, proceedings in courts in the cities of Chemnitz, Kaiserslautern, Saarbrücken, and especially Breslau ground to a virtual halt as a result of local initiatives in "racial" cleansing, or *Säuberungen*, as the antisemitic measures became euphemistically known. These mostly wanton acts can be described, in Fraenkel's parlance, as acts of a fledgling prerogative state. The Federation of National Socialist German Jurists (*Bund Nationalsozialistischer Deutscher Juristen*), or BNSDJ, fanned the flames by demanding, notably during its meeting in Leipzig on March 14, to remove with all deliberate speed Jewish judges and civil servants from their positions in German courts, to ban Jewish lawyers from representing clients, and to remove from the Bar any and all of these lawyers who were members of the SPD or the KPD.[15] This call paved the way for violent occupations of courts by local Nazi authorities and supporters in additional cities, including Oels, Gleiwitz, Görlitz, and Königsberg.[16]

Most interesting about these developments is the apparent discord inside the dictatorship over the most appropriate way forward. This discord echoed the at times vociferous disagreements among Nazi jurists debating the *Rechtsstaat*. It bears out Fraenkel's argument about an institutional dualism at the heart of the early Nazi state. As a civil servant with a certain respect for the rules and institutions of the normative state, Gürtner, whom we also encountered in the previous chapter, repeatedly insisted, especially when it came to the purification of the *Reichsgericht*, that the law was paramount and that local authorities ought to wait for the passage of legislation ("*was auf dem Wege des Gesetzes erfolge*") before embarking on a full-scale purification of the legal profession.[17] He was challenged by advocates of the gradually expanding prerogative state, notably by Hanns Kerrl, Hans Frank, and other heads of state judicial bureaucracies (*Landesjustizverwaltungen*). Kerrl and Frank in particular were pushing for what Lothar Gruchmann has termed a "radical solution" to the supposed problem of Jewish lawyers.[18] As ministers of justice in the large states of Prussia and Bavaria, respectively, they had clout. And their condoning and encouragement of random acts of intimidation and violence in their jurisdictions, not to mention their pursuit of unilateral and idiosyncratic practices, meant that they were formidable opponents.[19] Kerrl was a faithful member of the NSDAP and committed to the Nazification of the legal profession. Upon taking up the leadership of Prussia's ministry of justice, he bemoaned the fact that only a small number of the state's judges were NSDAP members.[20]

It was Gürtner who alerted Hitler to what he considered inappropriate and excessive initiatives from the periphery. Faced by "contradictory demands from Nazi radicals on the one hand and from his DNVP allies on the other," Hitler, on this occasion, sided with Gürtner, a DNVP member.[21] After a briefing by Franz Schlegelberger, state secretary in the Ministry of Justice, who maintained that the violent excesses in Prussia, Bavaria, and elsewhere necessitated the rapid adoption of a comprehensive and unified legal framework that would govern the displacement of Jews from legal life, and the subsequent presentation of draft legislation to this effect, Hitler reined in Kerrl, Frank, and their allies in the other state judicial bureaucracies. In doing so, he may have heeded considerations about the economic fallout of a radical solution. The Reich Association of Legal and Notary Employees *(Reichsvereinigung der Rechtsanwalts- und Notariatsangestellten)*, for example, had previously warned that a complete prohibition of Jewish legal activity would also spell unemployment for the more than 35,000 staff who were employed by Jewish law firms throughout Germany. Such an outcome, the Reich Association maintained, would burden "the already catastrophic labor market with another influx of job seekers."[22] In the end, the worst was averted in the spring of 1933, but the lobbying for a comprehensive cleansing of the legal profession did not abate. Increasingly, Jewish lawyers became ostracized, which threw their livelihoods into disarray. Political exclusion, social marginalization, and economic dislocation culminated in their outright ban in 1938. This worsening of conditions ultimately caused Fraenkel to flee his native Germany.

During the five interim years—that is, the period 1933–1938—Fraenkel was reluctantly afforded (a very uncomfortable and often dangerous) front row seat to the gradual destruction of the German *Rechtsstaat*. He had horrifying (but scholarly invaluable) access as a participant observer to one of the most far-reaching—and violent—legal transformations ever undertaken. *The Dual State* is the product of this extraordinary exposure to, and sustained reflection on, the legal origins of Nazi dictatorship. From his unique vantage point, and with a declining roster of clients, Fraenkel made theoretical sense, as best he could, of what was happening around him. Drawing on his disciplinary training in both law and history—and taking a leaf from the methodology of the social sciences that his imaginary wartime intellectual mentor, the lawyer and sociologist Max Weber—had propagated, Fraenkel embarked on what he conceived of as an exercise in the sociology of law.[23]

"THE THIRD REICH AS A DUAL STATE" (1937)

The concept of the dual state first found its way into print in 1937 in an article that Fraenkel wrote under the pseudonym "Conrad Jürgens" for the *Sozialistische Warte*, entitled "Das Dritte Reich as Doppelstaat" ("The Third Reich as a Dual State").[24] In this publication, Fraenkel chronicled the breakdown of democracy and the rise of dictatorship in Weimar Germany. He started with the observation that Nazi Germany, far from being the unitary state that the Hitler regime proclaimed it had established, consisted of two *parallel* and *contending* halves.[25] State power ("*Staatsgewalt*"), Fraenkel argued, resided in each of these halves. The institutional structures were located side-by-side ("*nebeneinander*") but operating at loggerheads ("*gegeneinander*").[26] But, and this is where Fraenkel's analysis departed from other critical perspectives on the Nazi state that existed at the time, the institutional divide that he thought to be most significant did not separate the Nazi state from the NSDAP. According to Fraenkel, state and party were institutionally fused, virtually indistinguishable in conceptual terms. More important than the superficial (and empirically meaningless) distinction between state and party, Fraenkel argued, was the division that existed *within* the state. He believed it essential to introduce a standard of institutional differentiation "into the structure of the state" ("*in das Gefüge des Staates*") itself.[27] In his first attempt at theorizing the nature of the Nazi state, Fraenkel distinguished between what he called "the state as political unity" ("*Staat als politische Einheit*") and "the state as technical apparatus" ("*Staat als technische[r] Apparat*").[28] These formulations were the precursors for Fraenkel's twin neologisms: the "*Maßnahmen-Staat*" (for which he subsequently adopted the spelling *Maßnahmenstaat* and rendered as "prerogative state" in the English translation that he would authorize in 1940) and the "*Normen-Staat*" (later spelled *Normenstaat* and translated as "normative state").[29]

Fraenkel traced the remote origins of the institutional bifurcation of the Nazi state back to the transition from "the bureaucratization of politics" ("*Bürokratisierung der Politik*") in Wilhelmine Germany to "the politicization of the bureaucracy" ("*Politisierung der Bürokratie*") in Weimar Germany.[30] The legacies of these countervailing developments in the late nineteenth and early twentieth centuries, he maintained, threw up a governance challenge that none of the preceding regimes in Germany had solved. "The problem became the Nazis's inheritance" ("*Das Problem blieb den Nationalsozialisten als Erbe.*").[31] The solution that the new authoritarian regime devised, according to Fraenkel, was to create an institutional dispensation in which political and technical logics of governance co-existed, albeit in an unequal fashion. The duality of the Nazi state was imbalanced, characterized as it was by the "primacy" ("*Primat*") of the political over the "technical apparatus" ("*technischen Apparat*") of the state.[32] As Fraenkel put it, "Germany today lives by dual law" ("*Deutschland lebt heute nach doppeltem Recht*").[33] But, as he hastened to add, it was not just a question of governance by two *types* of law; it also gave rise to governance by different *principles* of law.

What Fraenkel meant was that legal governance in the technical apparatus of state was structured by an elaborate and systematic set of established legal norms, rules, codes, and procedures. By contrast, legal governance in the "political state" ("*politischen Staat*") was not systematic, but wanton and senseless. In Fraenkel's reading, the few legal provisions that were explicitly crafted for the political state, and which, in theory at least, structured its operation, were "without exception so shallow in substantive terms that they amount to no more than the appearance of a legal norm" ("*ausnahmslos inhaltlich so farblos, daß sie lediglich den Schein einer Rechtsnorm darstellen*").[34] Another way of putting this is that the technical state (that is, the normative state) abided by the rule *of* law, whereas the political state (that is, the prerogative state) embodied rule *by* law. The former was governed by formal rationality, the latter by substantive rationality.[35] The primacy of the prerogative over the normative state, argued Fraenkel, was evidenced by the fact that the validity of the pre-Nazi legal norms, rules, codes, and procedures of the normative state was contingent; it was contingent on non-abrogation and non-suspension by the prerogative state.

The question arises why the Nazi regime did not do away with the remnants of the *Rechtsstaat* entirely? After all, as Fraenkel pointed out, the Nazis ridiculed any state that was "merely *Rechtsstaat*" ("*nichts als Rechtsstaat*"), this uniquely German variant of the rule-of-law state.[36] He reminded his readers that Ernst Forsthoff, one of the regime's young constitutional lawyers, had not long ago declared the pure *Rechtsstaat* to be a state lacking in "honor and dignity" ("*Ehre und Würde*").[37] But if the Nazis regarded the legacies of Weimar law as "law without value" ("*Recht ohne Wert*"), and if they were further convinced that the NSDAP's political manifesto was the instrument for injecting value into the (literally) meaningless legal order, why did the normative state of old survive? Indeed, why did this (in Nazi eyes) substantively hollow, formally rational state not only survive but occupy "a significant place" ("*einen bedeutenden Platz*") in the institutional architecture of the Nazi regime, as Fraenkel claimed it did?[38]

In this first stab at providing an answer, Fraenkel turned to orthodoxy. He believed that a dictator would not embrace a normative state for the sake of principle. It would always be a strategic choice.[39] One of the most immediate challenges the Nazis faced was how to ensure that the country would thrive economically in the midst of a social and racial revolution.[40] Upon seizing power, Hitler and his newly incumbent government continued on, and heavily fortified, the well-worn path toward state interventionism into the economy that governing elites in the Weimar Republic had established. But, as Adam Tooze has pointed out, "though it is important to do justice to the shift in power relations between state and business that undoubtedly occurred in the early 1930s, we must be careful to avoid falling into the trap of viewing German business merely as the passive object of the regime's draconian new system of regulation."[41] This brings us back to Fraenkel, who, in 1937, proffered a Marxist interpretation of the origins and logic of Nazi Germany's dual state.

It is worth reconstructing this interpretation in some detail because it all but disappeared, for reasons to be explained below, from the 1941 edition of *The Dual State*. In 1937, Fraenkel started with the assumption that capitalism had grown "economically and ideologically impotent."[42] He asserted that Germany's "high capitalism" of the 1920s was doomed to extinction unless revived by a strategic alliance with a racial state whose ambition to rearm the nation would inject the ailing economy with the funds necessary to secure its survival. With both the Nazi regime and the weakened "capitalist order," as Fraenkel called it, having an immediate interest in preserving the foundations of economic activity in Germany, it followed that the march of the prerogative state had to be slowed down. The temporary retention of the normative state served as the necessary break on the consolidation of totalitarianism in Nazi Germany. Here is how Fraenkel put it in 1937:

> If capitalism wants to remain capitalism, it requires at home a state apparatus that recognizes the rules of formal rationality, for without a predictability of opportunities, without legal certainty ("*Rechtssicherheit*"), capitalist planning is impossible. Capitalism today demands of the state a double ("*ein Doppeltes*"): Because capitalism is capitalism, it demands, first, the formally rational order of a technically intact state. Because capitalism is impotent, it demands, furthermore, a state that provides the political supports ("*politischen Stützen*") necessary to ensure its continued existence; a state with enemies against which capitalism is allowed to arm [...].[43]

The consequences of this capitalist alignment with the Nazi dictatorship produced positive externalities for political and economic elites alike: "What Hitler's regime positively enabled German business to do was to recover from the disastrous recession, to accumulate capital and to engage in high-pressure development of certain key technologies: the technologies necessary to achieve the regime's twin objectives of increased self-sufficiency (autarchy) and rearmament."[44] Fraenkel was convinced that Germany's capitalists sacrificed the well-being of the Nazis' real and imagined enemies on the altar of economic accumulation. As he put it, borrowing Marxist terminology, "the dual state is the ideological superstructure (*Überbau*) of a capitalism that thrives on politics because it is unable to exist any longer without politics."[45]

The root cause for this malaise Fraenkel detected in the changing character of politics, which he believed had been partially brought about by a radical transformation of the "concept of the political" ("*Begriff des Politischen*") in interwar Germany.[46] For him, the rise of the "political leadership state" ("*politische[r] Führer-Staat*"), the institutional antecedent of the full-blown prerogative state, was causally related to the redrawing of the boundaries of politics and of the political.[47] He wrote with concern about the "depoliticization of the state," a gradual process that he believed was hastened when the country's highest court, the *Reichsgericht*, the federal high court for civil and criminal matters, in a decision in which one of its chambers adjudicated the question of whether a member of the SA was, legally speaking, a civil servant. Its finding that the individual in question could not be considered a civil servant because his activities were of a political nature, and that only members of the normative state were bureaucrats, properly understood, Fraenkel found unpersuasive. He rejected the artificial distinction between Nazi state and Nazi party that underpinned the *Reichsgericht*'s reasoning. By relying on an impossibly narrow concept of the state (that is, the state as the technical apparatus of the normative state), the judges legitimated the Nazis' campaign to depoliticize the state. Their decision embodied the infamous Hitlerian injunction that the state did not govern the NSDAP, but the NSDAP the state.[48] This, said Fraenkel, was the institutional realization of a new concept of the political—that of Carl Schmitt.

In his first exposition of the dual-state-argument, Fraenkel described Schmitt as "the most prominent figure in the neo-German state theory" ("*der prominenteste Kopf der neudeutschen Staatsrechtslehre*").[49] He singled him out for opprobrium, holding the ambitious jurist to account for having paved the way with the publication of *Die geistesgeschichtliche Lage des heutigen Parlamentarismus* (*The Crisis of Parliamentary Democracy*) in 1923 for the rise of the "National-Socialist counter-state" ("*nationalsozialistische Gegenstaat*"). In addition to this failing, Fraenkel took Schmitt to task for having deliberately obscured the nature and meaning of political activity. As Fraenkel wrote, "It is not at all the case that the substance of politics ('*der Inhalt dessen, was Politik ist*') is explained by the concept of the political."[50] This is what Fraenkel called the "political function" ("*politische Funktion*") of Schmitt's concept of the political.[51] He warned that an insistence on the friend-enemy distinction as the defining attribute of the concept of the political enabled and legitimated "activity for activity's sake" ("*Aktivität um der Aktivität willen*") in the pursuit of contentious politics.[52] If politics is no longer about substantive issues, but only existential enemies, the road via the prerogative state looks less like a detour and more like a straight path to a more meaningful politics. Fraenkel paraphrased Schmitt: "It is of secondary importance who the enemy is. Key is that an enemy exists at all. Without an enemy, there is no politics [...]."[53] If we believe Fraenkel, what Schmitt concealed from his readers, was that capitalism, too, was dependent on a categorization of "the other," of a division of the world into friends and enemies: "Without a potential enemy, one against whom [the country] can be mobilized and armed, capitalism will cease to exist in Germany."[54]

Fraenkel was prescient about the political economy of dictatorship. He warned of the predictable consequences of collusion between big business and the racial state. The 1937 article ended on a rhetorically powerful note. Fraenkel declared that embedded in the "substantive rationality of National Socialism" was a desire for the destruction of the world. National Socialism was only "alive," he opined, because "it was readying itself to kill" *("[der Nationalsozialismus] nur dadurch zu leben vermag, daß er sich zum Töten vorbereitet")*.[55]

THE URDOPPELSTAAT (1938)

Fraenkel's first foray in the *Sozialistische Warte* quickly developed into a draft, clandestine manuscript, entitled *Der Doppelstaat: Ein Beitrag zur Staatslehre der deutschen Diktatur* (*The Dual State: A Contribution to the State Theory of the German Dictatorship*; hereinafter *Urdoppelstaat*).[56] The book-length treatment retained the unique blend of reason and emotion—of, on the one hand, dispassionate analysis that embodied the Weberian ideal of value neutrality, and, on the other, vociferous advocacy in opposition to the Nazi destruction of the *Rechtsstaat*. Given its explosive nature, one of Fraenkel's clients, Wilhelm Urban, a coal merchant active in the anti-Nazi resistance, temporarily hid the sensitive draft.[57] The book manuscript, written in German and only ever intended for an audience in his fatherland, found its way to the United States via France by way of a French embassy official.[58] One of Fraenkel's most trusted colleagues in this period—Fritz Eberhardt (the pseudonym of Hellmut von Rauschenplat)—was not only critical to the beginnings of the *Urdoppelstaat* but also to its survival. As Fraenkel recalled in his preface to the 1974 German edition:

> This book could not have been completed without the encouragement and continuous support of the *Internationaler Sozialistischer Kampfbund* (ISK, International Socialist Militant League), which was very active and exemplarily disciplined in the illegal underground movement. For years, I worked very closely with their Head of Domestic Affairs ("*Inlandsleiter*") Dr. Hellmut von Rauschenplat (Dr. Fritz Eberhardt), who was responsible for coordinating the movement's local resistance groups as well as for liaising with the Emigration Directorate ("*Emigrationsleitung*"), which was based in Paris. During long walks, we exchanged ideas about the meaning and purpose of illegal work ("*illegaler Arbeit*") and sought to gain greater clarity about the phenomenon of National Socialism. In the wake of such exchanges, I repeatedly dictated the conclusions we had reached in the

> form of short essays to Fritz Eberhardt who took stenographic notes ("*in das Stenogramm diktiert*"). They were intended for publication in the ISK journal *Sozialistische Warte*, which was published in Paris and subsequently distributed in Germany in the form of illegal flyers ("*illegale Flugblätter*"). [...] One of these articles contains the original version ("*Urfassung*") of *The Dual State*. It appeared under the pseudonym Conrad Jürgens.[59]

Throughout his life, Fraenkel told that the beginnings of the dual state concept lay in his personal encounters with the Hitler regime—as a lawyer, a social democrat, and a Jew. While allowed to practice law as a veteran of World War I, Fraenkel was simultaneously subjected to official and unofficial discrimination and intimidation. This schizophrenic experience prompted the idea of the dual state as a metaphor and concept—a state consisting of two halves, with conflicting imperatives. Fraenkel described the origins of his clandestine manuscript most eloquently (and comprehensively) in the preface to the 1974 German edition of *The Dual State*:

> The book is the result of internal emigration ("*innere Emigration*"). Its first version, which is also the foundation for this German edition, was written in an atmosphere of lawlessness and terror. It was based on sources that I collected in National Socialist Berlin, and on impressions that were forced upon me day in, day out ("*die sich mir tagtäglich aufgedrängt haben*"). It was conceived out of the need to make sense of these experiences theoretically in order to be able to cope with them. They stem mostly, though not exclusively, from my work as a practising lawyer in Berlin in the years 1933-1938. Despite being Jewish, I was permitted, due to my military service during the [First World] War, to practice at the bar even after 1933. The ambivalence of my bourgeois existence caused me to be particularly attuned to the contradictoriness ("*Widersprüchlichkeit*") of the Hitler regime. Though, legally speaking, an equal member of the bar, wherever I went, I was nonetheless subject to harassments, discriminations, and humiliations that emanated exclusively from the *staatstragende Partei* [literally: state-sustaining political party, i.e., the ruling Nazi party]. Anyone who did not shut his or her eyes to the reality of the Hitler dictatorship's administrative and judicial practices, must have been affected by the frivolous cynicism with which the state and the [Nazi] party called into question, for entire spheres of life, the validity of the legal order while, at the same time, applying, with bureaucratic exactness ("*mit bürokratischer Exaktheit*"), exactly the same legal provisions in situations that were said to be different ("*anders bewerteten Situationen*").[60]

In methodological terms, *The Dual State* is an excellent example of a practice that the political scientist David Collier has called "extracting new ideas at close range."[61] Participant observation aside, much of the research for the *Urdoppelstaat* was based on secondary sources as well as court cases. Fraenkel undertook it in Berlin's famous *Staatsbibliothek*, at the time the largest library in the German-speaking world. It dates back to 1661, when it was founded as the *Churfürstliche Bibliothek zu Cölln an der Spree*, a private library for the Prussian court. In 1918, the internationally renowned library was renamed the *Preußische Staatsbibliothek*. In 1905, its collection held more than one million titles; by 1939, the collection had mushroomed to three million, excluding 300,000 maps and other resources.[62] To wit, Fraenkel had access to all scholarly materials, legal and otherwise, that were available in Germany at the time, that is, to "all of the National-Socialist sources."[63] This excluded, as he noted in 1939, in the draft preface for the English edition, "the writings of the German political emigration and also of a considerable part of the non-German literature on the Third Reich which is not available in German libraries."[64] But Fraenkel appears not to have viewed the shortage of source materials as constraining. In the *Urdoppelstaat*, he declared that he had set himself the task of making "no claim about the legal and political order of National Socialism without demonstrating the validity of the claim with reference to National Socialist sources."[65]

It is important to fully appreciate Fraenkel's scholarly achievement: He managed to research and write—from within the belly of what his friend and colleague Franz Neumann, as we saw, dubbed a behemoth—a sophisticated analysis of the institutional formation, transformation, and deformation of the state in interwar Germany, and he did so by relying exclusively on participant observation and primary and secondary sources acceptable to the Nazis. And with little regard for his safety. When he told, years later, about his days of researching materials for the *Urdoppelstaat*, Fraenkel recalled that he tried to confuse and ditch Nazi spies in the *Staatsbibliothek* by ordering a slew of unrelated titles about every topic under the sun.

Despite the fact that Fraenkel's insurgent scholarship was taking up a great deal of his time, he continued to practice law in the courts of the Third Reich. He was in the habit of describing his role in the transition from authoritarianism to totalitarianism in Nazi Germany to friends as that of a "switchman" ("*Weichensteller*"):

> That is, I regarded it an essential part of my efforts to ensure that a given case was dealt with under the auspices of the "normative state," and not end up in the "prerogative state." Colleagues with whom I was on friendly terms confirmed that they, too, had repeatedly worked toward making sure that their clients were punished in a court of law ("*daß ihre Mandanten gerichtlich bestraft würden*") [rather than risking their arbitrary punishment in the prerogative state].[66]

Eventually, the prerogative state turned on Fraenkel himself. When, in 1935, his name appeared on a Gestapo list of thirteen lawyers whose representation of SPD defendants had rankled the Nazi authorities, Fraenkel and his wife began to think about emigration. They left Germany on September 20, 1938, a mere six weeks before the first systematic violent anti-Jewish pogrom—known by the euphemism "*Kristallnacht*"—in the course of which 267 synagogues were destroyed, an estimated 7,500 Jewish commercial establishments vandalized or looted or both, and 30,000 Jewish males rounded up and transferred to concentration camps. The violent campaign fundamentally changed the look of the latter. As Nikolaus Wachsmann has shown, "Never before had they held more inmates: within days the prisoner population doubled from twenty-four thousand to around fifty thousand. [...] Never before had there been as many Jews in the KL [the acronym for *Konzentrationslager*, the German word for concentration camp]: at the start of 1938, they had made up only around five percent of the prisoner population; now they were suddenly in the majority. And never before did as many prisoners die in the KL as in the weeks following the pogrom."[67]

After a brief stay in London, to where Fraenkel's fellow lawyer-friends Otto Kahn-Freund and Franz Neumann had previously emigrated, the Fraenkels fled to New York. Family connections meant that entry to the United States was assured and a visa easily obtained. Fraenkel's most important cargo—what he referred to as the *Urdoppelstaat*—made the journey by way of a French embassy official in Berlin. The brave diplomat, whom Eberhardt had drafted into the cause, hid the book manuscript in his diplomatic luggage and smuggled it to Paris—thus securing the work's survival. We now know that a carbon copy was buried for safekeeping in the garden of Otto and Susanne Suhr, but it was the well-travelled copy of the *Urdoppelstaat* that would serve as the foundation for the revision in exile.[68] This first draft ("*die erste Fassung*") was the nucleus of *The Dual State*.[69]

Long undiscovered, it turns out that Fraenkel, in 1957, had loaned a bound copy, printed on rough and absorbent paper, to the Otto-Suhr-Institut, the newly established Institute of Political Science at the Freie Universität in Berlin, where its library received the manuscript on October 9. On April 4, 1974, Fraenkel demanded the return of the manuscript, and the library has a record of this transaction as well.[70] From there, the bound version of the *Urdoppelstaat* eventually found its way to the Bundesarchiv, Germany's Federal Archives, along with another, unbound, and almost identical copy.[71] Both are believed to date from November 1938.[72] Fraenkel confirmed that he wrote the manuscript "in the years 1936–1938 in Germany."[73]

Alexander v. Brünneck, the editor of Fraenkel's collected writings from and about the Nazi period, has detected "significant differences" ("*signifikante Unterschiede*") between the *Urdoppelstaat* (completed in 1938) and *The Dual State* (completed in 1940). Fraenkel himself downplayed any such differences, suggesting they were about semantics rather than substance.[74] But v. Brünneck, a long-standing scholar and former student of Fraenkel, is undeniably correct. Four major differences stand out.

First, the *Urdoppelstaat* was shorter than *The Dual State*. By Fraenkel's own estimation, the *Urdoppelstaat* accounted for no more than sixty percent of the manuscript for *The Dual State*.[75] If we compare the length of both versions as they appear (in German) in the collected works, it is obvious that Fraenkel's estimation was off the mark.[76] Although it is true that the published (German) version of 1974 was longer than the *Urdoppelstaat*, the difference was less substantial than Fraenkel thought. Whereas the 1999 reprint in the collected works of the 1974 German translation (a retranslation of the 1941 OUP edition) comes in at 226 pages, the reprint of the *Urdoppelstaat* is 206 pages long. If the latter had comprised the sixty percent of *The Dual State* that Fraenkel thought it did, its reprint in the collected works should not have amounted to more than 136 pages.[77] In other words, the *Urdoppelstaat* was shorter than *The Dual State*, but only slightly so, not significantly, as Fraenkel had maintained.

These unexpected similarities in length aside, certain sections in *The Dual State* are more elaborate, others less so, than in the *Urdoppelstaat*. See Table 6.1. For the publication of *The Dual State*, Fraenkel substantially condensed Chapter 2 in Part II, which analyzed the Nazi onslaught on natural law in Germany. The revised analysis is five print pages shorter. Gone is the separate excursus on Hegel's influence on Nazi legal theory. Aspects of this account Fraenkel folded into the now extended analysis of what in 1941 he called "secular natural law" ("*das weltliche Naturrecht*")—and which he distinguished from "Christian natural law" ("*das christliche Naturrecht*").[78] More significant differences are noticeable in Part III. There, Fraenkel expanded his analysis of the political economy of the dual state. In the *Urdoppelstaat*, he had devoted eight pages to the topic, three years later the analysis was twice as long. This is interesting because of a second, substantive difference between the *Urdoppelstaat* and *The Dual State*.

There is diminished evidence in *The Dual State* of the functionalist, class-based analysis of law and society that characterized parts of the *Urdoppelstaat* as well as the 1937 article that had preceded it. The theoretical position of the original argument most certainly owed to Fraenkel's left-leaning socialization as well as to the ever-widening social inequality in interwar Germany that he was witnessing year in, year out. The turn to

Table 6.1 A Comparison of the *Urdoppelstaat* (1938) and *The Dual State* (1941): Structure, Organization, and Length

The *Urdoppelstaat* (1938)	*The Dual State* (1941)
Part I: *Die Rechtsordnung des Doppelstaates* (97 pages)	Part I: *Die Rechtsordnung des Doppelstaates* (103 pages)
Chapter 1: *Der Maßnahmenstaat* (52 pages)	Chapter 1: *Der Maßnahmenstaat* (57 pages)
Chapter 2: *Die Grenzen des Maßnahmenstaates* (8 pages)	Chapter 2: *Die Grenzen des Maßnahmenstaates* (6 pages)
Chapter 3: *Der Normenstaat* (33 pages)	Chapter 3: *Der Normenstaat* (36 pages)
Part II: *Die Rechtslehre des Doppelstaates* (49 pages)	Part II: *Die Rechtslehre des Doppelstaates* (45 pages)
Chapter 1: *Die Negation des rationalen Naturrechts durch den Nationalsozialismus* (6 pages)	Chapter 1: *Die Ablehnung des rationalen Naturrechts durch den Nationalsozialismus* (7 pages)
Chapter 2: *Der Nationalsozialismus im Kampf gegen die Restbestände des rationalen Naturrechts* (22 pages)	Chapter 2: *Der Nationalsozialismus im Kampf gegen das Naturrecht* (17 pages)
Chapter 3: *Nationalsozialismus und gemeinschaftliches Naturrecht* (17 pages)	Chapter 3: *Nationalsozialismus und gemeinschaftliches Naturrecht* (17 pages)
Part III: *Die Rechtswirklichkeit des Doppelstaates* (54 pages)	Part III: *Die Rechtswirklichkeit des Doppelstaates* (56 pages)
Chapter 1: *Die Rechtsgeschichte des Doppelstaates* (18 pages)	Chapter 1: *Die Rechtsgeschichte des Doppelstaates* (17 pages)
Chapter 2: *Die Oekonomie des Doppelstaates* (8 pages)	Chapter 2: Die ökonomischen Grundlagen des Doppelstaates (16 pages)
Chapter 3: *Die Soziologie des Doppelstaates* (24 pages)	Chapter 3: *Die Soziologie des Doppelstaates* (19 pages)

class as a conceptual variable came easily, but Fraenkel was more circumspect in his channeling of the materialist theory of history than some of his contemporaries, including Neumann.[79] For example, in a section of the *Urdoppelsaat* that did not make it into the 1941 book, Fraenkel explicitly distanced himself from mainstream, communist interpretations:

> We are far away from claiming that big agriculture ("*Großagrarier*") and heavy industry raised the Hitler movement as their vassal ("*Hausknecht*"), so to speak. The course of world history cannot be explained in such simple terms, nor can the materialist conception of history ("*die materialistische Geschichtsauffassung*") be applied in such a crude fashion.[80]

Fraenkel's take was more nuanced. He, too, believed that the peculiar logic of capitalism in Germany had played a role in the rise of the Nazis. However, his causal logic was less reductionist than that of Germany's communists. It was social-democratic in origin, infused with socialist ideas, not communist ones. For their elaboration, Fraenkel relied, among others, on the Austrian-born American economist Joseph Schumpeter, who would go on to publish, in 1942, *Capitalism, Socialism, and Democracy*.[81] In the *Urdoppelstaat*, Fraenkel invoked Schumpeter's article "The Sociology of Imperialisms."[82] In the 1918 essay, Schumpeter, while not unsympathetic, cast doubt on the explanatory power of "neo-Marxist theory" to account for the phenomenon of imperialist expansion.[83] With the help of a comparative historical analysis of empirical instances of imperialism, Schumpeter pierced the universalizing ambition of the materialist conception of history. Fraenkel applied the essence of Schumpeter's argument to the case of Nazism. Reasoning by analogy, he argued that National Socialism was not a product of capitalism; rather National Socialism (like nationalism and militarism in Schumpeter's case) was "capitalized," with the effect that National Socialism was recruiting its best personnel ("*beste Kräfte*") from the capitalist ranks.[84] Like Schumpeter, Fraenkel was influenced by Marxist thought. But neither man swallowed the theoretical framework whole. The relationship between capitalism and National Socialism, according to Fraenkel, was mutually constitutive: The former draws in the latter and thereby sustains it; the latter, in turn, gradually transforms the nature of the former.

Remnants of this interpretation can be found in the draft English translation (hereinafter the NYPL draft after the New York Public Library where it is held). In one part of the typed manuscript, for example, Fraenkel argued as follows:

> The legal order of the Third Reich is thoroughly rationalized in a functional sense with reference to the regulation of production and exchange in accordance with capitalistic methods. But late capitalistic economic activity is not substantially rational. For this reason it has had recourse to political methods, while giving to these methods the contentlessness [*sic*] of irrational activity. Capitalism at its high point was a system of substantial rationality which, relying on the prestabilised [*sic*] harmony which guided its destinies, exerted itself to remove irrational obstacles. When the belief in the substantial rationality of capitalism disappeared its functionally rationalized organizations still remained. What is the character of the tension which arises in consequence of this juxtaposition of a substantial rationality in a process of disappearance and maximally developed functional rationality?[85]

This section channeled both Marx and Weber. The approach was Marxist, the argumentation Weberian. But Fraenkel also made recourse to Karl Mannheim's recent work on the nature of rationality (which I discuss in more detail below), notably his argument about the economic origins of dictatorship and democracy in the case of Nazi Germany: "Faced with the choice between substantial rationality and substantial irrationality German capitalism cast its vote for the latter. It will accommodate itself to any substantial irrationality if only the necessary pre-requisites [*sic*] for its technically rational order are preserved. German capitalism has preferred [a] substantially irrational ideology which maintains the existing conditions of technical capitalistic rationality."[86] On the final page of the NYPL draft, Fraenkel concluded his fledgling book manuscript with another formulation that betrayed his socialist past, but which also invokes Weber's typology of law (to which I will also return below): "The foregoing again demonstrates that National-Socialism, although it passionately repudiates formal rationality in the application of the law as a leftover of a bygone age adheres to the principle of formal rationality when the case has a bearing on the capitalistic system. The capitalistic system cannot exist without a minimum of formal rationality."[87]

Fraenkel toned down this functional interpretation of Nazi dictatorship in the transition from *Urdoppelstaat* to *The Dual State*. Fraenkel, on his own accord or on the basis of conversations with mentors and colleagues, decided that the American audience he hoped to reach with the publication of an English edition might not appreciate an overtly Marxist interpretation of German history. This brings us to a third major difference between the *Urdoppelstaat* and *The Dual State*: the tone. The *Urdoppelstaat* was more passionate than *The Dual State*. Large chunks of it had more in common with Fraenkel's essayistic interventions on behalf of the ISK in the 1920s and 1930s than with the more detached analysis for which *The Dual State* became known. The change in tone was a consequence of the change in target audience. Whereas Fraenkel drafted the *Urdoppelstaat* with German readers in mind, he conceived *The Dual State* for a much broader readership. To this end, the language, terminology, empirical references, and even the argument needed to be rethought and tweaked. But the efforts were worth it. In the transition from *Urdoppelstaat* to *The Dual State*, an act of resistance turned into a contribution to scholarship.

Fourth, Fraenkel's translators, presumably in extensive conversation with the man himself, translated his concept of *Maßnahmenstaat* (literally: state of measures) as "prerogative state." In order to motivate this conceptual innovation and to avoid misunderstanding, Fraenkel included in the 1941 English edition a two-page discussion of John Locke's concept of the prerogative, with which his notion of the prerogative state must not be confused.[88] As Fraenkel wrote, "[A] connection might be presumed to exist between the neo-German constitutional doctrine [of the prerogative] and Locke's theory. Such a hypothesis would, however, be incorrect."[89] Fraenkel goes on to show how Locke's theory failed to make an impression on leading countries (England, France, United States) and leading thinkers (Thomas Jefferson, Montesquieu) alike. In *The Dual State*, Fraenkel quoted a passage from §158 in the Second Treatise of *Two Treatises of Civil Government* to capture Locke's definition of the concept: "Prerogative is nothing but the power of doing public good without a rule."[90] The bearer of the prerogative, in Locke's conception, governs "without the prescription of Law [...] and sometimes even against it".[91]

Despite conceptual similarities between Fraenkel's notion of the prerogative, of which more below, and Locke's, Fraenkel was adamant that he was not channeling Locke's doctrine of the separation of powers. And he was right to, for Locke's extra-legal power was not an arbitrary one.[92] Locke's understanding of the prerogative was imbued with values of paternity. Although the bearer of the prerogative decided the exception, it was a *benign* power. Fraenkel (and his translators) took a key Lockean term out of context, thereby turning the bearer of the prerogative into an utterly *malign* power—a power "tending to evil."[93]

THE DUAL STATE (1941)

In the United States, Fraenkel rewrote the *Urdoppelstaat* for American and English readers. His pathbreaking analysis would have aged considerably less well—and likely not be in need of republication in the twenty-first century—had Fraenkel not extensively revised it in exile. In the preface of the 1974 German edition (which appears in the 2017 edition of *The Dual State* in translation for the first time), he described the transition from *Urdoppelstaat* to OUP manuscript thus:

> In the drafting of the manuscript and its translation into English, special emphasis was placed on explaining the Third Reich's system of rule ("*Herrschaftsstruktur*") in academic categories that are familiar to the social-scientifically trained American reader—paraphrasing them, if necessary, to render them comprehensible. I need only point to such foundational terms as "*Ausnahmezustand*" [which most accurately translates as state of exception] and "Martial Law." A translation of the German text into English made sense only if it also involved a transposition ("*Transponierung*") of concepts from the National Socialist into the American system of government ("*Regierungssystem*").[94]

The resulting manuscript, translated into English by Edward A. Shils, a sociologist at the University of Chicago who later worked with Talcott Parsons, in collaboration with Edith Löwenstein (incorrectly spelled

Lowenstein on the frontispiece) and Klaus Knorr, combined in a compelling way an astute analysis of ethnographic (and other qualitative) data with a penchant for theoretical reasoning. It was a powerful analytic narrative of its time. After months of overhauling the *Urdoppelstaat*, Fraenkel secured a contract with Oxford University Press for its publication. Several organizations, institutions, and individuals provided subventions to aid the book's completion and production, including the American Guild for German Cultural Freedom, the Graduate Faculty at the New School for Social Research, and the International Institute of Social Research, the latter being the famous, exiled *Institut für Sozialforschung*, previously based in Frankfurt, Germany, and since mid-1934 housed at Columbia University.[95]

One would have thought that the large number of émigré scholars from Germany who had found refuge in New York City made for a stimulating intellectual environment in which to turn the *Urdoppelstaat* into *The Dual State*. After all, Fraenkel's had been a household name in Germany, and his Weimar-era publications are said to have reached more than 100,000 readers.[96] This was not to be. Fraenkel was in for a rude awakening. There was no interest on the part of the refuge community's leading intellectuals in a study of the legal origins of dictatorship and democracy. No-one seemed to think that a publication for the English-language market was a necessity. Max Horkheimer's positive, yet tepid response illustrates the general mood. In early 1939, Fraenkel had shared one of the versions of the book manuscript with Horkheimer. The latter replied on February 9: "But the work is not only important because it offers the first analysis of jurisprudence and scholarship. It also processes a wealth of empirical details ('*Fülle der Einzelheiten*') from a theoretical perspective that, in my opinion, is of decisive relevance ('*entscheidener Bedeutung*') not only for the production of knowledge ('*Erkenntnis*') but also for a critique of National Socialist viewpoints."[97] Horkheimer did not support the publication of *The Dual State*. Fraenkel was largely alone in thinking that an in-depth scholarly analysis of the transition *to* Nazi dictatorship was required, indeed essential, for planning for a transition *from* Nazi dictatorship. Notwithstanding the general indifference that had greeted him and his work in the United States, Fraenkel persevered. Several scholars commented on the manuscript-in-progress, including Max Rheinstein, Franz Neumann, and, perhaps most significantly, Carl F. Friedrich, one of the best-known and influential political scientists in the mid-twentieth century who at the time was Professor of Government at Harvard University. Friedrich's involvement with, and endorsement of, Fraenkel's project will not have hurt in OUP's deliberations about whether to publish *The Dual State*.

The New York Public Library holds a typescript of the manuscript for what eventually became the OUP book.[98] The typescript consists of a preface, a table of contents, and some chapters, with a large number of handwritten corrections.[99] The preface is dated November 2, 1939, with Chicago listed as the city where it was written. In terms of organization and substance, the typescript differs in minor rather than major ways from the published version. Inasmuch as the hundreds of additions, deletions, insertions, tweaks, and corrections altered the manuscript, mostly improving it, they did not fundamentally change the architecture and argument, save perhaps in Part III, Chapter 2 which in the manuscript of November 1939 was still entitled "The Economics of the Dual State," as it had been in the *Urdoppelstaat* ("*Die Oekonomie des Doppelstaates*").[100] In the 1941 published version, the chapter title was changed to "The Economic Background of the Dual State," a formulation that was changed to "The Economic Foundations of the Dual State" ("*Die ökonomischen Grundlagen des Doppelstaates*") in the retranslation for the 1974 German edition.[101] See also Table 6.1. Both changes could be seen as editorial. Alternatively, the first tweak can also be interpreted as a deliberative, *substantive* shift in emphasis with the intended effect of toning down, especially for American audiences, Fraenkel's economic interpretation of the rise and consequences of the dual state phenomenon in Nazi Germany. Support for this interpretation can be gleaned from a closer reading of the corrected typescript.

There, in several paragraphs crossed out by hand, we see Fraenkel soften the language of the original. Unlike in the *Urdoppelstaat*, the question of whether Nazism represented a form of capitalism was no longer at the forefront of the analysis in Part III, Chapter 2.[102] Fraenkel instead examined the economic determinants of the dual state in a less orthodox manner. It was a structuralist perspective still, but less overtly Marxist in conception. Accordingly, "the economic *structure* of the dual state" became "the economic *policy* of the dual state," a semantic change retained in the published book.[103] Here is another example of an omitted section from the same chapter that illustrates the kind of material that Fraenkel chose not to include in the OUP edition:

> In the present world situation, striving for an increase in power is identical with economic nationalism and imperialism. This force always works both externally and internally. Characteristically, force applied internally is considered [...] justified as a means to increase the strength of the group in group relations. The main task became to organize the economic system as [an] instrument for the increase and preservation of the power of the state and of the groups in which this power and this aspiration for greater power had been invested and centralized.[104]

The shift in tone and perspective—which, to be sure, was one of substance, not cosmetics—resulted in a nuanced analysis of economic developments in interwar Germany that was twice as long as it had been in the *Urdoppelstaat*. It was a sign of Fraenkel's analytical advancement, very likely in response to the conversations and exchanges he was having in the United States, especially in Chicago. In the preface to the 1941 typescript and book, for example, Fraenkel acknowledged Gerhard Meyer of the University of Chicago for having provided him with an "unpublished manuscript on the economic system of the Third Reich," a recognition that is worded even more profusely in the published acknowledgements.[105] It stands to reason that Fraenkel tempered his socialist zeal as a result of both the geographical and intellectual distance that he had put between himself and the country that persecuted him.

But there is another plausible explanation for the switch from "Economics of the Dual State" to "The Economic Background of the Dual State" as the title for Chapter 2 in Part III. The clue lays in an excised opening paragraph that was marked for deletion in the typescript. It reads as follows: "The following sketchy remarks do not pretend to provide final answers. Rather they are intende[d] to give a perspective to our chief results by way of presenting a series of questions and preliminary answers."[106] It was a weak opening paragraph and OUP's copy editor would have eventually got rid of the signposting. But it is equally plausible to assume that Fraenkel changed the chapter title because of the caveats expressed in the deleted opening sentences. If he indeed thought of his analysis as only tentative ("sketchy remarks;" "preliminary answers"), a punchy title like "The Economics of the Dual State" would have raised expectations on the part of his readers of analytical depth and breadth that Fraenkel may have been afraid of not meeting. A more prosaic chapter title like "The Economic Background of the Dual State," on the other hand, has the opposite effect: it reduces expectations.

In addition to the typescript of *The Dual State*, the NYPL holdings about Fraenkel include a folder of correspondence between him and David Riesman, Secretary of the American Committee for the Guidance of Professional Personnel (ACGPP), discussing the various placements that the committee arranged for Fraenkel. The Committee helped to relocate thirty-six German émigré scholars.[107] Aside from Riesman, who taught at Buffalo Law School at the time and subsequently at Harvard Law School, its selection panel included Carl J. Friedrich of the Department of Government at Harvard. Friedrich read the English manuscript of *The Dual State* in draft form and is also cited as a source for Fraenkel's discussion of the historical transformation of the separation-of-powers doctrine.[108]

Fraenkel appears to have submitted the typescript to the ACGPP in support of his fellowship application. In a cover letter to Riesman, dated November 17, 1939, that accompanied the submission, Fraenkel noted that the enclosed version was "revised by the translator once again," that is, presumably by Shils, Löwenstein, or Knorr, or a combination of those members of the translation team.[109] In the same letter, Fraenkel expressed regret for not being able to send the pre-print version: "Unfortunately I did not get the proofs."[110] The return address on the cover letter is 5723 Kimbark Avenue, Chicago, IL, which indicates that the bulk of the work involved in turning the *Urdoppelstaat* into *The Dual State* took place at the University of Chicago. This means that Fraenkel's ethnography of law, one of the most important books on Nazi dictatorship—and one of the most profound analyses of authoritarian rule anywhere—was finished while the author was in law school.[111]

7

"A Rational Core within an Irrational Shell": An Institutional Theory of Dictatorship

> Something is alive [...] only to the extent that
> it contains contradiction within itself [...]. [...]
> If [...] a concrete existent were not capable of [...]
> harboring contradiction within it,
> it would not be a living unity as such, [...]
> and in contradiction it would founder
> and sink to the ground.
>
> Georg Wilhelm Friedrich Hegel[1]

Fraenkel's principal argument in *The Dual State* had three parts.[2] The first part comprised several counterintuitive propositions about the nature of the institutional design of the Nazi political order. Fraenkel argued that this structure consisted of two interacting states: a prerogative and a normative state. The second part of his argument revolved around the institutional effects of this bifurcated state. Fraenkel claimed that it facilitated not only violent domination but *also* allowed for an orderly transition to and consolidation of authoritarian rule, notably by reducing incentives for exit from the Nazi polity on the part of so-called constructive forces, that is, societal groups and sectors, such as big business, that did not constitute or harbor real or imagined enemies of state. The third part of Fraenkel's argument concerned the institutional origins of the dual state. He was convinced that "[t]he root of the evil" had to be sought in the "community ideology" and "militant capitalism" that were holding sway in Nazi Germany.[3] I will elaborate each of these arguments in turn.

RIFLES AND RULES

With *The Dual State*, Fraenkel intervened into an ongoing debate about the nature of the Nazi state—and one that is continuing to this day.[4] It was his mission to correct what he believed were major misconceptions in this debate. He highlighted the most serious of these misconceptions in his Introduction to the 1941 edition of *The Dual State*: "A superficial view of the German dictatorship might be impressed either by its arbitrariness or by its efficiency based on order. It is the thesis of this book that the National-Socialist dictatorship is characterized by a combination of these two elements."[5] Fraenkel's lasting contribution to the debate was the ideal typical construction of the dual state as a conceptual variable.[6] The concept of the dual state—and the theoretical and empirical arguments that Fraenkel constructed around it—is, at first glance, simple and straightforward. In his preface to the 1974 German edition, Fraenkel explained how it came about: "Based on the insights into the functioning of the Hitler regime that I gleaned from my legal practice, I believed to have found a key to understanding the National Socialist system of rule ('*der nationalsozialistischen Herrschaftsordnung*') in the duality or concurrent existence ('*Nebeneinander*') of a 'normative state' ('*Normenstaat*') that generally respects its own laws, and a 'prerogative state' ('*Maßnahmenstaat*') that violates the very same laws."[7]

Fraenkel maintained that the early Nazi state was not a unitary state—as most of his contemporaries assumed—but, rather, two "simultaneous states."[8] Although a "line of division" kept these institutional loci apart, he argued that they were simultaneously tied to one another and "in constant friction."[9] As we have seen, he invented the memorable neologism of the "dual state" to name this mutually constitutive relationship between the prerogative and normative halves of the state.[10] It has been remarked, rather unkindly, that "the most accomplished" ("*das Gelungenste*") aspect of *The Dual State* was its title.[11] Spun more positively, we can think of the term as analytical shorthand ("*eine Art Chiffre*") for the institutional logic of a particular *kind* of rule, Nazi and otherwise.[12] Fraenkel made sense of this logic, which he thought of as dynamic, by adopting a perspective from methodological structuralism (as opposed to methodological individualism).

The hallmark of the prerogative state is arbitrary rule. Fraenkel argued that the phenomenon of the prerogative state derived from the institution of martial law and suggested that we think of it as "a continuous siege."[13] In the case of Nazi Germany, Fraenkel traced the rise of the prerogative state back, among other things, to the excessive use in the pre-Nazi years of Article 48 of the Weimar Constitution, which paved the way for presidential dictatorship in the Weimar Republic, and "totalitarian" dictatorship thereafter.[14] As a "governmental system," he wrote, the prerogative state exercised "unlimited arbitrariness and violence unchecked by any legal guarantees."[15] Its acts, or "measures" ("*Maßnahmen*") as Fraenkel called them, are self-legitimating, and thus self-enforcing: "The political sphere in the Third Reich is governed neither by objective nor by subjective law, neither by legal guarantees nor jurisdictional qualifications."[16] In other words, the prerogative state, as an idea, amounts to institutionalized lawlessness. The absence of boundaries is the essence of its nature. The prerogative state is what rulers make of it. To illustrate the pervasiveness of the phenomenon in Nazi Germany, Fraenkel analyzed briefly (and rather superficially) several agents of the prerogative state, what he called "instruments," and some of their practices. He singled out as key agents of the prerogative state the Gestapo (Secret State Police) and the NSDAP.[17] Notable practices, which Fraenkel exemplified with ample references to Nazi case law, ranged from the abolition of constitutional restraints to the abolition of restraints on the powers of the police, and from the abolition of judicial review to the negation of formal rationality.[18] In his argument, "[n]o sphere of social or economic life is immune from the inroads of the Prerogative State."[19]

Horst Dreier recently dissected what he termed the "phenomenology of the prerogative state."[20] He has introduced greater clarity into a conceptual analysis that in *The Dual State* occasionally left something to be desired. To sharpen the contours of the prerogative state as a conceptual variable, Dreier distinguished three different manifestations of the formally irrational half of the dual state. I base the following discussion on Dreier's useful analysis but elaborate on his observations and substitute my own categories for his. I differentiate three ideal types: (1) the prerogative state as a transgressive force; (2) the prerogative state as a restrictive force; and (3) the prerogative state as a constitutive force. What I call the prerogative state as a *transgressive force* refers to instances in which this boundless half of the dual state either undermines or overturns the operation or activities of the normative state. Fraenkel wrote passionately about this peculiar logic of domination in his 1937 article on the dual state: "Germany is a country in which thousands can be incarcerated for years without being convicted in a court of law, possessions can be seized without judicial authorization, and lives can be destroyed without recourse to law."[21]

The second subtype—the prerogative state as a *restrictive force*—by contrast, operates less overtly and in a less violent fashion. This variant of the prerogative state is less outcome-oriented, though as arbitrary in its raison d'état. Its operational logic revolves around long-term interventions into the affairs of the *Volk*. What Dreier, on whose discussion I draw, has in mind are instances in which agents and organizations of the Nazi state, especially from its normative half, respond with anticipatory obedience (what Germans call *vorauseilendem Gehorsam*) to presumed imperatives of what Carl Schmitt in the late 1920s had famously theorized as "the political."[22] Consider the following example: ordinary courts' voluntary abdication of their adjudicative power. Fraenkel focused especially on a case that the *Kammergericht*, the regional court of appeal for Prussia, had decided on May 31, 1935.[23] The judgment in the case concerned the legality of the executive decree (*Durchführungsverordnung*) required to implement in Prussia the notorious Decree of the Reich President for the Protection of *Volk* and State (*Verordnung des Reichspräsidenten zum Schutz von Volk und Staat*) of March 28, 1933. Fraenkel could not understand why the *Kammergericht* thought it necessary, at this very early stage of Nazi dictatorship, to rule in its judgment that the so-called Reichstag Fire Decree ("*Reichstagsbrandverordnung*"), as the national decree came to be known, "removes all federal and state restraints on the power of the police to whatever extent is required for the execution of the aims promulgated in the decree."[24] In addition to issuing a blank check to the powers at the helm of the prerogative state, the judges placed an arbitrary and immovable limitation on judicial review: "The question of appropriateness and necessity is not subject to appeal."[25] Fraenkel noted that other courts in the country were considerably more circumspect in their adoption of what he referred to as "[t]he constitutional charter of the Third Reich."[26]

The case before the *Kammergericht* was a flagrant example of what Dreier has discussed for the judiciary under the moniker of "self restriction" ("*Selbstrestriktion*," which he distinguishes from "restriction by another," or "*Fremdrestriktion*").[27] The first behavioral mode refers to judicial practices, interpretive or otherwise, that result in voluntary self-binding. Writes Dreier: "The possibility of judicial review gives way to judicial non-review."[28] By reducing from within the authority and jurisdiction of the judiciary, the power and reach of the prerogative state are also enhanced. Exemplary of the normative state's restriction from without, "by another," is a case concerning the institution of the Gestapo. On February 10, 1936, the Nazi regime passed the Law Concerning the Gestapo (*Gesetz über die Geheime Staatspolizei*). This important piece of legislation vastly restricted the powers of administrative review, de jure shielding the Gestapo from almost any form of judicial oversight. Prussia's regional court of appeal for administrative matters (*Oberverwaltungericht*) weighed in on the matter in a case concerning the legality of the expulsion of a missionary from a certain district in

Germany. The facts of the case need not concern us here.[29] What matters is that Prussia's highest administrative court seized the occasion of the particular, localized dispute to pronounce—on its own accord—on the *general* conditions under which Gestapo orders were subject to judicial review.[30] The panel held that very few such conditions existed. The organization of the prerogative state, it ruled, would *only* be subject to review in the event that acts of ordinary police (acting as auxiliary forces for the Nazi Secret Police) went above and beyond the orders they received from the Gestapo. Fraenkel described the institutional effect: "The significance of the decision cited above lies in the acknowledgment of the Gestapo's power to transfer entire spheres of life from the jurisdiction of the Normative State to the Prerogative State."[31] The Berlin proceeding highlights the power of the prerogative state as a restrictive force.

The prerogative state as a *constitutive force* represents the third and final subtype. Although related to the subtype just discussed, here the emphasis is on the manner in which the prerogative state, through its manifest facticity, reconstitutes the remnants of the normative state. The institution of the so-called *Sondergerichte* come to mind as an example, which, though located firmly inside the prerogative state, also had a bearing on Germany's culture of legality more generally.[32] The work of legal institutions in one half of the dual state (for example, the *Sondergerichte* in the prerogative state), Fraenkel believed, invariably rub off on the operation of legal institutions in the other half. We have since learned from the anthropology of law that Fraenkel was right to assume that legal mores (and the cultures to which they combine) do not exist in a vacuum, and, that they, like institutions and organizations, are subject to transformations and deformations in response to external stimuli.[33]

Having said that, not all legal institutions subsumed under the third subtype of the prerogative state were extra-judicial. In many cases the locus of (and scope for) action resided in the normative state itself. Numerous legal proceedings that Fraenkel examined in *The Dual State* drew attention to instances of self-immolation by the normative state. The difference with the second, just discussed subtype lies in the greater scope for discretion that was usually available to legal agents, notably judges, in these cases. The fact that lower-ranking courts in the Nazi judicial system, at least in the early years of dictatorship, regularly came to conclusions that differed in fundamental ways from those of courts of appeal demonstrates that such discretionary scope did indeed exist. This scope was not just a figment of Fraenkel's imagination, a logically conceivable but empirically unverifiable assumption of his theoretical model. Indeed, in these types of cases, court findings, decisions, and judgments often embodied the ethos of the surviving remnants of the *Rechtsstaat*.[34]

Fraenkel gave an example from the jurisprudence of Munich's regional court of appeal (*Oberlandesgericht*) to substantiate his contention that the really existing scope for discretion was often instrumentalized for the purpose of expanding the scope of the prerogative state—an example of what Otto Kirchheimer after the war came to refer to as "political justice," that is, "the utilization of judicial proceedings for political ends."[35]

The proceeding in question concerned the suspension of the principle of *ne bis in idem*, known as the prohibition of double jeopardy in the common law. It revolved around a defendant who had been convicted of (and already served his sentence for) an act of high treason, namely the distribution of illegal propaganda. When it was subsequently discovered that the defendant's conduct had been graver than previously thought, the judges of Munich's *Oberlandesgericht* convicted him a second time, and for the same underlying conduct, thus violating the principle of *ne bis in idem*.[36] Fraenkel used the example to illustrate the expanding reach of the prerogative state, its persistent advances into the province of the normative state. The example slots neatly into the third of the above subtypes—the prerogative state as a constitutive force—because the Bavarian court was neither coerced nor otherwise compelled to rule in the case the way it did. Rather, the judges, as nominal representatives of the normative state, had discretion in reaching their judgment. They used this discretion to further debase the legal foundations of the remnants of the normative state, even introducing from the bench a novel principle of law: "In serious cases of high treason," they held, "an adequate sentence has to be imposed in all circumstances regardless of all legal principles! The protection of state and people is more important than the adherence to formalistic rules of procedure which are senseless if applied without exception."[37] By internalizing the ethos of the prerogative state, the court, according to Fraenkel, "degraded its status to that of an instrument of the Prerogative State."[38] So much for the workings of the prerogative state, what Fraenkel once called the dual state's "irrational shell."[39]

I now turn to the "rational core" that he thought was contained within that irrational shell—the normative state.[40] Fraenkel grounded the concept of the dual state solidly in the theoretical scholarship of his time, drawing extensively on writings in philosophy, law, economics, and religion.[41] He also traced in some detail the historical roots of the dual state in Prussia, from the establishment of absolute monarchy to the prototype of the German *Rechtsstaat*. In thinking about the normative state, Fraenkel was heavily influenced by the history of the authoritarian regime of Frederick the Great, whose enlightened despotism laid the intellectual foundations for the more benign half, the institutional structure that Fraenkel saw at work in the Third Reich.[42] Fraenkel was particularly taken with the Prussian *Allgemeine Landrecht*, which, under the influence of Enlightenment precepts, fundamentally recast the nature and purpose of police powers.[43] Revolutionary for its time, this pre-German code of law drastically curtailed the powers of the police. Drawing on doctrines of natural law, the Prussian monarch placed far-reaching and unprecedented limits on his own erstwhile prerogative state.[44]

But it is important not to misconstrue Fraenkel's idea of the normative state. To be sure, the normative state is *not* akin to a rule-of-law state, what Germans call a *Rechtsstaat*.[45] Fraenkel distinguished very carefully between the concept of the rule-of-law state and that of the dual state. He pointed to the institution of extraordinary courts to drive home the conceptual difference: "The term Special Court [*Sondergericht* in German] sums up the difference between the Rule of Law State (*Rechtsstaat*) and the Dual State: the Rule of Law [State] refers political crimes to a *special* court despite the fact that they are questions of law; the Dual State refers political crimes to a special *court*, despite the fact that they are *political* questions."[46] In other words, the normative state is only ever as strong as the prerogative state permits it to be. In the case of the *Sondergerichte*, the prerogative state turned law from a *regulatory device* that reduced uncertainty into a *destructive force* that annihilated difference. As Nikolaus Wachsmann has shown, "the special courts were hailed as weapons to 'render harmless', 'eradicate' and 'exterminate' the political enemy."[47] As instruments of the prerogative state, the example of the *Sondergerichte* highlights the unknowable but really existing limits of the normative state. In Fraenkel's conception, the existence of these limits was a defining attribute of the dual state, a necessary condition for its existence. Here is a choice formulation that I quoted in a different context above: "The Normative State is a necessary complement to the Prerogative State and can be understood only in that light. Since the Prerogative and Normative States constitute an interdependent whole, consideration of the Normative State alone is not permissible."[48]

Fraenkel was at pains to establish this theoretical premise. In his argument, the normative state was at the beck and call of the prerogative state, so to speak. Law may have governed its practice, but it neither constituted nor legitimated it. Fraenkel put it concisely elsewhere in his book: "[S]ince the jurisdiction of the Prerogative State is not legally defined, there is no legal guarantee of the stability of the Normative State. The existence of the Normative State is not dependent on law. It depends on the complete permeation of the state by National-Socialist attitudes and ideas."[49] Here is Fraenkel once more, this time illustrating his theoretical argument with reference to one of the foundational principles of law-governed rule: "The complete abolition of the inviolability of law is the chief characteristic of the Prerogative State. [...] If inviolability within the sphere of the Normative State exists only under certain conditions, then it does not hold true as a principle, and conditional inviolability is necessarily the opposite of inviolability."[50] Here is the rub: Fraenkel distinguished between what we might call law-in-principle and law-in-practice. Just because the principles of the *Rechtsstaat* or the rule-of-law state are not sacrosanct in a given polity, he did not think it followed that agents could not behave *as if* they were; that they could not reach legal decisions under the influence of an imaginary rule of law.

After all, as he pointed out early on in *The Dual State*, "a nation of 80 million people can be controlled by a plan only if certain definite rules exist and are enforced according to which the relations between the state and its members, as well as the relations between the citizens themselves, are regulated."[51] Even precarious law can enable and constrain the behavior of agents. Unstable rules are generally less efficient than stable rules, but they are nonetheless useful, even in dictatorships. Such was Fraenkel's belief, bolstered by his unshakable faith in the power of procedure. As he once put it, "The significance of procedural questions is by no means inferior to those of substantive law."[52]

It is essential to be clear about the nature and purpose of Fraenkel's argument, to grasp fully what he wrote—and what he did not. Because those who invoke *The Dual State* sometimes do so very selectively, even in a manner that outright contradicts Fraenkel's theory of dictatorship.[53] Having laid out Fraenkel's conceptions of the two halves of his dual-state concept, what did he have to say about their interrelationship? What, exactly, is the logic of the hybrid regime that they co-constitute? The combination of the two notions—the prerogative state and the normative state—in one concept sets up a dynamic tension between these elements. The dual state has built into it what Reinhard Bendix termed "conflicting imperatives."[54] The normative state and the prerogative state, though complementary, also stand in tension with one another. The foundational relationship between the halves of the dual state—from which all dynamic interactions between them derive—can be stated thus: "the presumption of jurisdiction rests with the Normative State. The jurisdiction over jurisdiction rests with the Prerogative State."[55]

It was Emil Lederer who first inspired Fraenkel to embrace the idea of institutional hybridity. In 1915, Lederer had described the imperial state of Wilhelmine Germany as a two-pronged state. Fraenkel credited Lederer as being the first person to "depict the co-existence of the Normative State and the Prerogative State."[56] But the metaphor of a Janus-faced or dual-natured state predates even Lederer's conceptualization, as we saw in Chapter 4. In fact, it was Georg Jellinek who first theorized an institutional binary at the heart of the concept of the state, in his *Allgemeine Staatslehre* at the turn of the twentieth century.[57]

It bears emphasizing that in Fraenkel's argument, the distinction between the prerogative and normative halves of the dual state is not just a matter of degree, but of kind. For him the institutional differentiation was of a "qualitative" nature.[58] At the same time, he regarded the phenomenon of the dual state in Nazi Germany as anything but static. For Fraenkel it was durable for the time being because it represented a stable equilibrium. But he did not think of it as a permanent state of affairs. In the Introduction to the 1941 edition of *The Dual State*, Fraenkel left no doubt that he believed in the changing character of the dual state:

> It may be argued, both by those who are sympathetic with and by those who are opposed to National-Socialism, that the problem of the Dual State has no fundamental or permanent significance, that it is merely a transitory phenomenon. To those who think the Prerogative state transitory we point to the records of judicial proceedings in the Third Reich, which show that it is gaining rather than losing importance.[59]

This point is key because it is a response to those who erroneously claim that Fraenkel set out to capture the defining attributes of the Nazi state *as such*, that is, for the duration of its existence. Fraenkel had no such ambition. His was never going to be more than a snapshot of a state-in-formation—albeit one taken with enormous skill and from an exceptional vantage point.

Fraenkel twice illustrated the interactions between the prerogative state and the normative state with reference to generalized examples drawn from the universe of Nazi concentration camps. The first time, Fraenkel used the concentration camp setting to exemplify how favorable interventions by the normative state can be immediately undermined by the prerogative state: "The co-existence of legal and arbitrary actions," he wrote, is "most impressively demonstrated by the confinement in concentration camps of persons who have been acquitted by the courts."[60] The second example helped Fraenkel to illustrate the converse interaction between the two "simultaneous states": how a victim of the prerogative state could nonetheless benefit from the normative state. As Fraenkel wrote in his 1937 article on the dual-state concept: "[This is] a country in which it is possible that a concentration camp inmate can successfully file his tax complaints ('*Steuerbeschwerden*'). The prerogative state incarcerated him, the technical, normative state reviews his tax complaint as if nothing had happened, as if we all still lived in a *Rechtsstaat*."[61]

Looking back on the dual state's schizophrenic institutional design and its implications for everyday life many years later, Fraenkel declared that "[i]n the Third Reich, law did not determine what was 'political,' but politics determined what was legal."[62] Apropos of Fraenkel's implicit reference to Carl Schmitt—with whose concept of the political Fraenkel took issue repeatedly in *The Dual State*—another way of describing the essence of the dual state is to say that the prerogative state was the institutional embodiment of decisionism, the normative state the institutional expression of legalism.

STATE EFFECTS

The institutional effects of the dual state, as theorized by Fraenkel, were considerable and far-reaching. Some of these effects were direct, others indirect; some were of a short-term nature, others materialized over the long run. Most obviously, the institutionalized arbitrariness of the prerogative state depleted—and destroyed—an inordinate number of lives, Jewish and otherwise.[63] But Fraenkel was more concerned with the less obvious and hidden institutional effects of this state, for as he wrote, "we are not considering cases touching on the Jewish problem. To generalize from the treatment of the Jews [...] would be misleading."[64] For Fraenkel, *their* case was straightforward: "Once Jews had been eliminated from the economic life, it was possible to deprive them of all legal protection without adversely affecting the economic system," which is why the onset of more virulent forms of antisemitism "forced the Jews beyond the outer limits of the Normative State."[65]

Fraenkel had learned from personal experience that the dual state in the early years of Nazi dictatorship facilitated not only violent domination but also ensured an orderly transition to and consolidation of authoritarian rule, notably by reducing incentives for exit from the Nazi polity on the part of "constructive forces" in the Nazi universe, by which the Nazi jurist Werner Best, who coined the phrase, meant societal groups and sectors, such as big business, that did not constitute or harbor so-called enemies of state. Among the most notable institutional effects of the dual state Fraenkel counted (1) that the Nazis upheld "the institution of private property in general and of private ownership in the means of production [...] in principle and in fact;" and (2) that "income from private property is now, on the whole much safer than it was before."[66]

Fraenkel thought it especially remarkable that "[t]he principle of private ownership was upheld *even* for businesses towards which the National-Socialist program had shown some degree of antipathy, e.g., the department stores and banks."[67] Notwithstanding his comprehensive catalogue of consequential changes that Nazi authorities had made to the structure of the country's economic system and the members of its economic society—including the creation and proliferation of cartels and other monopolies; the steep increase in the rate of public investment financed by credit expansion; the buildout of public investment at the expense of private investment—Fraenkel was sufficiently detached analytically to appreciate that a considerable number of entrepreneurs, despite Nazi interference with the rules of the economic game, "even now [...] enjoy at least a comparative advantage."[68]

It was Fraenkel's great achievement—and, I suspect, one of the principal reasons for *The Dual State*'s negligible reception during the Cold War years—to have countered, in the substantive parts of his analysis, the scholarly trend of treating the German polity as if it were a totalitarian black box, to have resisted the moral urge to depict the emergent racial order as a monolithic garrison state that emerged fully formed.[69] What my analysis of Fraenkel's theory of dictatorship hopefully shows is that he reasoned and wrote like the analytically eclectic *social scientist* that he was.[70] He may have started out as a practicing lawyer, become a public intellectual, and briefly agitated as a social activist, but by the time he submitted his book manuscript to OUP's New York office, sometime in the summer or fall of 1940, Fraenkel was a different man. He was working with a greater degree of intellectual rigor: he was more analytically astute, theoretically sophisticated, and empirically innovative than he had ever been before—and, according to some, than he ever was again. *The Dual State* is testament to Fraenkel's intellectual feat, drafted on a dark continent in the middle of the twentieth century. What he brought to the shores of America was an intellectual diamond in the rough. Out of danger, he resized it, polished it. Shils and colleagues helped him make it sparkle. OUP offered it up in the marketplace of ideas, where demand, for a short while at least, was considerable.

William Scheuerman has remarked that he considers Fraenkel's pre-1945 writings "intellectually more creative and politically more provocative than his writings from the 1950s and 1960s. Although Fraenkel's later writings are hardly uninteresting, I suspect that we can learn a great deal more from those pieces written in the shadows of the 'state of emergency' conditions of Weimar and Nazi Germany than from Fraenkel's defensive and occasionally somewhat staid essays on liberal democracy from the Cold War period."[71] Like Scheuerman, I, too, find Fraenkel's pre-war writings more daring and compelling than his postwar oeuvre (which is, to be sure, nonetheless very impressive). And out of all of Fraenkel's pre-war writings, none was more creative than *The Dual State*. Fraenkel never bested that book's depth of insight and its breadth of knowledge, both of which he so painstakingly brought to bear on the subject of his life.[72]

To his lasting credit, Fraenkel, unlike other observers at the time, did not assume that the institutional logic of Nazi dictatorship did or would operate seamlessly and unchanged for the entirety of the Third Reich.[73] Fraenkel insisted "that the Third Reich cannot be interpreted as a 'totalitarian state' in an uncritical way."[74] Its changing character had to be taken as a given. Fraenkel told his readers that he "avoided using the term 'totalitarian state' because of its complex connotations."[75] This observation is related to the topic at hand—the institutional effects of the dual state, to which I now return.

Earlier I distinguished three subtypes of the prerogative state, one of which was the prerogative state as a constitutive force. Its operation sheds light on a causal mechanism that produced a number of institutional effects. I call this causal mechanism *institutional mimicking*. Fraenkel explained how it works: "Since the jurisdiction of the organs of the Prerogative State is unlimited, a certain tendency exists among the agencies of the Normative State to imitate this example and to enlarge the scope of their own discretion. Furthermore, since the Prerogative State has completely stifled all public opinion, resistance against such an encroachment was decisively weakened."[76] If we believe Fraenkel, one of the most significant institutional effects of the dual state in Nazi Germany was the homogenization of the institutions of rule—and of expectations about their rule. Channeling A. V. Dicey, Fraenkel argued that "the mere existence of governmental arbitrariness, as embodied in the Prerogative State, has dulled the sense of justice to such a degree that the existence of an agency with limited jurisdiction is considered as a legal institution even though the government exercised enormous discretionary power."[77]

A more indirect effect, a consequence of the uneven balance of power between the prerogative and normative halves of the Nazi state—which, as we have seen, is a defining, structural feature of the dual state—was the substitution of efficiency for liberty as raison d'état. "In National-Socialist Germany," Fraenkel observed, "the 'gospel of efficiency' has been substituted for the worship of liberty."[78] A concomitant effect of this substitution was the retention and continued maintenance (with a few notable exceptions to be discussed below) of the existing economic order. As the guardian of the economy, the normative state, in spite of its co-dependent relationship with the violent and overzealous prerogative state, managed to restore a sense of institutional normalcy and predictability in economic affairs, at least for a while. According to Fraenkel, "[i]n spite of the existing legal possibilities for intervention by the Prerogative State where and whenever it desires, the legal foundations of the capitalistic economic order have been maintained."[79] Drawing on an examination of the extant case law at the time, Fraenkel found that "[t]he legal institutions essential to private capitalism [...] still exist in Germany."[80] To substantiate his finding, he presented empirical evidence in the form of jurisprudence pertaining to freedom of enterprise, the sanctity of contracts, property rights, copyright, and the regulation of unfair competition, among others.[81]

Fraenkel's analysis of institutional effects of the Nazi dual state, notably its normative half, was most comprehensive for the economic realm. Incidentally, this is also the realm most relevant to Fraenkel's third and final argument. It was a response to a deceptively simple question: whence the dual state?

IMAGINED STATES

Part III, the final part of *The Dual State*, contains one of the most controversial chapters of the entire book—Chapter 2. There, Fraenkel attempted to make sense of the economic origins of Nazi dictatorship. Contrary to the *Urdoppelstaat*, where he possessed the courage of his convictions and stated his functionalist argument boldly, he introduced his revised position more gingerly in the opening pages of the 1941 book:

> We shall inquire whether the legal situation characterized as the Dual State is not the necessary consequence of a certain stage of crisis for the directing elements of capitalistic society. Perhaps it can be shown that they have lost confidence in rationality and have taken refuge in irrationality, at a time when it would seem that rationality is needed more than ever as a regulatory force within the capitalistic structure.[82]

This tentative introduction bespeaks Fraenkel's reservations about the materialist view of history. These reservations deepened in exile. As I explained above, Fraenkel substantially revised Part III, Chapter 2 as he moved from *Urdoppelstaat* to *The Dual State*.[83] Here is his argument in a nutshell: Fraenkel believed that the fundamental nature of Germany's economic order had been fundamentally altered in the transition from quasi-democracy to dictatorship. In his argument, the "organized private capitalism" of the Weimar era had been replaced in Nazi Germany with what he called "quasi-monopolistic capitalism."[84] It all started with the Great Depression, when "the power of the government in the economic sphere sharply increased."[85] The democratic state and its institutions behaved like "doctors at the sick-bed of capitalism," Fraenkel quoted a trade unionist as saying.[86] Extensive government interventions propped up ailing or failing economic sectors, notably banking and the steel industry. "The Reich," Fraenkel wrote, "extended its regulatory power to almost all aspects of economic activity, including wage levels."[87] Many of Fraenkel's contemporaries believed (as do economists and economic historians today) that state-led economic interventionism was necessary not least because, as Richard Overy has shown, in 1932, the year preceding the Nazi ascent of power, German business activity had been in a "disastrous trough."[88] This institutional transformation, however, had path-dependent consequences for the Nazi state, at least according to Fraenkel: "In many aspects, the economic policy of the Dual State seems a mere continuation, a somewhat more developed phase, of the 'organized capitalism' of the Weimar period."[89] Such was the opening salvo of Fraenkel's analysis. He supported his thesis about institutional and substantive continuities in the economic realm across two radically different political regimes with empirical evidence from various sectors of the economy.

But Chapter III, Part 2 is also about the origins of the dual state because it advances a theoretical argument as to why an authoritarian regime—such as the Nazi dictatorship—would have an interest in institutional self-binding. For this is precisely what, according to Fraenkel, transpired in the early 1930s:

> There still exist: capitalistic enterprises, markets in which these enterprises sell and buy, markets for property titles, private credit transactions and all kinds of accompanying disputes over claims and obligations. The system of private economic activities is surrounded, supported and limited by a vastly increased public bureaucracy which acts partly on the basis of generally clear, circumscribed laws and partly on the basis of more or less wide discretionary powers with the reservation that each matter may be regulated arbitrarily.[90]

Fraenkel showed that *despite* the Nazification of economic norms and institutions, and *despite* the comprehensive domination or violent destruction of other spheres of social life, a most remarkable situation existed in early Nazi Germany in which the supposedly constructive forces continued to enjoy the protection of the normative state, of these remnants of the *Rechtsstaat*. But what was "the precise function of the Normative State and what [were] the functions of the Prerogative State in the economic sphere?"[91]

In the governance of the economy, unlike in any other sphere of Nazi life, the prerogative state took a backseat to the normative state. Fraenkel hypothesized as follows: "If our analysis of the relations between the world of business and the Normative State is correct, then it follows, that the Prerogative State cannot be a direct and positively controlling power, but rather a limiting and indirectly supporting power."[92] But the prerogative state had roles to play nonetheless: *inter alia*, it protected economic life from political disturbances, by deterring or crushing protests and demonstrations; it held in check the underground trade union movement, thus suppressing open class struggle; and it enforced—through either the threat or application of violence—the more restrictive legal norms devised in the normative state for the regulation of the economy.[93] The normative state played a considerably larger role than the prerogative state in the economic reconstruction and development of Germany under the Nazi dictatorship. I have already discussed many of its functions in the foregoing analysis. According to the causal logic of Fraenkel's argument, the normative state administers and adjudicates the rules of the game for the participation of producers and consumers in the marketplace. It maintains "the legal frame-work [*sic*] for private property, market activities of the individual business units, all other kinds of contractual relations, and for the regulations of the control relations between government and business. Even if the rules of the game are changed by the lawmaker, some are indispensable in order to secure a minimum of predictability of the probable consequences of given economic decisions."[94] This will be the case, Fraenkel argued, whenever "the necessity of decentralization of certain functions in any large-scale society with advanced technology" arises.[95] It is for this reason that Fraenkel believed that "the field of economics remains the most important domain of the qualified 'Rule of Law' in present-day Germany."[96]

A seminal theoretical analysis of the institutional determinants of economic activity, with which Fraenkel's analysis of the normative state in Part III, Chapter 2 of *The Dual State* shares several traits is Douglass North's *Institutions, Institutional Change and Economic Performance*.[97] Consider, for example, the similarity between the just quoted passage from *The Dual State* with this well-known and oft-cited argument from North's 1990 book: "Institutions are the rules of the game in a society or, more formally, are the humanly devised constraints that shape human interaction."[98] Fraenkel and North, independently, both referred to the institutional framework governing social life as rules of the game. This superficial semblance, but even more so the considerable underlying similarities in the theories (and intellectual concerns) of both scholars, has prompted me to count Fraenkel's approach as one that belongs to what social scientists for more than thirty years have been calling the new institutionalism, an approach that North helped to pioneer. I pointed out in the Introduction that Fraenkel's way of seeing has a great deal in common with what has become known as historical institutionalism, a variant of the new institutionalism that emphasizes how institutions emerge from and are embedded in concrete temporal processes.[99] Given its approach to explanation and understanding, and its sophistication in the successful blending of nomothetic and ideographic reasoning, *The Dual State* deserves to be considered for inclusion in the annals of the historical institutionalism and its canon.

In his analysis of the normative state, in the economic or any other sphere, Fraenkel never proceeded far before reminding readers of the prerogative state's power of "jurisdiction over jurisdiction," that is, that organization's awesome ability to play overlord over the normative state, and, if necessary, to put the latter in its subordinate place in the institutional architecture of the Nazi state. He was convinced that it would be a grave mistake not to take seriously the nature and effects of an institutional structure—such as the dual state—just because its independence had been compromised in the process of its creation, and its members were known to have abused the institutional discretion that a prerogative state may have permitted them to exercise.[100] Scheuerman is correct, and he summarizes the underlying assumption of Fraenkel's theoretical argument pithily: "discretion is not wholesale arbitrariness."[101]

This brings us to the second aspect of Fraenkel's argument about "the economic background of the Dual State," specifically the question of why this institutional remnant of the *Rechtsstaat* survived in Nazi Germany. His answer: German capitalism needed "state aid."[102] Two types of aid were important, Fraenkel explained. I have given names to his types. I call them *violent aid* and *legal aid*. I take *violent aid* to refer to any and all activities by Nazi authorities, regardless of whether these authorities were housed in the normative state or the prerogative state, that were directed toward the elimination, in whatever form, of real or imagined enemies. Fraenkel vaguely wrote of "social enemies" in the context of this type of state aid, but then provided further particulars about exactly *who* German capitalism needed to extirpate "to guarantee its existence."[103] Capitalism's target, according to Fraenkel: "its socialist opponent."[104] The warnings from the 1920s by the harassed trade union movement—which had since been violently defeated by joint action of the normative and prerogative halves of the dual state—about the dire social and economic consequences of unfettered capitalism continued to reverberate in the working class and were also reaching the social-democratically inclined middle classes. Fraenkel reported that prior to the onset of Nazi dictatorship, "[t]he defenders of capitalism in post-[World War I] Germany were unable to convince the masses of the German people that it was the best of all economic systems. Capitalism had no chance in a democratic struggle against proletarian socialism, in whose extirpation its salvation lay."[105] This brings us to the supply—and demand—of violence.

In speaking of violent aid, my use of the adjective "violent" is deliberate, and I use it in a broad sense.[106] I take it to denote physical as well as non-physical violence. I purposely speak of violence in this context in order to draw attention to the frequently destructive consequences of acts (or omissions) perpetrated under the auspices of the dual state that on the surface are classified as being merely "administrative" or "bureaucratic" in nature (and thus supposedly less destructive), but which in reality often are equally devastating, and sometimes even more so. Fraenkel hypothesized that violent entrepreneurs were in demand from the agents of capitalism to defeat agitators on the left. Without the removal of these thorns in capitalism's side, so Fraenkel's argument went, the owners of the means of production would fail to convince the wretched masses of Germany "that 'private benefit is public benefit.' "[107] The prerogative state, in his view, was willing to supply whatever violent entrepreneurs were necessary to placate the concerns of the most valuable members of economic society, and to eventually co-opt them. But there was a twist to the argument.

The provision of state aid did not exhaust itself with the destruction of the "socialist opponent." If we believe Fraenkel, "[c]ontemporary German capitalism" also wanted to be supplied with a new enemy once the old socialist enemy was defeated. It was thus that capitalism was complicit in substituting the Jewish opponent (and others like it, such as purported foreign enemies) for the hurting and soon to be crushed socialist opponent. German capitalism, Fraenkel implied, was indifferent to the identity of its new opponent(s) as long as it would enable the economic sector to "arm itself as a *sine qua non* for its preservation."[108]

By *legal aid*, next, I mean the provision of legal norms and institutions that reduced uncertainty in the marketplace and facilitated the smooth functioning of economic exchange and accumulation (to the extent possible within the limits of Nazi ideology). Or, as Fraenkel put it in *The Dual State*, German capitalism needed state aid "in its role as guarantor of that legal order which is the pre-condition of exact calculability without which capitalist enterprise cannot exist. German capitalism requires for its salvation a dual, not a unitary state, based on arbitrariness in the political sphere and on rational law in the economic sphere. Contemporary German capitalism is dependent on the Dual State for its existence."[109]

Before I proceed, a clarification of terms is in order, terms that I have used throughout this book but whose meaning did not require elaboration until now. Because Fraenkel agreed "with many of the basic presuppositions of Weber's account of modern law," and, even more importantly, accepted "Weber's own normative preference for traditional formalistic legal mechanisms, as well as the verity of Weber's view that the demise

	Rational	**Irrational**
Formal	Formally rational	Formally irrational
Substantive	Substantively rational	Substantively irrational

Figure 7.1 Max Weber's Typology of Law

of legal formalism is likely to undermine legal rationality and security," it is essential that we gain clarity on what, exactly, Weber's contribution to the theory of law actually was.[110] I restrict myself to illuminating Weber's *conceptual* contribution. See Figure 7.1. Because this contribution is not easy to grasp, I offer a summation of Weber's typology of law:

> In general terms, *formal law* is internally legitimate because it is technically generalized and consistent, and *substantive law* is driven by extralegal motivations; and whereas *rational law* is controlled by the intellect, *irrational law* is governed by emotion.[111]

Weber, in other words, used two attributes (resulting in two separate binaries) to construct his ideal types. The first attribute produces a distinction between *form* and *substance*, resulting in the binary formal law/substantive law. The second attribute Weber used to construct a distinction between *rationality* and *emotion*, leading to the binary rational law/irrational law. The cross-tabulation of these attributes and binaries yields Weber's four ideal types of law:

> Law is *formally irrational* [...] when the adjudication of law is inspired by ordeals, oracles, or other prophetic revelations. The rigor with which these methods are applied may, however, exhibit formalism, and thus irrational law may nevertheless be formal. Law is *substantively irrational* [...] when enforcement officials make arbitrary decisions from case to case without recourse to general rules. The result of personal discretion, whether informed by political, moral, or other concerns, is unpredictable law. Weber chiefly used the example of qadi justice (*Kadijustiz*) to illustrate the point. [...] Law is *substantively rational* [...] when it is driven by, or the vehicle of, an extralegal moral, religious, or political ideology. Islamic law therefore qualifies as substantively rational, as it is infused with commands of the prophet Mohammed. [...] Law is *formally rational* [...], finally, when it forms a gapless system of abstract rules. For law to be formally rational it is necessary [according to Max Weber] that in "both substantive and procedural matters, only unambiguous general characteristics of the facts of the case are

> taken into account." Legal decisions in this type result from the application of a general rule of law—which is comprised of abstract legal concepts—to the particular facts of a case. Formally rational law, thus defined, explains the particular by recourse to the general in abstract form.[112]

Weber's preference for formally rational law over substantively rational law was also Fraenkel's. In many respects, the kinds of legal norms and institutions that Fraenkel attributed to the normative state represented formally rational law, as defined by Weber. Legal action that originated in, or emanated from, the prerogative state (a case in point are the *Sondergerichte*) would, in virtually all cases, have been both formally irrational as well as substantively irrational. See Figure 7.1 above.

In order to make sense of the role of rationalities in the *economic* sphere, Fraenkel turned to Karl Mannheim, the Hungarian-born sociologist who found refuge from the Nazi dictatorship at the LSE.[113] Mannheim's terminology is similar to Weber's but sufficiently different to warrant a brief account. Throughout *The Dual State*, Fraenkel wrote of "substantial rationality" (following Mannheim). According to Mannheim, "substantial rationality" in life and economics referred to action or thought "which reveals intelligent insight into the inter-relations of events in a given situation [. . .] whereas everything else which is either false or not an act of thought at all (for example drives, impulses, wishes, and feelings, both conscious and unconscious) will be called 'substantially irrational' "[114] Mannheim's concept of "functional rationality," next, referred to the calculability of social action. Social action became calculable, he theorized, "when viewed from the standpoint of an observer or a third person seeking to adjust himself to it."[115] Mannheim understood by "functional rationality" what is also known as instrumental rationality or means-ends rationality. Fraenkel applied the ideas of *both* Weber and Mannheim to the law and economics of Nazi dictatorship. What did he find?

William Scheuerman's account of the Fraenkel-Mannheim connection is helpful here. He posits, in *Mannheimian* terms, that "[t]he functional rationality of capitalist enterprise continues to requires [*sic*] some elements of legal calculability provided by traditional legal devices. At the same time, the preservation of this functional rationality now depends on political forms, the core of the prerogative state, substantially irrational in character."[116] Fraenkel was convinced that "[i]f such substantially irrational ideology is useful to capitalism, the latter is ready to accept the programmatic aims of this ideology."[117] He argued that capitalism played handmaiden to dictatorship; that it willfully embraced a violent, inhumane ideology of a racial regime because the powerful state that this regime commanded held out the promise to maintain "the existing conditions of technical rationality" that were indispensable to the maintenance of an economic order which resembled the unfettered capitalism of old.[118] In theoretical terms, a self-enforcing causal mechanism is at work: "In order to augment technical rationality, the irrationality of the ends is intensified; and the belt to attain the irrational ends, technical rationality, is heightened. For the sake of the armaments industries, armaments pile up; for the sake of armaments, armaments industries prosper."[119]

To conclude my account of Fraenkel's analysis of the economic background to the dual state, let me establish the link between economics and law in Fraenkel's argument. This means translating *Mannheimian* terms into *Weberian* ones. The "technical rationality" that Fraenkel saw the normative state providing, he showed to be an indispensable variable in the Nazi calculation for prosperity. The pursuit of prosperity (not to mention military preparedness), however, required at least a modicum of legal predictability. If we accept Weber's *normative* argument about modern law, the attainment of legal predictability, especially in the economic sphere, is typically associated with formally rational law. Translated into *Weberian* terms, Fraenkel's argument about the institutional foundations of Nazi economy can be restated thus: The remnants of formally rational law that were encased in the normative half of the dual Nazi state proved capable of providing a durable and predictable institutional framework with which the pursuit of Mannheim's technical rationality was inherently compatible, and within which economic actors felt sufficiently confident about the protection of their private property and associated right that they contributed, in an informal *quid pro quo* arrangement, to the maintenance and expansion of an inherently violent regime whose substantially irrational ideology they might not otherwise have countenanced.

In contradistinction to the law of the normative state, the law produced by the prerogative state was, in Weberian terms, substantively irrational: it was the result of Nazi officials making arbitrary decisions from case to case without recourse to general rules. But even though this prerogative state was driven by extralegal motivations *and* governed by emotion, and thus potentially detrimental to economic growth and expansions, the appeal of the normative institutional reserves in the "rational core" of an otherwise highly "irrational shell," to use Fraenkel's language, was sufficient to appease the fears of the country's wealthiest bankers and barons.

This brings us to the question of the relationship between authoritarian rule and economic performance. In pursuit of an answer, Fraenkel made use of a little known article by Hans Kelsen, published in 1936 in the long defunct LSE journal *Politica*. Kelsen had proposed that "[e]arly capitalism, still involved in the struggle with feudalism and only at the beginning of its technical development, alike with capitalism in its decadent period, characterized by a highly unstable social equilibrium, stands under the sign of state autocracy: to the one corresponds absolute monarchy, to the other party-dictatorship."[120] Fraenkel incorporated Kelsen's observation into his own empirical argument about Nazi dictatorship. He proposed that "the violence of the German tyranny" was a functional response to the new rulers' fear of losing political control of the changing—and economically hard hit—society.[121] The preservation of islands of legality in a sea of lawlessness was an integral part of this response, to soften the blow (for some) and to fund the consolidation of dictatorship. As Fraenkel wrote: "This symbiosis of capitalism and National-Socialism finds its institutional form in the Dual State. The conflict within society is expressed in the dual nature of the state. The Dual State is the necessary political outgrowth of a transitional period wrought with tension."[122] On the question of whether "the favors given to the more monopolistic sectors of the Germany economy" were an institutional by-product or the intended consequence of institutional design, Fraenkel equivocated.[123] Whereas his answer in the *Urdoppelstaat* had been unequivocal, in *The Dual State* of 1941, it was ambiguous:

> Although the present author is inclined to attach considerable importance to the salvation of the [...] capitalistic interests in the whole complex of National-Socialist objectives, it seems best to say that the National-Socialists have consistently acted *as if* the protection of monopolistic interests and the salvation of the most endangered sectors of the German economy were the most important objectives of their economic policy. It can [...] be left to further investigation, to determine how much historical truth is contained in the words "as if."[124]

Fraenkel *was* certain, however, that the country's monopoly capitalists were guilty of playing into (and exploiting) the political economy of transition: "When the threat [of international conflict] declined, it became necessary to invent a new one."[125] Why? For Fraenkel the answer was simple: because "[t]he defenders of capitalism in post-war Germany were unable to convince the masses [...] that it was the best of all economic systems."[126] And this is where the origins of the dual state become our concern again. To make some sort of sense of them, Fraenkel travelled back in time to what he called "the *furor politicus* in the debacle of 1918–19."[127] What he referenced was the utter disillusionment in society at large about the power of international institutions, from international law to international cooperation, that followed in the wake of the punitive peace after the end of World War I.[128] This conflagration cast a long shadow and loomed large in the minds of bankers and barons in 1930s, or so Fraenkel told: "German capitalism once sincerely believed that its own development would contribute to world peace, well-being and culture. Present-day German capitalism has lost this belief in its humanitarian mission. Having lost the belief in its own rationale, it elevates the cult of the irrational to the status of a modern religion."[129] In other words, the purported capitalist fear of its own insignificance, according to this argument, lessened leading entrepreneurs' concerns about the character of their political bedfellows.

This interpretation betrays traces of the more mechanistic argument about the political economy of Nazi dictatorship that Fraenkel had laid out in his 1937 article and the *Urdoppelstaat*. But as Scheuerman has pointed out, it still avoided the shortcomings of Franz Neumann's considerably more reductionist analysis of the economic dimensions of Nazi rule: "Fraenkel offers a gloss on this constellation of ideas that allows him to provide an interpretation of National Socialist law superior to Neumann's. Although Neumann and Fraenkel start from the same basic assumptions, Fraenkel's *[The] Dual State* is likely to prove of greater value for those still struggling to make sense of National Socialist legal practice and theory."[130] Fraenkel remained loyal to Weber's legacy in a way that Neumann did not.[131] He was careful to distance himself—explicitly—from more radical interpretations of Nazi dictatorship that in the 1930s were en vogue on the left: "There are many people who believe that National-Socialism is, so to speak, nothing but the house-servant of German monopoly capitalism. [...] These oversimplified theories tend quite unnecessarily to discredit the economic interpretation of fascism. Such an interpretation should be formulated in terms of far more minute and deeper reaching categories."[132]

Let me recap: Nazism gained (at least temporarily) from the dual state because it reduced domestic opposition to its authoritarian rule. It benefitted, furthermore, because private activities were "put to the service of political, chiefly military, expansion."[133] Capitalism gained (at least for a while) from the dual state because it was allowed (at least temporarily and in select sectors) to engage in economic activities without undue interference by the prerogative state. It was (almost) left to its own devices as long as political necessity or expediency did not demand otherwise, which is when the prerogative state rushed in. Capitalism also profited (in all senses of the word) from the Nazi regime's aggressive creation of new markets, especially in the armaments industry. The dual state's supply of violence was also beneficial because it made possible the defeat or destruction of those who stood in the path of Nazi Germany's monopoly capitalism.

At first glance, Fraenkel's argument about the political economy of dictatorship may appear anachronistic. Although not flawless, it provides, however, a theoretically plausible—and empirically verifiable—entry point into the ongoing, and highly policy-relevant debate about the economic origins of dictatorship and democracy.[134] It is a useful source for testable hypotheses. In fact *The Dual State* draws our attention to the rationality of institutions: "Rational actors also care about the future. This is where political institutions—which are durable and, consequently, have the capacity to influence political actions and political equilibria in the future—come in. Therefore we need to think seriously about political institutions in a dynamic setting; via the process, we can develop a theory of the emergence and, later, consolidation of democracy. Crucial to this is a notion of what political institutions do."[135] Not unlike twenty-first century political economists such as Daron Acemoglu and James Robinson, who wrote the just-quoted lines and whose mathematical models today dominate the study of dictatorship in the social sciences, Fraenkel (along with other left-leaning representatives of Weimar thought) also sought to come to terms with *homo economicus* and his role in institutional development. But unlike Acemoglu and Robinson, Fraenkel also knew that the ideology of the "one-dimensional man," which Herbert Marcuse famously critiqued in 1964 and to this day remains an important linchpin not just of contemporary capitalism but also of modern economics—and especially of game-theoretical accounts of dictatorship—was chimera.[136] Although he never made this explicit (presumably because he took it to be self-evident), Fraenkel assumed that humans were not automatons, and least of all in times of transition. They made means-ends calculations, he conceded, but he never doubted that norms and values mattered just as much as motivations for action. This is why, in *The Dual State*, Fraenkel acquainted us with another type of change agent, one almost as important to modern politics and society as the self-interested, utility-maximizing type: *homo juridicus*.[137]

8

The Decline of a Classic: Explaining the Reception of *The Dual State*, 1941–present

The reception of *The Dual State* has waxed and waned over the years, but it all began with a bang.[1] The pioneering analysis has found many adherents over the years, but none was more notable than one of the very first: Werner Best. Between 1935 and 1940, Best worked in the headquarters of the SS's *Sicherheitsdienst* (Security Service, SD) in Berlin. A legal advisor to the Gestapo and SS, he also served as deputy to both Reinhard Heydrich and Heinrich Himmler, who would go on to become principal architects of the Holocaust.[2] It turns out Best thought the concept of the dual state was a powerful heuristic for capturing the institutional logic of Nazi dictatorship, so much so that in a contribution to the *Jahrbuch der Akademie für Deutsches Recht*, the yearbook of the Academy for German Law, Best (albeit without using Fraenkel's terminology) sketched the dual existence of a normative state and a prerogative state in Nazi Germany. Best argued that the power of a state, with its legal status ("*Rechtsnatur*") grounded in the *Volk*, was inherently limitless.[3] At the same time, he insisted that this foundational principle of Nazi law did not amount to a blank check authorizing arbitrary rule. He denied that "any concrete statist activity (*konkrete staatliche Tätigkeit*) was permitted to be undertaken without regard to legal norms (*normenlos*)."[4] Arbitrary, discretionary rule, Best wrote, was costly in day-to-day governance. Here is an illuminating passage to that effect, one that contradicts *both* the widespread assumption of the existence of a total state as well as Neumann's argument of the non-state, and a depiction that Fraenkel explicitly invoked in *The Dual State*: "It is essential that many of the activities of the state should be carried out according to legal rules and that they should be calculable in advance, in order that the persons concerned may be able to orient themselves satisfactorily."[5] The second part of Best's argument is not dissimilar to what Friedrich Hayek, a few decades later, identified as the beating heart of the constitution of liberty: rules of legal order.[6] Best was no Hayek, however. In discussing the limits of the normative state, he left no doubt about his anti-liberal credentials: "The state's normative self-binding" ("*Selbstbeschränkung des Staates durch Normierung*"), Best wrote, was "generally appropriate vis-à-vis the *Volk*'s positive, constructive forces."[7] But, he hastened to add, as soon as the state was required to fight "destructive forces," a normative self-binding in the deployment of countermeasures was "out of the question."[8] Best's justification of the supremacy of the prerogative state was simple: Because adversaries did not legally constrain their behavior, the Nazi state could not do so either, for "every enactment of a legal norm (*Normierung*) also constitutes a bind (*Bindung*) and thus will result in a weakening of agents."[9]

Even more interesting than the fact that a leading Nazi jurist lent credence to the argument about the dual state is the story of how Best came about Fraenkel's institutional theory of dictatorship, which only existed in the form of a clandestine manuscript at the time. Fraenkel tells it in the preface to the German edition of *The Dual State*. It involved his good friend Martin Gauger, who at the time worked in the legal department of the *Bekennende Kirche* (Confessing Church), a break-away movement of the Protestant Church that opposed the Nazi government's attempts to "nazify" the Protestant Church in Germany. As part of his duties, Gauger lobbied the Gestapo for the return of previously confiscated funds. To this end, he thought it could be beneficial to try to finagle a meeting with the Gestapo's legal counsel: Best. "When, after many failed attempts, Gauger finally managed to arrange for a meeting with Best to demand the return of confiscated funds belonging to the Confessing Church," Fraenkel recalled, "he seized the opportunity to casually explain to Best the theory of the dual state."[10] Best was intrigued by the novel argument; so much so that, in the aforementioned contribution, he "developed an argument that largely rehearsed ideas that Gauger had shared with him."[11] It was thus that one of the first incarnations of Fraenkel's argument about the logic of Nazi dictatorship had a very unintended consequence: it found approbation inside the very dictatorship that it depicted. "We came to view it as a macabre confirmation of our theoretical efforts," Fraenkel recalled wryly.[12]

The next iteration of Fraenkel's underground project, the *Urdoppelstaat* had an unexpected readership as well. Apparently, a copy of the clandestine manuscript was quietly circulated in a department at the headquarters of the Nazi regime's *Oberkommando des Heeres* (OKH, Army High Command) in 1939.[13] The text in circulation was a typed manuscript without bibliographical information.[14] Because the OKH was not usually involved in the collection of domestic intelligence or analysis of "*staatsfeindliche*" publications (publications by enemies of the state), it stands to reason that Fraenkel's *Urdoppelstaat* did not surface at the OKH because its incendiary content had come to the attention of Nazi authorities, but because a few staff members deemed its unvarnished analysis such an important counterpoint to Nazi propaganda that they felt it was worth distributing even at the risk of losing their own lives.[15] According to Helmut Ridder, who relayed this early example of the reception of Fraenkel's extended treatment of the dual state, the book manuscript "made its way from one drawer to the next" ("*wanderte von einer Schublade zur anderen*").[16]

MADE IN AMERICA

Though imagined in Germany, *The Dual State*, as we know it, was made in America. As I have shown in Chapter 6, Fraenkel re-thought and re-wrote the *Urdoppelstaat* from the safety of his exile in the United States. It was at this point that Oxford University Press agreed to publish the revised manuscript. On December 20, 1940, the following notice appeared in the "Notes on Books and Authors" section of the *New York Times*:

> A practicing attorney in Berlin up to the latter part of 1938, Ernst Fraenkel had ample opportunity for observing the functioning of the Nazi state. In a book to be published by Oxford early in January he propounds the thesis of its dual character—that is, the traditional and administrative organs and courts continue to function but besides them a governmental system has arisen with unlimited and arbitrary powers. The author is now in this country. "The Dual State" will be the title.[17]

It was a remarkably accurate summary of Fraenkel's book. Two weeks later, the *New York Times* followed up the pre-publication announcement with a release notice in its section "Books Published Today."[18] Upon publication, *The Dual State* found immediate acclaim in the English-speaking world. It was reviewed in newspapers and learned journals alike, especially in the United States, where Fraenkel had begun to build a new life. He once quipped that he would rather live as an "immigrant" than an "emigrant."[19] Fraenkel was pleased that the reception of his book in the United States was so positive. In his correspondence with Otto Kahn-Freund, he mentioned with pride the book's review in many leading outlets of both law and political science.[20] Within the first two years of publication, Fraenkel's unorthodox account garnered more than a dozen favorable book reviews in high-ranking publications, including in the *Harvard Law Review* and the *American Political Science Review*, respectively America's leading law review and political science journal.[21]

The early reviews, save two, all paid tribute to Fraenkel's major theoretical and empirical achievement. The reviewer for the *Harvard Law Review*, Fritz Morstein Marx of Queens College, praised Fraenkel's "remarkable analysis of National Socialist statecraft" and found "[a]s a detailed record of what has happened to the *Rechtsstaat* under totalitarian auspices, the book is without rival."[22] He reserved special praise for the fact that Fraenkel "guards himself against overdoing the class angle," thereby validating Fraenkel's decision to revise the chapter that used to be called "the economics of the dual state."[23] George H. Sabine at Cornell University was less effusive but also found the account "of great interest and value," especially because "it contains a sort of information not readily available outside of Germany and not usually known to readers who have little acquaintance with German law."[24] Eric Voegelin also had some reservations about certain aspects of Fraenkel's analysis but, he, too, recognized the depth and breadth and danger of the field research that underpinned it:

> [T]he book is an important contribution to the understanding of the National Socialist régime, because it digests a wealth of materials which otherwise are difficult of access, such as certain types of periodical literature and civil, criminal, and administrative courts decisions. It is a book which could be written in this form only by a good lawyer who was, during the years 1933–1938, in intimate contact with these materials. The study gives first-hand knowledge of the sources below the level of general rules and standard treatises. [...] [T]he book is a penetrating, detailed analysis of National Socialist government in operation; it has, as far as I can see, no rival in the English language.[25]

In July 1941, Robert Kempner added his voice to the positive tenor of reviewers. Kempner's review stands out for several reasons. First, because Kempner had been chief legal adviser to the Prussian police in the Weimar Republic, he would have been intimately familiar with some of the source materials on which Fraenkel drew. Among other duties, Kempner partook in the investigation and prosecution of Adolf Hitler and Wilhelm Frick in the aftermath of the Munich Beer Hall Putsch of 1923, the failed Nazi overthrow of the regional government in Bavaria, intended as a prelude to a seizure of power of the national government in Berlin. Kempner's review is also interesting because, as we have seen in Chapter 3, he had been a regular contributor to *Die Justiz*, to which he contributed nine articles. He thus shared Fraenkel's general concerns about the gradual hollowing out of the *Rechtsstaat* in the Weimar Republic. Finally, Kempner's reaction is noteworthy because he went on to serve as Assistant U.S. Chief Counsel at the International Military Tribunal at Nuremberg, the IMT. There, he not only encountered Frick again but also Carl Schmitt, whose interrogations he conducted.[26] Presumably because of his personal familiarity with the law of the Third Reich, Kempner appreciated Fraenkel's contribution like few others, even though he made it plain that, inasmuch as "[t]he theory of the author is valid for the time between 1933 and 1939," "in the totalitarian state of 1941 there is no more room for struggling dualism. The resistance of the old judicial bodies was overthrown by the new ordinances of the totalitarian police power and by the influx of the young National Socialist generation of public officials."[27] But this caveat did not trouble Kempner:

> The importance of Fraenkel's study is not reduced by this statement [that is, Kempner's argument that the dual state no longer existed in 1941]. The book is valuable for its analysis of the internal struggle between the "Old Order" of democracy and fundamental rights, and the "New Order" of totalitarianism and police-omnipotence. A basic knowledge of this internal struggle against the "Old Order" is necessary in order to understand the external clash of today [presumably a reference to World War II] which is an outgrowth of it.[28]

Lawrence Preuss of the University of Michigan concurred in the *American Journal of International Law*: "Although the legal institutions of the Third Reich have been abundantly denounced as essentially lawless, no work in English up to the present time has provided a detailed and concrete analysis of their theory and functioning. This gap in the literature has now been filled by Dr. Fraenkel's penetrating study of the dualism between the 'Prerogative State' and the 'Normative State' in the emerging National Socialist legal system."[29] The reviews by Kempner and Preuss, both published in July 1941, were the most perceptive of the major reviews. They must have been gratifying to Fraenkel, whose life in the United States was far from stable. Unlike some other reviewers, who homed in on marginal rather than central concerns in *The Dual State* (such as the economic dimensions of Nazi rule), Preuss recognized, first, that Fraenkel was on a quest to solve a paradoxical puzzle—the "legalization of lawlessness;" and, second, that he was concerned with the "*emerging* National Socialist legal system," an important fact that many subsequent reviewers have failed to appreciate.[30]

In his review in the *University of Chicago Law Review*, Jerome Kerwin of the University of Chicago added another point worth mentioning. He drew attention to Fraenkel's style of analytical detachment: "Calm and objective treatises on National Socialism do not constitute a sizeable portion of our current literature."[31] Or, as Voegelin put it in his review of *The Dual State*, "While the enormous body of more or less emotional literature on totalitarian governments is enormous, the number of competent, well documented studies [of which he considered Fraenkel's to be an important example] is extremely small."[32] Another reviewer echoed the sentiment, remarking that Fraenkel's chapters "are written with insight, authority, and scholarship, and are indispensable to understanding the present Nazi system."[33]

Only two of the early reviews were critical—those by Erich Hula (in *Social Research*) and Otto Kirchheimer (in the *Political Science Quarterly*). Hula admitted that Fraenkel had written "a brilliant and interesting book," one crafted "with a broad knowledge of National Socialist doctrine [and] an intimate familiarity with the actual working of National Socialist legal machinery."[34] Yet, Hula exclaimed, the book was "as confusing as it was brilliant."[35] The cause for Hula's confusion was a supposed contradiction in Fraenkel's argument.[36] If, Hula asked, Fraenkel believed that the prerogative state marked "the complete abolition of the inviolability of law," how was it logically—and empirically—possible that a normative state, that is, "an administrative body endowed with elaborate powers for safeguarding the legal order as expressed in statutes, decisions of the courts, and activities of the administrative agencies," could exist alongside it.[37] A more careful read of *The Dual State* would have dispelled any confusion. Fraenkel, as we have seen, went to great lengths to get across his conceptual point that the normative state was "by no means identical with a state in which the 'Rule of Law' prevails, i.e., with the *Rechtsstaat* of the liberal period."[38] And yet Hula erroneously claimed that that was the premise on which Fraenkel had built his theoretical argument, a normative state "which the author pictures by and large as a *Rechtsstaat*, though one *sui generis*."[39] The subtlety and nuance of Fraenkel's argument were not just lost on Hula. They were also lost on Otto Kirchheimer, who was less kind.

At the time of his review, Kirchheimer, Schmitt's former doctoral student and a one-time friend to Fraenkel, was professor of political science at the New School for Social Research, where Fraenkel had hoped to secure employment but failed to make inroads. Kirchheimer acknowledged the fact that *The Dual State* was "the first attempt to provide a theoretical analysis of the German legal order," but he immediately faulted the "interesting" analysis for being "one-sided."[40] Like Hula, Kirchheimer was not convinced by the conceptual dichotomy, and especially the supposed role that the normative state was said by Fraenkel to have played in sustaining the capitalist economy in Nazi Germany. The law of the normative state was not law proper, Kirchheimer insisted, echoing the critique of *The Dual*

State by Franz Neumann, his friend and colleague: "This sphere of free judicial determination is lost when other state organs without any hindrance are able to change legal norms at their will."[41] Kirchheimer concluded in a dismissive manner: "That the German system is based on a dual policy of 'prerogative' constables and 'normative' judges [...] seems to be an application of cherished but antiquated doctrines to a radically changed reality."[42]

Like Neumann, the eminent Kirchheimer was unable to imagine in theory what Fraenkel had experienced in practice, which is why he missed entirely the pathbreaking insights about the complexity of authoritarian rule that *The Dual State* introduced into the study of dictatorship. It has become commonplace in the last few years to inquire into the nature and dynamics of the "authoritarian rule of law."[43] Fraenkel was the first theorist to identify this phenomenon, and, furthermore, the first to describe its logic and account for its rise. And he did so under some of the most difficult circumstances imaginable. For these reasons, and in spite of Kirchheimer's negative review, which irked Fraenkel, *The Dual State*, along with Neumann's *Behemoth*, was briefly recognized as a classic in the study of modern dictatorship, and of the early years of the Nazi dictatorship in particular. And yet, against hope, the publication of *The Dual State* and its very positive reception did not open any American doors for Fraenkel. With no teaching jobs on offer, he returned to legal practice. This eventually led to his participation—as a newly minted U.S. citizen—in the promotion of democracy abroad.

EXPORTING THE RULE OF LAW

In the fall of 1941, after completion of his J.D. at University Chicago Law School, Fraenkel was based for a few months in a Washington, D.C., law firm. Between January and October 1942, he held the position of Executive Secretary for the American Federation of Jews from Central Europe and concurrently worked for another refugee organization. David Riesman, of the American Committee for the Guidance of Professional Personnel, remained an ardent supporter of Fraenkel. He labored hard to secure for him a faculty position at a reputable U.S. university. The following excerpt from a letter that he sent on Fraenkel's behalf to Hans Staudinger at the New School for Social Research illustrates the high esteem in which Riesman held the author of *The Dual State*:

> Dr. Fraenkel was one of the first of the group of refugee lawyers re-trained under the auspices of the Committee of which I am secretary [...] and [I] found him at that time one of the best qualified of the European lawyers to

> undertake re-training in American law schools. He went to the University of Chicago Law School, where he was exceedingly well received both by students and faculty. [...] In my opinion, Dr. Fraenkel is the top man of the group of lawyers our Committee has assisted—not top-notch from the point of simple academic brilliance, but rather from the combination of insight into the social process with an unusually broad experience.[44]

Riesman's efforts did not result in a university appointment for Fraenkel, but in the fall of 1943 Fraenkel secured a research grant from the Carnegie Endowment for International Peace in association with the Institute of World Affairs. He was commissioned to write a report about the consequences of the occupation of the Rhineland by Entente powers in the aftermath of World War I. The research objective was to derive lessons for the expected Allied occupation of a defeated Nazi Germany. Fraenkel cherished the opportunity to conduct policy-relevant research unencumbered by constant worries about how to make ends meet. "It was my happiest time in America" ("*Es war meine schönste Zeit in Amerika*").[45] Even better, Fraenkel's work on what international lawyers today refer to as international territorial administration culminated in his second book, *Military Occupation and the Rule of Law*.[46] The illuminating but little-known book paved the way for Fraenkel's entry into government service in the spring of 1944. Concurrently, he was offered an adjunct teaching position at the École libre des hautes études—a university-in-exile for French refugee academics in New York, based at the Graduate Faculty of the New School for Social Research—where he taught comparative law, apparently with particular reference to "American legal terminology."[47] The teaching arrangement, during which Fraenkel was affiliated with the Institute of Comparative Law at the École libre, lasted until 1944.

Despite having two well-regarded English-language monographs with OUP to his name, a permanent faculty position was not on the cards for Fraenkel. He therefore decided to embark on a public service career, accepting, in the spring of 1944, a job at the newly established Foreign Economic Administration (FEA). The FEA operated under the auspices of the Office of Strategic Services (OSS), notably its Research and Analysis Branch, and Fraenkel's job description included the drafting of institutional designs for the postwar period in a liberated Germany.[48] U.S. troops had landed in Sicily in July 1943, and on the back of the Normandy landings of June 6, 1944, the U.S. government was mobilizing resources across the board for the military occupation of Europe. It was Hedwig Wachenheim, an erstwhile SPD activist, who had recruited Fraenkel.[49]

Hans Kelsen, too worked, for the FEA, and although Fraenkel liked the famous jurist as a person, he was not at all impressed with his proposals for the administration of postwar Germany, which Fraenkel thought ill-informed and too punitive.[50] Kelsen aside, Fraenkel was pessimistic about the potential for democracy in a liberated Germany. "The broad masses," he opined, would not be able to absorb the democratic ideals the Americans sought to instill in them, they were "too deeply poisoned by nationalistic feelings."[51] The, in his opinion, illusionary expectations of many other refugees that a revolution from below would do away with the vestiges of Nazi dictatorship, left him flabbergasted. Fraenkel had witnessed the abdication of responsibility of the working (not to mention middle) class for the rise of Nazi dictatorship in the mid-1930s. He had no reason to think that either would suddenly be ready for democracy, let alone be willing to go on the barricades for it.[52] But Fraenkel was equally dubious about the prospects of imposing democracy from above or outside, not least because of his in-depth, critical study of the interwar military occupation of the Rhineland. "Democracy cannot be improvised on the ruins of dictatorship," he wrote, adding that "[t]he real problem [in Germany] will be whether it is possible to shift the aim of planning from conquest to reconstruction."[53] Fraenkel was most concerned about reconstructing the *Rechtsstaat*, and about giving it the kind of social orientation that he and the Sinzheimer circle, influenced by Hermann Heller, had dreamt up at Frankfurt in the 1920s.[54] As Udi Greenberg observes, "To Fraenkel and émigrés like him, the future occupation was to be the fulfilment of Weimar's incomplete achievements."[55]

Unlike many of these émigrés, however, Fraenkel was mindful of how the U.S. occupying force would be received in a defeated Germany, and with what consequences for the reception and consolidation of democracy. He channeled his own experience of alienation vis-à-vis other German émigrés in the United States: "A deep gulf," he believed, separated anti-Nazis who survived inside the dictatorship from those, like him, who had managed to escape and looked on from without: "[T]he anti-Nazis inside Germany [by which he meant, on the one hand, German refugee scholars who were returning to help with the reconstruction and development of their country, albeit in U.S. uniforms, and, on the other, Germans who had survived and resisted the Hitler regime from within] will no longer understand one another because they speak different languages."[56] To facilitate the encounter, Fraenkel, alone or in collaboration, produced numerous FEA planning reports regarding the international administration of justice, including "Criminal Law" (March 1944), "On the Elimination of Nazi Law" (April 1944), "Adoption of the Constitution of the Courts and their Composition" (April 1944), "On Administration of Criminal Justice" (June 1944), "Property Controls under Present German Law as Related to Military Government" (June

1944), and, with Otto Kirchheimer who was based at the OSS, "U.S. Policy Towards German Cartels and Cartel-like Organizations during Allied Occupation" (April 1945).[57]

In 1945, Fraenkel was offered—but declined—a position in the U.S. military government for Germany, which in 1946 was consolidated as the Office of Military Government, United States, or OMGUS. He gave conflicting rationales for his decision. In a letter to the Suhr family of March 23, 1946, Fraenkel wrote that the Holocaust had made it impossible for him to return to Germany. When he first realized that the reports of Nazi genocide were not "propaganda communications" ("*Propagandamitteilungen*"), he consciously and deliberately "cut the ties between Germany and myself" and "resolved never to return to Germany ever again."[58] The letter was heartfelt, Fraenkel resolute:

> I feel no Jew can be expected to live in Germany in the future [...]. [...] I spent enough time in Germany to know that a very significant part ("*ein sehr erheblicher Teil*") of the German population condoned Hitler's measures ("*Maßnahmen*") against the Jews. Given that this campaign ("*Feldzug*") has resulted in annihilation, it is not permissible ("*angänging*") for me, as a Jew, to make the business of this people ("*die Sache dieses Volkes*") my own again.[59]

He put it even more starkly a few months later, on May 25, 1946, when he told Kahn-Freund how sickening the sight of perpetrators, bystanders, and other guilty Germans in the country of his birth would be for him: "That is unbearable to me; no Jew should be exposed to such an experience."[60] It was the only time that Fraenkel referenced the Holocaust. He never again invoked it as a motivation nor did he tackle it intellectually. To explain his refusal to help with the rebuilding of Germany on the ground, Fraenkel usually pointed to his principled reservations about U.S. policy planning.[61] This did not stop him from continuing to serve in the U.S. government. Following the dissolution of the OSS and FEA, Fraenkel, in October 1945, accepted an offer to serve as U.S. legal adviser in postwar Japan.[62] Yet shortly before his departure, new orders arrived: He would be stationed in Korea instead, to help with the promotion of democracy in the wake of Japanese occupation.[63]

Despite the existence of a veritable planning machinery in Washington, D.C., as well as in other Western capitals, *The Dual State*'s influence on the all-important postwar debate about the requisites of democracy, in Germany and elsewhere, was close to nil. Neither in scholarly nor in policy circles did Fraenkel's analysis leave much of a mark. Two explanations come to mind. First, the more forceful argument of Neumann's *Behemoth* quickly supplanted Fraenkel's analysis of the German case.

Second, Fraenkel's search for islands of rule-guided behavior in the violent sea of early Nazi law was out of step with the study of totalitarianism in the 1950s. I briefly consider these explanations in turn.

As discussed in Chapter 2, Neumann rejected the argument and findings of *The Dual State*. Here is a reprise of his assessment: "It has been maintained that National Socialism is a dual state, that is, in fact one state within which two systems are operating, one under normative law, the other under individual measures, one rational, the other the realm of the prerogative. We do not share this view because we believe that there is no realm of law in Germany, although there are thousands of technical rules that are calculable."[64] Neumann elaborated this claim by sketching an alternative institutional structure of the Third Reich. He rejected the label "state" for describing the Nazi polity's core: "Under National Socialism [...] the whole of society is organized into four solid, centralized groups, each operating under the leadership principle, each with a legislative, administrative, and judicial power of its own. Neither universal law nor a rationally operating bureaucracy is necessary for integration."[65] In other words, if we believe Neumann, there was no one structure at the apex of the Nazi regime, only an agent—Hitler—whose directives, however, ultimately were dependent on the leaders of the centralized groups:

> It is quite sufficient that the leadership of the four wings agree informally on a certain policy. The four totalitarian bodies will then explore it with the machinery at their disposal. There is no need for a state standing above all groups; the state may even be a hindrance to the compromises and to domination over rules classes. The decisions of the Leader are merely the result of the compromises among the four leaderships. [...] It is thus impossible to detect in the framework of the National Socialist political system any one organ which monopolizes political power.[66]

In the second, much expanded edition of *Behemoth*, published in 1944, Neumann asserted "German constitutional life is characterized by its utter shapelessness" and that, as such, "it is doubtful whether Germany can be called a state."[67] It was a restatement of his non-state-argument in the first edition, in which he concluded that it was "difficult to give the name state to four groups entering into a bargain."[68]

Neumann's rejection of the dual-state-argument had far-reaching consequences for Fraenkel. It was one of the key reasons why *Behemoth*, rather than Fraenkel's considerably more sophisticated analysis in *The Dual State*, came to dominate, until more comprehensive studies were available, the teaching and writing about Nazi dictatorship in the twentieth century. Neumann inaugurated a conceptual shift from a dual state to a totalitarian entity in descriptions of the regime. This depiction would become the standard one for several decades, although most observers did not think the regime to be quite as rudderless as Neumann made it out to be. Fraenkel's treatment in *The Dual State* was hamstrung by the fact that he had not taken into account empirical developments beyond the year 1938, the year he and his wife fled the ever-worsening state of dictatorship.

Whereas Neumann's book was up to date and seemed to have captured the essence of the Nazi state, Fraenkel's book, with its now more dispassionate tone, was seen by some to be lacking. Among other things, it was said to have failed to grasp the logic of categorical destruction at the regime's core. Consequently, Fraenkel's more subtle analysis, which he concluded several years prior to the regime's totalitarian turn in the late 1930s that featured so centrally in Neumann's *Behemoth*, was regularly—albeit wrongly—dismissed as having misunderstood the violent nature of Hitler's reign. It is obvious in retrospect that Fraenkel's analysis was more scholarly an achievement than Neumann's more popular, tendentious tome. Frankel avoided, also on account of his reworking of the *Urdoppelstaat*, Neumann's "inclination to ideological overreach" that, according to the historian Peter Hayes, mars *Behemoth*.[69] As a result, *The Dual State* has aged considerably better than *Behemoth*. A few years before her death, the political theorist Judith Shklar remarked that it was "one of the few older studies of the Third Reich that remain valid.[70]

In the immediate postwar period, *Behemoth* was vastly more influential than *The Dual State*. It was not just read in the academy but also in policy circles. Neumann's more conventional and orthodox account fit hand in glove with a new theoretical approach to Hitler's Germany that Hannah Arendt and Carl J. Friedrich were pioneering in the United States, where it gave rise—not long after World War II—to a field of inquiry known as the study of totalitarianism.[71] The totalitarian turn in the study of dictatorship arguably played an important role in the relative non-reception of *The Dual State* during the Cold War. The conceptual toolkit of the study of totalitarianism was different from the one that Fraenkel had used in the writing of *The Dual State*. And although leading historians of Nazi Germany like Martin Broszat, Hans Mommsen, and Ian Kershaw have always been skeptical of the totalitarianism concept, arguing that the Nazi state was institutionally too fractured to exhibit the kind of "near-complete monopoly of control" that Friedrich theorized as one of the defining attributes of the totalitarian state, the term dominated the social scientific approach to Nazi dictatorship in the 1950s and 1960s.[72] The approach was of a kind with Neumann's *Behemoth*. Neumann's case study and the theory of totalitarianism ensured that appreciation of *The Dual State*—after an initial spike in its international reception—declined markedly in the postwar years. Such was the influence of *The Dual State* in the United States, but what about the book's reception in Germany?

RETURNEE

In the preface to the 1974 German edition of *The Dual State*, Fraenkel gratefully acknowledged his wife, Hanna, for having supported him during the "difficult years of bureaucratic lawlessness" ("*schweren Jahre der bürokratischen Rechtlosigkeit*").[73] Yet for most of his postwar life, Fraenkel refused to reflect on—or otherwise relive—the violence of those years. He refused to have anything to do ever again with *The Dual State* or the topic that it addressed—Nazi dictatorship. Only Neumann's premature death in a car accident in 1954 momentarily pierced the protective shield that Fraenkel had erected around himself.[74]

A straight line can be drawn from Fraenkel's reluctance in the 1940s to become "a civil servant of the occupying power" ("*Beamte[r] der Okkupationsmacht*"), that is to join the U.S. military government of a defeated Germany, to his unwillingness to revisit the "difficult years of bureaucratic lawlessness."[75] Irritated by his close friend's steadfast refusal to try to make any sense at all of the Nazi past, Otto Kahn-Freund eventually sent a sarcastic missive (in French, no less) from the United Kingdom: "*La recherche du passé est interdite*" ("Research of the past is prohibited").[76] To no avail: Fraenkel did not relent. In his later years, Fraenkel spoke publicly about *The Dual State* only once. Given the vehemence and consistency of his avoidance, it is surprising, as Simone Ladwig-Winters recently discovered, that Fraenkel had been in advanced talks about directing a research project on the law of the Third Reich at the influential, Munich-based Institut für Zeitgeschichte—the respected institute for contemporary history that gained broad international renown in 2016 with the publication of a two-volume, scholarly and annotated edition of Hitler's *Mein Kampf*—a decade after his return to Germany.[77] It appears that Fraenkel was sickened by the continuity of judicial personnel between the Nazi and postwar dispensations and therefore sought to make a policy-relevant contribution by studying the legal origins of democracy and dictatorship in twentieth century Germany.

The historian Norbert Frei has described the widespread culture of impunity in newly democratizing Germany, in the judiciary and elsewhere, as the "triumph of silencing" ("*Triumph des Beschweigens*").[78]

Not surprisingly, neither Fraenkel's *The Dual State* nor Neumann's *Behemoth* were well received in the country whose descent into dictatorship they both documented.[79] Moreover, concern with really existing totalitarianism in the Soviet Union quickly supplanted concern with what many viewed as the distant totalitarianism of the Nazis.[80] In Bonn and other capitals of the so-called West, the rise of the study of totalitarianism (what became known and influential as "*Totalitarismusforschung*" in Germany) was fast-tracked at the expense of Holocaust studies, a field of inquiry that was universally postponed, not just in Germany, until another day.[81]

In postwar Germany only Alexander v. Brünneck recognized—and endeavored to spread the word about—the significance of *The Dual State*. In a sympathetic review in *Kritische Justiz*, a left-leaning law journal he made a case, in 1969, for the publication of a German edition. V. Brünneck highlighted Fraenkel's genuinely scholarly approach to a difficult topic: "Fraenkel is not content with moral condemnation or the non-theoretical stringing together ('*theorielose Aneinanderreihung*') of empirical facts."[82] This approach, argued v. Brünneck, was all the more important at a time when apologists were misrepresenting the logic of law in Nazi Germany for the purpose of alleviating the guilt of their own wrongdoing.

Leaving aside the deliberate sidelining and concomitant scarcity of research on the logic of both Nazi dictatorship and genocidal destruction in the first two decades following World War II, it is worth noting that Fraenkel also avoided the topic of Hitler's Germany for personal reasons. In a letter to Kahn-Freund about a former Ph.D. student, Wolfgang Scheffler, who had turned to researching and publishing about the Holocaust, Fraenkel wrote: "Scheffler [...] has been concerned with the problem of the 'Final Solution.' It is a mystery to me how one can deal [with that topic] without losing one's mind."[83] Fraenkel was adamant to spend his own time thinking about positive rather than negative models of governance.[84] This also explains why he, partly in tribute to the country (and nation) that had granted him exile in a time of desperate need, spent a good portion of his later years on the writing of his highly influential book (in Germany at least) about the U.S. political system, *Das amerikanische Regierungssystem*, which, certainly in Germany, is still better known (and taught more regularly) than *The Dual State*.[85] It is thus not surprising that Fraenkel refused to authorize a German edition of his most important book until the early 1970s. When he finally relented, he was adamant that he would not himself take on the translation.

In a revealing letter from his private correspondence, Fraenkel explained why he was unable—and unwilling—to do so:

> I will not undertake the translation myself. This is not just a question of time but also a question of my soul ("*ein seelisches Problem*"). For more than five years I was a practicing lawyer under the Nazi regime in Berlin, and I wrote *The Dual State* to unburden myself ("*aus der Seele geschrieben*"). At the outbreak of the war, I drew a line under my engagement with the Third Reich, and in the three decades since I have neither published on the topic nor read about National Socialism. By writing *The Dual State*, I have done my share to contribute to the theoretical clarification of this research problem ("*Fragenkomplex*"). I read the relevant literature until I was physically sickened ("*bis zum physischen Ekel*"), and I cannot bear to delve into this "subject" ("*Materie*") again. Yet doing so would be inevitable if I undertook the translation myself or even just contributed to it in any significant way.[86]

Even though Fraenkel was not interested in being a flag bearer for research on Hitler's Germany, the topic's neglect in the intellectual life of the early Federal Republic did not leave him cold: "The twelve years from 1933 until 1945 are treated in the German public sphere as if they never happened. [...] [But] twelve years cannot be cut from history ('*aus der Geschichte herausschneiden*')."[87] Presumably it was for this reason that he eventually became more involved in the production of the 1974 German edition than he ever thought possible. He edited and proofread the entire retranslated manuscript. Despite repeated bouts of illness, he worked hard to make sure that his theoretical ideas—and the intentions behind them—would be comprehensible to a new generation of readers. It was the final academic labor of his life.

Unlike the 1941 English edition, the 1974 translation was widely reviewed and positively received in Germany. The publication of the former had been a non-event in Germany (as, incidentally, had the publication of Neumann's *Behemoth*). Copies for purchase were hard to come by and even libraries struggled to procure the book via interlibrary loan.[88] Key works from the late 1960s, notably Karl Dietrich Bracher's *Die deutsche Dikatur* (*The German Dictatorship*) and Martin Broszat's *Der Staat Hitlers* (*The Hitler State*), both published in 1969, made passing references to *The Dual State* but failed to engage meaningfully with its theoretical argument.[89] Others, like Hans Buchheim, called into question Fraenkel's idea of institutional hybridity and introduced an alternative binary to capture the regime's institutional logic.[90] In the mid-1970s things were very different. At long last, Fraenkel's sophisticated analysis received the scholarly attention that it deserved in the country that had violently chased out its author. Bernhard Blanke's was the most comprehensive engagement.[91] It was an extended and careful explication and critique of a sophisticated argument. It was also refutation of Buchheim's more conventional, totalitarian account of Nazi dictatorship.[92] Blanke's was a very sympathetic reading of *The Dual State*, the first of its kind in any language that took its time to sift through the many interesting insights and observations contained in the book.

Wolfgang Luthardt, a few years later, continued in a similar vein in his comparative assessment of Fraenkel's argument.[93] He ventured that the relative neglect of *The Dual State* (and of Neumann and Kirchheimer and other scholars with left-leaning tendencies) in the first few decades of the postwar regime in Germany also had to do with a systematic bias in both the history and legal professions.[94] To help overcome this bias, he juxtaposed *The Dual State* with Neumann and Otto Kirchheimer's perspectives on the nature of the Nazi state in an attempt to create a wider readership for them.[95] According to Neumann and Kirchheimer, the Nazi state was an *Unrechtsstaat*, a state of lawlessness. Neumann went as far as referring to it as an "*Unstaat*" ("non-state"). Both disputed that a normative logic had ever operated inside it. Neumann argued, furthermore, that the Nazi justice system was a "part of the anti-state" ("*Teil des Anti-Staats*"), another name for the "counter state" ("*Gegenstaat*") that he believed the Nazis had built to weaken the fledgling democratic state.[96] Luthardt countered superficial criticisms of *The Dual State*, for example, the standard claim that the institutional structure of the Nazi state markedly changed after 1938. The fact that in the final analysis he thought Neumann's non-state-argument "theoretically more plausible" than Fraenkel's dual-state-argument did not detract from the deep and genuine appreciation that Luthardt felt for *The Dual State*.[97] Blanke's and Luthardt's extended, critical, but very serious treatments of *The Dual State* and several others like it re-legitimated Fraenkel's dual-state-argument in Germany, thereby also anchoring it in the historiography of Nazi dictatorship where it had at first been entirely overshadowed by Neumann's *Behemoth*.

In the most important standard accounts of National Socialism, Fraenkel's analysis is nowadays referenced extensively.[98] But inasmuch as the notion of "the dual state" is a deeply entrenched concept in the German academy, islands of indifference (and ignorance) persist in this sea of recognition. Horst Dreier has usefully surveyed references to Fraenkel in leading treatises, commentaries, and textbooks on what German lawyers call *Staatsrecht*, or, literally: state law. It turns out that most of the foundational texts that law students in Germany routinely use in the course of their studies gloss over Ernst Fraenkel's ethnography of law—despite it representing one of the most incisive analyses ever crafted about the uses of law in Germany.[99] Legal historians, with one exception, did not do much better than their practice- and doctrine-oriented colleagues.[100] Social historians, on the other hand, were quicker to recognize the analytical brilliance—and empirical validity—of Fraenkel's ethnography of law. The late Hans-Ulrich Wehler, in the fourth volume of his monumental *Deutsche Gesellschaftsgeschichte*, one of the most audacious and influential contributions to the study of German history, attested Fraenkel's "perceptiveness" ("*Hellsichtigkeit*") and relied on the idea of institutional hybridity to construct his own argument from, for a lack of a better term, "institutionalized charismatic authority," to wit, an account that advanced an argument located halfway between the explanatory poles of "monocracy" ("*Monokratie*") and "polycracy" ("*Polykratie*").[101] This was possible in no small measure due to Fraenkel's preparatory work. It is for this reason that another historian described *The Dual State* (along with Neumann's *Behemoth*) as "virtually the only pathbreaking contributions to the structuralist analysis of Nazi dictatorship" that were available in the mid- to late twentieth century.[102]

Despite the recognition, in the early 1970s, from Fraenkel's peers in the country in which he was born—and to which he once felt he belonged—all was not well. In his final years Fraenkel succumbed to bouts of severe depression.[103] His despair owed primarily to the unexpectedly negative treatment that he was receiving at the hands of the leftist student movement in Germany in the period 1967–1972.[104] Students at the FU Berlin labeled him and his theoretical ideas reactionary. Fraenkel was shocked, also unable to comprehend the pervasive lack of respect for authority that was a sign of the times. He even refused to participate in the celebrations in honor of his 75th birthday and the launch of the accompanying *Festschrift* for fear of student disturbances at the event.[105] Fraenkel often lost his nerve in this period, finding it hard to accept that the younger generation did not see him as a worthy (or even legitimate) interlocutor. In the fall of 1974, he confided to his friend Otto Kahn-Freund that he had resumed his correspondence with friends because he was "growing increasingly lonely" ("*ich doch zunehmend vereinsame*").[106] A broken man, Fraenkel died on March 28, 1975, three months after the publication of *Der Doppelstaat*, the first official German edition of *The Dual State*.

Ten years after Fraenkel's death, a mass-market reprint of the first German edition was published.[107] Michael Stolleis, the doyen of the historiography of Nazi law, reaffirmed on this occasion *The Dual State*'s status as a legal classic in a prominent law journal, the *Juristenzeitung*. He praised Fraenkel's "astonishing perceptiveness and precision" and concluded that *The Dual State* was "clearly superior" to most of the scholarship on the law of the Third Reich that had appeared since World War II.[108] Stolleis was not alone in his appreciation. Norberto Bobbio was similarly effusive in his praise. In his Introduction to *The Dual State*'s Italian edition, he declared Fraenkel to be Carl Schmitt's "principal antagonist," thus greatly contributing to Fraenkel's reception in Italy, where Schmitt was also enjoying a renaissance at the time.[109]

Two decades after the publication of the German edition, the concept of the dual state received practical acclamation: In a 1991 appeal judgment, Germany's *Bundessozialgericht* (Federal Social Court), held that the Nazi system of military justice (*Militärgerichtsbarkeit*) did not for the most part represent an institution of the normative state, but was overwhelmingly part and parcel of the prerogative state.[110] As the five-judge panel put it, "Only a limited portion of the jurisprudence at the time was in keeping with rule-of-law principles. Such judgments were attributable to the 'normative state,' that is, that part of the state that honored the kind of legal order appropriate to a civilized state."[111] A few data points illustrate the reach and destructive force of the prerogative state's role in the administration of military justice. In the period 1934–1945, more than 1,000 military courts administered more than 700,000 proceedings. In 50,000 cases, defendants (which also included civilians) received death sentences, of which an estimated fifty percent were carried out.[112]

In a momentous departure from its previous jurisprudence, the Federal Social Court ruled that death sentences handed down by German military courts during the Nazi dictatorship to punish deserters would henceforth be classified *categorically* as "manifest injustice" ("*offensichtliches Unrecht*"). Previously such death sentences had been found to constitute manifest injustice in exceptional circumstances only—to the chagrin of many widows of executed soldiers who were thus denied pensions, so-called *Witwenrenten*. The implications of the 1991 judgment were considerable: relatives of all German deserters sentenced by military courts, regardless of the nature of their supposed violation(s) of military discipline, were now entitled to receive compensation under the Federal Law Victims' Pension Act (*Bundesversorgungsgesetz*). As per the judges' ruling, "resistance fighters, non-political individuals, also 'cowards' and loyal footsoldiers in an illegal war (*einem völkerrechtswidrigen Krieg*)" who had fallen afoul of Nazi military authorities and been punished for desertion would have to be compensated equally in the future.[113] Legal outcomes produced by the Nazi's system of military justice, the judges declared, were—by definition and without exception—a product of the prerogative state, not the normative state.

By explicitly invoking his structuralist analysis, the Federal Social Court belatedly bestowed on Fraenkel the kind of public recognition that he deserved—and desired—during his lifetime.[114] It was a moment of posthumous justice for a courageous man whose final years were filled with despair about the country to which he had so reluctantly returned.[115]

9

Authoritarian Rule of Law

The rule of law can mean simply
a set of procedures rather than
a mechanism to produce substantive justice.
Indeed, in the context of neoliberalism,
this is increasingly what the rule of law means.

Sally Engle Merry[1]

A non-democratic legal system,
based on the denial of human rights,
on extensive poverty, on racial segregation,
sexual inequalities, and religious persecution may, in principle,
conform to the requirements of the rule of law
better than any of the legal systems of
the more enlightened Western democracies.

Joseph Raz[2]

What is at stake in revisiting the law of the Third Reich, in complicating the dominant narrative, as I have sought to do in this book? My answer turns on one of the most important debates in jurisprudence: that concerned with the relationship between law and morals. Made famous by the exchange between H. L. A. Hart and Lon Fuller in the pages of the *Harvard Law Review*, this debate always had a bearing on the real world. After all, it was the case of Nazi Germany, and Gustav Radbruch's philosophical argument about law and lawlessness in the Third Reich, that occasioned the Hart-Fuller debate. And the debate continues to matter in the twenty-first century. As Nicola Lacey wrote on the occasion of its fiftieth anniversary, "[T]he debate speaks to us, and to our students, in its direct engagement with two questions of genuinely timeless relevance: those of how far, and under what circumstances, law can be invoked to constrain political power and of how far we can expect it to be a force for good, or evil, in our complicated social world."[3] Arguably, Fraenkel's ethnography of Nazi law is more directly relevant to answering these questions than Hart and Fuller's contributions to the philosophy of law.

A TWITCH AND A WINK

An enduring metaphor to capture the essence of ethnography is one made famous by Clifford Geertz: "thick description."[4] It was actually Gilbert Ryle who coined the term.[5] Pondering Rodin's *le Penseur*, Ryle, a philosopher of language at the University of Oxford at the time, was contemplating the relationship between the observable and the concealed. The figure in Rodin's famous bronze sculpture mesmerized Ryle, causing him to muse about *le Penseur*: "What he is 'thinly' doing must have a 'thicker' description."[6] Keen to get at the underneath of things, Ryle came up with a thought experiment:

> Two boys fairly swiftly contract the eyelids of their right eyes. In the first boy this is only an involuntary twitch; but the other is winking conspiratorially to an accomplice. At the lowest or thinnest level of description the two contractions of the eyelids may be exactly alike. From a cinematograph-film of the two faces there might be no telling which contraction, if either, was a wink, or which, if either, was a mere twitch. Yet there remains the immense but unphotographable difference between a twitch and a wink.[7]

Telling this difference, Ryle was convinced, required special acumen: attunedness to context and the ability to appreciate and communicate the significance thereof. A thin description of a wink would state the obvious, that is, the observable: the physical act of the contraction of an eyelid. "For Ryle, thin description was an unadorned, first-order account of behavior, one that could be recorded just as well by a camera as by a human agent."[8] A thick description of a wink, by contrast, was knowing and elaborate and sophisticated. It would reveal the communicative function of the eyelid's movement and alert the reader to the social meaning for which it stands, be it arrogance or collusion, mimicry or rebellion, or any other state of being. Thick description, as Geertz understood it, is aimed at erecting "a stratified hierarchy of meaningful structures in terms of which twitches, winks, fake-winks, parodies [...] are produced, perceived, and interpreted, and without which they would not [...] in fact exist, no matter what anyone did or didn't do with his eyelids."[9]

What does this have to do with the law of the Third Reich? Quite a lot, as it turns out. Geertz believed the aim of ethnography was to draw large conclusions from small events all the while keeping in mind the inherent limitations of the exercise: "The essential vocation of interpretive anthropology is not to answer our deepest questions, but to make available to us answers that others, guarding other sheep in other valleys, have given, and thus to include them in the consultable record of what man [and woman] has said."[10] Fraenkel did just that in *The Dual State*. He interpreted memorably the webs of significance the Nazis had spun and showed how they became entangled with older such webs. Where Franz Neumann homogenized the law, Fraenkel disaggregated it, thereby providing us with a far subtler account of the violence of law in the Third Reich.

Deeply immersed in the everyday life of law, Fraenkel learned to tell the difference between a twitch and wink. He knew to distinguish the prerogative from the normative uses of law, knowing full well that *both* legal practices were serving the dictatorship that was out to destroy him.[11] And yet he thought it important to describe the inside of the Nazi dictatorship. Once again, he was not naïve. His account of ambivalence and dissonance in the legal norms and institutions of the Third Reich led to a far more accurate portrayal of the logic of authoritarian rule than monochrome accounts like Neumann's which sidestep the issue of institutional development.[12] Taking institutional historicity seriously, however, is essential for understanding law-in-society. For as Martin Krygier reminds us, "Law can ultimately serve bad purposes even if it does some good; indeed [. . .] doing good [by way of law] can be one way of doing bad because it legitimizes power, distances it from (its own) distasteful acts, can act as a pressure release valve."[13] This was precisely Fraenkel's point; the reason why he cautioned not to equate the Nazis' normative state with the *Rechtsstaat* of old.[14] This speaks to Krygier's point that legalism as a social practice of rule can have all kinds of institutional effects, intended and otherwise. Indeed, "sometimes, even in the midst of bad, doing good just does good; sometimes it is even intended to. We should leave conceptual space for those possibilities."[15] Neumann left no such space, which is why his description of the Nazi dictatorship looks so incredibly thin from the vantage point of the present.

Telling the difference between a twitch and a wink in the law of the Third Reich was no mean task for anyone, let alone a German Jew who leaned to the left.[16] In addition to having had to stare death in the face for years on end, as an ethnographer Fraenkel faced "a multiplicity of complex conceptual structures, many of them superimposed upon or knotted into one another, which are at once strange, irregular, and inexplicit, and which he must contrive somehow first to grasp and then to render."[17] Without intending to, Geertz with these words captured the exigencies of Fraenkel's life in the Third Reich, and that of other intellectuals, like Sebastian Haffner and Victor Klemperer, who, forty years before the publication of *The Interpretation of Cultures*, were searching for meaning amidst the mayhem, describing as thickly as they knew how the breakdown of democracy in Germany.[18] From Fraenkel one can learn, *pace* Neumann, that law is never just an instrument, never just a weapon of the strong. As E. P. Thompson put it in *Whigs and Hunters*, "If the law is evidently partial and unjust, then it will mask nothing, legitimize nothing, contribute nothing to any class's hegemony. The essential precondition for the effectiveness of law, in its function as ideology, is that it shall display an independence from gross manipulation and shall seem to be just."[19] My discursive analysis of the Nazi debate about the *Rechtsstaat* was designed to render visible some of the "actors, rules, and practices" involved in the Nazi reconstruction of legal thought and practice, and the desire of some notable Nazi jurists to not sacrifice (all of) law on the altar of authoritarian politics.

If my account of Fraenkel's institutional theory of dictatorship is correct, he had a better feel than most of his contemporaries for what it meant to be working in democracy's ruins. By piecing together in secret an ethnography of Nazi law, he contributed in large measure to the consultable record about the logic of law in one of the most violent of human institutions—dictatorship. His innovative solution to the methodological challenges involved in studying nondemocratic regimes also means that *The Dual State* is immediately relevant for making sense of twenty-first century authoritarianism. For contrary to the hopes of rule-of-law advocates in the international community, authoritarian rule is pervasive and durable. "Authoritarianism remained alive and well in the early twenty-first century," is how some have put it.[20] In the remainder of this chapter, I tease out the theoretical and empirical significance of my analysis by turning from the twentieth century to the twenty-first. In addition to this temporal leap, I make another: from one misunderstood manifestation of law to another, from the *Rechtsstaat* to the rule of law. My objective is to show that Fraenkel's ethnography of Nazi law is relevant beyond borders.

RECHTSSTAAT TO THE RULE OF LAW

In the late 1970s, Joseph Raz challenged conventional wisdom about the rule of law when he declared that the doctrine required of law nothing other than that it "be capable of guiding the behaviour of its subjects," and that the rule of law represented "just *one* of the virtues which a legal system may possess and by which it is to be judged."[21] Raz's defense of a procedural concept of the rule of law was fervent:

> Not uncommonly when a political ideal captures the imagination of large numbers of people its name becomes a slogan used by supporters of ideals which bear little or no relation to the one it originally designated. [...] In 1959 the International Congress of Jurists meeting in New Delhi gave official blessing to a similar perversion of the doctrine of the rule of law.[22]

Raz's critique of the incipient rule-of-law movement was no holds barred. Though plausible, it has had many detractors. The late Thomas Bingham, Lord Chief Justice of England and Wales, was among the most prominent critics to take issue with Raz's concept of the rule of law:

> While [...] one can recognize the logical force of Professor Raz's contention, I would roundly reject it in favour of a "thick" definition, embracing the protection of human rights within its scope. A state which savagely represses or persecutes sections of its people cannot in my view be regarded as observing the rule of law, even if the transport of the persecuted minority to the concentration camp or the compulsory exposure of female children on the mountainside is the subject of detailed laws duly enacted and scrupulously observed.[23]

The moralizing force of Lord Bingham's contention is a throwback to the progressive legal thought of Gustav Radbruch and Franz Neumann, which I critiqued in this book's early chapters.[24] It shows that the thorny questions thrown up by the case of Nazi Germany are neither confined to the civil law world, nor the sole preserve of the past. They are still with us today, perhaps more pressingly so than ever. As Sally Engle Merry writes from the perspective of the present: "Law is open to manipulation, but within limits. Where these limits are and when the features of the legal system itself obstruct its mobilization for political purposes is the most interesting aspect of the way law exercises power."[25] With the help of empirical vignettes about the authoritarian rule of law drawn from a handful of cases ranging from China to Spain, and from Russia to Singapore, I endeavor in the remainder to establish the dual state as a conceptual variable for the comparative historical analysis of authoritarianism.[26]

Many who have been wary of Fraenkel's argument about the normative state in Nazi Germany exhibited "rule skepticism." Hart famously used the term in *The Concept of Law*.[27] His mission was to overcome the belief that rules are epiphenomenal, a view held by American legal realists around Oliver Wendell Holmes, Jr. in the early twentieth century. Rule skeptics are convinced of two things: (1) that rules do not constrain social behavior; and (2) that they do not do so because legalism is in essence the rationalization of results brought about by other social practices, be they political or economic. Rule skeptics are even more doubtful about law's ability to have an independent effect in times of authoritarian rule. Marxists are notable rule skeptics, which partially explains why Neumann was so vociferous in his rejection of Fraenkel's selection of law as an intervening variable to explain the Nazi dictatorship. In order to respond to rule skeptics like Neumann, it is essential to work out what makes law distinctive. Frank Lovett did just that, and I will rely on his reformulation of the concept of law to deepen our understanding of the concept that I seek to define herein: that of the authoritarian rule of law.

We must begin with the question of law's domain. The task is to "define and delimit precisely the sphere of practical activity for which the practices distinctively characteristic of a legal system are the most appropriate method for organizing our activities."[28] Lovett does not think that a laundry list of principles such as generality, prospectivity, stability is particularly useful for demarcating the universe of law's reach, and I tend to agree: "Principles of legality do not themselves address the appropriate scope of law's domain."[29] This observation articulates a philosophical critique of ideal concepts of law, proponents of which included Radbruch, Fuller, and Neumann, whose treatments of Nazi law I juxtaposed with Fraenkel's and found wanting.

A Concept of Law

On the foundation of this critique, Lovett has crafted a new concept of law, one that I adopt:

> [A] set of social rules has the character of law (i.e., will be experienced as law and not something else) for those persons within the effective range of some public coercive agent when it is common knowledge that the rules in that set are supported, directly or indirectly, by that public coercive agent.[30]

This definition is sufficiently pragmatic to be usable in the real world. More important for the purpose of this book is the fact that Lovett is agnostic with respect to the aims of his public coercive agent. His conception of law "is not tethered to some particular view regarding its essential purpose or function—as, for example, that the function of law is to maintain social order or settle disputes."[31] Inasmuch as law everywhere fulfills regulatory and adjudicative functions, functional accounts of law are ill-suited to explain what is distinctive about law as a social phenomenon.[32] Yet gaining clarity about this distinctiveness is essential for clarifying the conditions under which law can matter under authoritarianism. Lovett's philosophical intervention raises questions about the analytical utility of the functional accounts of the authoritarian rule of law that recently saw the light of day.[33] I agree with Brian Tamanaha that the meaning of law must be articulated "*before* functional analysis can be engaged to inquire what it does, how it does it, and what its consequences are; we can instead posit the function—maintain social order—but then we must still come up with criteria to distinguish the distinctively 'legal' phenomena from among the others kinds of phenomena [...] which serve this function; which means, again, we must already know what law is."[34] Heeding this advice, I take Lovett's tripartite concept of the rule of law as my starting point for thinking about the authoritarian rule of law. With him, I assume the following:

> A society is ruled by law when no member of that society need fear being subject to coercive force, except as the public sanction attached to a known rule. This can only be the case when, roughly speaking, three broad criteria are satisfied, as follows:
> (1) Every use of coercive force in that society is governed by *rules*.
> (2) The rules governing the use of coercive force in that society must be *effective and reliable*.
> (3) It must be *common knowledge* in that society both (a) what rules govern the use of coercive force, and (b) that those rules are effective and reliable.[35]

This concept of the rule of law is reminiscent of Raz's better known formulation. But it is more useful for the comparative historical analysis of law because it offers a pared-down concept that can be operationalized more easily. It bears emphasizing that Lovett, in contrast to Tom Ginsburg and Tamir Moustafa, very deliberately equates the rule *of* law with rule *by* law, a practice that I follow.[36] Against this background, the value of the rule of law comes into view. It centers on law's ability to "govern the use of coercive force effectively and reliably in a way alternative practices cannot."[37] An *effective* rule of law, as I use the term, is one in which its norms and institutions actually temper agents, notably the manner in which they wield power; a *reliable* rule of law rule is one in which the probability of its norms and institutions being respected is suitably high across a wide range of substantive areas and social arenas.[38]

HYBRID REGIMES

I began Chapter 7 with a quote from G. W. F. Hegel about the idea of hybridity: "Something is alive [...] only to the extent that it contains contradiction within itself [...]."[39] Hegel, in *The Science of Logic*, also theorized about what happens when a Janus-faced phenomenon is unable to come to terms with the dissonance at its core: "If [...] a concrete existent were not capable of [...] harboring contradiction within it, it would not be a living unity as such, [...] and in contradiction it would founder and sink to the ground."[40] In the twentieth century, social scientists from Max Weber to Reinhard Bendix to Andrew Gould recovered this idea and emphasized the "conflicting imperatives" underlying all forms of social organization.[41] It is worth asking whether one of the reasons why the Nazi dictatorship proved to be unsustainable as a solution to the problem of *völkisch* order was its incapacity to contain the conflicting imperatives built into its dual state. From 1938 onward, the prerogative state began to eviscerate more forcefully than it had up until that point the surviving remnants of the *Rechtsstaat* in the Third Reich. Slowly but surely, the contradiction at the heart of the dictatorship was resolved in favor of the prerogative state. Although this did not mean the end of Nazi law, it resulted in a further devaluation of law as a means of authoritarian politics. A more violent dictatorship was the result. In the last few decades outcomes have been more mixed. In Chile and South Africa, largely successful transitions from authoritarian rule unfolded in the context of dual states.[42] Democratic rule has been sustained in both cases. Despite challenges to its consolidation, democracy has become self-enforcing.[43] In postcommunist Russia, by contrast, the transition from full authoritarianism to a dual state has been reversed. The Putin-led regime has reinforced the institutions of the prerogative state to such an extent that little institutional hybridity remains. Singapore and Hong Kong are two cases in which dual-state-rule has proved durable. In Kanishka Jayasuriya's reading,

> Singapore provides a good example of the dual state [...] as the hallmark of a regime of exception. The rule of law, the Singaporean leaders argue, is one of the defining features of the Singapore state, but it is a legalism that applies selectively to the economic or commercial sphere. The political arena [...] is regulated by executive prerogative power. In both colonial Hong Kong and independent Singapore, legalism has been used as a particularly effective weapon to depoliticise [...] society. Despite assumptions to the contrary, [the] new Chinese rulers in Hong Kong may find this form of authoritarian legalism quite handy. [...] Hong Kong exemplifies the kind of dual state that we have observed in Singapore.[44]

Given the temporary, post-handover institutional design for Hong Kong that was agreed between the United Kingdom and the People's Republic of China in the Sino-British Joint Declaration of 1984, one might say that Hong Kong represents a dual-state-enclave within China's full authoritarian regime.[45] The constitutional principle of "one country, two systems," formulated by Deng Xiaoping and valid until 2047, gives a sense of the large range of empirical settings to which the dual-state-concept is potentially applicable.

Fraenkel to Dahl

At the turn of the twenty-first century, Larry Diamond highlighted "a new wave of scholarly attention to the varieties of nondemocratic regimes and to the rather astonishing frequency with which contemporary authoritarian regimes manifest, at least superficially, a number of democratic features."[46] These "hybrid regimes," as he called them, are not a new fixture in the international system, but an increasingly prevalent one. "One of the most striking features of the 'late period' of the third wave has been the unprecedented growth in the number of regimes that are neither clearly democratic nor conventionally authoritarian."[47] This trend has not abated, as recent data from China to Venezuela, and even the United States, make clear.

These examples also show the democratizing bias that was inherent in early research on hybrid regimes. Steven Levitsky and Lucan Way have convincingly argued that "[s]uch characterizations are misleading. The assumption that hybrid regimes are (or should be) moving in a democratic direction lacks empirical foundation. Hybrid regimes followed diverse trajectories during the post-Cold War period. Although some of them democratized (e.g., Ghana, Mexico, and Slovakia), most did not. Many regimes remained stable (e.g., Malaysia and Tanzania) or became increasingly authoritarian (e.g., Belarus and Russia)."[48]

My analysis of the Nazi dictatorship is a case in point. There, the remnants of the *Rechtsstaat* confronted the worst excesses of the prerogative state for a short while, but the normative state was no match for the all-encompassing totalitarian dictatorship that consolidated itself in the late 1930s.[49] The Third Reich that Fraenkel knew firsthand was a hybrid regime on the path to totalitarianism. The case of Syria shows that transitions from hybrid to totalitarian rule are not a thing of the past.[50] When, after the death of Hafiz al-Asad, Bashar al-Asad assumed the presidency there in July 2000, he embarked on a modernization of his father's closed authoritarianism:

> Bashar al-Asad's project, on his accession to power, was to open the economy to the world market and adapt the country to the age of globalization through measures such as introduction of the internet. Ba'athist ideology was abandoned; yet, in the absence of a substitute blueprint, reform proceeded by trial and error, and incrementally to avoid destabilization

> and provoking enemies before Asad had built up his own reformist faction. His first priorities were to foster modernizing cadres and strengthen state institutions through administrative reform. In principle, the regime sought a "middle" way, expanding the private sector while reforming rather than privatizing the public sector, and maintaining social protection during economic liberalization, as embodied in the slogan of the "social market" economy adopted in 2005.[51]

The institutional effects of (fledgling) hybrid rule in Syria were not pathbreaking but noticeable. Freedom of expression was enhanced and "[c]ritics of the regime were treated more leniently, even encouraged to voice constructive criticism, albeit within boundaries highlighted by episodic instances of selective repression."[52] Syria's was a short-lived experiment in hybridity, however. Due to intra-regime competition from hardliners as well as continued discontent in the population, the hybrid regime ultimately proved unsustainable, which is what created the structural conditions for a worsening rather than softening of authoritarianism in times of crisis. The Arab uprising of 2011 was that crisis. Al-Asad chose violent repression over concession in response to the initially moderate demands of the peaceful demonstrators who gathered in Damascus and elsewhere. Outrage throughout the country about the disproportionate response "allowed what were localized protests demanding reform to spiral into a major uprising bent on overthrowing the regime."[53] It was the beginning of the end of authoritarianism in Syria and inaugurated a totalitarian turn that precipitated the country's descent into civil war. The scale of the collective violence that ensued is staggering: In a study for the UN High Commissioner for Human Rights, a team of scholars documented 191,369 conflict-related killings in Syria between March 2011 and April 2014.[54]

Unlike full authoritarian regimes, hybrid regimes allow for a modicum of contestation.[55] I distinguish, in the first instance, among two subtypes: electoral authoritarian regimes and competitive authoritarian regimes. Although the former subtype of authoritarianism has a long pedigree, Diamond believes the latter "is very much a product of the contemporary world."[56] In *electoral regimes*, contestation is centered on the institution of voting. Originally coined by Juan Linz, Andreas Schedler first conceptualized the term: "The notion of electoral authoritarianism takes seriously both the authoritarian quality these regimes possess and the electoral procedures they put into practice. The emphasis on authoritarianism serves to distinguish them from electoral democracies and the emphasis on elections to set them apart from 'closed' autocracies. Electoral democracies lack some attributes of liberal democracy (such as checks and balances, bureaucratic integrity, and an impartial judiciary), but they do conduct free and fair elections, which electoral authoritarian regimes don't."[57] The theoretical emphasis is on the ability to *vote* for power. For scholars who study *competitive regimes*, the ability to *vie* for power is more important. Levitsky and Way have come up with a useful definition of this second subtype:

> Competitive authoritarian regimes are civilian regimes in which formal democratic institutions exist and are widely viewed as the primary means of gaining power, but in which incumbents' abuse of the state places them at a significant advantage vis-à-vis their opponents. Such regimes are competitive in that opposition parties use democratic institutions to contest seriously for power, but they are not democratic because the playing field is heavily skewed in favor of incumbents. Competition is thus real but unfair.[58]

Where the concept of electoral authoritarianism prioritizes the question of access to power, the notion of competitive authoritarianism emphasizes the exercise of power in the classification of regimes.[59] The distinction between electoral regimes and competitive regimes can also be expressed in terms of the two dimensions of Robert Dahl's famous concept of polyarchy: participation and opposition.[60] Dahl regarded both as conditions *sine qua non* of what is more commonly known as procedural democracy. He alerted generations of political scientists to the fact that participation and opposition represented two sides of the same coin: "[I]n the absence of the right to oppose the right to 'participate' is stripped of a very large part of the significance it has in a country where public contestation exists. A country with universal suffrage and a completely repressive government would provide fewer opportunities for opposition, surely, than a country with a narrow suffrage but a highly tolerant government."[61]

Yet neither Schedler's electoral authoritarianism nor Levitsky and Way's competitive authoritarianism are capable of capturing the logic of hybridity at work in the early years of the Third Reich. Neither did the Hitler dictatorship permit elections nor did it countenance contestation by opposition parties. Nazi Germany's hybrid rule in the period 1933–1938 was schizophrenic in an altogether different way: it was *legal* more than it was electoral or competitive in the way it moderated its domination. Law plays a role in both of Dahl's dimensions of polyarchy, but it is also a phenomenon *sui generis*, which is why authoritarian regimes that are genuinely law-governed ought to be classified as a separate subtype: as *dual states*.[62] See Figure 9.1. If electoral regimes can be recognized by the electoral contestation they permit, and competitive regimes by the governmental contestation they allow, let us call legal contestation the practice of constraining full authoritarianism in dual states.[63]

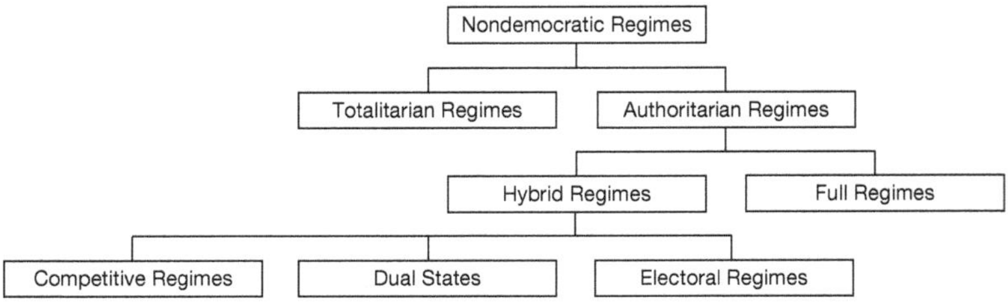

Figure 9.1 A typology of nondemocratic regimes

THE FORCE OF LAW

With their Janus-faced institutional design, dual states are the quintessential hybrid regimes. Inspired by Fraenkel's ethnography of law, I take dual states to refer to polities governed, in whole or in part, by an authoritarian rule of law. Dual states are useful indicators of the authoritarian rule of law, and vice versa. As a third subtype of hybrid authoritarianism, the category of dual states foregrounds the force of law as opposed to the force of other institutions (such as participation or opposition) in the logic of domination.[64] At the same time, it distinguishes this force from the force of physical violence. Dual states are instances of authoritarian rule in which a *legal* way of doing things co-exists with an alternative mode of behavior: a *violent* way of doing things. Life in dual states is perched on the precipice between the norm and the exception.

Like other ideal-type concepts, that of the dual state comprises "fundamental components that are mutually reinforcing *and* in tension with each other."[65] This conceptual strategy is analytically promising. It allows researchers interested in hybrid regimes to investigate the changing relationship between the normative and prerogative halves of really existing dual states, and to do so over time. It opens the door for dynamic analyses of institutional change over the *longue durée*.[66] Leaving aside its counterintuitive analytic narrative of Nazi dictatorship, *The Dual State* is also an insightful account of the structural transformation of a legal sphere—and one that can be replicated anywhere. But readying the concept of the dual state for replication—and for generalizations about the legal origins of dictatorship and democracy—necessitates a few friendly amendments.[67]

Mindful of Giovanni Sartori's so-called ladder of abstraction, I have tried to balance the amended concept's intension and extension so as to avoid conceptual stretching.[68] Given the clarity and parsimony of Fraenkel's original formulation, it would be counterproductive to alter the concept's basic set-up. In my effort to bring the dual state back in, I therefore retain but

Table 9.1 A Typology of Hybrid Regimes

Competitive Regimes	Dual States	Electoral Regimes
"Competitive authoritarian regimes are civilian regimes in which formal democratic institutions exist and are widely viewed as the primary means of gaining power, but in which incumbents' abuse of the state places them at a significant advantage vis-à-vis their opponents. Such regimes are competitive in that opposition parties use democratic institutions to contest seriously for power, but they are not democratic because the playing field is heavily skewed in favor of incumbents. Competition is thus real but unfair."[1]	Dual states are hybrid authoritarian regimes marked by the concurrent existence of a normative state that governs in accordance with legal norms and institutions, and a prerogative state that governs wantonly. Their constitutive halves are independent yet interrelated; as defining attributes they are necessary and sufficient. They stand for, and combine, two conflicting strategies of authoritarian rule: decisionism and legalism. Dual states are authoritarian in that they reign over a playing field violently skewed in favor of incumbents; they are legalist in that their authoritarianism is open to legal reasoning and legal disputing; and they are decisionist in that the sovereign will of their authoritarian ruler(s) is limitless and supreme.	"The notion of electoral authoritarianism takes seriously both the authoritarian quality these regimes possess and the electoral procedures they put into practice. The emphasis on authoritarianism serves to distinguish them from electoral democracies and the emphasis on elections to set them apart from 'closed' autocracies. Electoral democracies lack some attributes of liberal democracy (such as checks and balances, bureaucratic integrity, and an impartial judiciary), but they do conduct free and fair elections, which electoral authoritarian regimes don't."[2]

1. Steven Levitsky and Lucan A. Way, *Competitive Authoritarianism: Hybrid Regimes after the Cold War* (Cambridge: Cambridge University Press, 2010), p. 5.

2. Andreas Schedler, "The Logic of Electoral Authoritarianism," in idem., ed., *Electoral Authoritarianism: The Dynamics of Unfree Competition* (Boulder: Lynne Rienner, 2006), p. 5.

elaborate Fraenkel's minimal definition.[69] As I discussed in Chapter 7, the "key" for Fraenkel lay in "the duality or concurrent existence of a 'normative state' that generally respects its own laws, and a 'prerogative state' that violates the very same laws."[70] In dual states, a "line of division" keeps these constitutive loci apart.[71] And yet, following Fraenkel, as institutional halves of a greater whole, they are tied to one another and "in constant friction."[72] Important is the co-existence in dual states of "arbitrariness" (produced by the prerogative state) and "efficiency based on order" (provided by the normative state).[73] To qualify as dual states, authoritarian regimes must, I propose, definitionally contain a rational core within an irrational self. But more is needed to turn the dual state into a conceptual variable.

Let me define the prerogative state anew. As a form of institutionalized lawlessness, or wanton rule, the prerogative halves of dual states can be spotted by looking for evidence of "unlimited arbitrariness and violence unchecked by any legal guarantees."[74] This is not to say that prerogative states will continuously exercise their unfettered infrastructural power; the point is that they can and do, and that no sphere of life is immune from their interventions—neither politics and economics, nor law and society.[75] The prerogative half of dual states reminds of an ideal typical version of totalitarianism. Juan Linz's acclaimed take illustrates the point: "The dimensions [...] necessary to characterize a system as totalitarian are an ideology, a single mass party and other mobilizational organizations, and concentrated power in an individual and his collaborator or a small group that is not accountable to any large constituency and cannot be dislodged from power by institutionalized, peaceful means. Each of these elements can be found separately in other types of nondemocratic systems and only their simultaneous presence makes a system totalitarian."[76] The centrality of violence was also key for Linz: "The commitment to ideology, the desire for monopolistic control, and the fear of losing power [...] explain the propensity toward coercive methods in such systems and the likelihood for continuing terror. Therefore, terror [is one important factor that] distinguishes totalitarian systems from other nondemocratic systems."[77] Linz's focus on "terror" is similar to Fraenkel homing in on "continuous siege" as an indicator for the prerogative state.[78] It is logically conceivable, however, that a prerogative state rules ruthlessly and wantonly without the presence of an overriding ideology, a single mass party, or a total mobilization of society. The apartheid regime bears out this point. The regime was authoritarian, never totalitarian, and still a dual state. Another case in point is that of Singapore. The experience of postcommunist Russia also comes to mind, where the imperative of state-building in the transition to authoritarian rule trumped any allure of ideology.[79] What emerged was a veritable dual state, one in which refurbished remnants of the nineteenth century *Rechtsstaat* exerted institutional constraints.

It was the late Harold Berman who first drew attention to the idea of the *Rechtsstaat* in Russian legal culture.[80] Known as *pravovoe gosudarstvo* in Russian, it was a key trope of Mikhail Gorbachev's reformist agenda with roots in prerevolutionary Russia.[81] As a really existing institution, it gathered strength in the transition from communism to democracy but the idea of normative rule lost salience in the re-equilibration of authoritarianism that followed. Yet at the level of what Kathryn Hendley calls "everyday law," remnants of the *Rechtsstaat* have survived the attacks by Vladimir Putin's prerogative state.[82] Given the bifurcated nature of authoritarian rule in contemporary Russia, scholars like Hendley and Richard Sakwa have come to classify its hybrid regime as a dual state.[83] But it was Berman who originally transplanted the concept to eastern soil. In 1963, he highlighted the dual nature of the Soviet state, reporting that his evidence showed "a surprising degree of official compartmentalization of the legal and the extralegal."[84] Robert Sharlet concurred with this evaluation of the force of law, but reminded his readers that Berman's distinction had been "most effectively articulated in Ernst Fraenkel's concept of the Nazi legal order as a 'dual state.' "[85] Although Sharlet, like me, recommended several friendly amendments to make it usable as a conceptual variable, he believed that "the 'dual state' has heuristic value as a theoretical framework within which to analyze the continual tension between legality ('*zakonnost*') and party-orientation ('*partiinost*') in the administration of justice in the USSR."[86]

Hendley, Sakwa, and others have built on these earlier approaches to devise a more appropriate framework for studying the legal determinants of the Russian dictatorship than is commonly used.[87] As Hendley writes, rejecting the lawlessness narrative so widespread in popular and academic accounts of Putin's Russia, "Only by moving away from the rule-of-law versus rule-by-law debate and conceptualizing Russian law as dualistic can the full range of legal narratives be captured. This framework focuses our attention on the two extremes while leaving room for a wide range of other outcomes [...]."[88] But let me return to the theoretical issue at hand: the nature of the normative state.

For much of history, violent dictatorships were the norm, legal ones the exception. It is therefore not surprising that Fraenkel was vaguer when it came to the attributes of his normative-state-concept than in his treatment of the prerogative state. Given this vagueness at the heart of his theory, I advance what was undertheorized in Fraenkel's concept of the dual state. To begin with, I assume that an authoritarian regime is ruled by a normative state when members of that society can rely on the fact that a significant part of their everyday life is governed by remnants of the rule of law. This will be the case when, roughly speaking, three criteria are satisfied:

(1) A non-trivial portion of everyday life is governed by *legal rules*.

(2) The legal rules governing everyday life are *reasonably effective and reliable*.

(3) It is *common knowledge* (a) which legal rules continue to be operational, and (b) that these legal rules are reasonably effective and reliable.[89]

Taking a leaf from Dahl, I submit that the essence of the normative state, which for me is synonymous with the authoritarian rule of law, can be expressed in two dimensions: (1) *legal reasoning*, and (2) *legal disputing*. I have laid these out in Figure 9.2. An authoritarian regime may be located, theoretically, anywhere in the space bounded by these two

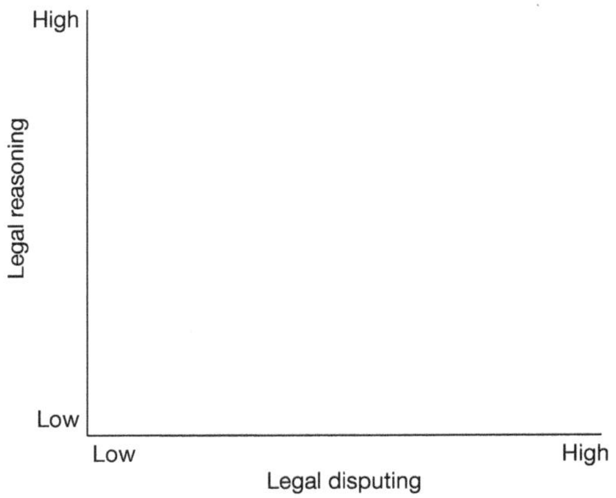

Figure 9.2 Two Theoretical Dimensions of The Authoritarian Rule of Law

dimensions. Now what does it mean for an authoritarian regime to be known for legal reasoning as I use the term?

Legal Reasoning

Legal reasoning in the common law tradition, as Edward Levi observed in a famous introductory text, stands for reasoning from part to part: "The basic pattern of legal reasoning is reasoning by example. It is reasoning from case to case. It is a three-step process described by the doctrine of precedent in which a proposition descriptive of the first case is made into a rule of law and then applied to a next similar situation. The steps are these: similarity is seen between cases; next the rule of law inherent in the first case is announced; then the rule of law is made applicable to the second case."[90] Legal reasoning in the common law is more dynamic than in the civil law tradition. Levi explained why: "[T]he rules change from case to case and are re-made with each case [...] because the scope of a rule of law, and therefore its meaning, depends upon a determination of what facts will be considered similar to those present when the rule was first announced. The finding of similarity or difference is the key step in the legal process."[91] In contrast to the civil law tradition, in which legal reasoning is, first and foremost, about the application of general rules to diverse facts, in the common law world, rules are in the eye of the legal beholder: "The determination of similarity or difference is the function of each judge. Where case law is considered, and there is no statute, he is not bound by the statement of the rule of law made by the prior judge even in the controlling case. [...] It is not what the prior judge intended that is of any importance; rather it is what the present judge, attempting to see the law as a fairly consistent whole, thinks should be the determining classification."[92] From Neil MacCormick's legal theory I borrow another element of legal reasoning: that of "giving (what are understood and presented as) good justifying reasons for claims, defences, or decisions."[93] MacCormick called this "the justificatory function of legal argumentation," and it is a further useful illumination of what legal reasoning, at a base level, entails.[94] As one of two dimensions of the authoritarian rule of law, let us refer to it as that mode of deliberation in which arguments derived from principles of law are systematically (and more or less consistently) brought to bear on questions of politics and society. At the most fundamental level, legal reasoning is the social practice known as playing by the rules.[95]

The ability to do so requires "a differentiated method of thinking, reasoning, and decision-making," according to Frederick Schauer.[96] Schauer illustrates his claim by recounting a well-known anecdote from English history that is worth hearing in full:

> [I]n 1607, Chief Justice Sir Edward Coke, one of the icons of the common law tradition, wrote, in defense of insisting that even the King would not be permitted as a judge in a legal case, that although "God had endowed his Majesty with excellent science and great endowments of nature," it was nevertheless true that "his Majesty was not learned in the laws of his realm of England, and causes which concern the life, or inheritance, or goods, or fortunes of his subjects, are not to be decided by natural reason but by the artificial reason and judgment of law, which law is an art which requires long study and experience, before that a man can attain to the cognizance of it.[97]

Coke's idea of "artificial reason" goes a long way toward clarifying what I regard as the first defining attribute of the normative state: a surviving institutionalized requirement of giving legal reasons in the creation, implementation, and adjudication of authoritarian rules. But seeing that we are talking about dual states, the requirement is not absolute: "In specifically political realms, power holders may directly apply administrative sanctions or extrajudicial force upon political adversaries, while they allow the rule of law to operate in less conflictive areas, such as the market or the repression of moderate opponents."[98] In the context of a nondemocratic regime, evidence of legal reasoning as I define it can be deduced from the extent to which legal rules regulate social life in a non-trivial fashion. A few examples may help to get the point across: If the drafting of legislation is, on balance, the preserve of technocrats not autocrats, legal reasoning is indicated.[99] If legal argumentation is an acceptable mode of communication, legal reasoning is prevalent. If constitutionalism has advocates, not just enemies, legal reasoning is alive. If any one of these or comparable scenarios obtain, law has the capacity to empower and constrain. To the extent that it does, law has authority, it has normativity.[100] It has force within unreason.

Legal Disputing

The second defining attribute of the normative state I call legal disputing. I chose the term to make the dual state amenable to the study of unfamiliar cultures in which "law" looks differently than it does in advanced industrialized settings such as Nazi Germany.[101] In order to ascertain the value of the normative state in a given society, we can ask how citizens, ordinary and otherwise, resolve quarrelsome situations. Do they prefer, naming, blaming, or claiming, as William Felstiner, Richard Abel, and Austin Sarat asked in their classic study of legal culture?[102] I propose that to the extent that grievances become disputes, and the members of a given population are not averse to becoming litigants in a court of law, and are permitted to seek institutionalized redress, legal norms and institutions are culturally significant. Because the naming of disputes, "the appropriate responses to disputing situations, and the remedies considered proper are inevitably informed by fundamental social values and even cultural identity," the nature and incidence of legal disputing in a given authoritarian society is a useful indicator of legal consciousness, and thus of a certain proclivity for a legal way of doing things, that is, the existence of a legal culture.[103]

Recall, for example, Fraenkel's ability to lodge in courts of Nazi law claims on behalf of his clients, often successfully so and almost up until his flight from the Third Reich in 1938.[104] Richard Abel compiled a trove of empirical evidence from court records to illustrate the power of cause lawyering under apartheid.[105] In less politically sensitive areas, such as the regulation of commercial and economic activity, the Nazi dictatorship expanded the reach of the normative state rather than curtailing it.[106] To strengthen this demarcated domain of the normative state, the institution of private property (*Eigentum*), contrary to conventional wisdom, remained largely sacrosanct in the Third Reich. It was beyond the reach of the prerogative state—as long as litigants were of Aryan descent.[107] The law of contracts was another remnant of the *Rechtsstaat*. Inasmuch as some theorists of Nazi law such as Karl Larenz and Rolf Michaelis clamored to introduce collectivist and racial ideas into the civil law code, the *Bürgerliches Gesetzbuch*, or BGB for short, the bulk of civil life was subject to formally rational law. Or, as one legal historian concluded in her in-depth analysis of the Nazi law of contracts: [W]ith the retention of [the institutions of the] contract and private property, the principle of bourgeois 'contractual society' was preserved."[108] Disputes arising from the interpretation of contracts were routinely handled by Nazi courts. Quarrels over patent infringement were also subject to legal disputing. The 1936 Patent Code meant that "employers could no longer deprive [Aryan] employees of authorship and block rewards by arguing that the company was the real inventor."[109] Patent reform paved the way for a sophisticated system of employee compensation that became the basis for postwar legislation. In other words, "the dictatorship, National Socialist rhetoric to the contrary notwithstanding, enacted a new Patent Code that borrowed much from older Anglo-American, liberal models favoring the individual inventor."[110] This is not to suggest that the consolidation of the rudimentary *Rechtsstaat* in the realm of patent law made for a more benign dictatorship. It did not. What the empirical vignette *is* meant to show is that law was structuring politics and society in decisive ways at a time when others thought lawlessness was the order of the day.

This brings me to the immediate present, and the continued relevance of the normative state as a conceptual variable therein. Hendley's comprehensive analysis of authoritarian legalism in Russia's lower level courts demonstrates how, and when, remnants of that country's *Rechtsstaat* allowed ordinary citizens to get justice and get even with the help of law—and in the shadow of Putin's powerful prerogative state.[111] Analyzing with the help of two national surveys, twenty-nine focus groups, and seventy-nine follow-up interviews as well as years of observational research Russians' general attitudes toward and concrete uses of the law (focusing on disputes involving mundane matters ranging from car accidents to water damage), Hendley has found ample evidence that the popular image of a state of lawlessness is misleading when it comes to Russia. Space constraints prevent me from delving more deeply into the data, but her conclusions are powerful and remind of the Nazi experience:

> What emerges is dualistic law: a legal system characterized by two basic realities. On the one hand, ordinary Russians are able to access their legal system with relative ease. Though not perfect, the courts resolve most disputes efficiently and, in doing so, judges are guided by the written law, both procedural and substantive. If assessed in terms of these mundane disputes, the Russian legal system would receive respectable scores on many elements of the rule of law. On the other hand, these routine cases, though representing the vast majority of cases brought to the courts, do not capture the full story of Russian law. Those who bring nonroutine disputes into the legal system (or have such cases brought against them) risk being swept into the shadowy world of telephone law. In such cases, the written law takes a back seat to brute power and any pretense of justice is absent.[112]

Perhaps the most notorious manifestation of law's violence in Russia to date was the prosecution of Mikhail Khodorkovsky, the former head of the Yukos Oil Company, who ran afoul of Putin and his *silovik* faction (associates with a strong connection to the security services). In Richard Sakwa's reading, the two trials "exposed the influence of telephone law and other limitations of judicial independence, and thus undermined the legitimacy of the regime in its entirety."[113] But other scholars have warned of reading too much into show trials like those of Khodorkovsky. Such trials, they say, are a poor indicator of law's meaning in everyday life, which is why Marina Kurkchiyan bemoans the "negative myth of the rule of law," proposing instead to rely on the concept of the dual state to capture the complicated role(s) of law in postcommunist Russia. "If the Russian legal system is neither fish nor fowl—neither a neat fit for 'rule of law' nor 'rule by law'—then how should we think about it? My first instinct is to advocate for doing away with these categories. But the multibillion-dollar industry that has grown up around the rule of law, which includes doling out aid based on countries' progress toward this elusive goal and the proliferation of indexes that purport to measure it, renders this proposal quixotic at best. [. . .] But maybe the time has come to step back from indexes and to encourage the sorts of thick description that better capture the everyday role of law."[114] This brings us back to Fraenkel.

Fraenkel was the first ethnographer of the authoritarian rule of law. In an era in which measuring the rule of law is seen as more important than understanding it—in the Weberian sense of interpreting it empathetically at the points of its practice—taking inspiration from Fraenkel's ethnography of Nazi law may help address the imbalance between desk research and field research in the study of authoritarianism, and, in the long run, lead to improved policy outcomes.[115] Without the kind of immersive research that Fraenkel was forced to conduct in the Third Reich, and Hendley chose to in Putin's Russia, the presence or absence of legal disputing in an authoritarian setting will not easily reveal itself. There is no substitute for observation to ascertain whether a given legal practice is real or mere façade, a Potemkin village of lawyers. The upshot of my illustrations from around the world is this: the ability to settle, and practice of settling, disputes in a legal setting is a useful indicator for the existence of a normative state in a hybrid authoritarian regime. Wherever legal reasoning and legal disputing are operative in more than an ad hoc fashion, a genuine commitment to at least a modicum of the rule of law can be said to exist. Like Dahl's dimensions of polyarchy, legal reasoning and legal disputing vary independently but are intertwined.

With this in mind, I present my amended definition of the dual state, recovered from Fraenkel's classic and made usable for comparative historical analysis: *Dual states are hybrid authoritarian regimes marked by the concurrent existence of a normative state that governs in accordance with legal norms and institutions, and a prerogative state that governs wantonly. Their constitutive halves are independent yet interrelated; as defining attributes they are necessary and sufficient. They stand for, and combine, two conflicting strategies of authoritarian rule: decisionism and legalism. Dual states are authoritarian in that they reign over a playing field violently skewed in favor of incumbents; they are legalist in that their authoritarianism is open to legal reasoning and legal disputing; and they are decisionist in that the sovereign will of their authoritarian ruler(s) is limitless and supreme.* See also Table 9.1.

I hope that my revised concept of the dual state will aid with the task of operationalization. The fact that the concept has "a lack of sharp denotational boundaries does not mean that the category is invalid."[116] Those for whom my re-conceptualization is insufficiently precise, or who are otherwise unconvinced about the dual state, I leave with the words of Edmund Burke. In 1874, the contrarian Irishman remarked with the wisdom that was his wont, "though no man can draw a stroke between the confines of night and day, still light and darkness are on the whole tolerably distinguishable."[117]

AUTHORITARIAN LEGALISM

Authoritarian legalism describes the social practice of conducting authoritarian politics by legal means. To the extent that authoritarian legalism is a recurring practice of authoritarian rule, and represents a defining feature of a hybrid regime, the authoritarian rule of law is present.[118] The institutional structure in which the authoritarian rule of law is embedded, I call a dual state, as re-conceptualized in the previous section. It denotes a hybrid authoritarian regime in which a normative state co-exists with a prerogative state.

The strength of the normative state is an empirical question; it cannot be determined in the abstract. The existence of authoritarian legalism does not say anything about the institutional strength of an authoritarian regime, for as the late Guillermo O'Donnell pointed out, "The distinctive mark of all kinds of authoritarian rule, even those that are highly institutionalized and legal[ly] formalized (a *Rechtsstaat*, in the original sense of the term), have somebody (a king, a junta, a party committee, or what not) that is sovereign in the classic sense: if and when they deem it necessary, they can decide without legal constraint."[119] This brings us back to my treatment of dual states as synthetic blends of decisionism and legalism. Dual states are distinguished from full authoritarian regimes in that legal norms and institutions exist with the help of which democracy-demanding forces can contest in a meaningful, if heavily circumscribed, way the politics of authoritarian rule. Although the playing field between adversaries is tilted heavily in favor of democracy-resisting forces, a space for legal contestation is preserved.

A good rule of thumb for assessing whether the ratio of normative rule to prerogative rule in a given authoritarian regime permits its classification as a dual state is to ask whether the available legal norms and institutions in that polity are sufficiently meaningful for dissenters, insurgents, or other opponents of dictatorship to take them seriously as swords or shields. In full authoritarian regimes, this will not usually be the case. More often than not, law is just a façade, which is why not all law-governed authoritarian regimes should automatically be classified as dual states. The case of post-genocide Rwanda is a case in point, and a rare find: a legalistic regime in which legal norms and institutions are virtually meaningless.[120]

In order for the operation of legal norms and institutions to rise to the level of the authoritarian rule of law (as opposed to representing merely a perfunctory use of rule by law), they need to be part of a legal culture. What I mean is that legal norms and institutions must have cultural resonance. This will be the case whenever a legal way of doing things is not alien but widespread in a given society. Something resembling a legal culture will usually lurk in the background of authoritarian settings governed by a dual state.[121] What such antecedents ensure is that legal enclaves of the kind Fraenkel theorized under the label of the normative state operate, until their demise or destruction, "on a repeated basis according to relatively fixed patterns of interactions that are valued for their own sake."[122] Such fidelity to law is a conceptual *sine qua non*. And yet it is not a given, and neither is the existence of a legal order, even though "[a] range of mainstream literatures in economics and politics [that] study law" start from that assumption, as Gillian Hadfield and Barry Weingast have noted: "Taken as a whole the institutional literatures continue to work with a highly abstract notion of law. At the extreme, they simply assume that a government that establishes a set of institutions characteristic of existing stable legal regimes—legal codes, well-trained judiciaries, enforcement agencies—will thereby institute the rule of law. But these accounts fail to explain why these institutions in many developing countries are hopelessly corrupt and ineffectual."[123]

The recognition and acknowledgment that there is something valuable about law *other* than its instrumental value for the pursuit of authoritarian politics is a scope condition for working with the concept of the dual state. There is no point to take law seriously as a conceptual variable unless there is a sense that legal consciousness is reasonably well developed in the empirical setting under investigation.[124] If law was never seriously embedded in a given society, it is unlikely that the dual-state-concept will be of much use for making sense of the logic of authoritarianism there. For as socio-legal scholars have insisted ever since Weber's sociology of law: "the law is connected to every aspect of society."[125] Where it isn't, other, better-established normative social orders will likely have greater institutional effects on political and economic outcomes than the rule of law, authoritarian or otherwise. My scope condition is another friendly amendment to Fraenkel's concept of the Janus-faced state.

Democracy promoters should not get their hopes up if they encounter the authoritarian rule of law. The empirical evidence to date suggests that authoritarian legalism is a self-reinforcing practice of nondemocratic rule; dual states are a durable subtype of authoritarianism. Yuhua Wang's quantitative evidence from China, where a dual state is holding sway, underscores this hypothesis. Wang's takeaway message: "promoting the partial rule of law does not undermine authoritarian rule in China."[126] The reconstruction of authoritarian legalism in China (after law was annihilated there during the Cultural Revolution) began in earnest in the 1990s when the country embarked on its "long march toward the rule of law" so as to attract more foreign direct investment.[127] Much of what goes on inside China's normative state has since been delegated to sub-national institutions: "To attract and retain foreign investors, Chinese local governments have taken deliberate actions to strengthen legal organizations. These include establishing more law schools, producing more professional lawyers and judges, enacting better laws to regulate the market economy, increasing court funding, and providing legal services to business."[128] But unlike the case of Nazi Germany, it appears that the commitment to law in China is purely instrumental with little expressive commitment to a legal way of doing things. As Wang has explained in an empirical analysis for his demand-side theory of the authoritarian rule of law, the push to legalize China's economy came from without, not from within. Domestic enterprises (both state-owned and private) as well as foreign enterprises owned by ethnic Chinese investors "have political connections in China and, therefore, prefer privilege to a level playing field. In contrast, foreign investors from outside the China circle lack the competitive advantage gained from building political connections with Chinese officials. They therefore have a strong preference for judicial impartiality."[129] Authoritarian legalism can be a barrier to arbitrariness, but it will never be more than a barrier to "facile change."[130] The specter of the prerogative state will generally loom too large for the authoritarian rule of law to amount to more than a weak institutional limit.

This brings us to the logic of the authoritarian rule of law. In abstract terms, the authoritarian rule of law holds the exercise of power at *t1* to the standard of choices about self-binding at *t0*. Barros puts it thus: "In general terms, [...] an institutional limit implies a legal standard, a mechanism of enforcement, a division among the authorities subject to the standard and those who uphold it, with the result that actors are constrained by prior decisions in the form of rules."[131] In a hybrid institutional design such as a dual state, law's constraining force is limited, and the power of prerogative in the final analysis absolute. And yet, as Robert Barros points out, "it is important not to conflate the argument that autocratic power is legally unbound with a claim that authoritarian power holders are free from all forms of constraint."[132] This is what most of Fraenkel's critics have overlooked. His institutional theory of dictatorship, with its account of the normative state as the guardian of the remnants of the *Rechtsstaat*, was not blind to Hitler's general omnipotence:

> The Normative State [...] is by no means identical with a state in which the "Rule of Law" prevails, i.e., with the *Rechtsstaat* of the liberal period. The Normative State is a necessary complement to the Prerogative State and can be understood only in that light. Since the Prerogative and Normative States constitute an independent whole, consideration of the Normative State alone is not permissible.[133]

It is worth reiterating the subservient relationship that exists between a normative state and the prerogative state on which it is dependent for toleration. Inasmuch as repression under a dual state may, normatively speaking, be preferable to a life under full authoritarianism or even totalitarianism, it is not a benign form of rule. As Jennifer Gandhi writes, "[n]ominally democratic institutions under dictatorship do matter but in ways that differ from their counterparts in democracies."[134] The same, I propose, goes for authoritarian legalism. The authoritarian rule of law places a modicum of institutional limits on violent rule, but it does not have the capacity to hold this rule in check. Theoretically speaking, "it is important to draw out the difference between material and political constraints and institutional limits because references to the former may lead readers to erroneously think that limited authoritarianism is relatively unproblematic."[135] It is not, as Fraenkel's personal fate in Nazi Germany demonstrates so very clearly.

Allow me to wind down this chapter with a thought experiment. I borrowed it from Lovett, and it illuminates much of what I discussed in this book. It sheds light on the presence and absence of law in a series of hypothetical interactions between two adversaries, "Andrea" and "Bob." By paying attention to what happens when the institution of law as an intervening variable is introduced into the basic structural set-up between these characters, we get a sense of what *can* happen when decisionism meets legalism under authoritarianism. In other words, the thought experiment cuts to the heart of the logic of the authoritarian rule of law, as I conceive of it:

> Imagine that Andrea is considerably stronger than Bob, and that they live in a world ungoverned by law. The probability *p* that Andrea will actually refrain from arbitrarily coercing Bob depends entirely on her subjective preferences and dispositions: if she is in the habit of respecting the personal integrity of others, the value of *p* might be reasonably high; if she has adopted "respect for the personal integrity of others" as a personal rule for herself, *p* might even approach 1. The difficulty is that, without having special insight into her private psychology, Bob cannot judge the reliability of her self-restraint. He is subject to domination.[136]

Now let us imagine the same scenario with law entering the world of Andrea's wanton rule: "The situation is transformed [...] once laws governing the use of coercive force are introduced," argues Lovett.[137] Their introduction may not spell the end of violence, but the transaction costs of Andrea's violence go up. The causal logic is straightforward:

> The constraints imposed by law supply publicly accessible reasons we can be confident will motivate across a wide range of contingent circumstances and psychologies, thus ensuring that the value of *p* will be reasonably high across a wide range of possible worlds. Notice here that the benefits of law are not reducible to predictability, which might be enhanced by raising the value of *p* alone: importantly, they involve broadening the robustness, so to speak, of that predictability. Of course, we cannot expect *p* to equal 1 in all possible worlds. There may be, for instance, a possible world in which it turns out that Andrea is an especially determined thug who cannot be deterred even by law. This only goes to show that we cannot hope to banish domination from human relations entirely.[138]

The contribution of law, therefore is constraining but limited:

> [T]he introduction of law significantly expands our freedom from domination by ensuring we will not be exposed to arbitrary coercive force: to the extent that we solve the problem of social order, only public coercive agents will be able to coerce us; and to the extent that we solve the problem

> of constitutionalism, the ability of public coercive agents to coerce us will, in turn, be reliably and effectively constrained to the enforcement of known rules of law.[139]

If we relate the imaginary world of "Andrea" and "Bob" to the real world of twenty-first century authoritarianism, both the promise and limits of authoritarian legalism come into view. Of course, Lovett's hypothetical scenario leaves out that it is public coercive agents, not private coercive agents like Andrea, that usually pose the greatest danger to freedom from domination under authoritarianism.

More interpretive research on the mechanisms and processes of authoritarian legalism is needed because the legalization of authoritarian politics—from China to Egypt to Hungary to Venezuela—is of immediate policy relevance at a time when "authoritarianism goes global."[140] Whether law is façade or foundation of authoritarian politics is a fundamental question of our time.[141] It is worth remembering in this context that authoritarian legalism was an evolutionary stage in the development of the rule of law—one that *preceded* the liberal ideal that has come to be cherished the world over. As Brian Tamanaha reminds us, "the rule of law ideal initially developed in non-liberal societies."[142] The rights and liberties for which it stood existed chiefly in the form of legal enclaves, and their reach was contingent on sovereign acquiescence.[143] This means, as Jothie Rajah has shown for the case of Singapore, "that authoritarianism and the 'rule of law' are not mutually incompatible."[144]

By recognizing the contribution of law to violence, and the violence that law itself inflicts, we are in a better position to understand the legal dimensions of dictatorship than by clinging, out of reverence, to an epistemologically problematic approach to authoritarian legalism in which the presence and absence of law is determined not by law's role in everyday life but by a moral determination about its worthiness. If we insist, with Radbruch and Neumann, that the abhorrent content of authoritarian legalism must lead to its classification as "non-law," an unintended consequence follows: disculpation. Talk of a "system failure" invariably deflects responsibility from individuals in authoritarian settings. Such an outcome is morally more problematic than the classification of an objectionable—but really existing—legal system as an authoritarian variant of the rule of law. Treating law as an institution like any other—rather than an ideal—allows us to see that even the most cherished achievements of civilization can be turned into weapons. By unpacking with the help of Fraenkel's institutional theory of dictatorship the cumulative radicalization of law in the Third Reich, I hope to have shed light on the logic of violence in law and the manner in which it can surface in transitions to authoritarian rule.

Fraenkel was not sitting in judgment as he tried to make sense of the changing character of law that was unfolding in front of his eyes. He was not proselytizing; he was analyzing. This restraint is a remarkable feat considering that he was in ever-present danger to his life at the time of his research and initial writing. Despite his being subjected to many of the excesses of the prerogative half of the Nazi state, Fraenkel brought his critical faculties to bear in a sophisticated and decidedly analytical manner. If for nothing else, *The Dual State* deserves to be re-read—and thus re-remembered—for the courage of his author's convictions.

At the time of Fraenkel's work as a cause lawyer in Weimar Germany, a term comparable to that of the dual state was invented in Spain: "*dictablanda*." In the context of that country's military junta, it was known as a pun on "*dictadura*" to describe the softening of the dictatorship under the leadership of Dámaso Berenguer who, at the behest of King Alfonso XIII, succeeded Primo de Rivera as prime minister in January 1930.[145] According to Juan Linz, remnants of the *Rechtsstaat* also partially constrained the Franco dictatorship. In the 1960s Linz argued that "the presence in the elite of men who have held power under states of law, and are themselves lawyers; or, if military, they share at least the military conception of law: legalism may not inhibit repression of the state's enemies, but it does lead to certain procedural rules, to an emphasis on actions rather than intentions" when it comes to their punishment.[146] If we believe Linz, whose interpretation of Fascist Spain has been met with resistance—just like Fraenkel's of Nazi Germany—for supposedly relativizing the brutality of the dictatorship, the regime's residual commitment to the idea of the *Rechtsstaat* meant that its courts frequently "question[ed] the decisions of the government, protect[ed] the rights of individuals and provid[ed] opportunities to the opposition to make itself heard."[147]

Linz went as far as claiming that authoritarian legalism occasionally had a constraining effect on the prerogative state even in political trials adjudicated by military tribunals (or by so-called public order tribunals), especially during the later years of the dictatorship: "In the context of some liberalization, with a tradition of judicial independence, a positivist interpretation of law that does not consider the intent as much as the nature of the act, and competent lawyers on the side of the defendants, the government or its supporters have lost a number of cases."[148] I am in no position to address the state of law in authoritarian Spain within the confines of this study. However, recent research on fascist legalism in Francoist Spain lends support to Linz's argument, though it attributes the rise of the authoritarian rule of law in the later years of the regime primarily to the diffusion in Spain of "new understandings" of law that

Spanish law students acquired in epistemic communities in the 1960s "through instruction, publication, and informal discussions."[149] As a result of this exposure, argues Lisa Hilbink, lawyers associated with *Justicia Democrática* (JD), a leftwing association comprised mostly of judges, openly challenged the authoritarian regime in the country's courtrooms. With the support of the Catholic Church, and emboldened by international alliances with like-minded jurists elsewhere, their presence inside the normative state kept Franco's prerogative state at bay, even though it was unable to shackle it. As Hilbink writes, "the young judges of JD became more risk accepting than the generations of magistrates who had preceded them, and they proactively worked to mitigate the threats from the institutional and political structures in which they functioned and ultimately, indeed, to change those structures."[150]

Could it be that John Austin had a point, when he exclaimed in *The Province of Jurisprudence Determined*, "the existence of law is one thing; its merit or demerit another"?[151] Fraenkel's ethnography of Nazi law unearthed compelling evidence to back up this assertion and to invalidate Radbruch's formula with which I opened this book. Regardless of the violence that the law of the Third Reich helped to inscribe, legitimate, and unleash, Fraenkel showed that, in Neil MacCormick's words, "[l]aws don't exist by virtue of being just, and don't stop existing by virtue of being unjust."[152] From the Nazi debate about the *Rechtsstaat* to the empirical vignettes drawn from the entire universe of legal practices in the Third Reich, I have marshalled evidence to show that, *pace* Radbruch, the idea of lawlessness is ill-suited for understanding the logic of Nazi dictatorship. And it has proved inadequate for making sense of hybrid regimes elsewhere.[153]

"That legalism can serve liberalism," Samuel Moyn opined, "does not mean it can't serve other things."[154] But the obverse is equally true, as the empirical vignette from Spain attests: that legalism can serve other things does not mean it can't serve liberalism. Holding *both* of these truths to be self-evident is what it takes to make sense of the authoritarian rule of law. A growing number of scholars are doing just that. They are stockpiling knowledge about practices of authoritarian legalism in all corners of the world. Alas, policy-makers are lagging behind, mostly unaware of how important the everyday is to establishing the rule of law. If we take the 2017 *World Development Report*, which addressed the subject of governance and the law, as our guide to the state of knowledge in the real world, it is instantly evident that more work remains to be done to show that the authoritarian rule of law is not a figment of the scholarly imagination, but a reality of rule in the twenty-first century.[155]

Notes

CHAPTER 1

1. "*Vollends sinnlos ist die Behauptung, daß in der Despotie keine Rechtsordnung bestehe, sondern Willkür des Despoten herrsche* [...]." Hans Kelsen, *Allgemeine Staatslehre* (Berlin: Springer, 1925), p. 335. Unless stated otherwise, all translations are mine. Kelsen omitted the aforementioned observation from the first English edition of his book: Hans Kelsen, *General Theory of Law and State* (Cambridge: Harvard University Press, [1925] 1949), p. 300. Leo Strauss was the first scholar to draw attention to this fact. See his *Natural Right and History* (Chicago: University of Chicago Press, [1950] 1965), p. 4, fn. 2. The omitted paragraph was reinserted into subsequent editions.
2. In November 1935, the *Reichsadler* became the official insignia of Nazi Germany. The emblem was a modified version of the insignia used in the Weimar Republic. Among other changes, the imperial eagle, with its wings spread, was now crouched on an oak wreath at the center of which was a swastika. The new *Reichsadler* mimicked, but did not quite replicate, the *Parteiadler* (Party Eagle), the official insignia of the National Socialist German Workers' Party. The distinguishing feature that differentiates the two insignia is the direction of the eagle's gaze. In the *Reichsadler*-design, the eagle's head is turned to its right, in the *Parteiadler*-design to its left.
3. For an analysis of Freisler's pivotal role in the intra-Nazi debate over the legalization of racial supremacy and the criminalization of so-called *Rassenschande*, or "racial treason," see Claudia Koonz, *The Nazi Conscience* (Cambridge: Belknap Press of Harvard University Press, 2003), Chapter 7.
4. Walter Wagner, *Der Volksgerichtshof im nationalsozialistischen Staat*, Expanded edition (Munich: Oldenbourg, 2011), p. 805.
5. An example of Freisler's call for substantively irrational law is his pamphlet *Etwas über Führertum in der Rechtspflege: Soll verantwortungsvolle Richterpersönlichkeit oder Abstimmungszahlenspiel Grundlage des Urteils sein?* (Berlin: Spaeth und Linde, 1935). See also idem., *Das Werden des Juristen im Dritten Reich* (Berlin: Junker und Dünnhaupt, 1933); idem., *Gedanken zum Schutz der Bewegung im neuen Strafrecht* (Berlin: Decker, 1936); idem., *Richter und Gesetz* (Berlin: Spaeth und Linde, 1937); idem., *Nationalsozialistisches Recht und Rechtsdenken* (Berlin: Spaeth und Linde, 1938); idem., *Gerichtliche Redekunst im Strafverfahren* (Jena: Biedermann, 1938); idem., *Widergeburt strafrechtlichen Denkens* (Berlin: Schenk, 1940); Roland Freisler and Justus Wilhelm Hedemann, *Deutsches Gemeinrecht im Werden* (Berlin: Decker, 1940). I discuss Weber's ideal types of law in Chapter 7.
6. Wagner, *Der Volksgerichtshof im nationalsozialistischen Staat*, p. 833.

7. The "German idea of the rule of law," Ralf Dahrendorf once quipped, is "one of the fetishes of German politics." Even Roland Freisler, he pointed out, embraced the idea, although, as Dahrendorf was quick to add, Freisler "went his own way in substance as well as language, in the National Socialist *Handbook of Legal Science*." Ralf Dahrendorf, *Society and Democracy in Germany* (London: Weidenfeld & Nicolson, 1968), p. 206.
8. Paul W. Kahn, *The Cultural Study of Law: Reconstructing Legal Scholarship* (New Haven: Yale University Press, 1999). See also Naomi Mezey, "Law as Culture," *Yale Journal of Law and the Humanities*, Vol. 13 (2001), pp. 35–67.
9. His was a conflicted life lived in a schizophrenic state. I do not here mean to suggest that Freisler had doubts about the course of the Third Reich: he was a committed servant of National Socialism and a rabid antisemite, as I explain in more detail in Chapter 5.
10. For a recent account of the Roman construction of the god of Janus, notably the archeological evidence pertaining to the shrine of Ianus Geminus in the Forum Romanum, see Rabun Taylor, "Watching the Skies: Janus, Auspication, and the Shrine in the Roman Forum," *Memoirs of the American Academy in Rome*, Vol. 45 (2000), pp. 1–40.
11. Ernst Fraenkel, *The Dual State: A Contribution to the Theory of Dictatorship*, translated by E. A. Shils, in collaboration with Edith Loewenstein and Klaus Knorr, with an Introduction by Jens Meierhenrich (Oxford: Oxford University Press, [1941] 2017).
12. Gustav Radbruch, "Gesetzliches Unrecht und übergesetzliches Recht," *Süddeutsche Juristen-Zeitung*, Vol. 1 (1946), reprinted in idem., *Rechtsphilosophie*, edited by Ralf Dreier and Stanley L. Paulson (Heidelberg: Müller, [1950] 2003), pp. 211–19. For an English translation by Bonnie Litschewski Paulson and Stanley L. Paulson, see Gustav Radbruch, "Statutory Lawlessness and Supra-Statutory Law," *Oxford Journal of Legal Studies*, Vol. 26 (2006), pp. 1–11. Leading commentary on Radbruch's formula includes Walter Ott and Franziska Buob, "Did Legal Positivism Render German Jurists Defenceless during the Third Reich?" *Social and Legal Studies*, Vol. 2 (1993), pp. 91–104; Stanley L. Paulson, "Lon L. Fuller, Gustav Radbruch, and the 'Positivist' Theses," *Law and Philosophy*, Vol. 13 (1994), pp. 313–59; idem., "Radbruch on Unjust Laws: Competing Earlier and Later Views?," *Oxford Journal of Legal Studies*, Vol. 15 (1995), pp. 489–500; Robert Alexy, "A Defence of Radbruch's Formula," in David Dyzenhaus, ed., *Recrafting the Rule of Law* (Oxford: Hart, 1999), pp. 15–39; Robert Alexy, *The Argument from Injustice: A Reply to Legal Positivism*, translated by Stanley L. Paulson and Bonnie Litschewski Paulson (Oxford: Oxford University Press, [1992] 2002), esp. pp. 40–68; Thomas Mertens, "Nazism, Legal Positivism, and Radbruch's Thesis on Statutory Injustice," *Law and Critique*, Vol. 14 (2003); Brian Bix, "Robert Alexy's Radbruch Formula, and the Nature of Legal Theory," *Rechtstheorie*, Vol. 37 (2006), pp. 139–49; Stanley L. Paulson, "On the Background and Significance of Gustav Radbruch's Post-War Papers," *Oxford Journal of Legal Studies*, Vol. 26 (2006), pp. 17–40; Torben Spaak, "Meta-Ethics and Legal Theory: The Case

of Gustav Radbruch," *Law and Philosophy*, Vol. 28 (2009), pp. 261–90; Brian H. Bix, "Radbruch's Formula and Conceptual Analysis," *American Journal of Jurisprudence*, Vol. 56 (2011), pp. 45–57; idem., "Radbruch's Formula, Conceptual Analysis, and the Rule of Law," in Imer B. Flores and Kenneth E. Himma, eds., *Law, Liberty, and the Rule of Law* (New York: Springer, 2013), pp. 65–76; and Douglas G. Morris, "Accommodating Nazi Tyranny? The Wrong Turn of the Social Democratic Legal Philosopher Gustav Radbruch after the War," *Law and History Review*, Vol. 34 (2016), pp. 649–88. For a more general treatment of Radbruch's concept of law, see Martin Borowski and Stanley L. Paulson, eds., *Die Natur des Rechts bei Gustav Radbruch* (Tübingen: Mohr, 2015).

13. Mertens, "Nazism, Legal Positivism, and Radbruch's Thesis on Statutory Injustice," p. 277.
14. H. L. A. Hart, "Positivism and the Separation of Law and Morals," *Harvard Law Review*, Vol. 71 (1958), pp. 593–629; Lon L. Fuller, "Positivism and Fidelity to Law: A Reply to Professor Hart," *Harvard Law Review*, Vol. 71 (1958), pp. 630–72. For a re-assessment, see, for example, the contributions to the special symposium "The Hart-Fuller Debate at Fifty," held at NYU Law School and published as *New York University Law Review*, Vol. 83 (2008).
15. For the most important examples of appellate jurisprudence from postwar Germany that turned on the application, and judicial affirmation, of Radbruch's formula, see BGHZ 3, 94 (*Haftung eines Volkssturmführers* Case); BVerfGE 3, 58 (*Beamtenverhältnisse* Case); BVerfGE 3, 225 (*Gleichberechtigung* Case); BVerfGE 6, 132 (*Gestapo* Case); BverfGE 23, 98 (*Ausbürgerung I* Case); BverfGE 54, 53 (*Ausbürgerung II* Case); BHGSt 39, 1 (*Mauerschützen I* Case); BGHSt 41, 101 (*Mauerschützen III* Case); and BVerfGE 95, 96 (*Mauerschützen* Case). The judgments—from 1951, 1953, 1957, 1968, 1980, 1992, 1995, and 1996, respectively—settled legal disputes relating to *both* of Germany's twentieth-century dictatorships, that of Nazi Germany and that of the German Democratic Republic.
16. Radbruch, "Statutory Lawlessness and Supra-Statutory Law," p. 7.
17. Radbruch, "Statutory Lawlessness and Supra-Statutory Law," p. 8.
18. Radbruch, "Statutory Lawlessness and Supra-Statutory Law," p. 11.
19. Frank Haldemann, "Gustav Radbruch vs. Hans Kelsen: A Debate on Nazi Law," *Ratio Juris*, Vol. 18 (2005), p. 165.
20. Manfred Walther, "Hat der juristische Positivismus die deutschen Juristen im 'Dritten Reich' wehrlos gemacht? Zur Analyse und Kritik der Radbruch-These," in Ralf Dreier and Wolfgang Sellert, eds., *Recht und Justiz im "Dritten Reich"* (Frankfurt: Suhrkamp, 1989), p. 353; Ingeborg Maus, "'Gesetzesbindung' der Justiz und die Struktur der nationalsozialistischen Rechtsnormen," in Ralf Dreier and Wolfgang Sellert, eds., *Recht und Justiz im "Dritten Reich"* (Frankfurt: Suhrkamp, 1989), pp. 102–3. For an account of the afterlives of Nazi lawyers in postwar Germany, see, for example, Ingo Müller, *Hitler's Justice: The Courts of the Third Reich*, translated by Deborah Lucas Schneider (Cambridge: Harvard University Press, [1987] 1991),

esp. pp. 201–98. More recently, see Manfred Görtemaker and Christoph Safferling, *Die Akte Rosenburg: Das Bundesministerium der Justiz und die NS-Zeit* (Munich: Beck, 2016).

21. Douglas Morris has shown that Radbruch's formula—notably the additional claim that legal positivism had rendered the German legal profession defenseless against the injustice of Nazi law—stemmed from a "historical misinterpretation of the Nazi judiciary," reflected "an atrophied political imagination," and resulted in a prescription for the new democracy that, tragically, "helped pollinate a postwar fascination with natural law thinking which served the purposes of judges who had once happily furthered Nazi discrimination, terror, and murder." Morris, "Accommodating Nazi Tyranny?," p. 686. For an earlier version of this argument, see Walther, "Hat der juristische Positivismus die deutschen Juristen im 'Dritten Reich' wehrlos gemacht?," p. 345.
22. It also deserves a closer look because its relevance is not confided to the German case; it can serve as a principle of transitional justice anywhere. As Brian Bix writes, "In practice, the Radbruch Formula is most likely applied where there has been some kind of transition in the relevant regime, such that a judge from one system or tradition is asked to apply (or not apply) the law of another system or tradition [...]." Bix, "Radbruch's Formula and Conceptual Analysis," p. 51.
23. Gustav Radbruch, "Die Erneuerung des Rechts," *Die Wandlung*, Vol. 2 (1947), as quoted in Paulson, "Lon L. Fuller, Gustav Radbruch, and the 'Positivist' Theses," p. 327.
24. Paulson, "Lon L. Fuller, Gustav Radbruch, and the 'Positivist' Theses," p. 333. For the most comprehensive refutation of Radbruch's exoneration thesis, see Bernd Rüthers, *Die unbegrenzte Auslegung: Zum Wandel der Privatrechtsordnung im Nationalsozialismus*, Sixth edition (Tübingen: Mohr, [1968] 2005). It was a forceful response to, among others, Hubert Schorn, a former Nazi judge, whose massive tome, *Der Richter im Dritten Reich: Geschichte und Dokumente* (Frankfurt: Klostermann, 1959), peddled the self-serving myth that judges in the Third Reich had fallen prey to legal positivism, and thus were individually blameless for any of their abhorrent conduct.
25. Paulson, "Lon L. Fuller, Gustav Radbruch, and the 'Positivist' Theses," pp. 331–2. Most recently, see Herlinde Pauer-Studer, "Einleitung: Rechtfertigungen des Unrechts," in Herlinde Pauer-Studer and Julian Fink, eds., *Rechtfertigungen des Unrechts: Das Rechtsdenken im Nationalsozialismus in Originaltexten* (Frankfurt: Suhrkamp, 2014), pp. 15–135.
26. Paulson, "Lon L. Fuller, Gustav Radbruch, and the 'Positivist' Theses," p. 332.
27. Carl Schmitt, *Staat, Bewegung, Volk: Die Dreigliederung der politischen Einheit* (Hamburg: Hanseatische Verlagsanstalt, 1933), p. 43. On this pamphlet, and what I call Carl Schmitt's "extremist institutionalism," see Jens Meierhenrich, "Fearing the Disorder of Things: The Development of Carl Schmitt's Institutional Theory, 1919–1942," in Jens Meierhenrich and Oliver Simons,

eds., *The Oxford Handbook of Carl Schmitt* (Oxford: Oxford University Press, 2016), pp. 171–216.

28. Schmitt, *Staat, Bewegung, Volk*, p. 43.
29. Roland Freisler, "Schutz des Volkes oder des Rechtsverbrechers? Fesselung des Verbrechers oder des Richters? Einiges über das zweckmäßige Maß der Bindung des Richters an gesetzliche Straftatbestände," *Deutsches Strafrecht*, Vol. 1 (1935), pp. 1–33. For an in-depth analysis of contending Nazi interpretations and extensions of the idea of the *Rechtsstaat*, see Chapter 5.
30. Paulson, "Lon L. Fuller, Gustav Radbruch, and the 'Positivist' Theses," p. 332. See also Gerhard Luf, "Zur Verantwortlichkeit des Rechtspositivismus für 'gesetzliches Unrecht': Überlegungen zur 'Radbruch-These,'" in Ulrike Davy, Helmut Fuchs, Herbert Hofmeister, Judith Marte and Ilse Reiter, eds., *Nationalsozialismus und Recht: Rechtssetzung und Rechtswissenschaft in Österreich unter der Herrschaft des Nationalsozialismus* (Vienna: Orac, 1990), pp. 18–37. For more definitive treatments of the substantively irrational dimensions of the Nazi legal system, see Diemut Majer, *Grundlagen des nationalsozialistischen Rechtssystems: Führerprinzip, Sonderrecht, Einheitspartei* (Stuttgart: Kohlhammer, 1987); and Klaus Anderbrügge, *Völkisches Rechtsdenken: Zur Rechtslehre in der Zeit des Nationalsozialismus* (Berlin: Duncker & Humblot, 1978).
31. On the topic more generally, see famously Jürgen Habermas, *Between Facts and Norms: Contributions to a Discourse Theory of Law and Democracy*, translated by William Rehg (Cambridge: MIT Press, [1992] 1996). In light of the issue at stake, it is perhaps worth noting that the title of the German original translates literally as "Facticity and Validity." See Jürgen Habermas, *Faktizitat und Geltung: Beiträge zur Diskurstheorie des Rechts und des demokratischen Rechtsstaats* (Frankfurt: Suhrkamp, 1992).
32. BVerfGE 54, 53, 54. On the implications of the Eleventh Decree to the Reich Citizenship Law, see Diemut Majer, *"Non-Germans" under the Third Reich: The Nazi Judicial and Administrative System in Germany and Occupied Eastern Europe, with Special Regard to Occupied Poland, 1939–1945*, translated by Peter Thomas Hill, Edward Vance Humphrey, and Brian Levin (Baltimore: Johns Hopkins University Press, 2003), pp. 160–1.
33. BVerfGE 54, 53, 68. More evocative than the language in the 1980 judgment is that which a panel of judges found in 1968, when the Federal Constitutional Court first pronounced on the legality of Nazi expulsions, in BVerfGE 23, 98 (the *Ausbürgerung I* Case), which is why I use it here. Stated in full, the orginal in which the quoted *obiter dictum* appeared reads as follows: "*Daher hat das Bundesverfassungsgericht die Möglichkeit bejaht, nationalsozialistischen 'Rechts'-Vorschriften die Geltung als Recht abzuerkennen, weil sie fundamentalen Prinzipien der Gerechtigkeit so evident widersprechen, daß der Richter, der sie anwenden oder ihre Rechtsfolgen anerkennen wollte, Unrecht statt Recht sprechen würde.*" BVerfGE 23, 98, 106. It is important to appreciate that the German word "*Unrecht*" has multiple connotations and presents a thorny challenge for any translator. It should therefore come as no surprise

that it has been translated in a variety of ways, each translation conjuring a very different meaning. For example, the legal philosopher Stanley Paulson, the most eminent of Radbruch's translators, together with his wife Bonnie Litschewski Paulson rendered the term "*Unrecht*" as "lawlessness," a practice that I follow. See Radbruch, "Statutory Lawlessness and Supra-Statutory Law." Note that alternative translations are occasionally used in the literature: "non-law," "false law," "flawed law," "injustice," and "despotism." Both of the latter, for example, appear in the English translation of Michael Stolleis's widely read collection of essays, *Recht im Unrecht: Studien zur Rechtsgeschichte des Nationalsozialismus* (Frankfurt: Suhrkamp, 1994), a semantic move with which Thomas Dunlap, the translator, unfortunately, obscured important nuances in Stolleis's historical argument. See Michael Stolleis, "General Introduction," in idem., *The Law under the Swastika: Studies on Legal History in Nazi Germany*, translated by Thomas Dunlap (Chicago: University of Chicago Press, 1998), esp. pp. 5, 8.

34. "*Die Staatsorgane der Bundesrepublik Deutschland können die Tatsachen nicht ungeschehen machen, die durch die Unrechtsmaßnahmen der Nationalsozialisten geschaffen worden sind.*" BVerfGE 54, 53, 69. Emphasis added in the English translation.
35. "*Die Ausbürgerung von Juden im Sinne der nationalsozialistischen Gesetzgebung bleibt ein historisches Geschehen, das als solches nicht nachträglich beseitigt werden kann.*" BVerfGE 54, 53, 69. Emphasis added in the English translation.
36. Here is the original, stated in full: "*Zwar mag das hier, wie auf manchen anderen Gebieten, vom Nationalsozialismus gesetzte Recht in einem höheren, philosophischen Sinne 'Unrecht' darstellen. Aber es würde eine in hohem Grade unrealistische Betrachtungsweise sein, diesen Gedanken positiv-rechtlich dahin auszubauen, daß dieses (formale) Recht ex post als nichtig und die dadurch bewirkte Umwandlung des Beamtenverhältnisses als nicht vorhanden betrachtet würde. Eine solche Auffassung würde übersehen, daß es auch eine 'soziologische' Geltung von Rechtsvorschriften gibt, die erst dort bedeutungslos wird, wo solche Vorschriften in so evidentem Widerspruch mit den alles formale Recht beherrschenden Prinzipien der Gerechtigkeit treten, daß der Richter, der sie anwenden oder ihre Rechtsfolgen anerkennen wollte, Unrecht statt Recht spräche.*" BVerfGE 3, 58, 118–19.
37. The same formulation also appeared in BVerfGE 3, 58, 119.
38. This reminds of John Finnis's argument from natural law. Concerning the topic of seriously unjust laws, he offered this solution: "If a course of reflection or discourse makes it appropriate to acknowledge the rule's 'settled' or 'posited' character as cognizable by reference to social-fact sources, one can say that it is legally valid though too unjust to be obeyed or applied." John Finnis, "Natural Law Theories," *Stanford Encyclopedia of Philosophy*, available at https://plato.stanford.edu/archives/win2016/entries/natural-law-theories/. Commenting on this solution, Brian Bix, returns us to the idea of Janus when he remarks that Finnis's analysis "is tied to his view that law

has a 'double life': as a history of official action, and as a normative system that plays a role in the practical reasoning of both citizens and judges." Bix, "Radbruch's Formula and Conceptual Analysis," p. 55. I am broadly sympathetic to the view that "the key conceptual point about unjust laws is not that they are not laws, but that they are not laws 'in the fullest sense,' including in the sense of creating reasons for judges to apply them (without modification) to legal disputes." Ibid. See also John Finnis, *Natural Law and Natural Rights*, Second edition (Oxford: Oxford University Press, 2011), esp. pp. 351–66.

39. Carsten Bäcker, *Gerechtigkeit im Rechtsstaat: Das Bundesverfassungsgericht an der Grenze des Grundgesetzes* (Tübingen: Mohr, 2015), p. 94. It is also worth highlighting that contemporary Anglo-American lawyers did not subscribe to the "perversion idea" of Nazi law as not law (which subsequently found philosophical expression in Radbruch's formula). David Fraser has shown that they "did not universally reject the German legal system after 1933 as being 'not law.' A careful examination of the legal discourse in English language countries, particularly the United States and Great Britain, indicates that the idea of a continuing law and legality operating within German society after 1933, was always present." David Fraser, " 'The Outsider Does Not See All the Game . . .': Perceptions of German Law in Anglo-American Legal Scholarship, 1933–1940," in Dieter Gosewinkel, ed., *Wirtschaftskontrolle und Recht in der nationalsozialistischen Diktatur* (Frankfurt: Klostermann, 2005), p. 343. See also Pauer-Studer, "Einleitung," esp. pp. 129–31. On the significance of this historical fact for the philosophical study of Nazi law (and by implication the status of Radbruch's formula), Fraser is unequivocal: "If coeval external understandings and constructions of the Nazi legal apparatus did not portray German law as 'not law,' as completely lacking in legitimacy, as 'beyond the pale' [. . .], basic questions about the jurisprudential nature of the Nazi state must be re-opened." Ibid.
40. As Stolleis explained in one of his best-known works, a collection of essays entitled, in the German original, *Recht im Unrecht*, or law amidst lawlessness: "By translating and interpreting texts, the legal historian seeks to observe how law functioned at various times, in different countries, and under different conditions. The approach is thus similar to that of an ethnologist, who seeks, through participatory observation, to decipher a cultural value system that is unfamiliar or appears familiar only by virtue of analogous elements. [. . .] It is obvious what kind of difficulties work against a stance of detached observation in dealing with National Socialism and the law that was in force in Germany between January 30, 1933, and May 8, 1945." Stolleis, "General Introduction," pp. 6–7.
41. Stolleis, "General Introduction," p. 9.
42. Stolleis, "General Introduction," p. 7.
43. Michael Stolleis, *A History of Public Law in Germany 1914–1945*, translated by Thomas Dunlap (Oxford: Oxford University Press, [1999] 2004), p. 249; Michael Stolleis, *Geschichte des öffentlichen Rechts in Deutschland*, vol.

3: *Staats- und Verwaltungswissenschaft in Republik und Diktatur 1914–1945* (Munich: Beck, 1999), p. 246.
44. Stolleis, *A History of Public Law in Germany 1914–1945*, p. 251.
45. "*Man darf nicht alles, was in Weimar und in den ersten Jahren des Dritten Reiches geschrieben worden ist, aus der wissenden Warte der Nachgeborenen und damit vom bekannt bösen Ende her interpretieren, sondern muß sich stets der Offenheit der historischen Situation bewußt bleiben, in der und in bezug auf die gedacht, gesprochen, geschrieben und gehandelt wurde.*" Horst Dreier, "Verfassungs- und Verwaltungsrecht 1914–1945," in idem., *Staatsrecht in Demokratie und Diktatur: Studien zur Weimarer Republik und zum Nationalsozialismus*, edited by Matthias Jestaedt and Stanley L. Paulson (Tübingen: Mohr, [2000] 2016), p. 411.
46. Dieter Simon, *Die Unabhängigkeit des Richters* (Darmstadt: Wissenschaftliche Buchgesellschaft, 1975), p. 54. Stolleis notes that prior to 1965, efforts at writing legal histories of the Nazi period were virtually non-existent. Only after the end of the so-called Adenauer era (named after postwar Germany's first chancellor), events such as the first Frankfurt Auschwitz trial of 1963–1965, combined with a generational change and the onset of university unrest created the necessary intellectual conditions for a scholarly turn to Nazi law. See Michael Stolleis, "Legal History during the Nazi Period: Outlines of a Scholarly Field," in idem., *The Law under the Swastika*, p. 42. On the controversial and large trial of mid- and low-level functionaries of the Auschwitz concentration and extermination camp held in Frankfurt, see, most important, Devin O. Pendas, *The Frankfurt Auschwitz Trial, 1963–1965: Genocide, History, and the Limits of the Law* (Cambridge: Cambridge University Press, 2006).
47. James G. March and Johan P. Olsen, "Elaborating the 'New Institutionalism,' " in R. A. W. Rhodes, Sarah A. Binder, and Bert A. Rockman, eds., *The Oxford Handbook of Political Institutions* (Oxford: Oxford University Press, 2006), p. 3.
48. For a discussion, see Robert E. Goodin, "Institutional Morality," in idem., ed., *The Theory of Institutional Design* (Cambridge: Cambridge University Press, 1996), pp. 126–53.
49. March and Olsen, "Elaborating the 'New Institutionalism,' " p. 4.
50. Nigel Simmonds, *Law as a Moral Idea* (Oxford: Oxford University Press, 2007), p. 6.
51. H. O. Pappe, "On the Validity of Judicial Decisions in the Nazi Era," *Modern Law Review*, Vol. 23 (1960), p. 270.
52. Robert Mohl, *Die Polizei-Wissenschaft nach den Grundsätzen des Rechtsstaates*, 2 volumes (Tübingen: Laupp, 1832). See also Rainer Grote, "The German Rechtsstaat in a Comparative Perspective," in James R. Silkenat, James E. Hickey Jr., and Peter D. Barenboim, eds., *The Legal Doctrines of the Rule of Law and the Legal State (Rechtsstaat)* (New York: Springer, 2014), p. 194.

53. For a basic account of the idea of the *Unrechtsstaat*, translations of which have ranged from "state of lawlessness" to "state of injustice," see David Johst, "Die Entdeckung des Unrechtsstaates," in Werner Konitzer, ed., *Moralisierung des Rechts: Kontinuitäten und Diskontinuitäten nationalsozialistischer Normativität* (Frankfurt: Campus, 2014), pp. 127–45.
54. Peter C. Caldwell, *Popular Sovereignty and the Crisis of German Constitutional Law: The Theory and Practice of Weimar Constitutionalism* (Durham: Duke University Press, 1997), p. xi.
55. Grote, "The German Rechtsstaat in a Comparative Perspective," p. 195. Emphasis added.
56. "*Vollends sinnlos ist die Behauptung, daß in der Despotie keine Rechtsordnung bestehe, sondern Willkür des Despoten herrsche [...] stellt doch auch der despotisch regierte Staat irgendeine Ordnung menschlichen Verhaltens dar [...]. Diese Ordnung ist eben die Rechtsordnung. Ihr den Charakter des Rechts abzusprechen, ist nur eine naturrechtliche Naivität oder Überhebung. [...] Was als Willkür gedeutet wird, ist nur die rechtliche Möglichkeit des Autokraten, jede Entscheidung an sich zu ziehen, die Tätigkeit der untergeordneten Organe bedingungslos zu bestimmen und einmal gesetzte Normen jederzeit [...] aufzuheben oder abzuändern. Ein solcher Zustand ist ein Rechtszustand, auch wenn er als nachteilig empfunden wird.*" Kelsen, *Allgemeine Staatslehre*, pp. 335–6.
57. Radbruch, "Statutory Lawlessness and Supra-Statutory Law," p. 7.
58. Alexy, *The Argument from Injustice*, pp. 66–7.
59. Alexy, *The Argument from Injustice*, p. 67.
60. On the debate's continued salience, see Peter Cane, ed., *The Hart-Fuller Debate in the Twenty-First Century* (Oxford: Hart, 2010).
61. D. N. MacCormick, "Law, Morality and Positivism," *Legal Studies*, Vol. 1 (1980), p. 139.
62. Fraenkel, *The Dual State*. Almost all leading theorists of dictatorship in the 1930s were lawyers. Most prominent among them were Hermann Heller, Hermann Kantorowicz, Hans Kelsen, Karl Loewenstein, and Carl Schmitt. The most influential non-lawyers were the political theorist Carl J. Friedrich, the historian Alfred Cobban, and the social scientist Sigmund Neumann. For the contributions of the aforementioned to the theory of dictatorship, see Carl Schmitt, *Dictatorship: From the Origin of the Modern Concept of Sovereignty to Proletarian Class Struggle*, translated by Michael Hoelzl and Graham Ward (Cambridge: Polity, [1921] 2014); Carl Joachim Friedrich, "Dictatorship in Germany?," *Foreign Affairs*, Vol. 9 (1930), pp. 118–32; Hermann Heller, "Rechtsstaat oder Diktatur?," in idem., *Gesammelte Schriften*, vol. 2: *Recht, Staat, Macht*, Second edition, edited by Christoph Müller (Tübingen: Mohr, [1930] 1992); Hermann Kantorowicz, "Dictatorships," *Politica*, Vol. 1 (1935), pp. 470–88; Hans Kelsen, "The Party-Dictatorship," *Politica*, Vol. 2 (1936), pp. 19–32; Karl Loewenstein, "Dictatorship and the German Constitution: 1933–1937," *University of Chicago Law Review*, Vol. 4 (1937), pp. 537–74; Alfred Cobban, *Dictatorship: Its History and Theory* (London: Jonathan Cape,

1939); and Sigmund Neumann, *Permanent Revolution: The Total State in a World at War* (New York: Harper, 1942). But see also Otto Forts-Battaglia and Huntley Paterson, *Dictatorship on Trial* (New York: Harcourt, Brace, 1931); Roy Pascal, *The Nazi Dictatorship* (London: Routledge, 1934); G. P. Gooch, *Dictatorship in Theory and Practice* (London: Watts & Co., 1935); J. A. R. Marriott, *Dictatorship and Democracy* (Oxford: Clarendon Press, 1935); Diana Spearman, *Modern Dictatorship* (London: Jonathan Cape, 1939); Frederick L. Schuman, *The Nazi Dictatorship: A Study in Social Pathology and the Politics of Fascism* (New York: Knopf, 1936); Albert H. Z. Carr, *Juggernaut: The Path of Dictatorship* (New York: Viking, 1939); and Guy Stanton Ford, ed., *Dictatorship in the Modern World* (London: Oxford University Press, 1939). For a useful analysis of interwar and wartime writings on dictatorship by authors from the German left such as Franz Borkenau, Ernst Fraenkel, Rudolf Hilferding, Max Horkheimer, Otto Kirchheimer, Karl Korsch, Richard Löwenthal, Herbert Marcuse, Franz Neumann, Sigmund Neumann, Arthur Rosenberg, and Karl August Wittfogel, see William David Jones, *The Lost Debate: German Socialist Intellectuals and Totalitarianism* (Urbana: University of Illinois Press, 1999).

63. Henry Sumner Maine, *Ancient Law: Its Connection with the Early History of Society, and Its Relation to Modern Ideas* (London: John Murray, 1861). For accounts of legal anthropology as a field of study, see Laura Nader, ed., *Law in Culture and Society* (Berkeley: University of California Press, [1969] 1997); Leonard J. Pospisil, *Anthropology of Law: A Comparative Theory* (New York: Harper & Row, 1971); Simon Roberts, *Order and Dispute: An Introduction to Legal Anthropology* (Harmondsworth: Penguin, 1979); June Starr and Jane F. Collier, eds., *History and Power in the Study of Law: New Directions in Legal Anthropology* (Ithaca: Cornell University Press, 1989); Lawrence Rosen, *Law as Culture: An Invitation* (Princeton: Princeton University Press, 2008); James M. Donovan, *Legal Anthropology: An Introduction* (Lanham: Rowman & Littlefield, 2008); Fernanda Pirie, *The Anthropology of Law* (Oxford: Oxford University Press, 2013); and Mark Goodale, *Anthropology and Law: A Critical Introduction* (New York: New York University Press, 2017). For a collection of classic and contemporary scholarship, see Sally Falk Moore, ed., *Law and Anthropology: A Reader* (Oxford: Blackwell, 2005).

64. Pirie, *The Anthropology of Law*, p. 23. One of the best introductions to the craft of ethnography remains Martyn Hammersly and Paul Atkinson, *Ethnography: Principles in Practice*, Third edition (London: Routledge, 2007). For a useful reflection on the task of understanding through observation, see Richard A. Shweder, "Anthropology's Romantic Rebellion against the Enlightenment, or There's More to Thinking than Reason and Evidence," in Richard A. Shweder and Robert A. LeVine, eds., *Culture Theory: Essays on Mind, Self, and Emotion* (Cambridge: Cambridge University Press, 1984), pp. 27–66.

65. Geertz was famously blunt about the centrality of inscription to participant observation: "The ethnographer 'inscribes' social discourse; he writes

it down." Clifford Geertz, "Thick Description: Toward an Interpretive Theory of Culture," in idem., *The Interpretation of Cultures: Selected Essays* (New York: Basic Books, 1973), p. 19. See also Roger Sanjek, ed., *Fieldnotes: The Makings of Anthropology* (Ithaca: Cornell University Press, 1990); Robert M. Emerson, Rachel I. Fretz, and Linda L. Shaw, *Writing Ethnographic Fieldnotes*, Second edition (Chicago: University of Chicago Press, 2011).

66. Paul Willis, *The Ethnographic Imagination* (Cambridge: Polity, 2000), p. 34.
67. Paul Bohannan, *Justice and Judgment among the Tiv* (London: Oxford University Press, 1957), p. 69. Bohannan's book was a sustained, though mostly oblique, critique of Max Gluckman's *The Judicial Process among the Barotse of Northern Rhodesia* (Manchester: Manchester University Press, 1955), which Bohannan considered to be a flawed work of legal ethnography. On the emic/etic dichotomy more generally, see, for example, Ward H. Goodenough, *Description and Comparison in Cultural Anthropology* (Cambridge: Cambridge University Press, 1970), Chapter 4.
68. Pirie, *The Anthropology of Law*, p. 12. See also Edward Schatz, ed., *Political Ethnography: What Immersion Contributes to the Study of Power* (Chicago: University of Chicago Press, 2009).
69. Pirie, *The Anthropology of Law*, p. 1.
70. Lawrence M. Friedman, "A Few Thoughts on Ethnography, History, and Law," in June Starr and Mark Goodale, eds., *Practicing Ethnography in Law: New Dialogues, Enduring Methods* (London: Palgrave, 2002), p. 186. For an important methodological intervention from a neighboring discipline, see Michael Burawoy, "Revisits: An Outline of a Theory of Reflexive Ethnography," *American Sociological Review*, Vol. 68 (2003), pp. 645–79. On observational field research in the social sciences more generally, see Paul S. Gray, John B. Williamson, David A. Karp, John R. Dalphin, *The Research Imagination: An Introduction to Qualitative and Quantitative Methods* (Cambridge: Cambridge University Press, 2007), pp. 179–210.
71. Ariel I. Ahram and J. Paul Goode, "Researching Authoritarianism in the Discipline of Democracy," *Social Science Quarterly*, Vol. 97 (2016), pp. 839–40.
72. Friedman, "A Few Thoughts on Ethnography, History, and Law," p. 186.
73. Bronislaw Malinowski, *Argonauts of the Western Pacific: An Account of Native Enterprise and Adventure in the Archipelagoes of Melanesian New Guinea* (London: Routledge and Kegan Paul, 1922); and idem., *Crime and Custom in Savage Society* (London: Routledge & Kegan Paul, 1926).
74. On the foundational significance of Malinowski's work for the anthropology of law, see, for example, John M. Conley and William M. O'Barr, "Back to the Trobriands: The Enduring Influence of Malinowski's *Crime and Custom in Savage Society*," *Law and Social Inquiry*, Vol. 27 (2002), pp. 847–74. For an early appreciation by a legal ethnographer who would come to stand on Malinowski's shoulders, see Max Gluckman, *An Analysis of the Sociological Theories of Bronislaw Malinowski* (London: Oxford University Press, 1949).
75. Malinowski, *Argonauts of the Western Pacific*, pp. 83–4.

76. On the rise and fall of legal primitivism, see, most recently, Kaius Tuori, *Lawyers and Savages: Ancient History and Legal Realism in the Making of Legal Anthropology* (London: Routledge, 2014).
77. Ernst Fraenkel, "Preface to the 1974 German Edition," in idem., *The Dual State*, pp. xv, xvii.
78. Pirie, *The Anthropology of Law*, p. 15.
79. Sally Engle Merry, "Ethnography in the Archives," in Starr and Goodale, eds., *Practicing Ethnography in Law*, esp. pp. 136–8.
80. Merry, "Ethnography in the Archives," p. 136.
81. Merry, "Ethnography in the Archives," p. 137.
82. Pirie, *The Anthropology of Law*, p. 24.
83. See Chapter 9 for a comprehensive discussion.
84. Most recently and generally, see Larry Diamond, Marc F. Plattner, and Christopher Walker, eds., *Authoritarianism Goes Global: The Challenge to Democracy* (Baltimore: Johns Hopkins University Press, 2016). For evidence from different parts of the world, see, for example, Marc J. Hetherington and Jonathan D. Weiler, *Authoritarianism and Polarization in American Politics* (Cambridge University Press, 2009); Joseph Sassoon, *Anatomy of Authoritarianism in the Arab Republics* (Cambridge: Cambridge University Press, 2016); Wenfang Tang, *Populist Authoritarianism: Chinese Political Culture and Regime Sustainability* (Oxford: Oxford University Press, 2016); Thobias Hagman and Filip Reyntjens, eds., *Aid and Authoritarianism in Africa: Development without Democracy* (London: Zed Books, 2016); Masha Gessen, *The Future Is History: How Totalitarianism Reclaimed Russia* (New York: Riverhead Books, 2017); and Achin Vanaik, *The Rise of Hindu Authoritarianism: Secular Claims, Communal Realities* (London: Verso, 2017).
85. Judith Goldstein, Miles Kahler, Robert O. Keohane, and Anne-Marie Slaughter, "Introduction: Legalization and World Politics," *International Organization*, Vol. 54 (2000), p. 388. As an example of a vast literature, see also Judith Goldstein, Miles Kahler, Robert O. Keohane, and Anne-Marie Slaughter, eds., *Legalization and World Politics* (Cambridge: MIT Press, 2001), previously published as a special—and very influential—issue of *International Organization*, of which the aforementioned article formed a part.
86. In political science, the *locus classicus* in the study of nondemocratic regimes remains Barrington Moor, Jr., *Social Origins of Dictatorship and Democracy: Lord and Peasant in the Making of the Modern World* (Boston: Beacon Press, 1966). But see also Juan J. Linz's, "Totalitarian and Authoritarian Regimes," in Fred I. Greenstein and Nelson W. Polsby, eds., *Handbook of Political Science*, vol. 3: *Macropolitical Theory* (Menlo Park: Addison-Wesley, 1975), pp. 175–411, whose in-depth concept analysis, 236 pages long, has had a considerable impact on the so-called democratization literature that began to emerge in the early 1980s. See, for example, Guillermo O'Donnell, Philippe C. Schmitter, and Laurence Whitehead, eds., *Transitions from Authoritarian Rule*, 4 volumes (Baltimore: Johns Hopkins

University Press, 1986); Samuel P. Huntington, *The Third Wave: Democratization in the Late Twentieth Century* (Norman: University of Oklahoma Press, 1991); Juan J. Linz and Alfred Stepan, *Problems of Democratic Transition and Consolidation: Southern Europe, South America, and Post-Communist Europe* (Baltimore: Johns Hopkins University Press, 1996). In recent decades, the totalitarian subtype in the universe of nondemocratic regimes has fallen by the wayside, also because of its rare occurrence. By contrast, the nondemocratic subtype of authoritarianism has been theorized extensively. Representative publications from a vast literature include, in chronological order, Mancur Olson, "Dictatorship, Democracy, and Development," *American Political Science Review*, Vol. 87 (1993), pp. 567–76; Mike Alvarez, José Antonio Cheibub, Fernando Limongi, Adam Przeworski, "Classifying Political Regimes," *Studies in Comparative International Development*, Vol. 31 (1996), pp. 3–36; Barbara Geddes, "What Do We Know about Democratization after Twenty Years?," *Annual Review of Political Science*, Vol. 2 (1999), pp. 115–44; Larry Diamond, "Thinking About Hybrid Regimes," *Journal of Democracy*, Vol. 13 (2002), pp. 21–35; Daron Acemoglu and James A. Robinson, *Economic Origins of Dictatorship and Democracy* (Cambridge: Cambridge University Press, 2006); Andreas Schedler, ed., *Electoral Authoritarianism: The Dynamics of Unfree Competition* (Boulder: Lynne Rienner, 2006); Jason Brownlee, *Authoritarianism in an Age of Democratization* (Cambridge: Cambridge University Press, 2007); Axel Hadenius and Jan Teorell, "Pathways from Authoritarianism," *Journal of Democracy*, Vol. 18 (2007), pp. 143–57; Jennifer Gandhi, *Political Institutions under Dictatorship* (Cambridge: Cambridge University Press, 2008); Mikael Wigell, "Mapping 'Hybrid Regimes': Regime Types and Concepts in Comparative Politics," *Democratization*, Vol. 15 (2008), pp. 230–50; Jason Brownlee, "Portents of Pluralism: How Hybrid Regimes Affect Democratic Transitions," *American Journal of Political Science*, Vol. 53 (2009), pp. 515–32; Jennifer Gandhi and Ellen Lust-Okar, "Elections under Authoritarianism," *Annual Review of Political Science*, Vol. 12 (2009), pp. 403–22; Steven Levitsky and Lucan A. Way, *Competitive Authoritarianism: Hybrid Regimes After the Cold War* (Cambridge: Cambridge University Press, 2010); José Antonio Cheibub, Jennifer Gandhi, James Raymond Vreeland, "Democracy and Dictatorship Revisited, *Public Choice*, Vol. 143 (2010), pp. 67–101; Leah Gilbert and Payam Mohseni, "Beyond Authoritarianism: The Conceptualization of Hybrid Regimes," *Studies in Comparative International Development*, Vol. 46 (2011), pp. 270–97; Milan W. Svolik, *The Politics of Authoritarian Rule* (Cambridge: Cambridge University Press, 2012); Yonatan L. Morse, "The Era of Electoral Authoritarianism," *World Politics*, Vol. 64 (2012), pp. 161–98; Carles Boix and Milan W. Svolik, "The Foundations of Limited Authoritarian Government: Institutions, Commitment, and Power-Sharing in Dictatorships," *Journal of Politics*, Vol. 75 (2013), pp. 300–16; Tom Ginsburg and Alberto Simpser, eds., *Constitutions in Authoritarian Regimes* (Cambridge: Cambridge University Press, 2014); Barbara Geddes, Erica Frantz, and Joseph G. Wright, "Military Rule," *Annual Review of Political*

Science, Vol. 17 (2014), pp. 147–62; Barbara Geddes, Joseph Wright, and Erica Frantz, "Autocratic Breakdown and Regime Transitions: A New Data Set," *Perspectives on Politics*, Vol. 12 (2014), pp. 313–31; Andreas Schedler, *The Politics of Uncertainty: Sustaining and Subverting Electoral Authoritarianism* (Oxford: Oxford University Press, 2015); Michael K. Miller, "Democratic Pieces: Autocratic Elections and Democratic Development since 1815," *British Journal of Political Science*, Vol. 45 (2015), pp. 501–30; Stephan Haggard and Robert R. Kaufman, *Dictators and Democrats: Masses, Elites, and Regime Change* (Princeton: Princeton University Press, 2016); Rory Truex, "Consultative Authoritarianism and Its Limits," *Comparative Political Studies*, Vol. 50 (2017), pp. 329–61; and Carl Henrik Knutsen, Håvard Mokleiv Nygård, and Tore Wig, "Autocratic Elections: Stabilizing Tool or Force for Change?," *World Politics*, Vol. 69 (2017), pp. 98–143. For a recent edited collection on the state of the art, see Aurel Croissant, Steffen Kailitz, Patrick Koellner, and Stefan Wurster, eds., *Comparing Autocracies in the Early Twenty-first Century*, 2 volumes (London: Routledge, 2014). The study of nondemocratic regimes in political science is not confined to the sub-field of comparative politics, however. It is also a staple of international relations scholarship, where the question of regime type for several decades has been deeply intertwined with research on the domestic sources of international conflict and international cooperation. Illustrative of this line of scholarship, with a particular focus on nondemocratic regimes, are Edward D. Mansfield and Jack Snyder, "Democratization and the Danger of War," *International Security*, Vol. 20 (1995), pp. 5–38; Brian Lai and Dan Slater, "Institutions of the Offensive: Domestic Sources of Dispute Initiation in Authoritarian Regimes, 1950–1992," *American Journal of Political Science*, Vol. 50 (2006), pp. 113–26; James Raymond Vreeland, "Political Institutions and Human Rights: Why Dictatorships Enter into the United Nations Convention against Torture," *International Organization*, Vol. 62 (2008), pp. 65–101; and Jessica L. Weeks, "Autocratic Audience Costs: Regime Type and Signaling Resolve," *International Organization*, Vol. 62 (2008), pp. 35–64. The subject of nondemocratic regimes has also been a recurring topic in the political theory sub-field of political science, where a long line of scholars, beginning with Carl J. Friedrich and Hannah Arendt, of whom more below, have wrestled with the institutional logic of repression, focusing in particular on the institution of dictatorship. See, among others, Clinton Rossiter, *Constitutional Dictatorship: Crisis Government in the Modern Democracies* (Princeton: Princeton University Press, 1948); Norberto Bobbio, *Democracy and Dictatorship: The Nature and Limits of State Power*, translated by Peter Kennealy (Cambridge: Polity, [1980] 1989); Melvin Richter, "Toward a Concept of Political Illegitimacy: Bonapartist Dictatorship and Democratic Legitimacy," *Political Theory*, Vol. 10 (1982), pp. 185–214; Claude Lefort, *The Political Forms of Modern Society: Bureaucracy, Democracy, and Totalitarianism*, edited and translated by John B. Thomson (Cambridge: MIT Press, 1986); Michael Halberstam, "Totalitarianism as a Problem for the Modern Conception of Politics," *Political Theory*, Vol. 26 (1998), pp. 459–88; Andrew Arato, "Good-bye to Dictatorships?," *Social*

Research, Vol. 67 (2000), pp. 925–55; Melvin Richter, "A Family of Political Concepts: Tyranny, Despotism, Bonapartism, Caesarism, Dictatorship, 1750–1917," *European Journal of Political Theory*, Vol. 4 (2005), pp. 321–48; Andreas Kalyvas, "The Tyranny of Dictatorship: When the Greek Tyrant Met the Roman Dictator," *Political Theory*, Vol. 35 (2007), pp. 412–42; and Mario Turchetti, " 'Despotism' and 'Tyranny,'" *European Journal of Political Theory*, Vol. 7 (2008), pp. 159–82.

87. Ahram and Goode, "Researching Authoritarianism in the Discipline of Democracy," p. 834.
88. Mine is a reference to Karl A. Schleunes's pathbreaking *The Twisted Road to Auschwitz: Nazi Policy toward German Jews 1933–1939*, with a Foreword by Hans Mommsen (Urbana: University of Illinois Press, [1970] 1990).
89. Baruch Fischhoff, "Hindsight ≠ Foresight: The Effect of Outcome Knowledge on Judgment under Uncertainty," *Journal of Experimental Psychology*, Vol. 1 (1975), pp. 288–99.
90. See, for example, Hartmut Blank, Jochen Musch, and Rüdiger F. Pohl, "Hindsight Bias: On Being Wise after the Event," *Social Cognition*, Vol. 25 (2007), pp. 1–9.
91. Hans Mommsen, "Foreword," in Schleunes, *The Twisted Road to Auschwitz*, p. ix.
92. Franz Neumann, *Behemoth: The Structure and Practice of National Socialism* (Toronto: Oxford University Press, 1942); idem., *Behemoth: The Structure and Practice of National Socialism 1933–1944* (Toronto: Oxford University Press, 1944). See also Michael D. Coogan, "Behemoth," in Bruce M. Metzger and Michael D. Coogan, eds., *The Oxford Guide to People and Places of the Bible* (New York: Oxford University Press, 2001), p. 33.
93. On the concept of the "genocidal regime," see Jens Meierhenrich, *Genocide: A Very Short Introduction* (Oxford: Oxford University Press, 2018), Chapter 2; and, for a more in-depth discussion, Jens Meierhenrich, *The Rationality of Genocide* (Princeton: Princeton University Press, forthcoming).
94. Eric D. Weitz, "Hans Mommsen, The Rise and Fall of Weimar Democracy" (Book review), *Central European History*, Vol. 31 (1998), p. 276.
95. Peter Fritzsche, "Did Weimar Fail?," *Journal of Modern History*, Vol. 68 (1996), p. 629.
96. It is worth noting that Fraenkel was a secular Jew, or, as he liked to say, "a Jew in the objective sense" ("*ein Jude im objektiven Sinne*"). According to Fraenkel, Jews in the subjective sense are those whose faith determines their being. By contrast, Jews in the objective sense, like him, were Jewish by dint of birth, not faith. As a result, Fraenkel argued, their Jewishness was largely externally determined. Even though Jewishness was incidental rather than integral to Fraenkel's identity, he nonetheless felt deep solidarity with other members of his inherited faith. See Winfried Steffani, "Ernst Fraenkel als Persönlichkeit," in Hubertus Buchstein and Gerhard Göhler, eds., *Vom Sozialismus zum Pluralismus: Beiträge zu Werk und Leben Ernst Fraenkels* (Baden-Baden: Nomos, 2000), p. 130.

97. Jakob Zollmann, "Alan E. Steinweis and Robert D. Rachlin, eds., The Law in Nazi Germany: Ideology, Opportunism, and the Perversion of Justice" (Book review), *German History*, Vol. 32 (2014), p. 496.
98. For overviews of the much-misunderstood conference, see Mark Roseman, *The Villa, The Lake, The Meeting: Wannsee and the Final Solution* (London: Penguin, 2003); Peter Longerich, *Wannseekonferenz: Der Weg zur "Endlösung"* (Munich: Pantheon, 2016); and Hans-Christian Jasch and Christoph Kreutzmüller, *Die Teilnehmer: Die Männer der Wannsee-Konferenz* (Berlin: Metropol, 2017). An exceedingly thorough, if controversial, account is Christian Gerlach, "The Wannsee Conference, the Fate of German Jews, and Hitler's Decision in Principle to Exterminate All European Jews," *Journal of Modern History*, Vol. 70 (1998), pp. 759–812.
99. It bears emphasizing that Fraenkel's analysis, unlike Neumann's, took into account *only* the regime's prewar years.
100. Stolleis, "General Introduction," p. 8.
101. See, most recently, Jens Meierhenrich and Oliver Simons, eds., *The Oxford Handbook of Carl Schmitt*. On the intellectual relationship between Fraenkel and Schmitt, see, for example, Michael Wildt, "Eine spannungsvolle Beziehung: Ernst Fraenkel und Carl Schmitt," in Robert Chr. van Ooyen and Martin H. W. Möllers, eds., *(Doppel-)Staat und Gruppeninteressen: Pluralismus–Parlamentarismus–Schmitt-Kritik bei Ernst Fraenkel* (Baden-Baden: Nomos, 2009), pp. 87–111.
102. Judith N. Shklar, "Political Theory and the Rule of Law," in idem., *Political Thinkers and Political Thought*, edited by Stanley Hoffmann (Chicago: University of Chicago Press, [1987] 1998), p. 37, fn. 10. In private correspondence, William Scheuerman has confirmed Shklar's admiration for *The Dual State*. Shklar was Scheuerman's doctoral supervisor in Harvard's Department of Government.

CHAPTER 2

1. Schleunes, *The Twisted Road to Auschwitz*, p. xiii. I adjusted the idiosyncratic spelling of the decades in the original.
2. Nathan Stoltzfus, *Hitler's Compromises: Coercion and Consensus in Nazi Germany* (New Haven: Yale University Press, 2016), p. 10.
3. Ian Kershaw, *Hitler 1889–1936: Hubris* (New York: Norton, 1999), p. xii.
4. Ian Kershaw, "Preface to the Bloomsbury Revelations Edition," in Ian Kershaw, *The Nazi Dictatorship: Problems and Perspectives of Interpretation* (London: Bloomsbury, 2015), p. ix.
5. Kershaw, "Preface to the Bloomsbury Revelations Edition," p. ix. Revised versions of the conference papers presented at Cumberland Lodge can be found in Gerhard Hirschfeld and Lothar Kettenacker, eds., *Der "Führerstaat": Mythos und Realität* (Stuttgart: Klett-Cotta, 1981).
6. For essential contributions from the second and third generations of historians studying the Third Reich, see, among others, Christopher R.

Browning, *The Origins of the Final Solution: The Evolution of Nazi Jewish Policy, September 1939–March 1942* (Lincoln: University of Nebraska Press, 2004); Jane Caplan, *Government without Administration: State and Civil Society in Weimar and Nazi Germany* (Oxford: Clarendon Press, 1988); Richard J. Evans, *The Third Reich in Power 1933–1939* (New York: Penguin, 2005); Robert Gellately, *The Gestapo and German Society: Enforcing Racial Policy 1933–1945* (Oxford: Clarendon Press, 1990); Ulrich Herbert, *Best: Biographische Studien über Radikalismus, Weltanschauung und Vernunft 1903–1989* (Munich: Beck, 2016); Ian Kershaw, *The "Hitler Myth": Image and Reality in the Third Reich* (Oxford: Clarendon Press, 1987); Claudia Koonz, *The Nazi Conscience* (Cambridge: Belknap Press of Harvard University Press, 2003); Michael Wildt, *Generation des Unbedingten: Das Führungskorps des Reichssicherheitshauptamtes* (Hamburg: Hamburger Edition, 2002); and Nikolaus Wachsmann, *KL: A History of the Nazi Concentration Camps* (New York: Little, Brown, 2015).

7. Martin Broszat, *Der Staat Hitlers: Grundlegung und Entwicklung seiner inneren Verfassung* (Munich: dtv, 1969), pp. 403–22. Notable specialist studies on law's role in Nazi Germany, in chronological order, are Horst Göppinger, *Juristen jüdischer Abstammung im "Dritten Reich": Entrechtung und Verfolgung*, Second, revised edition (Munich: Beck, [1963] 1990); Bernd Rüthers, *Die unbegrenzte Auslegung: Zum Wandel der Privatrechtsordnung im Nationalsozialismus*, Sixth, enlarged edition ([1968] 2005); Klaus Anderbrügge, *Völkisches Rechtsdenken: Zur Rechtslehre in der Zeit des Nationalsozialismus* (Berlin: Duncker & Humblot, 1978); Herbert Jäger, *Verbrechen unter totalitärer Herrschaft: Studien zur nationalsozialistischen Gewaltkriminalität* (Frankfurt: Suhrkamp, 1982); Diemut Majer, *Grundlagen des nationalsozialistischen Rechtssystems: Führerprinzip, Sonderrecht, Einheitspartei* (Stuttgart: Kohlhammer, 1987); Stefan König, *Vom Dienst am Recht: Rechtsanwälte als Strafverteidiger im Nationalsozialismus* (Berlin: De Gruyter, 1987); Ingo Müller, *Hitler's Justice: The Courts of the Third Reich*, translated by Deborah Lucas Schneider (Cambridge: Harvard University Press, [1987] 1991); Lothar Gruchmann, *Justiz im Dritten Reich 1933–1940: Anpassung und Unterwerfung in der Ära Gürtner*, Third edition (Munich: Oldenbourg, 2001); Bernd Rüthers, *Entartetes Recht: Rechtslehren und Kronjuristen im Dritten Reich*, Second, improved edition (Munich: Beck, 1989); Ralph Angermund, *Deutsche Richterschaft 1919–1945: Krisenerfahrung, Illusion, politische Rechtsprechung* (Frankfurt: Fischer, 1990); Martin Stolleis, *The Law under the Swastika: Studies on Legal History in Nazi Germany*, translated by Thomas Dunlap (Chicago: University of Chicago Press, [1994] 1998); Holger Schlüter, *Die Urteilspraxis des nationalsozialistischen Volksgerichtshofs* (Berlin: Duncker & Humblot, 1995); Christian Hilger, *Rechtsstaatsbegriffe im Dritten Reich: Eine Strukturanalyse* (Tübingen: Mohr, 2003); Nikolaus Wachsmann, *Hitler's Prisons: Legal Terror in Nazi Germany* (New Haven: Yale University Press, 2004); Manfred Messerschmidt,

Die Wehrmachtjustiz 1933–1945 (Paderborn: Schöningh, 2005); Bernd Mertens, *Rechtsetzung im Nationalsozialismus* (Tübingen: Mohr, 2009); and Maximilian Becker, *Mitstreiter im Volkstumskampf: Deutsche Justiz in den eingegliederten Ostgebieten 1939–1945* (Munich: Oldenbourg, 2014).

8. Thomas Childers and Jane Caplan, eds., *Reevaluating the Third Reich: New Controversies, New Interpretations* (New York: Holmes & Meier, 1993); Jane Caplan, ed., *Nazi Germany* (Oxford: Oxford University Press, 2008).
9. Peter Fritzsche, *Life and Death in the Third Reich* (Cambridge: Belknap Press of Harvard University Press, 2008); Evans, *The Third Reich in Power 1933–1939*; Thomas Childers, *The Third Reich: A History of Nazi Germany* (New York: Simon & Schuster, 2017); Hans-Ulrich Wehler, *Der Nationalsozialismus: Bewegung, Führerherrschaft, Verbrechen 1919–1945* (Munich: Beck, 2009); Robert Gellately, *Backing Hitler: Consent and Coercion in Nazi Germany* (Oxford: Oxford University Press, 2001); Koonz, *The Nazi Conscience*, Chapter 7. I comment on similar omissions in earlier scholarship in the pages to come.
10. Franz Neumann, *Behemoth: The Structure and Practice of National Socialism* (Toronto: Oxford University Press, 1942); idem., *Behemoth: The Structure and Practice of National Socialism 1933–1944* (Toronto: Oxford University Press, 1944). Lest I be misunderstood, law has played a secondary role in the analysis of the Third Reich for numerous reasons. My goal is not to lay the blame at Neumann's door. *Behemoth* undoubtedly hastened the turn away from law, but law's relative neglect in the historiography of Nazi Germany also has to do with the fact that, as a social phenomenon, it is often technical, tedious to study, and inaccessible to the non-lawyer. And for making sense of the Third Reich *tout court*, the explanatory power of variables other than the law is most certainly greater. I am very grateful to Douglas Morris for pushing me to clarify my argument.
11. Stoltzfus, *Hitler's Compromises*, p. 6.
12. Stoltzfus, *Hitler's Compromises*, p. 21.
13. Neumann, *Behemoth* [1942 edition], p. 459.
14. Neumann, "Note on the Name Behemoth," in idem., *Behemoth* [1942 edition], p. viii.
15. Franz Neumann, *Die Herrschaft des Gesetzes: Eine Untersuchung zum Verhältnis von politischer Theorie und Rechtssystem in der Konkurrenzgesellschaft*, edited with an Afterword by Alfons Söllner (Frankfurt: Suhrkamp, 1980), p. 343. Here Neumann described as a "circulis vitiosus," a vicious cycle, the Third Reich's elevation of Hitler decrees to the level of law, and Hitler's will as the supreme source of law.
16. Neumann, *Behemoth* [1942 edition], pp. 467–68.
17. Peter Hayes, "Introduction," in Franz Neumann, *Behemoth: The Structure and Practice of National Socialism 1933–1944* (Chicago: Ivan R. Dee, [1944] 2009), p. vii.
18. On the latter, see Chapter 8 below.

19. Examples of rational-choice approaches are Ronald Wintrope, *The Political Economy of Dictatorship* (Cambridge: Cambridge University Press, 1998); Jennifer Gandhi, *Political Institutions under Dictatorship* (Cambridge: Cambridge University Press, 2008).
20. Generally, see Charles S. Maier, *In Search of Stability: Explorations in Historical Political Economy* (Cambridge: Cambridge University Press, 1987), pp. 3–6.
21. On Neumann and the circle of critical theorists to which he belonged, see, for example, Moishe Postone, "Critique, State, and Economy," in Fred Rush, ed., *The Cambridge Companion to Critical Theory* (Cambridge: Cambridge University Press, 2004), pp. 165–93. See also Martin Jay, *The Dialectical Imagination. A History of the Frankfurt School and the Institute of Social Research 1923–1950*, Second edition (Berkeley: University of California Press, 1996); and Rolf Wiggershaus, *Die Frankfurter Schule: Geschichte, Theoretische Entwicklung, Politische Bedeutung* (Munich: Hanser, 1986); and Samuel Salzborn, ed., *Kritische Theorie des Staates: Staat und Recht bei Franz L. Neumann* (Baden-Baden: Nomos, 2009).
22. Postone, "Critique, State, and Economy," pp. 165, 166.
23. Neumann used the adjective "pragmatic" in *Behemoth* [1942 edition], p. 228.
24. The number of cartels in German industry grew rapidly between unification and the Nazi dictatorship. Whereas there were only 106 cartels in 1890, some 3,000 existed in 1926. Chris Thornhill, *Political Theory in Modern Germany: An Introduction* (Oxford: Polity, 2000), p. 101. The inflationary effects of the Great Depression further accelerated the speed of cartelization. By 1930, forty percent of Germany's industrial production was in the hands of cartels. Hartmut Bechtold, *Die Kartellierung der deutschen Volkswirtschaft und die sozialdemokratische Theorie-Diskussion vor 1933* (Frankfurt: Haag & Herchen, 1986), p. 242.
25. Neumann, *Behemoth* [1942 edition], p. 261. Neumann devoted four chapters, the entirety of Part II in *Behemoth*, to the development of this argument. See ibid, pp. 219–361. For the most comprehensive analysis of Neumann's analysis of varieties of capitalism in interwar Germany, see Jürgen Bast, *Totalitärer Pluralismus: Zu Franz L. Neumanns Analysen der politischen und rechtlichen Struktur der NS- Herrschaft* (Tübingen: Mohr, 1999), pp. 124–256.
26. Neumann, *Behemoth* [1942 edition], p. 469.
27. Hayes, "Introduction," p. x.
28. Neumann, *Behemoth* [1942 edition], p. 468.
29. Neumann, *Behemoth* [1942 edition], pp. 469–70.
30. Neumann, *Behemoth* [1942 edition], p. 469.
31. Bast, *Totalitärer Pluralismus*, esp. pp. 105–22, 299–303.
32. Neumann, *Behemoth* [1942 edition], p. 469. Cf. Neumann declaring in an early part of *Behemoth* "Adolf Hitler is top leader." Ibid, p. 84.
33. Thornhill, *Political Theory in Modern Germany*, p. 127.

34. Duncan Kelly, *The State of the Political: Conceptions of Politics and the State in the Thought of Max Weber, Carl Schmitt and Franz Neumann* (Oxford: Oxford University, 2003), p. 289.
35. As quoted in Neumann, *Behemoth* [1942 edition], p. 224. Note that Neumann misspelled Barth's first name. For the original source, see Eberhard Barth, *Wesen und Aufgaben der Organisation der gewerblichen Wirtschaft* (Hamburg: Hanseatische Verlagsanstalt, 1939), p. 107.
36. Neumann, Behemoth [1942 edition], p. 224.
37. Neumann, Behemoth [1942 edition], p. 361.
38. Neumann, Behemoth [1942 edition], p. 292.
39. Neumann, Behemoth [1942 edition], pp. 360–61.
40. For an illustration of Neumann's continued relevance, see, among others, Alfons Söllner, "Regression des Rechtsstaates? Zur Aktualität Franz L. Neumanns in der gegenwärtigen Diskussion," in Joachim Perels, ed., *Recht, Demokratie und Kapitalismus: Aktualität und Problem der Theorie Franz L. Neumanns* (Baden-Baden: Nomos, 1984), pp. 195–209; and William David Jones, *The Lost Debate: German Socialist Intellectuals and Totalitarianism* (Urbana: University of Illinois Press, 1999), p. 149.
41. Hayes, "Introduction," p. xv. For a case study proving Neumann wrong, see, for example, Kees Gispen, *Poems in Steel: National Socialism and the Politics of Inventing from Weimar to Bonn* (New York: Berghahn, 2002), esp. p. 6, where Gispen explicitly repudiates the cartelization-thesis.
42. Alfons Söllner, "Franz L. Neumann—Skizzen zu einer intellektuellen und politischen Biographie," in Franz L. Neumann, *Wirtschaft, Staat, Demokratie: Aufsätze 1940–1954*, edited by Alfons Söllner (Frankfurt: Suhrkamp, 1978), p. 19.
43. Postone, "Critique, State, and Economy," p. 179.
44. Ernst Fraenkel, "Vom monopol-kapitalistischen Charakter des Nazi-staatsgebildes: Das Produkt des Grosskapitals," in idem., *Gesammelte Schriften*, vol. 2: *Nationalsozialismus und Widerstand*, edited by Alexander v. Brünneck, Hubertus Buchstein, and Gerhard Göhler (Baden-Baden: Nomos, [1942] 1999), p. 576.
45. Fraenkel, "Vom monopol-kapitalistischen Charakter des Nazi-Staatsgebildes," p. 578.
46. Fraenkel, "Vom monopol-kapitalistischen Charakter des Nazi-Staatsgebildes," p. 578.
47. Doug McAdam, Sidney Tarrow, and Charles Tilly, *Dynamics of Contention* (Cambridge: Cambridge University Press, 2001).
48. Fraenkel, "Vom monopol-kapitalistischen Charakter des Nazi-Staatsgebildes," p. 578.
49. Fraenkel, "Vom monopol-kapitalistischen Charakter des Nazi-Staatsgebildes," p. 578.
50. Thornhill, *Political Theory in Modern Germany*, p. 95. Once in exile, Neumann began to distinguish between the German idea of the *Rechtsstaat* and the Anglo-American concept of the rule of law, most notably in his "The Concept of Political Freedom," *Columbia Law Review*, Vol. 53 (1953), pp. 901–35.

For the earliest articulation of this difference, see Neumann's second doctoral dissertation, "The Governance of the Rule of Law: An Investigation into the Relationship between Political Theories, the Legal System and the Social Background in the Competitive Society," Ph.D. dissertation, London School of Economics and Political Science, 1936. I am grateful to Douglas Morris for reminding me to highlight Neumann's preference for the rule of law later in life.

51. Kelly, *The State of the Political*, p. 272. Interestingly, Neumann synthesized insights from both Marxism *and* liberalism in his contribution to the theory of democracy.
52. For this argument, see, for example, Otto Kirchheimer, "Changes in the Structure of Political Compromise," *Studies in Philosophy and Social Science*, Vol. 9 (1941), pp. 264–89; and idem., "The Legal Order of National Socialism," *Studies in Philosophy and Social Science*, Vol. 9 (1941), pp. 456–75. Both essays are also available in Frederic S. Burin and Kurt L. Shell, eds., *Politics, Law, and Social Change: Selected Essays of Otto Kirchheimer* (New York: Columbia University Press, 1969).
53. For this claim, see Bast, *Totalitärer Pluralismus*, p. 287, who argues that Neumann did not think any "remnants" ("*Reste*") of the *Rechtsstaat* remained in Nazi Germany.
54. Neumann, *The Rule of Law*, p. 285. Not that Neumann was less disenchanted with the law of competitive capitalism. Thornhill reminds us that Neumann "ascribes positive qualities to liberal-capitalist law" but rejected "the legal order of monopoly capitalism, the advent of which Neumann identifies with the beginning of the Weimar Republic. [...] The law of the monopoly state, Neumann explains, abandons the rational universality of positive liberal law and replaces it with context-specific edicts, especially in the sphere of labor law." Thornhill, *Political Theory in Modern Germany*, p. 94. See also Franz L. Neumann, "The Change in the Function of Law in Modern Society," in William E. Scheuerman, The Rule of Law under Siege: Selected Essays of Franz L. Neumann and Otto Kirchheimer (Berkeley: University of California Press, [1937] 1996).
55. Carl Schmitt's Weimar-era writings had a profound effect on Neumann, as it had on almost every other German legal and political theorist of the interwar period, including Fraenkel. Neumann, for one, followed Schmitt in dismissing the nineteenth century idea of the liberal *Rechtsstaat*, of which more in Chapter 4, as the pathological manifestation of a self-interested bourgeois society in which the accumulation of private goods trumped any concern for the public good. This sentiment explains why Neumann, later in life, so fully embraced the idea of the rule of law. In a letter to Schmitt, dated September 7, 1932, Neumann named as "the decisive friend/foe grouping in Germany [...] that of labour and capital." As quoted in Keith Tribe, "Introduction," in idem., ed., *Social Democracy and the Rule of Law: Otto Kirchheimer and Franz Neumann*, translated by Leena Tanner and Keith Tribe (London: Allen and Unwin, 1987), p. 18. A complete reprint of the letter is available in Rainer Erd, ed., *Reform und Resignation: Gespräche über Franz L. Neumann*

(Frankfurt: Suhrkamp, 1985), pp. 79–80. Although both were existentialist communitarians of sorts, Schmitt and Neumann had *vastly* different ideas about how to solve the problem of social order in interwar Germany. Schmitt was convinced an identitarian society was needed, Neumann certain an egalitarian society was more urgent to establish. For a useful account of varieties of communitarianism, with particular reference to the German context, see Winfried Brugger, "Communitarianism as the Social and Legal Theory behind the German Constitution," *International Journal of Constitutional Law*, Vol. 2 (2004), pp. 431–60. On Franz Neumann's (ultimately disappointed) social-democratic zeal, see, most important, Peter Intelmann, *Franz L. Neumann: Chancen und Dilemma des politischen Reformismus* (Baden-Baden: Nomos, 1996), esp. pp. 152–223. Intelmann points out that Neumann in the early 1930s turned to considering dictatorship as a stop-gap-solution to the problem of Weimar democracy. Ibid, pp. 217–18. Neumann himself described "the creation of socialist dictatorship as a transitional state on the road to socialist democracy" ("*die Errichtung einer sozialistischen Diktatur als eines Übergangszustandes zur sozialistischen Demokratie*"). Franz L. Neumann, "Die Gewerkschaften in der Demokratie und in der Diktatur," in idem., eds., *Wirtschaft, Staat, Demokratie: Aufsätze 1930–1954*, edited by Alfons Söllner (Frankfurt: Suhrkamp, [1935] 1978), p. 219. Neumann shared his temporary faith in dictatorship as a means to making democracy work with none other than Schmitt. On the latter's prescription of "commissarial dictatorship," see, most recently, Duncan Kelly, "Carl Schmitt's Political Theory of Dictatorship," in Meierhenrich and Simons, eds., *The Oxford Handbook of Carl Schmitt* (Oxford: Oxford University Press, 2016), pp. 217–44; and Jens Meierhenrich, "Fearing the Disorder of Things: The Development of Carl Schmitt's Institutional Theory, 1919–1942," in Meierhenrich and Simons, eds., *The Oxford Handbook of Carl Schmitt*, pp. 171–216. For an excellent earlier analysis, see John P. McCormick, "From Constitutional Technique to Caesarist Ploy: Carl Schmitt on Dictatorship, Liberalism, and Emergency Powers," in Baehr and Richter, eds., *Dictatorship in History and Theory*, pp. 197–220.

56. Thornhill, *Political Theory in Modern Germany*, p. 125.
57. Primo Levi, *The Drowned and the Saved* (New York: Vintage, 1989), excerpted and annotated in Jens Meierhenrich, ed., *Genocide: A Reader* (Oxford: Oxford University Press, 2014), pp. 369–71. For a very useful recent treatment, see Sander H. Lee, "Primo Levi's Gray Zone: Implications for Post-Holocaust Ethics," *Holocaust and Genocide Studies*, Vol. 30 (2016), pp. 276–97.
58. For the most comprehensive overview of the Third Reich's legal machinery, see Gruchmann, *Justiz im Dritten Reich*.
59. On Schmitt's practice of categorical ordering, see Jens Meierhenrich and Oliver Simons, " 'A Fanatic of Order in an Epoch of Confusing Turmoil': The Political, Legal, and Cultural Thought of Carl Schmitt," in Meierhenrich and Simons, eds., *The Oxford Handbook of Carl Schmitt*, esp. pp. 12–21.

60. Ironically, Karl Korsch, a leading Marxist intellectual and figurehead of Germany's KPD in the 1920s, faulted Neumann's *Behemoth* not for its perfunctory treatment of the lived reality of law in the Third Reich, but for taking into account law as a conceptual variable at all. See idem., "The Structure and Practice of Totalitarianism," *New Essays*, Vol. 6 (1942), pp. 43–9. It appears that Neumann's "legalistic approach" also created distance between him and Max Horkheimer. See Jay, *The Dialectical Imagination*, p. 147. Although Neumann wrote *Behemoth* at the Institute for Social Research in New York, Horkheimer, its then director, ensured that the book did not have the Institute's official imprimatur. Joseph Maier in conversation with Rainer Erd, in Erd, ed., *Reform und Resignation*, p. 109. Between 1935 and 1938, Maier was a research assistant at the Institute for Social Research. On Horkheimer's complicated relationship with Neumann, see Leo Löwenthal in conversation with Rainer Erd, in Erd, ed., *Reform und Resignation*, p. 125. See also Martin Jay in conversation with Rainer Erd, in ibid, p. 125.
61. Neumann's argument can be found in his "The Change in the Function of Law in Modern Society," esp. p. 138.
62. Perels, "Adolf Arndt und Franz L. Neumann: Notizen zur Verdrängung sozialistischer Rechtstheorie," in idem., ed., *Recht, Demokratie und Kapitalismus*, p. 150.
63. Perels, "Adolf Arndt und Franz L. Neumann," pp. 151–2.
64. Perels, "Adolf Arndt und Franz L. Neumann," pp. 158, 159. Perels is particularly unimpressed by Neumann's ill-informed comments about the English common law.
65. Alfred Söllner in conversation with Rainer Erd, in Rainer Erd, ed., *Reform und Resignation*, p. 117.
66. William E. Scheuerman, *Between the Norm and the Exception: The Frankfurt School and the Rule of Law* (Cambridge: MIT Press, 1994), p. 127.
67. Alfred Söllner in conversation with Rainer Erd, p. 118.
68. Scheuerman, *Between the Norm and the Exception*, p. 128.
69. Neumann, *Behemoth* [1942 edition], pp. 469–70.
70. Neumann, *Behemoth* [1942 edition], p. 451.
71. Bast puts it slightly differently. In his reading, Neumann was concerned with the *formality* of law, whereas Fraenkel was more interested in the *validity* of law. See his *Totalitärer Pluralismus*, p. 281, fn. 32.
72. For a brief history of the *Rechtsstaat* in Germany up until 1933, see Chapter 4.
73. Franz L. Neumann, "Types of Natural Law," *Studies in Philosophy and Social Science*, Vol. 8 (1939), p. 361, reprinted in idem., *The Democratic and the Authoritarian State* (New York: Free Press, 1957), p. 90.
74. Lon L. Fuller, *The Morality of Law*, Revised edition (New Haven: Yale University Press, 1969), pp. 33–8.
75. Ronald Dworkin, "Philosophy, Morality, and Law—Observations Prompted by Professor Fuller's Novel Claim," *University of Pennsylvania Law Review*, Vol. 113 (1965), p. 676.

76. Dworkin, "Philosophy, Morality, and Law," pp. 676–7.
77. Kelsen, *Allgemeine Staatslehre*, p. 335.
78. Dworkin, "Philosophy, Morality, and Law," p. 678.
79. Douglas G. Morris, "The Dual State Reframed: Ernst Fraenkel's Political Clients and his Theory of the Nazi Legal System," *Leo Baeck Institute Year Book*, Vol. 58 (2013), p. 11. See also Klaus Behnken, ed., *Deutschland-Berichte der Sozialdemokratischen Partei Deutschlands (Sopade) 1934–1940*, 7 volumes (Frankfurt: Nettelbeck, 1980), which provided assessments, published by exiled social democrats in Prague, about political, legal, and economic developments in Nazi Germany that draw on first-hand accounts smuggled out of the Reich.
80. With a nod to his courtroom experience, Fraenkel included summaries of two of his cases as appendices in the first German edition of *The Dual State*. I recently translated these appendices, and they now form part of the expanded 2017 edition of *The Dual State*, where they appear for the first time in English.
81. Morris, "The Dual State Reframed," p. 20.
82. Morris, "The Dual State Reframed," p. 13.
83. Sebastian Haffner, *Defying Hitler: A Memoir*, translated by Oliver Pretzel (London: Weidenfeld and Nicolson, 2002), p. 89. Born Raimund Pretzel, Haffner, who for many years worked for *The Observer*, is revered in Germany, not least on account of his bestselling *Anmerkungen zu Hitler*, first released in 1978, and published in English as *The Meaning of Hitler*, translated by Ewald Osers (Cambridge: Harvard University Press, 1983). Interestingly, the title of Haffner's first book, *Germany: Jekyll and Hyde* (London: Secker and Warburg, 1940), like that of Fraenkel's, emphasized the two-sided nature of the Third Reich. If lore is to be believed, Winston Churchill told his war cabinet to read Haffner's eyewitness account to better understand the dictatorship across the channel. Apparently, David Astor, the longstanding editor of *The Observer*, considered Haffner to be one of the three most impressive individuals he ever encountered, on par with Churchill and Charles de Gaulle. As relayed by Joachim Fest in "Der fremde Freund," *Der Spiegel*, August 11, 2003.
84. Haffner, who was not Jewish, also chronicled the destruction of the *Rechtsstaat*, though unlike Neumann, he emphasized the processual character of law's marginalization, juxtaposing its blatant politicization with what he called "the triumphs of the older law." Haffner, *Defying Hitler*, p. 147.
85. Neumann, *Behemoth* [1942 edition], pp. 448, 450.
86. Morris, "The Dual State Reframed," p. 19.
87. Morris, "The Dual State Reframed," p. 17.
88. Morris, "The Dual State Reframed," p. 17.
89. Neumann, *Behemoth* [1942 edition], p. 447.
90. Neumann, *Behemoth* [1942 edition], p. 452.
91. Although Fraenkel only took into account evidence up until the beginning of World War II, we now know that his argument also held true for the war years during which select remnants of the *Rechtsstaat* continued to fulfill regulatory functions. For an excellent overview, see Dieter Gosewinkel, "Wirtschaftskontrolle und Recht in der nationalsozialistischen Diktatur: Forschung und

Forschungsperspektiven," in idem., ed., *Wirtschaftskontrolle und Recht in der nationalsozialistischen Diktatur* (Frankfurt: Klostermann, 2005), pp. ix-lix. For an in-depth case study, see Daniela Kahn, *Die Steuerung der Wirtschaft durch Recht im nationalsozialistischen Deutschland: Das Beispiel der Reichsgruppe Industrie* (Frankfurt: Klostermann, 2006).

92. The formulations are from Neumann, *Behemoth* [1942 edition], p. 440, where he conceded that his interpretation of law in Nazi Germany was idiosyncratic.
93. M. J. Bonn, "Franz Neumann, Behemoth: The Structure and Practice of National Socialism" (Book review), *Journal of Political Economy*, Vol. 51 (1943), p. 371.
94. I take holism to refer to approaches that reject methodological individualism in favor of structural variables such as class, race, gender, ideology, or the distribution of power in the international system as the starting point for the explanation of social phenomena (such as the law of the Third Reich). By functionalism I mean the explanation of social phenomena through a focus on the beneficial effects they have on something else (such as the Nazi dictatorship) or someone else (such as capitalists) rather than on the beliefs, preferences, strategies, and interactions of agents involved in the social construction of the thing to be explained.
95. Terry Lynn Karl, *The Paradox of Plenty: Oil Booms and Petro States* (Berkeley: University of California Press, 1997), pp. 10–11; Jens Meierhenrich, *The Legacies of Law: Long-Run Consequences of Legal Development in South Africa, 1652–2000* (Cambridge: Cambridge University Press, 2008), pp. 45–6.
96. Karl Marx, "The Eighteenth Brumaire of Louis Bonaparte," in idem., *Political Writings*, vol. 2: *Surveys from Exile*, edited and with an Introduction by David Fernbach (New York: Vintage, [1852] 1974), p. 146.
97. For a brief comparison between de Tocqueville and Marx and their respective methodologies, see Jon Elster, *Alexis de Tocqueville, the First Social Scientist* (Cambridge: Cambridge University Press, 2009), pp. 7–8.
98. On Neumann's "turning away" ("*Abkehr*") from reformism ("*Reformismus*"), see Intelmann, *Franz L. Neumann*, p. 217, who discusses Neumann's intellectual radicalization in the context of the so-called *Prager Manifest*, a manifestoed call for the revolutionary overthrow of the Nazi dictatorship authored by Rudolf Hilferding and released by Germany's Social Democratic Party (SPD) from its headquarters in exile on January 28, 1934. On the influence of Hilferding's economic writings about monopolistic theory and the role of financial capital on Neumann's argument about totalitarian monopoly capitalism, see Bast, *Totalitärer Pluralismus*, pp. 191–213. The other major theorist whose economic perspective left a deep mark on *Behemoth*, and on Neumann's thinking about capitalism more generally, was Karl Renner. Renner's sociological analysis of private legal institutions, notably of the institution of property, was first published in 1905 but received renewed attention in 1929, when a second edition was released. See Karl Renner, *Die Rechtsinstitute des Privatrechts und ihre soziale Funktion: Ein Beitrag zur Kritik des bürgerlichen Rechts*, Second edition (Tübingen: Mohr, [1905] 1929).

99. Koppel S. Pinson, "Franz Neumann, Behemoth: The Structure and Practice of National Socialism" (Book review), *Political Science Quarterly*, Vol. 57 (1942), p. 443.
100. Intelmann reckons that the differences between Neumann and Fraenkel are mere semantics. See his *Franz L. Neumann*, p. 277.
101. Neumann, *Behemoth* [1942 edition], p. 440. Neumann first introduced the distinction between a "political" concept of law and a "rational" one in 1937. His argument at the time sounded like this: "Not every measure of the sovereign, and not only measures of the sovereign, are law. [...] Law [...] is *ratio* and not necessarily *voluntas* at the same time." See Neumann, "The Change in the Function of Law in Modern Society," p. 104.
102. Neumann, *Behemoth* [1942 edition], p. 440.
103. Roger Cotterrell, "The Rule of Law in Corporate Society: Neumann, Kirchheimer and the Lessons of Weimar," *Modern Law Review*, Vol. 51 (1988), esp. pp. 132–5.
104. Cotterrell, "The Rule of Law in Corporate Society," p. 133.
105. Franz Neumann, "The Governance of the Rule of Law." The dissertation first appeared in print as Franz Neumann, *Die Herrschaft des Gesetzes: Eine Untersuchung zum Verhältnis von politischer Theorie und Rechtssystem in der Konkurrenzgesellschaft*, edited with an Afterword by Alfons Söllner (Frankfurt: Suhrkamp, 1980). The English edition that Cotterrell references has a more straightforward title: Franz Neumann, *The Rule of Law: Political Theory and the Legal System in Modern Society* (Leamington Spa: Berg, 1986). It is worth pointing out that with "The Governance of the Rule of Law," Neumann completed his *second* doctoral dissertation. He also held a doctorate in law, which he received in 1923, for a dissertation on punishment and the state. See Franz L. Neumann, "Rechtsphilosophische Einleitung zu einer Abhandlung über das Verhältnis von Staat und Strafe," Ph.D. dissertation, Universität Frankfurt, 1923. For a useful discussion of the dissertation's context and gestation, see Sascha Ziemann, "Relativismus in Zeiten der Krise: Franz L. Neumanns unveröffentlichte rechtsphilosophische Doktorarbeit von 1923," *Zeitschrift für Internationale Strafrechtsdogmatik*, Vol. 2 (2007), pp. 362–70.
106. William E. Scheuerman, "The Frankfurt School and the Rule of Law," in Jens Meierhenrich and Martin Loughlin, eds., *The Cambridge Companion to the Rule of Law* (Cambridge: Cambridge University Press, forthcoming). Scheuerman makes the important point that Neumann's faith in the ethical function of law set him apart from orthodox Marxists for whom the rule of law was nothing but a veil for capitalism, and thus epiphenomenal. Neumann discussed the ethical function of law explicitly in the following publications: *Die Herrschaft des Gesetzes*, pp. 354–5; "The Change in the Function of Law in Modern Society," pp. 117–18; *Behemoth* [1942 edition], pp. 442–4.

107. Cotterrell, "The Rule of Law in Corporate Society," p. 133.
108. Cotterrell, "The Rule of Law in Corporate Society," p. 133.
109. On the similarities and differences between the two neighboring concepts, see Jens Meierhenrich, "*Rechtsstaat* versus the Rule of Law," in Meierhenrich and Loughlin, eds., *The Cambridge Companion to the Rule of Law*.
110. Cotterrell, "The Rule of Law in Corporate Society," p. 133.
111. Cotterrell, "The Rule of Law in Corporate Society," p. 135.
112. Cotterrell, "The Rule of Law in Corporate Society," p. 135.
113. Ulrich K. Preuß, "Nachträge zur Theorie des Rechtsstaats," *Kritische Justiz*, Vol. 4 (1971), pp. 16–17.
114. See my discussion in Chapter 1.
115. On the upside, Neumann's argument that the Hitler regime lacked "a unified coercive machinery" laid the groundwork for pathbreaking analyses in the postwar period of the polycratic nature of the Third Reich. The most notable contribution was Peter Hüttenberger, "Nationalsozialistische Polykratie," *Geschichte und Gesellschaft*, Vol. 2 (1976), pp. 417–42. Martin Broszat and Hans Mommsen became the two most outspoken proponents of a structuralist interpretation of the Nazi state.
116. Heiko Maas, ed., *Furchtlose Juristen: Richter und Staatsanwälte gegen das NS-Unrecht* (Munich: Beck, 2017).
117. See Jens Meierhenrich, *Lawfare: A Genealogy* (Cambridge: Cambridge University Press, 2018).
118. Raul Hilberg, "The Relevance of *Behemoth* Today," *Constellations*, Vol. 10 (2003), p. 256. See also Raul Hilberg, *Politics of Memory: The Journey of a Holocaust Historian* (Chicago: Ivan R. Dee, 1996), esp. p. 89.
119. I had occasion to speak with Hilberg about Neumann and Fraenkel at the U.S. Holocaust Memorial Museum in 2005. It was palpable that he still felt indebted to his erstwhile mentor at Columbia University. On this debt more generally, see Jonathan A. Bush, "Raul Hilberg (1926–2007) in Memoriam," *Jewish Quarterly Review*, Vol. 100 (2010), pp. 661–88.
120. Raul Hilberg, *The Destruction of the European Jews*, 3 volumes, Third edition (New Haven: Yale University Press, [1961] 2003). In his *Debates on the Holocaust* (Manchester: Manchester University Press, 2010), Tom Lawson usefully situates Hilberg's trilogy in contemporary scholarship on the Nazi genocide. See esp. pp. 67–78. As is widely known, Hannah Arendt pilfered several of Hilberg's ideas and presented them as her own in her bestselling *Eichmann in Jerusalem: A Report on the Banality of Evil* (New York: Viking, 1963). Neither did she fully acknowledge her debt to Neumann's *Behemoth*, which she accrued in the writing of *The Origins of Totalitarianism*. See below for a brief discussion.
121. Browning read *The Destruction of the European Jews* during a long convalescence from mononucleosis. At a memorial service for Hilberg, he recalled the intellectual encounter with the three-volume set in dramatic terms: "Some people have religious conversion experiences; upon reading

Hilberg I had a life-changing academic conversion experience." As quoted in Nathaniel Popper, "A Conscious Pariah," *The Nation*, April 19, 2001.

122. Alfons Söllner, "Hannah Arendt's *The Origins of Totalitarianism* in its Original Context," *European Journal of Political Theory*, Vol. 3 (2004), p. 225.
123. On the metaphor, see the seminal analysis of Ernst H. Kantorowicz, *The King's Two Bodies: A Study in Mediaeval Political Theology* (Princeton: Princeton University Press, 1957).
124. As quoted in Intelmann, *Franz L. Neumann,* p. 46, fn. 237.
125. As quoted in Intelmann, *Franz L. Neumann*, p. 46, fn. 237.
126. Oscar Jászi, "Franz Neumann, Behemoth: The Structure and Practice of National Socialism; Rohan D'O. Butler: The Roots of National Socialism" (Book review), *American Political Science Review*, Vol. 36 (1942), p. 771.
127. Paul M. Sweezy, "Franz Neumann, Behemoth: The Structure and Practice of National Socialism" (Book review), *Science and Society*, Vol. 6 (1942), pp. 281, 286.
128. Waldemar Gurian, "Franz Neumann, Behemoth: The Structure and Practice of National Socialism" (Book review), *Review of Politics*, Vol. 4 (1942), p. 347; George Sabine, "Franz Neumann, Behemoth: The Structure and Practice of National Socialism" (Book review), *Philosophical Review*, Vol. 51 (1942), pp. 432, 434.
129. Robert A. Brady, "Franz Neumann, Behemoth: The Structure and Practice of National Socialism" (Book review), *American Economic Review*, Vol. 33 (1943), p. 389. Emphasis added.
130. Brady, "Franz Neumann, Behemoth," p. 389.
131. Pinson, "Franz Neumann, Behemoth," p. 441.
132. C. Wright Mills, "The Nazi Behemoth Dissected," *Partisan Review*, Vol. 9 (1942), pp. 432–6. As a Ph.D. student at the University of Wisconsin, Madison, Mills came under the tutelage of Hans Heinrich Gerth, a German refugee scholar and former student of Karl Mannheim and Karl Jaspers at Heidelberg. In 1958, Gerth and Mills translated and edited selected writings of Max Weber. The biographical connection may have sensitized Mills to the output of left-leaning émigré lawyers like Neumann. On Mills, see Daniel Geary, *Radical Ambition: C. Wright Mills, the Left, and American Social Thought* (Berkeley: University of California Press, 2009).
133. Mills, "The Nazi Behemoth Dissected," p. 437. Emphasis added.
134. Mills, "The Nazi Behemoth Dissected," p. 437. Emphasis added.
135. David Kettler, "Neumann, Franz," in William A. Darity, ed., *International Encyclopedia of the Social Sciences*, Second edition (London: Macmillan, 2008), p. 482. Kettler points out that Mills's *Power Elite* (New York: Oxford University Press, 1956) was in essence an application of Neumann's ideas to the case of the United States.
136. Talcott Parsons, *The Sociological Imagination* (New York: Oxford University Press, 1959), p. 57. See also idem., *The Social System* (Glencoe: Free Press, 1951); and idem., *On National Socialism*, edited with an Introduction by

Uta Gerhardt (New York: De Gruyter, 1993); as well as Uta Gerhardt, *Talcott Parsons: An Intellectual Biography* (Cambridge: Cambridge University Press, 2002), esp. pp. 58–128, in which the author analyzes Parsons's scholarship on the Nazi dictatorship.

137. Parsons, *The Sociological Imagination*, p. 59.
138. Moritz Julius Bonn, *So macht man Geschichte: Bilanz eines Lebens* (Munich: List, 1953), p. 330. The close relationship between Schmitt and Bonn, who mentored and supported Schmitt from the beginning of his career, came to an end in 1933, when Bonn's protégé threw his lot in with the Nazi dictatorship. See also my discussion in Chapter 5, where Schmitt resurfaces as one of the *dramatis personae* in the Nazi debate about the *Rechtsstaat*.
139. Bonn, "Franz Neumann, Behemoth", p. 371.
140. Bonn, "Franz Neumann, Behemoth", p. 371.
141. Dwight E. Lee, "Franz Neumann, Behemoth: The Structure and Practice of National Socialism" (Book review), *American Historical Review*, Vol. 48 (1943), p. 337.
142. Lee, "Franz Neumann, Behemoth" p. 338.
143. Lee, "Franz Neumann, Behemoth" p. 338.
144. Frederick H. Cramer, "Franz Neumann, Behemoth: The Structure and Practice of National Socialism" (Book review), *Journal of Modern History*, Vol. 15 (1943), pp. 156, 157.
145. Sweezy, "Franz Neumann," p. 285.
146. Generally, see, for example, Paul Pierson, *Politics in Time: History, Institutions, and Social Analysis* (Princeton: Princeton University Press, 2004). On the importance of taking Nazi institutions seriously, see, in the context of the Holocaust, Stefan Kühl, *Ganz normale Organisationen: Zur Soziologie des Holocaust* (Frankfurt: Suhrkamp, 2014).
147. C. H. Pegg, "Franz Neumann, Behemoth: The Structure and Practice of National Socialism" (Book review), *Social Forces*, Vol. 21 (1943), p. 364. Others agreed: "[T]he entire volume is permeated by a mechanical and outworn class interpretation of [N]ational [S]ocialism." Pinson, "Franz Neumann, Behemoth" p. 442.
148. Pegg, "Franz Neumann, Behemoth" p. 364.
149. Charles B. Robson, "Franz Neumann, Behemoth: The Structure and Practice of National Socialism" (Book review), *Journal of Politics*, Vol. 5 (1943), p. 71.
150. Carl Schorske in conversation with Rainer Erd, in Erd, ed., *Reform und Resignation*, p. 159.
151. Ernst Fraenkel, "Gedenkrede auf Franz L. Neumann," in idem., *Gesammelte Schriften*, vol. 6: *Internationale Politik und Völkerrecht, Politikwissenschaft und Hochschulpolitik*, edited by Hubertus Buchstein and Klaus-Gert Lutterbeck (Baden-Baden: Nomos, [1955] 1999), p. 365.
152. Neumann wrote the first edition of *Behemoth* in New York. The second edition benefitted from his access to additional documentation in the U.S. Library of Congress and at the OSS.

153. Josef L. Kunz, "Franz Neumann, Behemoth: The Structure and Practice of National Socialism, Second edition" (Book review), *American Political Science Review*, Vol. 39 (1945), p. 376.
154. Gurian, "Franz Neumann, Behemoth" p. 349. Emphasis added.
155. Gurian, "Franz Neumann, Behemoth" p. 349.
156. Kunz, "Franz Neumann, Behemoth" p. 377.
157. For an excellent, in-depth account of Neumann's standing at the Institute for Social Research, and his navigation of the New York émigré community, see Thomas Wheatland, "Franz L. Neumann: Negotiating Political Exile," in Jan Logemann and Mary Nolan, eds., *More Atlantic Crossings? European Voices and the Postwar Atlantic Community* (Washington: German Historical Institute, 2014), pp. 111–38. See also Martin Jay's *The Dialectical Imaginations*, esp. pp. 143–72.
158. Scheuerman, *Between the Norm and the Exception*, p. 123. See also Intelmann, *Franz L. Neumann*, pp. 47–52. More generally, see also Franz Neumann, Herbert Marcuse, and Otto Kirchheimer, *Secret Reports on Nazi Germany: The Frankfurt School Contribution to the War Effort*, edited by Raffaele Laudani (Princeton: Princeton University Press, 2013).
159. Scheuerman, *Between the Norm and the Exception*, p. 123.
160. Barry M. Katz, *Foreign Intelligence: Research and Analysis in the Office of Strategic Services 1942–1945* (Cambridge: Harvard University Press, 1989), p. 36. Cf. Neumann, *Behemoth* [1942 edition] and Neumann, *Behemoth* [1944].
161. Katz, *Foreign Intelligence*, p. 54.
162. Katz, *Foreign Intelligence*, p. 54.
163. Katz, *Foreign Intelligence*, p. 56. Also relevant are Mark Lewis, *The Birth of the New Justice: The Internationalization of Crime and Punishment, 1919–1950* (Oxford: Oxford University Press, 2014), pp. 167–73; and Shlomo Aronson, "Preparations for the Nuremberg Trial: The O.S.S., Charles Dwork, and the Holocaust," *Holocaust and Genocide Studies*, Vol. 12 (1998), pp. 257–81. On the long-run consequences of the introduction at the IMT of conspiracy and criminal organization as modes of collective responsibility, see Jens Meierhenrich, "Conspiracy in International Law," *Annual Review of Law and Social Science*, Vol. 2 (2006), pp. 341–57.
164. Katz, *Foreign Intelligence*, p. 56. Michael Salter reaches a similar conclusion in *Nazi War Crimes, U.S. Intelligence and Selective Prosecution at Nuremberg: Controversies Regarding the Role of the Office of Strategic Services* (London: Routledge, 2007), esp. pp. 307–46. See also idem., *U.S. Intelligence, the Holocaust and the Nuremburg Trials: Seeking Accountability for Genocide and Cultural Plunder*, vol. 2 (Boston: Nijhoff, 2009), pp. 594–636.
165. As quoted in Barry M. Katz, The Criticism of Arms: The Frankfurt School Goes to War," *Journal of Modern History*, Vol. 59 (1987), p. 447.
166. Klaus Epstein, *Vom Kaisserreich zum Dritten Reich: Geschichte und Geschichtswissenschaft im 20. Jahrhundert* (Frankfurt: Ullstein, 1973), p. 375.
167. John Herz in conversation with Rainer Erd, in Erd, ed., *Reform und Resignation*, p. 155.

168. Söllner, "Hannah Arendt's *The Origins of Totalitarianism* in its Original Context," p. 225.
169. Alfred Söllner in conversation with Rainer Erd, p. 117.
170. Hannah Arendt, *The Origins of Totalitarianism* (New York: Harcourt, Brace, 1951). The most famous critique (accompanied by Arendt's reply) remains Eric Voegelin, "The Origins of Totalitarianism," *Review of Politics*, Vol. 15 (1953), pp. 68–85. For a recent defense of Arendt's meandering analysis and theoretical incongruities, see Hans-Jörg Sigwart, "Political Characterology: On the Method of Theorizing in Hannah Arendt's *Origins of Totalitarianism*," *American Political Science Review*, Vol. 110 (2017), pp. 265–77. Note that even Sigwart is at pains to justify the book's shortcomings: "What the book cannot claim to be [...] is an exemplary case of a coherently organized study based on the systematic application of an attentively reflected theoretical framework and a corresponding method of inquiry. [...] Arendt's study is not very explicit with regard to its fundamental assumptions. At first sight it seems even to almost completely lack an explicitly reflected conceptual basis that would make it possible to locate it within the main methodological currents of the 20th-century contemporary theory debate." Ibid, p. 265. The description is apt (and reminds of Neumann's *Behemoth*). It does not invalidate the book as such. *The Origins of Totalitarianism* has inspired a whole host of worthy intellectual pursuits, including, most recently, the debate over the imperial dimensions of genocide, notably the Holocaust. But it does call into question the theoretical value (and empirical validity) of her argument (which she modelled on Neumann) about the Nazi dictatorship as a non-state. On the gestation of Arendt's classic, and an interesting explanation for its disjointed nature, see Roy T. Tsao, "The Three Phases of Arendt's Theory of Totalitarianism," *Social Research*, Vol. 69 (2002), pp. 579–619.
171. Vicky Iakovou, "Totalitarianism as a Non-State: On Hannah Arendt's Debt to Franz Neumann," *European Journal of Political Theory*, Vol. 8 (2009), pp. 429, 430.
172. Incidentally, Arendt borrowed extensively, often without attribution, not only from Neumann but also from Raul Hilberg, his student. She drew Hilberg's ire when, in 1959, she advised Princeton University Press not to publish his Holocaust trilogy and subsequently plagiarized—allegedly—key ideas from his book manuscript in her *Eichmann in Jerusalem* while dismissing others. For this allegation, see Raul Hilberg, *The Politics of Memory*, pp. 156–7. See also the enlightening obituary by Bush, "Raul Hilberg (1926–2007) in Memoriam," pp. 661–88.
173. Söllner, "Hannah Arendt's *The Origins of Totalitarianism* in its Original Context," pp. 219–38; Iakovou, "Totalitarianism as a Non-State", pp. 429–47.
174. William Selinger, "The Politics of Arendtian Historiography: European Federation and *The Origins of Totalitarianism*," *Modern Intellectual History*, Vol. 13 (2016), p. 435.

175. Armin Nolzen, "The Nazi Party and Its Violence against the Jews, 1933–1939: Violence as a Historiographical Concept," *Yad Vashem Studies*, Vol. 31 (2003), p. 246. Emphasis added.
176. "The Hundred Most Influential Books since the War," *Times Literary Supplement*, October 6, 1995.
177. They included Fritz Stern and Peter Gay, both of whom became eminent historians of Germany. Carl Schorske in conversation with Rainer Erd, in Erd, ed., *Reform und Resignation*, p. 158. Furthermore, *Behemoth* was influenced by, and gave impetus to, the evolving debate about totalitarianism in the period 1920–1960s, not least because of Neumann's analysis of Germany's "totalitarian monopolistic economy" that he laid out in Part II, Chapters 1–4 of *Behemoth*, and his depiction of the Nazi state as a "totalitarian state" in Chapter 1. On the legacy of Neumann's argument, see, for example, Walter Schlangen, *Die Totalitarismus-Theorie: Entwicklung und Probleme* (Stuttgart: Kohlhammer, 1976), pp. 33–5.
178. Hayes, "Introduction," p. xiii.
179. In his trenchant critique of functionalist explanations in the Marxist tradition, Jon Elster claimed that they "*postulate a purpose without a purposive actor*." Jon Elster, "The Case for Methodological Individualism," *Theory and Society*, Vol. 11 (1982), p. 454. Elster's point, which also applies to my critique of Neumann's *Behemoth*, is that methodological holism overlooks the actual incentives and collective action problems that really existing agents face in concrete social interactions. Or, as Elster writes: "Without a firm knowledge about the mechanisms that operate at the individual level, the grand Marxist claims about macrostructures and long-term change are condemned to remain at the level of speculation." Ibid.
180. Hayes, "Introduction," p. xiv.

CHAPTER 3

1. Stuart A. Scheingold and Austin Sarat, *Something to Believe in: Politics, Professionalism, and Cause Lawyering* (Stanford: Stanford University Press, 2004), p. 3.
2. Lisa Hajjar, "From the Fight for Legal Rights to the Promotion of Human Rights: Israeli and Palestinian Cause Lawyers in the Trenches of Globalization," in Austin Sarat and Stuart A. Scheingold, eds., *Cause Lawyering and the State in a Global Era* (New York: Oxford University Press, 2001), p. 68. More generally, see also Terence C. Halliday, "The Politics of Lawyers: An Emerging Agenda," *Law and Social Inquiry*, Vol. 24 (1999), pp. 1007–11.
3. For comprehensive accounts, see Jacob Katz, *Out of the Ghetto: The Social Background of Jewish Emancipation, 1770–1870* (Cambridge: Harvard University Press, 1973); Shulamit Volkov, *Die Juden in Deutschland 1780–1918*, translated by Simone Gundi (Munich: Oldenbourg, 2000). Going farther back in time are R. Po-Chia Hsia and Hartmut Lehmann, eds., *In and Out of the Ghetto: Jewish-Gentile Relations in Late Medieval*

and Early Modern Germany (Cambridge: Cambridge University Press, 1995) and Friedrich Battenberg, *Die Juden in Deutschland vom 16. bis zum Ende des 18. Jahrhunderts* (Munich: Oldenbourg, 2001). On the salience of, and relationship between, assimilation and antisemitism in the late nineteenth and early twentieth century Germany, see, most important, Shulamit Volkov, *Germans, Jews, and Antisemites: Trials in Emancipation* (Cambridge: Cambridge University Press, 2006). Useful synthetic treatments are Ruth Gay, *The Jews of Germany: A Historical Portrait* (New Haven: Yale University Press, 1991); and Peter Pulzer, *Jews and the German State: The Political History of a Minority* (Oxford: Blackwell, 1992).

4. Heinrich Heine, *On the History of Religion and Philosophy in Germany*, edited by Terry Pinkard (Cambridge: Cambridge University Press [1835], 2007), p. 69.
5. Ernst Fraenkel, "Anstatt einer Vorrede," in idem., *Reformismus und Pluralismus: Materialien zu einer ungeschriebenen Autobiographie*, edited by Falk Esche and Frank Grube (Hamburg: Hoffman und Campe, 1973), pp. 14–15.
6. Simone Ladwig-Winters, *Ernst Fraenkel: Ein politisches Leben* (New York: Campus Verlag, 2009), pp. 21–6.
7. Fraenkel, "Anstatt einer Vorrede," p. 18.
8. Fraenkel, "Anstatt einer Vorrede," p. 19.
9. Fraenkel, "Anstatt einer Vorrede," p. 14.
10. Hubertus Buchstein and Rainer Kühn, "Vorwort zu diesem Band," in Ernst Fraenkel, *Gesammelte Schriften*, vol. 1: *Recht und Politik in der Weimarer Republik*, edited by Hubertus Buchstein (Baden-Baden: Nomos, 1999), p. 17.
11. Fraenkel, "Anstatt einer Vorrede," p. 17. Epstein's father, Fraenkel's grandfather, in 1861 played a leading role, together with August Bebel and Karl Liebknecht, in the founding of the *Leipziger Arbeiterbildungsverein*, the first worker's educational association on German soil. Ibid, p. 16.
12. Fraenkel, "Anstatt einer Vorrede," p. 15. In his autobiographical reflections, Fraenkel recalled that in his family home "Russia was the enemy." His parents, wrote Fraenkel, deemed authoritarian Russia "rotten" because of the "barbaric antisemitic pogroms" taking place there. Accordingly, they celebrated with fanfare Japan's decisive victory in the May 1905 Battle of Tsushima, which effectively ended the Russo-Japanese war. Ibid, p. 14.
13. Fraenkel, "Anstatt einer Vorrede," p. 15.
14. For a reprint of Weber's article series, see his "Parliament and Government in Germany under a New Political Order," in Peter Lassman and Ronald Speirs, eds., *Weber: Political Writings* (Cambridge: Cambridge University Press, 1994), pp. 130–271.
15. Fraenkel, "Anstatt einer Vorrede," p. 20.
16. Fraenkel, "Anstatt einer Vorrede," p. 20.

17. Ernst Fraenkel, Letter to Ursula Schulz, May 12, 1974, as quoted in Ladwig-Winters, *Ernst Fraenkel*, p. 33.
18. Fraenkel, "Anstatt einer Vorrede," p. 20.
19. Fraenkel, "Anstatt einer Vorrede," p. 20.
20. Fraenkel, "Anstatt einer Vorrede," p. 21.
21. Fraenkel, "Anstatt einer Vorrede," p. 21; Ladwig-Winters, *Ernst Fraenkel*, pp. 34–5.
22. Ladwig-Winters, *Ernst Fraenkel*, p. 37.
23. Fraenkel, "Anstatt einer Vorrede," p. 21.
24. Fraenkel, "Anstatt einer Vorrede," p. 21.
25. Fraenkel, "Anstatt einer Vorrede," p. 23.
26. See Fraenkel, "Anstatt einer Vorrede," p. 25. Fraenkel's uncle cautioned that a degree in history would almost invariably lead to a teaching career and that such a career might not be the best choice for a Jew in Germany. Ibid, p. 24.
27. The *Reichsgericht* and *Staatsgerichtshof*, with which the former must not be confused, were the highest courts in Imperial Germany. Between 1877 and 1945, the *Reichsgericht*, or Reich Court, functioned as the federal high court for civil and criminal matters. By contrast, the *Staatsgerichtshof*, or State Court, served as the high court for constitutional matters. It was put to its test in the infamous case of *Preussen contra Reich* in the turbulent constitutional crisis of the early 1930s. The so-called *Preußenschlag*, the controversial political move in which Reich Chancellor Franz von Papen persuaded President Paul von Hindenburg to dissolve the subnational government of Prussia and seize power there in July 1932 plunged the Weimar Republic into disarray, and the *Staatsgerichtshof* was called upon to adjudicate the political intervention.
28. Ladwig-Winters, *Ernst Fraenkel*, pp. 46, 343, fn. 10.
29. For a history of *Öffentliches Recht* in early to mid-twentieth century Germany, see Michael Stolleis, *A History of Public Law in Germany, 1914–1945*, translated by Thomas Dunlap (Oxford: Oxford University Press, [1999] 2004).
30. Ladwig-Winters, *Ernst Fraenkel*, p. 343, fn. 9.
31. See Hugo Sinzheimer, "Was Wir Wollen," *Die Justiz*, No. 1 (1925), reprinted in Hugo Sinzheimer and Ernst Fraenkel, *Die Justiz in der Weimarer Republik: Eine Chronik*, edited by Thilo Ramm (Neuwied: Luchterhand, 1968), pp. 19–23.
32. Udi Greenberg, *The Weimar Century: German Émigrés and the Ideological Foundations of the Cold War* (Princeton: Princeton University Press, 2014), pp. 83–9. For a discussion of the idea of the "social *Rechtsstaat*," which Hermann Heller invented in 1930, and alternative conceptions of the *Rechtsstaat*, see the next chapter.
33. Ernst Fraenkel, "Vorwort zum Neudruck," in idem., *Gesammelte Schriften*, vol. 1: *Recht und Politik in der Weimarer Republik*, edited by Hubertus Buchstein (Baden-Baden: Nomos, [1968] 1999), p. 656.

34. On Morgenthau, see Michael C. Williams, ed., *Reconsidering Realism: The Legacy of Hans J. Morgenthau* (Oxford: Oxford University Press, 2007); and William E. Scheuerman, *Hans Morgenthau: Realism and Beyond* (Oxford: Polity, 2009). On Schmid, see Petra Weber, *Carlo Schmid, 1896–1979: Eine Biographie* (Munich: Beck, 1996).
35. On Neumann, see, most important, Rainer Erd, ed., *Reform und Resignation: Gespräche über Franz L. Neumann* (Frankfurt: Suhrkamp, 1985); Jürgen Bast, *Totalitärer Pluralismus: Zu Franz L. Neumanns Analysen der politischen und rechtlichen Struktur der NS-Herrschaft* (Tübingen, Mohr, 1999); Samuel Salzborn, ed., *Kritische Theorie des Staates: Staat und Recht bei Franz L. Neumann* (Baden-Baden: Nomos, 2009). For an early compilation of some of Neumann's shorter writings, see Franz L. Neumann, *Wirtschaft, Staat, Demokratie: Aufsätze 1930–1954*, edited by Alfons Söllner (Frankfurt: Suhrkamp, 1978). See also Duncan Kelly, *The State of the Political: Conceptions of Politics and the State in the Thought of Max Weber, Carl Schmitt and Franz Neumann* (Oxford: Oxford University, 2003), Chapter 5.
36. On this social democratic conception of law, see, most important, William E. Scheuerman, "Social Democracy and the Rule of Law: The Legacy of Ernst Fraenkel," in Peter C. Caldwell and William E. Scheuerman, eds., *From Liberal Democracy to Fascism* (Boston: Humanities Press, 2000), pp. 74–105. See also Keith Tribe, ed., *Social Democracy and the Rule of Law: Otto Kirchheimer and Franz Neumann*, translated by Leena Tanner and Keith Tribe (London: Allen & Unwin, 1987). On the topic more generally, see William E. Scheuerman, *Between the Norm and the Exception: The Frankfurt School and the Rule of Law* (Cambridge: MIT Press, 1994).
37. Ladwig-Winters, *Ernst Fraenkel*, p. 47.
38. For general accounts, see, esp. Martin Jay, *The Dialectical Imagination. A History of the Frankfurt School and the Institute of Social Research 1923–1950*, Second edition (Berkeley: University of California Press, 1996); David Held, *Introduction to Critical Theory: Horkheimer to Habermas* (Berkeley: University of California Press, 1980); and Rolf Wiggershaus, *Die Frankfurter Schule: Geschichte, Theoretische Entwicklung, Politische Bedeutung* (Munich: Hanser, 1986).
39. Ladwig-Winters, *Ernst Fraenkel*, pp. 52–4.
40. Ernst Fraenkel, "Der nichtige Arbeitsvertrag," in idem., *Gesammelte Schriften*, vol. 1: *Recht und Politik in der Weimarer Republik*, edited by Hubertus Buchstein (Baden-Baden: Nomos, [1923] 1999), pp. 69–120.
41. Ladwig-Winters, *Ernst Fraenkel*, pp. 56–7.
42. Thomas M. Hilbink, "You Know the Type . . . : Categories of Cause Lawyering," *Law and Social Inquiry*, Vol. 29 (2004), esp. pp. 673–81.
43. See Ernst Fraenkel, "Die Wirtschaftsschule des Deutschen Metallarbeiterverbandes in Bad Dürrenberg," in idem., *Gesammelte Schriften*, vol. 1: *Recht und Politik in der Weimarer Republik*, edited by Hubertus Buchstein (Baden-Baden: Nomos, [1926] 1999), pp. 163–6

44. Fraenkel, "Die Wirtschaftsschule des Deutschen Metallarbeiterverbandes in Bad Dürrenberg," p. 163.
45. Ladwig-Winters, *Ernst Fraenkel*, p. 58.
46. Ladwig-Winters, *Ernst Fraenkel*, pp. 59–60.
47. Ernst Fraenkel, *Zur Soziologie der Klassenjustiz*, in idem., *Gesammelte Schriften*, vol. 1: *Recht und Politik in der Weimarer Republik*, edited by Hubertus Buchstein (Baden-Baden: Nomos, [1927] 1999), pp. 177–211
48. Fraenkel, *Zur Soziologie der Klassenjustiz*, p. 177.
49. Greenberg, *The Weimar Century*, pp. 83–4. See also Douglas G. Morris, "Write and Resist: Ernst Fraenkel and Franz Neumann on the Role of Natural Law in Fighting Nazi Tyranny," *New German Critique*, Vol. 42 (2015), pp. 197–230.
50. Hermann Heller, "Rechtsstaat oder Diktatur?," in idem., *Gesammelte Schriften*, vol. 2: *Recht, Staat, Macht*, Second edition, edited by Christoph Müller (Tübingen: Mohr, [1930] 1992), pp. 443–62. Heller published a shorter version already in 1929. For an insightful overview of Heller's significance in German legal thought, see the contributions to Christoph Müller and Ilse Staff, eds., *Der soziale Rechtsstaat: Gedächtnisschrift für Hermann Heller 1891–1933* (Baden-Baden: Nomos, 1984).
51. Greenberg, *The Weimar Century*, p. 85.
52. Ladwig-Winters, *Ernst Fraenkel*, p. 65.
53. Ladwig-Winters, *Ernst Fraenkel*, p. 75. Most of these writings are available in Fraenkel, *Gesammelte Schriften*, vol. 1.
54. Ernst Fraenkel, "Kollektive Demokratie," in idem., *Gesammelte Schriften*, vol. 1: *Recht und Politik in der Weimarer Republik*, edited by Hubertus Buchstein (Baden-Baden: Nomos, [1929] 1999), pp. 343–57; Ernst Fraenkel, "Rechtssoziologie als Wissenschaft," in idem., *Gesammelte Schriften*, vol. 1: *Recht und Politik in der Weimarer Republik*, edited by Hubertus Buchstein (Baden-Baden: Nomos, [1929] 1999), pp. 370–9.
55. Ladwig-Winters, *Ernst Fraenkel*, p. 69.
56. Ernst Fraenkel, "Vorwort zum Neudruck," in Fraenkel, *Gesammelte Schriften*, vol. 1, p. 656. This is Fraenkel's preface to the 1968 edition of *Zur Soziologie der Klassenjustiz*.
57. See, for example, Ernst Fraenkel, "Antifaschistische Aufklärungsarbeit," in idem., *Gesammelte Schriften*, vol. 1: *Recht und Politik in der Weimarer Republik*, edited by Hubertus Buchstein (Baden-Baden: Nomos, [1930] 1999), pp. 410–17.
58. Fraenkel, "Kollektive Demokratie," p. 355.
59. Fraenkel, "Kollektive Demokratie," pp. 352, 356.
60. It is worth to recall that Max Weber's important contribution to the sociology of law, made in Chapter 7 of his magisterial *Economy and Society* was only published a few years earlier. Max Weber, *Wirtschaft und Gesellschaft: Grundriß der verstehenden Soziologie*, Fifth, revised edition, edited by Johannes Winckelmann (Tübingen: Mohr, [1922] 1972). The text only appeared posthumously, for the first time in 1922, then in enlarged editions in 1925, 1947, and 1956. See Simona Andrini, "Max Weber's Sociology

of Law as a Turning Point of his Methodological Approach," *International Review of Sociology*, Vol. 14 (2004), p. 143. I use the moniker "law-in-society" analogously to Joel Migdal's "state-in-society"-approach, which inspired my coinage. See his *State in Society: Studying How States and Societies Transform and Constitute One Another* (Cambridge: Cambridge University Press, 2001).

61. Fraenkel, "Rechtssoziologie als Wissenschaft," pp. 370–1.
62. Fraenkel, "Rechtssoziologie als Wissenschaft," p. 370.
63. Paul Laband, *Das Staatsrecht des deutschen Reiches*, 3 vol., Second edition (Tübingen: Mohr, 1888).
64. I quote Laband in the translation provided in Stefan Korioth, "The Shattering of Methods in Late Wilhelmine Germany," in Arthur J. Jacobson and Bernhard Schlink, eds., *Weimar: A Jurisprudence of Crisis* (Berkeley: University of California Press, 2000), p. 43.
65. Korioth, "The Shattering of Methods in Late Wilhelmine Germany," p. 43.
66. Karl Jaspers, *The Idea of the University*, edited by Karl W. Deutsch, translated by H. A. T. Reich and H. F. Vanderschmidt (London: Peter Owen, 1960), p. 37.
67. Anton Menger, *Das bürgerliche Recht und die besitzlosen Volksklassen* (Tübingen: Mohr, 1890); Eugen Ehrlich, *Grundlegung der Soziologie des Rechts* (Munich: Duncker & Humblot, 1913); Karl Renner, *Die Rechtsinstitute des Privatrechts und ihre soziale Funktion: Ein Beitrag zur Kritik des bürgerlichen Rechts* (Tübingen: Mohr, 1929).
68. Ehrlich, *Grundlegung der Soziologie des Rechts*, p. 172.
69. Fraenkel, "Rechtssoziologie als Wissenschaft," pp. 373–7.
70. Fraenkel, "Rechtssoziologie als Wissenschaft," p. 377.
71. Fraenkel, "Rechtssoziologie als Wissenschaft," pp. 378–9.
72. Ernst Fraenkel, *The Dual State: A Contribution to the Theory of Dictatorship*, translated by E. A. Shils, in collaboration with Edith Loewenstein and Klaus Knorr, with an Introduction by Jens Meierhenrich (Oxford: Oxford University Press, [1941] 2017), pp. ix–xi.
73. Fraenkel confirmed the use of evidence gleaned from participant observation in the preface to the 1974 German Edition of *The Dual State*. I recently translated this preface into English. It is available in the 2017 edition of his book. See Ernst Fraenkel, "Preface to the 1974 German Edition," in idem., *The Dual State: A Theory of Dictatorship*, translated by E. A. Shils, in collaboration with Edith Loewenstein and Klaus Knorr, with an Introduction by Jens Meierhenrich (Oxford: Oxford University Press, [1941] 2017), esp. p. xv.
74. Roger B. M. Cotterrell, "Interdisciplinarity: The Expansion of Knowledge and the Design of Research," *Higher Education Review*, Vol. 11 (1979), p. 55.
75. Otto Kirchheimer, "Einführung," in Hugo Sinzheimer and Ernst Fraenkel, *Die Justiz in der Weimarer Republik: Eine Chronik*, edited by Thilo Ramm with an Introduction by Otto Kirchheimer (Neuwied: Luchterhand, 1968), pp. 14–15.
76. Reprints of these essays are available in Sinzheimer and Fraenkel, *Die Justiz in der Weimarer Republik*. Gustav Radbruch and Hans Kelsen were even more prolific than Fraenkel. Radbruch contributed twenty-eight articles

(amounting to ninety-five pages) to *Die Justiz*, Kelsen three (totaling eighty-five pages). See Theo Rasehorn, *Justizkritik in der Weimarer Republik: Das Beispiel der Zeitschrift "Die Justiz"* (Frankfurt: Campus, 1985), p. 259. Another notable contributor was Robert Kempner who would go on to serves as Assistant U.S. Chief Counsel at the International Military Tribunal at Nuremberg. His occasional, pseudonymous writings in *Die Justiz* were in high demand on Weimar's marketplace of ideas, not least because Kempner wrote plainly, provocatively, and with the knowledge of an insider: Kempner was a high-ranking bureaucrat with Prussia's police as whose chief legal adviser (*Justitiar*) he served between 1928 and 1933.

77. Ernst Fraenkel, "Verfassungsreform und Sozialdemokratie," in idem., *Gesammelte Schriften*, vol. 1: *Recht und Politik in der Weimarer Republik*, edited by Hubertus Buchstein (Baden-Baden: Nomos, [1932] 1999), p. 523.
78. Karl Dietrich Bracher, *Die Auflösung der Weimarer Republik: Eine Studie zum Problem des Machtverfalls in der Demokratie* (Villingen: Ring, 1955), p. 34.
79. Fraenkel, "Verfassungsreform und Sozialdemokratie," p. 523.
80. Ernst Fraenkel, "XLIII," *Die Justiz*, February 1933, reprinted in Sinzheimer and Fraenkel, *Die Justiz in der Weimarer Republik*, p. 396.
81. Ladwig-Winters, *Ernst Fraenkel*, p. 92.
82. For a comprehensive overview, see Martin Dean, *Robbing the Jews: The Confiscation of Jewish Property in the Holocaust, 1933–1945* (Cambridge: Cambridge University Press, 2008).
83. Ladwig-Winters, *Ernst Fraenkel*, p. 99. See also Douglas Morris, "Discrimination, Degradation, Defiance: Jewish Lawyers in Nazi Germany," in Alan Steinweis and Robert D. Rachlin, eds., *The Law in Nazi Germany: Ideology, Opportunism, and the Perversion of Justice* (New York: Berghahn, 2013), pp. 105–35. On the political and legal background of these purification orders in the early years of Nazi dictatorship, see Horst Göppinger, *Juristen jüdischer Abstammung im 'Dritten Reich': Entrechtung und Verfolgung*, Second edition (Munich: Beck, 1990), pp. 45–76. For a gendered analysis, see Bundesministerium für Justiz und für Verbraucherschutz, ed., *Das Ende eines Aufbruchs: Jüdische Juristinnen und Juristinnen jüdischer Herkunft nach 1933* (Berlin: Bundesanzeiger, 2016).
84. Franz L. Neumann, "The Governance of the Rule of Law: An Investigation into the Relationship between the Political Theories, the Legal System, and the Social Background in the Competitive Society," Ph.D. dissertation, London School of Economics and Political Science, 1936. A book version was many years later published as *Die Herrschaft des Gesetzes: Eine Untersuchung zum Verhältnis von politischer Theorie und Rechtssystem in der Konkurrenzgesellschaft* (Frankfurt: Suhrkamp, 1980) in German; and as *The Rule of Law: Political Theory and the Legal System in Modern Society* (Leamington Spa: Berg, 1986) in English. Neumann had completed his first doctoral dissertation, in law, at the University of Frankfurt in 1923. See Sascha Ziemann, "Relativismus in Zeiten der Krise: Franz L. Neumanns

unveröffentlichte rechtsphilosophische Doktorarbeit von 1923," *Zeitschrift für internationale Strafrechtsdogmatik*, Vol. 9 (2007), pp. 362–70.

85. It bears emphasizing that Neumann's situation was different from Fraenkel's. He did not enjoy the limited and temporary privilege of a former *Frontsoldat*, which is why his situation in 1933 was more precarious than Fraenkel's.
86. For a brief discussion of the Gestapo's interest in Fraenkel's cause lawyering, see Stefan König, *Vom Dienst am Recht: Rechtsanwälte als Strafverteidiger im Nationalsozialismus* (Berlin: de Gruyter, 1987), pp. 85–6.
87. Fraenkel reflected on this time and its legal tactics, in a typically detached fashion, in "Auflösung und Verfall des Rechts im III. Reich," in idem., *Gesammelte Schriften*, vol. 2: *Nationalsozialismus und Widerstand*, edited by Alexander v. Brünneck, Hubertus Buchstein, and Gerhard Göhler (Baden-Baden: Nomos, [1960] 1999), pp. 617–18. For a discussion of specific cases, see Douglas G. Morris, "The Dual State Reframed: Ernst Fraenkel's Political Clients and His Theory of the Nazi Legal System," *Leo Baeck Institute Yearbook*, Vol. 58 (2013), pp. 5–21. For a recent account of a "humane" Nazi judge, in Fraenkel's parlance, see Herlinde Pauer-Studer and J. David Velleman, *Konrad Morgen: The Conscience of a Nazi Judge* (London: Palgrave, 2015). A judge in the *SS- und Polizeigerichtsbarkeit*, an intra-organizational system of justice that adjudicated violations by members of the SS or police, including the Gestapo (comparable to a system of military justice that hears cases involving military personnel), Morgen was put in charge, by Heinrich Himmler, of the investigation of SS corruption in Nazi concentration camps. But Morgen repeatedly exceeded his brief, instead bringing "charges of murder against the commandant of Buchenwald and the chief of the Gestapo at Auschwitz. He even sought a warrant to arrest Adolf Eichmann. Eventually, five concentration-camp commandants were charged, at least one of whom was eventually executed for his crimes." Pauer-Studer and Velleman, *Konrad Morgen*, pp. x–xi. The executed commandant was Karl Otto Koch, who had been in charge of Buchenwald concentration camp in the period 1937–1941, where he was notorious (together with his wife Ilse Koch) for the particularly cruel and violent treatment of inmates.
88. Ernst Fraenkel, "In der Maschine der politischen Strafjustiz des III. Reiches" [1934], in Fraenkel, *Gesammelte Schriften*, vol. 2, pp. 475–84. On the ISK's role and strategies of contention in the resistance to Nazism, see Sabine Lemke-Müller, ed. *Ethik des Widerstands: Der Kampf des Internationalen Sozialistischen Kampfbundes (ISK) gegen den Nationalsozialismus* (Bonn: Dietz, 1996).
89. Fraenkel, "In der Maschine der politischen Strafjustiz des III. Reiches" [1934], p. 475.
90. Ernst Fraenkel, "Der Sinn illegaler Arbeit," in idem., *Gesammelte Schriften, vol. 2: Nationalsozialismus und Widerstand*, edited by Alexander v. Brünneck, Hubertus Buchstein, and Gerhard Göhler (Baden- Baden: Nomos, [1935] 1999), pp. 491–7.

91. Ladwig-Winters, *Ernst Fraenkel*, p. 116.
92. Fraenkel, "Der Sinn illegaler Arbeit," p. 495.
93. Fraenkel, "Der Sinn illegaler Arbeit," p. 493.
94. Fraenkel, "Der Sinn illegaler Arbeit," p. 493.
95. Fraenkel, "Der Sinn illegaler Arbeit," p. 493.
96. Fraenkel, "Der Sinn illegaler Arbeit," pp. 495–6.
97. Fraenkel, "Der Sinn illegaler Arbeit," p. 497.
98. On the fate of Berlin's Jewish population in the period 1933–1945, see Beate Meyer, Hermann Simon, and Chana Schutz, eds., *Jews in Nazi Berlin: From Kristallnacht to Liberation* (Chicago: University of Chicago Press, 2009).
99. For an analysis of Gestapo interrogations of members of the leftist resistance, including those, like Fraenkel, who were active on behalf of the *Internationaler Sozialistischer Kampfbund*, see Isabel Richter, "Entwürfe des Widerstehens: Männer und Frauen aus dem linken Widerstand in Verhören der Gestapo (1934–1939)," *WerkstattGeschichte*, Vol. 26 (2000), pp. 47–70. The article draws on an archival subset of the 258 complete case files from the period 1934–39 that survived among the documents of the *Oberreichsanwalt* (attorney general of the German Reich) at the infamous *Volksgerichtshof*. The 50 interrogations that Richter sampled resulted in 159 judgments. In these proceedings alone, the court convicted 120 men and 39 women of *Landesverrat* (treason), a fate that would likely have awaited Fraenkel had the Nazis discovered his pseudonymous articles or clandestine manuscript.
100. Ladwig-Winters, *Ernst Fraenkel*, pp. 127–9.
101. Claus-Dieter Krohn, *Intellectuals in Exile: Refugee Scholars and the New School for Social Research*, translated by Rita and Robert Kimber (Amherst: University of Massachusetts Press, 1993).

CHAPTER 4

1. "*Man muß zunächst davon ausgehen, daß Wort und Begriff des 'Rechtsstaates' specifisch deutsch sind. Beide kommen weder in einer nicht deutschen Literatur vor, noch sind sie in einer nicht deutschen Sprache correct wieder zu geben.*" Lorenz von Stein, *Verwaltungslehre*, vol. 1: *Die vollziehende Gewalt*, Second edition (Stuttgart: Cotta: 1869), pp. 296–7.
2. Theodor Maunz and Reinhold Zippelius, *Deutsches Staatsrecht: Ein Studienbuch*, Twenty-eighth edition (Munich: Beck, 1991), p. 85. Theodor Maunz, who co-founded and co-edited the most important commentary on Germany's postwar constitution, the *Grundgesetz*, was previously an eminent law professor in Nazi Germany, where his studies of administrative law contributed in no small measure to securing the foundations of the racial state. The evidence is plentiful. Consider, for example, Maunz's participation in Carl Schmitt's infamous 1936 conference "Das Judentum in der Rechtswissenschaft" (literally: "Jewry in Legal Science"), where he decried "the fateful inclination of Jewish scholars of administrative law to subscribe to the liberal doctrine of the *Rechtsstaat*" ("*die verhängnisvolle Neigung*

jüdischer Verwaltungsrechtler zur liberalistischen Rechtsstaatsdoktrin"). Theodor Maunz, "Die Juden und die Verwaltungsrechtswissenschaft," as quoted in the conference report published in *Deutsche Juristenzeitung*, Vol. 41 (1936), p. 1230. In 1993, shortly after Maunz's death, it transpired that after World War II he had for decades advised a right-wing political party, the now defunct *Deutsche Volksunion*, and regularly contributed anonymously to their extremist publications. See Michael Stolleis, "Theodor Maunz—Ein Staatsrechtslehrerleben," *Kritische Justiz*, Vol. 26 (1993), pp. 393–6.

3. For a complete account, see Jens Meierhenrich, *The Idea of the* Rechtsstaat: *An Intellectual History*, Unpublished book manuscript, London School of Economics and Political Science, 2017.
4. Johann Wilhelm Petersen, *Litteratur der Staatslehre: Ein Versuch* (Stuttgart: Metzler, 1798).
5. Alexis de Tocqueville, *The Old Regime and the Revolution*, vol. 1: *The Complete Text*, edited with an Introduction and Critical Apparatus by François Furet and Françoise Mélonio, translated by Alan S. Kahan (Chicago: University of Chicago Press, [1856] 1998), p. 261. For a dated but still highly relevant analysis of the shifting discourse about, and development of, the *Rechtsstaat* in Prussia in the eighteenth and nineteenth century, see Otto Hintze, "Preußens Entwicklung zum Rechtsstaat," in idem., *Regierung und Verwaltung: Gesammelte Abhandlungen zur Staats-, Rechts- und Sozialgeschichte*, Second edition, edited with an Introduction by Gerhard Oestreich (Göttingen: Vandenhoeck & Ruprecht, [1920] 1967), pp. 97–163. For Hintze, the institutional development in Prussia resulted in a dispensation that satisfied "harmonically" the demands of state and of law ("*den Staatsgedanken mit dem Rechtsgedanken harmonisch verbindet*"). He termed this achievement the "*Rechtsstaat neueren Stils*," or "new-style *Rechtsstaat*," distinguishing it from the far more limited institutional design of the nineteenth century, what he called the "*Rechtsstaat älteren Stils*," or "old-style *Rechtsstaat*." Although the latter, according to Hintze, had placed checks on the *Polizeistaat* of the eighteenth century, in which the bureaucracy ran the state, the new *Justizstaat*, in which the judiciary ranked supreme, was structurally imbalanced and created a new set of problems for the governance of Prussia. If we believe Hintze, only the new-style *Rechtsstaat* of the early twentieth century, a normative state fashioned in the image of Rudolf Gneist—who had advocated the addition of a new adjudicative plank to the architecture of the *Rechtsstaat*, a system of administrative courts, the so-called *Verwaltungsgerichtsbarkeit*—finally made political order sustainable in Prussia. Ibid, pp. 161, 162. See also Rudolf Gneist, *Der Rechtsstaat* (Berlin: Springer, 1872); idem., *Der Rechtsstaat und die Verwaltungsgerichte in Deutschland*, Second edition (Berlin: Springer, 1879). For a more recent take, with particular reference to the rise of administrative law, see Kenneth F. Ledford, "Formalizing the Rule of Law in Prussia: The Supreme Administrative Law Court, 1876–1914," *Central European History*, Vol. 37 (2004), pp. 203–24.
6. Elisabeth Zoller, *Introduction to Public Law: A Comparative Study* (Leiden: Brill, 2008), p. 73. Wolfgang Wipperman concurs, arguing that the

Prussian state under Frederick II resembled more a prerogative state ("*singulärer Machtstaat*") than a truly normative state. See his *Preußen: Kleine Geschichte eines großen Mythos* (Freiburg: Herder, 2011), p. 41. For the argument that the General Law Code contained the seeds of the *Rechtsstaat*, see Detlef Merten, "Die Rechtsstaatlichkeit im Allgemeinen Landrecht," in Friedrich Ebel, ed., *Gemeinwohl-Freiheit-Vernunft-Rechtsstaat: 200 Jahre Allgemeines Landrecht für die Preußischen Staaten* (Berlin: De Gruyter, 1995), pp. 109–38.

7. de Tocqueville, *The Old Regime and the Revolution*, vol. 1, p. 261. Emphasis added.
8. Madame La Baronne de Staël Holstein, *De l'Allemagne*, Second edition (Paris: Nicolle, 1814), pp. 141–2.
9. de Tocqueville, *The Old Regime and the Revolution*, vol. 1, p. 262.
10. Heinrich Treitschke, *Deutsche Geschichte im neunzehnten Jahrhundert*, vol. 1: *Bis zum zweiten Pariser Frieden* (Leipzig: Hendel, 1927), p. 77; Hans Rosenberg, *Bureaucracy, Aristocracy, and Autocracy: The Prussian Experience 1660–1815* (Boston: Beacon Press, 1958), esp. pp. 46–56; Reinhart Koselleck, *Preußen zwischen Reform und Revolution: Allgemeines Landrecht, Verwaltung und soziale Bewegung von 1791 bis 1848* (Stuttgart: Klett-Cotta, 1965); Christopher Clark, *Iron Kingdom: The Rise and Downfall of Prussia, 1600–1947* (Cambridge: Belknap Press of Harvard University Press, 2006), pp. 281–3. As Clark writes, "The fascination of the General [Law] Code lies in the curiously unresolved portrait it offers of Prussia at the end of the eighteenth century. Peering at Prussia through its paragraphs is like using a pair of binoculars with different focal lengths." Ibid, p. 281. Peering at Nazi Germany in the early years through the debate about the *Rechtsstaat* creates a similar sensation, as I hope to show. On the one hand, there is evidence of a commitment to a legal way of doing things, but this is rivaled by contending commitments, notably to a violent way of doing things, both at home and abroad. See, for instance, Isabel V. Hull, *Absolute Destruction: Military Culture and the Practices of War in Imperial Germany* (Ithaca: Cornell University Press, 2005), esp. pp. 110–30. Yet one must be careful not to overstate the similarities. Prussia in the late 1790s and Nazi Germany in the early 1930s both offer portraits of authoritarian states in transition. But the logic and wages of violence were fundamentally different and must not be equated.
11. Petersen, *Litteratur der Staatslehre*, p. 73.
12. On the idea of "reequilibration" in transitions to and from authoritarian rule, see Juan J. Linz, *The Breakdown of Democratic Regimes: Crisis, Breakdown, and Reequilibration* (Baltimore: Johns Hopkins University Press, 1978), esp. pp. 87–98.
13. Adam Heinrich Müller, *Die Elemente der Staatskunst*, vol. 1: *Die Herdflamme*, edited by Othmar Spann (Jena: Fischer, [1809] 1922), pp. 196, 200.
14. Carl Theodor Welcker, *Die letzten Gründe von Recht, Staat und Strafe philosophisch und nach den Gesetzen der merkwürdigsten Völker entwickelt* (Gießen: Heyer, 1813), pp. 71–2. Johann Christoph Freiherr von Aretin also contributed to the emergence of a Kantian, liberal idea of the *Rechtsstaat*. See

his *Staatsrecht der konstitutionellen Monarchie: Ein Handbuch für Geschäftsmänner, studirende Jünglinge, und gebildete Bürger*, vol. 1 (Altenburg: Literatur-Comptoir, 1824), which Karl von Rotteck continued after the author's death.

15. Leonard Krieger, *The German Idea of Freedom: History of a Political Tradition* (Boston: Beacon Press, 1957), p. 253.
16. Robert Mohl, *Die Polizei-Wissenschaft nach den Grundsätzen des Rechtsstaates*, vol. 1 (Tübingen: Laupp, 1832), p. 5. According to Mohl, three other "types of states" ("*Staatsgattungen*") existed: "theocracy" is the institutional arrangement for the pursuit of religious ends, "despotism" suited to realize purely sensual objectives, and the "patriarchal state" reflective of a familial orientation. Ibid, pp. 5–6.
17. Mohl, *Die Polizei-Wissenschaft nach den Grundsätzen des Rechtsstaates*, vol. 1, p. 7.
18. Mohl, *Die Polizei-Wissenschaft nach den Grundsätzen des Rechtsstaates*, vol. 1, p. 7.
19. Mohl, *Die Polizei-Wissenschaft nach den Grundsätzen des Rechtsstaates*, vol. 1, p. 8. For an application of his theory to substantive areas of law, including property, agriculture, trade, and policing, see Robert Mohl, *Die Polizei-Wissenschaft nach den Grundsätzen des Rechtsstaates*, vol. 2 (Tübingen: Laupp, 1833).
20. Krieger, *The German Idea of Freedom*, p. 260.
21. Ingeborg Maus, "Entwicklung und Funktionswandel der Theorie des bürgerlichen Rechtsstaats," in idem., *Rechtstheorie und politische Theorie im Industriekapitalismus* (Munich: Fink, [1978] 1986), pp. 17–18.
22. "*Der ohnedem so oft mißverstandene und falsch angewendete Begriff des Rechtsstaates gibt eine Veranlassung weiter, nicht mehr zu thun, als was das äußere Gesetz verlangt, während dieses doch nur das Wenigste, nicht aber das Höchste befiehlt.*" Robert von Mohl, *Encyklopädie der Staatswissenschaften* (Tübingen: Laupp, 1859), p. 504.
23. von Mohl, *Encyklopädie der Staatswissenschaften*, p. 504.
24. von Mohl, *Encyklopädie der Staatswissenschaften*, p. 333.
25. von Mohl, *Encyklopädie der Staatswissenschaften*, p. 333.
26. "*Der Zweck des Rechtsstaates hat keineswegs eine bestimmte Form der Regierung zur nothwendigen Folge; vielmehr kann jede Gestaltung der Staatsgewalt, welche eine Förderung der sämmtlichen menschlichen Lebenszwecke erlaubt und in Aussicht stellt, rechtlich stattfinden.*" von Mohl, *Encyklopädie der Staatswissenschaften*, p. 333.
27. "*Es ist eine vollkommen verkehrte Auffassung, die Volksherrschaft als die einzig vollständig gerechtfertigte Form des Rechtsstaates zu betrachten.*" von Mohl, *Encyklopädie der Staatswissenschaften*, p. 345.
28. Mayer, *Deutsches Verwaltungsrecht*, vol. 1, p. 57.
29. Ernst-Wolfgang Böckenförde, "Entstehung und Wandel des Rechtsstaatsbegriffs," in idem., *Recht, Staat, Freiheit: Studien zu Rechtsphilosophie, Staatstheorie und Verfassungsgeschichte*, Expanded edition (Frankfurt: Suhrkamp, [1969] 2006), p. 151.
30. "*Der Staat soll Rechtsstaat sein, das ist die Losung und ist auch in Wahrheit der Entwicklungstrieb der neueren Zeit. Er soll die Bahnen und Grenzen*

seiner Wirksamkeit wie die freie Spähre seiner Bürger in der Weise des Rechts genau bestimmen und unverbrüchlich sichern. [...] Dies ist der Begriff des Rechtsstaates [...], er bedeutet überhaupt nicht Ziel und Inhalt des Staates, sondern nur Art und Charakter, dieselben zu verwirklichen." Friedrich Julius Stahl, *Die Philosophie des Rechts*, vol. 2: *Rechts- und Staatslehre auf der Grundlage christlicher Weltanschauung*, Third edition (Heidelberg: Mohr, 1856), §30. The critical characterization comes from Friedrich Christoph Dahlmann, as quoted in Klaus von Beyme, *Politische Theorien im Zeitalter der Ideologien* (Wiesbaden: Verlag für Sozialwissenschaften, 2002), p. 477.

31. Gneist, *Der Rechtsstaat und die Verwaltungsgerichte in Deutschland*, p. 62.
32. Rudolf Gneist, *Verwaltung–Justiz–Rechtsweg: Staatsverwaltung und Selbstverwaltung nach englischen und deutschen Verhältnissen mit besonderer Rücksicht auf Verwaltungsformen und Kreis-Ordnungen in Preußen* (Berlin: Springer, 1869), esp. p. 57. See also Böckenförde, "Entstehung und Wandel des Rechtsstaatsbegriffs," p. 153.
33. Ledford, "Formalizing the Rule of Law in Prussia," p. 207.
34. Michael Stolleis, *Geschichte des öffentlichen Rechts in Deutschland*, vol. 2: *Staatsrechtslehre und Verwaltungswissenschaft 1800–1914* (Munich: Beck, 1992), p. 457.
35. Paul Laband, *Das Staatsrecht des Deutschen Reiches*, vol. 2 (Tübingen: Laupp, 1878), p. 202.
36. On Laband's dominance as well as contending perspectives in German legal thought in the late nineteenth century, see Stolleis, *Geschichte des öffentlichen Rechts in Deutschland*, vol. 2, pp. 348–78.
37. "*Der Staat steht seinen Angehörigen nicht als gleichberechtigtes Subjekt gegenüber, sondern als der mit imperium ausgestattete Herr.*" Laband, *Das Staatsrecht des Deutschen Reiches*, vol. 2, p. 202.
38. Gustavo Gozzi, "*Rechtsstaat* and Individual Rights in German Constitutional History," in Pietro Costa and Danilo Zolo, eds., *The Rule of Law: History, Theory and Criticism* (Dordrecht: Springer, 2007), p. 247.
39. Martin Loughlin, *Foundations of Public Law* (Oxford: Oxford University Press, 2010), p. 320.
40. Loughlin, *Foundations of Public Law*, p. 321.
41. Manfred Friedrich, *Geschichte der deutschen Staatsrechtswissenschaft* (Berlin: Duncker & Humblot, 1997), p. 224.
42. Loughlin, *Foundations of Public Law*, p. 319. Michael Stolleis has suggested that in ordinary times the need for morals to attach to law may be less keenly felt than in extraordinary times, and, based on this assumption, accounted for the salience of legal positivism in the late nineteenth and early twentieth century. Stolleis, *Geschichte des öffentlichen Rechts in Deutschland*, vol. 2, p. 351.
43. As quoted in Otto Pflanze, *Bismarck: der Reichskanzler*, translated by Peter Hahlbrock (Munich: Beck, [1990] 1998), p. 447. On the reality of the *Rechtsstaat* in the era of Bismarck, see Erich Hahn, "Rudolf Gneist and the Prussian Rechtsstaat: 1862–78," *Journal of Modern History*, Vol. 49 (1977), pp. D1361–D1381.

44. As quoted in Pflanze, *Bismarck*, p. 447. Carl Schmitt refers to the "*Kunstausdruck des Herrn von Mohl*" ("Mr. von Mohl's term of art") in his Afterword to the published exchange in Nazi Germany between Günther Krauß and Otto von Schweinichen about the value of the *Rechtsstaat*, in which he credits Johannes Heckel, a notable scholar of church law, for having brought Bismarck's apparent quip to his attention. See Carl Schmitt, "Nachwort," in Günther Krauß and Otto von Schweinichen, *Disputation über den Rechtsstaat* (Hamburg: Hanseatische Verlagsanstalt, 1935), p. 85, fn. 1.
45. As quoted in Pflanze, *Bismarck*, p. 447.
46. Kenneth F. Ledford, *From General Estate to Special Interest: German Lawyers 1878– 1933* (Cambridge: Cambridge University Press, 1996), p. xix. Emphases added.
47. Ledford, *From General Estate to Special Interest*, p. xxvii.
48. David Blackbourn, "The Discreet Charm of the Bourgeoisie: Reappraising German History in the Nineteenth Century," in David Blackbourn and Geoff Eley, eds., *The Peculiarities of German History: Bourgeois Society and Politics in Nineteenth Century Germany* (Oxford: 1984), esp. pp. 190–5.
49. Michael F. John, "The Politics of Legal Unity in Germany, 1870–1896," *Historical Journal*, Vol. 28 (1985), p. 342. For a book-length treatment, see idem., *Politics and the Law in Late Nineteenth-Century Germany: The Origins of the Civil Code* (Oxford: Oxford University Press, 1989).
50. John, "The Politics of Legal Unity in Germany, 1870–1896," p. 353.
51. Ledford, *From General Estate to Special Interest*, p. xxvii.
52. Stefan Korioth, "The Shattering of Methods in Late Wilhelmine Germany," in Arthur J. Jacobson and Bernhard Schlink, eds., *Weimar: A Jurisprudence of Crisis* (Berkeley: University of California Press, 2000) p. 48.
53. Korioth, "The Shattering of Methods in Late Wilhelmine Germany," p. 49.
54. Max Weber, *Economy and Society: An Outline of Interpretive Sociology*, edited by Guenther Roth and Claus Wittich (Berkeley: University of California Press, [1922] 1978), pp. 657–8.
55. Korioth, "The Shattering of Methods in Late Wilhelmine Germany," p. 49.
56. Carl Schmitt, *Gesetz und Urteil: Eine Untersuchung zum Problem der Rechtspraxis*, Second edition (Munich: Beck, [1912] 1969).
57. Schmitt, *Gesetz und Urteil*, p. 11.
58. "*[E]ine richtige Meinung ist noch keine Erkenntnis*." Schmitt, *Gesetz und Urteil*, p. 17.
59. Schmitt, *Gesetz und Urteil*, p. 27.
60. Schmitt, *Gesetz und Urteil*, pp. 8, 94.
61. John P. McCormick, *Carl Schmitt's Critique of Liberalism: Against Politics as Technology* (Cambridge: Cambridge University Press, 1997), p. 209.
62. Schmitt, *Gesetz und Urteil*, p. 94.
63. McCormick, *Carl Schmitt's Critique of Liberalism*, p. 211.
64. Arthur J. Jacobson and Bernhard Schlink, "Constitutional Crisis: The German and the American Experience," in idem., eds., *Weimar: A Jurispruence of Crisis* (Berkeley: University of California Press, 2000), pp. 4–5.

65. Christoph Gusy, *Die Weimarer Reichsverfassung* (Tübingen: Mohr, 1997), is the best available account of the constitutional founding.
66. Jacobson and Schlink, "Constitutional Crisis," p. 8.
67. On the remnants of the prerogative state, see, for example, Mark Jones, *Founding Weimar: Violence and the German Revolution of 1918–1919* (Cambridge: Cambridge University Press, 2016).
68. Peter Caldwell, "National Socialism and Constitutional Law: Carl Schmitt, Otto Koellreutter, and the Debate over the Nature of the Nazi State, 1993–1937," *Cardozo Law Review*, Vol. 16 (1994), p. 401.
69. Note the dissimilarities between liberal and Nazi conceptions of the *Volk* in interwar Germany. For an excellent discussion in the context of the legal thought and practice of one of the Weimar Constitution's principal architects, see Peter C. Caldwell, "Hugo Preuss's Concept of the Volk: Critical Confusion or Sophisticated Conception?," *University of Toronto Law Journal*, Vol. 63 (2013), pp. 347–84.
70. For a comprehensive account, see my *The Idea of the* Rechtsstaat, Chapter 5. On Habermas's rethinking of Dolf Sternberger's notion of *Verfassungspatriotismus*, see Jürgen Habermas, "Über den doppelten Boden des demokratischen Rechtsstaates," in ibid, *Eine Art Schadensabwicklung: Kleine politische Schriften VI* (Frankfurt: Suhrkamp, 1987), pp. 18–23; and ibid, "Geschichtsbewußtsein und posttraditionale Identität: Die Westorientierung der Bundesrepublik," in ibid, *Eine Art Schadensabwicklung*, pp. 161–79. For a very useful discussion, see Jan-Werner Müller, *Constitutional Patriotism* (Princeton: Princeton University Press, 2007).
71. Ulrich Schellenberg, "Die Rechtsstaatskritik: Vom liberalen zum nationalen und nationalsozialistischen Rechtsstaat," in Ernst-Wolfgang Böckenförde, ed., *Staatsrecht und Staatsrechtslehre* (Heidelberg: Müller, 1985), p. 77.
72. Schellenberg, "Die Rechtsstaatskritik," p. 77.
73. David Dyzenhaus, *Legality and Legitimacy: Carl Schmitt, Hans Kelsen, and Hermann Heller in Weimar* (Oxford: Oxford University Press, 1997), p. 217. Heller was an intellectual opponent of Kelsen's, for whom, according to Heller, "every state is a *Rechtsstaat*" ("*ist doch jeder Staat ein Rechtsstaat*"). Hermann Heller, "Der Begriff des Gesetzes in der Reichsverfassung," in idem., *Gesammelte Schriften*, vol. 2: *Recht, Staat, Macht*, Second edition, edited by Christoph Müller (Tübingen: Mohr, [1928] 1992), p. 247. See also Hermann Heller, *Staatslehre*, Sixth edition (Tübingen: Mohr, [1934] 1983), reprinted in idem., *Gesammelte Schriften*, vol. 3: *Staatslehre als Politische Wissenschaft*, Second edition, edited by Christoph Müller (Tübingen: Mohr, [1934] 1992), pp. 81–410. For the most comprehensive and detailed account of positions in and disagreements among the progressive and democratic contributors to the subfield of *Staatsrechtslehre* prior to the Nazi dictatorship, see Kathrin Groh, *Demokratische Staatsrechtslehrer in der Weimarer Republik* (Tübingen: Mohr, 2010). But see also Joachim Blau, *Sozialdemokratische Staatslehre in der Weimarer Republik: Darstellung und Untersuchung der staatstheoretischen Konzeptionen von Hermann Heller, Ernst Fraenkel und Otto Kirchheimer* (Marburg: Verlag

Arbeiterbewegung und Gesellschaftswissenschaft, 1980); Manfred Gangl, ed., *Linke Juristen in der Weimarer Republik* (Frankfurt: Peter Lang, 2003); and, most recently, Andreas Anter, *Max Weber und die Staatsrechtslehre* (Tübingen: Mohr, 2016).

74. Dyzenhaus, *Legality and Legitimacy*, p. 163.
75. Heller, "Rechtsstaat oder Diktatur?," in idem., *Gesammelte Schriften, vol. 2: Recht, Staat, Macht*, Second edition, edited by Christoph Müller (Tübingen: Mohr, [1930] 1992) p. 445; Hermann Heller, "Europa und der Fascismus," in idem., *Gesammelte Schriften*, vol. 2: *Recht, Staat, Macht*, Second edition, edited by Christoph Müller (Tübingen: Mohr, [1929] 1992), p. 524.
76. "*Im Rechtsstaat sollte der Akt der Norm folgen.*" Heller, "Europa und der Fascismus," p. 528.
77. Heller, "Rechtsstaat oder Diktatur?," pp. 450–62.
78. Dyzenhaus, *Legality and Legitimacy*, p. 196.
79. References to the soul of the state as well as other anthropomorphic terminology appear throughout Heller's oeuvre. See, for example, Heller, "Rechtsstaat oder Diktatur?," p. 449.
80. Heller, "Europa und der Fascismus," p. 477.
81. Hermann Heller, "Die Souveränität: Ein Beitrag zur Theorie des Staats- und Völkerrechts," in idem., *Gesammelte Schriften*, vol. 2: *Recht, Staat, Macht*, Second edition, edited by Christoph Müller (Tübingen: Mohr, [1927] 1992), pp. 31–202. On Heller's admiration for the Fabian Society and his commitment to social democracy, see Christoph Müller, "Hermann Heller: Leben, Werk, Wirkung," in Hermann Heller, *Gesammelte Schriften*, vol. 3: *Staatslehre als Politische Wissenschaft*, Second edition, edited by Christoph Müller (Tübingen: Mohr, 1992), esp. 443–50. It is perhaps worth noting that Heller's critique of the liberal *Rechtsstaat* was less radical than that of some of his contemporaries on the Weimar left, including Neumann. See also the discussion in Chapter 4 above.
82. Heller, "Europa und der Fascismus," p. 475.
83. Heller, "Europa und der Fascismus," p. 475.
84. Heller, "Europa und der Fascismus," p. 475.
85. Heller, "Rechtsstaat oder Diktatur?," p. 449. On the cultural mentalities of the time, see Jeffrey Herf, *Reactionary Modernism: Technology, Culture, and Politics in Weimar and the Third Reich* (Cambridge: Cambridge University Press, 1984); and Helmuth Lethen, *Cool Conduct: The Cultural Distance in Weimar Germany*, translated by Don Reneau (Berkeley: University of California Press, [1994] 2002). On Schmitt in this context, see, most important, McCormick, *Carl Schmitt's Critique of Liberalism*, esp. Chapters 1–2. My analysis of Schmitt's take on the *Rechtsstaat* can be found in Chapter 5.
86. Hermann Heller, "Ziele und Grenzen einer deutschen Verfassungsreform," in idem., *Gesammelte Schriften*, vol. 2: *Recht, Staat, Macht*, Second edition, edited by Christoph Müller (Tübingen: Mohr, [1931] 1992), p. 416. In the same essay, an opinion piece for the *Frankfurter Zeitung*, Heller defined the *Volk* as the "carrier of certain culture-enabling values." Ibid, p. 414.

87. Stolleis, *Public Law in Germany*, p. 85; Dyzenhaus, *Legality and Legitimacy*, p. 198. See also Heller, "Die Souveränität," p. 126. In 1931, Heller lent support to the idea of an authoritarian state to steady the swaying Weimar Republic, but was eqally adamant in his resolve to "fight" ("*bekämpfen*") the rise of a total state. The difference between the two according to Heller: "*rechtsstaatliche Legalität*", the legality of the *Rechtsstaat*. Heller was wary of some comrades' plans to dispose of "the *Rechtsstaat* as such." Heller, "Ziele und Grenzen einer deutschen Verfassungsreform," pp. 413, 415, 416.
88. The relevant portion of the sentence in question reads "*die Staatsgewalt im positive Rechte nicht aufgeht.*" Heller, "Die Souveränität," p. 127, but see also the discussion on the pages preceding and subsequent to the cited passage.
89. Heller, "Die Souveränität," p. 126.
90. It was Ernst Fraenkel who first wrote of " 'concreteness' as a weapon against 'abstraction.' " He chided Schmitt not only for wielding it, but also for having stolen it from Hegel. Ernst Fraenkel, *The Dual State: A Contribution to the Theory of Dictatorship*, translated by E. A. Shils, in collaboration with Edith Loewenstein and Klaus Knorr, with an Introduction by Jens Meierhenrich (Oxford: Oxford University Press, [1941] 2017), p. 143. I owe this insight to McCormick, *Carl Schmitt's Critique of Liberalism*, p. 247, fn. 66.
91. On Heller's emphasis of concreteness, see, for example, his "Europa und der Fascismus," p. 476. On the arc from pragmatist institutionalism to extremist institutionalism in Schmitt's political thought, see Jens Meierhenrich, "Fearing the Disorder of Things: The Development of Carl Schmitt's Institutional Theory, 1919–1942," in Jens Meierhenrich and Oliver Simons, eds., *The Oxford Handbook of Carl Schmitt* (Oxford: Oxford University Press, 2016).
92. Wolfgang Schluchter, *Entscheidung für den sozialen Rechtsstaat: Hermann Heller und die staatstheoretische Diskussion in der Weimarer Republik*, Second edition (Baden-Baden: Nomos, 1983), p. 215.
93. Jo Eric Khushal Murkens, *From Empire to Union: Conceptions of German Constitutional Law since 1871* (Oxford: Oxford University Press, 2013), p. 19.
94. Georg Jellinek, *Allgemeine Staatslehre*, Third edition (Berlin: Häring, [1900] 1914), p. 12. On the interdependence between the factual and the normative halves of Jellinek's dual state-concept, see also Peter Badura, *Die Methoden der allgemeinen Staatslehre*, Second edition (Goldbach: Keip, [1959] 1998), p. 108.
95. "*Der Staat ist einmal ein gesellschaftliches Gebilde, sodann eine rechtliche Institution. Dementsprechend zerfällt die Staatslehre in die soziale Staatslehre und in die Staatsrechtslehre.*" Jellinek, *Allgemeine Staatslehre*, Third edition (Berlin: Häring, [1900] 1914), pp. 10–11. For a helpful introduction for the uninitiated to the confusing terminology of German legal thought, see Murkens, *From Empire to Union*, pp. 9–18, who teases out the relationships between and among *Staatslehre*, *Staatsrechtslehre*, *Allgemeine Staatslehre*, *Verfassungslehre*, and so forth.

96. Murkens, *From Empire to Union*, p. 18. See also Peter C. Caldwell, *Popular Sovereignty and the Crisis of German Constitutional Law: The Theory and Practice of Weimar Constitutionalism* (Durham: Duke University Press, 1997), pp. 34–35, 42–44.
97. Caldwell, *Popular Sovereignty and the Crisis of German Constitutional Law*, p. 41.
98. Jellinek, *Allgemeine Staatslehre*, p. 21.
99. Georg Jellinek, *Die rechtliche Natur der Staatenverträge: Ein Beitrag zur juristischen Construktion des Völkerrechts* (Vienna: Hölder, 1880), p. 32.
100. On "Jellinek's Paradox," see Caldwell, *Popular Sovereignty and the Crisis of German Constitutional Law*, p. 42.
101. On Weber's debt to Jellinek, see Stefan Breuer, *Georg Jellinek und Max Weber: Von der sozialen zur soziologischen Staatslehre* (Baden-Baden: Nomos, 1999); Duncan Kelly, *The State of the Political: Conceptions of Politics and the State in the Thought of Max Weber, Carl Schmitt and Franz Neumann* (Oxford: Oxford University, 2003), pp. 9, 93–108; and Anter, *Max Weber und die Staatsrechtslehre*, Chapter 2.
102. On Jellinek's role in the diffusion of Neo-Kantianism, see Oliver Lepsius, "Die Zwei-Seiten-Lehre des Staates," in Andreas Anter, ed., *Die normative Kraft des Faktischen: Das Staatsverständnis Georg Jellineks* (Baden-Baden: Nomos, 2004), esp. pp. 78–82. Generally, see Jonathan Trejo-Mathys, "Neo-Kantianism in the Philosophy of Law: Its Value and Actuality," in Nicolas de Warren and Andrea Staiti, eds., *New Approaches to Neo-Kantianism* (Cambridge: Cambridge University Press, 2015), pp. 147–70.
103. Jellinek, *Allgemeine Staatslehre*, p. 137.
104. See my discussion of Neumann's concept of law in Chapter 2.
105. Schluchter, *Entscheidung für den sozialen Rechtsstaat*, p. 215.
106. Jens Meierhenrich, *The Trilemma of Justice*, Unpublished book manuscript, Harvard University, 2004.
107. Note that the controversy centered on constitutional law, the most contested arena of law in the transition from monarchical to democratic rule. To get a sense of the kinds of barbs that were traded, see the recriminations between Heller and Kelsen, as recounted in Dyzenhaus, *Legality and Legitimacy*, pp. 161–2. For a helpful discussion of their frosty relationship, see also Christoph Müller, "Kritische Bemerkungen zur Auseinandersetzung Hermann Hellers mit Hans Kelsen," in Staff, ed., *Staatslehre in der Weimarer Republik*, pp. 128–57.
108. Stolleis, *Public Law in Germany*, p. 86. Note that Kelsen's pure theory of law was debated controversially by classical legal positivists.
109. Weber, *Economy and Society*, p. 312.
110. Hans Kelsen, "On the Borders between Legal and Sociological Method," in Arthur J. Jacobson and Bernhard Schlink, eds., *Weimar: A Jurispruence of Crisis* (Berkeley: University of California Press, [1911] 2000), p. 58.
111. Kelsen, "On the Borders between Legal and Sociological Method," p. 59.
112. Stolleis, *Public Law in Germany*, pp. 83–4.

113. Meierhenrich, "Fearing the Disorder of Things."
114. Jacobson and Schlink, "Constitutional Crisis," p. 17.
115. As mentioned earlier, two opposing camp faced off under the large tent of statutory positivism: Kelsen led the "logical" camp, which wanted its legal theory pure and neat; Anschütz and Thoma headed the "sociological" one, which was after a legal theory that was messy and concrete.
116. Korioth, "The Shattering of Methods in Late Wilhelmine Germany," p. 50.
117. Jacobson and Schlink, "Constitutional Crisis," p. 15.
118. Needless to say, the Nazi debate about the *Rechtsstaat*, as we shall see in Chapter 5, was racialized and exclusionary and thus did not meet the requirements of a rational discourse in legal argumentation. As Jürgen Habermas put it, "In rational discourse, we assume that conditions of communication obtain that (1) prevent a rationally unmotivated termination of argumentation, (2) secure both freedom in the choice of topics and inclusion of the best information and reasons through universal and equal access to, as well as equal and symmetrical participation in, argumentation, and (3) exclude every kind of coercion—whether originating outside the process of reaching understanding or within it—other than that of the better argument, so that all motives except that of the cooperative search for truth are neutralized." Jürgen Habermas, *Between Facts and Norms: Contributions to a Discourse Theory of Law and Democracy*, translated by William Rehg (Cambridge: MIT Press, [1992] 1996), p. 230.
119. The moniker "jurisprudence of crisis" is Jacobson and Schlink's.
120. Rudolf Smend, *Verfassung und Verfassungrecht* (Munich: Duncker & Humblot, 1928), reprinted in idem., *Staatsrechtliche Abhandlungen und andere Aufsätze*, Third edition (Berlin: Duncker & Humblot, [1955] 1994), pp. 119–276.
121. For a useful analysis of some of the critiques leveled against Laband, see Peter von Oertzen, *Die soziale Funktion des staatsrechtlichen Positivismus* (Frankfurt: Suhrkamp 1974), pp. 254–80.
122. Rudolf Smend, "Der Einfluß der deutschen Staats- und Verwaltungsrechtslehre des 19. Jahrhunderts auf das Leben in Verfassung und Verwaltung," *Deutsche Rechtswissenschaft*, Vol. 4 (1939), reprinted in idem., *Staatsrechtliche Abhandlungen und andere Aufsätze*, Third edition (Berlin: Duncker & Humblot, [1955] 1994), p. 335.
123. Generally and recently, see Robert Seyfert, *Das Leben der Institutionen: Zu einer allgemeinen Theorie der Institutionalisierung* (Weilerswist: Velbrück, 2011).
124. Otto von Gierke, "Labands Staatsrecht und die deutsche Rechtswissenschaft," *Schmollers Jahrbuch für Gesetzgebung, Verwaltung und Volkswirtschaft im Deutschen Reich*, Vol. 7 (1883), p. 1113.
125. Otto von Gierke, "Die Grundbegriffe des Staatsrechts und die neuesten Staatsrechtstheorien," *Zeitschrift für die gesamte Staatswissenschaft*, Vol. 30 (1874), esp. pp. 183–4.
126. Another target of Gierke's was Laband's brand of legal positivism. See Stolleis, *Geschichte des öffentlichen Rechts in Deutschland*, vol. 2, pp. 359–63.

127. Raimo Siltala, *Law, Truth, and Reason: A Treatise on Legal Argumentation* (New York: Springer, 2011), p. 188.
128. Stefan Korioth, "Rudolf Smend: Introduction," in Arthur J. Jacobson and Bernhard Schlink, eds., *Weimar: A Jurispruence of Crisis* (Berkeley: University of California Press, 2000), p. 211.
129. Anna-Maria Gräfin von Lösch, *Der nackte Geist: Die Juristische Fakultät der Berliner Universität im Umbruch von 1933* (Tübingen: Mohr, 1999), pp. 394–6.
130. Korioth, "Rudolf Smend," p. 211.

CHAPTER 5

1. On the concept of, and the discourse surrounding, the so-called *Machtergreifung*, see Norbert Frei, "'Machtergreifung': Anmerkungen zu einem historischen Begriff," *Vierteljahrshefte für Zeitgeschichte*, Vol. 31 (1983), pp. 136–45. For an account of the immediate run-up to the government takeover, see Henry Ashby Turner, Jr., *Thirty Days to Power: January 1933* (Reading: Addison-Wesley, 1996). Though slightly dated, the most comprehensive treatment of the early dictatorship remains Karl Dietrich Bracher, Wolfgang Sauer, and Gerhard Schulz, *Die nationalsozialistische Machtergreifung: Studien zur Errichtung des totalitären Herrschaftssystems in Deutschland 1933/34* (Cologne: Westdeutscher Verlag, 1960).
2. "*Dazu genügen nicht bloß Phrasen, sondern dazu bedarf es neben der geistigen Haltung auch des wissenschaftlichen Rüstzeuges.*" Otto Koellreutter, "Edgar Tatarin-Tarnheyden, Werdendes Staatsrecht" (Book review), *Archiv des öffentlichen Rechts*, Vol. 26 (1935), p. 128.
3. Carl Schmitt, "Nachwort," in Günther Krauß and Otto von Schweinichen, *Disputation über den Rechtsstaat* (Hamburg: Hanseatische Verlagsanstalt, 1935), p. 88.
4. "The Science of Administrative Law under National Socialism," in idem., *The Law under the Swastika: Studies on Legal History in Nazi Germany*, translated by Thomas Dunlap (Chicago: University of Chicago Press, [1985] 1998), p. 103.
5. Dieter Thomä, "The Difficulty of Democracy: Rethinking the Political in the Philosophy of the Thirties (Gehlen, Schmitt, Heidegger)," in Wolfgang Bialas and Anson Rabinbach, eds., *Nazi Germany and the Humanities: How German Academics Embraced Nazism* (London: Oneworld, 2007), p. 96.
6. Peter Caldwell, "National Socialism and Constitutional Law: Carl Schmitt, Otto Koellreutter, and the Debate over the Nature of the Nazi State, 1993–1937," *Cardozo Law Review*, Vol. 16 (1994), p. 400.
7. Caldwell, "National Socialism and Constitutional Law," p. 399.
8. Victor Klemperer, *LTI: Notizbuch eines Philologen*, Twenty-fifth edition (Stuttgart: Reclam, [1947] 2015).
9. In order to avoid confusion, a clarification of terms is in order, notably of *Staatslehre* (state theory), *Verfassungslehre* (constitutional theory), and *Staatsrechtslehre* (state law theory). At one point or another, each of these topoi stood for a distinct approach to the study of public law in modern

Germany. For a discussion, see Peter Häberle, "Allgemeines Staatsrecht, Verfassungslehre oder Staatsrechtslehre? Bemerkungen aus Anlaß der 5. Auflage der Allgemeinen Staatslehre von G. u. E. Küchenhoff (1964)," *Zeitschrift für Politik*, Vol. 12 (1965), pp. 381–95. The issue is also addressed throughout Martin Loughlin, *Foundations of Public Law* (Oxford: Oxford University Press, 2010); and Murkens, *From Empire to Union*. For an attempt to revive elements of early twentieth century Germany's *Staatsrechtslehre* for the study of constitutional law in the twenty-first century, see David Dyzenhaus, "The Idea of a Constitution: A Plea for *Staatsrechtslehre*," in David Dyzenhaus and Malcolm Thorburn, eds., *Philosophical Foundations of Constitutional Law* (Oxford: Oxford University Press, 2016), pp. 1–32.

10. Joachim Perels, "Zur Rechtslehre vor und nach 1945," in Eva Schumann, ed., *Kontinuitäten und Zäsuren: Rechtswissenschaft und Justiz im "Dritten Reich" und in der Nachkriegszeit* (Göttingen: Wallstein, 2008), p. 126.
11. Other leading representatives in the legal profession included Karl Larenz, Gerhard Dulckeit, and Martin Busse.
12. Julius Binder, "Der autoritäre Staat," *Logos*, Vol. 22 (1933), p. 153.
13. Binder, "Der autoritäre Staat," p. 156.
14. Binder, "Der autoritäre Staat," p. 158.
15. "*Die neue Lebenswertung hat den einzelnen von seinem Throne gestoßen. Er ist nicht um seiner selbst willen von Wert, er ist dienendes Glied der Gemeinschaft, ist ihr ein- und untergeordnet.*" Heinrich Lange, *Vom Gesetzesstaat zum Rechtsstaat: Ein Vortrag* (Tübingen: Mohr, 1934), p. 20.
16. Otto Koellreutter, *Grundriß der allgemeinen Staatslehre* (Tübingen: Mohr, 1933), p. 61.
17. See, most important, Michael Wildt, *Volksgemeinschaft als Selbstermächtigung. Gewalt gegen Juden in der deutschen Provinz 1919 bis 1939* (Hamburg: Hamburger Edition, 2007); Ian Kershaw, " 'Volksgemeinschaft': Potential und Grenzen eines neuen Forschungskonzepts," *Vierteljahrshefte für Zeitgeschichte*, Vol. 59 (2011), pp. 1–17; Michael Wildt, " 'Volksgemeinschaft': Eine Antwort auf Ian Kershaw," *Zeithistorische Forschungen*, Vol. 8 (2011), pp. 102–9; and the contributions in Martina Steber and Bernhard Gotto, eds., *Visions of Community in Nazi Germany: Social Engineering and Private Lives* (Oxford: Oxford University Press, 2014).
18. "*Das Recht ist nicht etwa dazu da, die sog. Individualsphäre zu sichern und damit das Privatleben zu umhegen. Das Recht des Staates als Lebensordnung der Volksgemeinschaft geht vielmehr vor.*" Wilhelm Glungler, *Theorie der Politik: Grundlehren einer Wissenschaft von Volk und Staat* (Munich: Voglrider, 1941), p. 301.
19. Hans Frank, "Eike von Repgow der Künder und Kämpfer des Rechts," *Deutsches Recht*, Vol. 6 (1936), p. 298.
20. Otto Koellreutter, "Volk und Staat in der Verfassungskrise: Zugleich eine Auseinandersetzung mit der Verfassungslehre Carl Schmitts," *Jahrbuch für politische Forschung*, Vol. 1 (1933), p. 36; Edgar Tatarin-Tarnheyden, *Werdendes Staatsrecht* (Berlin: Heymanns, 1934), p. 21; Lange, *Vom Gesetzesstaat zum Rechtsstaat: Ein Vortrag*, p. 14.

21. Helmut Nicolai, *Grundlagen der kommenden Verfassung: Über den staatsrechtlichen Aufbau des deutschen Reiches* (Berlin: Hobbing, 1933), p. 18.
22. Nicolai, *Grundlagen der kommenden Verfassung*, p. 19.
23. Peter C. Caldwell, *Popular Sovereignty and the Crisis of German Constitutional Law: The Theory and Practice of Weimar Constitutionalism* (Durham: Duke University Press, 1997), pp. 102–3.
24. Carl Schmitt, *Constitutional Theory*, translated and edited by Jeffrey Seitzer (Durham: Duke University Press, [1928] 2008), p. 176. Emphases added.
25. Martin Wittig, *Der Rechtsstaat im Wandel der Staatsformen* (Greifswald: Panzig, 1933), p. 32.
26. Lange, *Vom Gesetzesstaat zum Rechtsstaat: Ein Vortrag*, p. 6.
27. Günther Krauß, "These: Der Begriff des Rechtsstaats ist an die verfassungsrechtliche Lage des 19. Jahrhunderts gebunden; für den Staat des 20. Jahrhunderts hat er keine Berechtigung mehr," in Günther Krauß and Otto von Schweinichen, *Disputation über den Rechtsstaat* (Hamburg: Hanseatische Verlagsanstalt, 1935), pp. 22–4.
28. Schmitt, *Constitutional Theory*, p. 176.
29. Jens Meierhenrich, "Fearing the Disorder of Things: The Development of Carl Schmitt's Institutional Theory, 1919–1942," in Jens Meierhenrich and Oliver Simons, eds., *The Oxford Handbook of Carl Schmitt* (Oxford: Oxford University Press, 2016), esp. pp. 192–202.
30. Carl Schmitt, "Der Rechtsstaat," in Hans Frank, ed., *Nationalsozialistisches Handbuch für Recht und Gesetzgebung* (Munich: Zentralverlag der NSDAP, 1935), p. 9.
31. Schmitt, "Der Rechtsstaat," p. 9.
32. Helmut Nicolai, *Der Staat im nationalsozialistischen Weltbild* (Leipzig: Hirschfeld, 1933), p. 20.
33. Lange, *Vom Gesetzesstaat zum Rechtsstaat*, p. 15.
34. Friedrich Julius Stahl, *Die Philosophie des Rechts*, vol. 2: *Rechts- und Staatslehre auf der Grundlage christlicher Weltanschauung*, Third edition (Heidelberg: Mohr, 1856), §30.
35. Ernst Forsthoff, *Der totale Staat* (Hamburg: Hanseatische Verlagsanstalt, 1933), p. 13.
36. Carl Schmitt, "Was bedeutet der Streit um den 'Rechtsstaat'?," *Zeitschrift für die gesamte Staatswissenschaft*, Vol. 95 (1935), p. 192.
37. Hans Kelsen, *Vom Wesen und Wert der Demokratie*, Second edition (Tübingen, 1929), p. 79.
38. Forsthoff, *Der totale Staat*, p. 12.
39. Lange, *Vom Gesetzesstaat zum Rechtsstaat*, p. 13. Note, however, that both Forsthoff and Walz, despite their support for a distinct Nazi concept of law, had reservations about the centrality of the leadership principle in the legalization of the dictatorship. Forsthoff worried about the transient nature and finite duration of all leadership, Walz was not all too enamored with the "unmetaphysical" quality of any form of leadership. See Forsthoff, *Der totale Staat*, p. 31; Peter M. R. Stirk, *Twentieth-Century German Political Thought* (Edinburgh: Edinburgh University Press, 2006), p. 89.

40. Schmitt, *Political Theology*, p. 6.
41. Carl Schmitt, *Political Theology: Four Chapters on the Concept of Sovereignty*, translated by George Schwab (Chicago: University of Chicago Press, [1922] 2005), p. 13. For an early but still useful discussion of the relationship between norm and decision in Schmitt's thought, see Peter Schneider, *Ausnahmezustand und Norm: Eine Studie zur Rechtslehre von Carl Schmitt* (Stuttgart: Deutsche Verlags-Anstalt, 1957), pp. 259–66.
42. Schmitt, *Political Theology*, p. 7.
43. Schmitt, *Political Theology*, p. 6.
44. Schmitt, *Political Theology*, p. 10.
45. As Caldwell writes, "Schmitt's concept of the unpolitical bourgeois *Rechtsstaat* sought to theorize the refeudalized 'judicial' state that lacked a strong center. [...] The parliamentary component of the constitutional system [in the Weimar Republic], which Schmitt identified as part of the bourgeois *Rechtsstaat*, had failed to provide a unified political system." Caldwell, *Popular Sovereignty and the Crisis of German Constitutional Law*, pp. 112, 113–14.
46. Martin Loughlin, "Politonomy," in Jens Meierhenrich and Oliver Simons, eds., *The Oxford Handbook of Carl Schmitt* (Oxford: Oxford University Press, 2016), p. 582.
47. Schmitt, *Political Theology*, p. 13.
48. Caldwell, *Popular Sovereignty and the Crisis of German Constitutional Law*, p. 118.
49. Carl Schmitt, "Staatsethik und pluralistischer Staat" (1930), in idem., *Positionen und Begriffe im Kampf mit Weimar-Genf-Versailles 1923–1939*, Third edition (Berlin: Duncker & Humblot, [1940] 1994), p. 152. Emphasis added.
50. Generally, see John P. McCormick, *Carl Schmitt's Critique of Liberalism: Against Politics as Technology* (Cambridge: Cambridge University Press, 1997).
51. Carl Schmitt, "Nationalsozialistisches Rechtsdenken," *Deutsches Recht*, Vol. 4 (1934), pp. 225–9.
52. Günther Krauß, "These," p. 21.
53. Binder, "Der autoritäre Staat," pp. 126–60.
54. Krauß, "These," p. 21. On the appropriation of Hegelian thought by theorists in the Third Reich, including Julius Binder, see Ernst Topitsch, *Die Sozialphilosophie Hegels als Heilslehre und Herrschaftsideologie* (Neuwied: Luchterhand, 1967), pp. 63–88; Hubert Kiesewetter, *Von Hegel zu Hitler: Eine Analyse der Hegelschen Machtstaatsideologie und der politischen Wirkungsgeschichte des Rechtshegelianismus* (Hamburg: Hoffmann und Campe, 1974), esp. pp. 233–323; and Kluck, "Transpersonalismus," pp. 129–67.
55. Binder, "Der autoritäre Staat," p. 148.
56. Krauß, "These," p. 21.
57. For a general account that situates Stahl's scholarship and faith in historical perspective, see Doron Avraham, "The Idea of a Jewish Nation in the German Discourse about Emancipation," *Nations and Nationalism*, Vol. 22 (2016), pp. 505–23.

58. On the salience of antisemitism in German politics, society, and culture, with reference to elite constructions and everyday life, respectively, see Paul Lawrence Rose, *German Question/Jewish Question: Revolutionary Antisemitism in Germany from Kant to Wagner*, New edition (Princeton: Princeton University Press, 2006); Marion A. Kaplan, ed., *Jewish Daily Life in Germany, 1618–1945* (Oxford: Oxford University Press, 2005).
59. Krauß, "These," p. 14, fn. 1.
60. Heinrich Meier, *The Lesson of Carl Schmitt: Four Chapters on the Distinction between Political Theology and Political Philosophy*, Expanded edition (Chicago: University of Chicago Press, 2011), p. 152, fn. 78.
61. Most recently, see Raphael Gross, "The 'True Enemy': Antisemitism in Carl Schmitt's Life and Work," in Jens Meierhenrich and Oliver Simons, eds., *The Oxford Handbook of Carl Schmitt* (Oxford: Oxford University Press, 2016), pp. 96–116. See also Jens Meierhenrich, *In the Belly of the Fish: Carl Schmitt in Nazi Germany*, Unpublished book manuscript, London School of Economics and Political Science, 2016.
62. Meier, *The Lesson of Carl Schmitt*, p. 153.
63. "*Ein jüdischer Autor hat für uns keine Autorität, auch keine 'rein wissenschaftliche' Autorität. [...] Ein jüdischer Autor ist für uns, wenn er überhaupt zitiert wird, ein jüdischer Autor. Die Beifügung des Wortes und der Bezeichnung 'jüdisch' ist keine Äußerlichkeit, sondern etwas Wesentliches [...]. Sonst ist die Reinigung unserer Rechtsliteratur nicht möglich. Wer heute 'Stahl-Jolson' schreibt, hat dadurch in einer echt wissenschaftlichen klaren Weise mehr bewirkt, als durch große Ausführungen gegen die Juden, die sich in allgemeinen abstrakten Wendungen bewegen und durch die kein einizger Jude sich in concreto betroffen fühlt.*" Carl Schmitt, "Schlußwort des Reichsgruppenwalters Staatsrat Prof. Dr. Carl Schmitt," in idem., *Das Judentum in der Rechtswissenschaft*, vol. 1: *Die deutsche Rechtswissenschaft im Kampf gegen den jüdischen Geist* (Berlin: Deutscher Rechts-Verlag, 1936), pp. 29–30. Several of the presentations at the 1936 conference were subsequently published as short monographs. Nine of them appeared between 1936 and 1938.
64. Carl Schmitt, "Vorbemerkung," in Edgar Tatarin-Tarnheyden, *Das Judentum in der Rechtswissenschaft*, vol. 5: *Der Einfluß des Judentums in Staatsrecht und Staatslehre* (Berlin: Deutscher Rechts-Verlag, 1938), p. 4.
65. "*Wenn es aus einem sachlichen Grunde notwendig ist, jüdische Autoren zu zitieren, dann nur mit dem Zusatz 'jüdisch.' Schon von der bloßen Nennung des Wortes 'jüdisch' wird ein heilsamer Exorzismus ausgehen.*" Schmitt, "Schlußwort des Reichsgruppenwalters Staatsrat Prof. Dr. Carl Schmitt," p. 30.
66. Tatarin-Tarnheyden, *Das Judentum in der Rechtswissenschaft*, vol. 5. On the circumstances surrounding the 1936 conference, see Reinhard Mehring, *Carl Schmitt: Aufstieg und Fall* (Munich: Beck, 2009), pp. 372–8.
67. Tatarin-Tarnheyden, *Das Judentum in der Rechtswissenschaft*, vol. 5., p. 6.
68. Tatarin-Tarnheyden, *Das Judentum in der Rechtswissenschaft*, vol. 5., pp. 8, 11–12. Tatarin-Tarnheyden singled out Erich Kaufmann for a similar antisemitic treatment. See ibid, pp. 19–24.

69. Tatarin-Tarnheyden, *Das Judentum in der Rechtswissenschaft*, vol. 5., p. 15.
70. Tatarin-Tarnheyden, *Das Judentum in der Rechtswissenschaft*, vol. 5., p. 27.
71. Tatarin-Tarnheyden, *Das Judentum in der Rechtswissenschaft*, vol. 5., p. 27.
72. Krauß, "These," p. 23.
73. Hanns-Jürgen Wiegand, *Das Vermächtnis Friedrich Julius Stahls: Ein Beitrag zur Geschichte konservativen Rechts- und Ordnungsdenken* (Königstein: Athenäum, 1980), p. 22.
74. Tatarin-Tarnheyden, *Das Judentum in der Rechtswissenschaft*, vol. 5, p. 32. The play on words in the original is impossible to convey in translation.
75. Gavin I. Langmuir, *Toward a Definition of Antisemitism* (Berkeley: University of California Press, 1990), p. 328.
76. On the violence of language, see, for example, Thomas Pegelow Kaplan, *The Language of Nazi Genocide: Linguistic Violence and the Struggle of Germans of Jewish Ancestry* (Cambridge: Cambridge University Press, 2009).
77. For a useful and sophisticated discussion of the Hegelian concepts of "*Geist*" and "*Sittlichkeit*," which are relevant here, see, for example, Charles Taylor, *Hegel and Modern Society* (Cambridge: Cambridge University Press, 1979).
78. Nicolai, *Grundlagen der kommenden Verfassung*, p. 16.
79. "*Wir suchen eine Bindung, die zuverlässiger, lebendiger und tiefer ist als die trügerische Bindung an die verdrehbaren Buchstaben von tausend Gesetzesparagraphen. Wo anders könnte sie liegen als in uns selbst und in unserer eigenen Art?*" Carl Schmitt, *Staat, Bewegung, Volk: Die Dreigliederung der politischen Einheit* (Hamburg: Hanseatische Verlagsanstalt, 1933), p. 46.
80. Schmitt, *Staat, Bewegung, Volk*, esp. pp. 32–46.
81. Meierhenrich, "Fearing the Disorder of Things," p. 194.
82. Helmut Nicolai, *Die rassengesetzliche Rechtslehre: Grundzüge einer nationalsozialistischen Rechtsphilosophie*, Third edition (Munich: Eher, 1934). See also Helmut Nicolai, *Rasse und Recht: Vortrag gehalten auf dem deutschen Juristentage des Bundes nationalsozialistischer deutscher Juristen am 2. Oktober 1933 in Leipzig* (Berlin: Hobbing, 1933).
83. Helmut Nicolai, *Die rassengesetzliche Rechtslehre: Grundzüge einer nationalsozialistischen Rechtsphilosophie*, Second edition (Munich: Eher, 1933), p. 28.
84. Nicolai, *Die rassengesetzliche Rechtslehre*, p. 44.
85. Nicolai, *Die rassengesetzliche Rechtslehre*, p. 44.
86. Nicolai, *Die rassengesetzliche Rechtslehre*, p. 47.
87. On Frank's tendency to self-promotion and accumulation of titles and positions, see Dieter Schenk, *Hans Frank: Hitlers Kronjurist und Generalgouverneur* (Frankfurt: Fischer, 2006), pp. 117–28. See also Dietmar Willoweit, "Deutsche Rechtsgeschichte und nationalsozialistische Weltanschauung: das Beispiel Hans Frank," in Michael Stolleis and Dieter Simon, eds., *Rechtsgeschichte im Nationalsozialismus: Beiträge zur Geschichte einer Disziplin* (Tübingen: Mohr, 1989), pp. 25–42.
88. Schenk, *Hans Frank*, pp. 66–7, 127–8.
89. As quoted in Schenk, *Hans Frank*, p. 99.
90. Hans Frank, "Die Juden in der Rechtswissenschaft," *Deutsches Recht*, Vol. 6 (1936), p. 394.

91. Frank, "Die Juden in der Rechtswissenschaft," p. 394.
92. "Recht ist, was dem Volke nützt—Was dem Volke schädlich ist, muß Unrecht sein." Hans Frank, "Die Zeit des Rechts," p. 3.
93. Diemu Majer, *Grundlagen des nationalsozialistischen Rechtssystems: Führerprinzip, Sonderrecht, Einheitspartei* (Stuttgart: Kohlhammer, 1987), p. 25. On the "Kieler Schule," see Dieter Grimm, "Die 'Neue Rechtswissenschaft,'" in Peter Lundgren, ed., *Wissenschaft im Dritten Reich* (Frankfurt: Suhrkamp, 1985), pp. 31–54; and Christina Wiener, *Kieler Fakultät und "Kieler Schule": Die Rechtslehrer an der Rechts- und Staatswissenschaftlichen Fakultät zu Kiel in der Zeit des Nationalsozialismus und ihre Entnazifizierung* (Baden-Baden: Nomos, 2013).
94. Horst Dreier, "Die deutsche Staatsrechtslehre in der Zeit des Nationalsozialismus," in idem., *Staatsrecht in Demokratie und Diktatur: Studien zur Weimarer Republik und zum Nationalsozialismus*, edited by Matthias Jestaedt and Stanley L. Paulson (Tübingen: Mohr, [2001] 2016), p. 201.
95. Edin Šarčević, "Mißbrauch eines Begriffs–Rechtsstaat und Nationalsozialismus," *Rechtstheorie*, Vol. 24 (1993), p. 207.
96. For a well-known comparative account of Germany's earlier quests, see A. J. P. Taylor, *The Struggle for Mastery in Europe 1848–1918* (Oxford: Clarendon Press, 1954).
97. *Pars pro toto*, see Carsten Bäcker, *Gerechtigkeit im Rechtsstaat: Das Bundesverfassungsgericht an der Grenze des Grundgesetzes* (Tübingen: Mohr, 2015), p. 148.
98. Volker Neumann, *Carl Schmitt als Jurist* (Tübingen: Mohr, 2015, p. 341.
99. For an important, theoretical treatment of the relationship between identity and identification that is relevant here, see Rogers Brubaker and Frederick Cooper, "Beyond 'Identity,'" *Theory and Society*, Vol. 29 (2000), pp. 1–47.
100. Otto Koellreutter, *Grundriß der allgemeinen Staatslehre*, p. 74.
101. Koellreutter, "Volk und Staat in der Verfassungskrise;" Binder, "Der autoritäre Staat."
102. Koellreutter, *Grundriß der allgemeinen Staatslehre*, p. 74.
103. Mine is a play on Carl Schmitt's famous formula "Sovereign is he who decides on the exception." Schmitt, *Political Theology*, p. 5.
104. Otto Koellreutter, *Der nationale Rechtsstaat: Zum Wandel der deutschen Staatsidee* (Tübingen: Mohr, 1932); idem., "Der nationale Rechtsstaat," *Deutsche Juristen-Zeitung*, Vol. 38 (1933), pp. 517–24; idem., "Der nationalsozialistische Rechtsstaat," in Hans Heinrich Lammers and Hans Pfundtner, eds., *Die Verwaltungsakademie: Ein Handbuch für den Beamten im nationalsozialistischen Staat* (Berlin: Industrieverlag Spaeth und Linde, 1934), pp. 1–15.
105. Otto Koellreutter, "Quellen des nationalsozialistischen Staatsrechts," in Lammers and Pfundtner, eds., *Die Verwaltungsakademie*, p. 2.
106. Christian Hilger, *Rechtsstaatsbegriffe im Dritten Reich: Eine Strukturanalyse* (Tübingen: Mohr, 2003), p. 60.

107. Otto Koellreutter, "Der nationale Rechtsstaat," *Deutsche Juristen-Zeitung*, Vol. 38 (1933), p. 523.
108. Gesetz über Maßnahmen der Staatsnotwehr vom 3. Juli 1934, RGBl. 1933.
109. Koellreutter, "Der nationalsozialistische Rechtsstaat," pp. 6–7; Hilger, *Rechtsstaatsbegriffe im Dritten Reich*, p. 65.
110. Koellreutter, "Der nationalsozialistische Rechtsstaat," p. 6.
111. Otto Koellreutter, "Das Wesen des 'Politischen' in der öffentlichen Verwaltung," *Reichsverwaltungsblatt*, Vol. 54 (1933), p. 483.
112. Hilger, *Rechtsstaatsbegriffe im Dritten Reich*, p. 70.
113. Otto Koellreutter, "Recht und Richter in England und Deutschland," *Verwaltungsarchiv*, Vol. 47 (1942), p. 210. As Koellreutter's most formidable rival, Schmitt insisted that the word "*Rechtsstaat*" was not made for eternity ("*kein ewiges Wort sein kann*"). See his "Nachwort," p. 85.
114. I have borrowed the term "suggestive power" ("*suggestive Macht*") from Ulrich Schellenberg, "Die Rechtsstaatskritik: Vom liberalen zum nationalen und nationalsozialistischen Rechtsstaat," in Ernst-Wolfgang Böckenförde, ed., *Staatsrecht und Staatsrechtslehre* (Heidelberg: Müller, 1985), p. 71.
115. Stolleis, "The Science of Administrative Law under National Socialism," p. 102.
116. "Staat," in *Der große Brockhaus: Handbuch des Wissens in zwanzig Bänden*, Vol. 18 (Leipzig: Brockhaus, 1934), p. 7.
117. On this debate, see, among others, Jürgen Meinck, *Weimarer Staatslehre und Nationalsozialismus: Eine Studie zum Problem der Kontinuität im staats-rechtlichen Denken in Deutschland 1928 bis 1936* (Frankfurt: Campus, 1978); Gangl, ed., *Die Weimarer Staatsrechtsdebatte.*
118. Bodo Dennewitz, *Das nationale Deutschland ein Rechtsstaat: Die Rechtsgrundlagen des neuen deutschen Staates* (Berlin: Vahlen, 1933), pp. 7–8.
119. Dennewitz, *Das nationale Deutschland ein Rechtsstaat*, p. 9.
120. Dennewitz, *Das nationale Deutschland ein Rechtsstaat*, p. 7.
121. Dennewitz, *Das nationale Deutschland ein Rechtsstaat*, pp. 7, 8.
122. Dennewitz, *Das nationale Deutschland ein Rechtsstaat*, p. 7. This anticipates assumptions of historical institutionalism. See, for example, Pierson, *Politics in Time.*
123. Dennewitz, *Das nationale Deutschland ein Rechtsstaat*, p. 8.
124. Dennewitz, *Das nationale Deutschland ein Rechtsstaat*, p. 11.
125. Dennewitz, *Das nationale Deutschland ein Rechtsstaat*, p. 10.
126. Ernst Rudolf Huber, "Bedeutungswandel der Grundrechte," *Archiv des öffentlichen Rechts*, Vol. 62 (1933), pp. 1–98.
127. Bodo Dennewitz, *Staatslehre und nationalsozialistischer Staat* (Berlin: Vahlen, 1934), p. 18.
128. Dennewitz, *Das nationale Deutschland ein Rechtsstaat*, pp. 12–25.
129. Dennewitz, *Das nationale Deutschland ein Rechtsstaat*, p. 23.
130. Dennewitz, *Das nationale Deutschland ein Rechtsstaat*, p. 23.
131. Dennewitz, *Das nationale Deutschland ein Rechtsstaat*, p. 29.
132. Hilger, *Rechtsstaatsbegriffe im Dritten Reich*, p. 155.
133. Dennewitz, *Das nationale Deutschland ein Rechtsstaat*, p. 7.

134. Dennewitz, *Das nationale Deutschland ein Rechtsstaat*, pp. 7, 9.
135. Lange, *Vom Gesetzesstaat zum Rechtsstaat*, p. 10.
136. Lange, *Vom Gesetzesstaat zum Rechtsstaat*, p. 3.
137. Lange, *Vom Gesetzesstaat zum Rechtsstaat*, p. 4.
138. Hubert Kiesewetter, in a comprehensive, though not always fully convincing, analysis of the role of Hegelian ideas in the Third Reich, has described as "antipositivist metaphysics of law" the effort of integrating Hitler's racism and Hegel's idealism in Nazi legal thought, Kiesewetter, *Von Hegel zu Hitler*, p. 303.
139. Lange, *Vom Gesetzesstaat zum Rechtsstaat*, pp. 21, 40; Hilger, *Rechtsstaatsbegriffe im Dritten Reich*, p. 139.
140. Lange, *Vom Gesetzesstaat zum Rechtsstaat*, p. 21.
141. Lange, *Vom Gesetzesstaat zum Rechtsstaat*, p. 26.
142. Lange, *Vom Gesetzesstaat zum Rechtsstaat*, p. 27.
143. Lange, *Vom Gesetzesstaat zum Rechtsstaat*, p. 35.
144. Lange, *Vom Gesetzesstaat zum Rechtsstaat*, p. 30.
145. Lange, *Vom Gesetzesstaat zum Rechtsstaat*, p. 30.
146. Lange, *Vom Gesetzesstaat zum Rechtsstaat*, p. 30.
147. Lange, *Vom Gesetzesstaat zum Rechtsstaat*, p. 30.
148. Otto von Schweinichen, "Gegenthese: Das Wort Rechtsstaat kann so gebraucht warden, daß es den typischen Zusammenhang von Staat und Rechtsverwirklichung bezeichnet; dann hat es so viele Rechtsstaaten in der Geschichte gegeben wie es Staaten gegeben hat, in denen Recht in typischer Weise Geltung gefunden hat; von hier aus betrachtet, erscheint der Staat des 19. Jahrhunderts als typischer Gesetzesstaat, während der nationalsozialistische Staat Rechtsstaat im wahren Sinne ist," in Günther Krauß and Otto von Schweinichen, *Disputation über den Rechtsstaat* (Hamburg: Hanseatische Verlagsanstalt, 1935), pp. 39, 51.
149. von Schweinichen, "Gegenthese," p. 45.
150. von Schweinichen, "Gegenthese," pp. 40–1.
151. von Schweinichen, "Gegenthese," p. 41.
152. von Schweinichen, "Gegenthese," p. 42. Von Schweinichen borrowed the concept of "*Normanmaßung*" (which he contemplated retiring in favor of the term "*Normpotential*," or "norm potential") from the legal philosopher Carl August Emge, a member of the NSDAP since 1931. Ibid, p. 43, fn. 1. For Emge's contributions, see his *Vorschule der Rechtsphilosophie* (Berlin: Rothschild, 1925); and idem., *Geschichte der Rechtsphilosophie* (Berlin: Junker und Dünnhaupt, 1931).
153. von Schweinichen, "Gegenthese," p. 42.
154. Note that in both Wilhelmine Germany and Weimar Germany the principle of legality governed *only* executive (including administrative) action affecting individual freedom and private property. Gerhard Anschütz, *Die gegenwärtigen Theorien über den Begriff der gesetzgebenden Gewalt und den Umfang des königlichen Verordnungsrechts nach preußischem Staatsrecht*, Second edition (Tübingen: Mohr, 1901), p. 86; Neumann, *Carl Schmitt als Jurist*, p. 344.

155. Michael Stolleis, *Public Law in Germany: A Historical Introduction from the 16th to the 21st Century*, translated by Thomas Dunlap (Oxford: Oxford University Press, 2017) p. 69. Emphasis added.
156. Carl Schmitt, "Nationalsozialismus und Rechtsstaat," *Juristische Wochenschrift*, Vol. 63 (1934), p. 716.
157. Schmitt, "Neue Leitsätze für die Rechtspraxis," *Juristische Wochenschrift*, Vol. 62 (1933), p. 2793.
158. See, for example, Georg Dahm, Karl August Eckhardt, Reinhard Höhn, Paul Ritterbusch, and Wolfgang Siebert, "Leitsätze über die Stellung und Aufgaben des Richters," *Deutsche Rechtswissenschaft*, Vol. 1 (1936), pp. 123–4. The prohibition of judicial review was the third of five "guiding principles" that a working group under Georg Dahm's leadership drew up, and which Hans Frank proclaimed on January 14, 1936.
159. Carl Schmitt, "Die Rechtswissenschaft im Führerstaat," *Zeitschrift der Akademie für Deutsches Recht*, Vol. 2 (1935), p. 439. Larenz and Koellreutter used almost identical formulations as Schmitt. Larenz defined the statute as an "expression of the will of the leadership" ("*Ausdruck des Willens der Führung*"), Koellreutter as an "expression of the political will of the leadership" ("*Ausdruck des politischen Willens der Führung*"). Karl Larenz, *Rechts- und Staatsphilosophie der Gegenwart* (Berlin: Junker und Dünnhaupt, 1935), p. 155; Otto Koellreutter, *Deutsches Verfassungsrecht: Ein Grundriß* (Berlin: Junker und Dünnhaupt, 1935), p. 56.
160. Schmitt, "Nationalsozialismus und Rechtsstaat," p. 717.
161. For a seminal analysis of the politicization of *Generalklauseln* and the politics of legal interpretion in Nazi Germany, see Bernd Rüthers, *Die unbegrenzte Auslegung: Zum Wandel der Privatrechtsordnung im Nationalsozialismus*, Sixth edition (Tübingen: Mohr, [1968] 2005), esp. pp. 175–270. On prevalent methods of legal interpretation in the period 1850–1933, including a discussion of earlier responses to gaps in the law, see Jan Schröder, *Recht als Wissenschaft: Geschichte der juristischen Methodenlehre in der Neuzeit (1500–1933)*, Second, revised and expanded edition (Munich: Beck, 2012), pp. 329–92.
162. Schmitt, "Nationalsozialismus und Rechtsstaat," p. 717.
163. Rüthers, *Die unbegrenzte Auslegung*, pp. 262, 265.
164. On the Nazis' radical transformation of the nineteenth century idea of the statute, see also Ingeborg Maus, "'Gesetzesbindung' der Justiz und die Struktur der nationalsozialistischen Rechtsnormen," in Ralf Dreier and Wolfgang Sellert, eds., *Recht und Justiz im "Dritten Reich"* (Frankfurt: Suhrkamp, 1989), p. 84.
165. Schmitt, "Die Rechtswissenschaft im Führerstaat," p. 439. Note that Schmitt, as so often, distorted the meaning of Capitan's aphorism. The latter clearly envisaged a control function for parliament, something that Schmitt failed to acknowledge. René Capitan, *La réforme du parlamentarisme* (Paris: Recueil Sirey, 1934), p. 10.
166. Schmitt, "Die Rechtswissenschaft im Führerstaat," p. 439.

167. Ernst Rudolf Huber, *Verfassungsrecht des Großdeutschen Reiches*, Second edition (Hamburg: Hanseatische Verlagsanstalt, 1939), p. 237. Karl Loewenstein, the exiled political scientist, put it similarly at around the same time: "The law as a command of the Leader does not brook the control involved in judicial review." See his "Dictatorship and the German Constitution: 1933–1937," *University of Chicago Law Review*, Vol. 4 (1937), p. 565.
168. For a brief discussion, see also Dietrich Kirschenmann, *"Gesetz" im Staatsrecht und in der Staatsrechtslehre des NS* (Berlin: Duncker & Humblot, 1970), pp. 93–5.
169. Ulrich Scheuner, "Die deutsche Staatsführung im Kriege," *Deutsche Rechtswissenschaft*, Vol. 5 (1940), p. 34. For an in-depth assessment of the modes of Nazi lawmaking, see Bernd Mertens, *Rechtsetzung im Nationalsozialismus* (Tübingen: Mohr, 2009).
170. For a complete list of all unpublished *Führer* decrees issued during World War II, of which there were an estimated 400, see Martin Moll, ed., *Führer-Erlasse 1939–1945* (Stuttgart: Steiner, 1997).
171. Theodor Maunz, *Gestalt und Recht der Polizei* (Hamburg: Hanseatische Verlagsanstalt, 1943), esp. pp. 25–30; Johannes Heckel, "Wehrrecht und Wehrmachtbeamtentum," *Heeresverwaltung*, Vol. 6 (1941), p. 58. Cf. Loewenstein, "Dictatorship and the German Constitution," p. 562, who noted that whereas, in 1937, "[t]he customary distinction between formal statutory law, subject to parliamentary participation even if the content is no general rule but a political measure, and material statutory rule, meaning the establishment of general rules of law which are not necessarily subject to parliamentary participation is abandoned, [...] the traditional formalities of publication (*Verkündung*) and promulgation (*Ausfertigung*) are still observed." Emphases added. The marked decline in law's publicity is indicative of the progress that the Nazis made in the span of a few years in the de-institutionalization of the *Rechtsstaat*. It speaks to the importance of recognizing the Nazi dictatorship's institutional development in the realm of law. The institutional formation, deformation, and transformation of Nazi law was a dynamic process that neither a metatheoretical nor a macrohistorical account will be able to adequately represent.
172. Werner Weber, *Die Verkündung von Rechtsvorschriften* (Stuttgart: Kohlhammer, 1942), p. 7.
173. Weber, *Die Verkündung der Rechtsvorschriften*, p. 27.
174. Otto Koellreutter, "Recht und Richter in England und Deutschland," p. 228, fn. 44.
175. Otto Koellreutter, *Vom Sinn und Wesen der nationalen Revolution* (Tübingen: Mohr, 1933), p. 12.
176. "*Die Verkündung hat damit an Bedeutung zugenommen; sie erfüllt gewisse Funktionen nun allein, die früher auf eine Mehrzahl von Formelementen verteilt waren. Die Verkündung ist heute das Minimum an Form, auf das nicht verzichtet werden kann, wenn nicht überhaupt das Gesetz als*

Erscheinungsform des Rechts zertstört werden soll." Ernst Rudolf Huber, "Werner Weber, Die Verkündung von Rechtsvorschriften" (Book review), *Zeitschrift für die gesamte Staatswissenschaft*, Vol. 104 (1944), p. 336.

177. I owe this idea to Horst Dreier. See his "Rechtszerfall und Kontinuität," p. 58.
178. For a discussion of the cultural significance of "orderly thought" in the early twentieth century, see, for example, Frieder Günther, "Ordnen, gestalten, bewahren: Radikales Ordnungsdenken von deutschen Rechtsintellektuellen der Rechtswissenschaft 1920 bis 1960," *Vierteljahrshefte für Zeitgeschichte*, Vol. 59 (2011), pp. 353–84. See also Meierhenrich, "Fearing the Disorder of Things." More generally, see Andreas Anter, *Die Macht der Ordnung: Aspekte einer Grundkategorie des Politischen* (Tübingen: Mohr, 2004). One of the most influential arguments from the mid-twentieth century about the significance of institutional form for the creation and maintenance of political order is Samuel P. Huntington, *Political Order in Changing Societies* (New Haven: Yale University Press, 1968).
179. Carl Schmitt, "Kodifikation oder Novelle? Über die Aufgabe und Methode der heutigen Gesetzgebung," *Deutsche Juristen-Zeitung*, Vol. 40 (1935), pp. 924–5.
180. In his *Theory of Moral Sentiments*, Adam Smith famously invented the figure of the "impartial spectator" as the imaginary guardian of morally acceptable behavior, an observing self that is capable of detaching from our self-interested state of mind and of producing an unvarnished assessment of the extent to which our acts and omissions are praiseworthy or blameworthy: "Whenever I endeavor to examine my own conduct [...] I divide myself as it were into two persons: and that I, the examiner and judge, represent a different character from that other I, the person whose conduct is examined into and judged of. The first is the spectator [...]. The second is the agent." Adam Smith, *The Theory of Moral Sentiments*, edited by D. D. Raphael and A. L. Macfie (Oxford: Clarendon Press, [1759] 1976), III. 1.6. See also D. D. Raphael, *The Impartial Spectator: Adam Smith's Moral Philosophy* (Oxford: Oxford University Press, 2007).
181. In this context it is worth recalling that Smith spoke of the impartial spectator as "the voice of conscience," which he equated with "the voice of God." On the idea of "Nazi conscience," see Claudia Koonz, *The Nazi Conscience* (Cambridge: Belknap Press of Harvard University Press, 2003).
182. Schmitt, *Staat, Bewegung, Volk*, p. 46; Schmitt, "Kodifikation oder Novelle?," p. 921.
183. Schmitt, "Kodifikation oder Novelle?," pp. 922–3.
184. Schmitt, "Kodifikation oder Novelle?," p. 923.
185. On the institution of the *Richterbrief*, see Ralph Angermund, *Deutsche Richterschaft 1919–1945: Krisenerfahrung, Illusion, politische Rechtsprechung* (Frankfurt: Fischer, 1990), pp. 220–45; Heinz Boberach, ed., *Richterbriefe: Dokumente zur Beeinflussung der deutschen Rechtsprechung 1942–1944* (Boppard: Boldt, 1975).
186. Rüthers, *Die unbegrenzte Auslegung*, pp. 185–8, where he also examines three key interpretative techniques of Nazi law.

187. Kirschenmann, *"Gesetz" im Staatsrecht und in der Staatsrechtslehre des NS*, p. 107.
188. Ernst Rudolf Huber, "Reichsgewalt und Reichsführung im Kriege," *Zeitschrift für die gesamte Staatswissenschaft*, Vol. 101 (1941), p. 555.
189. Schmitt, "Der Zugang zum Machthaber, ein zentrales verfassungsrechtliches Problem," in idem., *Verfassungsrechtliche Aufsätze aus den Jahren 1924–1954: Materialen zu einer Verfassungslehre*, Fourth edition (Berlin: Duncker & Humblot, 2003), p. 436.
190. Schmitt, "Der Zugang zum Machthaber, ein zentrales verfassungsrechtliches Problem," p. 434.
191. "*Die Legalität ist ein Funktionsmodus jeder staatlichen Bürokratie. Deshalb trat die Notwendigkeit einer gewissen, wenigstens äußerlichen Legalität gerade an dieser Stelle in das Hitler-Regime ein, an dem Verbindungspunkt mit der großen Befehlsapparatur 'Staat' […].*" Schmitt, "Der Zugang zum Machthaber, ein zentrales verfassungsrechtliches Problem," p. 434.
192. Schmitt, "Der Zugang zum Machthaber, ein zentrales verfassungsrechtliches Problem," p. 433.
193. On the bureaucratic dimensions of the Nazi dictatorship, see, for example, Hans Mommsen, *Beamtentum im Dritten Reich: Mit ausgewählten Quellen zur nationalsozialistischen Beamtenpolitik* (Stuttgart: Deutsche Verlags-Anstalt, 1966); Jane Caplan, *Government without Administration: State and Civil Society in Weimar and Nazi Germany* (Oxford: Clarendon Press, 1988), esp. pp. 131–228; Dieter Rebentisch and Karl Teppe, eds., *Verwaltung contra Menschenführung im Staat Hitlers* (Göttingen: Vandenhoeck und Ruprecht, 1986); and, most recently, Sven Reichardt and Wolfgang Seibel, eds., *Der prekäre Staat: Herrschen und Verwalten im Nationalsozialismus* (Frankfurt: Campus, 2011).
194. Caplan, *Government without Administration*, p. 228.
195. Schmitt, "Der Zugang zum Machthaber, ein zentrales verfassungsrechtliches Problem," pp. 434, 436.
196. Caplan, *Government without Administration*, p. 200.
197. Caplan, *Government without Administration*, pp. 201–2.
198. Michael Stolleis, *Geschichte des öffentlichen Rechts in Deutschland*, vol. 3: *Staats- und Verwaltungsrechtswissenschaft in Republik und Diktatur 1914–1945* (Munich: Beck, 1999), p. 361.
199. Mommsen, *Beamtentum im Dritten Reich*, p. 121.
200. Mommsen, *Beamtentum im Dritten Reich*, pp. 121, 122–3.
201. Martin Stolleis, "Die Verwaltungsgerichtsbarkeit im Nationalsozialismus," in Bernhard Diestelkamp and Michael Stolleis, eds., *Justizalltag im Dritten Reich* (Frankfurt: Fischer, 1988), p. 36. On the role of judges across the entire universe of Nazi courts, see Angermund, *Deutsche Richterschaft 1919–1945*.
202. Mommsen, *Beamtentum im Dritten Reich*, p. 123. In the course of changing the way its bureaucracy worked, the Nazi regime replaced the principle of legality (*Prinzip der Gesetzmäßigkeit*) with the so-called principle of law (*Prinzip der Rechtmäßigkeit*). As a result, administrative action no longer had to be sanctioned by a statute; it sufficed that it was congruent

with the Nazi concept of law, as discussed above. For this argument, see Theodor Maunz, "Die Rechtmäßigkeit der Verwaltung," in Hans Frank, ed., *Deutsches Verwaltungsrecht* (Munich: Eher, 1937), pp. 51–65. Disturbingly, Maunz served as a prominent lawyer in *both* Nazi Germany and postwar Germany. For a brief, important discussion of the relationship between "new" (post-1933) and "old" (pre-1933) administrative law, see Stolleis, *Geschichte des öffentlichen Rechts in Deutschland*, vol. 3

203. Mommsen, *Beamtentum im Dritten Reich*, p. 123.
204. von Schweinichen, "Gegenthese," p. 36.
205. von Schweinichen, "Gegenthese," pp. 36, 39, 61, 69.
206. von Schweinichen, "Gegenthese," p. 50.
207. von Schweinichen, "Gegenthese," p. 53.
208. von Schweinichen, "Gegenthese," p. 61.
209. von Schweinichen, "Gegenthese," p. 56; 61.
210. von Schweinichen, "Gegenthese," p. 49.
211. He also used the terms "*unmittelbar gerechter Staat*," or inherently just state; "*Rechtswahrstaat*," a state committed to preserving law; and "*Rechtsgeltungsstaat*," a state committed to governing by law, to describe his conceptual alternative to that of the liberal *Rechtsstaat*. Von Schweinichen, "Gegenthese," pp. 53, 67, 69.
212. Günther Krauß, "Erwiderung: Als Antwort auf die Ausführungen meines Gegners gebe ich meiner These folgende Abwandlung: der Begriff des Rechtsstaates ist gerade als Allgemeinbegriff an die Verfassungslage des 19. Jahrunderts gebunden," in Günther Krauß and Otto von Schweinichen, *Disputation über den Rechtsstaat* (Hamburg: Hanseatische Verlagsanstalt, 1935), p. 83.
213. Roland Freisler, "Rechtsstaat: Eine staatsbiologische Betrachtung," *Völkischer Beobachter*, December 20/21, 1931.
214. Roland Freisler, "Der Rechtsstaat," *Deutsche Juristen-Zeitung*, Vol. 42 (1937), pp. 151–5.
215. Freisler, "Der Rechtsstaat," p. 152.
216. Freisler, "Der Rechtsstaat," p. 152.
217. "*Der nationalsozialistische Staat Adolf Hitlers, das Deutsche Reich, ist [...] kein Rechtsstaat [im liberalen] Sinne. Aber ein Rechtsstaat ist er doch, freilich in einem ganz anderen [...], höheren, innerlichen, natürlichen und damit wahren Sinne.*" Roland Freisler, "Rechtsstaat," in Erich Volkmar, Alexander Elster, and Günther Küchenhoff, eds., *Handwörterbuch der Rechtswissenschaft*, vol. 8: *Die Rechtsentwicklung der Jahre 1933 bis 1935/36* (Berlin: de Gruyter, 1937), p. 572.
218. "*Daß dieser Staat ein Rechtsstaat [...] ist, ist [...] eine Selbstverständlichkeit, mehr aber auch nicht.*" Freisler, "Der Rechtsstaat," p. 154.
219. Gustav Adolf Walz, "Autoritärer Staat, nationaler Rechtsstaat oder völkischer Führerstaat?," *Deutsche Juristen-Zeitung*, Vol. 38 (1933), pp. 1334–40. See also Thomas Ditt, "*Stoßtruppfakultät Breslau*": *Rechtswissenschaft im "Grenzland Schlesien" 1933–1945* (Tübingen: Mohr, 2011), esp. pp. 52–66.

220. Walz, "Autoritärer Staat, nationaler Rechtsstaat oder völkischer Führerstaat?," p. 1338.
221. Freisler, "Der Rechtsstaat," p. 154. Note that Freisler here borrowed explicitly from Hitler's *Mein Kampf*.
222. Gustav Adolf Walz, "Faschismus und Nationalsozialismus," *Deutsches Recht*, Vol. 5 (1935), pp. 315–19. See also idem., *Das Ende der Zwischenverfassung: Betrachtungen zur Entstehung des nationalsozialistischen Staates* (Stuttgart: Kohlhammer, 1933) p. 44.
223. Gustav Adolf Walz, "Autoritäre Staatsordnung und völkischer Führerstaat," *Bücherkunde*, Vol. 4 (1937), p. 77.
224. Herbert Krüger, a Smend pupil, was among those who believed that the "principle" of the authoritarian state represented "the constitution of the National Socialist state." Idem., "Das neue Staatsrecht des dritten Reiches," *Fischers Zeitschrift für Verwaltungsrecht*, Vol. 70 (1934), p. 291.
225. Walz, "Autoritärer Staat, nationaler Rechtsstaat oder völkischer Führerstaat?," p. 1338.
226. Stirk, *Twentieth-Century German Political Thought*, p. 88. Emphases added.
227. Roland Freisler, "Recht, Richter und Gesetz," *Deutsche Justiz*, Vol. 95 (1933), p. 696. I would be remiss if I did not point out that Freisler quickly changed his tune. By 1936, his idea of what was required in the interpretation of Nazi statutes had changed dramatically. Not law but ideology, he now argued, was what primarily bound judges in the racial dictatorship: "The binding nature of ideology gives the judge the freedom to interpret and apply statutes in a sovereign fashion." (*"Die Weltanschauungsgebundenheit gibt auch dem Richter die Freiheit souveräner Gesetzesauslegung und Gesetzesanwendung.") Roland Freisler, "Richter und Gesetz,"* in Hans Heinrich Lammers and Hans Pfundtner, eds., *Die Verwaltungs-Akademie: Ein Handbuch für den Beamten im nationalsozialistischen Staat*, vol. 1: *Grundlagen, Aufbau und Wirtschaftsordnung des nationalsozialistischen Staates* (Berlin: Industrieverlag Spaeth und Linde, 1936), p. 9. See also Maus, " 'Gesetzesbindung' der Justiz und die Struktur der nationalsozialistischen Rechtsnormen," pp. 88–9.
228. The analytical distinction between moderates and hardliners is a staple in the political science literature on democratization, first drawn by Adam Przeworski in the 1990s to facilitate game theoretical models of payoffs in transitions from authoritarian rule. Adam Przeworski, *Democracy and the Market: Political and Economic Reforms in Eastern Europe and Latin America* (Cambridge: Cambridge University Press, 1991). See also Josep M. Colomer, *Strategic Transitions: Game Theory and Democratization* (Baltimore: Johns Hopkins University Press, 2000). Volker Neumann has also cautioned against simplifying the complexity of the Nazi debate about the *Rechtsstaat*. See his *Carl Schmitt als Jurist* (Tübingen: Mohr, 2015), p. 341.
229. Stolleis, *Public Law in Germany*, p. 108.
230. Stolleis, *Public Law in Germany*, p. 112.
231. Stolleis, *Public Law in Germany*, pp. 113–14.
232. Stolleis, *Public Law in Germany*, p. 116.

233. My discussion of Wittig and Helfritz is indebted to Hilger, *Rechtsstaatsbegriffe im Dritten Reich*.
234. Wittig, *Der Rechtsstaat im Wandel der Staatsformen*, p. 16.
235. Wittig, *Der Rechtsstaat im Wandel der Staatsformen*, pp. 11–12, 40.
236. See Chapter 2 above.
237. Wittig, *Der Rechtsstaat im Wandel der Staatsformen*, p. 40.
238. Wittig, *Der Rechtsstaat im Wandel der Staatsformen*, p. 36.
239. Wittig, *Der Rechtsstaat im Wandel der Staatsformen*, pp. 37–8.
240. Wittig, *Der Rechtsstaat im Wandel der Staatsformen*, p. 42.
241. Hans Helfritz, "Rechtsstaat und nationalsozialistischer Staat," *Deutsche Juristen-Zeitung*, Vol. 39 (1934), pp. 425–33.
242. Helfritz, "Rechtsstaat und nationalsozialistischer Staat," p. 433.
243. Helfritz, "Rechtsstaat und nationalsozialistischer Staat," pp. 428–9.
244. "*Kein Staat hat sich damit begnügt, seinen Angehörigen nichts anderes zu bieten als eine Rechtsordnung und deren Aufrechterhaltung.*" Helfritz, "Rechtsstaat und nationalsozialistischer Staat," p. 431.
245. Helfritz, "Rechtsstaat und nationalsozialistischer Staat," p. 431.
246. Cf. Friedrich Darmstädter, *Rechtsstaat oder Machtstaat? Eine Frage nach der Geltung der Weimarer Verfassung* (Berlin: Rothschild, 1932).
247. Helfritz, "Rechtsstaat und nationalsozialistischer Staat," p. 431.
248. Helfritz, "Rechtsstaat und nationalsozialistischer Staat," p. 432.
249. Helfritz, "Rechtsstaat und nationalsozialistischer Staat," p. 430.
250. Helfritz, "Rechtsstaat und nationalsozialistischer Staat," p. 430.
251. Hilger, *Rechtsstaatsbegriffe im Dritten Reich*, p. 165.
252. Helfritz, "Rechtsstaat und nationalsozialistischer Staat," p. 433.
253. Hilger, *Rechtsstaatsbegriffe im Dritten Reich*, p. 167.
254. Stolleis, *Geschichte des öffentlichen Rechts in Deutschland*, vol. 3, p. 161, fn. 35.
255. See, for example, Walz, "Autoritärer Staat, nationaler Rechtsstaat oder völkischer Führerstaat?," pp. 1334–40. Despite his loss of the rectorship, Helfritz retained his professorship of law at Breslau university.
256. His insistence on the separation of law and morals stood in direct contrast to both Hitler's and Hans Frank's pronouncements on the nature of Nazi law, as Tatarin-Tarnheyden himself acknowledged. See *Werdendes Staatsrecht*, pp. 13–15.
257. Edgar Tatarin-Tarnheyden, "Staat und Sittlichkeit," *Kantstudien*, Vol. 35 (1930), p. 46; Tatarin-Tarnheyden, *Werdendes Staatsrecht*, p. 19.
258. Tatarin-Tarnheyden, *Werdendes Staatsrecht*, p. 19.
259. Tatarin-Tarnheyden, *Werdendes Staatsrecht*, p. 22.
260. Tatarin-Tarnheyden, *Werdendes Staatsrecht*, p. 22.
261. Tatarin-Tarnheyden, *Werdendes Staatsrecht*, p. 22.
262. Tatarin-Tarnheyden, *Werdendes Staatsrecht*, p. 23. Tatarin-Tarnheyden distinguished between "outer revolution" and "inner revolution," with the latter following on the heels of the former. The first revolutionary stage concerned the transition to dictatorship, the second the consolidation (and "material" grounding) of this dictatorship.

263. *"Es kommt darauf an, Normen zu schaffen, d.h., [...] die neue Staatsordnung auf ein wohlgefügtes gesetzliches Fundament zu stellen [...]. Man soll geformte Rechtsnormen nicht gering achten."* Tatarin-Tarnheyden, *Werdendes Staatsrecht*, p. 23.
264. Tatarin-Tarnheyden, *Werdendes Staatsrecht*, p. 18.
265. Tatarin-Tarnheyden, *Werdendes Staatsrecht*, p. 18.
266. Tatarin-Tarnheyden, *Werdendes Staatsrecht*, p. 151.
267. Tatarin-Tarnheyden, *Werdendes Staatsrecht*, p. 153.
268. Tatarin-Tarnheyden, *Werdendes Staatsrecht*, p. 152.
269. Tatarin-Tarnheyden, *Werdendes Staatsrecht*, pp. 154–9.
270. Edgar Tatarin-Tarnheyden, "Grundlagen des Verwaltungsrechts im neuen Staat," *Archiv des öffentlichen Rechts*, Vol. 24 (1934), p. 354.
271. Tatarin-Tarnheyden, *Werdendes Staatsrecht*, p. 153; Forsthoff, *Der totale Staat*, p. 42.
272. Tatarin-Tarnheyden, *Werdendes Staatsrecht*, pp. 157–8.
273. Tatarin-Tarnheyden, *Werdendes Staatsrecht*, p. 15.
274. Tatarin-Tarnheyden, *Werdendes Staatsrecht*, p. 5.
275. Tatarin-Tarnheyden, "Grundlagen des Verwaltungsrechts im neuen Staat," p. 349.
276. Tatarin-Tarnheyden, *Werdendes Staatsrecht*, p. 30.
277. *"[D]er Rechtsstaat als sozialer, die Willkür ausschließender Ordnungswert bedarf auch weiter einer festen und unverletzbaren Grundlage exakt geformten Rechtes."* Tatarin-Tarnheyden, *Werdendes Staatsrecht*, p. 30.
278. Tatarin-Tarnheyden, *Werdendes Staatsrecht*, p. 30.
279. Tatarin-Tarnheyden, *Werdendes Staatsrecht*, p. 30.
280. Tatarin-Tarnheyden, *Werdendes Staatsrecht*, p. 31.
281. Kurt Groß-Fengels, "Der Streit um den Rechtsstaat," Ph.D. dissertation, Universität Marburg, 1936.
282. Hilger, *Rechtsstaatsbegriffe im Dritten Reich*, p. 178.
283. Groß-Fengels, "Der Streit um den Rechtsstaat," p. 12.
284. Groß-Fengels, "Der Streit um den Rechtsstaat," p. 12.
285. Groß-Fengels, "Der Streit um den Rechtsstaat," p. 15.
286. Groß-Fengels, "Der Streit um den Rechtsstaat," p. 14.
287. Groß-Fengels, "Der Streit um den Rechtsstaat," p. 14.
288. Groß-Fengels, "Der Streit um den Rechtsstaat," p. 36.
289. Hilger, *Rechtsstaatsbegriffe im Dritten Reich*, p. 229.
290. On the violent dimensions of what he termed the Nazis' "substantalization of formal law," see Hubert Rottleuthner, "Die Substantialisierung des Formalrechts: Zur Rolle des Neuhegelianismus in der deutschen Juriprudenz," in Oskar Negt, ed., *Aktualität und Folgen der Philosophie Hegels* (Frankfurt: Suhrkamp, 1973), p. 258.
291. Carl Schmitt, "Das gute Recht der deutschen Revolution," *Westdeutscher Beobachter*, May 12, 1933.
292. Carl Schmitt, *Hugo Preuss: Sein Staatsbegriff und seine Stellung in der deutschen Staatslehre* (Tübingen: Mohr, 1930), p. 5. In the same passage, Schmitt continued thus: "Words such as 'sovereignty,' 'freedom,' '*Rechtsstaat*,'

and 'democracy,' obtain their precise meaning only through a concrete antithesis." Ibid.

293. Schmitt, "Nachwort," p. 85.
294. Cf. von Schweinichen, "Gegenthese," p. 36.
295. Carl Schmitt, "Neue Leitsätze zur Rechtspraxis," *Juristische Wochenschrift*, Vol. 62 (1933), p. 351.
296. Schmitt, "Neue Leitsätze zur Rechtspraxis," p. 351.
297. Schmitt, "Neue Leitsätze zur Rechtspraxis," p. 351.
298. Schmitt, "Was bedeutet der Streit um den 'Rechtsstaat'?," p. 200.
299. Schmitt, "Was bedeutet der Streit um den 'Rechtsstaat'?," p. 200.
300. On lawfare as a strategy of conflict, see Jens Meierhenrich, *Lawfare: A Genealogy* (Cambridge: Cambridge University Press, 2018).
301. Stirk, *Twentieth-Century German Political Thought* p. 86.
302. Schmitt, "Was bedeutet der Streit um den 'Rechtsstaat'?," p. 190.
303. Stirk, *Twentieth-Century German Political Thought*, p. 91.
304. I consider what I call "extremist legalism" to be a manifestation of the more genetal category of "extremist institutionalism," which I have defined elsewhere. See my "Fearing the Disorder of Things."
305. Krauß, "These," pp. 23, 24, 28–9.
306. Krauß, "These," p. 10.
307. Krauß, "These," p. 32.
308. Krauß, "These," p. 31.
309. "*Wenn wir an dem Begriff Rechtsstaat festhalten, wird der Führerstaat relativiert. Denn schließlich wird dann das 'Recht' wieder definiert als Selbstbeschränkung der Führung, Einhaltung des gesetzlichen Rechts [...].*" Krauß, "These," p. 31. In support of his argument, Krauß specifically invoked Walz, "Autoritärer Staat, nationaler Rechtsstaat oder völkischer Führerstaat?," p. 1338.
310. Krauß, "These," p. 30.
311. Ernst Forsthoff, "Otto Koellreutter, Der deutsche Führerstaat" (Book review), *Juristische Wochenschrift*, Vol. 63 (1934), p. 538.
312. Forsthoff, "Otto Koellreutter," p. 538.
313. On June 17, 1936, Hitler appointed Himmler *Reichsführer* (Reich Leader) SS and Chief of German Police. Himmer streamlined the dictatorship's police forces by creating two main offices, the *Hauptamt Sicherheitspolizei* (Security Police Main Office, headed by Heydrich, with Best as his deputy), and the *Hauptamt Ordnungspolizei* (Order Police Main Office, with Kurt Daluege in charge). The former was further divided into three additional offices: *Amt Verwaltung und Recht* (Office of Administration and Law, headed by Best), *Amt Politische Polizei* (Office of Political Police, run by Heydrich), and the *Kriminalpolizeiamt*, which governed the country's detective forces and was also overseen by Heydrich. For a quick overview, see Herbert, *Best*, p. 598, fn. 105.
314. In full, Best's definition reads as follows: " '*Polizei' ist alle staatliche Tätigkeit, die um der Erhaltung und Entfaltung des Volkes [...] willen nach selbständig festgelegter Notwendigkeit mit der Gewalt zur Anwendung von Zwang gegen*

Einzelmenschen und Mehrheiten solcher dem Schutze der Führungsund Gemeinschaftsordnung des Volkes gegen Störung und Zerstörung durch Einzelne und Mehrheiten solcher dient." As quoted in Best, Ulrich Herbert, *Best: Biographische Studien über Radikalismus, Weltanschauung und Vernunft 1903–1989* (Munich: Beck, 2016), p. 195.

315. Herbert, *Best*, p. 195.
316. Herbert, *Best*, p. 195.
317. "*Diese Selbstbeschränkung des Staates durch Normierung seiner künftigen Maßnahmen ist [...] im allgemeinen angebracht gegenber allen positiven aufbauenden Kräften des Volkes.*" *Werner Best, "Neubegründung des Polizeirechts,"* *Jahrbuch der Akademie für Deutsches Recht*, Vol. 4 (1937), pp. 132–8. For the sake of readability, I somewhat simplified the translation.
318. Best, "Neubegründung des Polizeirechts."
319. Herbert, *Best*, esp. pp. 195–213.
320. Herbert, *Best*, p. 183.
321. Peter Longerich, *Heinrich Himmler*, translated by Jeremy Noakes and Lesley Sharpe (Oxford: Oxford University Press, [2008] 2012), p. 196.
322. As quoted in Michael Stolleis, *A History of Public Law in Germany 1914–1945*, translated by Thomas Dunlap (Oxford: Oxford University Press, [1999] 2004), p. 347.
323. Hans Helfritz, "Rechtsstaat und nationalsozialistischer Staat," p. 427. Cf. Reinhard Höhn, *Der individualistische Staatsbegriff und die juristische Staatsperson* (Berlin: Heymann, 1935). See also Ronald Car, "Community of Neighbours vs Society of Merchants: The Genesis of Reinhard Höhn's Nazi State Theory," *Politics, Religion, and Ideology*, Vol. 16 (2015), pp. 1–22.
324. See, for example, Otto Koellreutter, "Führung und Verwaltung: Zum Problem einer neuen Begriffsjurisprudenz," in Roland Freisler, George A. Loening, H. C. Nipperdey, eds., *Festschrift für Justus Wilhelm Hedemann zum 60. Geburtstag* (Jena: Frommansche Buchhandlung, 1938), pp. 95–105.
325. Stolleis, *Geschichte des öffentlichen Rechts in Deutschland*, vol. 3, p. 329.
326. Stirk, *Twentieth-Century German Political Thought*, p. 90.
327. Anna- Maria Gräfin von Lösch, *Der nackte Geist: Die Juristische Fakultät der Berliner Universität im Umbruch von 1933* (Tübingen: Mohr, 1999), p. 402.
328. Mehring, *Carl Schmitt*, pp. 378–80.
329. Stolleis reports the use of this moniker, a reference to their ideological steadfastness, in *Geschichte des öffentlichen Rechts in Deutschland*, vol. 3, p. 322.
330. For a theoretical treatment, see Jens Meierhenrich, "The Presentation of Law in Everyday Life," Unpublished article manuscript, Harvard University, 2002.
331. Cass R. Sunstein, "On the Expressive Function of Law," *University of Pennsylvania Law Review*, Vol. 144 (1996), p. 2021.
332. Sunstein, "On the Expressive Function of Law," p. 2026. See also Lawrence Lessig, "The Regulation of Social Meaning," *University of Chicago Law Review*, Vol. 62 (1995), pp. 943–1045. For a discussion of varieties of expressive claims about law, see Richard H. McAdams, *The Expressive Powers of Law: Theories and Limits* (Cambridge: Harvard University Press, 2015).

333. Sunstein, "On the Expressive Function of Law," p. 2051.
334. Kenneth F. Ledford, *From General Estate to Special Interest: German Lawyers 1878–1933* (Cambridge: Cambridge University Press, 1996), p. 296.
335. Ledford, *From General Estate to Special Interest*, p. 299.
336. Stolleis, *Public Law in Germany*, p. 108.
337. Koonz, *The Nazi Conscience*.
338. Koonz, *The Nazi Conscience*, p. 168. Koonz did not address the operation of law outside of what the Nazi regime euphemistically called "the Jewish question." For a new assessment of the Nuremberg Race Laws, see Magnus Brechtken, Hans-Christian Jasch, Christoph Kreutzmüller, and Niels Weise, eds., *Die Nürnberger Gesetze–80 Jahre danach: Vorgeschichte, Entstehung, Auswirkungen* (Göttingen: Wallstein, 2017).
339. See, for example, Raphael Gross, *Anständig geblieben: Nationalsozialistische Moral* (Munich: Fischer, 2010); Wolfgang Bialas, *Moralische Ordnungen des Nationalsozialismus* (Göttingen: Vandenhoeck und Ruprecht, 2014); Werner Konitzer, ed., *Moralität des Bösen: Ethik und nationalsozialistische Verbrechen* (Frankfurt: Campus, 2009); Wolfgang Bialas and Lothar Fritze, eds., *Ideologie und Moral im Nationalsozialismus* (Göttingen: Vandenhoeck und Ruprecht, 2013); Werner Konitzer and David Palme, eds., *"Arbeit", "Volk", "Gemeinschaft": Ethik und Ethiken im Nationalsozialismus* (Frankfurt: Campus, 2016).
340. Koonz, *The Nazi Conscience*, p. 273.
341. Wolfgang Bialas, "Nationalsozialistische Ethik und Moral: Konzepte, Probleme, offene Fragen," in Bialas and Fritze, eds., *Ideologie und Moral im Nationalsozialismus*, pp. 23–63.
342. Kluck, "Transpersonalismus," p. 131. Note, however, that its effect on legal practice is in dispute. Taking opposing views are Ernst Topitsch, *Die Sozialphilosophie Hegels als Heilslehre und Herrschaftsideologie* (Neuwied: Luchterhand, 1967), who claims a central role for Neo-Hegelianism; and Rottleuthner, "Die Substantialisierung des Formalrechts," pp. 211–64, who doubts its relevance outside of Nazi legal thought.
343. For a contemporary account of the Hegel revival in German philosophy, see Heinrich Levy, *Die Hegel-Renaissance in der deutschen Philosophie: Mit besonderer Berücksichtigung des Neukantianismus* (Berlin: Heise, 1927).
344. Oliver Lepsius, *Die gegensatzaufhebende Begriffsbildung: Methodenentwicklungen in der Weimarer Republik und ihr Verhältnis zur Ideologisierung der Rechtswissenschaft unter dem Nationalsozialismus* (Munich: Beck, 1994), pp. 284–5.
345. Julius Binder, *Grundlegung zur Rechtsphilosophie* (Tübingen: Mohr, 1935); idem., *System der Rechtsphilosophie*, Second edition (Berlin: Stilke, 1937).
346. Lepsius, *Die gegensatzaufhebende Begriffsbildung*, p. 281.
347. Karl Larenz, *Rechts- und Staatsphilosophie der Gegenwart*, Second edition (Berlin: Junker und Dünnhaupt, 1935), p. 109.
348. Larenz, *Rechts- und Staatsphilosophie der Gegenwart*, p. 109.

349. Larenz, *Rechts- und Staatsphilosophie der Gegenwart*, p. 156.
350. Larenz, *Rechts- und Staatsphilosophie der Gegenwart*, p. 161.
351. Lepsius, *Die gegensatzaufhebende Begriffsbildung*, p. 281.
352. Steffen Kluck, "Transpersonalismus: Zur normativen Dimension der neuhegelianischen Rechtsphilosophie," in Werner Konitzer and David Palme, eds., *"Arbeit", "Volk", "Gemeinschaft": Ethik und Ethiken im Nationalsozialismus*, p. 130.
353. Michael Stolleis, *Gemeinwohlformeln im nationalsozialistischen Recht* (Berlin: Schweitzer, 1974), p. 196. For an overview of meanings and usages of the *Gemeinwohl*-concept in Nazi law, see idem., pp. 10–11.
354. Stolleis, *Gemeinwohlformeln im nationalsozialistischen Recht*, p. 297.
355. Stolleis, *Gemeinwohlformeln im nationalsozialistischen Recht*, p. 297.
356. Stolleis, *Gemeinwohlformeln im nationalsozialistischen Recht*, p. 297.
357. Stolleis, *Gemeinwohlformeln im nationalsozialistischen Recht*, p. 298.
358. Stolleis, *Gemeinwohlformeln im nationalsozialistischen Recht*, p. 300.
359. Stolleis, *Gemeinwohlformeln im nationalsozialistischen Recht*, p. 299.
360. Stolleis, *Gemeinwohlformeln im nationalsozialistischen Recht*, p. 300.
361. Stolleis, *Gemeinwohlformeln im nationalsozialistischen Recht*, p. 298. On room for judicial maneuver in the period 1942–1945, see Frank Laudenklos, *Die Autonomie des Rechts im Nationalsozialismus*, Ph.D. dissertation, Universität Frankfurt, 2003. Laudenklos has found evidence of *greater* judicial independence in everyday law at the time when judicial independence was further curtailed. During his three-year reign, Otto Georg Thierack, whom Hitler appointed as minister of justice on August 20, 1942, radicalized the law to an unprecedented degree. But, as Laudenklos has shown, the destruction of further conventions of legality inadvertently also created a degree of interpretive autonomy for judges that they did *not* possess during the early years of the dictatorship.
362. Hans Helfritz, "Rechtsstaat und nationalsozialistischer Staat," p. 426.
363. For a discussion, see Grimm, "Die 'Neue Rechtswissenschaft.'"
364. I treat Carl Schmitt as a *Schreibtischtäter* in Meierhenrich, *In the Belly of the Fish*, Chapter 4.
365. Koonz, *The Nazi Conscience*, p. 177.
366. Koonz, *The Nazi Conscience*, p. 176. Koonz borrowed the term "ethnocrats" from Michael Burleigh. On Nazi technocrats in the context of the "Jewish question" more generally, see also the controversial book by Götz Aly and Susanne Heim, *Architects of Annihilation: Auschwitz and the Logic of Destruction*, translated by A. G. Blunden (Princeton: Princeton University Press, [1991] 2002); and Stefan Kühl, *Ganz normale Organisationen: Zur Soziologie des Holocaust* (Frankfurt: Suhrkamp, 2014).
367. Koonz, *The Nazi Conscience*, p. 176.
368. Although he only joined the NSDAP in 1937, Gürtner played an active and important role in cementing the legal foundations of the Nazi dictatorship. A detailed and exhaustive account is Lothar Gruchmann, *Justiz im Dritten Reich, 1933–1940: Anpassung und Unterwerfung in der Ära Gürtner*, Third

edition (Munich: Oldenbourg, 2001). I develop the categories of extremist institutionalism and racial institutionalism in Meierhenrich, "Fearing the Disorder of Things," esp. pp. 172–3, 194–202.

369. Elsewhere I analyze the Nazi use of law to advance the persecution and destruction of Jews as an example of lawfare. See Meierhenrich, *Lawfare*.
370. Koonz, *The Nazi Conscience*, p. 188.
371. Koonz, *The Nazi Conscience*, p. 189.
372. I deliberately borrow here some of the language that Koonz uses to characterize the culmination of the internal Nazi debate over the creation of the 1935 Nuremberg Racial Laws. See Koonz, *The Nazi Conscience*, p. 188.
373. Koonz, *The Nazi Conscience*, p. 188.
374. Koonz, *The Nazi Conscience*, p. 188.
375. Sarah Schädler, *"Justizkrise" und "Justizreform" im Nationalsozialismus: Das Reichsministerium unter Reichsjustizminister Thierack (1942–1945)* (Tübingen: Mohr, 2009), p. 329. On Thierack's predecessor, the more moderate Franz Schlegelberger, who had served commissarially during the year after the death of Franz Gürtner, the previous Nazi minister of justice, see Michael Förster, *Jurist im Dienst des Unrechts: Leben und Werk des ehemaligen Staatssekretärs im Reichsjustizministerium, Franz Schlegelberger (1876–1970)* (Baden-Baden: Nomos, 1995).
376. Bible, Job 40: 15–18, New Revised Standard Version.
377. Stephen Holmes, "Introduction," in Thomas Hobbes, *Behemoth or The Long Parliament*, edited by Ferdinand Tönnies, with an Introduction by Stephen Holmes (Chicago: University of Chicago Press, [1682] 1990), p. ix.
378. Loewenstein, "Dictatorship and the German Constitution," p. 574. On the salience of Hobessian ideas in the interwar period, see, among others, David Dyzenhaus, "Leviathan in the 1930s: The Reception of Hobbes in the Third Reich," in John P. McCormick, ed., *Confronting Mass Democracy and Industrial Technology: Political and Social Theory from Nietzsche to Habermas* (Durham: Duke University Press, 2002), pp. 163–91; and Tomaz Mastnak, "Hobbes in Kiel, 1938: From Ferdinand Tönnies to Carl Schmitt," *History of European Ideas*, Vol. 41 (2015), pp. 966–91.
379. Loewenstein, "Dictatorship and the German Constitution," p. 574. Also interesting are the biographical entanglements: Loewenstein went on to interrogate Carl Schmitt on behalf of the U.S. prosecution team at the IMT in Nuremberg.
380. Lepsius, *Die gegensatzaufhebende Begriffsbildung*, pp. 381–2.
381. Jeffrey Herf, *Reactionary Modernism: Technology, Culture, and Politics in Weimar and the Third Reich* (Cambridge: Cambridge University Press, 1984), p. 28. Generally, see also Max Weinreich, *Hitler's Professors: The Part of Scholarship in Germany's Crimes against the Jewish People*, with an Introduction by Martin Gilbert (New Haven: Yale University Press, [1946] 1999); Andreas Flitner, ed., *Deutsches Geistesleben und Nationalsozialismus* (Tübingen: Wunderlich, 1965); Karl Corino, ed., *Intellektuelle im Bann des Nationalsozialismus* (Hamburg: Hoffmann und Campe, 1980); Peter Lundgren, ed., *Wissenschaft im Dritten Reich*; Notker Hammerstein, *Die Deutsche Forschungsgemeinschaft in der Weimarer Republik und im Dritten Reich: Wissenschaftspolitik in Republik und*

Diktatur (Munich: Beck, 1999); Wolfgang Bialas and Manfred Gangl, eds., *Intellektuelle im Nationalsozialismus* (New York: Lang, 2000). On Heidegger's involvement in the Third Reich, which has been studied extensively, see, most recently, Marion Heinz and Sidonie Kellerer, eds., *Martin Heideggers »Schwarze Hefte«: Eine philosophisch-politische Debatte* (Frankfurt: Suhrkamp, 2016).

382. The collaboration of Heidegger, Schmitt, and others with the Nazi regime did not lead to their being ostracized abroad. For the purpose of illustration, consider, for example, the legitimating role played by the world's most renowned university: Harvard University. "From 1933 through 1937, as the Nazi menace steadily increased and as Germany's savage persecution of Jews was widely reported in the United States, President [James Bryant] Conant's administration at Harvard was complicit in enhancing the prestige of the Hitler regime by seeking and maintaining friendly and respectful relations with Nazi universities and leaders." Stephen H. Norwood, *The Third Reich in the Ivory Tower: Complicity and Conflict on American Campuses* (Cambridge: Cambridge University Press, 2009), p. 73. If the President and Fellows of Harvard University were not going to look askance at Heidegger, Schmitt, et al. for supporting the Nazi dictatorship, what incentives—other than a commitment to human decency—did these theorists for the Reich have to disavow their *Führer*?
383. Herf, *Reactionary Modernism*, p. 29.
384. Koonz, *The Nazi Conscience*, p. 67.
385. Koonz, *The Nazi Conscience*, p. 68. Hilger distinguishes, among other things, between emotion-driven approaches and race-driven approaches to the concept of law by Nazi jurists involved in the debate about the Rechtsstaat. Hilger, *Rechtsstaatsbegriffe im Dritten Reich*, pp. 206–8.
386. Koonz, *The Nazi Conscience*, p. 68.
387. Cornelius Castoriadis, *L'Institution imaginaire de la societe* (Paris: Seuil, 1975).
388. John B. Thompson, "Ideology and the Social Imaginary: An Appraisal of Castoriadis and Lefort," *Theory and Society*, Vol. 11 (1982), p. 664.
389. Castoriadis, *L'Institution imaginaire de la societe*, p. 203, as quoted in Thompson, "Ideology and the Social Imaginary," p. 664.
390. As quoted in John B. Thompson, *Studies in the Theory of Ideology* (London: Wiley, 1984), p. 24.
391. In the index of Richard Bessel's well-known collection *Life in the Third Reich* (Oxford: Oxford University Press, 1987), the institution of law receives only two entries and four mentions. (Four additional entries reference specific legislation.)
392. Manfred B. Steger and Paul James, "Levels of Subjective Globalization: Ideologies, Imaginaries, Ontologies," *Perspectives on Global Development and Technology*, Vol. 12 (2013), p. 23.
393. David Fraser, *Law after Auschwitz: Towards a Jurisprudence of the Holocaust* (Durham: Carolina Academic Press, 2005), p. 28.
394. Peter Winch, *The Idea of a Social Science and Its Relation to Philosophy* (London: Routledge, 1958), p. 52.

395. Anthony King, *The Structure of Social Theory* (London: Routledge, 2004), pp. 58–9.
396. As Anthony King writes, "To follow a rule, and, therefore, to act appropriately in social life is not to apply a formula individually but to perform acts that others can understand." King, *The Structure of Social Theory*, p. 58.
397. Fraser, *Law after Auschwitz*, p. 23.
398. Loewenstein, "Dictatorship and the German Constitution," p. 538.
399. Friedrich Roetter, "The Impact of Nazi Law," *Wisconsin Law Review* (1945), p. 516.

CHAPTER 6

1. Fraenkel, "Preface to the 1974 German Edition," p. xiii.
2. For biographical sketches of left-leaning jurists in Weimar and Nazi Germany, see, most important, Kritische Justiz, ed., *Streitbare Juristen: Eine andere Tradition* (Baden-Baden: Nomos, 1988); and Bundesrechtsanwaltskammer, ed., *Anwalt ohne Recht: Schicksale jüdischer Anwälte in Deutschland nach 1933* (Berlin: be.bra Verlag, 2007).
3. Simone Ladwig-Winters believes that Fraenkel's marriage to his wife Hanna, who was classified as "Aryan" in the system of Nazi eugenics, also protected him and his legal practice. See Bundesrechtsanwaltskammer, ed., *Anwalt ohne Recht*, p. 48.
4. *Reichsgesetzblatt* 1938 I, pp. 1403–6. For a comprehensive compilation of Nazi decrees, legislation, and other legal instruments, see Ingo von Münch, ed., *Gesetze des NS-Staates: Dokumente eines Unrechtssystems*, Third, enlarged edition (Paderborn: Schöningh, 1994).
5. *Reichsgesetzblatt* 1933 I, pp. 175–7.
6. Ingo Müller, *Hitler's Justice: The Courts of the Third Reich*, translated by Deborah Lucas Schneider (Cambridge: Harvard University Press, 1991), p. 61. See also Fritz Osler, "Rechtsanwälte in der NS-Zeit: Fakten und Erinnerungen," *Anwaltsblatt*, Vol. 33 (1983), p. 59. Jarausch puts the number of attorneys and notaries who were practicing in Germany in 1933 at 19,364. On his count, the legal profession that year was comprised of 10,450 judges. See Konrad Jarausch, *The Unfree Professions: German Lawyers, Teachers, and Engineers, 1900–1950* (New York: Oxford University Press, 1990), p. 237. For an overview of the development of the German Bar from its establishment in 1878 until 1945, with particular reference to the period of Nazi dictatorship, see Kenneth C. H. Willig, "The Bar in the Third Reich," *American Journal of Legal History*, Vol. 20 (1976), pp. 1–14.
7. *Reichsgesetzblatt* 1933 I, pp. 188–9.
8. This exemption was included in the legislation at the urging of Reich President Paul von Hindenburg, who had had command of all German land forces in World War I. In a letter to Hitler, dated April 4, 1933, Hindenburg argued that if Jewish veterans "were worthy of fighting for Germany and bleeding for Germany, then they must also be considered worthy of continuing

to serve the Fatherland in their professions." See "Exchange of Letters Between Hindenburg and Hitler Concerning the Status of Jews who Served in the German Army," reprinted in Yitzhak Arad, Yisrael Gutman, and Abraham Margaliot, eds., *Documents on the Holocaust, Selected Sources on the Destruction of the Jews of Germany and Austria, Poland and the Soviet Union* (Jerusalem: Yad Vashem, 1981), pp. 37–9. A reprint of the German original is available in Walther Hubatsch, *Hindenburg und der Staat: Aus den Papieren des Generalfeldmarschalls und Reichspräsidenten von 1878 bis 1934* (Göttingen: Musterschmidt, 1966), pp. 375–6.

9. Jarausch, *The Unfree Professions*, p. 129.
10. Müller, *Hitler's Justice*, p. 61. See also Fritz Osler, "Rechstanwälte in der NS-Zeit," *Anwaltsblatt*, Vol. 33 (1983), p. 61.
11. Saul Friedländer, *Nazi Germany and the Jews*, vol. 1: *The Years of Persecution, 1933–1939* (London: Weidenfeld and Nicolson, 1997), p. 29. Friedländer works with a slightly higher starting figure than Müller, writing of 4,585 Jewish lawyers to begin with. Of these he believes, 3,167 initially retained their Bar membership. Out of 717 Jewish judges and state prosecutors, another 336 continued their work. Based on these figures, Friedländer claims that Jews, in June 1933, still comprised more than sixteen percent "of all practicing lawyers in Germany." Ibid, p. 29. For his figures, Friedländer draws on Avraham Barkai, *From Boycott to Annihilation: The Economic Struggle of German Jews, 1933–1943*, translated by William Templer (Hanover: University Press of New England, 1989), p. 4.
12. Friedländer, *Nazi Germany and the Jews*, vol. 1, p. 29.
13. As quoted in Jarausch, *The Unfree Professions*, p. 128.
14. Jarausch, *The Unfree* Professions, p. 128.
15. Founded on November 11, 1928, the BNSDJ was the brainchild of Hans Frank who acted at the behest of Hitler. A call for membership appeared in the *Völkischer Beobachter* on September 13, 1928.
16. Lothar Gruchmann, *Justiz im Dritten Reich 1933–1940: Anpassung und Unterwerfung in der Ära Gürtner*, Third edition (Munich: Oldenbourg, 2001), p. 125. The BNSDJ existed from 1928 until 1936, when it became the National Socialist Federation of Guardians of the Law *(Nationalsozialistischer Rechtswahrerbund)*, known by its acronym NSRB.
17. As quoted in Gruchmann, *Justiz im Dritten Reich 1933–1940*, p. 126.
18. Gruchmann, *Justiz im Dritten Reich 1933–1940*, p. 136.
19. For an exhaustive analysis of the intra-governmental and intra-organizational debates in the years 1933–1938 over the removal of Germany's Jews from legal life, see Gruchmann, *Justiz im Dritten Reich 1933–1940*, pp. 124–221. Interestingly, Gruchmann was a student of Fraenkel's. See Lothar Gruchmann, "Ernst Fraenkel zum 65. Geburtstag: Ein Gruß im Namen seiner Schüler," *Zeitschrift für Politik*, Vol. 12 (1964), pp. 303–8.
20. Bundesminister der Justiz, ed., *Im Names des Deutschen Volkes: Justiz und Nationalsozialismus* (Cologne: Verlag Wissenschaft und Politik, 1989), p. 272. For statistics on the Nazi proclivities of Germany's attorneys, see Jarausch, *The Unfree Professions*, p. 254.

21. Friedländer, *Nazi Germany and the Jews*, vol. 1, p. 29.
22. As quoted in Gruchmann, *Justiz im Dritten Reich 1933–1940*, p. 136.
23. Ernst Fraenkel, "Das Dritte Reich als Doppelstaat," in idem., *Gesammelte Schriften*, vol. 2: *Nationalsozialismus und Widerstand*, edited by Alexander v. Brünneck, Hubertus Buchstein, and Gerhard Göhler (Baden-Baden: Nomos, [1937] 1999), p. 504.
24. Fraenkel, "Das Dritte Reich als Doppelstaat," pp. 504–19.
25. Fraenkel, "Das Dritte Reich als Doppelstaat," p. 505.
26. Fraenkel, "Das Dritte Reich als Doppelstaat," p. 505.
27. Fraenkel, "Das Dritte Reich als Doppelstaat," p. 505.
28. Fraenkel, "Das Dritte Reich als Doppelstaat," p. 505.
29. For the original spelling, see Fraenkel, "Das Dritte Reich als Doppelstaat," pp. 509, 512, 514.
30. Fraenkel, "Das Dritte Reich als Doppelstaat," p. 507.
31. Fraenkel, "Das Dritte Reich als Doppelstaat," p. 507.
32. Fraenkel, "Das Dritte Reich als Doppelstaat," p. 508.
33. Fraenkel, "Das Dritte Reich als Doppelstaat," p. 509.
34. Fraenkel, "Das Dritte Reich als Doppelstaat," p. 509.
35. Fraenkel, "Das Dritte Reich als Doppelstaat," p. 510. See also my discussion of Weber's typology of law below, including Figure 7.1.
36. Fraenkel, "Das Dritte Reich als Doppelstaat," p. 510.
37. Ernst Forsthoff, *Der totale Staat* (Hamburg: Hanseatische Verlagsanstalt, 1933), p. 30.
38. Fraenkel, "Das Dritte Reich als Doppelstaat," p. 512.
39. For a counterargument that explores instrumental as well as expressive functions of institutional hybridity, see Jens Meierhenrich, *The Legacies of Law: Long-Run Consequences of Legal Development in South Africa, 1652–2000* (Cambridge: Cambridge University Press, 2008).
40. Generally, see Dan Silverman, *Hitler's Economy: Nazi Work Creation Programs, 1933–1936* (Cambridge: Harvard University Press, 1998).
41. Adam Tooze, *The Wages of Destruction: The Making and Breaking of the Nazi Economy* (London: Penguin, 2008), p. 114.
42. Fraenkel, "Das Dritte Reich als Doppelstaat," p. 517.
43. Fraenkel, "Das Dritte Reich als Doppelstaat," p. 518.
44. Tooze, *The Wages of Destruction*, p. 114.
45. Fraenkel, "Das Dritte Reich als Doppelstaat," p. 518.
46. Fraenkel, "Das Dritte Reich als Doppelstaat," p. 514.
47. Fraenkel, "Das Dritte Reich als Doppelstaat," p. 507.
48. Fraenkel, "Das Dritte Reich als Doppelstaat," p. 514.
49. Fraenkel, "Das Dritte Reich als Doppelstaat," p. 506. Carl Schmitt, *The Crisis of Parliamentary Democracy*, translated by Ellen Kennedy (Cambridge: MIT Press, [1923] 1988).
50. Fraenkel, "Das Dritte Reich als Doppelstaat," p. 515.
51. Fraenkel, "Das Dritte Reich als Doppelstaat," p. 515.
52. Fraenkel here invoked a formulation that Hermann Heller had used in *Europa und der Fascismus* (Berlin: De Gruyter, [1929] 2014), apparently a

fascist's response to the question of what characterized the nature of fascism. Fraenkel, "Das Dritte Reich als Doppelstaat," p. 515.

53. Fraenkel, "Das Dritte Reich als Doppelstaat," p. 517.
54. Fraenkel, "Das Dritte Reich als Doppelstaat," p. 517.
55. Fraenkel, "Das Dritte Reich als Doppelstaat," p. 519.
56. Ernst Fraenkel, *Der Urdoppelstaat*, in idem., *Gesammelte Schriften*, vol. 2: *Nationalsozialismus und Widerstand*, edited by Alexander v. Brünneck, Hubertus Buchstein, and Gerhard Göhler (Baden-Baden: Nomos, [1938] 1999), pp. 267–473.
57. Ernst Fraenkel, "Erklärung über die Tätigkeit des Herrn Wilhelm Urban in den Jahren 1933 bis 1938 vom 22. Oktober 1953," BArch N 1274 (Fraenkel, Ernst)/ 11, reprinted in idem., *Gesammelte Schriften*, vol. 2: *Nationalsozialismus und Widerstand*, edited by Alexander v. Brünneck, Hubertus Buchstein, and Gerhard Göhler (Baden-Baden: Nomos, 1999), p. 625.
58. As Fraenkel wrote, "At the time of writing, I never thought that the book, originally drafted in German, would ever be published in German." Ernst Fraenkel, "Preface to the 1974 German Edition," p. xiii.
59. Fraenkel, "Preface to the 1974 German Edition," p. xviii.
60. Fraenkel, "Preface to the 1974 German Edition," p. xv.
61. David Collier, "Data, Field Work, and Extracting New Ideas at Close Range," *APSA-CP: Newsletter of the Organized Section in Comparative Politics of the American Political Science Association*, No. 10 (1999), pp. 1–6.
62. Staatsbibliothek zu Berlin, http://staatsbibliothek-berlin.de/en/about-the-library/geschichte/
63. Ernst Fraenkel, "Preface" (1939), New York Public Library, Manuscripts and Archives Division, American Committee for the Guidance of Professional Personnel records, Box 2, Fraenkel, Ernst "The Dual State."
64. Ernst Fraenkel, "Preface."
65. Fraenkel, *Der Urdoppelstaat*, p. 359.
66. Fraenkel, "Preface to the 1974 German Edition," p. xix.
67. Nikolaus Wachsmann, *KL: A History of the Nazi Concentration Camps* (New York: Little, Brown, 2015), p. 181.
68. The source for the anecdote about the carbon copy is Wolfgang Müller. He made this claim on September 29, 2009, as quoted in Simone Ladwig-Winters, *Ernst Fraenkel: Ein politisches Leben* (New York: Campus, 2009), p. 357, fn. 148. Otto Suhr, a Social Democrat, was a lifelong friend of Fraenkel's. Between 1955 and his death in 1957, Suhr was mayor of West Berlin. In 1920, Suhr had founded the Deutsche Hochschule für Politik (DHfP), in effect the country's first department of political science. In 1940, the DHfP formally became a part of Berlin's Friedrich-Wilhelms-Universität (the forerunner of today's Humboldt Universität). In the wake of World War II, in 1948, Suhr's institution was re-established. Shortly thereafter it was integrated into the newly founded Freie Universität Berlin, or FU, the city's free university, and relocated from the city center to Dahlem in southwestern Berlin. The revived DHfP eventually merged with the FU's new Institut für politische Wissenschaft (IfpW), its Institute of Political Science. The resultant

institute was later renamed the Otto-Suhr-Institut, or OSI, and quickly grew into Germany's best-known and largest department of political science. All of this seemingly arcane information is relevant because it was Suhr (along with Neumann), who persuaded an ambivalent Fraenkel to bid farewell to the United States—his new home—and return to Germany to help in the reconstruction and development (not to mention democratization) of his first. And it was at the DHfP and FU, where Fraenkel resumed his academic career in 1951. To gain a glimpse of Fraenkel's esteem for Suhr, see Ernst Fraenkel, "Otto Suhr zum Gedächtnis," in idem., *Reformismus und Pluralismus: Materialien zu einer ungeschriebenen Biographie*, edited by Falk Esche and Frank Grube (Hamburg: Hoffman und Campe, [1957] 1973), pp. 369–88.

69. Fraenkel, "Preface to the 1974 German Edition," pp. xviii–xix.
70. Alexander v. Brünneck, "Vorwort zu diesem Band," in Ernst Fraenkel, *Gesammelte Schriften*, vol. 2: *Nationalsozialismus und Widerstand*, edited by Alexander v. Brünneck, Hubertus Buchstein, and Gerhard Göhler (Baden-Baden: Nomos, 1999), p. 14.
71. See BArch N 1274 (Fraenkel, Ernst)/151; BArch N 1274 (Fraenkel, Ernst)/152. Both are transfer prints; the original manuscript of the *Urdoppelstaat* is lost.
72. v. Brünneck, "Vorwort zu diesem Band" (vol. 2), pp. 14–15.
73. Ernst Fraenkel, Letter to Dr. Köhler, Director of the Library, Otto-Suhr-Institut, April 5, 1969, N 1274 (Fraenkel, Ernst)/62.
74. Fraenkel, "Preface to the 1974 German Edition," p. xiii.
75. Ernst Fraenkel, Letter to Alexander v. Brünneck, April 23, 1970, BArch N 1274 (Fraenkel, Ernst)/98. See also v. Brünneck, "Vorwort zu diesem Band" (vol. 2), p. 17.
76. Compare Fraenkel, *Der Urdoppelstaat*; and Ernst Fraenkel, *Der Doppelstaat*, in idem., *Gesammelte Schriften*, vol. 2: *Nationalsozialismus und Widerstand*, edited by Alexander v. Brünneck, Hubertus Buchstein, and Gerhard Göhler (Baden-Baden: Nomos, [1974] 1999), pp. 33–266. For the purpose of this exercise, I leave aside for the moment the editorial and substantive differences between the 1941 English edition and the 1974 German edition. The latter was the product of a slightly modified retranslation of the former. See further below for a discussion.
77. Ernst Fraenkel, *Der Doppelstaat*, in Fraenkel, *Gesammelte Schriften*, vol. 2, pp. 33–259 (excluding three appendices that were neither parts of the *Urdoppelstaat* nor the 1941 English edition); Ernst Fraenkel, *Der Urdoppelstaat*, in Fraenkel, *Gesammelte Schriften*, vol. 2, pp. 267–473. By way of comparison, the published English edition of 1941 was 248 pages long, including end matter.
78. Fraenkel, *Der Doppelstaat*, pp. 173–84; Fraenkel, *Der Urdoppelstaat*, pp. 384–400.
79. See, for example, Franz Neumann's glowing review of Harold Laski's 1935 *The State in Theory and Practice*, which he praised for coming to "a real Marxist conclusion." See also idem., "On the Marxist Theory of the State," in Keith Tribe, ed., *Social Democracy and the Rule of Law: Otto Kirchheimer and Franz Neumann* (London: Allen and Unwin, [1935] 1987), p. 76. For an influential

critique of functionalist, and especially class-based, analyses in the social sciences that focused on their lack of microfoundations, see Jon Elster, "Cohen on Marx's Theory of History: Review of G. A. Cohen, *Karl Marx's Theory of History*," *Political Studies*, Vol. 28 (1980), pp. 121–8; and, for a fuller statement, Jon Elster, *Making Sense of Marx* (Cambridge: Cambridge University Press, 1985).

80. Fraenkel, *Der Urdoppelstaat*, p. 441.
81. Joseph A. Schumpeter, *Capitalism, Socialism, and Democracy* (New York: Harper, 1942).
82. Joseph A. Schumpeter, "The Sociology of Imperialisms," in Joseph A. Schumpeter, *The Economics and Sociology of Capitalism*, edited by Richard Swedberg (Princeton: Princeton University Press, [1918] 1991), pp. 141–219.
83. Schumpeter, "The Sociology of Imperialisms," p. 144.
84. Fraenkel, *Der Urdoppelstaat*, p. 441.
85. New York Public Library, Manuscripts and Archives Division, American Committee for the Guidance of Professional Personnel records, Box 2, Fraenkel, Ernst "The Dual State." Here and in subsequent references to the NYPL draft, I silently incorporated all of Fraenkel's handwritten corrections into the excerpted section.
86. New York Public Library, Manuscripts and Archives Division, American Committee for the Guidance of Professional Personnel records, Box 2, Fraenkel, Ernst "The Dual State."
87. New York Public Library, Manuscripts and Archives Division, American Committee for the Guidance of Professional Personnel records, Box 2, Fraenkel, Ernst "The Dual State."
88. Ernst Fraenkel, *The Dual State: A Contribution to the Theory of Dictatorship*, translated by E. A. Shils, in collaboration with Edith Loewenstein and Klaus Knorr, with an Introduction by Jens Meierhenrich (Oxford: Oxford University Press, [1941] 2017), pp. 66–7. On Locke's concept of the prerogative, see, for example, Pasquale Pasquino, "Locke on King's Prerogative," *Political Theory*, Vol. 26 (1998), pp. 198–208. More generally, see Clement Fatovic, "The Political Theology of Prerogative: The Jurisprudential Miracle in Liberal Constitutional Thought," *Perspectives on Politics*, Vol. 6 (2008), pp. 487–501.
89. Fraenkel, *The Dual State*, p. 67.
90. Fraenkel, *The Dual State*, p. 66. See John Locke, *Two Treatises of Government*, edited by Peter Laslett (Cambridge: Cambridge University Press, [1690], 1988), p. 373, §158. In full, the relevant passage reads as follows: "*Prerogative* being nothing but a Power in the hands of the Prince to provide for the public good, in such Cases, which depending upon unforeseen and uncertain Occurrences, certain and unalterable Laws could not safely direct, whatsoever shall be done manifestly for the good of the People, and the establishing the Government upon its true Foundation, is, and always will be just *Prerogative*."
91. Locke, *Two Treatises of Government*, p. 375, §159.
92. Pasquino, "Locke on King's Prerogative," p. 205.

93. "Tending to evil" is the translation of the Latin term "*malignus*."
94. Fraenkel, "Preface to the 1974 German Edition," pp. xiii–xiv.
95. Fraenkel, *The Dual State*, p. v; Martin Jay, *The Dialectical Imagination. A History of the Frankfurt School and the Institute of Social Research 1923–1950*, Second edition (Berkeley: University of California Press, 1996), p. 39. See also my discussion of Neumann's association with the Institute for Social Research in Chapter 2.
96. The figure stems from Ladwig-Winters, *Ernst Fraenkel*, p. 140.
97. Max Horkheimer, Letter to Ernst Fraenkel, February 9, 1939, as quoted in Ladwig-Winters, *Ernst Fraenkel*, p. 148.
98. New York Public Library, Manuscripts and Archives Division, American Committee for the Guidance of Professional Personnel records, Box 2, Fraenkel, Ernst "The Dual State."
99. The corrections were done in different handwriting styles, one of which was likely Fraenkel's.
100. New York Public Library, Manuscripts and Archives Division, American Committee for the Guidance of Professional Personnel records, Box 2, Fraenkel, Ernst "The Dual State;" Fraenkel, *Der Urdoppelstaat* [1938], pp. 270, 440.
101. Fraenkel, *The Dual State*, pp. xi, 171; Fraenkel, *Der Doppelstaat*, pp. 36, 223.
102. Ladwig-Winters, *Ernst Fraenkel*, p. 144.
103. Cf. New York Public Library, Manuscripts and Archives Division, American Committee for the Guidance of Professional Personnel records, Box 2, Fraenkel, Ernst "The Dual State;" Fraenkel, *The Dual State*, p. 172. Emphases added.
104. New York Public Library, Manuscripts and Archives Division, American Committee for the Guidance of Professional Personnel records, Box 2, Fraenkel, Ernst "The Dual State."
105. New York Public Library, Manuscripts and Archives Division, American Committee for the Guidance of Professional Personnel records, Box 2, Fraenkel, Ernst "The Dual State;" Fraenkel, *The Dual State*, p. vi. In an aside, it is perhaps worth noting that Fraenkel's time at the University of Chicago overlapped with that of Friedrich Hayek, who was there completing the book that would make him a household name, *The Road to Serfdom* (London: Routledge, 1944).
106. New York Public Library, Manuscripts and Archives Division, American Committee for the Guidance of Professional Personnel records, Box 2, Fraenkel, Ernst "The Dual State."
107. Ladwig-Winters, *Ernst Fraenkel*, p. 151.
108. Fraenkel, *The Dual* State, pp. v, 66.
109. Ernst Fraenkel, Letter to David Riesmann [*sic*], November 17, 1939, New York Public Library, Manuscripts and Archives Division, American Committee for the Guidance of Professional Personnel records, Box 2, Fraenkel, Ernst "The Dual State."
110. Fraenkel, Letter to David Riesmann [*sic*].
111. Fraenkel received his J.D. from University of Chicago Law School on June 10, 1941.

CHAPTER 7

1. Georg Wilhelm Friedrich Hegel, *The Science of Logic*, translated and edited by George di Giovanni (Cambridge: Cambridge University Press, [1812–1831] 2010), pp. 382, 383.
2. I will not dwell in this chapter on Fraenkel's lengthy—and idiosyncratic—ruminations in *The Dual State* about the theory and history of the natural law tradition. See Ernst Fraenkel, *The Dual State: A Contribution to the Theory of Dictatorship*, translated by E. A. Shils, in collaboration with Edith Loewenstein and Klaus Knorr, with an Introduction by Jens Meierhenrich (Oxford: Oxford University Press, [1941] 2017), pp. 107–49. For a recent, comparative analysis, see Douglas G. Morris, "Write and Resist: Ernst Fraenkel and Franz Neumann on the Role of Natural Law in Fighting Nazi Tyranny," *New German Critique*, Vol. 126 (2015), pp. 197–230. See also William E. Scheuerman, "Social Democracy and the Rule of Law: The Legacy of Ernst Fraenkel," in Peter C. Caldwell and William E. Scheuerman, eds., *From Liberal Democracy to Fascism* (Boston: Humanities Press, 2000) pp. 76–85.
3. Fraenkel, *The Dual State*, p. 153.
4. The most comprehensive account of the Nazi debate is Christian Hilger, *Rechtsstaatsbegriffe im Dritten Reich: Eine Strukturanalyse* (Tübingen: Mohr, 2003). On one important sub-strand thereof, see Peter C. Caldwell, "National Socialism and Constitutional Law: Carl Schmitt, Otto Koellreutter, and the Debate over the Nature of the Nazi State, 1933–1937," *Cardozo Law Review*, Vol. 16 (1994), pp. 399–427. Helpful overviews are Michael Stolleis, "Im Bauch des Leviathan—Staatsrechtslehre im Nationalsozialismus," in Michael Stolleis, *Recht im Unrecht: Studien zur Rechtsgeschichte des Nationalsozialismus* (Frankfurt: Suhrkamp, [1989] 1994), pp. 126–46; and Michael Stolleis, *A History of Public Law in Germany, 1914–1945*, translated by Thomas Dunlap (Oxford: Oxford University Press, [1999] 2004), pp. 332–58. On the continuing, now purely scholarly debate about the nature of the Nazi state, see, among others, the following representative works from five different decades in the historiography of Germany: Hans Buchheim, Martin Broszat, Hans-Adolf Jacobsen, and Helmut Krausnick, eds., *Anatomie des SS-Staates*, Seventh edition (Munich: dtv, [1967] 1999); Martin Broszat, *Der Staat Hitlers: Grundlegung und Entwicklung seiner inneren Verfassung* (Munich: dtv, 1969); Peter Hüttenberger, "Nationalsozialistische Polykratie," *Geschichte und Gesellschaft*, Vol. 2 (1976), 417–42; Norbert Frei, *Der Führerstaat: Nationalsozialistische Herrschaft 1933 bis 1945* (Munich: dtv, 1987); Jane Caplan, *Government without Administration: State and Civil Service in Weimar and Nazi Germany* (Oxford: Clarendon Press, 1988); Michael Burleigh and Wolfgang Wippermann, *The Racial State: Germany 1933–1945* (Cambridge: Cambridge University Press, 1991); Ulrich von Hehl, *Nationalsozialistische Herrschaft* (Munich: Oldenbourg, 1996); and Mark Roseman, Devin O. Pendas, and Richard Wetzell, eds., *Beyond the Racial State* (Cambridge: Cambridge University Press, 2017). Useful overviews of the state of the scholarly debate include Robert Gellately, "Situating the

'SS-State' in a Social-Historical Context: Recent Histories of the SS, the Police, and the Courts in the Third Reich," *Journal of Modern History*, Vol. 64 (1992), pp. 338–65; and Ian Kershaw, "'Working Towards the Führer': Reflections on the Nature of the Hitler Dictatorship," *Contemporary European History*, Vol. 2 (1993), pp. 103–18.

5. Fraenkel, *The Dual State*, p. xvi.
6. Jens Meierhenrich, "Bringing the 'Dual State' Back In," Paper presented at the American Political Science Association Meeting, San Francisco, August 30–September 2, 2001.
7. Fraenkel, "Preface to the 1974 German edition," p. xv.
8. Fraenkel, *The Dual State*, p. xiii.
9. Fraenkel, *The Dual State*, p. xiii.
10. It is worth noting that the distinction between prerogative state and normative state is reminiscent of Immanuel Kant's distinction between "*Macht*" and "*Geist*." Seeing that "the dualistic tradition" of distinguishing between power and spirit has, according to Mary Fulbrook, "been popularized as one of the enduring features of subsequent German thought," it stands to reason that Fraenkel's conceptualization of institutional hybridity in the 1930s has theoretical antecedents stretching back to the eighteenth century. Mary Fulbrook, *A Concise History of Germany*, Second edition (Cambridge: Cambridge University Press, 2004), p. 92.
11. Helmut Ridder, "Der Doppelstaat: Die Ehe von Kapitalismus und NS-Diktatur," *Die Zeit*, June 12, 1970. Upon closer inspection, it becomes clear that Ridder's slight was unintentional; a poor choice of words rather than a dismissal of its significance. Indeed Ridder, in the same article, goes on to highlight what he considered several of the book's achievements (as well as a few shortcomings).
12. Horst Dreier, "Nachwort: Was ist doppelt am 'Doppelstaat'? Zu Rezeption und Bedeutung der klassischen Studie von Ernst Fraenkel," in Ernst Fraenkel, *Der Doppelstaat*, Third edition, edited with an Introduction by Alexander v. Brünneck, with an Afterword by Horst Dreier (Frankfurt: Europäische Verlagsanstalt, 2012), p. 300; Jens Meierhenrich, *The Legacies of Law: Long-Run Consequences of Legal Development in South Africa, 1652–2000* (Cambridge: Cambridge University Press, 2008), esp. pp. 3–5, 76–9.
13. Fraenkel, *The Dual State*, p. 24.
14. For a careful and detailed empirical account, see, for example, Hans Mommsen, *The Rise and Fall of Weimar Democracy*, translated by Elborg Forster and Larry Eugene Jones (Chapel Hill: University of North Carolina Press, 1996), esp. Chapters 11–13. Although critical of the concept of totalitarianism, Fraenkel, rather confusingly, used the adjective "totalitarian" nonetheless in the opening paragraph of *The Dual State* to describe the regime type of Hitler's Germany: "Totalitarian," he wrote, "is a word of many meanings too often inadequately defined. In this treatise we have tried to isolate one important characteristic of the totalitarian state in Germany, and by studying this fundamental aspect of the National-Socialist regime we hope to make clearer the legal reality of the Third Reich." Fraenkel, *The Dual State*, p. xiii.

15. Fraenkel, *The Dual State*, p. xiii.
16. Fraenkel, *The Dual State*, p. 3.
17. Fraenkel, *The Dual State*, pp. 9, 23, 33–7.
18. Fraenkel, *The Dual State*, pp. 14–33, 46–9.
19. Fraenkel, *The Dual State*, p. 44.
20. Horst Dreier, "Nachwort," pp. 282–95.
21. Ernst Fraenkel, "Das Dritte Reich als Doppelstaat," in idem., *Gesammelte Schriften, vol. 2: Nationalsozialismus und Widerstand*, edited by Alexander v. Brünneck, Hubertus Buchstein, and Gerhard Göhler (Baden-Baden: Nomos, [1937] 1999), pp. 513–14.
22. Dreier, "Nachwort," pp. 284–5; Carl Schmitt, *The Concept of the Political*, Expanded edition, translated with an Introduction and Notes by George Schwab (Chicago: University of Chicago Press, [1932] 2007). For key treatments of Schmitt's infamous concept, see Duncan Kelly, *The State of the Political: Conceptions of Politics and the State in the Thought of Max Weber, Carl Schmitt and Franz Neumann* (Oxford: Oxford University Press, 2003), Chapter 4; and Reinhard Mehring, ed., *Carl Schmitt, Der Begriff des Politischen: Ein kooperativer Kommentar* (Berlin: Akademie Verlag, 2003). Most recently, see also Jens Meierhenrich and Oliver Simons, "'A Fanatic of Order in an Epoch of Confusing Turmoil': The Political, Legal, and Cultural Thought of Carl Schmitt," in Jens Meierhenrich and Oliver Simons, eds., *The Oxford Handbook of Carl Schmitt* (Oxford: Oxford University Press, 2016), esp. pp. 21–5.
23. As quoted in Fraenkel, *The Dual State*, p. 16. The case was reported in *Deutsche Richter-Zeitung*, Vol. 27 (1935), p. 624.
24. As quoted in Fraenkel, *The Dual State*, p. 16.
25. Kammergericht, May 31, 1935.
26. Fraenkel, *The Dual State*, p. 3.
27. Dreier, "Nachwort," pp. 286–90.
28. Dreier, "Nachwort," p. 290.
29. For a brief summary, see Dreier, "Nachwort," pp. 81–3.
30. Fraenkel, *The Dual State*, p. 27.
31. Fraenkel, *The Dual State*, p. 28.
32. On the nature and function of the *Sondergerichte*, see the discussion below. For a comprehensive analysis of cultures of legality, their study and path dependent effects, see Meierhenrich, *The Legacies of Law*, pp. 219–64.
33. *Pars pro toto* of a vast body of increasingly interdisciplinary scholarship, see Fernanda Pirie, *Anthropology of Law* (Oxford: Oxford University Press, 2013). For a set of empirical investigations, see, among many others, Javier A. Couso, Alexandra Huneeus, and Rachel Sieder, eds., *Cultures of Legality: Judicialization and Political Activism in Latin America* (Cambridge: Cambridge University Press, 2010).
34. Dreier, "Nachwort," p. 291.
35. Otto Kirchheimer, "Politics and Justice," *Social Research*, Vol. 22 (1955), p. 377. For his famous book-length treatment, see idem., *Political Justice: The Use of Legal Procedure for Political Ends* (Princeton: Princeton University Press, 1961).

36. Fraenkel, *The Dual State*, p. 51.
37. *Oberlandesgericht* Munich, August 12, 1937, as quoted in *The Dual State*, p. 52. The case was reported in *Deutsche Justiz*, Vol. 100 (1938), p. 724.
38. Fraenkel, *The Dual State*, pp. 51–2.
39. Fraenkel, *The Dual State*, p. 206.
40. Fraenkel, *The Dual State*, p. 206.
41. See Fraenkel, *The Dual State*, Part II, Chapter 3; and Part III, Chapters 1, 2, and 3.
42. Fraenkel, *The Dual State*, p. 159.
43. See also my brief intellectual history of the *Rechtsstaat* in Chapter 4.
44. Otto Hintze traced the origins of the *Rechtsstaat* to this period. Otto Hintze, "Preußens Entwicklung zum Rechtsstaat," in idem., *Regierung Verwaltung: Gesammelte Abhandlungen zur Staats-, Rechts- und Sozialgeschichte*, edited by Gerhard Oestreich (Göttingen: Vandenhock und Ruprecht, 1967), esp. pp. 99–123. Another constitutional monarchy with a greater appetite for normative than prerogative rule was that of Austria under emperor Joseph II (1765–1790).
45. For a discussion of the *Rechtsstaat* concept, see, most important, Ernst-Wolfgang Böckenförde, "Entstehung und Wandel des Rechtsstaatsbegriffs" [1969], in idem., *Recht, Staat, Freiheit: Studien zur Rechtsphilosophie, Staatstheorie und Verfassungsgerichtsbarkeit* (Frankfurt: Suhrkamp, 1991), pp. 143–69. On the meaning(s) of the rule of law, see, for example, Allan C. Hutchinson and Patrick Monahan, eds., *The Rule of Law: Ideal or Ideology?* (Toronto: Carswell, 1987).
46. Fraenkel, *The Dual State*, pp. 50, 71. Pursuant to the Decree of the Reich President for the Defense against Malicious Attacks against the Government of the National Uprising (*Verordnung des Reichspräsidenten zur Abwehr heimtückischer Angriffe gegen die Regierung der nationalen Erhebung*) of March 21, 1933, a Nazi *Sondergericht* was established in each of Germany's judicial districts. See Nikolaus Wachsmann, *Hitler's Prisons: Legal Terror in Nazi Germany* (New Haven: Yale University Press, 2004), p. 114. For an overview, see also Hans Wüllenweber, *Sondergerichte im Dritten Reich: Vergessene Verbrechen der Justiz* (Munich: Luchterhand, 1993).
47. Wachsmann, *Hitler's Prisons*, p. 114.
48. Fraenkel, *The Dual State*, p. 71.
49. Fraenkel, *The Dual State*, p. 71.
50. Fraenkel, *The Dual State*, p. 107.
51. Fraenkel, *The Dual State*, p. xv.
52. Fraenkel, *The Dual State*, p. 51.
53. Dreier, "Nachwort," p. 270. Horst Möller, "Fraenkel—Analytiker von Demokratie und Diktatur," in Thomas Brechenmacher, ed., *Identität und Erinnerung: Schlüsselthemen deutsch-jüdischer Geschichte und Gegenwart* (Munich: Olzog, 2009), p. 168. One of the most flagrant misinterpretations has come from one of Germany's most respected historians, Karl Dietrich Bracher, who erroneously maintained that Fraenkel's Janus-faced concept referred to an institutional binary—state vs. party—that Fraenkel explicitly

and repeatedly insisted was *not* what he had in mind when speaking of the legal reality of the dual state. See Karl Dietrich Bracher, "Zusammenbruch des Versailler Systems und Zweiter Weltkrieg," in Golo Mann and August Nitschke, eds., *Propyläen Weltgeschichte: Eine Universalgeschichte*, vol. 9: *Das zwanzigste Jahrhundert* (Berlin: Propyläen, 1960), pp. 398–9. The concept of the dual state is entirely absent from Bracher's bestselling *The German Dictatorship: The Origins, Structure, and Effects of National Socialism*, translated from the German by Jean Steinberg, with an Introduction by Peter Gay (London: Weidenfeld and Nicolson, 1971). More recently, Robert O. Paxton also misread *The Dual State*. See his *The Anatomy of Fascism* (London: Penguin, 2005), pp. 119–27. Like Bracher, he completely misunderstood the essence of Fraenkel's argument, namely that "the line of division" between the prerogative and normative halves of the Nazi dual state is internal to the institutional structure of the state itself. Fraenkel insisted that "when we speak of the Dual State we do not refer to the co-existence of the state bureaucracy and the party bureaucracy. We do not place great importance on this feature of German constitutional law. [...] State and party are increasingly becoming identical, the dual organizational form is maintained merely for historical and political reasons." Fraenkel, *The Dual State*, p. xv. Or, as he put it later in the book, the NSDAP was neither identical *with* nor separate *from*, but rather "an instrument *of* the Prerogative State." Ibid, p. 33. Emphasis added.

54. See, for example, Reinhard Bendix, *Nation-Building and Citizenship*, Enlarged edition (Berkeley: University of California Press, 1977). Note that Bendix uses varying terms to refer to what he calls conflicting imperatives. More recently, see Andrew C. Gould, "Conflicting Imperatives and Concept Formation," *Review of Politics*, Vol. 61 (1999), pp. 439–63.
55. Fraenkel, *The Dual State*, p. 57.
56. Fraenkel, *The Dual State*, p. 168.
57. Georg Jellinek, *Allgemeine Staatslehre*, Third edition (Berlin: Häring, [1900] 1914).
58. Fraenkel, *The Dual State*, p. 69.
59. Ernst Fraenkel, "Introduction to the 1941 Edition," in idem., *The Dual State: A Contribution to the Theory of Dictatorship*, p. xxiv. Note that the pagination of the 2017 edition differs from that of the original OUP edition, though *only* for Fraenkel's brief Introduction. All other page numbers are identical. In the 1941 edition, the above quote appears on p. xiv.
60. Fraenkel, *The Dual State*, p. 39.
61. Fraenkel, "Das Dritte Reich als Doppelstaat," p. 514.
62. Ernst Fraenkel, "Auflösung und Verfall des Rechts im III. Reich," in idem., *Gesammelte Schriften*, vol. 2: *Nationalsozialismus und Widerstand*, edited by Alexander v. Brünneck, Hubertus Buchstein, and Gerhard Göhler (Baden-Baden: Nomos, [1960] 1999), p. 616.
63. For an account of the entire trajectory of Jewish suffering in particular—from persecution to destruction—at the hands of an ever expanding prerogative state in Nazi Germany, see, most recently, Christian Gerlach, *The*

Extermination of the European Jews (Cambridge: Cambridge University Press, 2016).

64. Fraenkel, *The Dual State*, p. 73.
65. Fraenkel, *The Dual State*, p. 90.
66. Fraenkel, *The Dual State*, p. 173.
67. Fraenkel, *The Dual State*, p. 173. Emphasis added.
68. Fraenkel, *The Dual State*, pp. 173, 176–82.
69. On the concept of the garrison state that was holding sway at the time, see Harold D. Lasswell, "The Garrison State," *American Journal of Sociology*, Vol. 46 (1941), pp. 455–68.
70. On analytical eclecticism as a research stance, see Rudra Sil and Peter J. Katzenstein, "Analytic Eclecticism in the Study of World Politics: Reconfiguring Problems and Mechanisms across Research Traditions," *Perspectives on Politics*, Vol. 8 (2010), pp. 411–31. For an interesting, retrospective recasting as a social scientist of another important theorist of institutions, see Jon Elster, *Alexis de Tocqueville: The First Social Scientist* (Cambridge: Cambridge University Press, 2009).
71. Scheuerman, "Social Democracy and the Rule of Law," p. 74, fn. 1. I venture that in contemporary Germany, many political scientists might disagree. There, for reasons that are beyond the scope of this chapter, Fraenkel's writings from the 1950s and 1960s have probably left more of a mark on the discipline than *The Dual State*. His most widely admired—and assigned—work is arguably *Deutschland und die westlichen Demokratien*, first published in 1964. See Ernst Fraenkel, *Deutschland und die westlichen Demokratien*, enlarged edition, edited by Alexander v. Brünneck (Frankfurt: Suhrkamp, [1964] 1991). For an insightful discussion of Fraenkel's postwar influence on the theory, practice, and study of democracy in the Federal Republic of Germany, see Alexander v. Brünneck, "Vorwort zu diesem Band," in Ernst Fraenkel, *Gesammelte Schriften*, vol. 5: *Demokratie und Pluralismus*, edited by Alexander v. Brünneck (Baden-Baden: Nomos, 2007), pp. 9–36, esp. 21–5.
72. Lest my allusion to the formulation's double meaning is lost, my point is this: The theory of dictatorship that Fraenkel developed in *The Dual State* was the *subject* of his life, but it was also the subject of his *life*.
73. As we have seen, the empirical coverage in *The Dual State* ended in the late 1930s, but Fraenkel's postwar commentary suggests he harbored no illusions about having produced an institutional analysis that was valid not only for the pre-war years but for the wars years as well.
74. Fraenkel, *The Dual State*, p. 59.
75. Fraenkel, *The Dual State*, p. 60.
76. Fraenkel, *The Dual State*, p. 70.
77. Fraenkel, *The Dual State*, p. 70; A. V. Dicey, *Introduction to the Study of the Law of the Constitution*, Eighth edition (London: Macmillan, 1926), p. 198.
78. Fraenkel, *The Dual State*, p. 71.
79. Fraenkel, *The Dual State*, p. 72.
80. Fraenkel, *The Dual State*, p. 73.
81. Fraenkel, *The Dual State*, pp. 73–82.

82. Fraenkel, *The Dual State*, p. xiv.
83. See my discussion in Chapter 6.
84. Fraenkel, *The Dual State*, pp. 171, 172.
85. On the economics of the interwar order, see Adam Tooze, *The Wages of Destruction: The Making and Breaking of the Nazi Economy* (London: Penguin, 2008); and Nicholas Crafts and Peter Fearon, eds., *The Great Depression of the 1930s: Lessons for Today* (Oxford: Oxford University Press, 2013).
86. Fraenkel, *The Dual State*, p. 172.
87. Fraenkel, *The Dual State*, p. 172.
88. Richard Overy, *The Nazi Economic Recovery 1932–1938*, Second edition (Cambridge: Cambridge University Press, 1996), p. 1.
89. Fraenkel, *The Dual State*, p. 172.
90. Fraenkel, *The Dual State*, p. 185.
91. Fraenkel, *The Dual State*, p. 185.
92. Fraenkel, *The Dual State*, p. 186.
93. Fraenkel, *The Dual State*, pp. 186–7.
94. Fraenkel, *The Dual State*, p. 185.
95. Fraenkel, *The Dual State*, p. 185.
96. Fraenkel, *The Dual State*, p. 185.
97. Douglass C. North, *Institutions, Institutional Change and Economic Performance* (Cambridge: Cambridge University Press, 1990). Whereas Fraenkel's book is a forgotten classic, North's book by the summer of 2016 had a racked up total of 48,038 citations on Google Scholar. See https://scholar.google.co.uk/citations?view_op=view_citation&hl=en&user=-LcMZqMAAAAJ&citation_for_view=-LcMZqMAAAAJ:u5HHmVD_uO8C, last accessed on July 24, 2016.
98. North, *Institutions, Institutional Change and Economic Performance*, p. 3.
99. For a solid overview, see Kathleen Thelen, "Historical Institutionalism in Comparative Politics," *Annual Review of Political Science*, Vol. 2 (1999), pp. 369–404. For a more recent set of treaments of historical institutionalism as an approach to, *inter alia*, the study of comparative politics, international relations, American politics, and European politics, see Orfeo Fioretos, Tulia G. Falleti, and Adam Sheingate, eds., *The Oxford Handbook of Historical Institutionalism* (Oxford: Oxford University Press, 2016).
100. See my discussion above and Fraenkel, *The Dual State*, p. 57.
101. Scheuerman, "Social Democracy and the Rule of Law," p. 90.
102. Fraenkel, *The Dual State*, p. 205.
103. Fraenkel, *The Dual State*, p. 205.
104. Fraenkel, *The Dual State*, p. 205.
105. Fraenkel, *The Dual State*, p. 203.
106. For a discussion of violence that is in line with my understanding of varieties of violence, see Charles Tilly, *The Politics of Collective Violence* (Cambridge: Cambridge University Press, 2003), esp. Chapter 1.
107. Fraenkel, *The Dual State*, p. 205.
108. Fraenkel, *The Dual State*, p. 205.

109. Fraenkel, *The Dual State*, pp. 205–6.
110. Scheuerman, "Social Democracy and the Rule of Law," p. 86.
111. Meierhenrich, *The Legacies of Law*, p. 17.
112. Meierhenrich, *The Legacies of Law*, pp. 17–20.
113. Karl Mannheim, *Man and Society in an Age of Reconstruction* (New York: Harcourt, Brace, and World, 1940).
114. Mannheim, *Man and Society in an Age of Reconstruction*, p. 53.
115. Mannheim, *Man and Society in an Age of Reconstruction*, p. 53.
116. Scheuerman, "Social Democracy and the Rule of Law," p. 93.
117. Fraenkel, *The Dual State*, p. 208.
118. Fraenkel, *The Dual State*, p. 208.
119. Fraenkel, *The Dual State*, p. 208.
120. Hans Kelsen, "The Party-Dictatorship, *Politica*, Vol. 2 (1936), p. 32.
121. Fraenkel, *The Dual State*, p. 203. Fraenkel described the "Nationalist-Socialist conception of politics" as revolving around one national interest, and one national interest only: "the central interest in power for the sake of power." Ibid, p. 202.
122. Fraenkel, *The Dual State*, p. 208.
123. It is unclear why Fraenkel equivocated. It may well have been out of caution. After all, he was desperately trying to make ends meet in a new and unfamiliar country. I am more inclined, however, to think that Fraenkel was undergoing an intellectual transformation. Under the influence of new ideas, his thought (and politics) gained new nuances. His lifelong admiration for, and the gratitude he felt he owed the United States for granting him refuge, are further suggestive of an expressive rather than instrumental reason for his rethinking the political economy of dictatorship. I thank Douglas Morris for pushing me to elaborate on the reasons for Fraenkel's equivocation.
124. The question has since been answered. Most important, see Tooze, *The Wages of Destruction*. For a pithy account, see Overy, *The Nazi Economic Recovery 1932–1938*.
125. Fraenkel, *The Dual State*, p. 203.
126. Fraenkel, *The Dual State*, p. 203.
127. Fraenkel, *The Dual State*, p. 202.
128. See, for example, Fraenkel, *The Dual State*, p. 197. For contending evaluations of the peace settlement and its consequences, see Patrick O. Cohrs, *The Unfinished Peace after World War I: America, Britain and the Stabilisation of Europe, 1919–1932* (Cambridge: Cambridge University Press, 2006); Manfred F. Boemeke, Gerald D. Feldman, and Elisabeth Glaser, eds., *The Treaty of Versailles: A Reassessment after 75 Years* (Cambridge: Cambridge University Press, 2008); Norman A. Graebner and Edward M. Bennett, *The Versailles Treaty and its Legacy: The Failure Of The Wilsonian Vision* (Cambridge: Cambridge University Press, 2011).
129. Fraenkel, *The Dual State*, p. 205.
130. Scheuerman, "Social Democracy and the Rule of Law," p. 88.
131. Scheuerman, "Social Democracy and the Rule of Law," p. 90. See also my critique of Neumann's *Behemoth* in Chapter 2.

132. Fraenkel, *The Dual State*, p. 183.
133. Fraenkel, *The Dual State*, p. 184.
134. For a much cited, but controversial contribution to this debate, see Daron Acemoglu and James A. Morrison, *Economic Origins of Dictatorship and Democracy* (Cambridge: Cambridge University Press, 2006), a response by two economists to Barrington Moore's social science classic, *Social Origins of Dictatorship and Democracy: Lord and Peasant in the Making of the Modern World* (Boston: Beacon Press, 1966).
135. Acemoglu and Morrison, *Economic Origins of Dictatorship and Democracy*, p. 173.
136. Herbert Marcuse, *One-Dimensional Man: Studies in the Ideology of Advanced Industrial Society* (Boston: Beacon Press, 1964). On game-theoretical accounts of dictatorship, see, among others, Mancur Olson, "Dictatorship, Democracy, and Development," *American Political Science Review*, Vol. 87 (1993), pp. 567–76; Roland Wintrope, *The Political Economy of Dictatorship* (Cambridge: Cambridge University Press, 1998); and Jennifer Gandhi, *Political Institutions under Dictatorship* (Cambridge: Cambridge University Press, 2008).
137. Generally, see Alan Supiot, *Homo Juridicus: On the Anthropological Function of the Law* (London: Verso, 2007).

CHAPTER 8

1. Ernst Fraenkel, "Das Dritte Reich als Doppelstaat," pp. 504–19.
2. From September 1939 to June 1940, Best also served as a section chief in the newly created *Reichssicherheitshauptamt* (Reich Security Main Office, RSHA), where he became involved in the administration of genocidal campaigns in Poland. Between June 1940 and the end of World War II, Best played leading roles in the Nazi occupation of France and Denmark. See the new edition of Ulrich Herbert, *Best: Biographische Studien über Radikalismus, Weltanschauung und Vernunft* (Munich: Beck, 2016) for an authoritative guide to Best's march through Nazi institutions.
3. Werner Best, "Neubegründung des Polizeirechts," *Jahrbuch der Akademie für Deutsches Recht*, Vol. 5 (1937), p. 133.
4. Best, "Neubegründung des Polizeirechts," p. 133. Note that this passage appears in a very different, less accurate translation in *The Dual State*. See Ernst Fraenkel, *The Dual State: A Contribution to the Theory of Dictatorship*, translated by E. A. Shils, in collaboration with Edith Loewenstein and Klaus Knorr, with an Introduction by Jens Meierhenrich (Oxford: Oxford University Press, [1941] 2017), p. 62.
5. As translated and quoted in Fraenkel, *The Dual State*, p. 62.
6. As Hayek writes, "The law tells him [a given individual] what facts he may count on and thereby extends the range within which he can predict the consequences of his actions. [...] Thus the rules under which the citizens act constitute an adaptation of the whole of society to its environment and to the general characteristics of its members. They serve, or should serve, to assist the individuals in forming plans of action that they will have a good

chance of carrying through. [...] Order with reference to society thus means essentially that individual action is guided by successful foresight, that people not only make effective use of their knowledge but can also foresee with a high degree of confidence [courtesy of extant rules] what collaboration they can expect from others." F. A. Hayek, *The Collected Works of F. A. Hayek*, vol. 17: *The Constitution of Liberty: The Definitive Edition*, edited by Ronald Hamowy (Chicago: University of Chicago Press, 2011), pp. 225, 226, 229.

7. Best, "Neubegründung des Polizeirechts," p. 133.
8. Best, "Neubegründung des Polizeirechts," p. 133.
9. Best, "Neubegründung des Polizeirechts," p. 133.
10. Fraenkel, "Preface to the 1974 German edition," p. xx.
11. Fraenkel, "Preface to the 1974 German edition," p. xx.
12. Fraenkel, "Preface to the 1974 German edition," p. xx.
13. Helmut Ridder, Letter to Ernst Fraenkel, October 16, 1969, N 1274 (Fraenkel, Ernst)/51.
14. Helmut Ridder, Letter to Alexander v. Brünneck, September 3, 1997, as quoted in Alexander v. Brünneck, "Ernst Fraenkels Urdoppelstaat von 1938 und der Doppelstaat von 1941/1974," in Hubertus Buchstein and Gerhard Göhler, eds., *Vom Sozialismus zum Pluralismus: Beiträge zu Werk und Leben Ernst Fraenkels* (Baden-Baden: Nomos, 2000), p. 41.
15. If Nazi authorities had been aware of the *Urdoppelstaat*'s existence, the avid readers at the OKH would most certainly have been subjected to the unlimited reach and arbitrary power of the regime's prerogative state. No such punishment was ever meted out, which lends further credence to Ridder's interpretation.
16. Ridder, Letter to Ernst Fraenkel.
17. "Notes on Books and Authors," *New York Times*, December 20, 1940.
18. "Books Published Today," *New York Times*, January 6, 1941.
19. As quoted in Simone Ladwig-Winters, *Ernst Fraenkel: Ein politisches Leben* (New York: Campus, 2009), p. 135.
20. See Ernst Fraenkel, Letter to Otto Kahn-Freund, May 20, 1941, London School of Economics and Political Science Archives, Otto Kahn-Freund Collection, Box 16.
21. Other notable reviews, albeit in lower-ranking journals, included Glenn Negley's review in the *American Bar Association Journal*, Vol. 28 (1942), pp. 74–5; and Heinz Guradze's assessment in *Washington University Law Review*, Vol. 27 (1942), pp. 603–7.
22. Fritz Morstein Marx, "Ernst Fraenkel, The Dual State: A Contribution to the Theory of Dictatorship" (Book review), *Harvard Law Review*, Vol. 54 (1941), pp. 1265, 1267.
23. Morstein Marx, "Ernst Fraenkel, The Dual State," p. 1266. Taylor Cole, though overall impressed with the book, was less enamored with Fraenkel's class-based analysis. See idem., "Ernst Fraenkel, The Dual State: A Contribution to the Theory of Dictatorship" (Book review), *Review of Politics*, Vol. 3 (1941), esp. pp. 255–6.

24. George H. Sabine, "Ernst Fraenkel, The Dual State: A Contribution to the Theory of Dictatorship" (Book review), *American Political Science Review*, Vol. 35 (1941), pp. 547, 548.
25. Eric Voegelin, "Ernst Fraenkel, The Dual State: A Contribution to the Theory of Dictatorship" (Book review), *Journal of Politics*, Vol. 4 (1942), pp. 271–2.
26. Helmut Quaritsch, ed., *Carl Schmitt: Antworten in Nürnberg* (Berlin: Duncker & Humblot, 2000); and Jens Meierhenrich, *In the Belly of the Fish: Carl Schmitt in Nazi Germany*, Unpublished book manuscript, London School of Economics and Political Science, 2016.
27. R. M. W. Kempner, "Ernst Fraenkel, The Dual State: A Contribution to the Theory of Dictatorship" (Book review), *Annals of the American Academy of Political and Social Science*, Vol. 216 (1941), p. 183.
28. Kempner, "Ernst Fraenkel, The Dual State," p. 183. Fraenkel, for reasons unknown, did not think very highly of Kempner, however. See Ladwig-Winters, *Ernst Fraenkel*, p. 209.
29. Lawrence Preuss, "Ernst Fraenkel, The Dual State: A Contribution to the Theory of Dictatorship" (Book review), *American Journal of International Law*, Vol. 35 (1941), p. 584.
30. Preuss, "Ernst Fraenkel, The Dual State," p. 584. Emphasis added.
31. Jerome G. Kerwin, "Ernst Fraenkel, The Dual State: A Contribution to the Theory of Dictatorship" (Book review), *University of Chicago Law Review*, Vol. 8 (1941), p. 616.
32. Voegelin, "Ernst Fraenkel, The Dual State," p. 269.
33. Harvey Pinney, "Ernst Fraenkel, The Dual State: A Contribution to the Theory of Dictatorship" (Book review), *Social Forces*, Vol. 20 (1942), p. 410.
34. Erich Hula, "Ernst Fraenkel, The Dual State: A Contribution to the Theory of Dictatorship" (Book review), *Social Research*, Vol. 9 (1942), pp. 271–2.
35. Hula, "Ernst Fraenkel, The Dual State," p. 272.
36. Hula also confessed to not being convinced by "the somewhat discredited economic interpretation of National Socialism." As he put it, "The 'dual state' is the legalistic formulation of the Marxist interpretation of National Socialism, but the concept does not substantiate the economic thesis." Hula, "Ernst Fraenkel, The Dual State," pp. 272, 273.
37. Hula, "Ernst Fraenkel, The Dual State," p. 272.
38. Fraenkel, *The Dual State*, p. 71.
39. Hula, "Ernst Fraenkel, The Dual State," p. 272.
40. Otto Kirchheimer, "Ernst Fraenkel, The Dual State: A Contribution to the Theory of Dictatorship" (Book review), *Political Science Quarterly*, Vol. 56 (1941), p. 434.
41. Kirchheimer, "Ernst Fraenkel, The Dual State," p. 436. On Neumann's rejection of Fraenkel's argument, see my extended discussion in Chapter 2.
42. Kirchheimer, "Ernst Fraenkel, The Dual State," p. 436.
43. See, for example, Robert Barros, *Constitutionalism and Dictatorship: Pinochet, the Junta, and the 1980 Constitution* (Cambridge: Cambridge University Press, 2007); Lisa Hilbink, *Judges beyond Politics in Democracy and Dictatorship:*

Lessons from Chile (Cambridge: Cambridge University Press, 2007); Tamir Moustafa, *The Struggle for Constitutional Power: Law, Politics, and Economic Development in Egypt* (Cambridge: Cambridge University Press, 2007); Jens Meierhenrich, *The Legacies of Law: Long- Run Consequences of Legal Development in South Africa, 1652–2000* (Cambridge: Cambridge University Press, 2008); Tom Ginsburg and Tamir Moustafa, eds., *Rule by Law: The Politics of Courts in Authoritarian Regimes* (Cambridge: Cambridge University Press, 2008); Jothie Rajah, *Authoritarian Rule of Law: Legislation, Discourse and Legitimacy in Singapore* (Cambridge: Cambridge University Press, 2012); Tom Ginsburg, *Constitutions in Authoritarian Regimes* (Cambridge: Cambridge University Press, 2013); Samuli Seppänen, *Ideological Conflict and the Rule of Law in Contemporary China: Useful Paradoxes* (Cambridge: Cambridge University Press, 2016). For a review of key scholarship, see Tom Ginsburg, "Courts and New Democracies: Recent Works," *Law and Social Inquiry*, Vol. 37 (2012), pp. 720–42.

44. David Riesman, Letter to Hans Staudinger, September 23, 1941, New York Public Library, Manuscripts and Archives Division, American Committee for the Guidance of Professional Personnel records, Box 6.
45. In the same letter, Fraenkel remarked that it was "at this time" ("*In dieser Zeit*") that he and his wife first heard about "the gas chambers in Auschwitz" ("*von den Gaskammern in Auschwitz*"). Ernst Fraenkel, "Brief vom 23. März 1946 an Familie Suhr," reprinted in Ernst Fraenkel, *Gesammelte Schriften*, vol. 3: *Neuaufbau der Demokratie in Deutschland und Korea*, edited by Gerhard Göhler (Baden-Baden: Nomos, 1999), p. 391.
46. Ernst Fraenkel, *Military Occupation and the Rule of Law: Occupational Government in the Rhineland, 1918–1923* (London: Oxford University Press, 1944). For recent, lawyerly accounts of international territorial administrations, see, most important, Ralph Wilde, *International Territorial Administration: How Trusteeship and the Civilizing Mission Never Went Away* (Oxford: Oxford University Press, 2008); Carsten Stahn, *The Law and Practice of International Territorial Administration: Versailles to Iraq and Beyond* (Cambridge: Cambridge University Press, 2008); and Gregory H. Fox, *Humanitarian Occupation* (Cambridge: Cambridge University Press, 2008).
47. Claude Lévi-Strauss was a founding member, in 1941, of what subsequently became, after its relocation to Paris, the École pratique des hautes études in 1947, and the École des hautes études en sciences sociales in 1975, one of France's foremost institutions of higher learning. For a brief summary of Fraenkel's time at the École libre des hautes études, see also Hans Staudinger, Letter to Ernst Fraenkel, July 9, 1956, BArch N 1274 (Fraenkel, Ernst)/19.
48. Generally, see Barry M. Katz, *Foreign Intelligence: Research and Analysis in the Office of Strategic Services, 1942–1945* (Cambridge: Harvard University Press, 1989).
49. Udi Greenberg, *The Weimar Century: German Émigrés and the Ideological Foundations of the Cold War* (Princeton: Princeton University Press, 2014), p. 93.
50. Ladwig-Winters, *Ernst Fraenkel*, pp. 196–7.

51. Ernst Fraenkel, Letter to Otto Kahn-Freund, December 25, 1942, London School of Economics and Political Science Archives, Otto Kahn-Freund Collection, Box 16.
52. For an insightful, pragmatic analysis of the promise, and limits, of relying on the German labor movement in the reconstruction and development of a defeated Germany, see Ernst Fraenkel, "Die künftige Organisation der deutschen Arbeiterbewegung," in idem., *Gesammelte Schriften*, vol. 3: *Neuaufbau der Demokratie in Deutschland und Korea*, edited by Gerhard Göhler (Baden-Baden: Nomos, [1943/1944] 1999), pp. 99–118.
53. Fraenkel, Letter to Otto Kahn-Freund, December 25, 1942.
54. See Chapters 3 and 4 above.
55. Greenberg, *The Weimar Century*, p. 94.
56. Ernst Fraenkel, Letter to Otto Kahn-Freund, July 22, 1945, London School of Economics and Political Science Archives, Otto Kahn-Freund Collection, Box 16. The slightly awkward formulations are Fraenkel's.
57. Gerhard Göhler and Dirk Rüdiger Schumann, "Vorwort zu diesem Band," in Fraenkel, *Gesammelte Schriften*, vol. 3, p. 15. For a recent collection of similar reports by other refugee scholars in the employ of the U.S. government, especially the OSS, see also Franz Neumann, Herbert Marcuse, and Otto Kirchheimer, *Secret Reports on Nazi Germany: The Frankfurt School Contribution to the War Effort*, edited by Raffaele Laudani (Princeton: Princeton University Press, 2013).
58. Fraenkel, "Brief vom 23. März 1946 an Familie Suhr," p. 391.
59. Fraenkel, "Brief vom 23. März 1946 an Familie Suhr," p. 392.
60. Ernst Fraenkel, Letter to Otto Kahn-Freund, May 25, 1946, London School of Economics and Political Science Archives, Otto Kahn-Freund Collection, Box 16.
61. Göhler and Schumann, "Vorwort zu diesem Band," p. 16.
62. Hiroshima and Nagasaki were destroyed by atomic bombs on August 6 and 9, 1945.
63. For a comprehensive discussion of Fraenkel's Korea years, see Ladwig-Winters, *Ernst Fraenkel*, pp. 210–38. For an overview of his output during this time, see Göhler and Schumann, "Vorwort zu diesem Band," pp. 16–19, 33–44.
64. Franz Neumann, *Behemoth* [1942 edition], pp. 467–8.
65. Neumann, *Behemoth* [1942 edition], p. 468.
66. Neumann, *Behemoth* [1942 edition], p. 469.
67. Neumann, *Behemoth* [1944 edition], p. 522.
68. Neumann, *Behemoth* [1942 edition], pp. 469–70.
69. Peter Hayes, "Introduction," in Franz Neumann, *Behemoth: The Structure and Practice of National Socialism*, with an Introduction by Peter Hayes (Chicago: Ivan R. Dee, [1942/1944] 2009), p. ix.
70. Judith Shklar, "Political Theory and the Rule of Law," in Allan C. Hutchinson and Patrick Monahan, eds., *The Rule of Law: Ideal or Ideology?* (Toronto: Carswell, 1987), p. 13. William E. Scheuerman confirmed Shklar's considerable admiration for Fraenkel's forgotten classic, a sentiment that her

brief mention of *The Dual State* in the above chapter did not fully convey. Correspondence with the author, May 6, 2014.

71. Note, however, that the study of totalitarianism has its origins in the inter-war era, notably in the writings of Luigi Storzo and Franz Borkenau. For an important overview of these pre-war debates, see Bernard Bruneteau, ed., *Le Totalitarisme: Origines d'un concept, genèse d'un débat, 1930–1942* (Paris: Cerf, 2010). Key publications that shaped the U.S. debate are Hannah Arendt, *The Origins of Totalitarianism* (New York: Harcourt, Brace, 1951); Carl J. Friedrich, ed., *Totalitarianism* (Cambridge: Harvard University Press, 1954); Carl J. Friedrich and Zbigniew K. Brzezinski, *Totalitarian Dictatorship and Autocracy* (Cambridge: Harvard University Press, 1956); and Carl J. Friedrich, Michael Curtis, and Benjamin R. Barber, eds., *Totalitarianism in Perspective: Three Views* (London: Pall Mall Press, 1969).
72. Carl J. Friedrich, "The Unique Character of Totalitarian Society," in idem., ed., *Totalitarianism*, p. 53.
73. Ernst Fraenkel, *Der Doppelstaat* (Frankfurt: Europäische Verlagsanstalt, 1974), dedication page.
74. In the heartfelt obituary to his old friend and erstwhile law partner, Fraenkel also provided a very rare personal-cum-professional account of his own life under the Nazi dictatorship. See Ernst Fraenkel, "Gedenkrede auf Franz L. Neumann," in Ernst Fraenkel, *Reformismus und Pluralismus: Materialien zu einer ungeschriebenen politischen Autobiographie*, edited by Falk Esche and Frank Grube (Hamburg: Hoffmann und Campe, [1955] 1973), pp. 168–79.
75. Fraenkel, "Brief vom 23. März 1946 an Familie Suhr," p. 394.
76. Otto Kahn-Freund, Letter to Ernst Fraenkel, January 25, 1960, BArch N 1274 (Fraenkel, Ernst)/33.
77. Ladwig-Winters, *Ernst Fraenkel*, p. 265.
78. Norbert Frei, *Vergangenheitspolitik: Die Anfänge der Bundesrepublik und die NS-Vergangenheit* (Munich: Beck, 1996), p. 15. See also Marc von Miquel, "Juristen," in Norbert Frei, ed. *Hitlers Eliten nach 1945* (Munich: dtv, 2003), pp. 165–217. For the first comprehensive account of impunity for, and continuity of, Nazi jurists in postwar Germany, see the influential and widely-read Ingo Müller, *Hitler's Justice: The Courts of the Third Reich*, translated by Deborah Lucas Schneider (Cambridge: Harvard University Press, 1991), pp. 201–98. For more recent perspectives, see Manfred Görtemaker and Christoph Safferling, eds., *Die Rosenburg: Das Bundesministerium der Justiz und die NS-Vergangenheit* (Vandenhoeck and Ruprecht, 2013); Manfred Görtemaker and Christoph Safferling, *Die Akte Rosenburg: Das Bundesministerium der Justiz und die NS-Zeit* (Munich: Beck, 2016); and also Edith Raim's very comprehensive *Justiz zwischen Diktatur und Demokratie: Wiederaufbau und Ahndung von NS-Verbrechen in Westdeutschland 1945–1949* (Berlin: De Gruyter, 2013); as well as Andreas Eichmüller, *Keine Generalamnestie: Die Strafverfolgung von NS-Verbrechen in der frühen Bundesrepublik* (Berlin: De Gruyter, 2012).
79. For this assessment, see, most recently, Christine Schoenmakers, *"Die Belange der Volksgemeinschaft erfordern … ": Rechtspraxis und Selbstverständnis von Bremer Juristen im "Dritten Reich"* (Paderborn: Schöningh, 2015), p. 24.

80. Generally, see Abbott Gleason, *Totalitarianism: The Inner History of the Cold War* (New York: Oxford University Press, 1995).
81. For a collection of previously published writings that helped to establish the study of totalitarianism more strongly in Germany than anywhere else, see Bruno Seidel and Siegfried Jenkner, ed., *Wege der Totalitarismus-Forschung* (Darmstadt: Wissenschaftliche Buchgesellschaft, 1968). The establishment, in 1993, of the Hannah-Arendt-Institut für Totalitarismusforschung, a research institute at the Technical University of Dresden, attests to the continued—and internationally exceptional—appeal that the concept of totalitarianism still holds in parts of German academia. Speaking to this scholarly tradition is Alfons Söllner, Ralf Walkenhaus, and Karin Wieland, eds., *Totalitarismus: Eine Ideengeschichte des 20. Jahrhunderts* (Munich: Oldenbourg, 1997).
82. Alexander v. Brünneck, "Ernst Fraenkel, The Dual State: A Contribution to the Theory of Dictatorship," (Book review), *Kritische Justiz*, Vol. 2 (1969), p. 320.
83. Ernst Fraenkel, Letter to Otto Kahn-Freund, n.d., BArch N 1274 (Fraenkel, Ernst)/62.
84. Ladwig-Winters, *Ernst Fraenkel*, p. 268. It is plausible that Fraenkel also created a certain distance between himself and his most famous book because he thought its anti-capitalist stance would sit uneasily with the influential theory of pluralism that he had developed in the postwar years. For this argument, see Alexander v. Brünneck, "Vorwort zu diesem Band," in Ernst Fraenkel, *Gesammelte Schriften, vol. 2: Nationalsozialismus und Widerstand*, edited by Alexander v. Brünneck, Hubertus Buchstein, and Gerhard Göhler (Baden-Baden: Nomos, 1999), p. 11.
85. Ernst Fraenkel, *Das amerikanische Regierungssystem: Eine politologische Analyse* (Opladen: Westdeutscher Verlag, 1962). On a personal note, I still possess the xeroxed copy of this title, which—alongside Fraenkel's other influential monograph, *Deutschland und die westlichen Demokratien*, edited by Alexander v. Brünneck (Frankfurt am Main: Suhrkamp, 1991)—was essential reading when I was an undergraduate student of law and of political science at the Universität Passau in the early 1990s. At the time, my fellow students and I neither knew nor were told by our professors that Fraenkel had also written *The Dual State*, a far more innovative book than either of the aforementioned titles. As far as I recall, neither the English edition from 1941 nor the German edition from 1974 was on any syllabus. Widely read and assigned instead were Fraenkel's influential (in postwar Germany at least) analysis of the U.S. system of government, his theory of pluralism, and his other contributions to democratic theory. For a collection of these writings, see Ernst Fraenkel, *Gesammelte Schriften*, vol. 4: *Amerikastudien*, edited by Hubertus Buchstein and Rainer Kühn (Baden-Baden: Nomos, 2000); Fraenkel, *Gesammelte Schriften*, vol. 5. For a very useful discussion of Fraenkel's role as a "bridge figure" in the postwar rapprochement between the United States and Germany, see Greenberg, *The Weimar Century*, pp. 107–19. The quote is from p. 113.
86. Ernst Fraenkel, Letter to Alexander v. Brünneck, April 8, 1970, BArch N 1274 (Fraenkel, Ernst)/98.

87. Ernst Fraenkel, "Startgleichheit und Klassenschichtung," in idem., *Gesammelte Schriften*, vol. 3: *Neuaufbau der Demokratie in Deutschland und Korea*, edited by Gerhard Göhler (Baden-Baden: Nomos, [1956] 1999), p. 628.
88. As relayed by Helmut Ridder, "Der Doppelstaat," *Die Zeit*, June 12, 1970.
89. Karl Dietrich Bracher, *Die deutsche Diktatur: Entstehung, Struktur, Folgen des Nationalsozialismus* (Köln: Kiepenheuer and Witsch, 1969), p. 235, fn. 22; Martin Broszat, *Der Staat Hitlers: Grundlegung und Entwicklung seiner inneren Verfassung* (Munich: dtv, 1969), p. 404. But see Gerhard Schulz, who took up Fraenkel's terminology in *Die nationalsozialistische Machtergreifung*, vol. 2: *Die Anfänge des totalitären Maßnahmenstaates* (Frankfurt: Ullstein, 1960). See also the discussion in Chapter 3 above.
90. In expert testimony for the Frankfurt Auschwitz Trial, 1963–1965, Buchheim of the Institut für Zeitgeschichte in Munich substituted a distinction between "statehood" ("*Staatlichkeit*") and the "extra-normative power of the Führer" ("*außernormative Führergewalt*") for Fraenkel's concept of the dual state. They maintained that the latter power existed *outside* of the state, which is why they faulted Fraenkel's institutionalist account, which assumed the existence of a duality *within* the Nazi state. Hans Buchheim, "Die SS—das Herrschaftsinstrument," in Hans Buchheim, Martin Broszat, Hans-Adolf Jacobsen, and Helmut Krausnick, eds., *Anatomie des SS-Staates*, Seventh edition (Munich: dtv, [1967] 1999), p. 21.
91. Bernhard Blanke, "Der deutsche Faschismus als Doppelstaat," *Kritische Justiz*, Vol. 6 (1975), pp. 221–43.
92. Blanke, "Der deutsche Faschismus als Doppelstaat," esp. pp. 231–2.
93. Wolfgang Luthardt, "Unrechtsstaat oder Doppelstaat? Kritisch-theoretische Reflektionen über die Struktur des Nationalsozialismus aus der Sicht demokratischer Sozialisten," in Hubert Rottleuthner, ed., *Recht, Rechtsphilosophie und Nationalsozialismus* (Wiesbaden: Steiner, 1983), pp. 197–209.
94. Luthardt, "Unrechtsstaat oder Doppelstaat?," pp. 198–9.
95. Note, however, that in his magnum opus, *Political Justice*, Kirchheimer moved considerably closer to the argument and historical institutionalism that was at the heart of *The Dual State*. See Otto Kirchheimer, *Political Justice: The Use of Legal Procedure for Political Ends* (Princeton: Princeton University Press, 1961).
96. Franz L. Neumann, "Die Gewerkschaften in der Demokratie und in der Diktatur," in Franz L. Neumann, *Wirtschaft, Staat, Demokratie: Aufsätze 1930–1954*, edited by Alfons Söllner (Frankfurt: Suhrkamp, [1935] 1978), pp. 113, 183.
97. Luthardt, "Unrechtsstaat oder Doppelstaat?," p. 209.
98. See, in order of publication, Klaus Hildebrand, *Das Dritte Reich*, Fifth edition (Munich: Oldenbourg, 1995); Ulrich von Hehl, *Nationalsozialistische Herrschaft* (Munich: Oldenbourg, 1996); Peter Reichel, Harald Schmid, and Peter Steinbach, *Der Nationalsozialismus: Die zweite Geschichte* (Munich: Beck, 2009); and Wehler, *Der Nationalsozialismus*.

99. See Horst Dreier, "Nachwort: Was ist doppelt am 'Doppelstaat'? Zu Rezeption und Bedeutung der klassischen Studie von Ernst Fraenkel," in Ernst Fraenkel, Der Doppelstaat, Third edition, edited with an Introduction by Alexander v. Brünneck, with an Afterword by Horst Dreier (Frankfurt: Europäische Verlagsanstalt, 2012) pp. 276–7, fn. 17. He neither found mentions of *The Dual State* in Rolf Grawert, "Die nationalsozialistische Herrschaft," in Josef Isensee and Paul Kirchhof, eds., *Handbuch des Staatsrechts der Bundesrepublik Deutschland: Grundlagen von Staat und Verfassung*, vol. 1, Third edition (Heidelberg: Müller, 2003), pp. 235–65; nor in Peter Badura, *Staatsrecht: Systematische Erläuterung des Grundgesetzes für die Bundesrepublik Deutschland*, Fourth edition (Munich: Beck, 2010). *The Dual State* is mentioned once under relevant literature but not discussed in Hartmut Maurer, *Staatsrecht I: Grundlagen, Verfassungsorgane, Staatsfunktionen*, Sixth edition (Munich: Beck, 2010). The only one of the four surveyed titles that included a very brief reference was Klaus Stern, *Das Staatsrecht der Bundesrepublik Deutschland*, vol. 5: *Die geschichtlichen Grundlagen des deutschen Staatsrechts* (Munich: Beck, 2000), p. 773.
100. From Werner Frotscher and Bodo Pieroth, *Verfassungsgeschichte*, Tenth edition (Munich: Beck, 2011), the book is missing. It is also missing from Karl Kroeschell, *Deutsche Rechtsgeschichte*, vol. 3: *Seit 1650*. Fifth edition (Cologne: Böhlau, 2008), which contains a separate (though brief) chapter of Nazi law. In Stolleis's *A History of Public Law in Germany, 1933–1945*, Fraenkel appears in passing on p. 376, as he does in Karl Kroeschell, *Rechtsgeschichte Deutschlands im 20. Jahrhundert* (Göttingen: Vandenhoeck und Ruprecht, 1992), p. 80. By contrast, more deliberate (albeit still brief) engagements can be found in Dietmar Willoweit, *Deutsche Verfassungsgeschichte: Vom Frankenreich bis zur Wiedervereinigung Deutschlands*, Sixth edition (Munich: Beck, 2009), p. 321; and Uwe Wesel, *Geschichte des Rechts: Von den Frühformen bis zur Gegenwart*, Third edition (Munich: Beck, 2006), pp. 511–12.
101. Hans-Ulrich Wehler, *Deutsche Gesellschaftsgeschichte*, vol. 4: *Vom Beginn des Ersten Weltkriegs bis zur Gründung der beiden deutschen Staaten 1914–1949* (Munich: Beck, 2003), esp. pp. 557–8, 623–6.
102. Möller, "Ernst Fraenkel," p. 155, 167.
103. Ladwig-Winters, *Ernst Fraenkel*, p. 333.
104. For a discussion, see Michael Wildt, "Die Angst vor dem Volk: Ernst Fraenkel in der deutschen Nachkriegsgesellschaft," in Monika Boll and Raphael Gross, eds., *"Ich staune, dass Sie in dieser Luft noch atmen können": Jüdische Intellektuelle in Deutschland nach 1945* (Frankfurt: Fischer, 2013), pp. 317–44.
105. Ernst Fraenkel, Letter to Winfried Steffani, December 6, 1973, reprinted in Steffani, "Ernst Fraenkel als Persönlichkeit," pp. 144–5. The *Festschrift* in question was Günther Doeker and Winfried Steffani, eds., *Klassenjustiz und Pluralismus: Festschrift für Ernst Fraenkel zum 75. Geburtstag* (Hamburg: Hoffmann und Campe, 1973).

106. Ernst Fraenkel, Letter to Otto Kahn-Freund, September 23, 1974, BArch N 1274 (Fraenkel, Ernst)/62.
107. The edition in question is Ernst Fraenkel, *Der Doppelstaat: Recht und Justiz im "Dritten Reich"* (Frankfurt: Fischer, 1984). Note the modified subtitle. A second and third edition of *The Dual State* have been published since: Ernst Fraenkel, *Der Doppelstaat*, Second edition, edited with an Introduction by Alexander v. Brünneck (Frankfurt: Europäische Verlagsanstalt, 2001); and Ernst Fraenkel, *Der Doppelstaat*, Third edition, edited with an Introduction by Alexander v. Brünneck, with an Afterword by Horst Dreier (Frankfurt: Europäische Verlagsanstalt, 2012). See also Giselher Schmidt, "Doppel- und Urdoppelstaat," *Die Zeit*, July 26, 2000.
108. Michael Stolleis, "Der Doppelstaat," *Juristenzeitung*, Vol. 39 (1984), p. 1097.
109. Norberto Bobbio, "Introduzione," in Ernst Fraenkel, *Il doppio Stato: Contributo alla teoria della dittatura*, translated by Pier Paolo Portinaro (Turin: Einaudi, 1983). For a more comprehensive analysis of *The Dual State* in the context of Italian political thought, see Franco De Felice, "Doppia lealtà e doppio Stato," *Studi Storici*, Vol. 30 (1989), pp. 493–563. See also Wolfgang Schieder, "Carl Schmitt und Italien," *Vierteljahrshefte für Zeitgeschichte*, Vol. 37 (1989), pp. 1–21; and Ilse Staff, *Staatsdenken im Italien des 20. Jahrhunderts: Ein Beitrag zur Carl Schmitt-Rezeption* (Baden-Baden: Nomos, 1991).
110. BSGE 69, 211.
111. "*Nur ein beschränkter Teil der damaligen Strafpraxis war rechtsstaatlich vertretbar. Solche Urteile waren dem 'Normenstaat' zuzurechnen, d.h. dem Teil der Staatsgewalt, der sich an eine im Kulturstaat vertretbare Rechtsordnung hielt.*" BSGE 69, 211, 216–17
112. See Hans Georg Bachmann, "Militärgerichtsbarkeit der deutschen Wehrmacht 1939–1945 und Wehrdienstgerichtsbarkeit in der Bundeswehr seit 1957: Eine Gegenüberstellung," *Unterrichtsblätter für die Bundeswehrverwaltung*, Vol. 11 (2009), pp. 409–11; Otto Hennicke and Fritz Wüllner, "Über die barbarischen Vollstreckungs-Methoden von Wehrmacht und Justiz im Zweiten Weltkrieg," in Wolfram Wette, ed., *Deserteure der Wehrmacht: Feiglinge–Opfer–Hoffnungsträger?* (Essen: Klartext, 1995), p. 74; and Manfred Messerschmidt and Fritz Wüllner: *Die Wehrmachtjustiz im Dienste des Nationalsozialismus: Zerstörung einer Legende* (Baden-Baden: Nomos, 1987), p. 49. For a comprehensive history of Nazi military justice, see Manfred Messerschmidt, *Die Wehrmachtjustiz 1933–1945* (Paderborn: Schöningh, 2005).
113. BSGE 69, 211, 216.
114. On the immediate reaction, much of it negative, to the 1991 judgment, see, however, Wolfgang Wette, "Deserteure der Wehrmacht rehabilitiert: Ein exemplarischer Meinungswandel in Deutschland (1980–2002)," *Zeitschrift für Geschichtswissenschaft*, Vol. 52 (2004), pp. 505–27, esp. 512–14.
115. The reception of *The Dual State* since the landmark judgment has been uneven, as the historian Michael Wildt pointed out. See Michael Wildt, "Ernst Fraenkel und Carl Schmitt: Eine ungleiche Beziehung," in Daniela Münkel and Jutta Schwarzkopf, eds., *Geschichte als Experiment: Studien zu Politik, Kultur und Alltag im 19. und 20. Jahrhundert* (Frankfurt: Campus, 2004), pp. 35–48.

CHAPTER 9

1. Sally Engle Merry, "The Rule of Law and Authoritarian Rule: Legal Politics in Sudan," *Law and Social Inquiry*, Vol. 41 (2016), p. 470.
2. Joseph Raz, *The Authority of Law: Essays on Law and Morality* (Oxford: Clarendon Press, 1979), p. 211.
3. Nicola Lacey, "Philosophy, Political Morality, and History: Explaining the Enduring Resonance of the Hart-Fuller Debate," *New York University Law Review*, Vol. 83 (2008), p. 1087.
4. Clifford Geertz, *The Interpretation of Cultures: Selected Essays* (New York: Basic Books, 1973), pp. 3–30.
5. Gilbert Ryle, "Thinking and Reflecting," in idem., *Collected Papers*, vol. 2: *Collected Essays, 1929–1968* (London: Routledge [1966/1967], 1971), pp. 479–93; and idem., "The Thinking of Thoughts: What Is 'Le Penseur' Doing?," in idem., *Collected Papers*, vol. 2: *Collected Essays, 1929–1968* (London: Routledge [1968], 1971), pp. 494–510.
6. Ryle, "Thinking and Reflecting," p. 493.
7. Ryle, "The Thinking of Thoughts," p. 494.
8. Heather Love, "Close Reading and Thin Description," *Public Culture*, Vol. 25 (2013), p. 403.
9. Geertz, *The Interpretation of Cultures*, p. 7.
10. Geertz, *The Interpretation of Cultures*, p. 30.
11. In addition to distinguishing the prerogative state from the normative *state* in Nazi Germany, Fraenkel also distinguished between the prerogative and normative uses of *law*. Unfortunately, the latter distinction is underdeveloped in *The Dual State*. Fraenkel only ever alluded to it in passing, as he did, for example, when he described the prerogative state "in operation," specifically in the context of the Nazi institution of *Sondergerichte*, of which Freisler's *Volksgerichtshof* was but the most notorious: "The People's Tribunal and the other Special Courts are the creation of the Prerogative State. The term Special Court sums up the difference between the Rule of Law State [...] and the Dual State: the Rule of Law [state] refers political crimes to a *special* court despite the fact that they are questions of law; the Dual State refers political crimes to a special *court*, despite the fact that they are *political* questions." Fraenkel, *The Dual State*, p. 50. Stated more plainly, Fraenkel's argument was this: Nazi Germany's legal institutions were not necessarily organs of the normative state. Whether they were or not depended on the extent of their commitment to a legal, that is, formally rational, way of doing things: "Courts making their decisions *only* in the light of political considerations, i.e., courts which recognize their own decisions only with reservations, cease to be judicial organs and their decisions are no longer real decisions; they are measures (*Massnahmen*). This distinction was formulated by Carl Schmitt very clearly in 1924." Fraenkel, *The Dual State*, p. 52. Emphasis added. See also Otto Kirchheimer, *Political Justice: The Use of Legal Procedure for Political Ends* (Princeton: Princeton University Press, 1961). I am grateful to Douglas Morris who persuaded me to clarify the difference between prerogative and normatives *states* and prerogative and normative uses of *law*. The distinction

is not trivial. Developing it further, as I have only begun to do, is directly related to the task of reconfiguring the dual state as a conceptual variable for the twenty-first century.

12. It is noteworthy that Neumann's idea of a democratic rule of law, which he honed over the course of his all-too-short life, was considerably more sophisticated than his treatment of law in *Behemoth* alone would suggest. Interested readers may want to consult, for example, Neumann, "The Concept of Political Freedom," prolegomena to a theory of democracy with three moving parts: juridical liberty, cognitive liberty, and volitional liberty.
13. Martin Krygier, "The Rule of Law between England and Sudan: Hay, Thompson, and Massoud," *Law and Social Inquiry*. Vol. 41 (2016), p. 486.
14. It is also the reason why I refer to "remnants" of the *Rechtsstaat*: to communicate in no uncertain terms that I consider the integrity of the *Rechtsstaat* to have been compromised to such an extent in 1933 that it would be a misnomer to speak of a supremacy of law after the Nazi seizure of power.
15. Krygier, "The Rule of Law between England and Sudan," p. 486.
16. See esp. Chapters 3 and 6 above.
17. Geertz, *The Interpretation of Cultures*, p. 10.
18. For autobiographical accounts by two of the most prominent members of the amorphous intellectual resistance, see Sebastian Haffner, *Defying Hitler: A Memoir*, translated by Oliver Pretzel (London: Weidenfeld and Nicolson, 2002); and Victor Klemperer, *I Will Bear Witness: A Diary of the Nazi Years 1933–1941*, translated and with a Preface by Martin Chalmers (New York: Random House, 1998).
19. E. P. Thompson, *Whigs and Hunters: The Origin of the Black Act* (New York: Pantheon, 1975), p. 263.
20. Steven Levitsky and Lucan A. Way, "Durable Authoritarianism," in Orfeo Fioretos, Tulia G. Falleti, and Adam Sheingate, eds., *The Oxford Handbook of Historical Institutionalism* (Oxford: Oxford University Press, 2016), p. 208. On the question of durability, see also Jennifer Gandhi, "Authoritarian Institutions and the Survival of Autocrats," *Comparative Political Studies*, Vol. 40 (2007), pp. 1279–301. For an overview of recent research on authoritarianism, see David Art's review article, "What Do We Know about Authoritarianism after Ten Years?," *Comparative Politics*, Vol. 44 (2012), pp. 351–73.
21. Raz, *The Authority of Law*, pp. 211, 214. Emphasis added.
22. Raz, *The Authority of Law*, p. 210.
23. Bingham, 2010, p. 67.
24. See Chapters 1 and 2 respectively.
25. Merry, "The Rule of Law and Authoritarian Rule," p. 468.
26. On the methodological demands of comparative historical analysis, see James Mahoney and Dietrich Rueschemeyer, eds., *Comparative Historical Analysis in the Social Sciences* (Cambridge: Cambridge University Press, 2003).
27. H. L. A. Hart, *The Concept of Law*, Second edition (Oxford: Clarendon Press, [1958] 1994), pp. 136–47.
28. Frank Lovett, *A Republic of Law* (Cambridge: Cambridge University Press, 2016), p. 13.

29. Lovett, *A Republic of Law*, pp. 13, 26. On the philosophy of legality, see Scott J. Shapiro, *Legality* (Cambridge: Harvard University Press, 2010).
30. Lovett, *A Republic of Law*, p. 68.
31. Lovett, *A Republic of Law*, p. 69. Lovett points to Eugen Ehrlich and Bronislaw Malinowski as legal theorists who believed law's function was to maintain social order, and to Henry Hart and Albert Sacks as well as Frederick Schauer as legal theorists who associated law with whatever norms and institutions settled disputes. Ibid, p. 69, fn. 11. See also Eugen Ehrlich, *Fundamental Principles of the Sociology of Law*, translated by Walter L. Moll (Cambridge: Harvard University Press, [1913] 1936); Bronislaw Malinowski, *Crime and Custom in Savage Society* (London: Routledge and Kegan Paul, 1926); Henry M. Hart, Jr. and Albert M. Sacks, *The Legal Process: Basic Problems in the Making and Application of Law* (Westbury: Foundation Press, [1951] 1994); and Frederick Schauer, *Playing by the Rules: A Philosophical Examination of Rule-Based Decision-Making in Law and in Life* (Oxford: Clarendon Press, 1993).
32. Lovett, *A Republic of Law*, p. 70.
33. Tamir Moustafa and Tom Ginsburg, "Introduction: The Functions of Courts in Authoritarian Politics," in Tom Ginsburg and Tamir Moustafa, eds., *Rule by Law: The Politics of Courts in Authoritarian Regimes* (Cambridge: Cambridge University Press, 2008), pp. 1–22; Tom Ginsburg, "Introduction: Constitutions in Authoritarian Regimes," in Ginsburg and Simpser, eds., *Constitutions in Authoritarian Regimes* (Cambridge: Cambridge University Press, 2014). For a mild defense with critical overtones, see Mark Tushnet, "Authoritarian Constitutionalism: Some Conceptual Issues," in Ginsburg and Simpser, eds., *Constitutions in Authoritarian Regimes*, esp. pp. 40–1.
34. Brian Z. Tamanaha, *Realistic Socio-Legal Theory: Pragmatism and a Social Theory of Law* (Oxford: Oxford University Press, 1997), p. 107.
35. Lovett, *A Republic of Law*, p. 128. This minimalist concept of the rule of law is preferable to substantive ones. Jeremy Waldron is right: "Once we open up the possibility of the Rule of Law's having a substantive dimension, we inaugurate a sort of competition in which everyone clamors to have their favorite political ideal incorporated as a substantive dimension of the Rule of Law. Those who favor property rights and market economy will scramble to privilege their favorite values in this regard. But so will those who favor human rights, or those who favor democratic participation, or those who favor civil liberties or social justice. The result is likely to be a general decline in political articulacy, as people struggle to use the same term to express disparate ideals." See his "The Rule of Law," *Stanford Encyclopedia of Philosophy* (2016), available at https://plato.stanford.edu/archives/fall2016/entries/rule-of-law/
36. Lovett, *A Republic of Law*, p. 113.
37. Lovett, *A Republic of Law*, p. 118.
38. See also Lovett, *A Republic of Law*, pp. 115–16. I was inspired by Martin Krygier to substitute the verb "temper" for my original choice: "constrain." I am grateful to him for the engaging conversation that persuded me to subtly alter what I expected of an affective rule of law. See also Martin Krygier, "Tempering Power," in Maurice Adams, Anne Meuwese, and Ernst Hirsch

Ballin, eds., *Constitutionalism and the Rule of Law: Bridging Idealism and Realism* (Cambridge: Cambridge University Press, 2017), pp. 34–59.

39. Georg Wilhelm Friedrich Hegel, *The Science of Logic*, translated and edited by George di Giovanni (Cambridge: Cambridge University Press, [1812–1831] 2010), p. 382.
40. Hegel, *The Science of Logic*, p. 383.
41. For a valuable discussion, see Andrew C. Gould, "Conflicting Imperatives and Concept Formation," *Review of Politics*, Vol. 61 (1999). See also Stephen E. Hanson, *Post-Imperial Democracies: Ideology and Party Formation in Third Republic France, Weimar Germany, and Post-Soviet Russia* (Cambridge: Cambridge University Press, 2010), pp. 21–2.
42. I provide empirical evidence in support of this argument for both cases in Jens Meierhenrich, *The Legacies of Law: Long-Run Consequences of Legal Development in South Africa, 1652–2000* (Cambridge: Cambridge University Press, 2008). On Chile, see also Robert Barros, *Constitutionalism and Dictatorship: Pinochet, the Junta, and the 1980 Constitution* (Cambridge: Cambridge University Press, 2007).
43. For a recent assessment, see, for example, Abraham F. Lowenthal and Sergio Bitar, "Getting to Democracy: Lessons from Successful Transitions," *Foreign Affairs*, Vol. 95 (2016), pp. 134–44.
44. Kanishka Jayasuriya, "The Exception Becomes the Norm: Law and Regimes of Exception in East Asia," *Asian-Pacific Law and Policy Journal*, Vol. 2 (2001), p. 121.
45. Some empirical evidence can be gleaned from an interesting collective case study overseen by Simon N. M. Young and Yashi Ghai. See idem., eds., *Hong Kong's Court of Final Appeal: The Development of the Law in China's Hong Kong* (Cambridge: Cambridge University Press, 2013).
46. Larry Diamond, "Thinking about Hybrid Regimes," *Journal of Democracy*, Vol. 13 (2002), p. 23. A few years earlier, Fareed Zakaria had coined the term "illiberal democracy" to capture a subset of the many hybrid regimes that emerged from the so-called third wave of democratization. See his "The Rise of Illiberal Democracy," *Foreign Affairs*, Vol. 76 (1997), pp. 22–43. I am concerned with the counterpart to Zakaria's concept: *liberal dictatorship*. Clinton Rossiter's concept of "constitutional dictatorship" is an example of this paradoxical institutional design. See Rossiter, *Constitutional Dictatorship*.
47. Diamond, "Thinking about Hybrid Regimes," p. 25. Subsequent research on hybrid regimes includes Mikael Wigell, "Mapping 'Hybrid Regimes': Regime Types and Concepts in Comparative Politics," *Democratization*, Vol. 15 (2008); Jason Brownlee, "Portents of Pluralism: How Hybrid Regimes Affect Democratic Transitions," *American Journal of Political Science*, Vol. 53 (2009); Leah Gilbert and Payam Mohseni, "Beyond Authoritarianism;" Matthijs Bogaards, "How to Classify Hybrid Regimes? Defective Democracy and Electoral Authoritarianism: The Conceptualization of Hybrid Regimes," *Studies in Comparative International Development*, Vol. 46 (2011); *Democratization*, Vol. 16 (2009), pp. 399–423; Andrea Cassani, "Hybrid

What? Partial Consensus and Persistent Divergence in the Analysis of Hybrid Regimes," *International Political Science Review*, Vol. 35 (2014), pp. 542–58.

48. Steven Levitsky and Lucan A. Way, *Competitive Authoritarianism: Hybrid Regimes after the Cold War* (Cambridge: Cambridge University Press, 2010), p. 4.
49. Robert Barros makes the important point, directly relevant here, that a conceptual distinction between regimes types "emphasizes differences in the forms that nondemocratic rule assumes, not a difference in the character of power in authoritarian and totalitarian regimes." Barros, *Constitutionalism and Dictatorship*, p. 12. This also helps explain why Linz, for example, never felt a need to change his original and controversial classification of Francoist Spain as an authoritarian regime.
50. Raymond Hinnebusch, "Syria: From 'Authoritarian Upgrading' to Revolution?," *International Affairs*, Vol. 88 (2012), pp. 95–113. On the origins and evolution of the Syrian dictatorship, see Steven Haydemann, *Authoritarianism in Syria: Institutions and Social Conflict, 1946–1970* (Ithaca: Cornell University Press, 1999).
51. Hinnebusch, "Syria," p. 98.
52. Hinnebusch, "Syria," p. 104.
53. Hinnebusch, "Syria," p. 106.
54. Megan Price, Anita Gohdes, and Patrick Ball, *Updated Statistical Analysis of Documentation of Killings in the Syrian Arab Republic* (August 2014), available at http://www.ohchr.org/Documents/Countries/SY/RDAGUpdatedReportAug2014.pdf. See also Megan Price, "Estimating the Human Toll in Syria," *Nature*, February 8, 2017.
55. I here follow Levitsky and Way, for whom "full authoritarianism" represents that set of nondemocratic regimes which "lack significant legal contestation for power." Levitsky and Way, *Competitive Authoritarianism*, p. 7, fn. 27. This category subsumes varieties of authoritarianism such as "closed regimes" and "hegemonic regimes." In keeping with the existing literature, I take closed authoritarian regimes to refer to those "in which a country's leaders are not selected through national elections, opposition political parties remain banned, political control is maintained through the use of repression, and there is little space for free media and civil society." Marc Morjé Howard and Philip G. Roessler, "Liberalizing Electoral Outcomes in Competitive Authoritarian Regimes," *American Journal of Political Science*, Vol. 50 (2006), p. 367. Whereas in closed regimes formal democratic institutions do not exist at all, in hegemonic regimes such institutions are nominally operational "but are reduced to façade status in practice." Levitsky and Way, *Competitive Authoritarianism*, p. 7.
56. Diamond, "Thinking about Hybrid Regimes," p. 24.
57. Andreas Schedler, "The Logic of Electoral Authoritarianism," in idem., ed., *Electoral Authoritarianism: The Dynamics of Unfree Competition* (Boulder: Lynne Rienner, 2006), p. 5. See also Juan J. Linz, *Totalitarian and Authoritarian Regimes* (Boulder: Lynne Rienner, [1975] 2000), pp. 33–4; Jennifer Gandhi and Ellen Lust-Okar, "Elections under Authoritarianism," *Annual Review*

of Political Science*, Vol. 12 (2009); Michael K. Miller, "Democratic Pieces: Autocratic Elections and Democratic Development since 1815," *British Journal of Political Science*, Vol. 45 (2015); and Carl Henrik Knutsen, Håvard Mokleiv, Nygård, and Tore Wig, "Autocratic Elections: Stabilizing Tool or Force for Change?," *World Politics*, Vol. 69 (2017).

58. Levitsky and Way, *Competitive Authoritarianism*, p. 5.
59. Schedler, "The Logic of Electoral Authoritarianism," p. 6.
60. Robert A. Dahl, *Polyarchy: Participation and Opposition* (New Haven: Yale University Press, 1971). Dahl himself used the term "competitive regime," the chance for the emergence of which rose, in his model, "[t]he more the costs of suppression exceed the costs of toleration." Ibid, p. 15. Emphasis removed.
61. Dahl, *Polyarchy*, p. 5.
62. Authoritarian regimes are genuinely law-governed if law is not just a façade.
63. The ability to facilitate a modicum of legal contestation is the hallmark of these states' normative halves.
64. For an incomplete account of "the world of dictatorial institutions," see Gandhi, *Political Institutions under Dictatorship*, pp. 1–4. Surprisingly, the institution of law does not feature in her account. This oversight may owe to the game-theoretical lens through which Gandhi views the logic of dictatorship. Her focus on dictators (from monarchical to military to civilian) has blinded her to the considerably larger universe of dictatorial institutions in which her world (and their rule) is embedded. The available data for the Third Reich are incontrovertible proof of my claim. With its reduction of empirical complexity, Gandhi's positive theory of dictatorship is reminiscent of the now defunct intentionalist approach to the Nazi dictatorship. Her model is too agentic to capture more than a sliver of the everyday life of dictatorship, then and now. For research that suffers from a similar shortcoming, and which also ignores legal institutions in favor of "authoritarian political institutions such as parties, legislatures and elections," see, *pars pro toto*, Joseph Wright and Abel Escribà-Folch, "Authoritarian Institutions and Regime Survival: Transitions to Democracy and Subsequent Autocracy," *British Journal of Political Science*, Vol. 42 (2011), pp. 283–309. Arguments from structured contingency, like Fraenkel's contribution to the theory of dictatorship, promise to paint a more accurate picture of authoritarianism, hybrid or otherwise, than formal approaches.
65. Gould, "Conflicting Imperatives and Concept Formation," p. 441. Gould believes that Weber's placement of conflicting imperatives at the core of some of his concepts did not mean that he thought empirical phenomena "that matched those concepts" were "in the process of being permanently undermined from within." Ibid, pp. 441–42, fn. 5.
66. See, for example, James Mahoney and Kathleen Thelen, eds., *Explaining Institutional Change: Ambiguity, Agency, and Power* (Cambridge: Cambridge University Press, 2009); Paul Pierson, *Politics in Time: History, Institutions, and Social Analysis* (Princeton: Princeton University Press, 2004).
67. Robert Adcock and David Collier, "Measurement Validity: A Shared Standard for Qualitative and Quantitative Research," *American Political*

Science Review, Vol. 95 (2001), p. 533. Defined by Adcock and Collier as a methodological strategy for improving concepts, and thus measurement validity, "'friendly amendments' occur when a scholar, out of a concern with validity, engages in further conceptual work to suggest refinements or make explicit earlier implicit assumptions. These amendments are friendly because they do not fundamentally challenge a systematized concept but instead push analysts to capture more adequately the ideas contained in it." Ibid. A typical example of a friendly amendment is the addition of one or more defining attributes to an existing concept.

68. Giovanni Sartori, "Concept Misformation in Comparative Politics," *American Political Science Review*, Vol. 64 (1970), pp. 1033–53; David Collier and James E. Mahon, Jr., "Conceptual 'Stretching' Revisited: Adapting Categories in Comparative Analysis," *American Political Science Review*, Vol. 87 (1993), pp. 845–55. "Extension" (or denotation) refers to the number of a concept's referents, that is, the range of cases to which it applies. The denotation of a word is the totality of objects indicated by that word. "Intension" (or connotation) refers to the number of a concept's defining attributes. The connotation of a word is the totality of characteristics anything must possess to be in the denotation of that word.
69. John Gerring has summarized the advantages of definitional minimalism in concept formation: "One long-standing definitional strategy seeks to identify the bare essentials of a concept, sufficient to differentiate it extensionally without excluding any of the phenomena generally understood as part of the extension. [...] Each attribute that defines a concept minimally is regarded as a necessary condition: all entities must possess this attribute in order to be considered a member of the set. Collectively, these attributes are jointly sufficient to bound the concept extensionally. Minimal definitions thus aim for crisp borders, allowing the classification of entities as 'in' or 'out.'" John Gerring, *Social Science Methodology: A Unified Framework*, Second edition (Cambridge: Cambridge University Press, 2012), pp. 135–6.
70. Fraenkel, "Preface to the 1974 German edition," p. xv.
71. Ernst Fraenkel, *The Dual State: A Contribution to the Theory of Dictatorship*, translated by E. A. Shils, in collaboration with Edith Loewenstein and Klaus Knorr, with an Introduction by Jens Meierhenrich (Oxford: Oxford University Press, [1941] 2017), p. xiii.
72. Fraenkel, *The Dual State*, p. xiii.
73. Fraenkel, *The Dual State*, p. xvi.
74. Fraenkel, *The Dual State*, p. xiii.
75. Fraenkel, *The Dual State*, p. 44.
76. Linz, "Totalitarian and Authoritarian Regimes," pp. 188–9.
77. Linz, "Totalitarian and Authoritarian Regimes," pp. 193, 217–28.
78. Fraenkel, *The Dual State*, p. 24.
79. Graeme Gill, *Building an Authoritarian Polity: Russia in Post-Soviet Times* (Cambridge: Cambridge University Press, 2015), esp. pp. 198–9; Graeme R. Robertson, *The Politics of Protest in Hybrid Regimes: Managing Dissent in Post-Communist Russia* (Cambridge: Cambridge University Press, 2011).

80. Harold J. Berman, "The Rule of Law and the Law-Based State (*Rechtsstaat*) (with Special Reference to Developments in the Soviet Union)," Paper presented at the Conference "In Search of the Law-Governed State: Political and Societal Reform under Gorbachev," Lehigh University, May 29-June 1, 1991, esp. pp. 1–5. Revised versions of the conference papers appeared in Donald D. Berry, ed., *Toward the "Rule of Law" in Russia: Political and Legal Reform in the Transition Period* (London: M.E. Sharpe, 1992).
81. For an important revisionist account that transcends conventional wisdom about the social meaning(s) of law in Tsarist Russia, see Jane Burbank, *Russian Peasants Go to Court: Legal Culture in the Countryside, 1905–1917* (Bloomington: Indiana University Press, 2004).
82. Kathryn Hendley, *Everyday Law in Russia* (Ithaca: Cornell University Press, 2017). On the fluctuations in Putin's authoritarianism, see William Zimmerman, *Ruling Russia: Authoritarianism from the Revolution to Putin* (Princeton: Princeton University Press, 2016), pp. 220–90.
83. Kathryn Hendley, "Rule of Law, Russian-Style," *Current History*, Vol. 108 (2009), pp. 339–40; Richard Sakwa, "The Dual State in Russia," *Post-Soviet Affairs*, Vol. 26 (2010), pp. 185–206; Richard Sakwa, *The Crisis of Russian Democracy: The Dual State, Factionalism and the Medvedev Succession* (Cambridge: Cambridge University Press, 2010). One of the first scholars to describe postcommunist Russia as a hybrid regime was Lilia Shevtsova. See her "Russia's Hybrid Regime," *Journal of Democracy*, Vol. 12 (2001), pp. 65–70; but see also Gordon B. Smith, *Reforming the Russian Legal System* (Cambridge: Cambridge University Press, 1996).
84. Harold J. Berman, *Justice in the USSR: An Interpretation of Soviet Law*, Revised edition (Cambridge: Harvard University Press, 1963), p. 8. A few years earlier, Barrington Moore, Jr. had noticed a similar dualism in the Soviet regime's institutional design. See his *Terror and Progress: Some Sources of Change and Stability in the Soviet Dictatorship* (Cambridge: Harvard University Press, 1954).
85. Robert Sharlet, "Stalinism and Soviet Legal Culture," in Robert C. Tucker, ed., *Stalinism: Essays in Historical Interpretation* (New York: Norton, 1977), p. 155.
86. Sharlet, "Stalinism and Soviet Legal Culture," pp. 155–6.
87. For the most recent applications of the dual-state-concept to contemporary Russia, see Richard Sakwa, "Systematic Stalemate: *Reiderstvo* and the Dual State," in Neil Robinson, ed., *The Political Economy of Russia* (Lanham: Rowman and Littlefield, 2013), pp. 59–96; Geir Flikke, "Resurgent Authoritarianism: The Case of Russia's New NGO Legislation," *Post-Soviet Affairs*, Vol. 32 (2016), pp. 103–31.
88. Hendley, *Everyday Law in Russia*, p. 235. Note that by limiting its application to the legal arena, Hendley, very deliberately, uses the concept of the dual state in a non-Fraenkelian way. See also ibid, p. 4, fn. 3. This usage is not unproblematic, but space constraints prevent me from addressing the analytical implications.
89. I have adapted Lovett's concept of the rule of law, discussed above, for my purposes.

90. Edward H. Levi, "An Introduction to Legal Reasoning," *University of Chicago Law Review*, Vol. 15 (1948), pp. 501–2.
91. Levi, "An Introduction to Legal Reasoning," p. 502.
92. Levi, "An Introduction to Legal Reasoning," p. 502.
93. Neil MacCormick, *Legal Reasoning and Legal Theory* (Oxford: Clarendon Press: 1978), p. 15. See also Frederick Schauer, "Giving Reasons," *Stanford Law Review*, Vol. 47 (1995), pp. 633–59. For an account of legal reasoning as decision-making (including fact-finding) in legal proceedings, see Barbara A. Spellman and Frederick Schauer, "Legal Reasoning," in Keith J. Holyoak and Robert G. Morrison, eds., *The Oxford Handbook of Thinking and Reasoning* (Oxford: Oxford University Press, 2012), pp. 719–35. Lest I be misunderstood, my focus in this chapter is on legal reasoning in a more general sense.
94. I do not propose to raise or engage herein the many challenging philosophical questions pertaining to the topic of legal reasoning. Aside from MacCormick's aforementioned text, two very useful treatments are Schauer, *Playing by the Rules: A Philosophical Examination of Rule-Based Decision-Making in Law and in Life*; and idem., *Thinking Like a Lawyer: A New Introduction to Legal Reasoning* (Cambridge: Harvard University Press, 2012). See also Robert Alexy, *A Theory of Legal Argumentation: The Theory of Rational Discourse as Theory of Legal Justification*, translated by Ruth Adler and Neil MacCormick (Oxford: Oxford University Press, [1978] 1989); and Neil MacCormick, *Rhetoric and the Rule of Law: A Theory of Legal Reasoning* (Oxford: Oxford University Press, 2005); Larry Alexander, *Demystifying Legal Reasoning* (Cambridge: Cambridge University Press, 2008). Also relevant is Friedrich V. Kratochwil, *Rules, Norms, and Decisions: On the Conditions of Practical and Legal Reasoning in International Relations and Domestic Affairs* (Cambridge: Cambridge University Press, 1991).
95. It was H. L. A. Hart who advanced the argument that legal systems are built on rules, not commands, as legal positivists from Thomas Hobbes to John Austin had thought. See Hart, *The Concept of Law*, Second edition.
96. Frederick Schauer, *The Force of Law* (Cambridge: Harvard University Press, 2015), p. 156. For a related account in which "legality becomes a place where processes are fair, decisions are reasoned, and the rules are known beforehand, at the same time as it is a place where justice is only partially achieved, if at all—where public defenders don't show up, sick old women cannot get disability benefits, judges act irrationally and with prejudice, and the haves come out ahead," see Susan S. Silbey, "Legal Culture and Cultures of Legality," in John R. Hall, Laura Grindstaff, and Ming-Cheng Lo, eds., *Handbook of Cultural Sociology* (London: Routledge, 2010), p. 476.
97. As quoted in Schauer, *The Force of Law*, p. 156.
98. Barros, *Constitutionalism and Dictatorship*, p. 25.
99. Or, as Judith Shklar quipped, "procedurally 'correct' repression is perfectly compatible with legalism." Shklar, *Legalism*, p. 17.
100. See also Lovett, *A Republic of Law*, p. 91.

101. By way of prominent examples, see John L. Comaroff and Simon Roberts, *Rules and Processes: The Culural Logic of Dispute in an African Context* (Chicago: University of Chicago Press, 1981); Simon Roberts and Michael Palmer, *Dispute Processes: ADR and the Primary Forms of Decision-Making*, Second edition (Cambridge: Cambridge University Press, 2005).
102. William L. F. Felstiner, Richard L. Abel, and Austin Sarat, "The Emergence and Transformation of Disputes: Naming, Blaming, Claiming ...," *Law and Society Review*, Vol. 15 (1980/1981), pp. 631–54.
103. Roberts and Palmer, *Dispute Processes*, p. 1.
104. See my discussion above, esp. in Chapter 4.
105. Richard L. Abel, *Politics by Other Means: Law and the Struggle against Apartheid* (London: Routledge, 1995).
106. Dieter Gosewinkel, "Wirtschaftskontrolle und Recht in der nationalsozialistischen Diktatur: Forschung und Forschungsperspektiven," in idem., ed., *Wirtschaftskontrolle und Recht in der nationalsozialistischen Diktatur* (Frankfurt: Klostermann, 2005), p. xxi.
107. On the dualism than ran through the Nazi law of private property, see Alexander v. Brünneck, "Die Eigentumsordnung im Nationalsozialismus,"in Redaktion Kritische Justiz, ed., *Der Unrechts-Staat*, vol. 2: *Recht und Justiz im Nationalsozialismus* (Baden-Baden: Nomos, 1984), pp. 9–30. A more recent and comprehensive study of the politicization of property law in the Third Reich is Jan Schleusener, *Eigentumspolitik im NS-Staat: Der staatliche Umgang mit Handlungs- und Verfügungsrechten über privates Eigentum 1933–1939* (Frankfurt: Lang, 2009).
108. Caroline Harth, *Der Mythos von der Zerstörung des Vertrages: Zur Vertragslehre im Nationalsozialismus* (Frankfurt: Lang, 2008), p. 146.
109. Kees Gispen, *Poems in Steel: National Socialism and the Politics of Inventing from Weimar to Bonn* (New York: Berghahn, 2002), p. 48.
110. Gispen, *Poems in Steel*, p. 6.
111. Hendley, *Everyday Law in Russia*, esp. Chapters 2–5. Generally, see Sally Engle Merry, *Getting Justice and Getting Even: Legal Consciousness among Working-Class Americans* (Chicago: University of Chicago Press, 1990).
112. Hendley, *Everyday Law in Russia*, p. 231.
113. Richard Sakwa, "The Trials of Khodorkovsky in Russia," in Jens Meierhenrich and Devin O. Pendas, eds., *Political Trials in Theory and History* (Cambridge: Cambridge University Press, 2016), p. 393. The term "telephone law" (sometimes translated as "telephone justice") refer to what Russians call "*telefonnoye pravo*," the practice of "making an informal command, request, or [sending a] signal in order to influence formal procedures or decision-making." Alena Ledeneva, "Telephone Justice in Russia," *Post-Soviet Affairs*, Vol. 24 (2008), p. 326. According to Ledeneva, "The term emphasizes the prevalence of oral commands over written instructions; refers to the culture of informality and self-censorship; points to the limitations of the judiciary vis-à-vis administrative power; hints at the use of legal institutions for extra-legal purposes; and implies that networking and [politically instrumental] mediation remain essential

instruments of governance." Ibid. For an updated analysis, see also idem., *Can Russia Modernise? Sistema, Power Networks and Informal Governance* (Cambridge: Cambridge University Press, 2013), Chapter 5.

114. Hendley, *Everyday Law in Russia*, pp. 230, 231.
115. On rule-of-law indexes and their critics, see, most recently, Mila Versteeg and Tom Ginsburg, "Measuring the Rule of Law: A Comparison of Indicators," *Law and Social Inquiry*, Vol. 42 (2017), pp. 100–37; Sally Engle Merry, Kevin Davis, and Benedict Kingsbury, eds., *The Quiet Power of Indicators: Measuring Governance, Corruption, and Rule of Law* (Cambridge: Cambridge University Press, 2015). On pathologies in the rule-of-law industry, see, among others, Stephen Humphreys, *Theatre of the Rule of Law: Transnational Legal Intervention in Theory and Practice* (Cambridge: Cambridge University Press, 2010).
116. Michael Stubbs, "Semantics," in Constant Leung and Brian V. Street, eds., *The Routledge Companion to English Studies* (London: Routledge, 2014), p. 220.
117. Edmund Burke, "Thoughts on the Cause of the Present Discontents," in idem., *Select Works*, vol. 1, edited with an Introduction and Notes by E. J. Payne, Fifth edition (Oxford: Clarendon Press, [1770] 1874), p. 39. Fittingly, given the institutional questions that I addressed throughout this book, Burke's pamphlet was an intervention into the eighteenth-century-debate about whether the crown or parliament controlled the executive in England. It was a rebuke of King George III, of whose attempt to re-assert the crown's prerogative (without reneging entirely on the 1689 Declaration of Right which had imposed institutional limits on royal power) Burke did not approve. His judgment was unequivocal: The King's sly attempt to strengthen the prerogative state at the expense of England's fledgling normative state may not have violated the letter of the constitution, but it certainly violated its spirit. That, he warned, was a sure way to sink the country "into the dead repose of despotism." Ibid p. 92. On England's Glorious Revolution generally, see, for example, Steve Pincus, *1688: The First Modern Revolution* (New Haven: Yale University Press, 2009). For a seminal institutionalist interpretation, see Douglass C. North and Barry Weingast, "Constitutions and Commitment: The Evolution of Institutions Governing Public Choice in Seventeenth-Century England," *Journal of Economic History*, Vol. 49 (1989), pp. 803–32. For a recent re-assessment of this seminal contribution, see Gary W. Cox, "Was the Glorious Revolution a Constitutional Watershed?," *Journal of Economic History*, Vol. 72 (2012), pp. 567–600.
118. Authoritarian legalism will be a recurring practice to the extent that it amounts to more than the occasional or ad hoc reliance on law as an instrument of rule; authoritarian legalism will be a defining feature of a hybrid authoritarian regime to the extent that its practice is an integral—not just incidental—feature of its institutional design.
119. Guillermo O'Donnell, "Polyarchies and the (Un)Rule of Law in Latin America: A Partial Conclusion." In Juan E. Méndez, Guillermo O'Donnell,

and Paulo Sérgio Pinheiro, eds., *The (Un)Rule of Law and the Underprivileged in Latin America* (Notre Dame: University of Notre Dame Press, 1999), p. 334.

120. I develop this argument at length in Meierhenrich, *The Violence of Law*, Unpublished book manuscript, Harvard University, 2009, a comparative historical analysis of the Rwandan case that ranges from pre-colonial to post-genocidal times. For similar critiques of post-genocidal legalism in Rwanda, see Filip Reyntjens, *Political Governance in Post-Genocide Rwanda* (Cambridge: Cambridge University Press, 2013); Timothy Longman, *Memory and Justice in Post-Genocide Rwanda* (Cambridge: Cambridge University Press, 2017).

121. I have analyzed the role of legal culture(s) under authoritarianism at length elsewhere. See my *The Legacies of Law*, esp. pp. 219–64. Relevant scholarship on the elusive concept of legal culture, in addition to Clifford Geertz's oeuvre, includes Lawrence M. Friedman, *The Legal System: A Social Science Perspective* (New York: Russell Sage Foundation, 1975); idem., *The Republic of Choice: Law, Authority, and Culture* (Cambridge: Harvard University Press, 1990); David Nelken, "Rethinking Legal Culture," in Michael Freeman, ed., *Law and Sociology* (Oxford: Oxford University Press, 2006), pp. 200–24; Silbey, "Legal Culture and Cultures of Legality;" and Sally Engle Merry, "What is Legal Culture? An Anthropological Perspective," *Journal of Comparative Law*, Vol. 5 (2010), pp. 40–58.

122. Bruce Gilley, "Democratic Enclaves in Authoritarian Regimes," *Democratization*, Vol. 17 (2010), p. 391. My use of the term "legal enclaves" was inspired by Gilley.

123. Gillian K. Hadfield and Barry R. Weingast, "Microfoundations of the Rule of Law," *Annual Review of Political Science*, Vol. 17 (2014), pp. 24, 30.

124. Of course, it is entirely conceivable that legal consciousness will develop after sufficient exposure to a legal way of doing things. For an example, see Mary E. Gallagher, "Mobilizing the Law in China: 'Informed Disenchantment' and the Development of Legal Consciousness," *Law and Society Review*, Vol. 40 (2006), pp. 783–816. On fluctuations in legal consciousness (and the existence of multiple "legal consciousnesses"), see also Hendley, *Everyday Law in Russia*, esp. Chapter 1.

125. Brian Z. Tamanaha, "The Primacy of Society and the Failure of Law and Development," *Cornell International Law Journal*, Vol. 44 (2011), p. 214.

126. Yuhua Wang, *Tying the Autocrat's Hands: The Rise of the Rule of Law in China* (Cambridge: Cambridge University Press, 2015), p. 155.

127. The first Chinese law on foreign direct investment dates back to 1979, but it proved insufficient to meet investor demands in the 1990s. See Jun Fu, *Institutions and Investments: Foreign Direct Investment in China during an Era of Reforms* (Ann Arbor: University of Michigan Press, 2000). The literature on Chinese legalism is sizable. Space constraints disallow me to do justice to it here. For reliable overviews, see Stanley B. Lubman, *Bird in a Cage: Legal Reform in China After Mao* (Stanford: Stanford University Press, 2000); idem., ed., *China's Legal Reforms* (Oxford: Oxford

University Press, 1996; Randall Peerenboom, *China's Long March toward the Rule of Law* (Cambridge: Cambridge University Press, 2002). More recently, see Rachel E. Stern, *Environmental Litigation in China: A Study in Political Ambivalence* (Cambridge: Cambridge University Press, 2013); Sida Liu and Terence C. Halliday, *Criminal Defense in China: The Politics of Lawyers at Work* (Cambridge: Cambridge University Press, 2016); and Kwai Ng and Xin He, *Judicial Decision-Making in China: Embedded Courts* (Cambridge: Cambridge University Press, 2017).

128. Wang, *Tying the Autocrat's Hands*, p. 43. Legal institutions at all levels of government are carefully monitored by *zhengfa wei*, the Communist Party's political and legal committees responsible for a given locality. They are the eyes and ears and muscle of the prerogative state in China. Their intervention can put a quick end to legalism, remind citizens of the supremacy of decisionism.
129. Wang, *Tying the Autocrat's Hands*, p. 37.
130. The term is Barros's. See *Constitutionalism and Dictatorship*, p. 20. Following Lovett, I take "arbitrariness" to refer to an institutional state of being in which power is or can be wielded free of "effective and reliable constraints that are common knowledge to all persons or groups concerned." It goes hand in hand with extreme forms of domination, "the uncontrolled ability to wield coercive force over others." Lovett, *A Republic of Law*, pp. 115, 116.
131. Barros, *Constitutionalism and Dictatorship*, p. 20.
132. Barros, *Constitutionalism and Dictatorship*, p. 25.
133. Fraenkel, *The Dual State*, p. 71. Note that Fraenkel's conception of the rule of law was a substantive one. It differed from my understanding of the rule of law.
134. Gandhi, *Political Institutions under Dictatorship*, p. xxiv.
135. Fraenkel, *The Dual State*, p. 27.
136. Lovett, *A Republic of Law*, p. 117.
137. Lovett, *A Republic of Law*, p. 117.
138. Lovett, *A Republic of Law*, p. 117.
139. Lovett, *A Republic of Law*, p. 117.
140. On China, see Mary E. Gallagher, *Authoritarian Legality in China: Law, Workers, and the State* (Cambridge: Cambridge University Press, 2017); on Egypt, see Moustafa, *The Struggle for Constitutional Power*; on Hungary, see Miklós Bánkuti, Gábor Halmai, and Kim Lane Scheppele, "Hungary's Illiberal Turn: Disabling the Constitution," *Journal of Democracy*, Vol. 23 (2012), pp. 138–46; on Venezuela, see Javier Corrales, "The Authoritarian Resurgence: Autocratic Legalism in Venezuela," *Journal of Democracy*, Vol. 26 (2015), pp. 37–51. On the first wave of authoritarianism in the twenty-first century, see Larry Diamond, Marc F. Plattner, and Christopher Walker, eds., *Authoritarianism Goes Global: The Challenge to Democracy* (Baltimore: Johns Hopkins University Press, 2016).
141. For an urgent answer from a different time, see Philippe Nonet and Philip Selznick, *Law and Society in Transition: Toward Responsive Law* (New York: Harper 1978).

142. Brian Z. Tamanaha, *On the Rule of Law: History, Politics, Theory* (Cambridge: Cambridge University Press, 2004), p. 5
143. Martin Loughlin, *Sword and Scales: An Examination of the Relationship between Law and Politics* (Oxford: Hart, 2000), p. 202.
144. Jothie Rajah, *Authoritarian Rule of Law: Legislation, Discourse and Legitimacy in Singapore* (Cambridge: Cambridge University Press, 2012), p. 8.
145. In Spanish, the suffix "*-blanda*" means "soft" as opposed to "*-dura*" in *dictadura*, which denotes hardness. The Portuguese equivalent of "*dictablanda*," which has been controversially applied to Brazil's dictatorship of 1964–1985, is "*ditabranda*" or "*ditamole*." The term has since been used to describe aspects of authoritarian rule in Mexico (1938–1968), Spain (1939–1975), and Chile (1973–1990). See, for example, Anthony W. Pereira, *Political (In) Justice: Authoritarianism and the Rule of Law in Brazil, Chile, and Argentina* (Pittsburgh: University of Pittsburgh Press, 2005); Paul Gillingham and Benjamin T. Smith, eds., *Dictablanda: Politics, Work, and Culture in Mexico, 1938–1968* (Durham: Duke University Press, 2014).
146. Juan J. Linz, "An Authoritarian Regime: The Case of Spain," in Erik Allardt and Yrjö Littunen, eds., *Cleavages, Ideologies, and Party Systems: Contributions to Contemporary Sociology* (Helsinki: Academic Bookstore, 1964), p. 267.
147. Juan J. Linz, "Opposition in and under an Authoritarian Regime: The Case of Spain," in Robert A. Dahl, ed., *Regimes and Oppositions* (New Haven: Yale University Press, 1973), p. 252.
148. Linz, "Opposition in and under an Authoritarian Regime," p. 253. For a re-conceptualization of political trials, see Jens Meierhenrich and Devin O. Pendas, "'The Justice of My Cause is Clear, but There's Politics to Fear': Political Trials in Theory and History", in idem., eds., *Political Trials in Theory and History*, pp. 1–64.
149. Lisa Hilbink, "The Origins of Positive Judicial Independence," *World Politics*, Vol. 64 (2012), p. 601.
150. Hilbink, "The Origins of Positive Judicial Independence," p. 603.
151. John Austin, *The Province of Jurisprudence Determined*, edited by H. L. A. Hart (London: Oxford University Press, 1954), pp. 184–5.
152. MacCormick, "Law, Morality and Positivism," p. 132.
153. Most recently, see Mark Fathi Massoud, *Law's Fragile State: Colonial, Authoritarian, and Humanitarian Legacies in Sudan* (Cambridge: Cambridge University Press, 2013); *Nick Cheesman, Opposing the Rule of Law: How Myanmar's Courts Make Law and Order* (Cambridge: Cambridge Uiversity Press, 2015).
154. Samuel Moyn, "Judith Shklar versus the International Criminal Court," *Humanity*, Vol. 4 (2013), p. 478.
155. World Bank, *World Development Report 2017: Governance and the Law* (Washington: World Bank, 2017). For a related argument as to why Fraenkel's institutional theory of dictatorship is relevant to making democracy work in the twenty-first century, see Lutz Oette, "Document and Analyze: The Legacy of Klemperer, Fraenkel, and Neumann for Contemporary Human Rights Engagment," *Human Rights Quarterly*, Vol. 39 (2017), pp. 832–59.

According to Oette, empirically thick scholarship like Fraenkel's (and that of Franz Neumann and Victor Klemperer) amounts to "a call from the past to be rigorous in analyzing how a [given] regime or system operates and how it impacts individuals, institutions, and society at large." Ibid., p. 858. Among other things, writes Oette, "[t]his requires "paying close attention to language and documents, i.e., to take the outputs of a regime seriously." Ibid. Klemperer did this masterfully, dissecting in his diaries and elsewhere, the presentation of dictatorship in everyday life. In 1995, thirty-five years after his death, and to much acclaim, his clandestine observations were posthumously published. They have been hailed the world over. See, for example, Omer Bartov, "The Last German," *The New Republic*, December 28, 1998. Fraenkel was no less masterful than Klemperer in making sense of the unthinkable. His work, like Klemperer's, "underscores the power of documentation and analysis as praxis of resistance." Oette, "Document and Analyze," p. 858.

Bibliography

Abel, Richard L., *Politics by Other Means: Law and the Struggle against Apartheid* (London: Routledge, 1995)

Acemoglu, Daron, and James A. Morrison, *Economic Origins of Dictatorship and Democracy* (Cambridge: Cambridge University Press, 2006)

Adcock, Robert, and David Collier, "Measurement Validity: A Shared Standard for Qualitative and Quantitative Research," *American Political Science Review*, Vol. 95 (2001), pp. 529–46

Ahram, Ariel I., and J. Paul Goode, "Researching Authoritarianism in the Discipline of Democracy," *Social Science Quarterly*, Vol. 97 (2016), pp. 834–49

Alexander, Larry, *Demystifying Legal Reasoning* (Cambridge: Cambridge University Press, 2008)

Alexy, Robert, *A Theory of Legal Argumentation: The Theory of Rational Discourse as Theory of Legal Justification*, translated by Ruth Adler and Neil MacCormick (Oxford: Oxford University Press, [1978] 1989)

Alexy, Robert, *The Argument from Injustice: A Reply to Legal Positivism*, translated by Stanley L. Paulson and Bonnie Litschewski Paulson (Oxford: Oxford University Press, [1992] 2002)

Alexy, Robert, "A Defence of Radbruch's Formula," in David Dyzenhaus, ed., *Recrafting the Rule of Law* (Oxford: Hart, 1999), pp. 15–39

Alvarez, Mike, José Antonio Cheibub, Fernando Limongi, and Adam Przeworski, "Classifying Political Regimes," *Studies in Comparative International Development*, Vol. 31 (1996), pp. 3–36

Aly, Götz, and Susanne Heim, *Architects of Annihilation: Auschwitz and the Logic of Destruction*, translated by A. G. Blunden (Princeton: Princeton University Press, [1991] 2002)

Anderbrügge, Klaus, *Völkisches Rechtsdenken: Zur Rechtslehre in der Zeit des Nationalsozialismus* (Berlin: Duncker and Humblot, 1978)

Andrini, Simona, "Max Weber's Sociology of Law as a Turning Point of his Methodological Approach," *International Review of Sociology*, Vol. 14 (2004), pp. 143–50

Angermund, Ralph, *Deutsche Richterschaft 1919–1945: Krisenerfahrung, Illusion, politische Rechtsprechung* (Frankfurt: Fischer, 1990)

Anschütz, Gerhard, *Die gegenwärtigen Theorien über den Begriff der gesetzgebenden Gewalt und den Umfang des königlichen Verordnungsrechts nach preußischem Staatsrecht*, Second edition (Tübingen: Mohr, 1901)

Anter, Andreas, *Die Macht der Ordnung: Aspekte einer Grundkategorie des Politischen* (Tübingen: Mohr, 2004)

Anter, Andreas, *Max Weber und die Staatsrechtslehre* (Tübingen: Mohr, 2016)

Arad, Yitzhak, Yisrael Gutman, and Abraham Margaliot, eds., *Documents on the Holocaust: Selected Sources on the Destruction of the Jews of Germany and Austria, Poland and the Soviet Union* (Jerusalem: Yad Vashem, 1981)

Arato, Andrew, "Good-bye to Dictatorships?," *Social Research*, Vol. 67 (2000), pp. 925–55

Arendt, Hannah, *The Origins of Totalitarianism* (New York: Harcourt, Brace, 1951)

Arendt, Hannah, *Eichmann in Jerusalem: A Report on the Banality of Evil* (New York: Viking, 1963)

Aretin, Johann Christoph Freiherr von, *Staatsrecht der konstitutionellen Monarchie: Ein Handbuch für Geschäftsmänner, studirende Jünglinge, und gebildete Bürger*, vol. 1 (Altenburg: Literatur-Comptoir, 1824)

Aronson, Shlomo, "Preparations for the Nuremberg Trial: The O.S.S., Charles Dwork, and the Holocaust," *Holocaust and Genocide Studies*, Vol. 12 (1998), pp. 257–81

Art, David, "What Do We Know about Authoritarianism after Ten Years?," *Comparative Politics*, Vol. 44 (2012), pp. 351–73

Austin, John, *The Province of Jurisprudence Determined*, edited by H. L. A. Hart (London: Oxford University Press, 1954)

Avraham, Doron, "The Idea of a Jewish Nation in the German Discourse about Emancipation," *Nations and Nationalism*, Vol. 22 (2016), pp. 505–23

Bachmann, Hans Georg, "Militärgerichtsbarkeit der deutschen Wehrmacht 1939–1945 und Wehrdienstgerichtsbarkeit in der Bundeswehr seit 1957: Eine Gegenüberstellung," *Unterrichtsblätter für die Bundeswehrverwaltung*, Vol. 11 (2009), pp. 409–11

Bäcker, Carsten, *Gerechtigkeit im Rechtsstaat: Das Bundesverfassungsgericht an der Grenze des Grundgesetzes* (Tübingen: Mohr, 2015)

Badura, Peter, *Die Methoden der allgemeinen Staatslehre*, Second edition (Goldbach: Keip, [1959] 1998)

Badura, Peter, *Staatsrecht: Systematische Erläuterung des Grundgesetzes für die Bundesrepublik Deutschland*, Fourth edition (Munich: Beck, 2010)

Bánkuti, Miklós, Gábor Halmai, and Kim Lane Scheppele, "Hungary's Illiberal Turn: Disabling the Constitution," *Journal of Democracy*, Vol. 23 (2012), pp. 138-46

Barkai, Avraham, *From Boycott to Annihilation: The Economic Struggle of German Jews, 1933–1943*, translated by William Templer (Hanover: University Press of New England, 1989)

Barros, Robert, *Constitutionalism and Dictatorship: Pinochet, the Junta, and the 1980 Constitution* (Cambridge: Cambridge University Press, 2007)

Barth, Eberhard, *Wesen und Aufgaben der Organisation der gewerblichen Wirtschaft* (Hamburg: Hanseatische Verlagsanstalt, 1939)

Bast, Jürgen, *Totalitärer Pluralismus: Zu Franz L. Neumanns Analysen der politischen und rechtlichen Struktur der NS-Herrschaft* (Tübingen: Mohr, 1999)

Battenberg, Friedrich, *Die Juden in Deutschland vom 16. bis zum Ende des 18. Jahrhunderts* (Munich: Oldenbourg, 2001)

Bechtold, Hartmut, *Die Kartellierung der deutschen Volkswirtschaft und die sozialdemokratische Theorie-Diskussion vor 1933* (Frankfurt: Haag & Herchen, 1986)

Becker, Maximilian, *Mitstreiter im Volkstumskampf: Deutsche Justiz in den eingegliederten Ostgebieten 1939–1945* (Munich: Oldenbourg, 2014)

Behnken, Klaus, ed., *Deutschland-Berichte der Sozialdemokratischen Partei Deutschlands (Sopade) 1934–1940*, 7 volumes (Frankfurt: Nettelbeck, 1980)

Bendix, Reinhard, *Nation-Building and Citizenship*, Enlarged edition (Berkeley: University of California Press, 1977)

Berman, Harold J., *Justice in the USSR: An Interpretation of Soviet Law*, Revised edition (Cambridge: Harvard University Press, 1963)

Berman, Harold J., "The Rule of Law and the Law-Based State (*Rechtsstaat*) (with Special Reference to Developments in the Soviet Union)," Paper presented at the Conference "In Search of the Law-Governed State: Political and Societal Reform under Gorbachev," Lehigh University, May 29–June 1, 1991

Berry, Donald D., ed., *Toward the "Rule of Law" in Russia: Political and Legal Reform in the Transition Period* (London: M.E. Sharpe, 1992)

Bessel, Richard, *Life in the Third Reich* (Oxford: Oxford University Press, 1987)

Best, Werner, "Neubegründung des Polizeirechts," *Jahrbuch der Akademie für Deutsches Recht*, Vol. 4 (1937), pp. 132–8

Beyme, Klaus von, *Politische Theorien im Zeitalter der Ideologien* (Wiesbaden: Verlag für Sozialwissenschaften, 2002)

Bialas, Wolfgang, *Moralische Ordnungen des Nationalsozialismus* (Göttingen: Vandenhoeck und Ruprecht, 2014)

Bialas, Wolfgang, "Nationalsozialistische Ethik und Moral: Konzepte, Probleme, offene Fragen," in Wolfgang Bialas and Lothar Fritze, eds., *Ideologie und Moral im Nationalsozialismus* (Göttingen: Vandenhoeck und Ruprecht, 2013), pp. 23–63

Bialas, Wolfgang, and Manfred Gangl, eds., *Intellektuelle im Nationalsozialismus* (New York: Lang, 2000)

Bialas, Wolfgang, and Lothar Fritze, eds., *Ideologie und Moral im Nationalsozialismus* (Göttingen: Vandenhoeck und Ruprecht, 2013)

Binder, Julius, "Der autoritäre Staat," *Logos*, Vol. 22 (1933), pp. 126–60

Binder, Julius, *Grundlegung zur Rechtsphilosophie* (Tübingen: Mohr, 1935)

Binder, Julius, *System der Rechtsphilosophie*, Second edition (Berlin: Stilke, 1937)

Bix, Brian H., "Robert Alexy's Radbruch Formula, and the Nature of Legal Theory," *Rechtstheorie*, Vol. 37 (2006), pp. 139–49

Bix, Brian H., "Radbruch's Formula and Conceptual Analysis," *American Journal of Jurisprudence*, Vol. 56 (2011), pp. 45–57

Bix, Brian H., "Radbruch's Formula, Conceptual Analysis, and the Rule of Law," in Imer B. Flores and Kenneth E. Himma, eds., *Law, Liberty, and the Rule of Law* (New York: Springer, 2013), pp. 65–76

Blackbourn, David, "The Discreet Charm of the Bourgeoisie: Reappraising German History in the Nineteenth Century," in David Blackbourn and Geoff Eley, eds., *The Peculiarities of German History: Bourgeois Society and Politics in Nineteenth Century Germany* (Oxford: 1984), pp. 159–292

Blank, Hartmut, Jochen Musch, and Rüdiger F. Pohl, "Hindsight Bias: On Being Wise after the Event," *Social Cognition*, Vol. 25 (2007), pp. 1–9

Blanke, Bernhard, "Der deutsche Faschismus als Doppelstaat," *Kritische Justiz*, Vol. 6 (1975), pp. 221–43

Blau, Joachim, *Sozialdemokratische Staatslehre in der Weimarer Republik: Darstellung und Untersuchung der staatstheoretischen Konzeptionen von Hermann Heller, Ernst Fraenkel und Otto Kirchheimer* (Marburg: Verlag Arbeiterbewegung und Gesellschaftswissenschaft, 1980)

Bobbio, Norberto, *Democracy and Dictatorship: The Nature and Limits of State Power*, translated by Peter Kennealy (Cambridge: Polity, [1980] 1989)

Bobbio, Norberto, "Introduzione," in Ernst Fraenkel, *Il doppio Stato: Contributo alla teoria della dittatura*, translated by Pier Paolo Portinaro (Turin: Einaudi, 1983), pp. ix–xxiv

Boberach, Heinz, ed., *Richterbriefe: Dokumente zur Beeinflussung der deutschen Rechtsprechung 1942–1944* (Boppard: Boldt, 1975)

Böckenförde, Ernst-Wolfgang, "Entstehung und Wandel des Rechtsstaatsbegriffs," in idem., *Recht, Staat, Freiheit: Studien zur Rechtsphilosophie, Staatstheorie und Verfassungsgerichtsbarkeit* (Frankfurt: Suhrkamp, [1969] 1991), pp. 143–69

Boemeke, Manfred F., Gerald D. Feldman, and Elisabeth Glaser, eds., *The Treaty of Versailles: A Reassessment after 75 Years* (Cambridge: Cambridge University Press, 2008)

Bogaards, Matthijs, "How to Classify Hybrid Regimes? Defective Democracy and Electoral Authoritarianism," *Democratization*, Vol. 16 (2009), pp. 399–423

Bohannan, Paul, *Justice and Judgment among the Tiv* (London: Oxford University Press, 1957)

Boix, Carles, and Milan W. Svolik, "The Foundations of Limited Authoritarian Government: Institutions, Commitment, and Power-Sharing in Dictatorships," *Journal of Politics*, Vol. 75 (2013), pp. 300–16

Bonn, Moritz Julius, "Franz Neumann, Behemoth: The Structure and Practice of National Socialism" (Book review), *Journal of Political Economy*, Vol. 51 (1943), p. 371

Bonn, Moritz Julius, *So macht man Geschichte: Bilanz eines Lebens* (Munich: List, 1953)

Borowski, Martin, and Stanley L. Paulson, eds., *Die Natur des Rechts bei Gustav Radbruch* (Tübingen: Mohr, 2015)

Bracher, Karl Dietrich, *Die Auflösung der Weimarer Republik: Eine Studie zum Problem des Machtverfalls in der Demokratie* (Villingen: Ring, 1955)

Bracher, Karl Dietrich, "Zusammenbruch des Versailler Systems und Zweiter Weltkrieg," in Golo Mann and August Nitschke, eds., *Propyläen Weltgeschichte: Eine Universalgeschichte*, vol. 9: *Das zwanzigste Jahrhundert* (Berlin: Propyläen, 1960), pp. 398–9

Bracher, Karl Dietrich, *Die deutsche Diktatur: Entstehung, Struktur, Folgen des Nationalsozialismus* (Köln: Kiepenheuer and Witsch, 1969)

Bracher, Karl Dietrich, *The German Dictatorship: The Origins, Structure, and Effects of National Socialism*, translated from the German by Jean Steinberg, with an Introduction by Peter Gay (London: Weidenfeld and Nicolson, [1969] 1971)

Bracher, Karl Dietrich, Wolfgang Sauer, and Gerhard Schulz, *Die nationalsozialistische Machtergreifung: Studien zur Errichtung des totalitären Herrschaftssystems in Deutschland 1933/34* (Cologne: Westdeutscher Verlag, 1960)

Brady, Robert A., "Franz Neumann, Behemoth: The Structure and Practice of National Socialism" (Book review), *American Economic Review*, Vol. 33 (1943), pp. 386–9

Brechtken, Magnus, Hans-Christian Jasch, Christoph Kreutzmüller, and Niels Weise, eds., *Die Nürnberger Gesetze–80 Jahre danach: Vorgeschichte, Entstehung, Auswirkungen* (Göttingen: Wallstein, 2017)

Breuer, Stefan, *Georg Jellinek und Max Weber: Von der sozialen zur soziologischen Staatslehre* (Baden-Baden: Nomos, 1999)

Broszat, Martin, *Der Staat Hitlers: Grundlegung und Entwicklung seiner inneren Verfassung* (Munich: dtv, 1969)

Browning, Christopher R., *The Origins of the Final Solution: The Evolution of Nazi Jewish Policy, September 1939–March 1942* (Lincoln: University of Nebraska Press, 2004)

Brownlee, Jason, *Authoritarianism in an Age of Democratization* (Cambridge: Cambridge University Press, 2007)

Brownlee, Jason, "Portents of Pluralism: How Hybrid Regimes Affect Democratic Transitions," *American Journal of Political Science*, Vol. 53 (2009), pp. 515–32

Brubaker, Rogers, and Frederick Cooper, "Beyond 'Identity,' " *Theory and Society*, Vol. 29 (2000), pp. 1–47

Brugger, Winfried, "Communitarianism as the Social and Legal Theory behind the German Constitution," *International Journal of Constitutional Law*, Vol. 2 (2004), pp. 431–60

Bruneteau, Bernard, ed., *Le Totalitarisme: Origines d'un concept, genèse d'un débat, 1930–1942* (Paris: Cerf, 2010)

Brünneck, Alexander v., "Ernst Fraenkel, The Dual State: A Contribution to the Theory of Dictatorship" (Book review), *Kritische Justiz*, Vol. 2 (1969), pp. 319–21

Brünneck, Alexander v., "Die Eigentumsordnung im Nationalsozialismus," in Redaktion Kritische Justiz, ed., *Der Unrechts-Staat*, vol. 2: *Recht und Justiz im Nationalsozialismus* (Baden-Baden: Nomos, 1984), pp. 9–30

Brünneck, Alexander v., "Vorwort zu diesem Band," in Ernst Fraenkel, *Gesammelte Schriften*, vol. 2: *Nationalsozialismus und Widerstand*, edited by Alexander v. Brünneck, Hubertus Buchstein, and Gerhard Göhler (Baden-Baden: Nomos, 1999), pp. 7–32

Brünneck, Alexander v., "Ernst Fraenkels Urdoppelstaat von 1938 und der Doppelstaat von 1941/1974," in Hubertus Buchstein and Gerhard Göhler, eds., *Vom Sozialismus zum Pluralismus: Beiträge zu Werk und Leben Ernst Fraenkels* (Baden-Baden: Nomos, 2000), pp. 29–42

Brünneck, Alexander v., "Vorwort zu diesem Band," in Ernst Fraenkel, *Gesammelte Schriften*, vol. 5: *Demokratie und Pluralismus*, edited by Alexander v. Brünneck (Baden-Baden: Nomos, 2007), pp. 9–36

Buchheim, Hans, "Die SS—das Herrschaftsinstrument," in Hans Buchheim, Martin Broszat, Hans-Adolf Jacobsen, and Helmut Krausnick, eds., *Anatomie des SS-Staates*, Seventh edition (Munich: dtv, [1967] 1999), pp. 15–212

Buchheim, Hans, Martin Broszat, Hans-Adolf Jacobsen, and Helmut Krausnick, eds., *Anatomie des SS-Staates*, Seventh edition (Munich: dtv, [1967] 1999)

Buchstein, Hubertus, and Rainer Kühn, "Vorwort zu diesem Band," in Ernst Fraenkel, *Gesammelte Schriften*, vol. 1: *Recht und Politik in der Weimarer Republik*, edited by Hubertus Buchstein (Baden-Baden: Nomos, 1999), pp. 15–54

Bundesminister der Justiz, ed., *Im Names des Deutschen Volkes: Justiz und Nationalsozialismus* (Cologne: Verlag Wissenschaft und Politik, 1989)

Bundesministerium für Justiz und für Verbraucherschutz, ed., *Das Ende eines Aufbruchs: Jüdische Juristinnen und Juristinnen jüdischer Herkunft nach 1933* (Berlin: Bundesanzeiger, 2016)

Bundesrechtsanwaltskammer, ed., *Anwalt ohne Recht: Schicksale jüdischer Anwälte in Deutschland nach 1933* (Berlin: be.bra Verlag, 2007)

Burawoy, Michael, "Revisits: An Outline of a Theory of Reflexive Ethnography," *American Sociological Review*, Vol. 68 (2003), pp. 645–79

Burbank, Jane, *Russian Peasants Go to Court: Legal Culture in the Countryside, 1905–1917* (Bloomington: Indiana University Press, 2004)

Burin, Frederic S., and Kurt L. Shell, eds., *Politics, Law, and Social Change: Selected Essays of Otto Kirchheimer* (New York: Columbia University Press, 1969)

Burke, Edmund, "Thoughts on the Cause of the Present Discontents," in idem., *Select Works*, vol. 1, edited with an Introduction and Notes by E. J. Payne, Fifth edition (Oxford: Clarendon Press, [1770] 1874), pp. 69–156

Burleigh, Michael, and Wolfgang Wippermann, *The Racial State: Germany 1933–1945* (Cambridge: Cambridge University Press, 1991)

Bush, Jonathan A., "Raul Hilberg (1926–2007) in Memoriam," *Jewish Quarterly Review*, Vol. 100 (2010), pp. 661–88

Caldwell, Peter C., "National Socialism and Constitutional Law: Carl Schmitt, Otto Koellreutter, and the Debate over the Nature of the Nazi State, 1993–1937," *Cardozo Law Review*, Vol. 16 (1994), pp. 399–427

Caldwell, Peter C., *Popular Sovereignty and the Crisis of German Constitutional Law: The Theory and Practice of Weimar Constitutionalism* (Durham: Duke University Press, 1997)

Caldwell, Peter C., "Hugo Preuss's Concept of the Volk: Critical Confusion or Sophisticated Conception?," *University of Toronto Law Journal*, Vol. 63 (2013), pp. 347–84

Cane, Peter, ed., *The Hart-Fuller Debate in the Twenty-First Century* (Oxford: Hart, 2010)

Capitan, René, *La réforme du parlamentarisme* (Paris: Recueil Sirey, 1934)

Caplan, Jane, *Government without Administration: State and Civil Society in Weimar and Nazi Germany* (Oxford: Clarendon Press, 1988)

Caplan, Jane, ed., *Nazi Germany* (Oxford: Oxford University Press, 2008)

Car, Roland, "Community of Neighbours vs Society of Merchants: The Genesis of Reinhard Höhn's Nazi State Theory," *Politics, Religion, and Ideology*, Vol. 16 (2015), pp. 1–22

Carr, Albert H. Z., *Juggernaut: The Path of Dictatorship* (New York: Viking, 1939)

Cassani, Andrea, "Hybrid What? Partial Consensus and Persistent Divergence in the Analysis of Hybrid Regimes," *International Political Science Review*, Vol. 35 (2014), pp. 542–58

Castoriadis, Cornelius, *L'Institution imaginaire de la societe* (Paris: Seuil, 1975)

Cheesman, Nick, *Opposing the Rule of Law: How Myanmar's Courts Make Law and Order* (Cambridge: Cambridge Uiversity Press, 2015)

Cheibub, José Antonio, Jennifer Gandhi, and James Raymond Vreeland, "Democracy and Dictatorship Revisited, *Public Choice*, Vol. 143 (2010), pp. 67–101

Childers, Thomas, *The Third Reich: A History of Nazi Germany* (New York: Simon and Schuster, 2017)

Childers, Thomas, and Jane Caplan, eds., *Reevaluating the Third Reich: New Controversies, New Interpretations* (New York: Holmes and Meier, 1993)

Clark, Christopher, *Iron Kingdom: The Rise and Downfall of Prussia, 1600–1947* (Cambridge: Belknap Press of Harvard University Press, 2006)

Cobban, Alfred, *Dictatorship: Its History and Theory* (London: Jonathan Cape, 1939)

Cohrs, Patrick O., *The Unfinished Peace after World War I: America, Britain and the Stabilisation of Europe, 1919–1932* (Cambridge: Cambridge University Press, 2006)

Cole, Taylor, "Ernst Fraenkel, The Dual State: A Contribution to the Theory of Dictatorship" (Book review), *Review of Politics*, Vol. 3 (1941), pp. 254–6

Collier, David, "Data, Field Work, and Extracting New Ideas at Close Range," *APSA-CP: Newsletter of the Organized Section in Comparative Politics of the American Political Science Association*, No. 10 (1999), pp. 1–6

Collier, David, and James E. Mahon, Jr., "Conceptual 'Stretching' Revisited: Adapting Categories in Comparative Analysis," *American Political Science Review*, Vol. 87 (1993), pp. 845–55

Colomer, Josep M., *Strategic Transitions: Game Theory and Democratization* (Baltimore: Johns Hopkins University Press, 2000)

Comaroff, John L., and Simon Roberts, *Rules and Processes: The Culural Logic of Dispute in an African Context* (Chicago: University of Chicago Press, 1981)

Conley, John M., and William M. O'Barr, "Back to the Trobriands: The Enduring Influence of Malinowski's *Crime and Custom in Savage Society*," *Law and Social Inquiry*, Vol. 27 (2002), pp. 847–74

Coogan, Michael D., "Behemoth," in Bruce M. Metzger and Michael D. Coogan, eds., *The Oxford Guide to People and Places of the Bible* (New York: Oxford University Press, 2001), p. 33

Corino, Karl, ed., *Intellektuelle im Bann des Nationalsozialismus* (Hamburg: Hoffmann und Campe, 1980)

Corrales, Javier, "The Authoritarian Resurgence: Autocratic Legalism in Venezuela," *Journal of Democracy*, Vol. 26 (2015), pp. 37–51

Cotterrell, Roger, "Interdisciplinarity: The Expansion of Knowledge and the Design of Research," *Higher Education Review*, Vol. 11 (1979), pp. 47–56

Cotterrell, Roger, "The Rule of Law in Corporate Society: Neumann, Kirchheimer and the Lessons of Weimar," *Modern Law Review*, Vol. 51 (1988), pp. 126–40

Couso, Javier A., Alexandra Huneeus, and Rachel Sieder, eds., *Cultures of Legality: Judicialization and Political Activism in Latin America* (Cambridge: Cambridge University Press, 2010)

Cox, Gary W., "Was the Glorious Revolution a Constitutional Watershed?," *Journal of Economic History*, Vol. 72 (2012), pp. 567–600

Crafts, Nicholas, and Peter Fearon, eds., *The Great Depression of the 1930s: Lessons for Today* (Oxford: Oxford University Press, 2013)

Cramer, Frederick H., "Franz Neumann, Behemoth: The Structure and Practice of National Socialism" (Book review), *Journal of Modern History*, Vol. 15 (1943), pp. 156–7

Croissant, Aurel, Steffen Kailitz, Patrick Koellner, and Stefan Wurster, eds., *Comparing Autocracies in the Early Twenty-first Century*, 2 volumes (London: Routledge, 2014)

Dahl, Robert A., *Polyarchy: Participation and Opposition* (New Haven: Yale University Press, 1971)

Dahm, Georg, Karl August Eckhardt, Reinhard Höhn, Paul Ritterbusch, and Wolfgang Siebert, "Leitsätze über die Stellung und Aufgaben des Richters," *Deutsche Rechtswissenschaft*, Vol. 1 (1936), pp. 123–4

Dahrendorf, Ralf, *Society and Democracy in Germany* (London: Weidenfeld and Nicolson, 1968)

Darmstädter, Friedrich, *Rechtsstaat oder Machtstaat? Eine Frage nach der Geltung der Weimarer Verfassung* (Berlin: Rothschild, 1932)

Dean, Martin, *Robbing the Jews: The Confiscation of Jewish Property in the Holocaust, 1933–1945* (Cambridge: Cambridge University Press, 2008)

Dennewitz, Bodo, *Das nationale Deutschland ein Rechtsstaat: Die Rechtsgrundlagen des neuen deutschen Staates* (Berlin: Vahlen, 1933)

Dennewitz, Bodo, *Staatslehre und nationalsozialistischer Staat* (Berlin: Vahlen, 1934)

Diamond, Larry, "Thinking about Hybrid Regimes," *Journal of Democracy*, Vol. 13 (2002), pp. 21–35

Diamond, Larry, Marc F. Plattner, and Christopher Walker, eds., *Authoritarianism Goes Global: The Challenge to Democracy* (Baltimore: Johns Hopkins University Press, 2016)

Dicey, A. V., *Introduction to the Study of the Law of the Constitution*, Eighth edition (London: Macmillan, 1926)

Ditt, Thomas, "*Stoßtruppfakultät Breslau*": *Rechtswissenschaft im "Grenzland Schlesien" 1933–1945* (Tübingen: Mohr, 2011)

Doeker, Günther, and Winfried Steffani, eds., *Klassenjustiz und Pluralismus: Festschrift für Ernst Fraenkel zum 75. Geburtstag* (Hamburg: Hoffmann und Campe, 1973)

Donovan, James M., *Legal Anthropology: An Introduction* (Lanham: Rowman and Littlefield, 2008)

Dreier, Horst, "Verfassungs- und Verwaltungsrecht 1914–1945," in idem., *Staatsrecht in Demokratie und Diktatur: Studien zur Weimarer Republik und zum Nationalsozialismus*, edited by Matthias Jestaedt and Stanley L. Paulson (Tübingen: Mohr, [2000] 2016), pp. 397–420

Dreier, Horst, "Die deutsche Staatsrechtslehre in der Zeit des Nationalsozialismus," in idem., *Staatsrecht in Demokratie und Diktatur: Studien zur Weimarer Republik und zum Nationalsozialismus*, edited by Matthias Jestaedt and Stanley L. Paulson (Tübingen: Mohr, [2001] 2016), pp. 185–259

Dreier, Horst, "Nachwort: Was ist doppelt am 'Doppelstaat'? Zu Rezeption und Bedeutung der klassischen Studie von Ernst Fraenkel," in Ernst Fraenkel, *Der Doppelstaat*, Third edition, edited with an Introduction by Alexander v. Brünneck, with an Afterword by Horst Dreier (Frankfurt: Europäische Verlagsanstalt, 2012), pp. 274–300

Dworkin, Ronald, "Philosophy, Morality, and Law—Observations Prompted by Professor Fuller's Novel Claim," *University of Pennsylvania Law Review*, Vol. 113 (1965), pp. 668–90

Dyzenhaus, David, *Legality and Legitimacy: Carl Schmitt, Hans Kelsen, and Hermann Heller in Weimar* (Oxford: Oxford University Press, 1997)

Dyzenhaus, David, "Leviathan in the 1930s: The Reception of Hobbes in the Third Reich," in John P. McCormick, ed., *Confronting Mass Democracy and Industrial Technology: Political and Social Theory from Nietzsche to Habermas* (Durham: Duke University Press, 2002), pp. 163–91

Dyzenhaus, David, "The Idea of a Constitution: A Plea for *Staatsrechtslehre*," in David Dyzenhaus and Malcolm Thorburn, eds., *Philosophical Foundations of Constitutional Law* (Oxford: Oxford University Press, 2016), pp. 1–32

Ehrlich, Eugen, *Grundlegung der Soziologie des Rechts* (Munich: Duncker and Humblot, 1913)

Ehrlich, Eugen, *Fundamental Principles of the Sociology of Law*, translated by Walter L. Moll (Cambridge: Harvard University Press, [1913] 1936)

Eichmüller, Andreas, *Keine Generalamnestie: Die Strafverfolgung von NS-Verbrechen in der frühen Bundesrepublik* (Berlin: De Gruyter, 2012)

Elster, Jon, "Cohen on Marx's Theory of History: Review of G. A. Cohen, *Karl Marx's Theory of History*," *Political Studies*, Vol. 28 (1980), pp. 121–8

Elster, Jon, "The Case for Methodological Individualism," *Theory and Society*, Vol. 11 (1982), pp. 453–82

Elster, Jon, *Making Sense of Marx* (Cambridge: Cambridge University Press, 1985)

Elster, Jon, *Alexis de Tocqueville, the First Social Scientist* (Cambridge: Cambridge University Press, 2009)

Emerson, Robert M., Rachel I. Fretz, and Linda L. Shaw, *Writing Ethnographic Fieldnotes*, Second edition (Chicago: University of Chicago Press, 2011)

Emge, Carl August, *Vorschule der Rechtsphilosophie* (Berlin: Rothschild, 1925)

Emge, Carl August, *Geschichte der Rechtsphilosophie* (Berlin: Junker und Dünnhaupt, 1931)

Epstein, Klaus, *Vom Kaisserreich zum Dritten Reich: Geschichte und Geschichtswissenschaft im 20. Jahrhundert* (Frankfurt: Ullstein, 1973)

Erd, Rainer, ed., *Reform und Resignation: Gespräche über Franz L. Neumann* (Frankfurt: Suhrkamp, 1985)

Evans, Richard J., *The Third Reich in Power 1933–1939* (New York: Penguin, 2005)

Fatovic, Clement, "The Political Theology of Prerogative: The Jurisprudential Miracle in Liberal Constitutional Thought," *Perspectives on Politics*, Vol. 6 (2008), pp. 487–501

Felice, Franco de, "Doppia lealtà e doppio Stato," *Studi Storici*, Vol. 30 (1989), pp. 493–563

Felstiner, William L. F., Richard L. Abel, and Austin Sarat, "The Emergence and Transformation of Disputes: Naming, Blaming, Claiming . . . ," *Law and Society Review*, Vol. 15 (1980/1981), pp. 631–54

Fest, Joachim, "Der fremde Freund," *Der Spiegel*, August 11, 2003

Finnis, John, *Natural Law and Natural Rights*, Second edition (Oxford: Oxford University Press, 2011)

Finnis, John, "Natural Law Theories," *Stanford Encyclopedia of Philosophy*, available at https://plato.stanford.edu/archives/win2016/entries/natural-law-theories/

Fioretos, Orfeo, Tulia G. Falleti, and Adam Sheingate, eds., *The Oxford Handbook of Historical Institutionalism* (Oxford: Oxford University Press, 2016)

Fischhoff, Baruch, "Hindsight ≠ Foresight: The Effect of Outcome Knowledge on Judgment under Uncertainty," *Journal of Experimental Psychology*, Vol. 1 (1975), pp. 288–99

Flikke, Geir, "Resurgent Authoritarianism: The Case of Russia's New NGO Legislation," *Post-Soviet Affairs*, Vol. 32 (2016), pp. 103–31

Flitner, Andreas, ed., *Deutsches Geistesleben und Nationalsozialismus* (Tübingen: Wunderlich, 1965)

Ford, Guy Stanton, ed., *Dictatorship in the Modern World* (London: Oxford University Press, 1939)

Förster, Michael, *Jurist im Dienst des Unrechts: Leben und Werk des ehemaligen Staatssekretärs im Reichsjustizministerium, Franz Schlegelberger (1876–1970)* (Baden-Baden: Nomos, 1995)

Forsthoff, Ernst, *Der totale Staat* (Hamburg: Hanseatische Verlagsanstalt, 1933)

Forsthoff, Ernst, "Otto Koellreutter, Der deutsche Führerstaat" (Book review), *Juristische Wochenschrift*, Vol. 63 (1934), p. 538

Forts-Battaglia, Otto, and Huntley Paterson, *Dictatorship on Trial* (New York: Harcourt, Brace, 1931)

Fox, Gregory H., *Humanitarian Occupation* (Cambridge: Cambridge University Press, 2008)

Fraenkel, Ernst, "Der nichtige Arbeitsvertrag," in idem., *Gesammelte Schriften*, vol. 1: *Recht und Politik in der Weimarer Republik*, edited by Hubertus Buchstein (Baden-Baden: Nomos, [1923] 1999), pp. 69–120

Fraenkel, Ernst, "Die Wirtschaftsschule des Deutschen Metallarbeiterverbandes in Bad Dürrenberg," in idem., *Gesammelte Schriften*, vol. 1: *Recht und Politik in der Weimarer Republik*, edited by Hubertus Buchstein (Baden-Baden: Nomos, [1926] 1999), pp. 163–6

Fraenkel, Ernst, *Zur Soziologie der Klassenjustiz*, in idem., *Gesammelte Schriften*, vol. 1: *Recht und Politik in der Weimarer Republik*, edited by Hubertus Buchstein (Baden-Baden: Nomos, [1927] 1999), pp. 177–211

Fraenkel, Ernst, "Rechtssoziologie als Wissenschaft," in idem., *Gesammelte Schriften*, vol. 1: *Recht und Politik in der Weimarer Republik*, edited by Hubertus Buchstein (Baden-Baden: Nomos, [1929] 1999), pp. 370–9

Fraenkel, Ernst, "Kollektive Demokratie," in idem., *Gesammelte Schriften*, vol. 1: *Recht und Politik in der Weimarer Republik*, edited by Hubertus Buchstein (Baden-Baden: Nomos, [1929] 1999), pp. 343–57

Fraenkel, Ernst, "Antifaschistische Aufklärungsarbeit," in idem., *Gesammelte Schriften*, vol. 1: *Recht und Politik in der Weimarer Republik*, edited by Hubertus Buchstein (Baden-Baden: Nomos, [1930] 1999), pp. 410–17

Fraenkel, Ernst, "Verfassungsreform und Sozialdemokratie," in idem., *Gesammelte Schriften*, vol. 1: *Recht und Politik in der Weimarer Republik*, edited by Hubertus Buchstein (Baden-Baden: Nomos, [1932] 1999), pp. 516–29

Fraenkel, Ernst, "XLIII," *Die Justiz*, reprinted in Hugo Sinzheimer and Ernst Fraenkel, *Die Justiz in der Weimarer Republik: Eine Chronik*, edited by Thilo Ramm with an Introduction by Otto Kirchheimer (Neuwied: Luchterhand, [1933] 1968), pp. 395–9

Fraenkel, Ernst, "In der Maschine der politischen Strafjustiz des III. Reiches," in idem., *Gesammelte Schriften*, vol. 2: *Nationalsozialismus und Widerstand*, edited by Alexander v. Brünneck, Hubertus Buchstein, and Gerhard Göhler (Baden-Baden: Nomos, [1934] 1999), pp. 475–84

Fraenkel, Ernst, "Der Sinn illegaler Arbeit," in idem., *Gesammelte Schriften*, vol. 2: *Nationalsozialismus und Widerstand*, edited by Alexander v. Brünneck, Hubertus Buchstein, and Gerhard Göhler (Baden-Baden: Nomos, [1935] 1999), pp. 491–7

Fraenkel, Ernst, "Das Dritte Reich als Doppelstaat," in idem., *Gesammelte Schriften*, vol. 2: *Nationalsozialismus und Widerstand*, edited by Alexander v. Brünneck, Hubertus Buchstein, and Gerhard Göhler (Baden-Baden: Nomos, [1937] 1999), pp. 504–19

Fraenkel, Ernst, *Der Urdoppelstaat*, in idem., *Gesammelte Schriften*, vol. 2: *Nationalsozialismus und Widerstand*, edited by Alexander v. Brünneck, Hubertus Buchstein, and Gerhard Göhler (Baden-Baden: Nomos, [1938] 1999), pp. 267–473

Fraenkel, Ernst, *The Dual State: A Contribution to the Theory of Dictatorship*, translated by E. A. Shils, in collaboration with Edith Loewenstein and Klaus Knorr, with an Introduction by Jens Meierhenrich (Oxford: Oxford University Press, [1941] 2017)

Fraenkel, Ernst, "Vom monopol-kapitalistischen Charakter des Nazi-Staatsgebildes: Das Produkt des Grosskapitals," in idem., *Gesammelte Schriften*, vol. 2: *Nationalsozialismus und Widerstand*, edited by Alexander v. Brünneck, Hubertus Buchstein, and Gerhard Göhler (Baden-Baden: Nomos, [1942] 1999), pp. 576–9

Fraenkel, Ernst, "Die künftige Organisation der deutschen Arbeiterbewegung," in idem., *Gesammelte Schriften*, vol. 3: *Neuaufbau der Demokratie in Deutschland und Korea*, edited by Gerhard Göhler (Baden-Baden: Nomos, [1943/1944] 1999), pp. 99–118

Fraenkel, Ernst, *Military Occupation and the Rule of Law: Occupational Government in the Rhineland, 1918–1923* (London: Oxford University Press, 1944)

Fraenkel, Ernst, "Brief vom 23. März 1946 an Familie Suhr," reprinted in idem., *Gesammelte Schriften*, vol. 3: *Neuaufbau der Demokratie in Deutschland und Korea*, edited by Gerhard Göhler (Baden-Baden: Nomos, [1946] 1999), pp. 389–95

Fraenkel, Ernst, "Erklärung über die Tätigkeit des Herrn Wilhelm Urban in den Jahren 1933 bis 1938 vom 22. Oktober 1953," BArch N 1274 (Fraenkel, Ernst)/ 11, reprinted in idem., *Gesammelte Schriften*, vol. 2: *Nationalsozialismus und Widerstand*, edited by Alexander v. Brünneck, Hubertus Buchstein, and Gerhard Göhler (Baden-Baden: Nomos, [1953] 1999), pp. 624–5

Fraenkel, Ernst, "Gedenkrede auf Franz L. Neumann," in idem., *Gesammelte Schriften*, vol. 6: *Internationale Politik und Völkerrecht, Politikwissenschaft und Hochschulpolitik*, edited by Hubertus Buchstein and Klaus-Gert Lutterbeck (Baden-Baden: Nomos, [1955] 1999), pp. 362–73

Fraenkel, Ernst, "Startgleichheit und Klassenschichtung," in idem., *Gesammelte Schriften*, vol. 3: *Neuaufbau der Demokratie in Deutschland und Korea*, edited by Gerhard Göhler (Baden-Baden: Nomos, [1956] 1999), pp. 625–9

Fraenkel, Ernst, "Otto Suhr zum Gedächtnis," in idem., *Reformismus und Pluralismus: Materialien zu einer ungeschriebenen Biographie*, edited by Falk Esche and Frank Grube (Hamburg: Hoffman und Campe, [1957] 1973), pp. 369–88

Fraenkel, Ernst, "Auflösung und Verfall des Rechts im III. Reich," in idem., *Gesammelte Schriften*, vol. 2: *Nationalsozialismus und Widerstand*, edited by Alexander v. Brünneck, Hubertus Buchstein, and Gerhard Göhler (Baden-Baden: Nomos, [1960] 1999), pp. 608–21

Fraenkel, Ernst, *Das amerikanische Regierungssystem: Eine politologische Analyse* (Opladen: Westdeutscher Verlag, 1962)

Fraenkel, Ernst, *Deutschland und die westlichen Demokratien*, enlarged edition, edited by Alexander v. Brünneck (Frankfurt: Suhrkamp, [1964] 1991)

Fraenkel, Ernst, "Vorwort zum Neudruck," in idem., *Gesammelte Schriften*, vol. 1: *Recht und Politik in der Weimarer Republik*, edited by Hubertus Buchstein (Baden-Baden: Nomos, [1968] 1999), pp. 654–61

Fraenkel, Ernst, "Anstatt einer Vorrede," in idem., *Reformismus und Pluralismus: Materialien zu einer ungeschriebenen Autobiographie*, edited by Falk Esche and Frank Grube (Hamburg: Hoffman und Campe, 1973), pp. 11–26

Fraenkel, Ernst, *Der Doppelstaat* (Frankfurt: Europäische Verlagsanstalt, 1974)

Fraenkel, Ernst, *Der Doppelstaat*, in idem., *Gesammelte Schriften*, vol. 2: *Nationalsozialismus und Widerstand*, edited by Alexander v. Brünneck, Hubertus Buchstein, and Gerhard Göhler (Baden-Baden: Nomos, [1974] 1999), pp. 33–266

Fraenkel, Ernst, "Preface to the 1974 German Edition," in idem., *The Dual State: A Theory of Dictatorship*, translated by E. A. Shils, in collaboration with Edith Loewenstein and Klaus Knorr, with an Introduction by Jens Meierhenrich (Oxford: Oxford University Press, [1941] 2017), pp. xiii–xxi

Fraenkel, Ernst, *Der Doppelstaat: Recht und Justiz im "Dritten Reich"* (Frankfurt: Fischer, 1984)

Fraenkel, Ernst, *Gesammelte Schriften*, vol. 4: *Amerikastudien*, edited by Hubertus Buchstein and Rainer Kühn (Baden-Baden: Nomos, 2000)

Fraenkel, Ernst, *Der Doppelstaat*, Second edition, edited with an Introduction by Alexander v. Brünneck (Frankfurt: Europäische Verlagsanstalt, 2001)

Fraenkel, Ernst, *Der Doppelstaat*, Third edition, edited with an Introduction by Alexander v. Brünneck, with an Afterword by Horst Dreier (Frankfurt: Europäische Verlagsanstalt, 2012)

Frank, Hans, "Der deutsche Rechtsstaat Adolf Hitlers," *Deutsches Recht*, Vol. 4 (1934), pp. 120–3

Frank, Hans, "Die Zeit des Rechts," *Deutsches Recht*, Vol. 6 (1936), pp. 1–3

Frank, Hans, "Eike von Repgow der Künder und Kämpfer des Rechts," *Deutsches Recht*, Vol. 6 (1936), pp. 297–9

Frank, Hans, "Die Juden in der Rechtswissenschaft," *Deutsches Recht*, Vol. 6 (1936), pp. 393–5

Fraser, David, *Law after Auschwitz: Towards a Jurisprudence of the Holocaust* (Durham: Carolina Academic Press, 2005)

Fraser, David, "'The Outsider Does Not See All the Game . . .': Perceptions of German Law in Anglo-American Legal Scholarship, 1933–1940," in Dieter Gosewinkel, ed., *Wirtschaftskontrolle und Recht in der nationalsozialistischen Diktatur* (Frankfurt: Klostermann, 2005), pp. 341–67

Frei, Norbert, "'Machtergreifung': Anmerkungen zu einem historischen Begriff," *Vierteljahrshefte für Zeitgeschichte*, Vol. 31 (1983), pp. 136–45

Frei, Norbert, *Der Führerstaat: Nationalsozialistische Herrschaft 1933 bis 1945* (Munich: dtv, 1987)

Frei, Norbert, *Vergangenheitspolitik: Die Anfänge der Bundesrepublik und die NS-Vergangenheit* (Munich: Beck, 1996)

Freisler, Roland, "Rechtsstaat: Eine staatsbiologische Betrachtung," *Völkischer Beobachter*, December 20/21, 1931

Freisler, Roland, *Das Werden des Juristen im Dritten Reich* (Berlin: Junker und Dünnhaupt, 1933)

Freisler, Roland, "Recht, Richter und Gesetz," *Deutsche Justiz*, Vol. 95 (1933), pp. 694–6

Freisler, Roland, *Etwas über Führertum in der Rechtspflege: Soll verantwortungsvolle Richterpersönlichkeit oder Abstimmungszahlenspiel Grundlage des Urteils sein?* (Berlin: Spaeth und Linde, 1935)

Freisler, Roland, "Schutz des Volkes oder des Rechtsverbrechers? Fesselung des Verbrechers oder des Richters? Einiges über das zweckmäßige Maß der Bindung des Richters an gesetzliche Straftatbestände," *Deutsches Strafrecht*, Vol. 1 (1935), pp. 1–33

Freisler, Roland, *Gedanken zum Schutz der Bewegung im neuen Strafrecht* (Berlin: Decker, 1936)

Freisler, Roland, "Richter und Gesetz," in Hans Heinrich Lammers and Hans Pfundtner, eds., *Die Verwaltungs-Akademie: Ein Handbuch für den Beamten im nationalsozialistischen Staat*, vol. 1: *Grundlagen, Aufbau und Wirtschaftsordnung des nationalsozialistischen Staates* (Berlin: Industrieverlag Spaeth und Linde, 1936), Heft 17

Freisler, Roland, *Richter und Gesetz* (Berlin: Spaeth und Linde, 1937)

Freisler, Roland, "Der Rechtsstaat," *Deutsche Juristen-Zeitung*, Vol. 42 (1937), pp. 151–5

Freisler, Roland, "Rechtsstaat," in Erich Volkmar, Alexander Elster, and Günther Küchenhoff, eds., *Handwörterbuch der Rechtswissenschaft*, vol. 8: *Die Rechtsentwicklung der Jahre 1933 bis 1935/36* (Berlin: de Gruyter, 1937), pp. 568–77

Freisler, Roland, *Nationalsozialistisches Recht und Rechtsdenken* (Berlin: Spaeth und Linde, 1938)

Freisler, Roland, *Gerichtliche Redekunst im Strafverfahren* (Jena: Biedermann, 1938)

Freisler, Roland, *Widergeburt strafrechtlichen Denkens* (Berlin: Schenk, 1940)

Freisler, Roland, and Justus Wilhelm Hedemann, *Deutsches Gemeinrecht im Werden* (Berlin: Decker, 1940)

Friedländer, Saul, *Nazi Germany and the Jews*, vol. 1: *The Years of Persecution, 1933–1939* (London: Weidenfeld and Nicolson, 1997)

Friedman, Lawrence M., *The Legal System: A Social Science Perspective* (New York: Russell Sage Foundation, 1975)

Friedman, Lawrence M., *The Republic of Choice: Law, Authority, and Culture* (Cambridge: Harvard University Press, 1990)

Friedman, Lawrence M., "A Few Thoughts on Ethnography, History, and Law," in June Starr and Mark Goodale, eds., *Practicing Ethnography in Law: New Dialogues, Enduring Methods* (London: Palgrave, 2002), pp. 185–201

Friedrich, Carl J., "Dictatorship in Germany?," *Foreign Affairs*, Vol. 9 (1930), pp. 118–32

Friedrich, Carl J., ed., *Totalitarianism* (Cambridge: Harvard University Press, 1954)

Friedrich, Carl J., "The Unique Character of Totalitarian Society," in idem., ed., *Totalitarianism* (Cambridge: Harvard University Press, 1954), pp. 47–60

Friedrich, Carl J., and Zbigniew K. Brzezinski, *Totalitarian Dictatorship and Autocracy* (Cambridge: Harvard University Press, 1956)

Friedrich, Carl J., Michael Curtis, and Benjamin R. Barber, eds., *Totalitarianism in Perspective: Three Views* (London: Pall Mall Press, 1969)

Friedrich, Manfred, *Geschichte der deutschen Staatsrechtswissenschaft* (Berlin: Duncker and Humblot, 1997)

Fritzsche, Peter, "Did Weimar Fail?," *Journal of Modern History*, Vol. 68 (1996), pp. 629–56

Fritzsche, Peter, *Life and Death in the Third Reich* (Cambridge: Belknap Press of Harvard University Press, 2008)

Frotscher, Werner, and Bodo Pieroth, *Verfassungsgeschichte*, Tenth edition (Munich: Beck, 2011)

Fu, Jun, *Institutions and Investments: Foreign Direct Investment in China during an Era of Reforms* (Ann Arbor: University of Michigan Press, 2000)

Fulbrook, Mary, *A Concise History of Germany*, Second edition (Cambridge: Cambridge University Press, 2004)

Fuller, Lon L., "Positivism and Fidelity to Law: A Reply to Professor Hart," *Harvard Law Review*, Vol. 71 (1958), pp. 630–72

Fuller, Lon L., *The Morality of Law*, Revised edition (New Haven: Yale University Press, 1969)

Gallagher, Mary E., "Mobilizing the Law in China: 'Informed Disenchantment' and the Development of Legal Consciousness," *Law and Society Review*, Vol. 40 (2006), pp. 783–816

Gallagher, Mary E., *Authoritarian Legality in China: Law, Workers, and the State* (Cambridge: Cambridge University Press, 2017)

Gandhi, Jennifer, "Authoritarian Institutions and the Survival of Autocrats," *Comparative Political Studies*, Vol. 40 (2007), pp. 1279–301

Gandhi, Jennifer, *Political Institutions under Dictatorship* (Cambridge: Cambridge University Press, 2008)

Gandhi, Jennifer, and Ellen Lust-Okar, "Elections under Authoritarianism," *Annual Review of Political Science*, Vol. 12 (2009), pp. 403–22

Gangl, Manfred, ed., *Linke Juristen in der Weimarer Republik* (Frankfurt: Lang, 2003)

Gangl, Manfred, ed., *Die Weimarer Staatsrechtsdebatte: Diskurs- und Rezeptionsstrategien* (Baden-Baden: Nomos, 2011)

Gay, Ruth, *The Jews of Germany: A Historical Portrait* (New Haven: Yale University Press, 1991)

Geary, Daniel, *Radical Ambition: C. Wright Mills, the Left, and American Social Thought* (Berkeley: University of California Press, 2009)

Geddes, Barbara, "What Do We Know about Democratization after Twenty Years?," *Annual Review of Political Science*, Vol. 2 (1999), pp. 115–44

Geddes, Barbara, Erica Frantz, and Joseph G. Wright, "Military Rule," *Annual Review of Political Science*, Vol. 17 (2014), pp. 147–62

Geddes, Barbara, Joseph Wright, and Erica Frantz, "Autocratic Breakdown and Regime Transitions: A New Data Set," *Perspectives on Politics*, Vol. 12 (2014), pp. 313–31

Geertz, Clifford, "Thick Description: Toward an Interpretive Theory of Culture," in idem., *The Interpretation of Cultures: Selected Essays* (New York: Basic Books, 1973), pp. 3–30

Geertz, Clifford, *The Interpretation of Cultures: Selected Essays* (New York: Basic Books, 1973)

Gellately, Robert, *The Gestapo and German Society: Enforcing Racial Policy 1933–1945* (Oxford: Clarendon Press, 1990)

Gellately, Robert, "Situating the 'SS-State' in a Social-Historical Context: Recent Histories of the SS, the Police, and the Courts in the Third Reich," *Journal of Modern History*, Vol. 64 (1992), pp. 338–65

Gellately, Robert, *Backing Hitler: Consent and Coercion in Nazi Germany* (Oxford: Oxford University Press, 2001)

Gerhardt, Uta, *Talcott Parsons: An Intellectual Biography* (Cambridge: Cambridge University Press, 2002)

Gerlach, Christian, "The Wannsee Conference, the Fate of German Jews, and Hitler's Decision in Principle to Exterminate All European Jews," *Journal of Modern History*, Vol. 70 (1998), pp. 759–812

Gerlach, Christian, *The Extermination of the European Jews* (Cambridge: Cambridge University Press, 2016)

Gerring, John, *Social Science Methodology: A Unified Framework*, Second edition (Cambridge: Cambridge University Press, 2012)

Gessen, Masha, *The Future Is History: How Totalitarianism Reclaimed Russia* (New York: Riverhead Books, 2017)

Gierke, Otto von, "Die Grundbegriffe des Staatsrechts und die neuesten Staatsrechtstheorien," *Zeitschrift für die gesamte Staatswissenschaft*, Vol. 30 (1874), pp. 265–335

Gierke, Otto von, "Labands Staatsrecht und die deutsche Rechtswissenschaft," *Schmollers Jahrbuch für Gesetzgebung, Verwaltung und Volkswirtschaft im Deutschen Reich*, Vol. 7 (1883), pp. 1097–1195

Gilbert, Leah, and Payam Mohseni, "Beyond Authoritarianism: The Conceptualization of Hybrid Regimes," *Studies in Comparative International Development*, Vol. 46 (2011), pp. 270–97

Gill, Graeme, *Building an Authoritarian Polity: Russia in Post-Soviet Times* (Cambridge: Cambridge University Press, 2015)

Gilley, Bruce, "Democratic Enclaves in Authoritarian Regimes," *Democratization*, Vol. 17 (2010), pp. 389–415

Gillingham, Paul, and Benjamin T. Smith, eds., *Dictablanda: Politics, Work, and Culture in Mexico, 1938–1968* (Durham: Duke University Press, 2014)

Ginsburg, Tom, "Courts and New Democracies: Recent Works," *Law and Social Inquiry*, Vol. 37 (2012), pp. 720–42

Ginsburg, Tom, "Introduction: Constitutions in Authoritarian Regimes," in Tom Ginsburg and Alberto Simpser, eds., *Constitutions in Authoritarian Regimes* (Cambridge: Cambridge University Press, 2014), pp. 1–17

Ginsburg, Tom, and Tamir Moustafa, eds., *Rule by Law: The Politics of Courts in Authoritarian Regimes* (Cambridge: Cambridge University Press, 2008)

Ginsburg, Tom, and Alberto Simpser, eds., *Constitutions in Authoritarian Regimes* (Cambridge: Cambridge University Press, 2014)

Gispen, Kees, *Poems in Steel: National Socialism and the Politics of Inventing from Weimar to Bonn* (New York: Berghahn, 2002)

Gleason, Abbott, *Totalitarianism: The Inner History of the Cold War* (New York: Oxford University Press, 1995)

Gluckman, Max, *An Analysis of the Sociological Theories of Bronislaw Malinowski* (London: Oxford University Press, 1949)

Gluckman, Max, *The Judicial Process among the Barotse of Northern Rhodesia* (Manchester: Manchester University Press, 1955)

Glungler, Wilhelm, *Theorie der Politik: Grundlehren einer Wissenschaft von Volk und Staat* (Munich: Voglrider, 1941)

Gneist, Rudolf, *Verwaltung–Justiz–Rechtsweg: Staatsverwaltung und Selbstverwaltung nach englischen und deutschen Verhältnissen mit besonderer Rücksicht auf Verwaltungsformen und Kreis-Ordnungen in Preußen* (Berlin: Springer, 1869)

Gneist, Rudolf, *Der Rechtsstaat* (Berlin: Springer, 1872)

Gneist, Rudolf, *Der Rechtsstaat und die Verwaltungsgerichte in Deutschland*, Second edition (Berlin: Springer, 1879)

Göhler, Gerhard, and Dirk Rüdiger Schumann, "Vorwort zu diesem Band," in Ernst Fraenkel, *Gesammelte Schriften*, vol. 3: *Neuaufbau der Demokratie in Deutschland und Korea*, edited by Gerhard Göhler (Baden-Baden: Nomos, 1999), pp. 9–49

Goldstein, Judith, Miles Kahler, Robert O. Keohane, and Anne-Marie Slaughter, "Introduction: Legalization and World Politics," *International Organization*, Vol. 54 (2000), pp. 385–99

Goldstein, Judith, Miles Kahler, Robert O. Keohane, and Anne-Marie Slaughter, eds., *Legalization and World Politics* (Cambridge: MIT Press, 2001)

Gooch, G. P., *Dictatorship in Theory and Practice* (London: Watts and Co., 1935)

Goodale, Mark, *Anthropology and Law: A Critical Introduction* (New York: New York University Press, 2017)

Goodenough, Ward H., *Description and Comparison in Cultural Anthropology* (Cambridge: Cambridge University Press, 1970)

Goodin, Robert E., "Institutional Morality," in idem., ed., *The Theory of Institutional Design* (Cambridge: Cambridge University Press, 1996), pp. 126–53

Göppinger, Horst, *Juristen jüdischer Abstammung im "Dritten Reich": Entrechtung und Verfolgung*, Second, revised edition (Munich: Beck, [1963] 1990)

Görtemaker, Manfred, and Christoph Safferling, eds., *Die Rosenburg: Das Bundesministerium der Justiz und die NS-Vergangenheit* (Vandenhoeck and Ruprecht, 2013)

Görtemaker, Manfred, and Christoph Safferling, *Die Akte Rosenburg: Das Bundesministerium der Justiz und die NS-Zeit* (Munich: Beck, 2016)

Gosewinkel, Dieter, "Wirtschaftskontrolle und Recht in der nationalsozialistischen Diktatur: Forschung und Forschungsperspektiven," in idem., ed., *Wirtschaftskontrolle und Recht in der nationalsozialistischen Diktatur* (Frankfurt: Klostermann, 2005), pp. ix–lix

Gould, Andrew C., "Conflicting Imperatives and Concept Formation," *Review of Politics*, Vol. 61 (1999), pp. 439–63

Gozzi, Gustavo, "*Rechtsstaat* and Individual Rights in German Constitutional History," in Pietro Costa and Danilo Zolo, eds., *The Rule of Law: History, Theory and Criticism* (Dordrecht: Springer, 2007), pp. 237–60

Graebner, Norman A., and Edward M. Bennett, *The Versailles Treaty and its Legacy: The Failure of The Wilsonian Vision* (Cambridge: Cambridge University Press, 2011)

Grawert, Rolf, "Die nationalsozialistische Herrschaft," in Josef Isensee and Paul Kirchhof, eds., *Handbuch des Staatsrechts der Bundesrepublik Deutschland: Grundlagen von Staat und Verfassung*, vol. 1, Third edition (Heidelberg: Müller, 2003), pp. 235–65

Gray, Paul S., John B. Williamson, David A. Karp, John R. Dalphin, *The Research Imagination: An Introduction to Qualitative and Quantitative Methods* (Cambridge: Cambridge University Press, 2007), pp. 179–210

Greenberg, Udi, *The Weimar Century: German Émigrés and the Ideological Foundations of the Cold War* (Princeton: Princeton University Press, 2014)

Grimm, Dieter, "Die 'Neue Rechtswissenschaft,'" in Peter Lundgren, ed., *Wissenschaft im Dritten Reich* (Frankfurt: Suhrkamp, 1985), pp. 31–54

Groh, Kathrin, *Demokratische Staatsrechtslehrer in der Weimarer Republik* (Tübingen: Mohr, 2010)

Gross, Raphael, *Anständig geblieben: Nationalsozialistische Moral* (Munich: Fischer, 2010)

Gross, Raphael, "The 'True Enemy': Antisemitism in Carl Schmitt's Life and Work," in Jens Meierhenrich and Oliver Simons, eds., *The Oxford Handbook of Carl Schmitt* (Oxford: Oxford University Press, 2016), pp. 96–116

Groß-Fengels, Kurt, "Der Streit um den Rechtsstaat," Ph.D. dissertation, Universität Marburg, 1936

Grote, Rainer, "The German Rechtsstaat in a Comparative Perspective," in James R. Silkenat, James E. Hickey Jr., and Peter D. Barenboim, eds., *The Legal Doctrines of the Rule of Law and the Legal State (Rechtsstaat)* (New York: Springer, 2014), pp. 193–207

Gruchmann, Lothar, "Ernst Fraenkel zum 65. Geburtstag: Ein Gruß im Namen seiner Schüler," *Zeitschrift für Politik*, Vol. 12 (1964), pp. 303–8

Gruchmann, Lothar, *Justiz im Dritten Reich 1933–1940: Anpassung und Unterwerfung in der Ära Gürtner*, Third edition (Munich: Oldenbourg, 2001)

Günther, Frieder, "Ordnen, gestalten, bewahren: Radikales Ordnungsdenken von deutschen Rechtsintellektuellen der Rechtswissenschaft 1920 bis 1960," *Vierteljahrshefte für Zeitgeschichte*, Vol. 59 (2011), pp. 353–84

Guradze, Heinz, "Ernst Fraenkel, The Dual State: A Contribution to the Theory of Dictatorship" (Book review), *Washington University Law Review*, Vol. 27 (1942), pp. 603–7

Gurian, Waldemar, "Franz Neumann, Behemoth: The Structure and Practice of National Socialism" (Book review), *Review of Politics*, Vol. 4 (1942), pp. 347–52

Gusy, Christoph, *Die Weimarer Reichsverfassung* (Tübingen: Mohr, 1997)

Habermas, Jürgen, "Über den doppelten Boden des demokratischen Rechtsstaates," in idem., *Eine Art Schadensabwicklung: Kleine politische Schriften VI* (Frankfurt: Suhrkamp, 1987), pp. 18–23

Habermas, Jürgen, "Geschichtsbewußtsein und posttraditionale Identität: Die Westorientierung der Bundesrepublik," in idem., *Eine Art Schadensabwicklung: Kleine politische Schriften VI* (Frankfurt: Suhrkamp, 1987), pp. 161–79

Habermas, Jürgen, *Faktizitat und Geltung: Beiträge zur Diskurstheorie des Rechts und des demokratischen Rechtsstaats* (Frankfurt: Suhrkamp, 1992)

Habermas, Jürgen, *Between Facts and Norms: Contributions to a Discourse Theory of Law and Democracy*, translated by William Rehg (Cambridge: MIT Press, [1992] 1996)

Hadenius, Axel, and Jan Teorell, "Pathways from Authoritarianism," *Journal of Democracy*, Vol. 18 (2007), pp. 143–57

Hadfield, Gillian K., and Barry R. Weingast, "Microfoundations of the Rule of Law," *Annual Review of Political Science*, Vol. 17 (2014), pp. 21–42

Häberle, Peter, "Allgemeines Staatsrecht, Verfassungslehre oder Staatsrechtslehre? Bemerkungen aus Anlaß der 5. Auflage der Allgemeinen Staatslehre von G. u. E. Küchenhoff," *Zeitschrift für Politik*, Vol. 12 (1965), pp. 381–95

Haffner, Sebastian, *Germany: Jekyll and Hyde* (London: Secker and Warburg, 1940)

Haffner, Sebastian, *The Meaning of Hitler*, translated by Ewald Osers (Cambridge: Harvard University Press, 1983)

Haffner, Sebastian, *Defying Hitler: A Memoir*, translated by Oliver Pretzel (London: Weidenfeld and Nicolson, 2002)

Haggard, Stephan, and Robert R. Kaufman, *Dictators and Democrats: Masses, Elites, and Regime Change* (Princeton: Princeton University Press, 2016)

Hagman, Thobias, and Filip Reyntjens, eds., *Aid and Authoritarianism in Africa: Development without Democracy* (London: Zed Books, 2016)

Hahn, Erich, "Rudolf Gneist and the Prussian Rechtsstaat: 1862–78," *Journal of Modern History*, Vol. 49 (1977), pp. D1361–D1381

Hajjar, Lisa, "From the Fight for Legal Rights to the Promotion of Human Rights: Israeli and Palestinian Cause Lawyers in the Trenches of Globalization," in Austin Sarat and Stuart A. Scheingold, eds., *Cause Lawyering and the State in a Global Era* (New York: Oxford University Press, 2001), pp. 68–95

Halberstam, Michael, "Totalitarianism as a Problem for the Modern Conception of Politics," *Political Theory*, Vol. 26 (1998), pp. 459–88

Haldemann, Frank, "Gustav Radbruch vs. Hans Kelsen: A Debate on Nazi Law," *Ratio Juris*, Vol. 18 (2005), pp. 162–78

Halliday, Terence C., "The Politics of Lawyers: An Emerging Agenda," *Law and Social Inquiry*, Vol. 24 (1999), pp. 1007–11

Hammersly, Martyn, and Paul Atkinson, *Ethnography: Principles in Practice*, Third edition (London: Routledge, 2007)

Hammerstein, Notker, *Die Deutsche Forschungsgemeinschaft in der Weimarer Republik und im Dritten Reich: Wissenschaftspolitik in Republik und Diktatur* (Munich: Beck, 1999)

Hanson, Stephen E., *Post-Imperial Democracies: Ideology and Party Formation in Third Republic France, Weimar Germany, and Post-Soviet Russia* (Cambridge: Cambridge University Press, 2010)

Hart, H. L. A., *The Concept of Law*, Second edition (Oxford: Clarendon Press, [1958] 1994)

Hart, H. L. A., "Positivism and the Separation of Law and Morals," *Harvard Law Review*, Vol. 71 (1958), pp. 593–629

Hart, Henry M., Jr., and Albert M. Sacks, *The Legal Process: Basic Problems in the Making and Application of Law* (Westbury: Foundation Press, [1951] 1994)

Harth, Caroline, *Der Mythos von der Zerstörung des Vertrages: Zur Vertragslehre im Nationalsozialismus* (Frankfurt: Lang, 2008)

Haydemann, Steven, *Authoritarianism in Syria: Institutions and Social Conflict, 1946–1970* (Ithaca: Cornell University Press, 1999)

Hayek, Friedrich A., *The Collected Works of F. A. Hayek*, vol. 17: *The Constitution of Liberty: The Definitive Edition*, edited by Ronald Hamowy (Chicago: University of Chicago Press, [1960] 2011)

Hayes, Peter, "Introduction," in Franz Neumann, *Behemoth: The Structure and Practice of National Socialism*, with an Introduction by Peter Hayes (Chicago: Ivan R. Dee, [1942/1944] 2009), pp. vii–xvii

Heckel, Johannes, "Wehrrecht und Wehrmachtbeamtentum," *Heeresverwaltung*, Vol. 6 (1941), pp. 57–62

Hegel, Georg Wilhelm Friedrich, *The Science of Logic*, translated and edited by George di Giovanni (Cambridge: Cambridge University Press, [1812–1831] 2010)

Hehl, Ulrich von, *Nationalsozialistische Herrschaft* (Munich: Oldenbourg, 1996)

Heine, Heinrich, *On the History of Religion and Philosophy in Germany*, edited by Terry Pinkard (Cambridge: Cambridge University Press, [1835] 2007)

Heinz, Marion, and Sidonie Kellerer, eds., *Martin Heideggers »Schwarze Hefte«: Eine philosophisch-politische Debatte* (Frankfurt: Suhrkamp, 2016)

Held, David, *Introduction to Critical Theory: Horkheimer to Habermas* (Berkeley: University of California Press, 1980)

Helfritz, Hans, "Rechtsstaat und nationalsozialistischer Staat," *Deutsche Juristen-Zeitung*, Vol. 39 (1934), pp. 425–33

Heller, Hermann, *Die Souveränität: Ein Beitrag zur Theorie des Staats- und Völkerrechts*, in idem., *Gesammelte Schriften*, vol. 2: *Recht, Staat, Macht*, Second edition, edited by Christoph Müller (Tübingen: Mohr, [1927] 1992), pp. 31–202

Heller, Hermann, "Der Begriff des Gesetzes in der Reichsverfassung," in idem., *Gesammelte Schriften*, vol. 2: *Recht, Staat, Macht*, Second edition, edited by Christoph Müller (Tübingen: Mohr, [1928] 1992), pp. 203–47

Heller, Hermann, *Europa und der Fascismus*, in idem., *Gesammelte Schriften*, vol. 2: *Recht, Staat, Macht*, Second edition, edited by Christoph Müller (Tübingen: Mohr, [1929] 1992), pp. 463–609

Heller, Hermann, "Rechtsstaat oder Diktatur?," in idem., *Gesammelte Schriften*, vol. 2: *Recht, Staat, Macht*, Second edition, edited by Christoph Müller (Tübingen: Mohr, [1930] 1992), pp. 443–62

Heller, Hermann, "Ziele und Grenzen einer deutschen Verfassungsreform," in idem., *Gesammelte Schriften*, vol. 2: *Recht, Staat, Macht*, Second edition, edited by Christoph Müller (Tübingen: Mohr, [1931] 1992), pp. 411–17

Heller, Hermann, *Staatslehre*, in idem., *Gesammelte Schriften*, vol. 3: *Staatslehre als Politische Wissenschaft*, Second edition, edited by Christoph Müller (Tübingen: Mohr, [1934] 1992), pp. 81–410

Hendley, Kathryn, "Rule of Law, Russian-Style," *Current History*, Vol. 108 (2009), pp. 339–40

Hendley, Kathryn, *Everyday Law in Russia* (Ithaca: Cornell University Press, 2017)

Hennicke, Otto, and Fritz Wüllner, "Über die barbarischen Vollstreckungs-Methoden von Wehrmacht und Justiz im Zweiten Weltkrieg," in Wolfram Wette, ed., *Deserteure der Wehrmacht: Feiglinge–Opfer–Hoffnungsträger?* (Essen: Klartext, 1995), pp. 74–94

Herbert, Ulrich, *Best: Biographische Studien über Radikalismus, Weltanschauung und Vernunft 1903–1989* (Munich: Beck, 2016)

Herf, Jeffrey, *Reactionary Modernism: Technology, Culture, and Politics in Weimar and the Third Reich* (Cambridge: Cambridge University Press, 1984)

Hetherington, Marc J., and Jonathan D. Weiler, *Authoritarianism and Polarization in American Politics* (Cambridge University Press, 2009)

Hilberg, Raul, *The Destruction of the European Jews*, 3 volumes, Third edition (New Haven: Yale University Press, [1961] 2003)

Hilberg, Raul, *Politics of Memory: The Journey of a Holocaust Historian* (Chicago: Ivan R. Dee, 1996)

Hilberg, Raul, "The Relevance of *Behemoth* Today," *Constellations*, Vol. 10 (2003), pp. 256–63

Hilbink, Lisa, *Judges beyond Politics in Democracy and Dictatorship: Lessons from Chile* (Cambridge: Cambridge University Press, 2007)

Hilbink, Lisa, "The Origins of Positive Judicial Independence," *World Politics*, Vol. 64 (2012), pp. 587–621

Hilbink, Thomas M., "You Know the Type ... : Categories of Cause Lawyering," *Law and Social Inquiry*, Vol. 29 (2004), pp. 657–98

Hildebrand, Klaus, *Das Dritte Reich*, Fifth edition (Munich: Oldenbourg, 1995)

Hilger, Christian, *Rechtsstaatsbegriffe im Dritten Reich: Eine Strukturanalyse* (Tübingen: Mohr, 2003)

Hinnebusch, Raymond, "Syria: From 'Authoritarian Upgrading' to Revolution?," *International Affairs*, Vol. 88 (2012), pp. 95–113

Hintze, Otto, "Preußens Entwicklung zum Rechtsstaat," in *idem., Regierung und Verwaltung: Gesammelte Abhandlungen zur Staats-, Rechts- und Sozialgeschichte*, Second edition, edited with an Introduction by Gerhard Oestreich (Göttingen: Vandenhoeck und Ruprecht, [1920] 1967), pp. 97–163

Hirschfeld, Gerhard, and Lothar Kettenacker, eds., *Der "Führerstaat": Mythos und Realität* (Stuttgart: Klett-Cotta, 1981)

Höhn, Reinhard, *Der individualistische Staatsbegriff und die juristische Staatsperson* (Berlin: Heymann, 1935)

Holmes, Stephen, "Introduction," in Thomas Hobbes, *Behemoth or The Long Parliament*, edited by Ferdinand Tönnies, with an Introduction by Stephen Holmes (Chicago: University of Chicago Press, [1682] 1990), pp. vii–l

Howard, Marc Morjé, and Philip G. Roessler, "Liberalizing Electoral Outcomes in Competitive Authoritarian Regimes," *American Journal of Political Science*, Vol. 50 (2006), pp. 365–81

Hsia, R. Po-Chia, and Hartmut Lehmann, eds., *In and Out of the Ghetto: Jewish-Gentile Relations in Late Medieval and Early Modern Germany* (Cambridge: Cambridge University Press, 1995)

Hubatsch, Walther, *Hindenburg und der Staat: Aus den Papieren des Generalfeldmarschalls und Reichspräsidenten von 1878 bis 1934* (Göttingen: Musterschmidt, 1966)

Huber, Ernst Rudolf, "Bedeutungswandel der Grundrechte," *Archiv des öffentlichen Rechts*, Vol. 62 (1933), pp. 1–98

Huber, Ernst Rudolf, *Verfassungsrecht des Großdeutschen Reiches*, Second edition (Hamburg: Hanseatische Verlagsanstalt, 1939)

Huber, Ernst Rudolf, "Reichsgewalt und Reichsführung im Kriege," *Zeitschrift für die gesamte Staatswissenschaft*, Vol. 101 (1941), pp. 530–79

Huber, Ernst Rudolf, "Werner Weber, Die Verkündung von Rechtsvorschriften" (Book review), *Zeitschrift für die gesamte Staatswissenschaft*, Vol. 104 (1944), pp. 336–9

Hula, Erich, "Ernst Fraenkel, The Dual State: A Contribution to the Theory of Dictatorship" (Book review), *Social Research*, Vol. 9 (1942), pp. 271–3

Hull, Isabel V., *Absolute Destruction: Military Culture and the Practices of War in Imperial Germany* (Ithaca: Cornell University Press, 2005)

Humphreys, Stephen, *Theatre of the Rule of Law: Transnational Legal Intervention in Theory and Practice* (Cambridge: Cambridge University Press, 2010)

Huntington, Samuel P., *Political Order in Changing Societies* (New Haven: Yale University Press, 1968)

Huntington, Samuel P., *The Third Wave: Democratization in the Late Twentieth Century* (Norman: University of Oklahoma Press, 1991)

Hutchinson, Allan C., and Patrick Monahan, eds., *The Rule of Law: Ideal or Ideology?* (Toronto: Carswell, 1987)

Hüttenberger, Peter, "Nationalsozialistische Polykratie," *Geschichte und Gesellschaft*, Vol. 2 (1976), 417–42

Iakovou, Vicky, "Totalitarianism as a Non-State: On Hannah Arendt's Debt to Franz Neumann," *European Journal of Political Theory*, Vol. 8 (2009), pp. 429–47

Intelmann, Peter, *Franz L. Neumann: Chancen und Dilemma des politischen Reformismus* (Baden-Baden: Nomos, 1996)

Jacobson, Arthur J., and Bernhard Schlink, "Constitutional Crisis: The German and the American Experience," in idem., eds., *Weimar: A Jurispruence of Crisis* (Berkeley: University of California Press, 2000), pp. 1–39

Jäger, Herbert, *Verbrechen unter totalitärer Herrschaft: Studien zur nationalsozialistischen Gewaltkriminalität* (Frankfurt: Suhrkamp, 1982)

Jarausch, Konrad, *The Unfree Professions: German Lawyers, Teachers, and Engineers, 1900–1950* (New York: Oxford University Press, 1990)

Jasch, Hans-Christian, and Christoph Kreutzmüller, *Die Teilnehmer: Die Männer der Wannsee-Konferenz* (Berlin: Metropol, 2017)

Jaspers, Karl, *The Idea of the University*, edited by Karl W. Deutsch, translated by H. A. T. Reich and H. F. Vanderschmidt (London: Peter Owen, 1960)

Jászi, Oscar, "Franz Neumann, Behemoth: The Structure and Practice of National Socialism; Rohan D'O. Butler: The Roots of National Socialism" (Book review), *American Political Science Review*, Vol. 36 (1942), pp. 771–4

Jay, Martin, *The Dialectical Imagination. A History of the Frankfurt School and the Institute of Social Research 1923–1950*, Second edition (Berkeley: University of California Press, 1996)

Jayasuriya, Kanishka, "The Exception Becomes the Norm: Law and Regimes of Exception in East Asia," *Asian-Pacific Law and Policy Journal*, Vol. 2 (2001), pp. 108–24

Jellinek, Georg, *Die rechtliche Natur der Staatenverträge: Ein Beitrag zur juristischen Construktion des Völkerrechts* (Vienna: Hölder, 1880)

Jellinek, Georg, *Allgemeine Staatslehre*, Third edition (Berlin: Häring, [1900] 1914)

John, Michael F., "The Politics of Legal Unity in Germany, 1870–1896," *Historical Journal*, Vol. 28 (1985), pp. 341–55

John, Michael F., *Politics and the Law in Late Nineteenth-Century Germany: The Origins of the Civil Code* (Oxford: Oxford University Press, 1989)

Johst, David, "Die Entdeckung des Unrechtsstaates," in Werner Konitzer, ed., *Moralisierung des Rechts: Kontinuitäten und Diskontinuitäten nationalsozialistischer Normativität* (Frankfurt: Campus, 2014), pp. 127–45

Jones, Mark, *Founding Weimar: Violence and the German Revolution of 1918–1919* (Cambridge: Cambridge University Press, 2016)

Jones, William David, *The Lost Debate: German Socialist Intellectuals and Totalitarianism* (Urbana: University of Illinois Press, 1999)

Kahn, Daniela, *Die Steuerung der Wirtschaft durch Recht im nationalsozialistischen Deutschland: Das Beispiel der Reichsgruppe Industrie* (Frankfurt: Klostermann, 2006)

Kahn, Paul W., *The Cultural Study of Law: Reconstructing Legal Scholarship* (New Haven: Yale University Press, 1999)

Kalyvas, Andreas, "The Tyranny of Dictatorship: When the Greek Tyrant Met the Roman Dictator," *Political Theory*, Vol. 35 (2007), pp. 412–42

Kantorowicz, Ernst H., *The King's Two Bodies: A Study in Mediaeval Political Theology* (Princeton: Princeton University Press, 1957)

Kantorowicz, Hermann, "Dictatorships," *Politica*, Vol. 1 (1935), pp. 470–88

Kaplan, Marion A., ed., *Jewish Daily Life in Germany, 1618–1945* (Oxford: Oxford University Press, 2005)

Kaplan, Thomas Pegelow, *The Language of Nazi Genocide: Linguistic Violence and the Struggle of Germans of Jewish Ancestry* (Cambridge: Cambridge University Press, 2009)

Karl, Terry Lynn, *The Paradox of Plenty: Oil Booms and Petro States* (Berkeley: University of California Press, 1997)

Katz, Barry M., "The Criticism of Arms: The Frankfurt School Goes to War," *Journal of Modern History*, Vol. 59 (1987), pp. 439–78

Katz, Barry M., *Foreign Intelligence: Research and Analysis in the Office of Strategic Services 1942–1945* (Cambridge: Harvard University Press, 1989)

Katz, Jacob, *Out of the Ghetto: The Social Background of Jewish Emancipation, 1770–1870* (Cambridge: Harvard University Press, 1973)

Kelly, Duncan, *The State of the Political: Conceptions of Politics and the State in the Thought of Max Weber, Carl Schmitt and Franz Neumann* (Oxford: Oxford University, 2003)

Kelly, Duncan, "Carl Schmitt's Political Theory of Dictatorship," in Jens Meierhenrich and Oliver Simons, eds., *The Oxford Handbook of Carl Schmitt* (Oxford: Oxford University Press, 2016), pp. 217–44

Kelsen, Hans, "On the Borders between Legal and Sociological Method," in Arthur J. Jacobson and Bernhard Schlink, eds., *Weimar: A Jurispruence of Crisis* (Berkeley: University of California Press, [1911] 2000), pp. 57–63

Kelsen, Hans, *Allgemeine Staatslehre* (Berlin: Springer, 1925)

Kelsen, Hans, *General Theory of Law and State* (Cambridge: Harvard University Press, [1925] 1949)

Kelsen, Hans, *Vom Wesen und Wert der Demokratie*, Second edition (Tübingen, 1929)

Kelsen, Hans, "The Party-Dictatorship," *Politica*, Vol. 2 (1936), pp. 19–32

Kempner, R. M. W., "Ernst Fraenkel, The Dual State: A Contribution to the Theory of Dictatorship" (Book review), *Annals of the American Academy of Political and Social Science*, Vol. 216 (1941), p. 183

Kershaw, Ian, *The "Hitler Myth": Image and Reality in the Third Reich* (Oxford: Clarendon Press, 1987)

Kershaw, Ian, "'Working Towards the Führer': Reflections on the Nature of the Hitler Dictatorship," *Contemporary European History*, Vol. 2 (1993), pp. 103–18

Kershaw, Ian, *Hitler 1889–1936: Hubris* (New York: Norton, 1999)

Kershaw, Ian, "'Volksgemeinschaft': Potential und Grenzen eines neuen Forschungskonzepts," *Vierteljahrshefte für Zeitgeschichte*, Vol. 59 (2011), pp. 1–17

Kershaw, Ian, "Preface to the Bloomsbury Revelations Edition," in idem., *The Nazi Dictatorship: Problems and Perspectives of Interpretation* (London: Bloomsbury, 2015), pp. viii–xii

Kerwin, Jerome G., "Ernst Fraenkel, The Dual State: A Contribution to the Theory of Dictatorship" (Book review), *University of Chicago Law Review*, Vol. 8 (1941), pp. 616–18

Kettler, David, "Neumann, Franz," in William A. Darity, ed., *International Encyclopedia of the Social Sciences*, Second edition (London: Macmillan, 2008). pp. 481–3

Kiesewetter, Hubert, *Von Hegel zu Hitler: Eine Analyse der Hegelschen Machtstaatsideologie und der politischen Wirkungsgeschichte des Rechtshegelianismus* (Hamburg: Hoffmann und Campe, 1974)

King, Anthony, *The Structure of Social Theory* (London: Routledge, 2004)

Kirchheimer, Otto, "Changes in the Structure of Political Compromise," *Studies in Philosophy and Social Science*, Vol. 9 (1941), pp. 264–89

Kirchheimer, Otto, "The Legal Order of National Socialism," *Studies in Philosophy and Social Science*, Vol. 9 (1941), pp. 456–75

Kirchheimer, Otto, "Ernst Fraenkel, The Dual State: A Contribution to the Theory of Dictatorship" (Book review), *Political Science Quarterly*, Vol. 56 (1941), pp. 434–6

Kirchheimer, Otto, "Politics and Justice," *Social Research*, Vol. 22 (1955), pp. 377–98

Kirchheimer, Otto, *Political Justice: The Use of Legal Procedure for Political Ends* (Princeton: Princeton University Press, 1961)

Kirchheimer, Otto, "Einführung," in Hugo Sinzheimer and Ernst Fraenkel, *Die Justiz in der Weimarer Republik: Eine Chronik*, edited by Thilo Ramm with an Introduction by Otto Kirchheimer (Neuwied: Luchterhand, 1968), pp. 7–15

Kirschenmann, Dietrich, *"Gesetz" im Staatsrecht und in der Staatsrechtslehre des NS* (Berlin: Duncker and Humblot, 1970)

Klemperer, Victor, *LTI: Notizbuch eines Philologen*, Twenty-fifth edition (Stuttgart: Reclam, [1947] 2015)

Klemperer, Victor, *I Will Bear Witness: A Diary of the Nazi Years 1933–1941*, translated and with a Preface by Martin Chalmers (New York: Random House, 1998)

Kluck, Steffen, "Transpersonalismus: Zur normativen Dimension der neuhegelianischen Rechtsphilosophie," in Werner Konitzer and David Palme, eds., *"Arbeit", "Volk", "Gemeinschaft": Ethik und Ethiken im Nationalsozialismus* (Frankfurt: Campus, 2016), pp. 129–67

Knutsen, Carl Henrik, Håvard Mokleiv Nygård, and Tore Wig, "Autocratic Elections: Stabilizing Tool or Force for Change?," *World Politics*, Vol. 69 (2017), pp. 98–143

Koellreutter, Otto, *Der nationale Rechtsstaat: Zum Wandel der deutschen Staatsidee* (Tübingen: Mohr, 1932)

Koellreutter, Otto, *Grundriß der allgemeinen Staatslehre* (Tübingen: Mohr, 1933)

Koellreutter, Otto, *Vom Sinn und Wesen der nationalen Revolution* (Tübingen: Mohr, 1933)

Koellreutter, Otto, "Der nationale Rechtsstaat," *Deutsche Juristen-Zeitung*, Vol. 38 (1933), pp. 517–24

Koellreutter, Otto, "Volk und Staat in der Verfassungskrise: Zugleich eine Auseinandersetzung mit der Verfassungslehre Carl Schmitts," *Jahrbuch für politische Forschung*, Vol. 1 (1933), pp. 7–38

Koellreutter, Otto, "Das Wesen des 'Politischen' in der öffentlichen Verwaltung," *Reichsverwaltungsblatt*, Vol. 54 (1933), pp. 481–3

Koellreutter, Otto, "Der nationalsozialistische Rechtsstaat," in Hans Heinrich Lammers and Hans Pfundtner, eds., *Die Verwaltungsakademie: Ein Handbuch für den Beamten im nationalsozialistischen Staat* (Berlin: Industrieverlag Spaeth und Linde, 1934), pp. 1–15

Koellreutter, Otto, *Deutsches Verfassungsrecht: Ein Grundriß* (Berlin: Junker und Dünnhaupt, 1935)

Koellreutter, Otto, "Edgar Tatarin-Tarnheyden, Werdendes Staatsrecht" (Book review), *Archiv des öffentlichen Rechts*, Vol. 26 (1935), pp. 127–8

Koellreutter, Otto, "Recht und Richter in England und Deutschland," *Verwaltungsarchiv*, Vol. 47 (1942), pp. 208–46

Koellreutter, Otto, "Quellen des nationalsozialistischen Staatsrechts," in Hans-Heinrich Lammers and Hans Pfundtner, eds., *Die Verwaltungsakademie: Ein Handbuch für den Beamten im nationalsozialistischen Staat* (Berlin: Industrieverlag Spaeth und Linde, 1935), Heft 16

Koellreutter, Otto, "Führung und Verwaltung: Zum Problem einer neuen Begriffsjurisprudenz," in Roland Freisler, George A. Loening, H. C. Nipperdey, eds., *Festschrift für Justus Wilhelm Hedemann zum 60. Geburtstag* (Jena: Frommansche Buchhandlung, 1938), pp. 95–105

König, Stefan, *Vom Dienst am Recht: Rechtsanwälte als Strafverteidiger im Nationalsozialismus* (Berlin: de Gruyter, 1987)

Konitzer, Werner, ed., *Moralität des Bösen: Ethik und nationalsozialistische Verbrechen* (Frankfurt: Campus, 2009)

Konitzer, Werner, ed., and David Palme, eds., *"Arbeit", "Volk", "Gemeinschaft": Ethik und Ethiken im Nationalsozialismus* (Frankfurt: Campus, 2016)

Koonz, Claudia, *The Nazi Conscience* (Cambridge: Belknap Press of Harvard University Press, 2003)

Korioth, Stefan, "The Shattering of Methods in Late Wilhelmine Germany," in Arthur J. Jacobson and Bernhard Schlink, eds., *Weimar: A Jurisprudence of Crisis* (Berkeley: University of California Press, 2000), pp. 41–57

Korioth, Stefan, "Rudolf Smend: Introduction," in Arthur J. Jacobson and Bernhard Schlink, eds., *Weimar: A Jurispruence of Crisis* (Berkeley: University of California Press, 2000), pp. 207–13

Korsch, Karl, "The Structure and Practice of Totalitarianism," *New Essays*, Vol. 6 (1942), pp. 43–9

Koselleck, Reinhart, *Preußen zwischen Reform und Revolution: Allgemeines Landrecht, Verwaltung und soziale Bewegung von 1791 bis 1848* (Stuttgart: Klett-Cotta, 1965)

Kratochwil, Friedrich V., *Rules, Norms, and Decisions: On the Conditions of Practical and Legal Reasoning in International Relations and Domestic Affairs* (Cambridge: Cambridge University Press, 1991)

Krauß, Günther, "These: Der Begriff des Rechtsstaats ist an die verfassungsrechtliche Lage des 19. Jahrhunderts gebunden; für den Staat des 20. Jahrhunderts hat er keine Berechtigung mehr," in Günther Krauß and Otto von Schweinichen, *Disputation über den Rechtsstaat* (Hamburg: Hanseatische Verlagsanstalt, 1935), pp. 9–32

Krauß, Günther, "Erwiderung: Als Antwort auf die Ausführungen meines Gegners gebe ich meiner These folgende Abwandlung: der Begriff des Rechtsstaates ist gerade als Allgemeinbegriff an die Verfassungslage des 19. Jahrunderts gebunden," in Günther Krauß and Otto von Schweinichen, *Disputation über den Rechtsstaat* (Hamburg: Hanseatische Verlagsanstalt, 1935), pp. 70–83

Krieger, Leonard, *The German Idea of Freedom: History of a Political Tradition* (Boston: Beacon Press, 1957)

Kritische Justiz, ed., *Streitbare Juristen: Eine andere Tradition* (Baden-Baden: Nomos, 1988)

Kroeschell, Karl, *Rechtsgeschichte Deutschlands im 20. Jahrhundert* (Göttingen: Vandenhoeck und Ruprecht, 1992)

Kroeschell, Karl, *Deutsche Rechtsgeschichte*, vol. 3: *Seit 1650*, Fifth edition (Cologne: Böhlau, 2008)

Krohn, Claus-Dieter, *Intellectuals in Exile: Refugee Scholars and the New School for Social Research*, translated by Rita and Robert Kimber (Amherst: University of Massachusetts Press, 1993)

Krüger, Herbert, "Das neue Staatsrecht des dritten Reiches," *Fischers Zeitschrift für Verwaltungsrecht*, Vol. 70 (1934), pp. 289–315

Krygier, Martin, "The Rule of Law between England and Sudan: Hay, Thompson, and Massoud," *Law and Social Inquiry*, Vol. 41 (2016), pp. 480–8

Krygier, Martin, "Tempering Power," in Maurice Adams, Anne Meuwese, and Ernst Hirsch Ballin, eds., *Constitutionalism and the Rule of Law: Bridging Idealism and Realism* (Cambridge: Cambridge University Press, 2017), pp. 34–59

Kühl, Stefan, *Ganz normale Organisationen: Zur Soziologie des Holocaust* (Frankfurt: Suhrkamp, 2014)

Kunz, Josef L., "Franz Neumann, Behemoth: The Structure and Practice of National Socialism, Second edition" (Book review), *American Political Science Review*, Vol. 39 (1945), pp. 375–7

Laband, Paul, *Das Staatsrecht des Deutschen Reiches*, vol. 2 (Tübingen: Laupp, 1878)

Laband, Paul, *Das Staatsrecht des Deutschen Reiches*, 3 volumes, Second edition (Tübingen: Mohr, 1888)

Lacey, Nicola, "Philosophy, Political Morality, and History: Explaining the Enduring Resonance of the Hart-Fuller Debate," *New York University Law Review*, Vol. 83 (2008), pp. 1059–87

Ladwig-Winters, Simone, *Ernst Fraenkel: Ein politisches Leben* (New York: Campus, 2009)

Lai, Brian, and Dan Slater, "Institutions of the Offensive: Domestic Sources of Dispute Initiation in Authoritarian Regimes, 1950–1992," *American Journal of Political Science*, Vol. 50 (2006), pp. 113–26

Lange, Heinrich, *Vom Gesetzesstaat zum Rechtsstaat: Ein Vortrag* (Tübingen: Mohr, 1934)

Langmuir, Gavin I., *Toward a Definition of Antisemitism* (Berkeley: University of California Press, 1990)

Larenz, Karl, *Rechts- und Staatsphilosophie der Gegenwart*, Second edition (Berlin: Junker und Dünnhaupt, 1935)

Lasswell, Harold D., "The Garrison State," *American Journal of Sociology*, Vol. 46 (1941), pp. 455–68

Laudenklos, Frank, *Die Autonomie des Rechts im Nationalsozialismus*, Ph.D. dissertation, Universität Frankfurt, 2003

Lawson, Tom, *Debates on the Holocaust* (Manchester: Manchester University Press, 2010)

Ledeneva, Alena, "Telephone Justice in Russia," *Post-Soviet Affairs*, Vol. 24 (2008), pp. 324–50

Ledeneva, Alena, *Can Russia Modernise? Sistema, Power Networks and Informal Governance* (Cambridge: Cambridge University Press, 2013)

Ledford, Kenneth F., *From General Estate to Special Interest: German Lawyers 1878–1933* (Cambridge: Cambridge University Press, 1996)

Ledford, Kenneth F., "Formalizing the Rule of Law in Prussia: The Supreme Administrative Law Court, 1876–1914," *Central European History*, Vol. 37 (2004), pp. 203–24

Lee, Dwight E., "Franz Neumann, Behemoth: The Structure and Practice of National Socialism" (Book review), *American Historical Review*, Vol. 48 (1943), pp. 337–8

Lee, Sander H., "Primo Levi's Gray Zone: Implications for Post-Holocaust Ethics," *Holocaust and Genocide Studies*, Vol. 30 (2016), pp. 276–97

Lefort, Claude, *The Political Forms of Modern Society: Bureaucracy, Democracy, and Totalitarianism*, edited and translated by John B. Thomson (Cambridge: MIT Press, 1986)

Lemke-Müller, Sabine, ed., *Ethik des Widerstands: Der Kampf des Internationalen Sozialistischen Kampfbundes (ISK) gegen den Nationalsozialismus* (Bonn: Dietz, 1996)

Lepsius, Oliver, *Die gegensatzaufhebende Begriffsbildung: Methodenentwick lungen in der Weimarer Republik und ihr Verhältnis zur Ideologisierung der Rechtswissenschaft unter dem Nationalsozialismus* (Munich: Beck, 1994)

Lepsius, Oliver, "Die Zwei-Seiten-Lehre des Staates," in Andreas Anter, ed., *Die normative Kraft des Faktischen: Das Staatsverständnis Georg Jellineks* (Baden-Baden: Nomos, 2004), pp. 63–88

Lessig, Lawrence, "The Regulation of Social Meaning," *University of Chicago Law Review*, Vol. 62 (1995), pp. 943–1045

Lethen, Helmuth, *Cool Conduct: The Cultural Distance in Weimar Germany*, translated by Don Reneau (Berkeley: University of California Press, [1994] 2002)

Levi, Edward H., "An Introduction to Legal Reasoning," *University of Chicago Law Review*, Vol. 15 (1948), pp. 501–74

Levi, Primo, *The Drowned and the Saved* (New York: Vintage, 1989)

Levitsky, Steven, and Lucan A. Way, *Competitive Authoritarianism: Hybrid Regimes after the Cold War* (Cambridge: Cambridge University Press, 2010)

Levitsky, Steven, "Durable Authoritarianism," in Orfeo Fioretos, Tulia G. Falleti, and Adam Sheingate, eds., *The Oxford Handbook of Historical Institutionalism* (Oxford: Oxford University Press, 2016), pp. 208–22

Levy, Heinrich, *Die Hegel-Renaissance in der deutschen Philosophie: Mit besonderer Berücksichtigung des Neukantianismus* (Berlin: Heise, 1927)

Lewis, Mark, *The Birth of the New Justice: The Internationalization of Crime and Punishment, 1919–1950* (Oxford: Oxford University Press, 2014)

Linz, Juan J., "An Authoritarian Regime: The Case of Spain," in Erik Allardt and Yrjö Littunen, eds., *Cleavages, Ideologies, and Party Systems: Contributions to Contemporary Sociology* (Helsinki: Academic Bookstore, 1964), pp. 291–341

Linz, Juan J., "Opposition in and under an Authoritarian Regime: The Case of Spain," in Robert A. Dahl, ed., *Regimes and Oppositions* (New Haven: Yale University Press, 1973), pp. 171–259

Linz, Juan J., "Totalitarian and Authoritarian Regimes," in Fred I. Greenstein and Nelson W. Polsby, eds., *Handbook of Political Science*, vol. 3: *Macropolitical Theory* (Menlo Park: Addison-Wesley, 1975), pp. 175–411

Linz, Juan J., *Totalitarian and Authoritarian Regimes* (Boulder: Lynne Rienner, [1975] 2000)

Linz, Juan J., *The Breakdown of Democratic Regimes: Crisis, Breakdown, and Reequilibration* (Baltimore: Johns Hopkins University Press, 1978)

Linz, Juan J., and Alfred Stepan, *Problems of Democratic Transition and Consolidation: Southern Europe, South America, and Post-Communist Europe* (Baltimore: Johns Hopkins University Press, 1996)

Liu, Sida, and Terence C. Halliday, *Criminal Defense in China: The Politics of Lawyers at Work* (Cambridge: Cambridge University Press, 2016)

Locke, John, *Two Treatises of Government*, edited by Peter Laslett (Cambridge: Cambridge University Press, [1690] 1988)

Loewenstein, Karl, "Dictatorship and the German Constitution: 1933–1937," *University of Chicago Law Review*, Vol. 4 (1937), pp. 537–74

Longerich, Peter, *Heinrich Himmler*, translated by Jeremy Noakes and Lesley Sharpe (Oxford: Oxford University Press, [2008] 2012)

Longerich, Peter, *Wannseekonferenz: Der Weg zur "Endlösung"* (Munich: Pantheon, 2016)

Longman, Timothy, *Memory and Justice in Post-Genocide Rwanda* (Cambridge: Cambridge University Press, 2017)

Lösch, Anna-Maria Gräfin von, *Der nackte Geist: Die Juristische Fakultät der Berliner Universität im Umbruch von 1933* (Tübingen: Mohr, 1999)

Loughlin, Martin, *Sword and Scales: An Examination of the Relationship between Law and Politics* (Oxford: Hart, 2000)

Loughlin, Martin, *Foundations of Public Law* (Oxford: Oxford University Press, 2010)

Loughlin, Martin, "Politonomy," in Jens Meierhenrich and Oliver Simons, eds., *The Oxford Handbook of Carl Schmitt* (Oxford: Oxford University Press, 2016), pp. 570–91

Love, Heather, "Close Reading and Thin Description," *Public Culture*, Vol. 25 (2013), pp. 401–34

Lovett, Frank, *A Republic of Law* (Cambridge: Cambridge University Press, 2016)

Lowenthal, Abraham F., and Sergio Bitar, "Getting to Democracy: Lessons from Successful Transitions," *Foreign Affairs*, Vol. 95 (2016), pp. 134–44

Lubman, Stanley B., ed., *China's Legal Reforms* (Oxford: Oxford University Press, 1996)

Lubman, Stanley B., *Bird in a Cage: Legal Reform in China After Mao* (Stanford: Stanford University Press, 2000)

Luf, Gerhard, "Zur Verantwortlichkeit des Rechtspositivismus für 'gesetzliches Unrecht': Überlegungen zur 'Radbruch-These,'" in Ulrike Davy, Helmut Fuchs, Herbert Hofmeister, Judith Marte and Ilse Reiter, eds., *Nationalsozialismus und Recht: Rechtssetzung und Rechtswissenschaft in Österreich unter der Herrschaft des Nationalsozialismus* (Vienna: Orac, 1990), pp. 18–37

Lundgren, Peter, ed., *Wissenschaft im Dritten Reich* (Frankfurt: Suhrkamp, 1985)

Luthardt, Wolfgang, "Unrechtsstaat oder Doppelstaat? Kritisch-theoretische Reflektionen über die Struktur des Nationalsozialismus aus der Sicht demokratischer Sozialisten," in Hubert Rottleuthner, ed., *Recht, Rechtsphilosophie und Nationalsozialismus* (Wiesbaden: Steiner, 1983), pp. 197–209

Maas, Heiko, ed., *Furchtlose Juristen: Richter und Staatsanwälte gegen das NS-Unrecht* (Munich: Beck, 2017)

McAdams, Richard H., *The Expressive Powers of Law: Theories and Limits* (Cambridge: Harvard University Press, 2015)

McCormick, John P., *Carl Schmitt's Critique of Liberalism: Against Politics as Technology* (Cambridge: Cambridge University Press, 1997)

McCormick, John P., "From Constitutional Technique to Caesarist Ploy: Carl Schmitt on Dictatorship, Liberalism, and Emergency Powers," in Peter Baehr and Melvin Richter, eds., *Dictatorship in History and Theory* (Cambridge: Cambridge University Press, 2004), pp. 197–220

MacCormick, Neil, *Legal Reasoning and Legal Theory* (Oxford: Clarendon Press: 1978)

MacCormick, Neil, "Law, Morality and Positivism," *Legal Studies*, Vol. 1 (1980), pp. 131–45

MacCormick, Neil, *Rhetoric and the Rule of Law: A Theory of Legal Reasoning* (Oxford: Oxford University Press, 2005)

Mahoney, James, and Dietrich Rueschemeyer, eds., *Comparative Historical Analysis in the Social Sciences* (Cambridge: Cambridge University Press, 2003)

Mahoney, James, and Kathleen Thelen, eds., *Explaining Institutional Change: Ambiguity, Agency, and Power* (Cambridge: Cambridge University Press, 2009)

Maier, Charles S., *In Search of Stability: Explorations in Historical Political Economy* (Cambridge: Cambridge University Press, 1987)

Maine, Henry Sumner, *Ancient Law: Its Connection with the Early History of Society, and Its Relation to Modern Ideas* (London: John Murray, 1861)

Majer, Diemut, *Grundlagen des nationalsozialistischen Rechtssystems: Führerprinzip, Sonderrecht, Einheitspartei* (Stuttgart: Kohlhammer, 1987)

Majer, Diemut, *"Non-Germans" under the Third Reich: The Nazi Judicial and Administrative System in Germany and Occupied Eastern Europe, with Special Regard to Occupied Poland, 1939–1945*, translated by Peter Thomas Hill, Edward Vance Humphrey, and Brian Levin (Baltimore: Johns Hopkins University Press, 2003)

Malinowski, Bronislaw, *Argonauts of the Western Pacific: An Account of Native Enterprise and Adventure in the Archipelagoes of Melanesian New Guinea* (London: Routledge and Kegan Paul, 1922)

Malinowski, Bronislaw, *Crime and Custom in Savage Society* (London: Routledge and Kegan Paul, 1926)

Mannheim, Karl, *Man and Society in an Age of Reconstruction* (New York: Harcourt, Brace, and World, 1940)

Mansfield, Edward D., and Jack Snyder, "Democratization and the Danger of War," *International Security*, Vol. 20 (1995), pp. 5–38

March, James G., and Johan P. Olsen, "Elaborating the 'New Institutionalism,' " in R. A. W. Rhodes, Sarah A. Binder, and Bert A. Rockman, eds., *The Oxford Handbook of Political Institutions* (Oxford: Oxford University Press, 2006), pp. 3–20

Marcuse, Herbert, *One-Dimensional Man: Studies in the Ideology of Advanced Industrial Society* (Boston: Beacon Press, 1964)

Marriott, J. A. R., *Dictatorship and Democracy* (Oxford: Clarendon Press, 1935)

Marx, Fritz Morstein, "Ernst Fraenkel, The Dual State: A Contribution to the Theory of Dictatorship" (Book review), *Harvard Law Review*, Vol. 54 (1941), pp. 1264–7

Marx, Karl, "The Eighteenth Brumaire of Louis Bonaparte," in idem., *Political Writings*, vol. 2: *Surveys from Exile*, edited and with an Introduction by David Fernbach (New York: Vintage, [1852] 1974), pp. 143–249

Massoud, Mark Fathi, *Law's Fragile State: Colonial, Authoritarian, and Humanitarian Legacies in Sudan* (Cambridge: Cambridge University Press, 2013)

Mastnak, Tomaz, "Hobbes in Kiel, 1938: From Ferdinand Tönnies to Carl Schmitt," *History of European Ideas*, Vol. 41 (2015), pp. 966–91

Maunz, Theodor, "Die Rechtmäßigkeit der Verwaltung," in Hans Frank, ed., *Deutsches Verwaltungsrecht* (Munich: Eher, 1937), pp. 51–65

Maunz, Theodor, *Gestalt und Recht der Polizei* (Hamburg: Hanseatische Verlagsanstalt, 1943)

Maunz, Theodor, and Reinhold Zippelius, *Deutsches Staatsrecht: Ein Studienbuch*, Twenty-eighth edition (Munich: Beck, 1991)

Maurer, Hartmut, *Staatsrecht I: Grundlagen, Verfassungsorgane, Staatsfunktionen*, Sixth edition (Munich: Beck, 2010)

Maus, Ingeborg, "Entwicklung und Funktionswandel der Theorie des bürgerlichen Rechtsstaats," in idem., *Rechtstheorie und politische Theorie im Industriekapitalismus* (Munich: Fink, [1978] 1986), pp. 11–82

Maus, Ingeborg, "'Gesetzesbindung' der Justiz und die Struktur der nationalsozialistischen Rechtsnormen," in Ralf Dreier and Wolfgang Sellert, eds., *Recht und Justiz im "Dritten Reich"* (Frankfurt: Suhrkamp, 1989), pp. 81–103

Mehring, Reinhard, ed., *Carl Schmitt, Der Begriff des Politischen: Ein kooperativer Kommentar* (Berlin: Akademie Verlag, 2003)

Mehring, Reinhard, ed., *Carl Schmitt: Aufstieg und Fall* (Munich: Beck, 2009)

Meier, Heinrich, *The Lesson of Carl Schmitt: Four Chapters on the Distinction between Political Theology and Political Philosophy*, Expanded edition (Chicago: University of Chicago Press, 2011)

Meierhenrich, Jens, "Bringing the 'Dual State' Back In," Paper presented at the American Political Science Association Meeting, San Francisco, August 30–September 2, 2001

Meierhenrich, Jens, "The Presentation of Law in Everyday Life," Unpublished article manuscript, Harvard University, 2002

Meierhenrich, Jens, *The Trilemma of Justice*, Unpublished book manuscript, Harvard University, 2004

Meierhenrich, Jens, "Conspiracy in International Law," *Annual Review of Law and Social Science*, Vol. 2 (2006), pp. 341–57

Meierhenrich, Jens, *The Legacies of Law: Long-Run Consequences of Legal Development in South Africa, 1652–2000* (Cambridge: Cambridge University Press, 2008)

Meierhenrich, Jens, *The Violence of Law*, Unpublished book manuscript, Harvard University, 2009

Meierhenrich, Jens, ed., *Genocide: A Reader* (Oxford: Oxford University Press, 2014)

Meierhenrich, Jens, "Fearing the Disorder of Things: The Development of Carl Schmitt's Institutional Theory, 1919–1942," in Jens Meierhenrich and Oliver Simons, eds., *The Oxford Handbook of Carl Schmitt* (Oxford: Oxford University Press, 2016), pp. 171–216

Meierhenrich, Jens, *In the Belly of the Fish: Carl Schmitt in Nazi Germany*, Unpublished book manuscript, London School of Economics and Political Science, 2016

Meierhenrich, Jens, *The Idea of the* Rechtsstaat: *An Intellectual History*, Unpublished book manuscript, London School of Economics and Political Science, 2017

Meierhenrich, Jens, *Lawfare: A Genealogy* (Cambridge: Cambridge University Press, 2018)

Meierhenrich, Jens, *Genocide: A Very Short Introduction* (Oxford: Oxford University Press, 2018)

Meierhenrich, Jens, "*Rechtsstaat* versus the Rule of Law," in Jens Meierhenrich and Martin Loughlin, eds., *The Cambridge Companion to the Rule of Law* (Cambridge: Cambridge University Press, forthcoming)

Meierhenrich, Jens, *The Rationality of Genocide* (Princeton: Princeton University Press, forthcoming)

Meierhenrich, Jens, and Devin O. Pendas, "'The Justice of My Cause is Clear, but There's Politics to Fear': Political Trials in Theory and History," in idem., eds., *Political Trials in Theory and History* (Cambridge: Cambridge University Press, 2016), pp. 1–64

Meierhenrich, Jens, and Oliver Simons, "'A Fanatic of Order in an Epoch of Confusing Turmoil': The Political, Legal, and Cultural Thought of Carl Schmitt," in Jens Meierhenrich and Oliver Simons, eds., *The Oxford Handbook of Carl Schmitt* (Oxford: Oxford University Press, 2016), pp. 3–70

Meierhenrich, Jens, and Oliver Simons, eds., *The Oxford Handbook of Carl Schmitt* (Oxford: Oxford University Press, 2016)

Meinck, Jürgen, *Weimarer Staatslehre und Nationalsozialismus: Eine Studie zum Problem der Kontinuität im staatsrechtlichen Denken in Deutschland 1928 bis 1936* (Frankfurt: Campus, 1978)

Menger, Anton, *Das bürgerliche Recht und die besitzlosen Volksklassen* (Tübingen: Mohr, 1890)

Merry, Sally Engle, *Getting Justice and Getting Even: Legal Consciousness among Working-Class Americans* (Chicago: University of Chicago Press, 1990)

Merry, Sally Engle, "Ethnography in the Archives," in June Starr and Mark Goodale, eds., *Practicing Ethnography in Law: New Dialogues, Enduring Methods* (London: Palgrave, 2002), pp. 128–42

Merry, Sally Engle, "What is Legal Culture? An Anthropological Perspective," *Journal of Comparative Law*, Vol. 5 (2010), pp. 40–58

Merry, Sally Engle, "The Rule of Law and Authoritarian Rule: Legal Politics in Sudan," *Law and Social Inquiry*, Vol. 41 (2016), pp. 465–70

Merry, Sally Engle, Kevin Davis, and Benedict Kingsbury, eds., *The Quiet Power of Indicators: Measuring Governance, Corruption, and Rule of Law* (Cambridge: Cambridge University Press, 2015)

Merten, Detlef, "Die Rechtsstaatlichkeit im Allgemeinen Landrecht," in Friedrich Ebel, ed., *Gemeinwohl–Freiheit–Vernunft–Rechtsstaat: 200 Jahre Allgemeines Landrecht für die Preußischen Staaten* (Berlin: De Gruyter, 1995), pp. 109–38

Mertens, Bernd, *Rechtsetzung im Nationalsozialismus* (Tübingen: Mohr, 2009)

Mertens, Thomas, "Nazism, Legal Positivism, and Radbruch's Thesis on Statutory Injustice," *Law and Critique*, Vol. 14 (2003), pp. 277–95

Messerschmidt, Manfred, *Die Wehrmachtjustiz 1933–1945* (Paderborn: Schöningh, 2005)

Messerschmidt, Manfred, and Fritz Wüllner, *Die Wehrmachtjustiz im Dienste des Nationalsozialismus: Zerstörung einer Legende* (Baden-Baden: Nomos, 1987)

Meyer, Beate, Hermann Simon, and Chana Schutz, eds., *Jews in Nazi Berlin: From Kristallnacht to Liberation* (Chicago: University of Chicago Press, 2009)

Mezey, Naomi, "Law as Culture," *Yale Journal of Law and the Humanities*, Vol. 13 (2001), pp. 35–67

Migdal, Joel S., *State in Society: Studying How States and Societies Transform and Constitute One Another* (Cambridge: Cambridge University Press, 2001)

Miller, Michael K., "Democratic Pieces: Autocratic Elections and Democratic Development since 1815," *British Journal of Political Science*, Vol. 45 (2015), pp. 501–30

Mills, C. Wright, "The Nazi Behemoth Dissected," *Partisan Review*, Vol. 9 (1942), pp. 432–7

Mills, C. Wright, *Power Elite* (New York: Oxford University Press, 1956)

Miquel, Marc von, "Juristen," in Norbert Frei, ed., *Hitlers Eliten nach 1945* (Munich: dtv, 2003), pp. 165–217

Mohl, Robert von, *Die Polizei-Wissenschaft nach den Grundsätzen des Rechtsstaates*, vol. 1 (Tübingen: Laupp, 1832)

Mohl, Robert von, *Die Polizei-Wissenschaft nach den Grundsätzen des Rechtsstaates*, vol. 2 (Tübingen: Laupp, 1833)

Mohl, Robert von, *Encyklopädie der Staatswissenschaften* (Tübingen: Laupp, 1859)

Moll, Martin, ed., *Führer-Erlasse 1939–1945* (Stuttgart: Steiner, 1997)

Möller, Horst, "Fraenkel—Analytiker von Demokratie und Diktatur," in Thomas Brechenmacher, ed., *Identität und Erinnerung: Schlüsselthemen deutsch-jüdischer Geschichte und Gegenwart* (Munich: Olzog, 2009), pp. 155–72

Mommsen, Hans, *Beamtentum im Dritten Reich: Mit ausgewählten Quellen zur nationalsozialistischen Beamtenpolitik* (Stuttgart: Deutsche Verlags-Anstalt, 1966)

Mommsen, Hans, "Foreword," in Karl A. Schleunes, *The Twisted Road to Auschwitz: Nazi Policy Toward German Jews 1933–1939*, with a Foreword by Hans Mommsen (Urbana: University of Illinois Press, [1970] 1990), pp. vii–xi

Mommsen, Hans, *The Rise and Fall of Weimar Democracy*, translated by Elborg Forster and Larry Eugene Jones (Chapel Hill: University of North Carolina Press, 1996)

Moore, Sally Falk, ed., *Law and Anthropology: A Reader* (Oxford: Blackwell, 2005)

Moore, Barrington, Jr., *Terror and Progress: Some Sources of Change and Stability in the Soviet Dictatorship* (Cambridge: Harvard University Press, 1954)

Moore, Barrington, Jr., *Social Origins of Dictatorship and Democracy: Lord and Peasant in the Making of the Modern World* (Boston: Beacon Press, 1966)

Morris, Douglas G., "The Dual State Reframed: Ernst Fraenkel's Political Clients and His Theory of the Nazi Legal System," *Leo Baeck Institute Yearbook*, Vol. 58 (2013), pp. 5–21

Morris, Douglas G., "Discrimination, Degradation, Defiance: Jewish Lawyers in Nazi Germany," in Alan Steinweis and Robert D. Rachlin, eds., *The Law in Nazi Germany: Ideology, Opportunism, and the Perversion of Justice* (New York: Berghahn, 2013), pp. 105–35

Morris, Douglas G., "Write and Resist: Ernst Fraenkel and Franz Neumann on the Role of Natural Law in Fighting Nazi Tyranny," *New German Critique*, Vol. 126 (2015), pp. 197–230

Morris, Douglas G., "Accommodating Nazi Tyranny? The Wrong Turn of the Social Democratic Legal Philosopher Gustav Radbruch after the War," *Law and History Review*, Vol. 34 (2016), pp. 649–88

Morse, Yonatan L., "The Era of Electoral Authoritarianism," *World Politics*, Vol. 64 (2012), pp. 161–98

Moustafa, Tamir, *The Struggle for Constitutional Power: Law, Politics, and Economic Development in Egypt* (Cambridge: Cambridge University Press, 2007)

Moustafa, Tamir, and Tom Ginsburg, "Introduction: The Functions of Courts in Authoritarian Politics," in Tom Ginsburg and Tamir Moustafa, eds., *Rule by Law: The Politics of Courts in Authoritarian Regimes* (Cambridge: Cambridge University Press, 2008), pp. 1–22

Moyn, Samuel, "Judith Shklar versus the International Criminal Court," *Humanity*, Vol. 4 (2013), pp. 473–500

Müller, Adam Heinrich, *Die Elemente der Staatskunst*, vol. 1: *Die Herdflamme*, edited by Othmar Spann (Jena: Fischer, [1809] 1922)

Müller, Christoph, "Kritische Bemerkungen zur Auseinandersetzung Hermann Hellers mit Hans Kelsen," in Christoph Müller and Ilse Staff, eds., *Staatslehre in der Weimarer Republik: Hermann Heller zu ehren* (Frankfurt: Suhrkamp, 1985), pp. 128–57

Müller, Christoph, "Hermann Heller: Leben, Werk, Wirkung," in Hermann Heller, *Gesammelte Schriften*, vol. 3: *Staatslehre als Politische Wissenschaft*, Second edition, edited by Christoph Müller (Tübingen: Mohr, 1992), esp. 443–50

Müller, Christoph, and Ilse Staff, eds., *Der soziale Rechtsstaat: Gedächtnisschrift für Hermann Heller 1891–1933* (Baden-Baden: Nomos, 1984)

Müller, Ingo, *Hitler's Justice: The Courts of the Third Reich*, translated by Deborah Lucas Schneider (Cambridge: Harvard University Press, [1987] 1991)

Müller, Jan-Werner, *Constitutional Patriotism* (Princeton: Princeton University Press, 2007)

Münch, Ingo von, ed., *Gesetze des NS-Staates: Dokumente eines Unrechtssystems*, Third, enlarged edition (Paderborn: Schöningh, 1994)

Murkens, Jo Eric Khushal, *From Empire to Union: Conceptions of German Constitutional Law since 1871* (Oxford: Oxford University Press, 2013)

Nader, Laura, ed., *Law in Culture and Society* (Berkeley: University of California Press, [1969] 1997)

Negley, Glenn, "Ernst Fraenkel, The Dual State: A Contribution to the Theory of Dictatorship" (Book review), *American Bar Association Journal*, Vol. 28 (1942), pp. 74–5

Nelken, David, "Rethinking Legal Culture," in Michael Freeman, ed., *Law and Sociology* (Oxford: Oxford University Press, 2006), pp. 200–24

Neumann, Franz L. "Rechtsphilosophische Einleitung zu einer Abhandlung über das Verhältnis von Staat und Strafe," Ph.D. dissertation, Universität Frankfurt, 1923

Neumann, Franz L., "On the Marxist Theory of the State," in Keith Tribe, ed., *Social Democracy and the Rule of Law: Otto Kirchheimer and Franz Neumann* (London: Allen and Unwin, [1935] 1987), pp. 75–84

Neumann, Franz L., "Die Gewerkschaften in der Demokratie und in der Diktatur," in idem., eds., *Wirtschaft, Staat, Demokratie: Aufsätze 1930–1954*, edited by Alfons Söllner (Frankfurt: Suhrkamp, [1935] 1978), pp. 145–222

Neumann, Franz L., "The Governance of the Rule of Law: An Investigation into the Relationship between Political Theories, the Legal System and the Social Background in the Competitive Society," Ph.D. dissertation, London School of Economics and Political Science, 1936

Neumann, Franz L., "The Change in the Function of Law in Modern Society," in William E. Scheuerman, The Rule of Law under Siege: Selected Essays of Franz L. Neumann and Otto Kirchheimer (Berkeley: University of California Press, [1937] 1996), pp. 101–41

Neumann, Franz L., "Types of Natural Law," *Studies in Philosophy and Social Science*, reprinted in idem., *The Democratic and the Authoritarian State* (New York: Free Press, [1939] 1957), pp. 69–95

Neumann, Franz L., *Behemoth: The Structure and Practice of National Socialism* (Toronto: Oxford University Press, 1942)

Neumann, Franz L., *Behemoth: The Structure and Practice of National Socialism 1933–1944*, Second edition (Toronto: Oxford University Press, 1944)

Neumann, Franz L., "The Concept of Political Freedom," *Columbia Law Review*, Vol. 53 (1953), pp. 901–35

Neumann, Franz L., *Wirtschaft, Staat, Demokratie: Aufsätze 1930–1954*, edited by Alfons Söllner (Frankfurt: Suhrkamp, 1978)

Neumann, Franz L., *Die Herrschaft des Gesetzes: Eine Untersuchung zum Verhältnis von politischer Theorie und Rechtssystem in der Konkurrenzgesellschaft*, edited with an Afterword by Alfons Söllner (Frankfurt: Suhrkamp, 1980)

Neumann, Franz L., *The Rule of Law: Political Theory and the Legal System in Modern Society* (Leamington Spa: Berg, 1986)

Neumann, Franz L., Herbert Marcuse, and Otto Kirchheimer, *Secret Reports on Nazi Germany: The Frankfurt School Contribution to the War Effort*, edited by Raffaele Laudani (Princeton: Princeton University Press, 2013)

Neumann, Sigmund, *Carl Schmitt als Jurist The Total State in a World at War* (New York: Harper, 1942)

Neumann, Volker, *Carl Schmitt als Jurist* (Tübingen: Mohr, 2015)

Ng, Kwai, and Xin He, *Judicial Decision-Making in China: Embedded Courts* (Cambridge: Cambridge University Press, 2017)

Nicolai, Helmut, *Der Staat im nationalsozialistischen Weltbild* (Leipzig: Hirschfeld, 1933)

Nicolai, Helmut, *Grundlagen der kommenden Verfassung: Über den staatsrechtlichen Aufbau des deutschen Reiches* (Berlin: Hobbing, 1933)

Nicolai, Helmut, *Rasse und Recht: Vortrag gehalten auf dem deutschen Juristentage des Bundes nationalsozialistischer deutscher Juristen am 2. Oktober 1933 in Leipzig* (Berlin: Hobbing, 1933)

Nicolai, Helmut, *Die rassengesetzliche Rechtslehre: Grundzüge einer nationalsozialistischen Rechtsphilosophie*, Second edition (Munich: Eher, 1933)

Nicolai, Helmut, *Die rassengesetzliche Rechtslehre: Grundzüge einer nationalsozialistischen Rechtsphilosophie*, Third edition (Munich: Eher, 1934)

Nolzen, Armin, "The Nazi Party and Its Violence against the Jews, 1933–1939: Violence as a Historiographical Concept," *Yad Vashem Studies*, Vol. 31 (2003), pp. 245–85

Nonet, Philippe, and Philip Selznick, *Law and Society in Transition: Toward Responsive Law* (New York: Harper 1978)

North, Douglass C., *Institutions, Institutional Change and Economic Performance* (Cambridge: Cambridge University Press, 1990)

North, Douglass C., and Barry Weingast, "Constitutions and Commitment: The Evolution of Institutions Governing Public Choice in Seventeenth-Century England," *Journal of Economic History*, Vol. 49 (1989), pp. 803–32

Norwood, Stephen H., *The Third Reich in the Ivory Tower: Complicity and Conflict on American Campuses* (Cambridge: Cambridge University Press, 2009)

O'Donnell, Guillermo, "Polyarchies and the (Un)Rule of Law in Latin America: A Partial Conclusion," in Juan E. Méndez, Guillermo O'Donnell, and Paulo

Sérgio Pinheiro, eds., *The (Un)Rule of Law and the Underprivileged in Latin America* (Notre Dame: University of Notre Dame Press, 1999), pp. 303–37

O'Donnell, Guillermo, Philippe C. Schmitter, and Laurence Whitehead, eds., *Transitions from Authoritarian Rule*, 4 volumes (Baltimore: Johns Hopkins University Press, 1986)

Oertzen, Peter von, *Die soziale Funktion des staatsrechtlichen Positivismus* (Frankfurt: Suhrkamp 1974)

Oette, Lutz, "Document and Analyze: The Legacy of Klemperer, Fraenkel, and Neumann for Contemporary Human Rights Engagment," *Human Rights Quarterly*, Vol. 39 (2017), pp. 832–59

Olson, Mancur, "Dictatorship, Democracy, and Development," *American Political Science Review*, Vol. 87 (1993), pp. 567–76

Osler, Fritz, "Rechtsanwälte in der NS-Zeit: Fakten und Erinnerungen," *Anwaltsblatt*, Vol. 33 (1983), pp. 50–9

Ott, Walter, and Franziska Buob, "Did Legal Positivism Render German Jurists Defenceless during the Third Reich?" *Social and Legal Studies*, Vol. 2 (1993), pp. 91–104

Overy, Richard, *The Nazi Economic Recovery 1932–1938*, Second edition (Cambridge: Cambridge University Press, 1996)

Pappe, H. O., "On the Validity of Judicial Decisions in the Nazi Era," *Modern Law Review*, Vol. 23 (1960), pp. 260–74

Parsons, Talcott, *The Social System* (Glencoe: Free Press, 1951)

Parsons, Talcott, *The Sociological Imagination* (New York: Oxford University Press, 1959)

Parsons, Talcott, *On National Socialism*, edited with an Introduction by Uta Gerhardt (New York: De Gruyter, 1993)

Pascal, Roy, *The Nazi Dictatorship* (London: Routledge, 1934)

Pasquino, Pasquale, "Locke on King's Prerogative," *Political Theory*, Vol. 26 (1998), pp. 198–208

Pauer-Studer, Herlinde, "Einleitung: Rechtfertigungen des Unrechts," in Herlinde Pauer-Studer and Julian Fink, eds., *Rechtfertigungen des Unrechts: Das Rechtsdenken im Nationalsozialismus in Originaltexten* (Frankfurt: Suhrkamp, 2014), pp. 15–135

Pauer-Studer, Herlinde, and J. David Velleman, *Konrad Morgen: The Conscience of a Nazi Judge* (London: Palgrave, 2015)

Paulson, Stanley L., "Lon L. Fuller, Gustav Radbruch, and the 'Positivist' Theses," *Law and Philosophy*, Vol. 13 (1994), pp. 313–59

Paulson, Stanley L., "Radbruch on Unjust Laws: Competing Earlier and Later Views?," *Oxford Journal of Legal Studies*, Vol. 15 (1995), pp. 489–500

Paulson, Stanley L., "On the Background and Significance of Gustav Radbruch's Post-War Papers," *Oxford Journal of Legal Studies*, Vol. 26 (2006), pp. 17–40

Paxton, Robert O., *The Anatomy of Fascism* (London: Penguin, 2005)

Peerenboom, Randall, *China's Long March toward the Rule of Law* (Cambridge: Cambridge University Press, 2002)

Pegg, C. H., "Franz Neumann, Behemoth: The Structure and Practice of National Socialism" (Book review), *Social Forces*, Vol. 21 (1943), p. 364

Pendas, Devin O., *The Frankfurt Auschwitz Trial, 1963–1965: Genocide, History, and the Limits of the Law* (Cambridge: Cambridge University Press, 2006)

Pereira, Anthony W., *Political (In)Justice: Authoritarianism and the Rule of Law in Brazil, Chile, and Argentina* (Pittsburgh: University of Pittsburgh Press, 2005)

Perels, Joachim, "Adolf Arndt und Franz L. Neumann: Notizen zur Verdrängung sozialistischer Rechtstheorie," in idem., ed., *Recht, Demokratie und Kapitalismus: Aktualität und Problem der Theorie Franz L. Neumanns* (Baden-Baden: Nomos, 1984), pp. 137–44

Perels, Joachim, "Zur Rechtslehre vor und nach 1945," in Eva Schumann, ed., *Kontinuitäten und Zäsuren: Rechtswissenschaft und Justiz im "Dritten Reich" und in der Nachkriegszeit* (Göttingen: Wallstein, 2008), pp. 123–40

Petersen, Johann Wilhelm, *Litteratur der Staatslehre: Ein Versuch* (Stuttgart: Metzler, 1798)

Pflanze, Otto, *Bismarck: der Reichskanzler*, translated by Peter Hahlbrock (Munich: Beck, [1990] 1998)

Pierson, Paul, *Politics in Time: History, Institutions, and Social Analysis* (Princeton: Princeton University Press, 2004)

Pincus, Steve, *1688: The First Modern Revolution* (New Haven: Yale University Press, 2009)

Pinney, Harvey, "Ernst Fraenkel, The Dual State: A Contribution to the Theory of Dictatorship" (Book review), *Social Forces*, Vol. 20 (1942), pp. 409–10

Pinson, Koppel S., "Franz Neumann, Behemoth: The Structure and Practice of National Socialism" (Book review), *Political Science Quarterly*, Vol. 57 (1942), pp. 441–3

Pirie, Fernanda, *The Anthropology of Law* (Oxford: Oxford University Press, 2013)

Pospisil, Leonard J., *Anthropology of Law: A Comparative Theory* (New York: Harper & Row, 1971)

Popper, Nathaniel, "A Conscious Pariah," *The Nation*, April 19, 2001

Postone, Moishe, "Critique, State, and Economy," in Fred Rush, ed., *The Cambridge Companion to Critical Theory* (Cambridge: Cambridge University Press, 2004), pp. 165–93

Preuss, Lawrence, "Ernst Fraenkel, The Dual State: A Contribution to the Theory of Dictatorship" (Book review), *American Journal of International Law*, Vol. 35 (1941), pp. 584–5

Preuß, Ulrich K., "Nachträge zur Theorie des Rechtsstaats," *Kritische Justiz*, Vol. 4 (1971), pp. 16–44

Price, Megan "Estimating the Human Toll in Syria," *Nature*, February 8, 2017

Price, Megan, Anita Gohdes, and Patrick Ball, *Updated Statistical Analysis of Documentation of Killings in the Syrian Arab Republic* (August 2014), available at http://www.ohchr.org/Documents/Countries/SY/HRDAGUpdatedReportAug2014.pdf

Przeworski, Adam, *Democracy and the Market: Political and Economic Reforms in Eastern Europe and Latin America* (Cambridge: Cambridge University Press, 1991)

Pulzer, Peter, *Jews and the German State: The Political History of a Minority* (Oxford: Blackwell, 1992)

Quaritsch, Helmut, ed., *Carl Schmitt: Antworten in Nürnberg* (Berlin: Duncker and Humblot, 2000)

Radbruch, Gustav, "Gesetzliches Unrecht und übergesetzliches Recht," *Süddeutsche Juristen-Zeitung*, Vol. 1 (1946), reprinted in idem., *Rechtsphilosophie*, edited by Ralf Dreier and Stanley L. Paulson (Heidelberg: Müller, [1950] 2003), pp. 211–19

Radbruch, Gustav, "Statutory Lawlessness and Supra-Statutory Law," *Oxford Journal of Legal Studies*, Vol. 26 (2006), pp. 1–11

Raim, Edith *Justiz zwischen Diktatur und Demokratie: Wiederaufbau und Ahndung von NS-Verbrechen in Westdeutschland 1945–1949* (Berlin: De Gruyter, 2013)

Rajah, Jothie, *Authoritarian Rule of Law: Legislation, Discourse and Legitimacy in Singapore* (Cambridge: Cambridge University Press, 2012)

Raphael, D. D., *The Impartial Spectator: Adam Smith's Moral Philosophy* (Oxford: Oxford University Press, 2007)

Rasehorn, Theo, *Justizkritik in der Weimarer Republik: Das Beispiel der Zeitschrift "Die Justiz"* (Frankfurt: Campus, 1985)

Raz, Joseph, *The Authority of Law: Essays on Law and Morality* (Oxford: Clarendon Press, 1979)

Rebentisch, Dieter, and Karl Teppe, eds., *Verwaltung contra Menschenführung im Staat Hitlers* (Göttingen: Vandenhoeck und Ruprecht, 1986)

Reichardt, Sven, and Wolfgang Seibel, eds., *Der prekäre Staat: Herrschen und Verwalten im Nationalsozialismus* (Frankfurt: Campus, 2011)

Reichel, Peter, Harald Schmid, and Peter Steinbach, *Der Nationalsozialismus: Die zweite Geschichte* (Munich: Beck, 2009)

Reyntjens, Filip, *Political Governance in Post-Genocide Rwanda* (Cambridge: Cambridge University Press, 2013)

Renner, Karl, *Die Rechtsinstitute des Privatrechts und ihre soziale Funktion: Ein Beitrag zur Kritik des bürgerlichen Rechts*, Second edition (Tübingen: Mohr, [1905] 1929)

Richter, Melvin, "Toward a Concept of Political Illegitimacy: Bonapartist Dictatorship and Democratic Legitimacy," *Political Theory*, Vol. 10 (1982), pp. 185–214

Richter, Melvin, "A Family of Political Concepts: Tyranny, Despotism, Bonapartism, Caesarism, Dictatorship, 1750–1917," *European Journal of Political Theory*, Vol. 4 (2005), pp. 321–48

Richter, Isabel, "Entwürfe des Widerstehens: Männer und Frauen aus dem linken Widerstand in Verhören der Gestapo (1934–1939)," *WerkstattGeschichte*, Vol. 26 (2000), pp. 47–70

Ridder, Helmut, "Der Doppelstaat: Die Ehe von Kapitalismus und NS-Diktatur," *Die Zeit*, June 12, 1970

Roberts, Simon, *Order and Dispute: An Introduction to Legal Anthropology* (Harmondsworth: Penguin, 1979)

Roberts, Simon, and Michael Palmer, *Dispute Processes: ADR and the Primary Forms of Decision-Making*, Second edition (Cambridge: Cambridge University Press, 2005)

Robertson, Graeme R., *The Politics of Protest in Hybrid Regimes: Managing Dissent in Post-Communist Russia* (Cambridge: Cambridge University Press, 2011)

Robson, Charles B., "Franz Neumann, Behemoth: The Structure and Practice of National Socialism (Book review)," *Journal of Politics*, Vol. 5 (1943), pp. 70–2

Roetter, Friedrich, "The Impact of Nazi Law," *Wisconsin Law Review* (1945), pp. 516–62

Rose, Paul Lawrence, *German Question/Jewish Question: Revolutionary Antisemitism in Germany from Kant to Wagner*, New edition (Princeton: Princeton University Press, 2006)

Roseman, Mark, *The Villa, The Lake, The Meeting: Wannsee and the Final Solution* (London: Penguin, 2003)

Roseman, Mark, Devin O. Pendas, and Richard Wetzell, eds., *Beyond the Racial State* (Cambridge: Cambridge University Press, 2017)

Rosen, Lawrence, *Law as Culture: An Invitation* (Princeton: Princeton University Press, 2008)

Rosenberg, Hans, *Bureaucracy, Aristocracy, and Autocracy: The Prussian Experience 1660–1815* (Boston: Beacon Press, 1958)

Rossiter, Clinton, *Constitutional Dictatorship: Crisis Government in the Modern Democracies* (Princeton: Princeton University Press, 1948)

Rottleuthner, Hubert, "Die Substantialisierung des Formalrechts: Zur Rolle des Neuhegelianismus in der deutschen Juriprudenz," in Oskar Negt, ed., *Aktualität und Folgen der Philosophie Hegels* (Frankfurt: Suhrkamp, 1973), pp. 211–64

Rüthers, Bernd, *Die unbegrenzte Auslegung: Zum Wandel der Privatrechtsordnung im Nationalsozialismus*, Sixth, enlarged edition (Tübingen: Mohr, [1968] 2005)

Rüthers, Bernd, *Entartetes Recht: Rechtslehren und Kronjuristen im Dritten Reich*, Second, improved edition (Munich: Beck, 1989)

Ryle, Gilbert, "Thinking and Reflecting," in idem., *Collected Papers*, vol. 2: *Collected Essays*, 1929–1968 (London: Routledge [1966/1967], 1971), pp. 479–93

Ryle, Gilbert, "The Thinking of Thoughts: What Is 'Le Penseur' Doing?," in idem., *Collected Papers*, vol. 2: *Collected Essays, 1929–1968* (London: Routledge [1968], 1971), pp. 494–510

Sabine, George, "Franz Neumann, Behemoth: The Structure and Practice of National Socialism" (Book review), *Philosophical Review*, Vol. 51 (1942), pp. 432–5

Sakwa, Richard, *The Crisis of Russian Democracy: The Dual State, Factionalism and the Medvedev Succession* (Cambridge: Cambridge University Press, 2010)

Sakwa, Richard, "The Dual State in Russia," *Post-Soviet Affairs*, Vol. 26 (2010), pp. 185–206

Sakwa, Richard, "Systematic Stalemate: *Reiderstvo* and the Dual State," in Neil Robinson, ed., *The Political Economy of Russia* (Lanham: Rowman and Littlefield, 2013), pp. 59–96

Sakwa, Richard, "The Trials of Khodorkovsky in Russia," in Jens Meierhenrich and Devin O. Pendas, eds. *Political Trials in Theory and History* (Cambridge: Cambridge University Press, 2016), pp. 369–93

Salter, Michael, *Nazi War Crimes, U.S. Intelligence and Selective Prosecution at Nuremberg: Controversies Regarding the Role of the Office of Strategic Services* (London: Routledge, 2007)

Salter, Michael, *U.S. Intelligence, the Holocaust and the Nuremburg Trials: Seeking Accountability for Genocide and Cultural Plunder*, vol. 2 (Boston: Nijhoff, 2009)

Salzborn, Samuel, ed., *Kritische Theorie des Staates: Staat und Recht bei Franz L. Neumann* (Baden-Baden: Nomos, 2009)

Sanjek, Roger, ed., *Fieldnotes: The Makings of Anthropology* (Ithaca: Cornell University Press, 1990)

Šarčević, Edin, "Mißbrauch eines Begriffs–Rechtsstaat und Nationalsozialismus," *Rechtstheorie*, Vol. 24 (1993), pp. 205–33

Sartori, Giovanni, "Concept Misformation in Comparative Politics," *American Political Science Review*, Vol. 64 (1970), pp. 1033–53

Sassoon, Joseph, *Anatomy of Authoritarianism in the Arab Republics* (Cambridge: Cambridge University Press, 2016)

Schädler, Sarah, *"Justizkrise" und "Justizreform" im Nationalsozialismus: Das Reichsministerium unter Reichsjustizminister Thierack (1942–1945)* (Tübingen: Mohr, 2009)

Schatz, Edward, ed., *Political Ethnography: What Immersion Contributes to the Study of Power* (Chicago: University of Chicago Press, 2009)

Schauer, Frederick, *Playing by the Rules: A Philosophical Examination of Rule-Based Decision-Making in Law and in Life* (Oxford: Clarendon Press, 1993)

Schauer, Frederick, "Giving Reasons," *Stanford Law Review*, Vol. 47 (1995), pp. 633–59

Schauer, Frederick, *Thinking Like a Lawyer: A New Introduction to Legal Reasoning* (Cambridge: Harvard University Press, 2012)

Schauer, Frederick, *The Force of Law* (Cambridge: Harvard University Press, 2015)

Schedler, Andreas, "The Logic of Electoral Authoritarianism," in idem., ed., *Electoral Authoritarianism: The Dynamics of Unfree Competition* (Boulder: Lynne Rienner, 2006), pp. 1–23

Schedler, Andreas, ed., *Electoral Authoritarianism: The Dynamics of Unfree Competition* (Boulder: Lynne Rienner, 2006)

Schedler, Andreas, *The Politics of Uncertainty: Sustaining and Subverting Electoral Authoritarianism* (Oxford: Oxford University Press, 2015)

Scheingold, Stuart A., and Austin Sarat, *Something to Believe in: Politics, Professionalism, and Cause Lawyering* (Stanford: Stanford University Press, 2004)

Schellenberg, Ulrich, "Die Rechtsstaatskritik: Vom liberalen zum nationalen und nationalsozialistischen Rechtsstaat," in Ernst-Wolfgang Böckenförde, ed., *Staatsrecht und Staatsrechtslehre* (Heidelberg: Müller, 1985), pp. 71–88

Schenk, Dieter, *Hans Frank: Hitlers Kronjurist und Generalgouverneur* (Frankfurt: Fischer, 2006)

Scheuerman, William E., *Between the Norm and the Exception: The Frankfurt School and the Rule of Law* (Cambridge: MIT Press, 1994)

Scheuerman, William E., "Social Democracy and the Rule of Law: The Legacy of Ernst Fraenkel," in Peter C. Caldwell and William E. Scheuerman, eds., *From Liberal Democracy to Fascism* (Boston: Humanities Press, 2000), pp. 74–105

Scheuerman, William E., *Hans Morgenthau: Realism and Beyond* (Oxford: Polity, 2009)

Scheuerman, William E., "The Frankfurt School and the Rule of Law," in Jens Meierhenrich and Martin Loughlin, eds., *The Cambridge Companion to the Rule of Law* (Cambridge: Cambridge University Press, forthcoming)

Scheuner, Ulrich, "Die deutsche Staatsführung im Kriege," *Deutsche Rechtswissenschaft*, Vol. 5 (1940), pp. 1–43

Schieder, Wolfgang, "Carl Schmitt und Italien," *Vierteljahrshefte für Zeitgeschichte*, Vol. 37 (1989), pp. 1–21

Schlangen, Walter, *Die Totalitarismus-Theorie: Entwicklung und Probleme* (Stuttgart: Kohlhammer, 1976)

Schleunes, Karl A., *The Twisted Road to Auschwitz: Nazi Policy toward German Jews 1933–1939*, with a Foreword by Hans Mommsen (Urbana: University of Illinois Press, [1970] 1990)

Schleusener, Jan, *Eigentumspolitik im NS-Staat: Der staatliche Umgang mit Handlungs- und Verfügungsrechten über privates Eigentum 1933–1939* (Frankfurt: Lang, 2009)

Schluchter, Wolfgang, *Entscheidung für den sozialen Rechtsstaat: Hermann Heller und die staatstheoretische Diskussion in der Weimarer Republik*, Second edition (Baden-Baden: Nomos, 1983)

Schlüter, Holger, *Die Urteilspraxis des nationalsozialistischen Volksgerichtshofs* (Berlin: Duncker and Humblot, 1995)

Schmidt, Giselher, "Doppel- und Urdoppelstaat," *Die Zeit*, July 26, 2000

Schmitt, Carl, *Gesetz und Urteil: Eine Untersuchung zum Problem der Rechtspraxis*, Second edition (Munich: Beck, [1912] 1969)

Schmitt, Carl, *Dictatorship: From the Origin of the Modern Concept of Sovereignty to Proletarian Class Struggle*, translated by Michael Hoelzl and Graham Ward (Cambridge: Polity, [1921] 2014)

Schmitt, Carl, *Political Theology: Four Chapters on the Concept of Sovereignty*, translated by George Schwab (Chicago: University of Chicago Press, [1922] 2005)

Schmitt, Carl, *The Crisis of Parliamentary Democracy*, translated by Ellen Kennedy (Cambridge: MIT Press, [1923] 1988)

Schmitt, Carl, *Constitutional Theory*, translated and edited by Jeffrey Seitzer (Durham: Duke University Press, [1928] 2008)

Schmitt, Carl, *Hugo Preuss: Sein Staatsbegriff und seine Stellung in der deutschen Staatslehre* (Tübingen: Mohr, 1930)

Schmitt, Carl, "Staatsethik und pluralistischer Staat," in idem., *Positionen und Begriffe im Kampf mit Weimar–Genf–Versailles 1923–1939*, Third edition (Berlin: Duncker and Humblot, [1930] 1994), pp. 151–65

Schmitt, Carl, *The Concept of the Political*, Expanded edition, translated with an Introduction and Notes by George Schwab (Chicago: University of Chicago Press, [1932] 2007)

Schmitt, Carl, *Staat, Bewegung, Volk: Die Dreigliederung der politischen Einheit* (Hamburg: Hanseatische Verlagsanstalt, 1933)

Schmitt, Carl, "Das gute Recht der deutschen Revolution," *Westdeutscher Beobachter*, May 12, 1933

Schmitt, Carl, "Neue Leitsätze für die Rechtspraxis," *Juristische Wochenschrift*, Vol. 62 (1933), pp. 2793–4

Schmitt, Carl, "Nationalsozialismus und Rechtsstaat," *Juristische Wochenschrift*, Vol. 63 (1934), pp. 713–18

Schmitt, Carl, "Nationalsozialistisches Rechtsdenken," *Deutsches Recht*, Vol. 4 (1934), pp. 225–9

Schmitt, Carl, "Was bedeutet der Streit um den 'Rechtsstaat'?," *Zeitschrift für die gesamte Staatswissenschaft*, Vol. 95 (1935), pp. 189–201

Schmitt, Carl, "Der Rechtsstaat," in Hans Frank, ed., *Nationalsozialistisches Handbuch für Recht und Gesetzgebung* (Munich: Zentralverlag der NSDAP, 1935), pp. 3–10

Schmitt, Carl, "Kodifikation oder Novelle? Über die Aufgabe und Methode der heutigen Gesetzgebung," *Deutsche Juristen-Zeitung*, Vol. 40 (1935), pp. 919–25

Schmitt, Carl, "Die Rechtswissenschaft im Führerstaat," *Zeitschrift der Akademie für Deutsches Recht*, Vol. 2 (1935), pp. 435–40

Schmitt, Carl, "Nachwort," in Günther Krauß and Otto von Schweinichen, *Disputation über den Rechtsstaat* (Hamburg: Hanseatische Verlagsanstalt, 1935), pp. 84–8

Schmitt, Carl, "Schlußwort des Reichsgruppenwalters Staatsrat Prof. Dr. Carl Schmitt," in idem., *Das Judentum in der Rechtswissenschaft*, vol. 1: *Die deutsche Rechtswissenschaft im Kampf gegen den jüdischen Geist* (Berlin: Deutscher Rechts-Verlag, 1936), pp. 28–34

Schmitt, Carl, "Vorbemerkung," in Edgar Tatarin-Tarnheyden, *Das Judentum in der Rechtswissenschaft*, vol. 5: *Der Einfluß des Judentums in Staatsrecht und Staatslehre* (Berlin: Deutscher Rechts-Verlag, 1938), pp. 3–4

Schmitt, Carl, "Der Zugang zum Machthaber, ein zentrales verfassungsrechtliches Problem," in idem., *Verfassungsrechtliche Aufsätze aus den Jahren 1924–1954: Materialen zu einer Verfassungslehre*, Fourth edition (Berlin: Duncker and Humblot, [1947] 2003), pp. 430–9

Schneider, Peter, *Ausnahmezustand und Norm: Eine Studie zur Rechtslehre von Carl Schmitt* (Stuttgart: Deutsche Verlags-Anstalt, 1957)

Schoenmakers, Christine, *"Die Belange der Volksgemeinschaft erfordern …": Rechtspraxis und Selbstverständnis von Bremer Juristen im "Dritten Reich"* (Paderborn: Schöningh, 2015)

Schorn, Hubert, *Der Richter im Dritten Reich: Geschichte und Dokumente* (Frankfurt: Klostermann, 1959)

Schröder, Jan, *Recht als Wissenschaft: Geschichte der juristischen Methodenlehre in der Neuzeit (1500–1933)*, Second, revised and expanded edition (Munich: Beck, 2012)

Schulz, Gerhard, *Die nationalsozialistische Machtergreifung*, vol. 2: *Die Anfänge des totalitären Maßnahmenstaates* (Frankfurt: Ullstein, 1960)

Schuman, Frederick L., *The Nazi Dictatorship: A Study in Social Pathology and the Politics of Fascism* (New York: Knopf, 1936)

Schumpeter, Joseph A., "The Sociology of Imperialisms," in Joseph A. Schumpeter, *The Economics and Sociology of Capitalism*, edited by Richard Swedberg (Princeton: Princeton University Press, [1918] 1991), pp. 141–219

Schumpeter, Joseph A., *Capitalism, Socialism, and Democracy* (New York: Harper, 1942)

Schweinichen, Otto von, "Gegenthese: Das Wort Rechtsstaat kann so gebraucht warden, daß es den typischen Zusammenhang von Staat und Rechtsverwirklichung bezeichnet; dann hat es so viele Rechtsstaaten in der Geschichte gegeben wie es Staaten gegeben hat, in denen Recht in typischer Weise Geltung gefunden hat; von hier aus betrachtet, erscheint der Staat des 19. Jahrhunderts als typischer Gesetzesstaat, während der nationalsozialistische Staat Rechtsstaat im wahren Sinne ist," in Günther Krauß and Otto von Schweinichen, *Disputation über den Rechtsstaat* (Hamburg: Hanseatische Verlagsanstalt, 1935), pp. 33–69

Seidel, Bruno, and Siegfried Jenkner, ed., *Wege der Totalitarismus-Forschung* (Darmstadt: Wissenschaftliche Buchgesellschaft, 1968)

Selinger, William, "The Politics of Arendtian Historiography: European Federation and *The Origins of Totalitarianism*," *Modern Intellectual History*, Vol. 13 (2016), pp. 417–46

Seppänen, Samuli, *Ideological Conflict and the Rule of Law in Contemporary China: Useful Paradoxes* (Cambridge: Cambridge University Press, 2016)

Seyfert, Robert, *Das Leben der Institutionen: Zu einer allgemeinen Theorie der Institutionalisierung* (Weilerswist: Velbrück, 2011)

Shapiro, Scott J., *Legality* (Cambridge: Harvard University Press, 2010)

Sharlet, Robert, "Stalinism and Soviet Legal Culture," in Robert C. Tucker, ed., *Stalinism: Essays in Historical Interpretation* (New York: Norton, 1977), pp. 155–79

Shevtsova, Lilia, "Russia's Hybrid Regime," *Journal of Democracy*, Vol. 12 (2001), pp. 65–70

Shklar, Judith N., "Political Theory and the Rule of Law," in Allan C. Hutchinson and Patrick Monahan, eds., *The Rule of Law: Ideal or Ideology?* (Toronto: Carswell, 1987), pp. 1–16

Shklar, Judith N., "Political Theory and the Rule of Law," in idem., *Political Thinkers and Political Thought*, edited by Stanley Hoffmann (Chicago: University of Chicago Press, [1987] 1998), pp. 21–37

Shweder, Richard A., "Anthropology's Romantic Rebellion against the Enlightenment, or There's More to Thinking than Reason and Evidence," in Richard A. Shweder and Robert A. LeVine, eds., *Culture Theory: Essays on Mind, Self, and Emotion* (Cambridge: Cambridge University Press, 1984), pp. 27–66

Sigwart, Hans-Jörg, "Political Characterology: On the Method of Theorizing in Hannah Arendt's *Origins of Totalitarianism*," *American Political Science Review*, Vol. 110 (2017), pp. 265–77

Sil, Rudra, and Peter J. Katzenstein, "Analytic Eclecticism in the Study of World Politics: Reconfiguring Problems and Mechanisms across Research Traditions," *Perspectives on Politics*, Vol. 8 (2010), pp. 411–31

Silbey, Susan S., "Legal Culture and Cultures of Legality," in John R. Hall, Laura Grindstaff, and Ming-Cheng Lo, eds., *Handbook of Cultural Sociology* (London: Routledge, 2010), pp. 470–9

Siltala, Raimo, *Law, Truth, and Reason: A Treatise on Legal Argumentation* (New York: Springer, 2011)

Silverman, Dan, *Hitler's Economy: Nazi Work Creation Programs, 1933–1936* (Cambridge: Harvard University Press, 1998)

Simmonds, Nigel, *Law as a Moral Idea* (Oxford: Oxford University Press, 2007)

Simon, Dieter, *Die Unabhängigkeit des Richters* (Darmstadt: Wissenschaftliche Buchgesellschaft, 1975)

Sinzheimer, Hugo, "Was Wir Wollen," *Die Justiz*, reprinted in Hugo Sinzheimer and Ernst Fraenkel, *Die Justiz in der Weimarer Republik: Eine Chronik*, edited by Thilo Ramm with an Introduction by Otto Kirchheimer (Neuwied: Luchterhand, [1925] 1968), pp. 19–23

Smith, Adam, *The Theory of Moral Sentiments*, edited by D. D. Raphael and A. L. Macfie (Oxford: Clarendon Press, [1759] 1976)

Smith, Gordon B., *Reforming the Russian Legal System* (Cambridge: Cambridge University Press, 1996)

Smend, Rudolf, *Verfassung und Verfassungrecht*, in idem., *Staatsrechtliche Abhandlungen und andere Aufsätze*, Third edition (Berlin: Duncker and Humblot, [1928] 1994), pp. 119–276

Smend, Rudolf, "Der Einfluß der deutschen Staats- und Verwaltungsrechtslehre des 19. Jahrhunderts auf das Leben in Verfassung und Verwaltung," in idem., *Staatsrechtliche Abhandlungen und andere Aufsätze*, Third edition (Berlin: Duncker and Humblot, [1939] 1994), pp. 326–45

Söllner, Alfons, "Franz L. Neumann—Skizzen zu einer intellektuellen und politischen Biographie," in Franz L. Neumann, *Wirtschaft, Staat, Demokratie: Aufsätze 1940–1954*, edited by Alfons Söllner (Frankfurt: Suhrkamp, 1978), pp. 7–56

Söllner, Alfons, "Regression des Rechtsstaates? Zur Aktualität Franz L. Neumanns in der gegenwärtigen Diskussion," in Joachim Perels, ed., *Recht, Demokratie und Kapitalismus: Aktualität und Problem der Theorie Franz L. Neumanns* (Baden-Baden: Nomos, 1984), pp. 195–209

Söllner, Alfons, "Hannah Arendt's *The Origins of Totalitarianism* in its Original Context," *European Journal of Political Theory*, Vol. 3 (2004), pp. 219–38

Söllner, Alfons, Ralf Walkenhaus, and Karin Wieland, eds., *Totalitarismus: Eine Ideengeschichte des 20. Jahrhunderts* (Munich: Oldenbourg, 1997)

Spaak, Torben, "Meta-Ethics and Legal Theory: The Case of Gustav Radbruch," *Law and Philosophy*, Vol. 28 (2009), pp. 261–90

Spearman, Diana, *Modern Dictatorship* (London: Jonathan Cape, 1939)

Spellman, Barbara A., and Frederick Schauer, "Legal Reasoning," in Keith J. Holyoak and Robert G. Morrison, eds., *The Oxford Handbook of Thinking and Reasoning* (Oxford: Oxford University Press, 2012), pp. 719–35

Staël Holstein, Madame La Baronne de, *De l'Allemagne*, Second edition (Paris: Nicolle, 1814)

Staff, Ilse, *Staatsdenken im Italien des 20. Jahrhunderts: Ein Beitrag zur Carl Schmitt-Rezeption* (Baden-Baden: Nomos, 1991)

Stahl, Friedrich Julius, *Die Philosophie des Rechts*, vol. 2: *Rechts- und Staatslehre auf der Grundlage christlicher Weltanschauung*, Third edition (Heidelberg: Mohr, 1856)

Stahn, Carsten, *The Law and Practice of International Territorial Administration: Versailles to Iraq and Beyond* (Cambridge: Cambridge University Press, 2008)

Starr, June, and Jane F. Collier, eds., *History and Power in the Study of Law: New Directions in Legal Anthropology* (Ithaca: Cornell University Press, 1989)

Steber, Martina, and Bernhard Gotto, eds., *Visions of Community in Nazi Germany: Social Engineering and Private Lives* (Oxford: Oxford University Press, 2014)

Steffani, Winfried, "Ernst Fraenkel als Persönlichkeit," in Hubertus Buchstein and Gerhard Göhler, eds., *Vom Sozialismus zum Pluralismus: Beiträge zu Werk und Leben Ernst Fraenkels* (Baden-Baden: Nomos, 2000), pp. 125–47

Steger, Manfred B., and Paul James, "Levels of Subjective Globalization: Ideologies, Imaginaries, Ontologies," *Perspectives on Global Development and Technology*, Vol. 12 (2013), pp. 17–40

Stein, Lorenz von, *Verwaltungslehre*, vol. 1: *Die vollziehende Gewalt*, Second edition (Stuttgart: Cotta: 1869)

Stern, Klaus, *Das Staatsrecht der Bundesrepublik Deutschland*, vol. 5: *Die geschichtlichen Grundlagen des deutschen Staatsrechts* (Munich: Beck, 2000)

Stern, Rachel E., *Environmental Litigation in China: A Study in Political Ambivalence* (Cambridge: Cambridge University Press, 2013)

Stirk, Peter M. R., *Twentieth-Century German Political Thought* (Edinburgh: Edinburgh University Press, 2006)

Stolleis, Michael, *Gemeinwohlformeln im nationalsozialistischen Recht* (Berlin: Schweitzer, 1974)

Stolleis, Michael, "Der Doppelstaat," *Juristenzeitung*, Vol. 39 (1984), p. 1097

Stolleis, Michael, "The Science of Administrative Law under National Socialism," in idem., *The Law under the Swastika: Studies on Legal History in Nazi Germany*, (translated by Thomas Dunlap (Chicago: University of Chicago Press, [1985] 1998), pp. 102–14

Stolleis, Michael, "Die Verwaltungsgerichtsbarkeit im Nationalsozialismus," in Bernhard Diestelkamp and Michael Stolleis, eds., *Justizalltag im Dritten Reich* (Frankfurt: Fischer, 1988), pp. 26–38

Stolleis, Michael, "Im Bauch des Leviathan—Staatsrechtslehre im Nationalsozialismus," in Michael Stolleis, *Recht im Unrecht: Studien zur Rechtsgeschichte des Nationalsozialismus* (Frankfurt: Suhrkamp, [1989] 1994), pp. 126–46

Stolleis, Michael, "Legal History during the Nazi Period: Outlines of a Scholarly Field," in idem., *The Law under the Swastika: Studies on Legal History in Nazi Germany*, translated by Thomas Dunlap (Chicago: University of Chicago Press, [1989] 1998), pp. 40–7

Stolleis, Michael, *Geschichte des öffentlichen Rechts in Deutschland, vol. 2: Staatsrechtslehre und Verwaltungswissenschaft 1800–1914* (Munich: Beck, 1992)

Stolleis, Michael, "Theodor Maunz—Ein Staatsrechtslehrerleben," *Kritische Justiz*, Vol. 26 (1993), pp. 393–6

Stolleis, Michael, *Recht im Unrecht: Studien zur Rechtsgeschichte des Nationalsozialismus* (Frankfurt: Suhrkamp, 1994)

Stolleis, Michael, "General Introduction," in idem., *The Law under the Swastika: Studies on Legal History in Nazi Germany*, translated by Thomas Dunlap (Chicago: University of Chicago Press, [1994] 1998), pp. 5–22

Stolleis, Michael, *Geschichte des öffentlichen Rechts in Deutschland*, vol. 3: *Staats- und Verwaltungswissenschaft in Republik und Diktatur 1914–1945* (Munich: Beck, 1999)

Stolleis, Michael, *A History of Public Law in Germany 1914–1945*, translated by Thomas Dunlap (Oxford: Oxford University Press, [1999] 2004)

Stolleis, Michael, *Public Law in Germany: A Historical Introduction from the 16th to the 21st Century*, translated by Thomas Dunlap (Oxford: Oxford University Press, 2017)

Stoltzfus, Nathan, *Hitler's Compromises: Coercion and Consensus in Nazi Germany* (New Haven: Yale University Press, 2016)

Strauss, Leo, *Natural Right and History* (Chicago: University of Chicago Press, [1950] 1965)

Stubbs, Michael, "Semantics," in Constant Leung and Brian V. Street, eds., *The Routledge Companion to English Studies* (London: Routledge, 2014), pp. 215–28

Sunstein, Cass R., "On the Expressive Function of Law," *University of Pennsylvania Law Review*, Vol. 144 (1996), pp. 2021–53

Supiot, Alan, *Homo Juridicus: On the Anthropological Function of the Law* (London: Verso, 2007)

Svolik, Milan W., *The Politics of Authoritarian Rule* (Cambridge: Cambridge University Press, 2012)

Sweezy, Paul M. "Franz Neumann, Behemoth: The Structure and Practice of National Socialism" (Book review), *Science and Society*, Vol. 6 (1942), pp. 281–6

Tamanaha, Brian Z., *Realistic Socio-Legal Theory: Pragmatism and a Social Theory of Law* (Oxford: Oxford University Press, 1997)

Tamanaha, Brian Z., *On the Rule of Law: History, Politics, Theory* (Cambridge: Cambridge University Press, 2004)

Tamanaha, Brian Z., "The Primacy of Society and the Failure of Law and Development," *Cornell International Law Journal*, Vol. 44 (2011), pp. 209–48

Tang, Wenfang, *Populist Authoritarianism: Chinese Political Culture and Regime Sustainability* (Oxford: Oxford University Press, 2016)

Tatarin-Tarnheyden, Edgar, "Staat und Sittlichkeit," *Kantstudien*, Vol. 35 (1930), pp. 42–59

Tatarin-Tarnheyden, Edgar, *Werdendes Staatsrecht* (Berlin: Heymanns, 1934)

Tatarin-Tarnheyden, Edgar, "Grundlagen des Verwaltungsrechts im neuen Staat," *Archiv des öffentlichen Rechts*, Vol. 24 (1934), pp. 345–58

Taylor, A. J. P. Taylor, *The Struggle for Mastery in Europe 1848–1918* (Oxford: Clarendon Press, 1954)

Taylor, Charles, *Hegel and Modern Society* (Cambridge: Cambridge University Press, 1979)

Taylor, Rabun, "Watching the Skies: Janus, Auspication, and the Shrine in the Roman Forum," *Memoirs of the American Academy in Rome*, Vol. 45 (2000), pp. 1–40

Thelen, Kathleen, "Historical Institutionalism in Comparative Politics," *Annual Review of Political Science*, Vol. 2 (1999), pp. 369–404

Thomä, Dieter, "The Difficulty of Democracy: Rethinking the Political in the Philosophy of the Thirties (Gehlen, Schmitt, Heidegger)," in Wolfgang Bialas and Anson Rabinbach, eds., *Nazi Germany and the Humanities: How German Academics Embraced Nazism* (London: Oneworld, 2007), pp. 75–100

Thompson, E. P., *Whigs and Hunters: The Origin of the Black Act* (New York: Pantheon, 1975)

Thompson, John B., "Ideology and the Social Imaginary: An Apprisal of Castoriadis and Lefort," *Theory and Society*, Vol. 11 (1982), pp. 659–81

Thompson, John B., *Studies in the Theory of Ideology* (London: Wiley, 1984)

Thornhill, Chris, *Political Theory in Modern Germany: An Introduction* (Oxford: Polity, 2000)

Tilly, Charles, *The Politics of Collective Violence* (Cambridge: Cambridge University Press, 2003)

Tilly, Charles, Sidney Tarrow, and Doug McAdam, *Dynamics of Contention* (Cambridge: Cambridge University Press, 2001)

Tocqueville, Alexis de, *The Old Regime and the Revolution*, vol. 1: *The Complete Text*, edited with an Introduction and Critical Apparatus by François Furet and Françoise Mélonio, translated by Alan S. Kahan (Chicago: University of Chicago Press, [1856] 1998)

Tooze, Adam, *The Wages of Destruction: The Making and Breaking of the Nazi Economy* (London: Penguin, 2008)

Topitsch, Ernst, *Die Sozialphilosophie Hegels als Heilslehre und Herrschaftsideologie* (Neuwied: Luchterhand, 1967)

Treitschke, Heinrich, *Deutsche Geschichte im neunzehnten Jahrhundert*, vol. 1: *Bis zum zweiten Pariser Frieden* (Leipzig: Hendel, 1927)

Trejo-Mathys, Jonathan, "Neo-Kantianism in the Philosophy of Law: Its Value and Actuality," in Nicolas de Warren and Andrea Staiti, eds., *New Approaches to Neo-Kantianism* (Cambridge: Cambridge University Press, 2015), pp. 147–70

Tribe, Keith, "Introduction," in idem., ed., *Social Democracy and the Rule of Law: Otto Kirchheimer and Franz Neumann*, translated by Leena Tanner and Keith Tribe (London: Allen and Unwin, 1987), pp. 1–26

Tribe, Keith, ed., *Social Democracy and the Rule of Law: Otto Kirchheimer and Franz Neumann*, translated by Leena Tanner and Keith Tribe (London: Allen and Unwin, 1987)

Truex, Rory, "Consultative Authoritarianism and Its Limits," *Comparative Political Studies*, Vol. 50 (2017), pp. 329–61

Tsao, Roy T., "The Three Phases of Arendt's Theory of Totalitarianism," *Social Research*, Vol. 69 (2002), pp. 579–619

Tuori, Kaius, *Lawyers and Savages: Ancient History and Legal Realism in the Making of Legal Anthropology* (London: Routledge, 2014)

Turchetti, Mario, "'Despotism' and 'Tyranny,'" *European Journal of Political Theory*, Vol. 7 (2008), pp. 159–82

Turner, Henry Ashby, Jr., *Thirty Days to Power: January 1933* (Reading: Addison-Wesley, 1996)

Tushnet, Mark, "Authoritarian Constitutionalism: Some Conceptual Issues," in Tom Ginsburg and Alberto Simpser, eds., *Constitutions in Authoritarian Regimes* (Cambridge: Cambridge University Press, 2014), pp. 36–49

Vanaik, Achin, *The Rise of Hindu Authoritarianism: Secular Claims, Communal Realities* (London: Verso, 2017)

Versteeg, Mila, and Tom Ginsburg, "Measuring the Rule of Law: A Comparison of Indicators," *Law and Social Inquiry*, Vol. 42 (2017), pp. 100–37

Voegelin, Eric, "Ernst Fraenkel, The Dual State: A Contribution to the Theory of Dictatorship" (Book review), *Journal of Politics*, Vol. 4 (1942), pp. 269–72

Voegelin, Eric, "The Origins of Totalitarianism," *Review of Politics*, Vol. 15 (1953), pp. 68–85

Volkov, Shulamit, *Die Juden in Deutschland 1780–1918*, translated by Simone Gundi (Munich: Oldenbourg, 2000)

Volkov, Shulamit, *Germans, Jews, and Antisemites: Trials in Emancipation* (Cambridge: Cambridge University Press, 2006)

Vreeland, James Raymond, "Political Institutions and Human Rights: Why Dictatorships Enter into the United Nations Convention against Torture," *International Organization*, Vol. 62 (2008), pp. 65–101

Wachsmann, Nikolaus, *Hitler's Prisons: Legal Terror in Nazi Germany* (New Haven: Yale University Press, 2004)

Wachsmann, Nikolaus, *KL: A History of the Nazi Concentration Camps* (New York: Little, Brown, 2015)

Wagner, Walter, *Der Volksgerichtshof im nationalsozialistischen Staat*, Expanded edition (Munich: Oldenbourg, 2011)

Waldron, Jeremy, "The Rule of Law," *Stanford Encyclopedia of Philosophy* (2016), available at https://plato.stanford.edu/archives/fall2016/entries/rule-of-law/

Walther, Manfred, "Hat der juristische Positivismus die deutschen Juristen im 'Dritten Reich' wehrlos gemacht? Zur Analyse und Kritik der Radbruch-These," in Ralf Dreier and Wolfgang Sellert, eds., *Recht und Justiz im "Dritten Reich"* (Frankfurt: Suhrkamp, 1989), pp. 323–54

Walz, Gustav Adolf, *Das Ende der Zwischenverfassung: Betrachtungen zur Entstehung des nationalsozialistischen Staates* (Stuttgart: Kohlhammer, 1933)

Walz, Gustav Adolf, "Autoritärer Staat, nationaler Rechtsstaat oder völkischer Führerstaat?," *Deutsche Juristen-Zeitung*, Vol. 38 (1933), pp. 1334–40

Walz, Gustav Adolf, "Faschismus und Nationalsozialismus," *Deutsches Recht*, Vol. 5 (1935), pp. 315–19

Walz, Gustav Adolf, "Autoritäre Staatsordnung und völkischer Führerstaat," *Bücherkunde*, Vol. 4 (1937), pp. 76–9

Wang, Yuhua, *Tying the Autocrat's Hands: The Rise of the Rule of Law in China* (Cambridge: Cambridge University Press, 2015)

Weber, Max, "Parliament and Government in Germany under a New Political Order," in Peter Lassman and Ronald Speirs, eds., *Weber: Political Writings* (Cambridge: Cambridge University Press, [1918] 1994), pp. 130–271

Weber, Max, *Wirtschaft und Gesellschaft: Grundriß der verstehenden Soziologie*, Fifth, revised edition, edited by Johannes Winckelmann (Tübingen: Mohr, [1922] 1972)

Weber, Max, *Economy and Society: An Outline of Interpretive Sociology*, edited by Guenther Roth and Claus Wittich (Berkeley: University of California Press, [1922] 1978)

Weber, Petra, *Carlo Schmid, 1896–1979: Eine Biographie* (Munich: Beck, 1996)

Weber, Werner, *Die Verkündung von Rechtsvorschriften* (Stuttgart: Kohlhammer, 1942)

Weeks, Jessica L., "Autocratic Audience Costs: Regime Type and Signaling Resolve," *International Organization*, Vol. 62 (2008), pp. 35–64

Wehler, Hans-Ulrich, *Deutsche Gesellschaftsgeschichte*, vol. 4: *Vom Beginn des Ersten Weltkriegs bis zur Gründung der beiden deutschen Staaten 1914–1949* (Munich: Beck, 2003)

Wehler, Hans-Ulrich, *Der Nationalsozialismus: Bewegung, Führerherrschaft, Verbrechen 1919–1945* (Munich: Beck, 2009)

Weinreich, Max, *Hitler's Professors: The Part of Scholarship in Germany's Crimes against the Jewish People*, with an Introduction by Martin Gilbert (New Haven: Yale University Press, [1946] 1999)

Weitz, Eric D., "Hans Mommsen, The Rise and Fall of Weimar Democracy" (Book review), *Central European History*, Vol. 31 (1998), pp. 273–7

Welcker, Carl Theodor, *Die letzten Gründe von Recht, Staat und Strafe philosophisch und nach den Gesetzen der merkwürdigsten Völker entwickelt* (Gießen: Heyer, 1813)

Wesel, Uwe, *Geschichte des Rechts: Von den Frühformen bis zur Gegenwart*, Third edition (Munich: Beck, 2006)

Wette, Wolfgang, "Deserteure der Wehrmacht rehabilitiert: Ein exemplarischer Meinungswandel in Deutschland (1980–2002)," *Zeitschrift für Geschichtswissenschaft*, Vol. 52 (2004), pp. 505–27

Wheatland, Thomas, "Franz L. Neumann: Negotiating Political Exile," in Jan Logemann and Mary Nolan, eds., *More Atlantic Crossings? European Voices and the Postwar Atlantic Community* (Washington: German Historical Institute, 2014), pp. 111–38

Wiegand, Hanns-Jürgen, *Das Vermächtnis Friedrich Julius Stahls: Ein Beitrag zur Geschichte konservativen Rechts- und Ordnungsdenken* (Königstein: Athenäum, 1980)

Wiener, Christina, *Kieler Fakultät und "Kieler Schule": Die Rechtslehrer an der Rechts- und Staatswissenschaftlichen Fakultät zu Kiel in der Zeit des Nationalsozialismus und ihre Entnazifizierung* (Baden-Baden: Nomos, 2013)

Wigell, Mikael, "Mapping 'Hybrid Regimes': Regime Types and Concepts in Comparative Politics," *Democratization*, Vol. 15 (2008), pp. 230–50

Wiggershaus, Rolf, *Die Frankfurter Schule: Geschichte, Theoretische Entwicklung, Politische Bedeutung* (Munich: Hanser, 1986)

Wilde, Ralph, *International Territorial Administration: How Trusteeship and the Civilizing Mission Never Went Away* (Oxford: Oxford University Press, 2008)

Wildt, Michael, *Generation des Unbedingten: Das Führungskorps des Reichssicherheitshauptamtes* (Hamburg: Hamburger Edition, 2002)

Wildt, Michael, "Ernst Fraenkel und Carl Schmitt: Eine ungleiche Beziehung," in Daniela Münkel and Jutta Schwarzkopf, eds., *Geschichte als Experiment: Studien zu Politik, Kultur und Alltag im 19. und 20. Jahrhundert* (Frankfurt: Campus, 2004), pp. 35–48

Wildt, Michael, *Volksgemeinschaft als Selbstermächtigung: Gewalt gegen Juden in der deutschen Provinz 1919 bis 1939* (Hamburg: Hamburger Edition, 2007)

Wildt, Michael, "Eine spannungsvolle Beziehung: Ernst Fraenkel und Carl Schmitt," in Robert Chr. van Ooyen and Martin H. W. Möllers, eds., *(Doppel-) Staat und Gruppeninteressen: Pluralismus–Parlamentarismus–Schmitt-Kritik bei Ernst Fraenkel* (Baden-Baden: Nomos, 2009), pp. 87–111

Wildt, Michael, "'Volksgemeinschaft': Eine Antwort auf Ian Kershaw," *Zeithistorische Forschungen*, Vol. 8 (2011), pp. 102–9

Wildt, Michael, "Die Angst vor dem Volk: Ernst Fraenkel in der deutschen Nachkriegsgesellschaft," in Monika Boll and Raphael Gross, eds., "*Ich staune, dass Sie in dieser Luft noch atmen können*": *Jüdische Intellektuelle in Deutschland nach 1945* (Frankfurt: Fischer, 2013), pp. 317–44

Williams, Michael C., ed., *Reconsidering Realism: The Legacy of Hans J. Morgenthau* (Oxford: Oxford University Press, 2007)

Willig, Kenneth C. H., "The Bar in the Third Reich," *American Journal of Legal History*, Vol. 20 (1976), pp. 1–14

Willis, Paul, *The Ethnographic Imagination* (Cambridge: Polity, 2000)

Willoweit, Dietmar, "Deutsche Rechtsgeschichte und nationalsozialistische Weltanschauung: das Beispiel Hans Frank," in Michael Stolleis and Dieter Simon, eds., *Rechtsgeschichte im Nationalsozialismus: Beiträge zur Geschichte einer Disziplin* (Tübingen: Mohr, 1989), pp. 25–42

Willoweit, Dietmar, *Deutsche Verfassungsgeschichte: Vom Frankenreich bis zur Wiedervereinigung Deutschlands*, Sixth edition (Munich: Beck, 2009)

Winch, Peter, *The Idea of a Social Science and Its Relation to Philosophy* (London: Routledge, 1958)

Wintrope, Roland, *The Political Economy of Dictatorship* (Cambridge: Cambridge University Press, 1998)

Wittig, Martin, *Der Rechtsstaat im Wandel der Staatsformen* (Greifswald: Panzig, 1933)

World Bank, *World Development Report 2017: Governance and the Law* (Washington: World Bank, 2017)

Wright, Joseph, and Abel Escribà-Folch, "Authoritarian Institutions and Regime Survival: Transitions to Democracy and Subsequent Autocracy," *British Journal of Political Science*, Vol. 42 (2011), pp. 283–309

Wüllenweber, Hans, *Sondergerichte im Dritten Reich: Vergessene Verbrechen der Justiz* (Munich: Luchterhand, 1993)

Young, Simon N. M. Young and Yashi Ghai. See idem., eds., *Hong Kong's Court of Final Appeal: The Development of the Law in China's Hong Kong* (Cambridge: Cambridge University Press, 2013)

Zakaria, Fareed, "The Rise of Illiberal Democracy," *Foreign Affairs*, Vol. 76 (1997), pp. 22–43
Ziemann, Sascha, "Relativismus in Zeiten der Krise: Franz L. Neumanns unveröffentlichte rechtsphilosophische Doktorarbeit von 1923," *Zeitschrift für Internationale Strafrechtsdogmatik*, Vol. 2 (2007), pp. 362–70
Zimmerman, William, *Ruling Russia: Authoritarianism from the Revolution to Putin* (Princeton: Princeton University Press, 2016)
Zoller, Elisabeth, *Introduction to Public Law: A Comparative Study* (Leiden: Brill, 2008)
Zollmann, Jakob, Alan E. Steinweis and Robert D. Rachlin, eds., "The Law in Nazi Germany: Ideology, Opportunism, and the Perversion of Justice" (Book review), *German History*, Vol. 32 (2014), pp. 494–6

Index

The manufacturer's authorised representative in the EU for product safety is Oxford University Press España S.A. of el Parque Empresarial San Fernando de Henares, Avenida de Castilla, 2 – 28830 Madrid (www.oup.es/en or product.safety@oup.com). OUP España S.A. also acts as importer into Spain of products made by the manufacturer.

www.ingramcontent.com/pod-product-compliance
Ingram Content Group UK Ltd.
Pitfield, Milton Keynes, MK11 3LW, UK
UKHW021002310326
469541UK00006B/16
* 9 7 8 0 1 9 8 8 1 4 4 1 2 *